RICHARD WAGNER
HIS LIFE IN HIS WORK

RICHARD WAGNER

From " Richard Wagner," published by Messrs. Friedrich Bruckmann, A.G., Verlag Müncken. The original photograph was taken in Paris in 1861.

RICHARD WAGNER
HIS LIFE IN HIS WORK

BY PAUL BEKKER

TRANSLATED BY
M. M. BOZMAN

 BOOKS FOR LIBRARIES PRESS
FREEPORT, NEW YORK

First Published 1931
Reprinted 1970

STANDARD BOOK NUMBER:
8369-5176-X

LIBRARY OF CONGRESS CATALOG CARD NUMBER:
70-107792

PRINTED IN THE UNITED STATES OF AMERICA

AUTHOR'S PREFACE

FOR the man and woman of to-day the life and personality of Richard Wagner belong already to the region of myth, while his art continues as heretofore to rule the stage and to compel attempts at analysis. Wagnerian literature hitherto has been a battle-ground of Wagnerians and anti-Wagnerians, a polemic, more or less objective, of contending theories and opinions. Neither panegyric nor deliberately hostile attack tend to a better knowledge of the true nature of a great art. There may be certain deep-seated reasons why it has not been possible to reach some critical standpoint above and beyond absolute acceptance or absolute rejection. Perhaps the stimulating contrast of a new art was needed for a true understanding of Wagner's work with all its greatness and its limitations.

For the existence of this book I have to thank present-day music, the legitimate offspring of Wagnerian art, to which its tendencies are opposed upon matters of the first importance. An attempt to understand this contradiction drew me on to examine the nature of the conflicting phenomena and so to consider the meaning of certain æsthetic terms current in the speech of the day. Among designations for the most part ordinary in their application, I found the concept *expressionist art* by far the most illuminating. It is one of the most popular in present-day critical terminology and shares thereby the fate of all such—namely, that little attempt is made to reflect upon its meaning, its bases, its qualities and delimitations. This I' have endeavoured to do.

The more closely I approached Wagner's work, taking this idea of expressionist art as my base, the more convinced I became that it was not only a most stimulating but indeed the only practicable standpoint whence to reach an understanding of his personality and art. Wagner's works, his character, even his writings, usually regarded as a troublesome side-issue, revealed themselves to me more and more readily, and the unity of Wagner's whole being took an air of

v

persuasive completeness. It was necessary to remain constantly aware that the will to expression has a merely relative value as a formative principle in art. From this standpoint the critic's task seemed to consist not in detailed criticism but rather in a critical understanding of that one underlying idea, for, its presuppositions and consequences once clearly set forth, the tree of Wagnerian personality and work must stand revealed from its roots to its topmost branches.

In this idea arose my book, and the plan of my book. I could not consider the life, writings and works of art separately, since the human, literary and artistic expressions of each phase of Wagner's development are but manifestations on different levels of the same will to expression and illuminate one another. For this reason the book bears the sub-title *His Life in His Work*; and for this reason also I have dealt with the writings as being, in my opinion, neither more nor less than dramaturgical allegories, always and exclusively concerned with the individual work which they immediately precede. On the same grounds I have found it necessary to take the works in strict chronological order, not discussing the *Venusberg* together with the *Tannhäuser* of the Dresden period, nor the third act of *Siegfried* and *The Dusk of the Gods* with the antecedent portions of *The Ring*. If considerations of chronology or stylistic criticism alone forbade such grouping they might have been ignored, but in any attempt to interpret Wagner's life and art as manifestations of Expressionism, consideration of the inner nature of the works themselves must make it as impossible to place the later parts of *The Nibelungs* side by side with the earlier as it was to Wagner to compose them in this order.

Once I had recognised the elemental unity in all Wagner's life and work I found it equally impracticable to write of him merely as a musician. Wagner's music may be examined as such, and Ernst Kurth has done so in exemplary fashion in his book on Romantic harmony. Such a work, however, is a specialised study in which the artist from whom examples are drawn remains but a subsidiary subject. And the whole subject of Wagner could never be understood by means of an empirical examination of his music. On the other hand I believe that through the avenues opened to me by means of a critical examination of the idea of *Expressionism* I have been able to interpret Wagner's work in such a way that new light is shed even on his music. Since I hold Wagnerian dramatic action to be a drama of musical notes and their interrelations, projected in a symbolic allegorical scenic picture, I believe that in contemplating his drama we are contemplating his music, and that every performance of his music is a dramatic performance. A deliberate sundering of the pair in favour of either would be an act of violence, would be misleading, and would frustrate my endeavour, which is to show the natural union of the two. The idea of " musical action made visible "—*the* fundamental idea of all Wagner's art—has not been allowed hitherto its full significance and consequence. Its presentation demonstrates the fruitfulness of the idea of Expressionism.

I have naturally read much about Wagner, and some of what I have read may have remained in my mind without my being able to assign it to its proper source. But I have intentionally consulted only Glasenapp's biography in addition to Wagner's own scores, letters and papers. In saying this I do not intend to disparage other works, and on the contrary feel bound to thank all who have handled the subject before me. But I felt that it was beside my purpose to examine earlier works ; my object was merely to show what my particular view-point had enabled me to see of Wagner. If my work presents a picture, if it stimulates others to look, it will have fulfilled its purpose, though other observers may see differently from myself. I hope it may appear that my fundamental object in this book has been to observe and to note down, uninfluenced by the desire to prove any case. Thus we may learn to love and admire Wagner and his art, for the very reason that he and it already belong as it were to another planet. The light which that planet sheds upon us will help us to see our own path, for the clearer and more reverent our knowledge of the past the better shall we understand the present.

PAUL BEKKER.

HOFHEIM I. T.,
June 1924.

TRANSLATOR'S NOTE

THE translator has thought it advisable to retain the original German of all verse quotations, with English translations appended in most instances. The English of lines from *The Flying Dutchman*, *Tannhäuser*, *The Mastersingers of Nuremberg*, *The Ring* cycle and *Parsifal* is from Mr. Ernest Newman's translations, that of lines from *Lohengrin* and *Tristan and Isolda* from Messrs. Corders' translations. These versions are in the first instance " singable " and are therefore not always literal. For permission to quote from them acknowledgments are due to Messrs. Breitkopf & Härtel and Mr. Ernest Newman.

The English of passages from *Rienzi* and the lesser operas, of passages eventually deleted by Wagner from the libretti of the greater operas, and of lines from non-Wagnerian works has been supplied by the translator.

The translator wishes to thank Mr. Eric Blom for most kind assistance in revising a number of technical or semi-technical passages of musical description and criticism.

CONTENTS

Foreword

PART I
EXPRESSIONISM

PART ONE: EXPRESSIONISM

CHAPTER I

A SENSE OF THEATRE

RICHARD WAGNER came of a theatrical family. His father, who was born in 1770 (the year of Beethoven's birth), and who was Clerk of the Court in Leipzig, was a zealous supporter of amateur theatricals in that city, and liked to associate with professional actors. His stepfather, Ludwig Geyer, whom he himself regarded as his real father and whose name he bore till his fourteenth year, was an actor, singer, and painter. Of his six surviving brothers and sisters, four went on the stage. Albert, the eldest, became a singer, and was father of the afterwards celebrated Johanna Jachmann-Wagner. Two sisters, Rosalie and Louisa, were actresses; Clara was a singer. Richard, born on May 22, 1813, six months before his father's death, was on familiar terms with the stage from early childhood, owing to his stepfather's profession. Heredity and early environment thus combined to evoke and foster a propensity destined to govern the whole course of Wagner's life and art—a propensity to see and feel in terms of the theatre.

The idea of an effective scene, the instinct to translate each imaginative impulse into external, visual drama, is the source of Wagner's art. His childish pleasure in watching and imitating stage matters soon grew into a desire to invent and shape for himself. He possessed innate verbal facility. When one of his schoolfellows died and the boys were set to compose verses on the occasion, the prize went to the twelve-year-old Wagner, whose lines, purged of some bombastic pathos, actually attained the dignity of print. Such a success might seem to betoken a poetic vocation, yet it is only as a maker of dramatic scenes that Wagner can rank as a poet. His next literary ventures were a series of dramatic scenes, based on classical subjects learned in school. These were followed a year later by a full-length tragedy, inspired by his first introduction to Shakespeare. Behind all this work is the idea of dramatic effect, the attempt to invent theatrically impressive characters and situations, or what appealed as such to the imagination of a thirteen-year-old boy. "Forty-two characters died in the course of that piece, and I found it necessary to bring most of them on again as ghosts!" said the grown-up Wagner later. That this was humorous exaggeration is proved by a rough draft of *Leubald*, since discovered, and found to bear a strong resemblance to Kleist's *Familie Schroffenstein*. Nevertheless Wagner's memory had retained the essential quality of the work, showing the propensity of his fancy to theatrical effect, to the bold presentation of stirring and sensational incident.

The boy's talent for music developed considerably later than his "taste for play-acting"—a taste, be it noted, for making, not for acting plays. In music Wagner was no *enfant prodigue*, and as a child he showed no particular aptitude for it. No one instrument attracted him more than another, nor did he indulge his imagination musically. This is the more surprising because at the theatre he had opportunities of hearing not only drama but opera. After his mother's second marriage in 1814, the family moved to Dresden, where Carl Maria Weber had been active since 1817. The first performance of *Der Freischütz* was given in 1822. Wagner, then nine years old, was not present, as, following his stepfather's death, he had been sent to stay for a few months with relatives in Eisleben. Shortly after his return, however, he heard the new work and received his first deep impression of dramatic music. He was then taking pianoforte lessons, and tried, secretly, to get the *Freischütz* overture by heart. He asked his mother for money to buy score paper so that he could copy out "Lützow's wilde Jagd," and got up a performance of the "Wolf-schlucht" scene among his schoolfellows, assigning himself the part of Kasper, in which rôle, as he recalled later, he "adopted a perfectly diabolic tone of voice and gesture for an effective rendering of the 'Hier im ird'schen Jammertal.'" Such were some of the after-effects of the impression made by *Der Freischütz*. They differed from those arising out of drama. Opera stirred him merely to imitative *reproduction*; as yet there was no manifest impulse to *create* on similar

lines. His recorded impression of Weber's personality confirms this :
" Not a king, not an emperor, but able to stand there and conduct
like that ! " Once again, Wagner's most vivid impression is of the
musical *gesture*, whether seen in dramatic action on the stage, or in the
commanding attitude of the conductor as he controls the whole performance. " To conduct like that " now became Wagner's ambition.
" To compose like that " was as yet, perhaps, beyond the scope of his
wishes. Yet, as later events prove, it was not recognition of his own
technical incapacity that set bounds to his desires—the youthful fantast
was capable of launching into an operatic score even when he scarcely
knew how to write the notes. It was not courage he lacked, but the
compulsion of desire. His interest in music had not as yet got beyond
a dawning realisation of its dramatic expressiveness—an admiration
for *Der Freischütz* and *Preciosa* as " good theatre." He soon abandoned
methodical study of the pianoforte, the results being as disappointing
as those of the violin lessons begun in 1827 after the removal to Leipzig.
Nevertheless it was the move to Leipzig, the city of the Gewandhaus
concerts, that, in another way, aroused the dormant musical feeling
in Wagner. In his fourteenth year he heard Beethoven's symphonies
in the Gewandhaus, and the *Egmont* music in the theatre. This twofold experience of the emotional power of music and of its capacity for
enhancing dramatic action did what Weber's *Freischütz* had failed to
do—it awoke the musician in Wagner. He realised in a flash that his
still unfinished tragedy needed music ; and, as he had usually found
himself able to do what he set his mind to do, he determined to become
a musician.

The beginning of Wagner's career as a creative and formative
artist was thus characteristic and in accordance with what we learn
of him in all his later works. The theatre is his world. It is to him
axiomatic. In it alone he lives and moves. Dramatic action stands
for him in place of the gestures and processes of real life ; he can think
and feel only in an imaginary world of theatrically ordered events.
Yet these events acquire direction and significance for him only
through music—music, it is true, in quite a new acceptation of the
term. Music as a pattern in tone, formal music, music appealing solely
to the ear, he ignored. These aspects of music made no impression
on him. He lacked the musical instincts of the executively gifted
child. Musical tone made no appeal to him at all till the crisis of
puberty, when he suddenly awoke to the emotional significance of

tone. Something was liberated in him at that time which had given no sign of its existence during childhood, and he accepted music from the first as the voice of passion. He was naturally so constituted that he could receive music only as an echo of the passionate ebullitions arising in his own awakening emotional instincts. As these instincts became increasingly dominant, musical impulses gradually took possession of the pictorial dramatic world in which dwelt his mind. Into the innate, and cultivated, theatrical imagination of the boy there flowed, with dawning manhood, music, to be henceforward its very life-blood, to give sustenance and form and the rhythm of life to his imaginative creations.

The very curious time and manner of Wagner's first approach to music are indicative of the peculiarities of his talent. There is no parallel instance in the history of music. The normal approach to music is by way of pleasure in the evocation and arrangement of musical sounds : a pleasure bound up with instrumental (or in earlier times vocal) technique—that is to say, with the executive function. This is the avenue of approach followed by all great musicians before Wagner, and by all talented ones since ; the dormant emotions of the child are stirred by delight in tune and harmony and by the imitative instinct, both being nourished on classical models till the moment when the individual creative instinct awakes. Yet can we say that the lack in Wagner of any youthful impulse to play with musical sounds betokened any lack of musical talent ? The genius of the creator of *Tristan* and *The Mastersingers* is surely at least as remarkable as that of his contemporary who at seventeen years of age wrote the *Midsummer Night's Dream* overture. It is irrelevant to plead that the latter ripened exceptionally early, the former exceptionally late. These are mere superficial facts that explain nothing. The true explanation lies elsewhere. *Wagner's musical talent appeared quite as early as that of other composers,* but it was not exercised, as was theirs, in play with musical sounds, because *sound* was not the key to Wagner's musical sensibilities. It was exercised rather in play with scenic images. In Wagner's development as a composer the stage and its phenomena hold the place occupied by the clavier and the laws of musical form in that of Mendelssohn or Chopin. From the very first, music, to Wagner, was gesture in sound. For him, action and visual drama emanate naturally and directly from a passage of music. When Wagner as a boy wrote plays it was because they meant to him what piano-fantasias meant to the twelve-year-old Beethoven. The boy Beethoven came to know music through imitative handling of musical sounds, the boy Wagner through imitative handling of emotionally effective gesture. In both the musical impulse was present while original creative ability was still latent, but in Wagner's case the musical impulse underlying the emotional gesture did not become apparent till the moment when the law of physical development set his ability free. Wagner then recognised that the forms he visualised were by themselves incomplete—were, in fact, mute music, without valid existence until that music was awakened. For Wagner the visual image is the fixation of what he conceives as the essence of music—its expression, and expression is the one true fount from which music can spring. The basis of his art, therefore, is not formal design in tone nor the natural pleasure of the ear, but a music with an expressive significance as precise as that presented by the visual concept. Following the blind impulses of childhood, Wagner at first produced mere modes of expression, as yet unrealised musically, airy phantasms of the goal towards which his wish-fantasies strove. With the awakening powers of manhood he was destined to find a path that actually led to that goal.

Music considered as expression is the legacy of the eighteenth century to the nineteenth, of the Classics to the Romantics, of art conditioned by form to art conditioned by feeling. The act of creation is divested of its objective function; it assumes emotional significance, begins to lay bare the inward creative impulse, to understand psychological causes, to make intimate confessions. This mutation of the creative force into a realisation of subjective emotional processes begins in the second half of the eighteenth century. It goes hand in hand with the increasing recognition of the importance of individuality and emotion which is generally characteristic of the age. Thus the sonata form is preferred and cultivated because, in contrast to the typical forms of the earlier polyphony, it is particularly suited to the expression of subjective emotion, while a slackening of the dynamic element in music, coincident with modifications and enlargements of musical language affording finer shades of tone-colour and increased possibilities of delicacy in execution, are cumulative symptoms of a profound change in musical conceptions. Music ceases to be primarily sound-building and becomes a method of emotional representation. *Expression*, the reflection or exteriorisation of subjective, interior processes, now becomes the criterion, and the individual begins to claim attention for those experiences—or reactions to experience—which form increasingly the subject-matter of artistic exposition. A change in musical conceptions answers to a changed outlook on life, and to a change in the artist's critical perception of events within and around him: for on this critical perception depends his theme.

Classical music marks the psychological point of departure for this change. Classical music, which had strength enough in itself to hold the balance between objective and subjective art, between form-building and emotional expression (indeed, in this compromise resides its surpassing excellence), eventually assured the predominance of the music of expression, for in Beethoven expressionist music tips the scale. The more triumphantly Beethoven's own strength of personality raised the subjective element in emotional representation above the mere record of experience into higher and more objective spheres, the more powerfully the new element, coming to birth in him, worked upon generations to come. This new element consists in revelation of emotional events, in emphasis upon the parallelism between musical and psychological processes, in recognition of the *espressivo* character of musical sound. Sensuous excitement and emotional significance become increasingly the sole end of artistic creation. This form of art logically induces a desire to exploit the sensuous and exciting possibilities of its themes to the utmost, and a tendency to regard completeness of expression as in itself constituting the true value of a work.

The " Will to Expression " for its own sake thus dominates the music of the nineteenth century. It is commonly called " Romanticism," and makes subjectivity the basis of art. Some emotional state, some mental chimera, presses for expression, and the artist's essential problem is to project a reflection of that interior event upon the exterior surface afforded by musical sound. A variety of methods of thus externalising the inner vision are exemplified in the music that followed Beethoven's death. Berlioz, in his programme music, does so in the form of a commentary on a series of outward events. Liszt, in his symphonic poems, casts it in the form of poetic meditation. Other methods are shown in Mendelssohn's musical landscapes and *genre* art, in Schubert's lyrical fantasies and Schumann's temperamental confessions. Ways and means differ, but all show a like trend towards the expressionist goal, involving emphasis on the dramatic significance of a musical composition, its definition as a psychological event.

The change from a conception of music as a natural acoustic phenomenon to a conception of it as symbolically significant sound extended an influence beyond the purely cultural and aesthetic spheres. It reacted strongly upon the organic structure of the very stuff in which the musician works, introducing new, foreign elements, at once fructifying and disruptive. The musical note, conceived no longer as a natural, self-subsistent *noise* but as an expression-value, gained thereby definite significance, a significance conditioned, however, by ideas directly connected with the intelligible, external world. An idea seeking expression and striving to find sensuous embodiment in music may be outside the reach of thought that can be put into words : in making itself intellectually recognisable, however dimly, it is bound to exhaust and use up the inherent force, the purely natural activity, of sound, in like measure as it enhances its specific significance. Sound in itself is inexpressive ; it is a natural fact, not a symbol, and it assumes form in accordance with the natural laws of its substance. Sound as expression, on the other hand, is simply the vehicle of something other than sound, and is shaped in servitude to the emotion the artist seeks to express. The will to display a non-tonal emotion by means of tone now determines the shape of the sound-organism, and thereby conditions the character of the creative impulse itself, which ceases to be a distinctively *musical* impulse, springing up spontaneously, forcing an outlet, and carving for itself the channel of musical form, and becomes instead an *emotional* impulse, which makes use of sound as a means of expression. Accordingly great creative artists in sound give place to great masters of the art of emotional expression ; masculine, formative natures give place to feminine, emotional natures. But in Beethoven the two natures are combined. His musicianship is tonally elemental, though not quite so intact as that of Bach, Haydn, and Mozart, but he influences his immediate successors chiefly through the *ethos* and pathos of his emotion. In these successors music as a purely natural sound-phenomenon ceases to be ; emotion is now the law-giver, and drives them along its own appointed paths.

Wagner's nature was thus governed by emotion. He was primarily neither musician nor poet, but like Berlioz, Liszt, Schubert, Mendelssohn, and Schumann, he was primarily an expressionist. Nourished on dramatic stage scenes, his youthful imagination conceived expression almost as a self-subsistent phenomenon, and, groping after the media of expression, found enlightenment at last through Beethoven's music, which appealed to him, as to his contemporaries, chiefly as a manifestation of the " Will to Expression " and stirred him most profoundly where it was linked with drama, as in *Egmont* and *Fidelio*. At the same time this union of music and drama revealed to Wagner the representational power of expressionist art in its most vivid form— that is, in the quasi-theatrical play of musical tones.   His natural genius now suggested to him how to make the very most of his expressionist instinct—how he might draw upon all the resources of imagination and make expression so exact that there could be no doubt as to the basic intention, creating in the process a wealth of expressive symbols to cover the whole ground, and so achieve an expressive synthesis of universal significance.   For such a purpose representational methods bound up with the earlier, purely natural, musical forms were insufficient.   In these older forms, even where transfigured by the audacity of a Berlioz or a Liszt, there remained an unreconciled contradiction between their organic structure and the brilliant arbitrariness of the use to which they were put.   Where, on the other hand, the customary limits were respected, as in the work of Schubert, Mendelssohn, and Schumann, the " Will to Expression " was cramped by subordination to the conventions of traditional musical form.   In both cases the " Will to Expression " was imperfectly represented.

Now the " Will to Expression " tends inevitably towards the concrete image as its most complete manifestation, while, conversely, this image requires simultaneous emotional justification through music. Consequently there was a revulsion from purely instrumental music, as at best a makeshift, spoken drama having already been discarded because therein the " Will to Expression " is obstructed in its quest for scenic externalisation by intellectual processes and extra-emotional phenomena.   Each of these methods was therefore by itself unsuitable and insufficient, but the two combined offered a prospect of a more perfect embodiment of the " Will to Expression " through a synchronisation of music's acoustic intimations of emotional stresses with visible dramatic action.

Thus was born the idea of an art transcending music and spoken drama, while using both as media.   The aim, and also the subject, of the artist's vision is to be the rendering of emotional expression. To this end he is to use music and scenic tableaux, while the dramatic form becomes merely the machinery by means of which the varied flow of expression-sequences is effected. Emotion becomes a charm to conjure cognition ; it becomes the fundamental law of all artistic activity. Such a concept exalts the artist's own personality to be the norm of artistic creation : for what is the expression of emotion but a reflection of phenomena as mirrored in the individual ? This reflection, detached from the object which originally cast it, a mere echo of what actually *is*, is henceforth to be the subject of artistic treatment. The transference of the psychological fulcrum of all events to the individual forces on him the struggle to make terms between himself and the universe—a struggle leading, in the sphere of philosophy, to the proclamation of Will as a " thing in itself," a " world-sustaining power," and, in the region of aesthetics, to the doctrine that expression is the direct projection of Will and the highest possible criterion of creative achievement. Will-expression, accordingly, governs the form of a work of art which, though superficially associated with a particular medium and appearing to develop it organically, actually transmutes it entirely in order to embody and reveal the new artistic impulse.

It took Wagner nearly half a lifetime to attain a clear intellectual grasp of that union of music with scenic tableaux in the service of expression which he had from the first envisaged intuitively. Not till after his flight from Dresden in 1849, when he was thirty-six years of age, did the crisis in his life which the Dresden revolution had precipitated reach its climax, compelling him, during the long cessation of creative activity that followed the composition of *Lohengrin*, to apply himself to theoretic and aesthetic research into the nature of his task. During the earlier half of his life he wrestled with a form of art which seemed at first to offer in outline exactly what he wanted, though gradually, as he progressed from work to work, he discovered its inadequacy to meet his expressionist demands. Opera, in which music and drama coalesce and complement each other to form a new artistic vehicle, was, in fact, a foreshadowing of what he needed, and so far instinct indicated unerringly the gateway of the path along which his genius was destined to travel.

From his nineteenth year, when he wrote the libretto of *Die Hochzeit*, Wagner had no doubt as to the form his artistic activity was to take.

Far as he had to travel from this early attempt by way of *Die Feen* and *Das Liebesverbot* to *Rienzi*, and again from *Rienzi* by way of *The Flying Dutchman*, *Tannhäuser*, and *Lohengrin* to *The Ring*, *Tristan*, *The Master-singers*, and, ultimately, *Parsifal*, the inner unity of his work was established from the very first. It was a unity independent of any particular aesthetic dogma or intellectual theory, and it was not broken by external dissimilarities or changes of artistic method. It sprang from the individual—the intensely individual—laws of Wagner's own psyche, which impelled him to strive for the visual presentation of expression in drama conditioned by music.

Opera, as Wagner found it when first his creative faculties awoke, and as he came to know it from personal experience during the first half of his life as Kapellmeister in various German provincial theatres, and in Riga, Paris, and Dresden, offered a great variety of models and types. Mozart and Gluck were commonly accorded the places of honour, the former through the power of his music, the latter because of his dramatic force. Closely associated with Gluck was French *grand opéra*, represented by the operas of Halévy and Spontini ; while at no great distance came lesser works, derived from the *Singspiel*, some comic, some lyric, represented by the German *Spieloper* and French *opéras comiques* of Weigl, Winter, Lortzing, Cherubini, Boieldieu, Méhul, and Auber; Italian song-opera, represented by Rossini, Bellini, and Donizetti ; and, finally, a mixture of the heroic and pathetic styles, represented by Rossini's *Guglielmo Tell*, Auber's *Muette de Portici*, and an assortment of works by German imitators, internationalised by Meyerbeer. Various as were these types in kind and in importance, they were fundamentally alike in treating opera as primarily a musical form. The drama served as a stimulus and supplied the composer with the bare outline of figures, scenes and incidents, which in turn drew sensuous life from the music and found justification as musical form-impulses. Artists and audiences alike regarded music as the predominant factor, and even when dramatic action was of high im-portance, as in Gluck's work, its translation into terms of pure musical form was regarded as the composer's proper aim.

A single exception attracted Wagner's attention. Weber, who, in contrast to Wagner, began his musical career as an executive virtuoso (and even in that sphere aimed very palpably at expressionism), was the first operatic composer who, instead of writing "pure" music and regarding the libretto as a stimulus to begin composition, set to work

the other way round, and, starting with music, used drama to exter-
nalise the music's meaning. Weber's arias, choruses, and finales are not
" pieces of music " in the same sense as those of Mozart, Beethoven,
and Spontini. Indeed, his music as such was felt to lack body, and
Weber was confronted by an accusation, subsequently often made
against Wagner—an accusation, levelled by serious professional
musicians—that his music was " amateurish." This reproach was not
directed against any obvious, palpable structural details. It was
evoked by a recognition, quite just in itself, that the music under
discussion is not " pure tone " but is impregnated through and
through with ideas from outside which disturb the natural, organic
structure of musical form. The *Wolfschlucht*, the *Hunting Chorus*,
the *Jungfernkranz*, Agatha's song *Leise, leise*, and Max's *Durch die
Wälder, durch die Auen*, are not tonally organic musical compositions,
complete in themselves, even though crystallised about some scenic
suggestion. They owe their charm to the simplicity and purity with
which they display *through* music the emotions as such evoked by the
beauties of nature or by love. The success of *Der Freischütz*, therefore,
was not, intrinsically, a triumph of German over Italian art, though
certain incidents at that time, such as the rivalries of Spontini in Berlin
and Morlacchi in Dresden, stamped that character upon it. That,
however, was a side issue, and many German composers, such as
E. T. A. Hoffmann and Spohr, held quite a contrary opinion. Actually
Weber's success was a triumph of pictorial, emotional music over
formal, acoustic music, and marked the acceptance of naturalistic
expressionism as the signpost to a new art. A talent for naturalistic
representation is apparent in all Weber's work and gives it its musical
character. Even such a song as " Lützow's wilde Jagd " owes its
success to the fresh spontaneity and vigour with which rhythm and
harmony are combined to paint a picture, to express the non-musical,
visual world of the poem by musical means.

Weber's peculiar gift—a very beautiful one—is his capacity for
painting in this way subjects within the scope of popular appreciation.
His simple, straightforward nature lacks strength to cope with scenes
from other and greater worlds. He failed in *Euryanthe*, where ambition
urged him to aim higher. The fact of the librettist's failure in this
work is really immaterial, for Weber failed initially in his whole conception of his task, which he approached as a musician only, and not
as an artist in expression. Within the narrow range of *Der Freischütz*
he had succeeded in combining both faculties, but in the more spacious

Euryanthe, with its greater wealth of contrast, though his skill in musical characterisation was probably adequate, his representational powers were not. The world of great passions upon which he ventured in *Euryanthe* was outside his scope. He succeeded, indeed, in writing rich and lovely music of the older type in a new manner. But the problem before him here was not to write good music in contradistinction to bad : it was to catch accurately the *expression* of his scenes and characters in the medium of music, as in the " Laughing Chorus " and Kasper's " Drinking Song." *Der Freischütz* was criticised as unmusicianly and amateurish. In *Euryanthe* Weber proved his professional musicianship all too conclusively ; here he showed too little of the " amateurishness " of which his critics had accused him.

The true, active, creative principle in the new art is the " Will to Expression." For this the artist needs, primarily, neither musical inspiration nor poetic idea, but *experience* of emotional storm and stress, acting upon a nature capable of savouring it emotionally and of reproducing it through the medium of art. A high degree of impressionability, intense receptivity, are essential if the individual is to become a creative echo. For *ex*pression—that is, the forcing outwards of something within—is truly the echo of *im*pression. Thus in the new art the source of the creative impulse is in the artist's capacity for absorbing impressions, in susceptibility, in emotional response to experience to the end that it may be expressed with heightened intensity. If the artist must experience before he can create, a talent for experience is as necessary to him as creative ability. Where then should we look for expressionist genius if not in a man who, from instinctive craving for ever keener sensibilities, ever-increasing wealth of expression, will probe his own nature to its depths and deliberately shape his own destiny to provide ever-recurrent stimuli to his mental and emotional life ? Where is the proper home of expressionist art if not in a temperament able to test the whole gamut of sensuous experience, to realise in itself to the full the passions of love and ambition, and of every stage of the ethical life, culminating in the heights of religious ecstasy ? Expressionism was the result of a general increase of interest in the personal and individual, but expressionism could never attain the stature of a great art-form save through individual artists bold to range through heaven, earth, and hell so that in expressing what was within them they might mirror a universe.

It could never be claimed that Weber was such an one. He was an ordinary man with some imaginative gifts. When urged by ambition to try higher flights his expressionist talent broke down, and he had to fall back on "pure" music. Wagner lacked Weber's simple warmth and sincerity, his frank popular sentiment. Also his connection with music was looser than Weber's. But he was endowed by nature with capacity for an experience of life almost exceeding in startling contrast and incident that of the great eighteenth-century adventurers, that of the martyrs in passion and suffering, that of the wildest revellers and debauchees in hot-blooded sensuality, that of the mediaeval enthusiasts in ecstatic intensity. This rich experience, however, was not bound up with Wagner's development as a man in the ordinary sense. His manhood, as such, stood aside, while the artist in him gained from his experience an ever-increasing quality of resonance—the power to transform and transmit experience. And yet it would be misleading to say that his experience made his art. Rather, the artist's "Will to Expression" determined what the man was to experience as prelude to the conception and mastery of an expressionist vision of life, of which, cast in the form of scenic concepts, he himself first became fully cognisant through the secondary, sympathetic emotion of the spectator.

This remarkable process, repeated each time with growing intensity, marked the young Wagner's transition as an artist from appeal through scenic imagery to appeal through music—the emotional expressionist urge gathering force on each occasion till it discharged itself, through experience, in musical tone. A life such as Wagner's, therefore, cannot rightly be described as "tragic" or "fatal" in the primary sense of those terms, for it was passed in the *use* of tragedy and fatality for the purposes of creative art. Impelled by necessities rooted deep in the law of his being, Wagner, the expressionist artist, shaped the course and events of his own life in such a way as to elicit his own creative powers. Only by living as he did could he create, and only as a creator could he live. His will was ruled by a powerful *daemon*, and his genius appeared in his ability to give expression to that *daemon's* inspirations. Life, like music, was to him simply a medium of expression, and each had need of the other. The "Will to Expression" commanded and Life obeyed that it might be transmuted to Art. Wagner the man was subjected by life to stresses of joy and pain that he might have strength and resilience to produce his work. As the "Will to Expression" grew, the stresses imposed by experience became fiercer and deeper, the objective of his artistic aspirations became higher, and his power of achievement increased to meet the increased demand.

CHAPTER II

THE WAY OF EXPERIENCE

SUCH was the natural bent which led the youthful Wagner to opera. His art was not to be music, still less poetry, but rather expressionist representation of a life experienced emotionally. Drama gave back its reflection, but the sensuous intensity with which Wagner experienced it drove him to music. Music, however, was music to him only in so far as it added emotional emphasis to the dramatic scene. This conception bears no real relation to the old idea of opera as the art of dramatically inspired musical form. On the other hand, Wagner found points of contact with the new Romantic opera, whose mood and scope closely corresponded with his experience as a youth. The promptings of his hot-blooded, sensual temperament found him subjects to suit this urge for experience, and his imagination embodied situations revealing the strongly erotic tendencies of his mental life. His earliest psychological problems and stresses were occasioned by sexual instinct, and of these the young artist unburdened himself in three sketches which followed each other in quick succession : *Die Hochzeit*,[1] written at nineteen years of age in the style of a penny dreadful ; *Die Feen*,[2] a fairy play, written very shortly afterwards ; and *Das Liebesverbot*[3] (after Shakespeare's *Measure for Measure*), written in praise of irresponsible enjoyment of life.

Unlike as are these three works in mood and musical expression, all three spring from the same experience—erotic tension that finds expressive representation in three different ways. *Die Hochzeit* (a fragment) and *Die Feen* spring from the soil of German Romanticism. The characters, the situations, the ideals embodied in the action, reproduce types created by Weber and his successor Marschner. A non-musical idea governs the whole work—the idea of the *guiltiness* of love, an idea induced by conflict between natural sexual instinct and

---

[1] *The Wedding.*   [2] *The Fairies.*   [3] *The Decree Against Love.*

the social order it disturbs.   It expresses the emotional problem of a
young man—Wagner himself—on feeling within him the upsurge of
irresistible forces at enmity with the moral and social code.   Wagner
found himself the plaything of these forces, yet denied the right by
current opinion to give them play, so that they appeared to him in the
guise of tragic guilt.   This fundamental discord in his nature suggested
the rather crude situation of *Die Hochzeit*, in which a stranger climbs
to the bridal chamber and is thrown down from the window by the
resisting bride, who herself perishes upon his corpse.   The same
fundamental discord drew him to Gozzi's legend of a marriage between
a guilty mortal and a fairy, of the man's punishment and the expiation
of his sins through a series of supernatural ordeals.   A time came,
however, when the life-instinct refused any longer to allow the sex-
instinct to be regarded as sinful ; rather, the code that would have it so
must be hypocritical, and the life-giving power of the love-instinct is
triumphantly affirmed in *Das Liebesverbot*.   The conception of this
work was doubly important for Wagner.   In it he discards ideas of
love guilt and love expiation in favour of joy in life and love, thereby
parting company with German Romantic opera, which was wholly
based on these critical and ethical conceptions of the sexual emotion.
All Weber's work from *Euryanthe* and *Der Freischütz* to *Oberon*, and all
Marschner's from *Der Vampyr* and *Der Templer* to *Hans Heiling*, rests
on the fundamental notion of the guilt of love and is wholly devoted
to its emotional presentation.   It is therefore no accident that in the
libretto of *Das Liebesverbot* a German is compared with a southerner
to the former's disadvantage.   It represents the natural reaction of a
nature struggling to free itself from convention.   Wagner burst the
bonds of Romantic expressionism and turned impetuously to celebrate
unrestrained sensual enjoyment—to a point of view, in fact, which
underlay the typical French and Italian musical drama of the day.

   This reaction, important as a revelation of Wagner's personality,
and emancipation from German Romantic ideas, was no more than
a bold youthful incursion into territory hitherto forbidden or regarded
with obstinate prejudice.   Had Wagner been a musician of the Italian
type he would have been well satisfied to go on exploiting this territory.
But mere primitive affirmation of *eros* was as inadequate as the Romantic
conception of love guilt permanently to satisfy Wagner's natural thirst
for experience.   He needed some new and stimulating problem to
enhance the first two, some experience more profound than either love

guilt or love indulgence in their simple form. He now added to his naïve conceptions of the attraction between the sexes a vision of the external world, peopled with conflicting personalities engaged in active struggle for *power*. The appetite for power is not one of the fundamental human instincts, and is therefore incapable of stirring the deepest powers of the psyche. Nevertheless it lends grandeur to human gesture, far-reaching external significance to human action, and splendour to human bearing. Wagner found all these things in grand opera as cultivated by Italians and French, and as developed by the German Jew, Meyerbeer. Yet Wagner's connection with grand opera was not more organic, more real, than his connection with early German Romanticism (as seen in *Die Hochzeit* and *Die Feen*) or with the song-opera of Bellini, Auber, and Donizetti (as reflected in *Das Liebesverbot*). In each instance his growing instinct for expression appropriated the means lying nearest to hand, and, while his nature interpenetrated the borrowed form, transmuted it into personal experience.

In grand opera the erotic motive was never, as in German and Italian opera, the central theme. The love element in *Rienzi* is, accordingly, of secondary importance, and is left to minor characters. Rienzi himself is in love with Rome only, and proudly proclaims the fact. The main interest is centred in external events, and we are given mass movements, portraying revolution, war, peace celebrations, conspiracies, turmoil, prayer, pantomime and dance. Characters in the drama make their most poignant appeal in moments of malediction, prayer or praise. A general survey of this work, incomparably more vital than its predecessors, shows that it differs from them chiefly by an increase of pathos, both in scheme and execution. Pathos is made possible by the composer's adherence to the form of grand opera, but the underlying impulse springs from a new development in Wagner's own nature—from the " Will to Ethics."

With the emergence of this " Will to Ethics " Wagner's nature swings over to its opposite pole. Though directly opposed to the erotic instinct, it is, none the less, conditioned by it and forms its normal counterpoise. Wagner's ethic rests on no intellectual arguments and is never propounded by him as an abstract dogma. It is the organic complement of his eroticism, and must be judged according to its origin and essence, not as a considered opinion but as an emotional force that sets the man's whole nature swinging in unstable equilibrium. Eroticism alone had failed to do this ; it had reached the limit of its unaided influence in *Die Feen* and *Das Liebesverbot*. As a source of experience eroticism needed to be raised to the pathetic level. This could only be done by a blend of the erotic with the ethical sense and by the intensification of expressionist tension resulting from the union. In *Rienzi*, however, an ethical intention predominates. " This fellow Rienzi, his heart and head crammed with noble thoughts amid vile and brutal surroundings," makes Wagner's " every nerve quiver with sympathy and love." In *Das Liebesverbot* the intention was purely erotic. Despite Shakespeare, ethical treatment of the subject had been deliberately excluded. In *Rienzi* the erotic element is confined strictly to episodes. Thereafter the two elements are found enhancing each other in Wagner's work. The lyric note of amorous desire deepens to epic pathos, and, moreover, is shown in conjunction with other vital motive forces, while the ethical element, no longer expressed merely in declamatory phrases totally lacking in sensuous appeal, reveals itself as the erotic impulse in its highest form. Wagner returned to the " Romantic " subject of love guilt, but he was no longer content to solve its problems by appeal to a moral code imposed by external, superior authority (as by the Hermit in *Der Freischütz*, the Mountain Queen in *Hans Heiling*, and the Sorcerer, Groma, in *Die Feen*). Enlightenment, the ethical solution, had now to be sought within. By working through the older forms of opera and gaining experimental understanding of the forces moving them Wagner reached the point of evolving a new operatic form. Italian opera's naïve eroticism, French opera's ethical pathos, German opera's theme of sin and expiation, were now to be combined in grand *Romantic* opera, a form uniting in itself spheres of expression hitherto divided.

Wagner had now realised two elements in his will—firstly eroticism, the natural urge to action, and secondly the ethical sense, eroticism's opposite, the power that binds and looses. In so doing he completed the stage of mere youthful experiment and set the expressionist powers of his imagination free for action. He had no more to learn from the past. He had taken all it had to offer him—that " all " being little more than, metaphorically speaking, a flinty surface against which his creative genius had struck and caught fire. He had no occasion as yet to pause and ponder on his work's likeness to, or divergence from, that of his contemporaries who remained in the beaten paths, but he did notice that his own progress as a composer was marked by an odd series of leaps. After a somewhat rackety beginning as conductor of the chorus and Kapellmeister in several small German provincial theatres, he had, at the age of twenty-three, married a young actress when out of work in Königsberg, and had subsequently gone to Riga to take up an appointment there as director of music. Fleeing thence from his creditors, he reached Paris after an adventurous sea voyage, and lived there in extreme poverty till the production of *Rienzi* in Dresden brought him sudden renown and an appointment as Court Kapellmeister in that city. But the work Wagner regarded, and intended, as a mere prelude to greater successes long remained his only success. *Rienzi* was keyed according to the prevailing mode. By virtue of its young composer's naïve enthusiasm it " got away with " many faults of immaturity and became the success of the day. The works that followed were far less appreciated, and the last he wrote in Dresden was not even produced there.

During the Dresden years Wagner came very keenly to feel that he was but a stranger and a sojourner—an alien, both by nature and by a relentless destiny that drove him from city to city and imposed on him a poverty which was not only pecuniary but spiritual. He had dreamed he could win the world's friendship by admitting it to share his experience as expressed in his art, but no sooner had he found his true artistic self than he felt the world's rebuff. His earliest self-discovery had been through an imperious desire for love, expressed sentimentally in *Die Feen*, passionately and rebelliously in *Das Liebesverbot*. He had found himself a second time through emotional dreams of the glory and freedom of man, proclaimed in *Rienzi*. And now when that same self, with its demand for love and its message of good tidings to humanity, was ready to lavish itself upon the world through a synthesis of these impulses, it was misunderstood : the world insisted on regarding as " theatre " in the ordinary sense what was for Wagner an expression of his very life.

The sense that he was misunderstood was, however, in itself a new experience. It gave birth in Wagner's imagination to shadowy outlines of three figures, all strangers, all wanderers in search of home and love, all aliens and fugitives in the world, all misunderstood by the world. The first comes from over the sea, like the sea restless and storm-driven. The second comes a fugitive from the kingdom of

sensual love, still harried and enslaved by lawless passions.   The third
descends from the heaven of a creative artist's ecstasy, ready and eager
to give himself in loving trust to the world, but betrayed and rejected
by the world.   Each figure is a fresh embodiment of the *eros*-instinct
that woke the artist in Wagner, and each reflects the actual experience
of life immediately preceding its creation.   *The Flying Dutchman* was
composed in Paris before the completion of *Rienzi*.   It is Wagner's
first really penetrating collocation of past experience, and at the same
time it is prophetic of the future.   It is the cry of a soul tormented by
a demon of unrest and yearning to find rest in the bosom of love.
Tannhäuser, first offspring of Wagner's illusory prosperity in Dresden,
is inspired by conflict in a soul torn between idle enjoyment of the
pleasure of love and the call to action with all the suffering action
entails.   It marks Wagner's final breach with the past—a breach even
with what was then his present.   *Lohengrin* tells how Genius descends
from heaven out of love to mankind, yet is rejected of men.   Its
theme is the loneliness of the creative spirit.   All three works show
sexual instinct as subordinate to individual ethical instinct, the motive
inspiring each work being the conflict between these two forces.   The
Flying Dutchman's curse is the curse of creative genius; only the magic
of love can overcome it.   The fires that burn in Tannhäuser's veins
are the fires that consume the slave of lust ; only love's sacrifice can
buy him freedom.   Lohengrin, though he has passed into the supernatural order, is bound by love to mankind.   He is lonely because he
obeys the moral law to express love in action, and his withdrawal when
his trust is betrayed, while it punishes his faithless lover, is a damning
judgment upon himself.

The sources of these three dramas in Wagner's own experience are
easily traced.   All are self-revelations of a man whose life was ruled
by a ruthless urge to *experience* in order that he might *reveal*.   We are
face to face here with the fundamental difference between confession
extorted by real spiritual necessity and confession used as a medium of
expressionist art.   The difference is that between great tragic poetry
and great opera.   Where the former keeps actual experience in the
background and affords merely an echo or suggestion of it, the latter
strives to outdo it.   This difference does not spring from choice of
artistic medium : on the contrary, choice of artistic medium is determined by difference of view-point and aim.   The very spirit and essence
of Wagner's three great Romantic operas lies in their erotic basis, in

their expression of desire. The moral trend is something superadded which nevertheless penetrates the erotic material of the work, shaping and colouring it, giving it complexity and variety. The composer, having suffered himself, idealises himself in his heroes. His yearning for love is magnified into the sorrow of a world, and the dramatic picture he paints of his sufferings as he sees them is the imaginatively magnified expression of his will—the dream-like wrestling of his ego with the universe.

By blending the erotic and ethical motives Wagner found a new method of artistic treatment in which psychological problems occupied a foremost place. The older type of opera had had no room for psychology as a dramatic factor. It was confined to musical delineation of conventionalised types. Any attempt at psychological presentation of character or incident would have obstructed the free flow of the music and subjected it to the dominion of an essentially alien power. The new conception of music, however, as a means of expression, and its enlistment as a method of embodying experience, required of it psychological characterisation, thus according with the tendency of the time to make personality the fulcrum of artistic treatment.

In *The Flying Dutchman, Tannhäuser,* and *Lohengrin,* the action is essentially psychological. In all three dramas the conflict portrayed is fundamentally the same, though differences arise in the varying characters and temperaments of the several protagonists which assign to each his individual sphere, his individual impulses, his individual battle-ground. Since the dramatic action from first to last turns upon psychological events in the soul of the hero, new laws of dramatic construction are called for to suit the new conception of the hero's psychology as the only proper subject-matter. The unity underlying the action must be a *psychological* unity, the characters in the drama must be *psychologically* conceived, so that, necessarily, a new impulse guides the choice and presentation of external incident upon the stage. The varied field of human psychology invites the artist to concentrate his creative genius upon a variety of metamorphoses and stages of development. His imagination continually receives fresh impetus to invent some new psychological variation, to express artistically the many varieties of experience. With the introduction of the psychological motive as formative principle, a new and fructifying power entered opera. In the conscious exploitation of this power Wagner travelled even further beyond the type of his latest synthesis (" grand Romantic opera," or the blend of Romantic, Italian, and grand opera as exemplified in *The Flying Dutchman, Tannhäuser*, and *Lohengrin*) than he had therein travelled beyond its predecessors. The expressionist impulse urged him unceasingly forward. Wagner's life as a man continued to present him with an increasing number of psychological problems, and the psychological view-point entered increasingly into his work.

In *The Flying Dutchman, Tannhäuser*, and *Lohengrin*, Wagner realised his experience of man as a stranger, a seeker, a rejected outcast, in three several inflections of the " Will to Expression." In each the ego was the central figure in the drama, and the clash between erotic impulse and ethical sense formed the motive of plots which were, even at this date, conceived emotionally, though not yet consciously and intellectually, as *psychological*. Widely as Wagner's three heroes differ in circumstance, character, and temperament, they betray their common origin in one respect—that is, in their demand that other men should believe in their integrity and their mission. By faith Senta calls the Flying Dutchman from over the sea, by faith Elsa brings Lohengrin from Montsalvat, by faith Elizabeth draws Tannhäuser from the arms of Venus and causes leaves to bud on the pilgrim's staff. The very existence of these three voyagers from the Land of Genius depends on belief in their existence. Faith alone renders them visible to human eyes and active in human affairs. If erotic feeling and the ethical sense form the basis of experience underlying Wagner's art, belief in the greatness of that art is the response he demands from the world. Such faith was accorded him temporarily when, still a young man, he returned from romantic wanderings abroad and produced his *tour de force, Rienzi*. But it quickly weakened and disappeared. Was Wagner's failure wholly due to the short-sightedness and narrowness of his world ? It was a question he had to ask himself. He answered it, perhaps, as an artist, in *Lohengrin,* but the spirit of resignation there expressed—praise of the Grail's unapproachable glory, abandonment of this world for another—offered no practical, workable solution. Without the faith of others to arouse it to life and activity, Wagner's creative impulse came to a standstill. A period of reflection set in. Who and what was he ? he asked himself. Why had he this need of the faith of others ? Why was it denied him ? Who and what were they that denied it ? Faith implies a yearning for things as yet unknown. Did any such yearning exist in the world ? He saw it, and yet he did not see it. He divined a dim surge of longing in one section of mankind, yet felt that like a wave it spent itself vainly against the strong wall of the past. He himself was ensconced upon that ancient, indestructible wall. The wave was Revolution. He thought he saw the meaning of the force that moved it. What else, indeed, could it be but an expression of the yearning that filled his soul, impelling him to preach the gospel implicit in his art ? A thirst for experience had guided his footsteps, and the expression of experience had become his art. That his art happened also to be music seemed to him of far less moment than that it was expression of experience, for he could only appreciate music, intellectually or emotionally, as a means to that end.

The art of expression of experience, however, demanded an audience ready and willing to experience the expression. For this Wagner's audiences showed as yet not the least desire. They continued to ask for something that to Wagner was merely incidental, a means to an end : they asked for music. They felt no need of faith where they felt no desire, and the name and fame of the Kapellmeister who composed *Rienzi* were not impressive enough to sway them. Wagner scrutinised his public closely. They rejected, it seemed, belief in experience as a basis of art, and their rejection seemed to him a shameful weakness. Yet these people with their incapacity for experience, their unwillingness to believe, were the very people who stood with him upon the wall against which the aspirations of the revolutionaries surged like a wave.

Wagner began to trace a correspondence between certain subjective and certain external events. It seemed to him that the faith that lay behind the forces of Revolution was that very faith for which he thirsted and which alone could nourish his creative powers. The aspiration which underlies any new social movement seemed to him to correspond with the aspiration of his own soul. Life, from which Lohengrin had withdrawn into idle, loveless loneliness, suddenly offered the brooding visionary a new experience. His natural instinct to take part in any dramatic scene fired him to a new form of activity. When at last the floods rose high and threatened to sweep away the wall, he cast himself recklessly into the turbulent waters. Their rapid ebb tore him from all his former holds—from theatre, from home, from friends—and swept him out into exile. The Flying Dutchman's earth-bound spirit was set free ; Tannhäuser threw off the fleshly shackles ; Lohengrin set his helm for a far country, guided by a dove, the messenger of the promises of faith.   Wagner's human and artistic destinies unrolled in perfect accord, and a new realm of experience lay open before him.

It was some time before the new experience could be sufficiently ordered and digested for transmutation into art.   The new material was so vast that more than an inspirational artistic process was necessary before Wagner could come to terms with it as a man, or shape it as an artist.   He needed now a process of conscious intellectual clarification, meditation on past events, and deliberate elucidation of future aims. Wagner was faced with the fact that his " bourgeois " career as an artist was shattered, but in his heart he could not regard this as a catastrophe.   It was a natural consequence of his spiritual alienation from that kind of life, an alienation necessary to his development as an artist.   The stark realities now confronting him had appeared in answer to the needs of his own being.   When he wrote his three grand Romantic operas he had been obliged to help out his art by inventing a romantic apotheosis for his heroes, but now actual experience had overtaken that forward leap of the imagination.   He was himself now an outlaw, banished and deprived of his goods, but neither embittered nor complaining.   Fate, he felt, had provided the only escape from entanglements in which the contradiction between what he was and what he willed to be had involved him.

The new vision had, none the less, proved deceptive.   The Revolution which had seemed to mirror his aspirations, and in which he had put his trust, had passed, leaving not so much as an afterglow of vain heroism behind it.   He had no regrets for the old faith, but he had not found a new one.   As an artist he was confronted with a spiritual vacuum : the question of his own aims and ideals occupied him perforce.   The creative impulse, by its nature optimistic, might have enabled him to set aside questions of the why, the wherefore, and the how, had not the artist's will to communicate to others constantly revived them.   The answers would determine whether he had indeed reached an *impasse*, or whether he was merely halting at the beginning of a new path—whether Lohengrin would withdraw for ever from mankind to some inconceivable distance, or whether he would one day return from his solitary journey to Montsalvat to answer the call of faith and vision and to sojourn again amongst men.

A vast complexity of questions, concepts, needs arose at this juncture, all intimately interwoven and prolific of new problems. Wagner wrote essays, pamphlets, and books in his effort to correlate them, and to clear his mind (as he supposed) as to the intellectual basis of the artistic activities which had placed him where he was. He believed that he was looking at himself objectively and analysing himself scientifically. Yet the basic standard of reference by which he observed and evaluated was conditioned (though of this he was unconscious) by those same laws of his personality which governed his life and work from the first. He set out to understand himself and his art in relation to history and to life in general, but he succeeded only in manipulating history and life to fit in with the law of his own being and of his work as an artist. That law was *expression of experience*, and Wagner accordingly measured and judged the universe, mankind and art, by the strength with which they evinced the "Will to Experience" and by the power with which they were able to express this "Will to Experience" in life or in art.

It was thus a foregone conclusion that the world in which Wagner found himself would fail to pass the tests he applied, for he would not otherwise have felt impelled to conduct his inquiry. But even Art in its most exalted manifestations could not satisfy his demand for absolute faithfulness in the expression of experience. To do so it must rest, as did his, upon the widest possible realisation of all sources of experience. Modern art, however, was (in his view) always sectional, and even within its chosen sections subjected the "Will to Expression" to the tyranny of petty conventions. Whether or not the presentation of the "Will to Expression" is actually the first commandment of creative art, whether or not artistic work is justified only in so far as it is an echo of experience, whether or not works of art which Wagner judged imperfect by this standard may not, perhaps, rest on laws of a kind quite other than those he presupposes, are questions which for him did not and could not arise. For himself, he accepted experience as the condition of his art. In his hunger for enriching his creative capacity he gradually absorbed all the external relationships of his life into his work, and was inevitably driven, by need of increased experience, to reach out beyond his individual being and to recognise in that of the community, the folk, a compendium of all the sources of experience. He thus arrived at the view that the artist, being possessed by a spirit of prophecy and endowed with enhanced sensibilities, experiences sympathetically all that the creatures of his imagination experience, till he himself embodies the idea of a People.

Wagner believed that such a collective spirit is manifested in the popular art of ancient Greece, and that expressionist art was perfectly developed there. Later ages, in his opinion, mistook the means for the end, and, while cultivating various branches of art in isolation, neglected the true meaning and goal of *Art*. Thus, spoken drama was imperfect because lack of music precluded the immediate presentation of emotion. Opera, again, had erred from the true way through disesteem of expression of experience as its essential purpose, and through preponderance of interest in such side issues as formal music and song. The representative and plastic arts had wandered down barren side-tracks, and, forgetting the common aim and exaggerating their individual importance, had developed one-sidedly. Properly, however, there were no *arts*, but only *Art*. Those things which men called " the Arts " and cultivated as such during a long period of misdirected development—spoken drama, opera, painting and sculpture —were only means to this one Art. Wagner excused this departmentalism up to a point as an effort to increase the expressive power of the various artistic media. Now, however, each "art" by itself had become sterile. Spoken poetry was barren ; opera, dancing, the pictorial and plastic arts had faded out ; music had achieved all of which it was capable as an independent art in Beethoven. The time had come for these " arts " to be recalled to their original use as means to a common end. That end, the only true art, was *drama*, in the sense of the " collective work of art," a form in which the full expressive powers of an artistically minded people would be able to mirror the whole of experience.

By his theory of the " collective work of art " Wagner lifted himself above the chaos of recent experience. To him it was a key opening the way for further artistic work, a fresh view-point from which to take a comprehensive survey of past experiences. The usual lyrical treatment could not suffice for such a summation. Wagner found the portrayal of life reflected in grand Romantic opera small and narrow indeed compared with that which he now began dimly to envisage. Love, the ethical sense, the appeal for faith—these could not fully express the new interior world to which new experience, and hard thinking about that experience, had opened Wagner's eyes.

There must be some stronger and deeper power behind these others. And the power which Wagner began at this time to recognise as the strongest motive force in his nature, the power to which he owed all he had accomplished in life and art—and therefore presumably the dominating force of the universe—was the power of Will. Will was the fundamental human emotional impulse, manifesting itself primarily in the erotic and ethical senses, but extending universal sway beyond these things. Will sustained the universe in being and was the most absolute expression of the individual. Will, again, was the absolute creative principle, and it alone, therefore, could endow the " collective work of art " with content, form and motion. Wagner's experience of Will strove for embodiment, and the result was the great expressionist artist's picture of the universe in *The Ring of the Nibelungs*.

Wagner's conception of this work was not complete from the first, nor was its execution uninterrupted. It is remarkable that an interval of some years occurred, during which criticism and reflection took the place of creation, yet there is no real break in continuity. Wagner took up his work at the point where he had laid it down, but his manner of doing so reveals the new impulse as clearly as his previous cessation revealed the reason for the interruption. Lohengrin, betrayed by love and appealing vainly for faith, was not Wagner's final inspiration in the Dresden period. The completion of that opera was followed by the conception and execution of the libretto of a fourth grand Romantic opera, *The Death of Siegfried*. The plot is developed on much the same lines as that of *Lohengrin*, though the critical moments are more heavily underlined. Siegfried, like Lohengrin, enters the world as a stranger, offering grace from on high in the form of mighty deeds, and, like Lohengrin, asking for nothing in return but the response of unquestioning faith. Like Lohengrin he is disillusioned and loses not only love and happiness but life itself. The parallel with *Lohengrin* is as unmistakable as the parallel with Wagner's own fate, which was approaching its crisis when this sketch was drafted. The former argument with the universe is repeated, this time on a sharper note of complaint and reproach, and there is greater self-apotheosis, but in this variation on an autobiographical theme there is no new creative note. Wagner carried the draft with him to Zurich, and there, in a clearer atmosphere, the hostile powers that had frowned on the old life lost their portentous aspect. The only element

of all those that had gone to make the sketch that retained vitality
and continued to grow was a sense, embodied in Siegfried, of power,
of joy in action, of all-conquering fearlessness, an apprehension of
a new beginning and a new dispensation. This mood, however,
accorded ill with the subject of Siegfried's *death*. Siegfried must live
and be filled with the joy of life. Therefore, in the new conception,
the bliss of mere being, of easy triumph over all obstacles, predominates, and Wagner imagines a new poem, celebrating the origin and
deeds of young Siegfried and his winning a bride from a fortress of
flame which he alone can penetrate. In this, as in his earlier works,
Wagner is intensely autobiographical, yet he is no longer occupied
with the lyrical plaints of a misunderstood and thwarted personality,
but with a man of free action, one who makes no moral appeal to
the world to believe in him, but acts fearlessly according to the dictates
of his own nature.

At this stage, however, a higher artistic impulse took charge and
mere youthful delight in life and action became but a link in the chain
forged by Will. Wagner experienced the emotional cataclysm of a
new love affair. He met again a young woman who had admired him
in Dresden days and who, while living a somewhat humdrum married
life in Bordeaux, had joined a group of friends, led by an older woman,
Julie Ritter, to assist the composer with money. Closer acquaintance
resulted in mutual passion and the pair decided to elope. Their plan
was, however, frustrated, and Wagner returned to Zurich in a state
of emotional upheaval. Thus Jessie Laussot and Wagner, " Bringer
of disaster," became prototypes of Sieglinde and Siegmund, from
whose union, so cruelly cut short, sprang Siegfried's free and glorious
youth. Life had already forged for Wagner another link in the chain;
the problem of the sanctity of marriage, which forms the framework
of the *Valkyrie* plot, echoes a problem in Wagner's own history.

The idea of Will, which underlies the whole work and gives it
impetus and direction, is embodied in the figure of Wotan, the Stranger,
the Wanderer, the God of Wishes, who roves the world and holds
converse with each and every inhabitant. In his hand he grasps the
Spear of Authority, signifying the law underlying all existence, yet he
yearns for possession since this alone can secure his power. But
possession means renunciation of love. This, for Will, is the stumb-
ling-block, for Will wills to have both love and possession. Wotan,
primaeval Will, thus violates the law of righteousness, and Siegfried,

love-begotten, breaks the enfeebled spear, though even he falls victim at last to the Will that wills incompatibilities. Possession and power dissolve back into the elements whence they sprang, and all-reconciling love rises purified to the heights.

Will represents, in essence, that strong creative impulse in the artist soul whence an almost inexhaustible variety of expressionist manifestations may take rise. Yet strive as Wagner may to portray it as the *instinctive*, primaeval life-impulse, an intractable *intellectual* residuum remains. In the Wotan drama as laid down in *The Rhinegold* (which was first in order, though last composed, of the *Ring* series and was designed as substructure for the whole) Wagner ceases to give free expression to experience and verges on the intellectual and purposive. The colossal proportions of the form which Wagner— working from the end backwards—found himself compelled to use, threatened to prove too much for his expressive powers. The theory of the " collective work of art," designed to integrate and com- prehend, was in some danger of disintegrating through too much subordinate detail, not merely of an expressionist, but even of an intellectual kind. Wagner felt that his theme was growing top-heavy and that he needed to return to fresher and more immediate sources of expression. The tremendous tract he had marked out for himself in his sketch of the libretto—covering no less than the beginning, the course, and the end of the entire world-process—was far too vast to be traversed in a stride. A concentration of his will had enabled him to survey it prophetically, but by no effort of his expressionist powers could he give life and form to the whole varied series of phenomena which it contained. *The Rhinegold* was conceived in the first plenitude of inspiration and material. *The Valkyrie* arose in the impulse to express a recent experience ; *Young Siegfried* in lust for action and a sense of freedom. Up to this point Wagner's experience sufficed. He knew in his own person the power of Will, the heat of a forbidden passion which had flamed up and burned down to ashes, the sensation of renewed joy and purpose in life. Faced with the problem, however, of portraying Siegfried's escape from loneliness, his conquest of wealth and love, and the intricate causes of his downfall, Wagner grew dis- couraged. The reason was not, as he supposed, realisation of the practical uselessness of his project, but a lack of spiritual experience which for the time being left him at a loss in the world he had con- ceived. While the emotional expressionist impulse necessary to fill in its bare outlines was absent he could get no further.   His vision of the Nibelungen world grew dim, the great impulse of his will remained unfulfilled, and the " collective work of art " began to appear no more than a gigantic phantasm.   Such for a time it remained.

A new psychic tide had, however, begun to rise in Wagner's soul— a tide destined to overwhelm and obliterate the rational and intel- lectual landmarks left by its predecessor.   Fate aimed a blow more sharp than the self-conceived torments of the Romantic expressionist : a blow that brushed aside the theories of the philosophic aesthete, the dreams of the worshipper of will and power ; a blow that at last pierced the real man and extorted a cry of real pain.   For the first time in his life Wagner experienced love in the true meaning of the word.   He had thought that he had discovered the fundamental secret of life in all-creative Will-power.   Now, when his own will was tested to the uttermost, he was ripe for the revelation that Will itself is derived from love.   This vision had been foreshadowed in the "love-curse" attach- ing to the treasure, in Brynhilda's final song in *The Death of Siegfried.* There it had only been glimpsed at the close of the work ; now it was made the very centre, the essential content of the drama.   An interior process brought this to pass.   Some last veil was withdrawn from the soul's vision ; the artist in Wagner came to a perfect flowering.

The personal and biographical aspect of this experience is, by comparison with its spiritual significance, of slight import.   Wagner's nature was hotly sensual and therefore, naturally enough, though women as mere creatures of sex played an important part in his life, as *persons* they affected him little.   Minna Planer, whom he married at twenty-three, appears to have possessed a combination of qualities which bound Wagner to her erotically for many years, and the fact that later, notwithstanding the change in his character which she found so incomprehensible, she was unwilling to relinquish him and did all she could to compensate for waning feminine charm by domestic and maternal solicitude, proves that some strong bond held the pair together in defiance of intellectual estrangement.   Wagner's portrait of Minna as Fricka in *The Ring*, showing how she tries to hold her man by " blissful domesticity," while also insisting jealously on her marriage rights, displays, notwithstanding his emphasis on the narrow- ness of her understanding, no mean estimate of her essential humanity. This, however, is the only echo of Wagner's relations with Minna to be found in his work. The women of the three grand Romantic operas are artificial figures, masculine conceptions of typical femininity. Ortrud is more demon than woman, and the only grandly conceived female figure of this period, Venus in *Tannhäuser*, was not rendered fully intelligible till after the completion of *Tristan*. Among the women of *The Ring* Sieglinde is the first to embody a new experience. Freia is a lay-figure in the Romantic manner. Brynhilda is at first merely a female projection of Wotan's desire. The real woman in her lies sleeping and unrevealed within the as yet impenetrable ring of flame. This flame still had power to scorch Wagner, but as yet he had found no creature of the opposite sex whom he could embody in his work as a *personality*. The women he loved were to him but fuel to the flame that consumed him and them—mere objects against which his desires again and again struck fire, their individualities remaining phantasmal and without living reality.

Even Mathilde Wesendonk was a phantom to Wagner. None the less she had for him a significance and an effect unlike that of any of her predecessors. Because in loving him she put the artist first, and because as a woman she gave him the pure, unconditional faith of his unrealised romantic dreams, she gave him power to sublimate his *eros* in his art. This *eros*, denied on the human side and thrown back on art, drew Wagner's whole capacity for experience within its glowing orbit; he found untrammelled outlet for the full sensuality of his nature, not, however, by satisfaction of desire in the ordinary way, but by a conscious and deliberate acceptance of non-reality, of an agonised yet ecstatic vision of love as an elemental force. Mathilde's significance for Wagner lay in the fact that she was a woman who denied herself and him, not through pride, but through aspiration towards an emotion surpassing desire. Her personality in the fuller sense did not influence the situation. Wagner, however, would have failed to grasp the essential meaning of this experience had it not come to him in a moment when inevitable reaction from exaggerated concentration upon *Will* forced him to seek in *Love* the highest possible experience, the true meaning of existence.

The world of actualities vanished; day gave place to a night lit only by the torch of love. Life's intricate web, which had recently seemed to him expressible only in terms of conflicting and tangled interrelationships, suddenly appeared quite simple. Only two figures matter—Man and Woman. They love, but consciousness of the world of actualities clouds their minds, so that the Woman thinks it her duty to hate the Man, the Man feels constrained to renounce the Woman. Nevertheless the emotion of love is between them. In the cold light of day this is mere desire for sensual gratification, but as they gaze at one another it takes on a more gracious aspect. Consciousness of the individual, the physical, the visible, fades away. Daylight reawakens this consciousness; therefore it is an illusion. A so-called " reality " deceives the sense. There is only one Truth— Love beyond the bounds of the physical world. For all who live exiled in the world of phenomena there is but one way to find and know this Love, and that way lies through the night of death.

It is a concept that exalts the sensuous to the level of the non-sensuous and can only be explained by Wagner's state of lonely ecstasy. Circumstances at that time made it seem unlikely that he would again mingle with the world, and the childlike faith of a woman who honoured him passionately as an artist, nourished in him a conception of the sexual instinct which, by its deliberate denial of reality, produced a most sublime manifestation of expressionist art. The metaphysical eroticism of *Tristan* represents reaction from the tremendous effort of Will expressed in *The Nibelungs*, but it is a reinterpretation of the love-instinct as a joy to be won only through pain that, in its turn, swiftly gave place to an uprush of unbridled desire. Life, from which the banished outlaw believed himself for ever excluded, called to him again. By command of the Emperor Napoleon III Wagner visited Paris to produce *Tannhäuser* at the Opéra. The desireless night of *Tristan* made way for the dawn of a new day, and the homeless exile found himself suddenly in the thick of men and affairs. The life he had lately pronounced a deceitful dream surged about his path in greater luxuriance than ever, and its goddess, she who had once before lured Tannhäuser to her embraces, held out her arms to him again. Never had her charms made so intense an appeal to Wagner, for the death ecstasy of *Tristan* had left him highly susceptible to the joys of life. He reacted violently from unreality back to reality. Venus, bestower of sensual joys, reappears in an orgy of lustful fantasy that has, in its naked fleshliness, something sinister and terrible, explicable only by reference to the equally sinister and terrible enchantment of the *Liebestod* that preceded it.

Wagner, however, was once more fooled by a trick of destiny. The faith the world now offered him was not the faith in his mission for which he asked. It was simply belief in his abilities as an operatic composer—the very thing he was determined not to be. Once more Tannhäuser turned his back on the Venusberg, this time without interior conflict. The fever of desire which had possessed him was simply the result of the sudden impact on his unreal dream-world of outward reality in its most stimulating form. Its influence could not endure, but it had done good. It had brought Wagner back from night to day ; it had taught him afresh the joys of daylight. It was then that his sentence of banishment was repealed and he was allowed to re-enter German territory. Wagner returned to the old world in the mood of the discoverer of a new one. Matters that had once seemed gravely important to him, now seemed trivial and paltry, but with the charm of homeliness. The *Tannhäuser* drama was re-enacted. Former enemies, he found, were ready to welcome him on condition that he " came in peace," and he thought the old quarrel safely buried. He looked out on the world in a mood of pleasant melancholy. An idea, long dormant, stirred in his mind—a plan for a companion piece to the Song Contest scene in *Tannhäuser*, but in a comedy vein and with a happy ending. He had sketched a rough draft of *The Mastersingers* during the Dresden period, and Mathilde wrote recalling it to his mind. In that night she had been his guiding star; now she pointed the way back to daylight. Wagner realised the significance of the gesture. It meant that he must part with something that had never properly belonged to him. It meant that he must abandon dreams about Will and Love and search for reality in the whole ordered and interrelated scheme of being. It meant that he must be reconciled with the past and settle down in quiet content to work. The fruit of this was a new Romantic opera, like *Tristan* conceived *as* an opera. In it the exaggerated stresses of past experience were equalised. A mood of wild exaltation was appropriate to cast wild experience into artistic form, but such a mood was not now a necessary condition of creation. The " collective work of art " receded further and further into the background. Will had an acknowledged place as the ordering and organising force upon which all phenomena rest, but not as their source and origin. Wotan has become Hans Sachs. A thread of psychological development, carried on from Romantic opera, into the grand tapestry of *The Nibelungs*, spun into exquisite tenuity and woven into the fabric of *Tristan*, remains still unexhausted and unbroken to be worked in *The Master-*

singers into a pattern of the older operatic type.   The characters in *The Mastersingers*, with the exception of one who towers effortless above the rest, are unimportant.   The real hero of the piece is Art itself, whose praises are sung by the home-returning artist at the flood-tide of patriotic pride in his German blood.   The experience presented in this work must not be sought in plot, incident or action, but rather in the recognition, the renewed acknowledgment of that reality of which our senses tell us, the earth in which all things grow, and the soil which nourishes all that the earth brings forth.

Wagner had traversed a new cycle of experience.   He had been led out from the dreamland of Romanticism that he might drink the heady draughts of Will and Love ; he had been awakened to the broad light of day and brought back, both as man and artist, to an old world that yet was new.   The Revolution had been fought out, and Wagner's efforts at speculative self-analysis had brought enlightenment.   In the works of Schopenhauer he found confirmation of his intuitive perception that Music is the immediate expression of the Universal Will that begets and upholds all things, and that other arts belong to the world of concepts, being mere reflections, not absolute but mediate. From Will and Concept, however, springs something which Wagner recognised as his ultimate gaol—a pure, unified art-form to which " the arts " should be auxiliary.   Wagner's mind was once more obsessed with the vision of the " collective work of art."   His great scheme was still incomplete, for Will alone could not call it into being, and Love—the love that was the slave of rapturous self-contemplation and led to desireless night—was equally incapable of consummation, for it lacked the power of self-giving.   Even less adequate to the task was Wagner's new-won world of actuality, for though pleasant enough in aspect, it repelled, as formerly, any claim upon its faith and trust. Brynhilda still slept upon her rock.   Fafner still guarded the treasure. Siegfried dreamed beneath the lime-tree, and no bird called in the forest stillness.

Then, once again, Wagner's impulse to experience waxed strong. The world's faith and love are sources of power which the man of action carries within himself and upon which he can call, yet nothing short of a spell can make them effective—and that spell is *miracle*. A miracle must not be looked for save where need is extreme.   Wagner, therefore, both as man and artist, now set about providing the

D

necessary condition. He reached a state of destitution unparalleled in his life hitherto and stood on the verge of utter ruin. Apart from a few isolated moments of success, Wagner's position in Germany had been growing steadily worse. The *Rhinegold* and *The Valkyrie* proved labour lost, and preparations for the promised production of *Tristan*, first in Carlsruhe and then in Vienna, after dragging on for a time were eventually abandoned. Certain sources of monetary support failed him and no new source of income was forthcoming. *Tristan's* creator lived like a swindler on the money of creditors whom he was forced to deceive with promises he could not hope to redeem. He separated from Minna who settled in Dresden and depended on him for a livelihood. He had lost all taste for the bourgeois comforts of her menage, but he had acquired one for secret luxury, and he added zest to life by a series of petty amours. The problem of making ends meet, of avoiding actual starvation, grew more and more insoluble. Wagner's sense, however, of the disproportion between the value of his message to the world and his " worth " in actual cash, prevented him from regarding the struggle as a moral question. The moralist, had, in fact, become a cynic, and lamentations gave place to mocking laughter. It was a critical period for Wagner as an artist, for he was tempted to think that all he had ever willed, hoped or created was but a cruel illusion of the fancy, a piece of self-deception, and to cast all, with a despairing gesture, into the abyss—himself after it.

It was then that the miracle happened. An enthusiastic boy of eighteen ascended the Bavarian throne, bent on devoting all his power to Wagner's service. The composer, a fugitive, and discredited debtor, was discovered by the King's emissaries with difficulty and became, overnight as it were, a king's master. A fairy-tale had come true. Wagner had found faith at last, a royal faith, rooted in a new world of feeling and desire such as he once hoped Revolution would bring, a faith carrying stored within it ample power for fulfilment. Strangely, almost inconceivably, Wagner's wildest dreams were realised. For to the miracle of a king's faith was added a second—the miracle of a woman's love. The woman was the wife of Wagner's friend. He was called on to take her not, as with Jessie Laussot or Mathilde, in face of a hostile society, but in defiance of loyalty and friendship. But Wagner is no longer Wehwalt der Wälsung, he is no longer Tristan, dying before the miracle of love unveiled. He is Siegfried who once had dreamed beneath the lime-tree but is ready now to slay Mime and Fafner.   Effortless he wins the treasure, and not the treasure only but the Ring that confers " boundless power." Last of all he wins the woman, Wotan's daughter, who can teach him to read the runes of life's primaeval wisdom.   With the new-forged sword that conquered the treasure he shatters the spear of the old dispensation.   He breaks through the flames of desire which consume all mortal flesh, and now, ringed about by their glow, Siegfried and Brynhilda stand united, singing in praise of the love that is both understanding and fulfilment.

The " collective work of art " was finished, but not as originally planned.   *Tristan* and *The Mastersingers* had purged the earlier conception of the speculative element.   A reminiscent echo of the idea of Wotan as embodied Will lingers on, and *The Dusk of the Gods* bears out, superficially, the earlier scheme, but in style the old " new opera " again becomes prominent.   Organic development can be traced here also in the way the later work links on to the earlier.   This piece was the starting-point.   It began as *The Death of Siegfried* in the " operatic " period and to this period it now led back after the stylistic changes of intervening years had been worked through.   On the creative side also it represents a synthesis.   Siegfried as an active force recedes into the background and his death is no longer the climax of the work. His place is taken by the heroine, Brynhilda, the woman deceived by love ; and not the human herd's jealousy of great deeds but Siegfried's own fatal and fated betrayal of love brings about his fall.   He is driven against his will to that betrayal by world forces, but he is part of the world, and a world in which love is not the first law is doomed to destruction.

A deep yearning, built into the very foundations of this work, is embodied in Brynhilda, the woman who awakens Siegfried to manhood and who is his true mate.   It is a yearning for a new world beyond this present order which involves even the pure in heart in its treacheries. Valhalla, Will's self-builded stronghold, is doomed to fiery destruction ; but far from Valhalla, in a distant land, is another stronghold " called Montsalvat," the Fortress of Faith, and to this trusting love points the way.   The Ring, the ring of royal power, was torn from Wagner's grasp and was dissolved in the elements from which it came. His hope of setting up a new art, a new world in place of the old, of realising the theatre of his dreams, had come to naught.   He saw the inevitability of failure, the powerlessness of power in a world where love is betrayed. He was forced to flee from Munich. But when power proved treacherous, faith and love stood firm, and faith and love together can build a temple beyond the world's end, a stronghold where the imagination finds peace—that lofty fortress whence Lohengrin came to dwell with men—a place not to be approached by those who are entangled in the world's deceits, but open to those who possess the faith that is rooted in love. The temple-fortress where the creator spirit alights like a dove to feed his elect became, indeed, an actuality, for through the flames of burning Valhalla shone the star of Bayreuth.

The House was built at last, and, deeply moved, Wagner saw the miracle that desire, will, faith and love had accomplished. Beholding it he took stock of his whole life. He saw himself first as the Stranger, the Unknown, coming into the world, himself unconscious of his mission. He heard the cry of anguish wrung from the sinner who, though enticed to his fall by lust, must yet guard the sanctuary. He watched the awful Exposition of the Grail ; the Vision plucked at his heart-strings, but as yet he could not interpret it ; the inwardness of that holy mystery was hidden from him because as yet he knew not unholiness. Beyond the fortress he found the enchanted gardens of pleasure where Tannhäuser strayed and where Venus spreads her seductions, not by her own will but under compulsion of her sex. Suddenly he understood the meaning of the cries of that lust-tortured soul. The seductive illusion broke, but the curse of thwarted desire drove out the soul that had resisted to wander upon the face of the earth. Only through supreme anguish could it find its way back to the Holy Place, there to find Lust metamorphosed to ministering Love, and the stern guardian of the faith who before had tested and rejected it changed to a loving and understanding friend. The once despised outcast now bore the Spear of Royal Authority. Purged by humble love, consecrated by faith and trust, he might enter at last the citadel of the fortress, the Holy of Holies, where the miracle of ultimate revelation is fulfilled.

Nothing more remained to be experienced or expressed. Wagner died.

CHAPTER III

In the foregoing chapters I have attempted to trace the course of Wagner's life in relation to his art ; it must be emphasised, however, that that life was not the source of that art.   Rather we have to deal with an art whose expressionist demands shaped and moulded a man's life and experience.   Yet the goal of that art must be sought elsewhere than in the experience it generated.   It was not desire, will, faith or love : these merely supplied motive power.   It was not opera, drama or music : these were merely machinery to make that power effective. The goal itself was, simply, *theatre*.

Modern theatrical art, evolving from the form-culture of the eighteenth century, is based on conscious make-believe—the deliberate building up of an illusion to form an artistic counterpart to reality. The erection of a stage, representing a world set apart from the real world, and the necessity for presenting scenes under artificial lighting effects, are conditions which make this inevitable.   Indeed, these two conditions—separation of stage from auditorium, and display of persons and events in the glamour of pseudo-magical light—render it impossible to make any true comparison between the modern theatre and that of classical antiquity or of the Middle Ages, or between the different artistic methods employed in each.

Stage and artificial lighting make non-actuality the first law for the characters and events presented in the modern theatre, thereby forcing it to impose a like non-actuality on the creative art associated with it.   The more strictly this condition is observed, the more perfect is the harmony between means and end, the more complete the organic unity between the subject and its presentation.   The search for such unity gave rise to opera, where transference of the action to the musical sphere adds yet a third element of non-actuality (that of vocal and instrumental tone) to those already imposed by stage demarcation and artificial lighting.   Song as a substitute for spoken words forms a barrier against temptations to despise a fundamental aesthetic law of the modern theatre and to trespass on realism, while pure music absolutely precludes realistic representation.   Opera is the characteristic art-form of the modern theatre and conforms in all its methods to the requirements of non-actuality.   In opera, musical form with structural laws of its own, combined with an entirely non-realistic treatment of plot and character, carries anti-realism to extremes.   Actually, the more completely music took charge in this sphere, vigorously developing forms of its own and surcharging all the other elements in the drama with tonal life, the more valuable it became as a theatrical medium. Mozartian opera is the most perfect artistic achievement extant, or indeed conceivable, not in music only but in theatrical art as a whole. Here non-actuality is frankly accepted *as* non-actual—as something wholly divorced from actualities.   Perfect artificiality used in the service of illusion, an ideal congruity between means and end, is the *ethos* of Mozart's work.

Wagner's stands at the opposite pole.   The exclusion of realism from plot, character, incident or stage effect, though in fact dictated by the profoundest wisdom, seemed to Wagner an imperfection. Even he, it is true, recognised that illusion is fundamentally necessary in stage-craft, yet far from endeavouring to maintain consciousness of illusion in the style of his work for the stage, he attempts to make us forget that it *is* illusion.   He seeks to provide an illusion of reality as a substitute for conscious, deliberate make-believe, and to this end he handles the mechanism of scenery and staging in a manner hitherto undreamt.   Wagner's scenic effects, such, for example, as the Flying Dutchman's storm-tossed ship, the aqueous activities of the Rhine maidens in the depths of their stream, the flaming circle round Brynhilda's rock, the fires of burning Valhalla, the thunder and the rainbow of *The Rhinegold*, all portray natural phenomena with a realism unknown till his day.   In the past effects of this kind were sometimes used for scenic display, but were regarded as symptoms of artistic inferiority, rather to be avoided than cultivated.   They were introduced into grand opera at times for the sake of pageantry, but Wagner was the first artist to use them strictly organically as a means of expression. Wotan's journey with Loki down the Rhine to Nibelheim and back to the Land of the Gods, and the transformation scenes in *Parsifal*, are devices to make the incredible credible.   Wagner's scenic directions constantly insist on the utmost fidelity to nature, though to-day

some of his more naïvely thorough-going instructions as to detail
—for instance, the clatter of hoofs at the opening of the last scene in
Lohengrin—are very commonly ignored.

Wagner held that the illusory character of the stage scene should
be forgotten rather than accepted. The development of this conviction explains his increasing polemic against opera, his growing preference for drama as more realistic in treatment than opera, and his
rejection, in middle life, of strict musical forms, and of any aspect of
song as an end to be cultivated for its own sake. It was also ultimately
the reason why he crystallised each of his dramas upon an actual
experience, the effective expression of which governs the whole work
from first to last. Wagner looked upon the theatre not only (as did
Schiller) as a school of ethics, but, quite frankly, as a religious cult.
He believed in Art (by which he always meant the " collective work of
art " as defined by himself) as the appointed method for the regeneration of mankind, and he assessed the value of all things human in their
relation to this central conception of art.

If we regard Wagner's work from this standpoint, if we consider
his dramas according to his intention as expressions of spiritual truth,
his plots as pictures of human destiny, his writings in prose and verse
as gospels and creeds, we seem to be faced with a piece of monstrous
self-delusion. Wagner's theories were based on the fundamental
error of believing that deliberate deception can ever amount to absolute
truth. The modern theatre is deliberate deception, and the more,
as in Mozart's work, it emphasises this fact and moulds itself accordingly, the more likely is it to achieve *artistic* truth ; while the more, as
in Wagner's work, it employs the methods of deception to create an
actual illusion of reality (as by the use of naturalistic scenery and plot
and the embodiment of actual experience in the drama), making belief
in the reality of a mere illusion an aesthetic postulate, the more readily
it succumbs to the *falsity* which underlies all illusion.

Wagner erred theoretically through failure to appreciate the inherent falsity of the theatre. A similar misunderstanding is the basis
of a controversy to which Wagner and his works have given rise.
Disciples accept illusion for truth on the strength of Wagner's own
interpretation, opponents reject it as false by appeal to the same
authority. Actually, the ground for this controversy disappears if
we turn from an intellectual to an imaginative appreciation of Wagner's
work and personality. We see him then as the greatest theatrical

genius of the modern stage, and even his error as a theorist is perceived to be an indispensable premise of his activity as a creative artist. If Wagner gave his very life to his art, if he believed, and required that others should believe, in that art's abolute veracity, whereas it was, in reality, all illusion and deception in the service of " theatre," if thereby the passions and ecstasies of a lifetime became merely so much dramatic copy, it was because thus and only thus could he bring a new and a great art into the theatre. We may catch echoes of experience, it is true, in Mozart's *Figaro, Don Juan, Cosi fan tutte*, and *The Magic Flute*, but these echoes are never more than accidental, anecdotal, and even when most prominent are not the true end and object of the work. Mozart approached the theatre by way of music, whereas Wagner reached music by way of theatre. Thus the mimic life of the boards, ever recognised by Mozart as illusory, formal and conventional, was accepted by Wagner as truth in order that he might charge his radically theatrical genius with music. And yet it is through his predilection for music, conceived by him as the best artistic medium to convey sheer emotion, the most powerful to create illusion, that Wagner betrays the unreality on which his art is based, and proves that his mission is not to be a moralist or reformer but a man of the theatre, to whom nature gave an illusion of truth in order that he might successfully achieve dramatic illusion.

Since Wagner's aim was *theatre*, he needed some means of creating illusion, and therefore he needed music. Again, needing music, he required expressionist impulse, and because expression demands experience, Wagner, at the behest of his creative *daemon*, staked his life to gain experience. Such is the chain. The importance of its several links depends on their relation to one another, their effect on the ultimate goal. Expression is a reflex of the stimulus supplied by experience. If it is to be conveyed to others, however, it must find a channel, a means of egress, of *liberation*. That channel, that door, that *liberation* is music. Wagner's expressionist urge, stimulated by theatrical emotion, is liberated through music, and it is only as a *liberator* in this sense that he thinks of music at all. Music opens the door ; she sets free. That is the central fact in both the form and the substance of Wagnerian drama. The idea of a way out, a release, a deliverance, permeates and dominates all Wagner's work from *Die Feen* to *Parsifal*. But this idea of deliverance must not be classed with emotional motives of drama, the experience-stimuli of desire, will,

faith, and love.   The liberation-idea, sustaining and informing all
Wagner's work, is not of psychological origin.   Independent of subject in the narrower sense, it is organic in the creative process itself.
It is a functional idea.   It is in essence neither more nor less than a
discharge of psychic expressionist impulse through musical movement.

Wagner's whole conception and practice of the art of music is
based on this function of tone as a liberating power.   It accounts
at once for the fact that his music has no organic independence.
Wagnerian music is not a synthetised embodiment of dynamic, rhythmic
and melodic impulses, but is made to serve as a channel for conveying
its composer's emotionally stimulated " Will to Expression " to his
audience, for making it real to them, so that they may have an illusion
that they actually experience what is expressed.   Thus it is a music
whose real object is to beget illusion.   In Wagner the expressionist
impulse, the drama, and, finally, music (as simply another weapon in
his theatrical armoury), are all equally at the service of illusion.   This
essentially illusory character of Wagnerian music governs it in two
relations—in its relation to *the spoken word*, and in its relation to
instrumental tone.

Wagner wrote his own libretti.   His case is thus historically
remarkable—the more so that he was not driven to this course by
unfortunate experiences with librettists, but took to it quite naturally
from the first.   The unusualness of such an ostensibly double talent,
the extreme effectiveness of his plots, and, on the other hand, the
adverse criticism levelled at Wagner's work from a literary standpoint,
have raised the question whether Wagner was in any sense a poet.
Literary authority is generally agreed that he was not.   But one might
just as well ask whether Wagner was a musician, and with equal
justification accept a negative reply.   Both questions are beside the
point, for neither his poetry nor his music are required to stand alone ;
both are merely servants of *theatre*.   Word and thought are indissolubly
wedded to the musical note, and are only to be understood in this
relation.   Wagner's words, therefore, must not be compared either
with literary poetry, or with the libretti of the older type of opera.
The latter served merely as initial inspiration for a form of music
which was complete and independent in itself.   Wagner's libretto on
the other hand is simply part of the process of *liberation* through music.
The intellectual sense of the words, the rational content of the dramatic

theme, the poetry *per se* of the diction, take secondary places. Wagner uses words for the oral fixation of expression, just as he uses notes for the musical fixation of expression. Spoken word and musical note are each subject to his demand that his music shall effectively evoke illusion. It is only because Wagner conceives word and note as of common origin, because he deals neither in the literary forms of the poet nor in the tone forms of the musician but in the word-tone forms of the theatrical artist, that he succeeds in creating the illusion which provides the one true outlet for his creative impulse and conveys it truly to his audience. Music, in Wagner's sense, is neither more nor less than a method of evoking theatrical illusion. In the light of this fundamental concept he regards all musical phenomena, and on this basis he works out every detail of his art.

The natural lines of Wagnerian art, independent of theory or conscious design, appear very clearly in the unerring instinct with which Wagner took his own way even in his earliest youthful experiments. He was drawn first to the theatre, and the immature boy found the theatrical scene all-sufficing. From scene he passed to dramatic dialogue as the next most obvious theatrical medium, and from dialogue to music. He did not doubt that these things had a common origin, but it was only gradually that he came to understand the radical connection between sound in words and sound in musical notes. The libretti of the earlier works, up to and including *Lohengrin*, are conceived very much on the model of the older operatic libretti. They are based in each case on an outlined scenarium, from which emerge first dramatic situations, and from these again the characters of the drama. Wagner was as yet unconscious of any compulsion to proceed on these lines. He thought of himself simply as an operatic composer who made libretti for his own use because his own ideas pleased him best, and because no one else was likely to do the work so much to his satisfaction, and he regarded his turn for writing both words and music as a highly convenient endowment, enabling him on occasion to offer one of his libretti to some less usefully gifted musician for composition. Actually only one man, Wagner's boyhood friend Johann Kittl, who took the " book " of *Die Hohe Braut*, ever made use of such an offer. Others realised that a Wagner libretto was very different from one by Metastasio or Da Ponte. There were many composers able to put to music the words of the old Italian librettists, who supplied merely a formal stimulus to composition, but only a composer of Wagnerian music could properly deal with a Wagnerian libretto, because it was conceived on lines that anticipated its musical expression.

This peculiarity gradually dawned on Wagner when hostility to his work and the accidents of destiny forced him to reflect on the nature of his work. Believing as he did that expression was the true end of theatrical art, and that spoken drama and music were simply means to that end, he soon decided that an independent libretto as such was unthinkable ; that, in fact, word-sound and note-sound were but different aspects of tone, and were both of musical origin. Then, looking back, he realised for the first time that his apparently double talent was a true unity, and that, aiming at musical externalisation, it used words to bridge the gulf between music and the visual.

Wagner's realisation of this connection synchronised with his more general recognition of the expressionist character of his work, and of the reasons which forced it to diverge from the older operatic form which was based on quite different laws. His instinct for self-justification led him into an objective error of judgment in considering those laws in themselves unsound, but this error of judgment does not invalidate Wagner's subjective conclusions. These did not stop short at aesthetic generalisation, but dealt at once with particular questions arising out of the organic structure of the work of art. It was of the first importance that there should be a fresh recognition of the relationship between words and music. That their union could alone produce what Wagner understood as music, he took to be conclusively proved by his own history. For the same reason he felt that Beethoven ought to be acclaimed as the prophet of the one true art ; for where Beethoven touches the summit of instrumental music in the Ninth Symphony he resorts to words to complete his expression. Wagner found a parallel here with his own work—a use of words, not (as in operatic libretto) as a set scaffolding for music, but as a final revelation, welling up from music, of musical expression. The *liberator-idea* was developing ; · if music set free the expressionist impulse, words, within the sphere of music, delivered tone from musical abstraction, making it a vehicle for the intelligible revelation of emotion.

Words arise in tone. Like tone they are in origin musical, and amongst the various means of visualisation offer the most direct interpretation of the musical illusion. When a composer sets down the words and lines of his libretto he is laying down his first musical sketch as surely as the symphonist when he jots down the main outlines of his symphony in a score of one or two lines only. The principal melody of the work to be lies hidden in the words, its character being broadly indicated by their arrangement. That arrangement should be based on musical (not on verbal) laws, so that there may be real unity between the word-sound and the note-sound. In this way the impulse to elucidate music led Wagner to a new method of handling words. Rime and the metrical laws of poetic diction he jettisoned as non-musical. In *The Ring*, which bears the strongest impress of Wagner's application of his theories, he uses alliteration, believing this to be the best way of welding speech and tone together. In *Tristan* he abandons this particular device ; there the words well up in an emotional stream without regard to logical thought, pulsating with the expressionist impulse and blending perfectly with the melodic line in absolute accord with the musical concept. Reaction sets in in *The Mastersingers* ; here there is some restraint upon the too heady surge of emotionalism, there is plastic economy, and a return (as indeed in *Tristan*) in defiance of the theories of *The Ring*, to the use of rime. Wagner uses the latter to lend point to his diction, having discovered that it enhances realism by increase of emphasis, in contrast to the flowing language of *Tristan*. In the second part of *Siegfried* and in *The Dusk of the Gods* many draft changes were made before the work was complete, but in *Parsifal* Wagner garners his full harvest of experience, using alliteration, end-rime, metrical verse (as in *The Mastersingers*), or free verse (as in *Tristan*), in accordance with the expressionist purpose of the moment. But the significance of word-sounds as organically complementary to note-sounds, the recognition that music is formed of both, persists throughout Wagner's work. Even in the earlier, and still conventional, pieces this theory is applied with instinctive certainty of touch in accordance with Wagner's " Will to Expression " at that stage, and its application grows with the growing expressionist urge to present an externalised, concrete image of the music.

Word-sound is Wagner's melody. This is true in an actual, not a metaphorical sense. To Wagner melody is not a recurrent pulsation of rhythmic and dynamic musical phrases, as it is in Mozart's music, nor is it a euphonious musical line, born of instinctive vocal technique, as in the Italian school, nor a declamatory phrase, borrowed from oratorical pathos, as in grand opera. Elements of these varying

melodic types distil over into his work and emerge on occasion
without exercising anything more than an episodic influence on his
style. But to Wagner melody is essentially an emotion-charged,
concrete revelation of music. It arises on the frontiers of emotion
and thought, where word and note blend. Melody represents the
summit of music, achieved when the striving " Will to Expression "
takes form, climbs the final step towards manifestation, and gains that
peak where inarticulate sound becomes articulate—where note-sound
becomes word-sound.

The Romantic school's conception of music was an essentially
visual one. Berlioz and Brahms differ greatly as men, and whereas the
former naturally writes " shockers," the latter as naturally deals in
secrets of the soul too delicate for external dramatisation. Yet this
implies no difference in their view of their art. Each, in his work,
presents us with some event, using music to mediate the expressionist
vision. Whether that vision be of an obvious, physical fact or of
something more ethereal is fundamentally unimportant. The essential
is that a third factor interposes between the artist and his music, and
this third factor is the " Will to Expression " which governs the musical
structure. In each case the music becomes a picture, an illusion, and
only the subject of the picture varies according to the artist's temperament and choice. Wagner bases his theory of the " collective work
of art " on the belief that the theatre offers the most forceful method
of representation. Music can help in this representation. The whole
musical organism is subject to the " Will to Representation," but since
melody is music at its most concentrated, the full force of the expressionist impulse must be concentrated in it. It must be transmuted
into speech and thence into gesture. But if the resultant word-melody
is to exercise its representational power to the full, it must be supported
by a musical organism that will enhance its prominence and make it
appear the really logical and inevitable result of the whole musical
process. In these conditions the older conception of a musical form
as a self-subsistent organism no longer suffices. An entirely different
musical world must be created, founded on different laws and governed
by different impulses. This world must approximate to the visual
world, it must be understood visually, and its motive forces must
correspond with those of the visual world which it seeks to represent.
Word-melody, representing music's furthest reach towards visual

form, must be able to move, as in a room, through the length, breadth and height of the musical organism in which it arises. Hence emerges the idea of a kind of magical tone-space. A musical structure becomes a picture, an illusion of an actual, visual, dimensional world. The process by which it is possible to express such a spatial concept in music is *harmony*.

Wagner experiences melody as *form*, and harmony as *space*. It is his revelation of these two original modes of musical experience which (if it may be detached from his work as a whole) is Wagner's chief claim to importance as a composer. It is easy, when analysing his melodic style in detail, to see what he owes to his period, his sympathies, his affinities. There are striking parallels to be found with Weber, Marschner, and more particularly with Mendelssohn, until we come to *The Ring*. These simply prove that Wagner as a musician was a man of his age and had a closer connection with it than is generally allowed. But superficial resemblances only serve to throw the difference into higher relief. That difference is felt at first as a want of technique, and when Schumann speaks of Wagner's " incompetence " in four-part choral writing, his lack of fluency in harmonic phrasing (in *Tannhäuser*), the criticism, from the professional musician's viewpoint, is confirmed by the facts. There is much in Wagner that is " incompetent " in this sense, not however from lack of ability, but because his art has nothing whatever to do with that sort of competence. Melody and harmony as musical ends in themselves are as indifferent to Wagner as " musical " opera or " literary " drama. To him melody and harmony are representative devices. They could not have served him as such had they been employed with the professional competence demanded by the musicians. Wagner created for himself the technique he needed, based on laws very different from any the professional musician of his day knew or could conceive. As he improved this technique its suggestive power increased, and the receptive powers of audiences developed proportionately to recognise and receive impressions of *melodic form* and *harmonic space* which revealed a new charm in music—namely, its power of illusionist representation.

Wagner's harmonic sense developed by the same stages as his receptivity of experience and his skill in modelling speech-melody. The space-illusion conjured by his harmony is not, however, illustrative of the visible space of the stage. There is plenty of illustration, it is true, in Wagner, as witness the wave-figures that recur in his work from *The Flying Dutchman* to *The Rhinegold*, besides flicker of flame, rainbows, forest murmurs, and innumerable other details where the music unmistakably paints pictures answering to dramatic scenery and action. Such features must not be overlooked, signifying as they do an intermediate stage at which the illusionist impulse uses the methods of the tone-painter, or where the subject-matter to be represented possesses too little psychic interest, or is too definitely pictorial, to admit of more than simply illustrative expression. These passages are, however, mere episodes in the scheme of Wagnerian music. They can no more lay bare the fundamental laws of his harmonic architecture than can isolated instances of mimetic gesture in his speech-melody disclose the secrets of his melodic sculpture. The space-concept upon which Wagner's harmony is based and which constitutes the world in which his melody moves is the emotional sphere of his characters. It represents the expressionist domain in which the work has taken rise, a domain whose extent, frontiers, natural features, climate and fertility are harmonically portrayed to accord with the temper and quality of the melodic " characters " who live and move there.

The illusionist powers of harmony had been recognised by the earlier Romantics, and their cultivation had been the chief task of the Romantic as opposed to the Classic musician, with his predominantly melodic interests. Harmony, connected in a tone-physiological sense with the development of a spatial-acoustic conception of *depth*, is comparable with perspective in drawing. Like the latter it is concerned with objects in their relations rather than in themselves. Harmony, therefore, is an expression of tone relationships. A sense of musical notes, not as a series of individual sounds but as acquiring certain values in relation to each other, is thus the origin of a mode of musical expression corresponding with architectonic conceptions in the spatial arts. The four opening chords of the *Midsummer Night's Dream* overture build up a tone-spatial concept of the elfin world in which the drama is to be subsequently unfolded. The first eight bars of the *Euryanthe* overture, with their simple harmonic alternations from tonic to dominant and from dominant to tonic in triple rhythm, give a vision of the colour and movement of the days of chivalry. In these and many similar instances the melody is no more than an external link, a surface reflection. The expressionist's main task is to make us free, by means of harmony, of the tone-spatial world in which

his drama is set. What distinguishes Wagner's conception and handling of harmony from those of his predecessors is simply the conscious
purposiveness, the dogged persistence, by means of which he succeeded
in making it serve the theatrical "Will to Illusion," and thereby
greatly enhanced the capacity of harmony for creating expressionist
illusion.

With an innate feeling for speech-melodic structure Wagner combined an equally instinctive sense of harmonic emotional tone-space.
This instinct was, of course, subject to modification and progress as
his imaginative space-concept broadened, deepened, grew more varied
and more lucid in detail and outline. The overtures and preludes
which introduce his dramas show the tone-spatial use of harmony
very clearly, for it is their task to reveal, in a few bars, the world in
which the coming drama is set. The imaginative world of *Die Feen*
is not envisioned objectively ; it is, rather, conceived lyrically. Yet
even here the half-bar harmonies of the prelude, changing from the
E major chord in a sequence of dominants of B, F sharp, C sharp
to G sharp, and suddenly back again to E (reminding us of Mendelssohn's *Midsummer Night's Dream* overture), indicate the appropriate
world of magic and fantastic metamorphoses to which the tale and
characters belong. A contrast to this world of mood, harmonically
expressed, is afforded by the overture to *Das Liebesverbot*, which
reminds the hearer of Hérold's *Zampa* and shows a marked tendency
towards homophonic song-melody. The harmony in this case is no
more than a sketchy groundwork of thematic contrasts, ultimately
resolved in a fanfare of trumpets. *Rienzi* opens with the commanding resonant A of the trumpet call, which echoes gently in *crescendo*
and *diminuendo* between treble and bass, and where the wide unbridged
gaps in the harmonic register excite anticipation of that clash of
contrasts with which the great historical drama is concerned.
Actuality, space, depth are lacking as yet ; their place is occupied by
mere " scenery "—wings and a backcloth. The harmony is superficial
and there is no perspective. Even the flat surface is done with
conventional, if effective, strokes of the brush.

The first trace of something deeper is found in the stormy seascape of *The Flying Dutchman*. Here the imaginative appeal, though
still primarily illustrative, has a real inner connection with the motives
of the action and of the actors. From the broken chords of the storm

harmonies rises the Flying Dutchman motif, to be resolved and transfigured at last in the D major apotheosis of the close. Here is something more than the mere " atmosphere " of *Die Feen,* or the one-dimensional, pictorial appeal of *Rienzi.* The passionate wave theme in D minor sets the scene of action for the music-drama and finds psychological resolution in the harmonically developed *leit-motivs* of the Flying Dutchman and of Senta. In *Tannhäuser* the process is carried further. Starting from the key-note in E major, a contrast is presented between the chorale with its marching rhythm, simply diatonic at first and later developing chromatically, and the dazzling brilliance of the Venusberg. Both themes are developed on visual lines, the former by the device of gradual approach and withdrawal, the latter by a suggestion of figures in turbulent motion on the spot. The whole overture is built on ideas of advance and retreat as between the opposing forces of the drama. Contrast is obtained by varied handling of harmony. Nevertheless, the sense of three-dimensional space, of journeyings to and fro, is conveyed less by the specifically harmonic device of modulation than by contrasts of rhythm and dynamic. Variations in the dynamic and in the tonal shading of the harmony as a whole represent *perspective* in the emotional world in which the melodic characters move and act.

This line of development culminates in *Lohengrin.* There, too, the harmonic " space " is revealed by musical dynamic, though the sense of direction conveyed is different from that in *Tannhäuser.* *Tannhäuser* is built upon ideas of *near* and *far* whereas the *Lohengrin* score is informed by conceptions of *high* and *low*. The extreme of *height* is defined by the A major harmonies of the Grail Vision, the extreme of *depth* by the A minor harmonies of the Forbidden Question. As before, Wagner succeeds in building up the idea by instrumental and dynamic means. In the prelude he carries his harmony from high to low and up to high again. The emotional drama of *Lohengrin* is contained in this harmonic rise and fall, just as that of *Tannhäuser* is contained in harmonic approach and withdrawal, and that of *The Flying Dutchman* in passionate harmonic turbulence. The idea underlying all three is the same—an effort to wrest a tone-spatial concept from a basically musical dramatic impulse which first organises the harmonic elements and finally shapes for itself characters through whose speech-melodic utterance it finds its ultimate self-revelation. In its striving towards exteriorisation this same musical dramatic

E

impulse creates the overture.   Like that of Weber and Mendelssohn
the Wagnerian overture is programmatic in the sense of being a résumé
not of the plot but of the expression.   In *The Flying Dutchman* overture
Wagner equals his model, Weber, in *Tannhäuser* he surpasses him, and
in *Lohengrin* he far outstrips him.   In each case he uses harmony to
create a tone-spatial illusion.   The melodic contour, on the other hand,
which stands out boldly in *The Flying Dutchman*, is in *Tannhäuser* woven
deep into the harmonic texture, while in *Lohengrin*, ripest work of the
three, it becomes a tenuous thread running through and connecting
the harmonies and existing solely for this purpose—only a flower now,
not a root.

Wagner's harmony has shown itself hitherto as a self-contained
whole, subject to tonal and dynamic alterations of register, to rhythmic
consolidation and resolution, but suffering comparatively little change
or modification in itself.   As his experience widened, however, and
his conception of speech-melody underwent a change, his harmony
also could not remain unaltered.   He ceased to accept the harmonic
complex as a simple unity and began to examine its component parts
and their relationships.   He now ordered the individual notes of the
chord on the same perpendicular and horizontal plan on which he
had ordered the harmonies.   Modulation, used as a means of forcing
entrance into the magic realm of space-harmony, began to take on
independent importance as an expressive medium.   The relation of
thirds and fifths to the key-note acquired significance as a space-
illusory device and each of these notes carried in itself the possibility
of innumerable new relationships.

We come thus to *The Rhinegold* prelude.   The combined originality
of thought and simplicity of method with which Wagner here identifies
certain organic musical tone-relations with certain illusionary concepts
place this work among his most daring inspirations.   He gets his
effect by merely exploiting the E flat major chord from lowest register
to highest, dispensing altogether with the use of dynamic, though there
is a gradual introduction of instrument after instrument in a series of
ascending parts, so that the music calls up a vision of space, and of a
new universe rising in pristine purity and strength from the abyss.
Finally, when the whole is filled and sustained by the power of music,
the singing voice appears and crowns primaeval Being with conscious
Life.

Wagner was now fully aware that he could use harmony, and the relative " height " and " depth " of the individual notes which form it, to build a striking illusion of space, and at the beginning of a new creative period he produced an almost perfect example of this procedure. The vividness of the nature pictures in *The Ring* is very largely due to the illusionary power of harmony thus directed to visual ends in *The Rhinegold*, *The Valkyrie*, and *Young Siegfried*. *The Ring*, incomplete as the world-system which Wagner intended it to be, is based, in so far as it expresses individual temperamental experience, on Siegfried's dawning sense of power, his consciousness of will. Its speech-melodic formation springs from Wagner's growing awareness of unity between word and note as melody's source. Style and execution express tone-pictorial renderings of a sublime vision of nature. It opens up avenues of harmonic development but dimly guessed hitherto, leading to recognition of the tone-physiological possibilities inherent in it. A grasp of the primary significance of harmonic relationships is the very basis of all musical suggestiveness ; it is the manner in which chords are set off against each other that creates scenic illusion. In *The Ring* harmony stands for the fundamental natural laws which determine the varied aspects, the growth and conduct of all nature's phenomena.

This harmonic picture of nature is followed by a picture of wild passion. The calm reflection is broken up, nature's pure note dies away, chords fall asunder and are never reconstructed, notes grope towards and flee one another or overlap—all to form a picture of eternal, insatiable, ever-unsatisfied desire. Even where a key-foundation is attained the ceaseless struggle goes on in a series of endless sequence passages—the chromaticism of *Tristan*—the *Liebestod*. Here again it is harmony that defines the emotional sphere—a sphere of unreality, of negation. What else, indeed, is harmony itself but a world of unreality, of negation ? For it is the most powerful of all the weapons of illusion, an actualisation of that which is not, a vision of the invisible, a night in which all the threads of daylight existence become wildly entangled and are yet at the same time more clearly traceable than by daylight. The harmony of *Tristan*, the human counterpart in its revelation of dreamlike, exaggerated subjectivity of the nature symbolism of the harmony of *The Ring*, represents Wagner's farthest musical reach ; after this he ceased to grow, though he continued to ripen.

Wagner's harmony, like his drama and speech-melody, was subject to regressions. A bacchanalian reflex of *Tristan* ecstasies appears in the second version of the Venusberg orgies. This second version, while retaining the old theme, succeeds, where the first did not, in conveying a true emotional picture of the Venusberg's sensual delights by means of a new-won rhythmic and chromatic harmonic freedom. Suddenly the tempestuous, concupiscent, baroque harmonies shrivel and die, a simple C major is heard, and there is a return to the earlier non-chromatic, unified harmony, dominated by the unity-symbolism of the triad. Yet the resemblance to an earlier stage is no more than superficial. The harmony of *The Mastersingers* does not consist, as does that of *The Ring*, in a symbolic use of intervals to portray the harmony of Nature, nor, as does that of *Tristan*, in a chromatic confusion of interval relations to evoke a world of pure emotion. Still less, however, is it simply a return to the purely tonal and dynamic harmony of Wagner's Romantic period. In *The Mastersingers* he no longer splits the harmony into its component parts, but divides it polyphonically. The polyphonic formation makes it possible to secure a double effect : first through harmony as a whole, and secondly through the sum of its independent yet closely related parts. It supersedes both the naturalism of *The Ring* and the emotional fantasy of *Tristan* and the *Venusberg*. Polyphonic harmony offers, in place of an alternately tightening and slackening single complex of tone-relationships, a new form of " musical space," realistically plastic and objective. A very free treatment of harmonic perspective becomes possible and the " space " can be foreshortened, lengthened, deepened or extended to match the relationships of the figures in the drama. Change of harmony, and of the interval-relations underlying it, is developed to give tone-spatial realism in the individual, as well as in the general, sphere, and the illusion-building power of harmony results in an entirely objective tone-picture.

The Mastersingers marks Wagner's furthest point of advance towards his goal. All that follows is the cultivation, the confirmation, the complete exploitation, of territory already won. Polyphonic diatonic harmony, used to present plastic space-concepts, is henceforth Wagner's stylistic basis. The second part of *Siegfried*, and *The Dusk of the Gods*, show how Wagner's new harmonic method encroaches upon and almost entirely supersedes the old nature-symbolic harmony of *The*

Ring. While the earlier thematic ideas are not discarded, their presentation is subject to modification in accordance with the newer harmony, as in the Venusberg scene from *Tannhäuser*. The difference is plain if we compare, for instance, the Rhine maiden scenes in *The Rhinegold* and in *The Dusk of the Gods*. In the former we find simple songs of the *Lieder* type, homophonic melodies simply harmonised and based on the clear use of the pure sound of all the intervals. In the latter we find involved polyphonic writing, vocal and orchestral, freely sprinkled with chromatic melodic distortions, and harmonic indications of an expressive phrase related only through chance external similarities with that which preceded it. The change indubitably accords well with the march of the drama towards its climax, yet it is equally certain that it could not have been effected without the discovery of new harmonic laws made through *Tristan* and *The Mastersingers*. The result is to break the original unity of the *The Ring* into two distinct sections : the first, a nature drama, a nature illusion in chords ; the second a human drama, a stylistic illusion in polyphony.

Wagner's later art became purely stylistic. *Parsifal* is a work of retrospective experience. Both speech-melody and harmony in this work are a compendium, a blend. Tracing the line of development backwards, we recognise a premonition of the opening notes of the *Parsifal* prelude in the first trumpet call of *Rienzi*. The advancing and retreating motion of the *Tannhäuser* chorus re-echoes in the gradual approaching chords of the wind in the *Parsifal* Faith theme, and the dynamic rise and fall of the Miracle theme in *Lohengrin* is recalled by the changing pitch of the Grail theme in the architectonic stairway of the Grail chorus. The chromaticism of *Tristan*, the glittering harmonies of the Venusberg, live again in Klingsor's magic garden and the lamentations of Amfortas. The harmonic nature-symbolism of *The Ring* reappears in the first act of *Parsifal*, and the polyphonic style of the later works from *The Mastersingers* to *The Dusk of the Gods* runs through the whole. Yet these many affinities notwithstanding, there is no mere readaptation of the old—a new light illumines all. The harmony of Parsifal, though consciously and deliberately compiled by the ageing composer from a blend of his earlier concepts of space and action, expresses, through the true unification of these elements, a new, mystic vision. Wagner returns once again to the sphere of purely emotional drama, though it is one very different from that of *Tristan*. *Tristan* is characterised by ecstatic exaggeration and confusion of interval relationships, whereas in *Parsifal* alternations of harmonic method reveal the inter-relations of the impulses from which they derive. In *Parsifal*, apart from episodes, there is no clearly-defined emotional spatial world, but instead there is consciousness of a mystical sphere embracing both Klingsor's tower and Titurel's fortress. The pictures melt one into another, the boundaries of time and space are indistinct, harmonic expression assumes first one guise and then another, none dictated objectively, but all employed as stylistic media so that the mind is led beyond sensuous space concepts into a world of supersensuous events.

Melody and harmony, in the state in which classical music bequeathed them to Romantic, are employed by Wagner as exhibitive devices in the service of illusionary, theatrical art. Melody becomes a character of the drama portrayed in speech-tone, harmony builds the world in which that character moves and suffers. The third element required to create perfect illusion is *time*, and a sense of *time* is achieved by the linking of memory and anticipation through the *motif*.

Here again the earlier Romantics pointed the way. As all intellectual activity is dependent on the faculty of memory, which constructs a logical unity from a time-sequence of ideas and impressions, so music, striving towards actuality, makes use of memory. Memory can place the various stages of an event side by side, and their conjunction awakes associated ideas. The motif was well known to early Romantic opera as an expressive fixation of emotionally pregnant moments, of dramatic situations, of characters, and it was deliberately employed by Wagner as early as *Die Feen* to link up ideas. As, however, his musical structure became increasingly visual, he strove harder to give the musical organism structural features which would make it seem to represent a real lapse of time. Even in *The Flying Dutchman*, *Tannhäuser* and *Lohengrin*, the reminiscent motif is handled with a precision far in advance of any former use and appropriate to the psychological basis of these works. None the less these early motifs, despite clever links and cross-references, are no more than lyrically reminiscent. Wagner had not yet learnt to make them carry the whole work ; they affirm and confirm but do not direct.

The crisis in Wagner's career as an artist at the time of the Dresden Revolution and his adoption of a new model of theatrical art as the highest form of expressionism, shed new light for him on the problems of constructive dynamic. Wagner supported his theories of word-melody, of the derivation of the words from that which the music sought to reveal, by an appeal to Beethoven, and again it was from the motival life of Beethoven's symphonies that he learned the way to a further development of the musical organism. By blending the organic formative principle of the motival theme in Beethoven with the reminiscent motif of Romantic visual music, Wagner obtained a new formative method for the formal development of his music-drama—namely, the motival, associative tone-symbol. Fundamentally similar to the reminiscent theme of the Romantics, but shorter, more forceful and more malleable, it was capable of symphonic use as active principle in the harmonic process.

In this way Wagner found the third great implement of illusionary expressionist music. Of these the first and most prominent is speech-melody, which gives the expressionist impulse intelligible shape ; the second is harmony, which defines the appropriate emotional-spatial world ; and the third is motival association, which actualises the sequence of events. This last answers to the gradual unfolding in the psychic sphere of the " Will to Expression " and makes the emotional development psychologically intelligible. Conscious employment of the motif symbol to exhibit the passage of time runs parallel with conscious analysis of the harmonic complex and recognition of the spatial significance of interval relations. Only the mutual co-operation of tone-temporal and tone-spatial illusion could make possible word-tone-melody, which is the immediate bridge with the intellectually comprehensible, visible world, making attainable a most convincing illusion of actuality, a scenic picture, in which action, elucidated in speech, achieves a final expression of experience.

Thus word-tone-melody and the harmonic spatial concept, set in motion by motival presentation of the dramatic time-series, are mutually dependent and inseparable. Stylistic changes in one involve stylistic changes in the others. Not one of the three is of organic musical origin. All are devices by which music is made to illustrate the expressionist impulse, by which sound acquires visual, pictorial values. Wagner's motivation, therefore, is subject to the same stylistic changes as his melody and harmony. In *The Ring* it appears simply as a chord-symbol of natural processes and primitive emotions. In *Tristan's* unearthly love-night it is seen as a chromatically distorted line, groping and wavering through the harmonies.　In the Venusberg scene (second version) it is made to don the outer garment of Wagner's earlier, reminiscent melody, though within all is fantastic, feverish nightmare.　It conforms to the plastic realism of *The Mastersingers*, adapting itself to the new polyphonic harmonic construction, sacrificing its previous independence and prominence to the stricter form, while at the same time giving individual character to the parts.　In the latter half of *The Ring*, as a naturalistic mode of presentation gives place to a stylistic one, it supplies the life-blood of scenic expression. Finally, in *Parsifal*, it varies its aspect as the work as a whole reverts first to one, then to another, of the earlier types of melody and harmony. The reminiscent atmosphere here recalls the old reminiscent motif, and Parsifal's swan carries us back to Lohengrin's.　There is an echo of the *Dresden Amen* Faith motif, and voices of the Knights of the Grail have the very cadence of an earlier work of the *Tannhäuser* period—*The Love-Feast of the Apostles*.　In *Parsifal*, as harmonic space-representation passes over into mystical regions, so motival portrayal of time becomes purely symbolic.　Psychological conceptions are transcended, giving place to a deeper insight into mystical correspondences between events.　When the Parsifal motif flowers in the melody of the Good Friday music, the change reveals the secret meaning of the highest miracle faith and love can compass—" the redemption of the redeemer."

" Music is a woman."

Thus wrote Wagner in 1851 (he was then thirty-eight years of age) in the first part of his *Opera and Drama*.

But music is not a woman when it determines its own formative laws, when its form is self-begotten, and such is the music of Bach and Handel, such is the music upon which they built, and such is the music of the great classical period, even though in its final transfigured manifestations it appears to borrow certain alien sources of power— a matter, however, merely of appearance, which must not deceive us as to its essentially self-determining, self-creative, masculine nature.

But Wagner's music is indeed a woman.　It receives the fructifying seed of expressionism, and its offspring is a form of visual art.　This sexual inversion results in a curious transformation of music's whole character and activity.　Pure music is a sensuous activity, as remote from the visual sense as from the conceptual, or from any visual

realisation of the forces that direct it.   Such is music when independent
and free.   Wagner, however, presses it into the service of expressionism, making it exchange freedom for servitude, unreality for
reality.   We no longer contemplate a dance of the elemental powers of
music but an illusion of emotional experience.   Upon music, thus
womanised, is forcibly begotten a truth opposed to the deepest truth
of its own being.   Yet some mysterious, irresistible law brings just
retribution.   Expressionist truth is after all nothing but *theatrical*
truth—a new method of liberating the eternal mimetic impulse of the
theatre.   The violator, the deceiver, is himself deceived.   His work,
the work to which he sacrifices his life and strength, is truth, perhaps,
to him ; indeed, he can only produce his work because he believes in
it with the whole power of his will.   The arts, however, which he
thinks of as mere means to his end, the arts he conjures to serve him
with his heart's blood, are too strong for him.   They are elemental.
He can call upon them, but he cannot change the everlasting laws of
their being.   Drama, music, apparently in vassalage to expressionism,
draw the would-be magician into their own magic circle and make
new play with *him*.   The sacred and the profane, the sublime and the
foolish, the visionary and the absurd, strip off their masks of experience
and what remains, to be stored for ever in the treasury of art, is not
realism, experience, knowledge, but an eternal procession of primaeval
forces, outside and beyond the world of appearances.   The *ethos* of
that great movement is something more exalted than the most exalted
ethic of life-intoxicated, reason-enslaved, illusion-thirsty man.

In his old age Wagner saw a wondrous vision.   High upon a
tower stands a Magician, gazing upon a domain peopled by the power
of his magic art—heroes ensnared by cunning wiles sporting with
maidens born of enchanted blossoms.   To this land there comes a
young Knight from a far country.   Seeing him the Magician lays his
spell upon a Woman.   Goddess of lust, yet servant of God as she is,
the spirit that rules her compels her to entice the stranger Knight and
to conquer him by the power of sex.   But the Knight resists, seizes
the Magician's wand and shatters his realm of illusion.   The Woman
is now his slave and he dedicates her to the service of the sanctuary.
The vision is an allegory, not only of a life but of an art.   The
Woman is music as Wagner understood it—a creature who wakes in
tears from her magic sleep, who does not seek to seduce yet is forced

to do so. The armed knights in the magic garden have been subdued through her wiles to the Magician, and to him she is merely a serving-maid. But Klingsor, Amfortas, and Parsifal, stand for three aspects of the creative artist. The first scorns holiness and misuses the power of the Spear. The second sets out to defeat evil, yet receives in his body the wound of lust. The third resists the wiles of the Woman and sets her free from the evil spell. The figures of Klingsor and Amfortas are confessional, Parsifal embodies an aspiration. The parallel with Wagner's art is complete. Music, with twofold nature, serves, and the " Will to Expression," enlightened through compassion, commands. Art is that holy thing revealed through the miracle of creation to the pure in heart who surrender all and suffer for the sake of the vision.

Such was Wagner's vision, and so it was fulfilled. But the truth therein enshrined is not the story as Wagner told it, nor the aspiration embodied in the figure of the " *reiner Tor.*" It is to be found rather in those two types of experience, Kundry's victim smarting from unholy wounds, and the Demon Magician, Kundry's master with the magic wand. Herein is expressed the very nature of music, goddess and slave, woman the incomprehensible, who ever abjures, yet is ever again driven to solicit, the embrace. The Temple of the Grail grows a little dim amidst the clouds of incense, a mere fading theatrical effect, but Klingsor's magic garden, the creation of desire and imagination, peopled with the life forces that strive for ever amidst new delusions and new miracles, is a vision of the artist's deepest, most transcendent wisdom.

PART II
OPERA

CHAPTER I

EARLY WORKS

" I WELL remember," writes Wagner to Mathilde Wesendonk in
1862, " how, when I was about thirty, I used to ask myself whether
after all I had the stuff in me to do really individual work. I could
still see influence and imitation in everything of mine, and could only
venture an anxious hope that I might some day develop as a truly
original artist." Doubts and questions of this sort are symptoms
that attend every artist's development. They usually become conscious at the moment when the man of real originality pauses to look
back upon the road he has traversed before striking out on his own
way into the unknown. Wagner's confession, made long after the
time to which it relates, though it refers, on the face of it, to a stage
very commonly preceding the full flowering of genius, is, none the
less, a very acute piece of self-criticism. There is more in the reference
to " influence and imitation " in his work than mere over-scrupulosity.
There is a true statement of fact. The fact has, however, no bearing
on the question of the *greatness* of his talent, but on its peculiar *nature*.
Wagner's genius was imitative *in kind*. But he never realised this so
acutely as up to, and during, his thirtieth year, when his absolute
dependence on models became very clear to him. Afterwards his
dependence *in externals* became less obvious. The imitative tendency
withdrew from the surface and entrenched itself deep in the imagination
itself. Imitation took place henceforth increasingly in the imaginative
province, assuming the guise of creative incentive, and clothing
itself more and more effectually in original ideas. Wagner's artistic
genius expanded in this work of transformation. But its true foundation is still the imitative impulse which underlies all expressionist art.

In another passage Wagner emphasises the *value* of imitation to
his art, thus supplementing and completing his confession to Mathilde.
In *Mitteilung an meine Freunde* he declares that he can conceive of the
artistic faculty only as the " power of receptivity." The artistic

temperament depends on the capacity for surrender without reserve " to impressions sympathetic to the artist's perceptive faculty." The depth of such impressions depends on the strength of the receptive faculty, and " the communicative urge comes into play only when the receptive faculty is surcharged with impressions." The artistic impulse is " neither more nor less than the artist's need to relieve himself of his too luxuriant conceptions by communication." If the artist is capable of receiving only *artistic* impressions, his art will develop only on the " absolute " side, will remain apart from life's realities, will become *literature*, whether in the form of poetry, music or painting. If, on the other hand, he receives his impressions not only from art but from life, " life itself will eventually afford artistic impressions, and the strong urge to communicate, which springs from the superfluity of such impressions, is the only true poetic force. This latter is not cut off from life but strives to overtake life through artistic form."

Wagner believes he is justified in describing this urge to create, inspired equally by art and life, as " the masculine, procreative type of art " as opposed to the " absolute " impulse, governed by artistic impressions only, which is the " purely feminine " type of art. As a matter of fact the picture that he draws is typical of a receptive, conceptive, feminine form of art, wholly dependent on acceptance of impressions, whether of purely artistic or of living origin. It is the preliminary need for impressions of any sort, the definition of creative art as the reproduction of impressions, that is the crux of the matter. That which is to issue in *ex*pression, must first make *im*pression upon the artist's imagination, whose anterior activity must therefore be to gather, to fill itself to overflowing, with impressions, while its subsequent, creative, function is to *present* these impressions, whether gathered from " pure " art, or from living experience. Such art is essentially reproductive. It reproduces an impression, which serves as a model to be imitated, represented, expressed. Without antecedent impressions this art can do nothing ; indeed, as an art it only exists to receive impressions and reproduce them ; its power is that of the mime who gathers his effects, correlates them, and presents them to his audience.

Seen in this light Wagner's confession to Mathilde gains significance. Until his thirtieth year or thereabouts, Wagner was troubled by his own dependence on impressions of purely artistic origin.

Lacking the individual turn supplied by real life they proclaim themselves imitations very plainly, and Wagner saw this. Doubts of his
own talent awoke, spurring him on from imitation to imitation,
making him strive towards an ever wider range of impressions, till
his artistic models were all exhausted. It was now the turn of living
experience, and here too he sought continually for change and ventured
on bolder and bolder combinations. In all this he was remorselessly
driven by his need to acquire new impressions.

The effect upon Wagner's early works is twofold ; they show a
remarkable lack of absolute artistic value, and an equally remarkable
variety in style. He seems to have made random choice of very varying models. His fancy strays from classic sonatas and symphonies to
Beethoven's poetic overtures, from Weber's and Marschner's fairy-
tale Romanticism to the melodious voluptuousness of Italian song-
opera, from that again to the solemn pathos of grand opera. These
changes are due to the very nature of imitative art, to the urge to amass
impressions. With Wagner, apparent aimlessness becomes a stern
inner law. The musical studies which preceded these creative attempts
were equally varied. He showed no interest in any instrument for
purely musical purposes. Neither his pianoforte lessons in Dresden
nor his violin lessons in Leipzig made a performer of him. Even
lessons in musical theory awakened little enthusiasm. When *Egmont*
first made the boy realise that his *Leubald* was incomplete without
music he knew nothing of the technique of composition. Like the
young Schumann, however, he saw no particular difficulty in acquiring
it. To him it was simply a way of writing, of setting down expression,
which could not, therefore, be hard to learn. Another point of likeness between Wagner and Schumann is that both thought at first that
they could teach themselves and both, when this method unexpectedly
proved insufficient, took a sort of " cramming " course from a sound
practical teacher of musical theory. And, indeed, in a very true sense,
it *is* a " method of writing " that both practise. It serves them to
express their thoughts, but it has no connection with the thoughts
themselves. Neither is ever conscious of that which is proper to
music in the form he has chosen, of the tone-born art of composition, for neither feels a primarily musical impulse. They use music
for the ulterior purpose of expression. But expression, says Schumann,
is " broadly speaking, the distinct emergence of thoughts, emotions,
and passions in tone, whether by means of rhythm, melody, harmony,

the skill of the executant, the special timbre of the instrument, or a mingling of all these." Wagner, like Schumann, aims at the " distinct emergence of thoughts, emotions and passions." Both started with scarcely an inkling of that tone-organic element in musical form which was foreign to their natures.

Shortly after the Wagner family's removal to Leipzig and the failure of Richard's first attempt to teach himself, he took a course of lessons in elementary theory from the organist, Gottlieb Müller. The course was never finished, but, in conjunction with Wagner's own studies, it bore fruit in a pianoforte arrangement of the Ninth Symphony, a sonata, a quartet, an aria, a pastoral (half Goethe and half Pastoral Symphony) and, first and foremost, an Overture in B flat major. This work was actually performed in the Leipzig theatre under Heinrich Dorn where it was laughed out of court for the obstinate drum-tap which monotonously recurs every four bars. Wagner has overdone the expression business and has clothed it very primitively and inadequately in musical garb. He recognised his failure, however, saw that his mastery of the mechanism of tone was insufficient for his purposes, and returned to his lessons, this time with more serious application. A kindly schoolmaster named Weinlig, a cantor in S. Thomas church, taught the eighteen-year-old boy the technique of musical form and script. Under Weinlig's guidance Wagner composed a pianoforte sonata, a polonaise arranged as a pianoforte duet, and, on his own initiative, a pianoforte fantasia in F sharp minor, a second sonata and a concert overture in D minor. He studied Mozart as a model in form, but, emotional enthusiast that he was, Beethoven's Ninth Symphony remained his gospel. Then his impressions again sought an outlet and gave rise to a fresh series of compositions, this time unmistakably dramatic in inspiration. Raupach's tragedy, *King Enzio*, inspired the overture and finale of that name, and this was followed by a grand concert overture in C, a " Scene and Aria," seven compositions for Goethe's *Faust*, and a symphony. From *Enzio* onward these works belong to 1832, and in the autumn of that year Wagner made his first real début in theatrical music with *Die Hochzeit*.

It is an astonishing thing that Wagner, when scarcely nineteen years of age, succeeded in getting most of these pieces performed— that is to say, his overture with the drum-tap, his *Enzio* music, his two

1832 concert overtures, and even his symphony—either in the theatre, or in the Euterpe Concert Society, a private society at which works were tried out for the Gewandhaus. Wagner's orchestral works were performed in both places soon after their composition. The *Enzio* music was retained for the theatre and Wagner composed the " Scene and Aria " for a special evening recital to take place there. The *Faust* music alone got no performance. The family's wide circle of acquaintance, the public's memories of Ludwig Geyer, Albert and Louisa, and the present activities of the young composer's sister Rosalie probably created prejudice in his favour. It may be, moreover, that there·was little difficulty in getting even a symphony performed in music-loving Leipzig, especially when local pride in a family of artists overcame many of the usual obstacles. None the less the fact that the works were performed shows that they were performable—that they satisfied customary demands. There is something arresting in the fact that— eccentricities of intention apart—the conventions *were* met. The idea of performance on one or other of the city's platforms, either at the theatre or in the Gewandhaus, seems to have played a part from the first in each work's conception. This reveals an important Wagnerian characteristic—namely, his close association of the idea of performance with the original plan of a work, his dislike of purely academic efforts, his view of production not as a detached and separate goal, but as a reciprocal result of the set conditions of performance and of the use the artist makes of these. We have here the germ of an idea that recurs constantly later, the idea that a work is incomplete until it is actually performed, and that consequently the conditions of performance must be taken into account from the first. Accordingly these early works are not designed at random. Wagner uses the pianoforte alone for intimate experiment and that in one instance only, the F sharp major fantasia, which expresses a personal artistic impulse. Work not written for the pianoforte is calculated from the outset for performance ; it is deliberately designed to suit either the theatre or the Gewandhaus programme. It is platform music, and the reason for this must be sought not in the young composer's ambition but in a temperamental peculiarity ; the instinct to make the machinery at his disposal *work* impels him to seek the formula most likely to set it in motion.

This impulse constitutes the active principle in these early works. They are outlets less for the " Will to Creation " than for the " Will to Performance," production being merely one of the methods of

F

achieving representation. This explains the curious dual nature of these works, the strange mixture of maturity in externals with immaturity, almost amounting to inanity, on the inspirational side. In "A Note upon the revival of an early work," written in 1882, Wagner relates how the aged Rochlitz, after looking through the score of one of his symphonies, exclaimed in astonishment when Wagner came to visit him, " But how is this ? You are quite a young man ? I had expected a much older and much more experienced composer ! " The old man's words exactly express the situation. The remarkable thing about this work is that in it a young man uses conventional musical speech to convey to us not music, but experience—an experience of the representational possibilities associated with the form and the expressive resources of the symphonic orchestra. This may possibly explain Mendelssohn's silence at a later date when Wagner gave him a score to look at. Mendelssohn no doubt felt a natural antipathy to art of a kind which must have seemed to him to display nothing but superficial dexterity. He himself had had no difficulty in mastering the secrets of organic musical form, and he discerned in this clever imitation nothing but the hollow mask of a symphony. The contrast between formal pretentiousness and musical vacuity must have struck him as dishonest, while he was unable to discover the impulse therein active to create a " performable form."

Wagner's apprentice years can only be understood by reference to this yearning of his to imitate external impressions. He did not seek to write music ; he sought to reproduce an effect produced on himself in such a way that it might have the same effect on others. The impulse to produce is a reaction from the reception of an impression, while the imitative instinct prompts him to seize upon those means which created the impression. There, it seemed to him, lay the cause, and he did not look for the cause behind the cause. It is here that Wagner's line of development parts company with that of the very similarly disposed Schumann. In Schumann the fundamental expressionist impulse became closely associated with a dawning critical consciousness of the tone-organic functions of musical phenomena, and led to a gradual crippling of the creative faculty. In Wagner, on the other hand, the imitative instinct continued to dominate, driving him to seek ever higher and higher models to copy. First in this series were the musical forms to which Weinlig introduced him.

We have no exact account of these lessons apart from a conversational remark of Wagner's in which he emphasises the "practical" side of Weinlig's teaching. "He would choose a particular work, usually one of Mozart's, draw attention to the structure of the whole, the range and the interrelations of the individual sections, the principal modulations, the number and quality of the themes and the general character of their movement and development. He would then set an exercise, telling his pupil to write, roughly, so many bars, divide them into so and so many sections with corresponding modulations, with so and so many themes of such and such a character. In the same way he would set exercises in counterpoint, canons and fugues. He would analyse some model down to the least detail, and then give plain directions to the student as to how he should carry out his task. The most important part of his teaching, however, was his careful and painstaking correction of exercises. He took endless trouble to track down every mistake and to show why and to what end an amendment was necessary. I could see at once what he objected to and would soon amend it to his satisfaction. Some such simple plan is the only way to teach music. In singing, playing or composing, however elementary and however advanced, there is nothing like a plain example and careful correction of mistakes in the attempt to follow it."

Apart from the correction of mistakes in musical syntax Wagner here portrays a system of teaching based on purely imitative lines. This method passes over the fundamental laws of form and concentrates on the resultant phenomena, of which the pupil is expected to make a fair copy. Weinlig, in common with his contemporaries, no doubt based his ideas of polyphony and counterpoint (as the reference to Mozart suggests) on a primarily harmonic, anti-polyphonic conception of music. But previous essays and practical experience had brought his eighteen-year-old pupil to a stage when he found little difficulty in grasping and imitating the models his master explained so clearly. It is not difficult to see, therefore, why the six months' course was completed with satisfaction to both parties, and why Wagner thought it the only adequate system of teaching. Before that time his reading of Hoffmann had taught him to think of the still unknown domain of music as alive with phantasmal, mysterious figures : "In my daydreams I used to have visions in which the keynote, thirds and fifths used to appear to me in bodily form and reveal their character and significance." He set about writing his "drum-tap" overture in inks of three different colours—"red for the strings, green for the wood-wind, black for the brass "—and each group, with a theme of its own, was to engage in a kind of combat with the others. These ideas, of which the earliest mention occurs in the autobiographical sketches of 1842, must have been very deeply rooted in Wagner, for many years later, in 1879, a biographical note for an American paper tells how the " interrelations and movements of notes seemed to his youthful imagination to be ghostly living creatures whose actual personalities emerged in a thrilling phantasmagoria." This almost physical apprehension of tonal life persisted in Wagner. Even Weinlig's tuition did not destroy it ; on the contrary, the advantage of his teaching was just that it left his pupil's individual attitude towards music absolutely untouched. At the same time the mystery of tone ceased for him to be unintelligible, giving place to a conscious mastery of technical form, which his hungry imagination received in plastic and pictorial terms and placed at the disposal of his imitative instinct.

Wagner's early instrumental works obey imitative, visual conceptions of thematic construction, in which the idea of *performance* is linked with visual ideas of tonal drama. The most important of these, and the most finished in execution, is the C major symphony. " Let me tell you that Herr Wagner has outsoared you ! " writes the twelve-year-old Clara Wieck to Schumann in December 1832. " There has been a symphony of his performed that is said to be as like as two pins to Beethoven's A major symphony. Father says that Friedrich Schneider's symphony, performed at the Gewandhaus, is like a loaded wagon rumbling safely along the road to Wurzen and taking two days to get there, but Wagner drives a fast dog-cart over stocks and stones, turns over in the ditch a dozen times, yet gets to Wurzen none the less in a single day, black and blue all over ! " Mention of Beethoven's Seventh Symphony occurs in all the really favourable contemporary criticism of this work. Wagner himself recognised the resemblance. It is most striking in the andante, the melody of which, in Wagner's own words, " would probably never have seen the light of day but for the andante of the C minor Symphony and the allegretto of the A major Symphony," but which seems to have impressed him as late as 1882 with his own " proficiency in the elegiac vein as long as fifty years ago." Actually, this A minor melody, which Wagner quotes at the end of his account, is the most individual melodic feature in the whole work and a most eloquent witness to Wagner's musical skill. It shows no trace of immaturity, awkwardness, or, externally, of lack of originality. Its debts to the C minor andante in the matter of rhythmic structure and to the A minor allegretto in the matter of melody are confined to a few obvious turns in the melodic line itself, by no means amounting to plagiarism ; there are similarities of the kind to be found in plenty between the mature works of Brahms and Beethoven. The interest does not lie in these external marks of origin, but in the remarkable way in which Beethoven's gestures of expression are imitated. The imitation is as whole-hearted as it is successful. In this movement the artist's intention is plainly revealed as the " Will to Imitation," and his power of achievement is shown in the success of his imitation. He has succeeded perfectly in reproducing an " impression " of one of Beethoven's typical forms. He has achieved his artistic object in a perfect reproduction, undistorted by any impulse of his own such as might have falsified his model. By using Beethoven's methods he has produced a mask of Beethoven to deceive the beholder. The success of the mask testifies to Wagner's rising genius.

The impression, however, is reproduced with illusory completeness only in the one movement whose *pastiche* mood is furthest removed from Wagner's own emotional nature, and is therefore least difficult for him to apprehend objectively. The young imitator's immaturity is more apparent in the quicker movements, and is he is most at a loss in the finale. This is an aimlessly sprightly rondo, in which artificial vivacity and vigorous development-work fail to compensate for a lack of plastic design. The preceding scherzo is nearer the model, though it does not hit it off so perfectly as the andante. As a personal revelation the first movement is the most significant. Even here the influence of the model is unmistakable, but, just as the quicker forms elude imitation, so here a more personal stamp is inevitable. The action is on a larger scale so that there is more room for the expression of personal impulses. The result is that though this movement is less skilful as a piece of musical portraiture than the andante, it is important as a first attempt to infuse original ideas into musical material. Though veiled as yet under conventional methods of theme-building, we have here for the first time the alphabet, as it were, of the musical language which was to be Wagner's very own— the lay-out of the principal subject, in broken chords, the chromatic line in the interwoven parts of the introduction, the pathetic lilt in the song-like phrase, with the characteristic turn which recurs so often from

Rienzi to *The Dusk of the Gods*. Even more remarkable, however, than such rhetorical emphasis in a work at once mature and immature, is the skilful handling of the orchestration. The individual timbre of each instrument is fully understood and appropriately applied in greater or lesser strength according to the effect desired, even while there is as yet no sign of any actual personal impulse behind the method of treatment. The representational resources of the whole battery of music, from formal theme-building and development-work to the technique of each individual instrument is clearly grasped, and the resulting symphony reproduces Wagner's impression of the " effect of an orchestral work " in the abstract. Wagner, having experienced such an impression, proceeded to reflect his experience in a portrait of a symphony.

The effect of this particular art-form on his receptive faculty was then exhausted and Wagner composed no more strictly instrumental music. Later overtures arose in particular circumstances and in isolated instances. Two years later he began a symphony in E major but got no further than a sketch for the second movement. He had succeeded in imitating the greatest of the instrumental forms ; it had given him what he was able to receive from it—interpretative pathos, thematic types, skill in movement, a growing variety of developments, the sound apparatus of an orchestra. What it could *not* give—personal significance to thematic figures, an organic law to their relations and development, a method of formal construction capable of transcending its pattern—this had to be supplied elsewhere. Symphonic music merely gave Wagner the key to the theatre.

Before writing the symphony Wagner had already written two works for the theatre, an overture and finale for *King Enzio*, and seven incidental pieces for *Faust*. Both, probably, were instigated by Rosalie Wagner's connection with the stage, so that Wagner wrote them as occasional pieces, whereas it was ambition that spurred him to attempt a symphony as the greatest and most solemn form of concert music and as therefore more likely to command attention. Wagner at nineteen was determined to arouse interest, thus groping his way along the path he dimly discerned as his destiny. Once entered at the University as " *Stud. mus.*," however, he threw himself light-heartedly into the gay student life, made merry with his friends of the *Burschenschaft*, and, for the rest, let himself drift with the stream. His music study under Weinlig was the first definite undertaking of his life, and it was a surprise to his family. They began to think that music, the only one of his many and varied talents with a basis in solid application, might be Richard's future profession. A man who was meant to be a musician, however, must give serious attention to concert music; the earlier theatrical pieces were regarded as comparatively unimportant though they possessed far more individual character than the symphony. In *King Enzio* the impress of the themes, the contrast of melodic expression-characters, the compactness of construction, show a far firmer hand than even the first movement of the symphony. The debt to Beethoven, to a blend of the *Egmont* and *Coriolanus* overtures with thematic elements from the pianoforte sonatas, is as obvious as in the andante of the symphony, but, apart from this reliance on an indispensable pattern, there is independent inspiration derived from the subject of the play. The *Faust* pieces, also, songs and choruses for incidental use, show a surprisingly unforced simplicity in music-pictorial illustration. The development of the plot is effortlessly rendered through plastic rhythms and vivacious melodic accentuation, and in the "Ach neige, du Schmerzensreiche" appears an eloquent lyrical expression-melody which recurs shortly afterwards in *Die Feen*.

Compared with his theatre music, the symphony falls far short in freshness and spontaneity of expression. The *Polonia* overture, which was sketched at this time, is an attempt, like the *Rule, Britannia!* overture, written four years later in Königsberg, to substitute song-characters for thematic content, in order by this means to enliven the neutral symphonic thematic structure with concepts of concrete significance. Though Wagner no longer had visions of musical intervals in bodily shape, of or themes engaged in a battle of coloured inks, his musical imagination was in reality no less concrete than before. It was incapable of receiving and retaining impressions save from concrete, visually conceived subjects. His strongest impressions of concrete actuality were derived from the works of two creative artists, one of whom directed his attention to the theatre, the other to music. It was Shakespeare who drew him to the theatre and Wagner's reading of the plays resulted in the *Leubald* sketch, representing a general survey of Shakespearean tragedy from *Hamlet*, *Othello* and *Macbeth* to *Lear*. It was Beethoven who drew him to music and whose strains were destined to lend the characters in *Leubald* supplementary justification, making the imitator of Shakespeare an imitator of Beethoven, a composer of symphonies and overtures. Wagner no longer found poetry practicable without music. Literature as such lay outside his sphere of interest, and where it was associated with drama it spurred him to musical imitation. But music without the stage was for him equally impracticable. Alone it could not supply any initial formative impulse, and tended to grope towards the theatre, or at least to a ballad-like contrast of themes. A union of poetry and music in spoken drama seemed equally inadequate, for it provided the musician with merely episodic opportunities and subordinated him to the poet. Wagner tried all these forms, including the play with appropriate incidental music and overture and the pure symphony without any underlying dramatic and poetic idea. His desires reached out to both these spheres, attempting to comprehend in one the worlds of Shakespeare and of Beethoven, to make the drama emit sound, the music appear on the stage. In opera these things were possible. Wagner went to Vienna and to Prague, where old Dionys Weber's talk of his acquaintance with Mozart, his praise of the young composer's symphony and his arrangement for its performance by the Conservatoire orchestra, stimulated his youthful enthusiasm to a bold decision. Wagner wrote his first operatic sketch and began at once upon its composition.

The subject he chose was wildly fantastic and little less gruesome than the blood-and-thunder romanticism of *Leubald.* " A demented lover climbs to the bed-chamber where his friend's bride awaits the bridegroom's coming ; the bride struggles with him and hurls him down to his death in the courtyard below. At the funeral the bride throws herself with a cry upon the corpse and expires." The framework of the action was supplied by Büsching's book on chivalry, by Wagner's own experience of jealousy in a love affair at Prague, and by Immermann's *Cardenio and Celinde.* The motive is a typically Romantic one—the idea of the guilt of errant love and " the mystic strength of concealed passion." It is an idea that lived on in Wagner, reappearing in *Tristan,* and even in *The Dusk of the Gods.* Wagner at first intended to make a short story of the subject, whose crude contrasts stimulated his interest and very quickly impelled him to musical composition. The work opens with a solemn chorus whose middle section, assigned to female voices, foreshadows the Messengers of Peace chorus in *Rienzi,* while the alternating passages for male and female voices which surround it are reminiscent of the second *Fidelio* finale. Between this chorus and the concluding septet (which reverts again to Beethoven's diction) is a characteristic recitative in which the " stranger guest " is portrayed by a very pregnant, rhythmical, motive-like, recurrent bass phrase.

When the work had got thus far, Wagner tore up the libretto and the score was never finished. His sister Rosalie, who was his adviser in all theatrical questions, objected to the subject for its crude situations. Wagner abandoned his project, though Weinlig was particularly pleased with the septet " on account," says the Autobiography, " of its clarity and singableness."

Was it indeed, as Wagner represented later, Rosalie's dislike for his plot that determined its rejection ? Was it not rather that the slight prospect of so outspoken a story's ever being actually produced on any stage was supplemented by some even deeper reason for its abandonment ? Wagner himself draws attention to a connection between the sketch for *Die Hochzeit* and the earlier *Leubald* plan. Both are the outcome of a theatrical emotional conception which obsessed Wagner—the conception of the love-emotion astray in the everyday world, and of the victory of feeling over the deceptive world of phenomena. That Wagner derived this subject of drama purely from his theatrical instinct and not in the least from actual experience is proved by its very early appearance, first in the " shocker," *Leubald*, and next in *Die Hochzeit*, a more closely knit piece of drama than the former though still full of boyish delight in horror for horror's sake. It was a subject upon which Shakespeare and Beethoven (as Wagner understood them) found common ground—Shakespeare, the dramatist of the fantastic and monstrous, Beethoven, expressing the wildest transports of passion in music. Striking economy is observed in the elements of the plot, and Wagner is justified in speaking of his " scorn of all extraneous operatic decoration " in his sketch for *Die Hochzeit*. Here, too, we catch the first hint of conflict between the young composer and his environment. Rosalie missed just those things which he had purposely omitted ; she wanted " the simple facts " to be " developed and embellished to give more varied and more sympathetic situations." The family verdict on the sketch for *Die Hochzeit* foreshadows future conflicts, and might well cause the nineteen-year-old Wagner to ask himself how far he was qualified to solve the problem before him. This was the second time it had presented itself, evoked

rather by the rash courage of his theatrical instincts than by any deep
interior urge. For the moment his creative impulse was satisfied with
having begun the musical execution of the sketch, but there was need
of some model to complete it and to form the kernel of the whole work.
Where, in opera, was he to find an example of that which he envisaged?

This is but the first instance of an oft-repeated incident in Wagner's
career ; he conceives some theatrical vision, sets it down in outline,
writes the libretto, begins to compose—and leaves it for a time incomplete. In addition to the theatrical idea he needs something more—
some impression, some experience of life itself—to arouse in him
emotion—his only avenue to music. The emotional *gesture* is present
to his visual imagination, but the emotional *tone* refuses to sound in his
auditory imagination. It is a process typical of the theatrical musician.
He envisages the situation scenically and in action, but the vitalising
motive power is absent, and this can only be supplied as he gradually
discovers his own powers of emotional receptivity. Thus ended this
second glimpse of one of the basic situations of Wagnerian drama—
—ended not because of his sister's opposition, not because performance
was unlikely, but because he himself failed a second time to retain it
and to realise it, because he had not as yet gathered sufficient impressions for " enraptured overflow " in expression.

The impressions, when they came, came both from the actualities
of the stage and the realities of life. Wagner at this time came into
touch with the liberal revolutionary circles of " Young Germany,"
with Heinrich Laube at their head. Laube was then editing his
Zeitung für die Elegante Welt in Leipzig and, as a critic, soon got to
know the Wagner family. Wagner and he discussed a plan for col-
laborating in an opera, *Kosziusko*, inspired, no doubt, by the Polish
rising. They talked at large of philosophy, art, music, and life. To
Wagner, still a somewhat nebulous-minded and happy-go-lucky
youth, Laube's wide experience, confident judgments, breadth of
outlook, and true sense of proportion in both practical and intellectual
matters, were a revelation of what a secure and resolute personality
might be. This new friend quite eclipsed the amiable figure of Uncle
Adolf, brother of Wagner's father and acknowledged head and
adviser of the family, with his little book-shop, his dislike of the
theatre, his romantically studious literary dilettantism. Actually, it
was less Laube's conversation than the brilliant figure he cut as a man
who had early won fame and commanded respect which excited and

stimulated Wagner at a time when his self-consciousness and ambition were heightened by the forthcoming performance of his symphony at the Gewandhaus in January 1833. Previous experiences made it quite certain that his next venture would be a theatrical one. The draft of *Die Hochzeit* faithfully indicated in what direction the venture would lie, though in this case the path selected had proved impassable. The actual stage offered a number of other models. Heinrich Marschner had followed in the footsteps of the Weber of the *Freischütz* songs, of the chivalry of *Euryanthe*, of the fairy magic of *Oberon*. Marschner's *Vampire, The Templar and the Jewess, The Falconer's Bride*, had added a new realm of passion-charged magic to the emotional theatre. Visions of enchantment and of the uncanny, unknown to Beethoven, went some way to supplant in Wagner the crude excess of passion underlying *Die Hochzeit*. Impressions received from this new species of opera directed his thirst for strange plots and stirring scenes into a fairy-tale world. One of Gozzi's poems suggested a suitable outline and he laid out the plan of *Die Feen*.

Outward circumstances lent aid. Wagner's brother, Albert, who was employed as a singer and producer in Würzburg, got him an invitation from the Würzburger Musikverein to go there and produce an overture, doubtless with some idea of keeping the black sheep of the family under his own eye and putting him in the way of a profession. A few days after the performance of the symphony at the Gewandhaus, in January 1833, Wagner set out for Würzburg. There he was offered the post of choirmaster in the theatre at a small salary, the first step in the practical career of a professional Kapellmeister. During the summer vacation his married brother went for a holiday, leaving Wagner to look after the children, so that he stayed on in Würzburg and resumed his work at the opening of the new season. On his hurried return to Leipzig, early in January 1834, he carried with him the score of a new three-act opera, intending to get it produced in that city forthwith.

" Beethoven and Weber were my models," writes Wagner, referring to *Die Feen* in his 1842 autobiographical sketch. The *Mitteilung an meine Freunde* is more detailed. " Weber's romantic opera, predominant at that time, and the work of Marschner which was just then becoming known in my own city, Leipzig, spurred me to imitation. I made myself exactly the operatic text I wanted and set it to music in accordance with impressions gained from Beethoven, Weber and Marschner (who has been very unjustly called an imitator of Weber). Nevertheless I was drawn to Gozzi's fairy-tale not merely because I found it very suitable for an operatic libretto, but because of the vivid appeal of the story itself." Wagner then briefly summarises the action of the plot. " A fairy renounces her immortality for the sake of her mortal lover, but she can only attain mortality upon certain hard conditions, whose non-fulfilment, on her mortal lover's part, must subject her to a most terrible fate. The lover fails in the test, which was that he must never lose faith in the fairy in howsoever cruel and evil a guise she might (under magic compulsion) appear to him. In Gozzi's story the fairy is changed into a serpent, the repentant lover breaks the spell by kissing the snake and thus wins her to wife. I altered this conclusion. The fairy, having been changed to stone, is released by the mortal's yearning love-song, and for this deed he is admitted by the Fairy King to the immortal joys of fairy-land—not sent back to earth with the bride he has won. Even now I think the point not unimportant. It was suggested at the time by the music and the usual operatic conventions, but it contained in germ an important element in my whole course of development."

This retrospective estimate, written in 1851, of the *Die Feen* plan is a full statement of the case. Characteristic, however, is Wagner's emphasis not only on his alteration in the conclusion of the poem, but on his choice and execution of the subject itself, regarded as scenic and musical form. His reference to Weber and Marschner as his more immediate sources of inspiration, and his less emphatic mention of Beethoven by way of completing the tale of youthful influences, is also very just. The drop of Beethoven which he had absorbed, overflowing in his desire to impart to others his own experience of Beethoven, influenced him from the symphony to the sketch for *Die Hochzeit*, when it suddenly disappeared below the surface to run like an underground stream in the deeps of his soul, and to well up to daylight once more in the stormy music of *The Flying Dutchman*. Wagner's new interest in opera fed his imagination with a series of new impressions. Faced with two possible methods of expressionist art— passionate emotion working from within outwards, and illuminating tone-formation shining inwards from without—the romantic operatic view-point influenced him to choose the latter. Opera of this type is a picture-show, a story—a play of external contrasts in light and colour, in which the human motive is subordinate to the working of non-human natural and supernatural forces. The strongest and most mysterious of these forces is, however, music. Music is power made audible ; it subdues all to its spell ; its notes determine the incidents which enmesh the figures of the drama, making them mere tools without will of their own. When Oberon winds his magic horn all who hear it are forced to obey.

This conception of music as *primal magic* came to Wagner from the romantic operas of Weber and Marschner, wooing him from the interior music of passion whose language he had learned from Beethoven. The plot of *Die Feen* shows no individual passions, and scarcely an individual figure. Its charm, as Wagner says, consists in the interweaving of a variety of fantastic situations. Only music's magic can call these into being, ravel and unravel them. Music is thus the central interest of the whole process. Musical sound itself is made the subject of drama, and the magic in the plot is simply the magic of the world of tone in which it is unfolded. Music acquires content by transposition into a world of concrete phenomena, and the outward story or fable that inspires this content must, for its part, dissolve completely into the musical atmosphere which envelops it. The instinct which led Wagner to aim at this dissolution and prompted the changed ending of the story, Ada's disenchantment through Arindal's song and the acceptance of Arindal into the world of the immortals, is indeed " an important element " in Wagner's development. It must not, however, be confused with the " liberation idea," intellectually understood. It is part of a more general tendency of all concrete phenomena to dissolve in the element of sound which is the life and meaning of the whole work.

Die Feen is Wagner's earliest, premonitory attempt to build a concrete world out of the world of sound. He goes to foreign sources for his plot, and is inevitably completely dominated by the models he enumerates in plot-construction, characterisation, musico-scenic forms, and even melody. His *method* of imitation, however, makes his Romantic opera appear as mask-like as the former symphonic imitation of Beethoven. Yet because Wagner has concentrated on the theatrical effectiveness of the structural formulae he borrows from his models, he succeeds for the first time in achieving those types of musical expression through which music becomes incarnate in the dramatic scene. His peculiar gift of musical visualisation, which showed very early and gave rise to fantastic visions of sound, finds expression at last in a work bearing the outward semblance of Romantic opera, and lends this work—the first in which libretto and music are by a single hand—the strange double character of a plot which is in reality music, and a score which is in reality dramatic incident.

The author was unaware of either of these facts, believing that he was writing " Romantic opera." They were equally hidden from his contemporaries, who, such as heard the work at all, saw nothing in it but imitation. Subsequent developments alone could reveal the peculiarities of this work, and these show *Die Feen* to have been the starting point of a cycle which runs through Wagner's work, embracing *Rienzi, Lohengrin, The Nibelungs,* and closing in the first and last acts of *Parsifal.* This cycle comprises the phenomena of a diatonic harmony, which is displayed in its twofold function as a harmonic complex, and as melody analysed diatonically and in chords. Harmony as an unbroken whole finds representation in the scenic idea of a mystery, a guarded secret. Melody, rising and falling by intervals, strives to attain to the marvel of the mystic chord, and has all the time a parallel in the accompanying dramatic action. The idea of these musical movements as being interchangeable with dramatic incidents, of tone as visible and of the visible as tonal, leads to the establishment of certain basic musico-scenic types. Absolute harmony (portraying the sphere of the miraculous) cannot retain its rounded integrity if questions intrude upon it ; it is represented in *Die Feen* by introductory major triads, with their fivefold modulation through upper dominants. From these emerges a melodic line, ascending through the chord, which is a feature in Wagner's work from the beginning of the overture of *Die Feen* to the epilogue of the Messengers of Peace chorus, the *Faust* overture, the surging love- and fire-magic of Brynhilda and the Good Friday music in *Parsifal,* and which forms his basic musico-scenic symbol of aspiration towards harmonic fulfilment. These chordal formations are supplemented by melodic types that rise and fall step by step. In *Die Feen* the ascending line leads from the opening choral romance to the solemn closing song " Gegrüsst sei Arindal im hohen Feenreiche " ; it reappears in Senta's tender duet " Er steht vor mir mit leidenvollen Zügen," in the Grace theme in *Tannhäuser,* and thereafter in many guises up to the Grail theme in *Parsifal.* The descending, diatonic, line, first found in the overture of *Die Feen,* appears in the stretto of *The Flying Dutchman* duet, in Tannhäuser's " Ha, jetzt erkenne ich sie wieder," in the Brynhilda melodies, and so, through continual changes in rhythmic and tonal accent, persists in Wagner's last work, *Parsifal.*

These recurrent resemblances, more or less striking, are never fortuitous. A world of harmonic tone, based on the fundamental concept of the wonder-working pure chord, is sub-divided into a number of set action-types, whose acoustic and scenic characters tally perfectly. This idea, seen for the first time under the mask of Romantic opera in *Die Feen,* thereafter gradually reveals its significance in increasing precision of expression. The movements used are functionally the simplest possible within the harmonic space. In a symphony they would appear musically meaningless and insipid, but united, as they are, with the stage, their dynamic significance affects the imagination pictorially. Through this the musical theme at once acquires a plasticity of dramatic expression which Wagner could not achieve in a purely instrumental sphere.

The most important gain to Wagner from this work was his acquisition, through the impression made on his mind by Romantic opera, of certain basic types of musico-scenic expression. He also got practical experience of vocal composition, receiving valuable criticisms and suggestions from his brother Albert on the construction of the big concerted forms, especially in the elaborate second finale. There are also certain scenes in the work which foreshadow future mature successes in the construction of effective climaxes. Certain musical details in Arindal's mad scene point directly to Sieglinde's mad scene. The youthful composer had suddenly struck down to the foundations of his own genius. In *Die Feen* he succeeded in casting the creatures of a boy's dreams in the reality of musical form, and he infused into the work all that seemed to him worth preserving from his earlier essays. The pianoforte fantasia in F sharp minor, written when under Weinlig's tutelage, furnishes several melodic features, and even the *Faust* occasional music pays tribute in Gretchen's melodramatic " Ach neige, du Schmerzensreiche," now changed from the minor to the major and used as a subordinate theme in the overture.

The work as a whole, prolix and disconnected in plot and reminiscent in its melodic character, its flowery connecting passages, its instrumentation, now in Weber's phraseology, now in Marschner's rigid rhythms and cruder harmony, forms an imposing score, and

Wagner, returning home after a year's absence, might well present the three fat volumes to " a highly delighted mother and sister " in an " uncommonly self-confident and satisfied humour." His work contained everything that could be expected of a proper romantic, fairy-tale opera—decorative scenes, as pretty or as horrible as such scenes could be, and, mingled with the human actors, fays and gnomes and strange creatures made of bronze, spirits visible and invisible, peasants and warriors, and all the implements of wizardry in the greatest variety—a magic sword and shield and lyre, a singing stone, and a fiery grot into which the children of the lovers are cast by their own mother. All devices to excite the fancy used in opera from *The Magic Flute* to *The Vampire* are here assembled. Grotesque as this display of magic may be in itself, the skill with which everything available in that kind is introduced, and to some extent ordered, is truly astonishing. Notwithstanding Rosalie's active exertions, however, Wagner found difficulties in getting the work accepted. To explain this there is no need of Wagner's story of the Mendelssohn-loving manager Hauser's hostility to his " tendencies." No intrigue is needed to account for an opposition which was due to the character of the work. From a contemporary point of view not only was it an exaggerated hotch-potch of operatic effects in inartistic combination, but it lacked attractions for the actor and producer. Wagner had made scenes and pictures, he had called upon music to conjure a luxuriant sequence of fantastic stage events, he had written choruses, arias and ensembles in the approved style, but the figures he had placed within this setting and to whom he had entrusted the action were something less than the mere types used by those he imitated. They were nothing but vocally endowed shadows, designed to illustrate a story, and they lacked any sort of individuality, even a purely theatrical one.

This deficiency was inherent in Wagner's initial approach to his task. He was imitating a *form* of art, and an interpretative personality was as yet outside the range of his experience. The experience came to him, however, within a few weeks of his return home. In March 1834 Wilhelmina Schroeder-Devrient came to Leipzig to sing as Romeo in Bellini's opera. Wagner had heard this great singer some years previously as Fidelio, but not till now did the magic spell of her personality have practical results. Wagner received from her the most powerful impression he ever received from any artistic effort, an impression that was repeated every time he came in contact with this artist. " The most distant contact with this remarkable woman was to me electrical," writes Wagner, " and to this very day I invariably see, hear and feel her whenever I feel the urge to artistic creation." Wagner's uniformly enthusiastic references to Schroeder-Devrient from their first meeting to the *Parsifal* period prove that she made an impression on his receptive faculties comparable for depth and power with that made by two other artists only—Beethoven and Shakespeare. Indeed, in certain ways the former exceeded the latter, for it united them and gave them immediacy and objectivity. The secrets of those two great artists of the past, only revealed through imitative imagination, became in her part of a living, speaking present. Wagner felt the power which an inspired theatrical artist exerts through the emotional appeal of music. Here was the very mystery of passion revealed to all the senses simultaneously—through visible gesture, through the sound of the voice ; here was the creative art of plastic imagery giving ultimate expression to the artistic vision. Expression itself acquired form, mimic genius became a natural force incarnate in this singing, acting woman. In the greatest woman artist he ever encountered, Wagner suddenly saw revealed the true nature of inter-pretative genius. His human experience at this time matched his revolutionary experience as an artist. " For me," says Wagner, " woman began to exist." On the one hand there came to him with the consciousness of manhood the awakening demands and joys of the senses, on the other this phenomenal artist whose interpretation made something great and heart-shaking out of the trivial Italian music that she sang. Romantic opera now seemed a shadowy thing and Wagner woke to music not as a spell to conjure imaginary worlds and scenes, but as the voice of the sensuous tumult in the blood—not of that great, pathetic passion expressed by Beethoven, but of bodily desire. Here was a new basis of drama, centring in, and swayed by, sensual woman conceived on heroic lines. Music becomes identi-fied with such a woman ; all the elements and complications of the drama must originate in her. The world of harmonic, diatonic types fades, giving place to one dominated by personal, passion-inspired melody, a language of complicated modulation and chromatic accen-tuation. Thus begins the *second* cycle of expression, linking *Tann-häuser, Tristan,* and the Venusberg music with the second act of *Parsifal.* The point of departure is *Das Liebesverbot.*

G

The sudden and stormy revulsion which reversed Wagner's previous orientation found expression not only in but also outside his changed attitude to music. He found that Laube's poor opinion of German Romantic opera was fully justified ; in fact, he felt impelled to express this opinion himself. In the June number of the *Zeitung für die elegante Welt*, that is to say barely six months after the completion of *Die Feen*, Wagner wrote an article on " German Opera " in which he embraced in one sweeping condemnation Weber (" who cannot write vocal parts ") as " a purely lyrical genius," unequal to opera, *Euryanthe* as " a piece of petty sophistry," and German opera *in toto* as foolish pedantry. " We must shake off this rubbish that is threatening to choke us, get rid of a good deal of affected counterpoint, cease to regard fifths and augmented ninths as reprehensible, and become real *men*. . . . Why is it that no German opera-composer has come to the fore for so long ? Because none can speak with the people's voice— that is to say, because none lays hold of life as it is, real and warm. . . . We must lay hold on the time and try genuinely to cultivate its new forms. The new operatic master will write not Italian or French, but German."

The words " lay hold on " are the key to this article, and they are used by Wagner in almost the same way a few months later, in November 1834, in the *Pasticcio* published as a *canto spianato* in Schumann's *Neue Zeitschrift für Musik*. " Our modern romantic grimaces are foolish phantoms. Away with them—lay hold of real passion ! Man can only feel for what is human, and the dramatic singer can represent none but human emotions. It has been said often enough, though you will not believe it, that one thing only is requisite in opera, and that is *poetry* !—words and notes are merely its expression."

Such were the stormy petrels that heralded *Das Liebesverbot*. Wagner is not very precise as to what he means by *poetry* in the last sentence, though it is clear from what follows that he does not mean versification. He means that which *grips*, that which has just been revealed to him in the example of a great operatic and dramatic singer—the concrete impact of the drama as it flows from the flesh-and-blood actor. Meanwhile the mighty wave that had carried him so far beyond his own immediate past had not left his personal life unaffected. In June, while on holiday in Teplitz, he planned *Das Liebesverbot* after Shakespeare's *Measure for Measure*. A month later he took up his first independent post as Music-director of the Bethmann company, which played during the summer in Lauchstädt and Rudolstadt and had permanent winter headquarters in Magdeburg. Wagner, at twenty-one years old, now found himself artistically and financially his own master. He was swept into the whirlpool of theatrical life, his longed-for world of *Zampa* and *Tancred* and *Fra Diavolo*, of rehearsals and performances, of larks and escapades. Schroeder-Devrient herself came to sing under his direction and actually assisted at a benefit concert on his behalf in which he tried in vain to " grip " the Magdeburg public with Beethoven's *Battle of Vittoria*. He opened the year 1835 at his theatre with a New Year cantata, in which his beloved andante theme from the symphony reappeared to symbolise the Old Year. The summer brought practical worries. The finances of the theatre were precarious and Wagner's own gay life had heaped up debts. There was a violent and mortifying quarrel with his rich brother-in-law, Friedrich Brockhaus. Wagner's mother attempted admonishments and reconcilements. He went again to Teplitz under pretext of looking round for actors on behalf of the manager, proceeded to Karlsbad and Prague, and returned by way of Nuremberg, where his sister Clara and her husband had an engagement. With the opening of the new season the financial position of the management went from bad to worse. They could scarcely struggle through the season. The last performance took place on March 29, 1836. A repetition fixed for the 30th was cancelled owing to a quarrel among the actors themselves. The work thus victimised after a single performance was *Das Liebes-verbot*. The benefit performance that failed to come off was to have helped the twenty-two-year-old composer to clear his debts. The somewhat frivolous view of art which Wagner had adopted after his return from Würzburg had reacted upon his more mundane affairs. He found himself Kapellmeister to a bankrupt theatrical company, engaged to a pretty actress, like himself out of a job, deeply in debt without prospect of new employment, author of several articles deriding Romantic opera, and composer of a work of which the manager of the Leipzig theatre said that " the Town Council would never give permission for the performance of such a thing ! "

" It was Isabella who inspired me—a girl-novice who leaves her convent to beg from a hard-hearted governor pardon for her brother who, under a draconian law, has been condemned to death for an illicit love affair. In the presence of the cold judge Isabella's chaste soul finds such cogent reasons for the forgiveness of this crime, and her intense emotion enables her to present her reasons with such persuasive warmth, that the severe moralist finds himself seized with passion for this glorious woman, and his suddenly kindled flame prompts him to promise pardon for the brother at the price of the lovely sister's favours. Horrified by these proposals, Isabella resorts to a trick to unmask the hypocrite and save her brother. Shakespeare settles the conflict by the return in public of the Prince who has been watching all the proceedings incognito. I, on the other hand, unravel the knot without the intervention of a Prince, by means of a revolution. I change the scene to the Sicilian capital so that I may have the support of the hot southern temperament. I make the governor, a puritanical German, forbid a carnival for which the people are preparing. A desperate young man, in love with Isabella, urges the populace to mask and hold their swords in readiness :

> " Wer sich nicht freut bei unser Lust,
>   Dem stosst dass Messer in die Brust ! "
> (" He who disdains our joy to feel
>   Shall in his breast receive the steel ! ")

The governor, persuaded by Isabella to come masked to a rendezvous, is discovered, unmasked and laughed to scorn. The brother is rescued, just in time, by force of arms from his impending execution. Isabella renounces her novitiate and gives her hand to the wild young leader of the carnival. The whole masked populace advances to meet the returning Prince, who, one supposes, is not so mad as his governor."

This account is taken from *Mitteilung an meine Freunde*. It makes no mention of the broad *buffo* scenes interspersed throughout the opera, in which the true basis of the work is revealed as rough-and-tumble comedy, bordering on farce. This strolling-player spirit is the origin both of the uncouth jesting of the *buffo* marionettes and the heroics of the central feminine figure. The *stage*, no longer a magic mirror of musical action, but a focus of mimetic gesture governed by music, is the origin and end of the whole work. Wagner's musical form no longer wears the mask of Romanticism, but is moulded in the image of the then fashionable song-opera upon which his sketch is based. " The *Liebesverbot* music, also, exercised in advance a formative and selective influence on the plot, and this music was none other than the reflex upon my excited sensual perceptions of modern French influences and (as regards melody) of Italian opera."

The process is exactly the same as with the symphony and *Die Feen* ; only the occasions differ. Wagner's receptive faculty first seeks some impression. Whether this is derived from Beethoven, from Weber and Marschner, or from Donizetti and Auber, is of secondary importance. Proof of the essential unity and consistency of the recipient's nature does not rest on similarity in the matter reproduced. Rather does that nature show its transmogrifying power by the contrasts between its chosen models. Sudden and violent changes are necessary to its activities. It must be continually refilled with new material in order, by the method of reproduction, to show its peculiar quality— that is, a capacity for assuming a series of masks, and permeating its material according to the canons of representational art.

The music of *Das Liebesverbot*, accordingly, has a formal structure diametrically opposed to that of *Die Feen*. The latter is crystallised about the miraculous phenomenon of harmony, whose analysis gives rise to diatonic and progressive melodic types, while in *Das Liebesverbot* the human singing voice, directed to dramatic effect, forms the fulcrum of the work. In this opera we have song as an expression of individual character at the basis of musical expression— song as a demonstration of the personal and human, linked with the temperament and passion of the singer. Here, too, emerge the two main types under which Wagner conceives the expressive capacity of the human voice. The baritone, full of passionate yearning appeal, is the vocal type that represents the masculine character ; it appears here in the governor, Friedrich, and later in the Flying Dutchman, Wotan, Hans Sachs, and Amfortas. Contrasted with the baritone is the dramatic soprano, vocal type of the feminine character, exemplified in all Wagner's heroic female figures from Isabella to Kundry. Thus Wagner sets up the elemental figures in his vocal drama in accordance with the elemental emotions associated with their peculiar turn of expression. He recognises and uses the effective possibilities of these voices as contrasting dramatic characters—the aria-like, declamatory monologue of the man, the passionate song of the woman, the union of the two in the duet. In *Das Liebesverbot* all this is accomplished within the framework of Franco-Italian opera, but the form that outwardly dominates this work has as little to do with its artistic essence as has the form and manner of Romantic opera with the essence of *Die Feen*.   None the less, in the former work as in the latter, the form does very effectively conceal the essence.

The establishment, as here, of certain vocal dramatic types to represent *Man* and *Woman* was to dominate all Wagner's work.   It was to give rise to new and greater conceptions, just as the types of musical movement in *Die Feen* were to reappear, in various guises, throughout his work.   The representational vocal type led to a special method of melodic stylisation, not harmonic and orchestral, but chromatic and vocal, the laws of expressive vocalisation causing it to contrast, as a living, intensive, human sound, with the abstract sounds of the orchestra.   Nearly all these melodies show a chromatic texture, which, assigned them as an element of development and prolongation, also constitutes the backbone of the melodic line. This is strikingly concise as compared with the broad periodisation of the melody of *Die Feen*.   The Italianate structure serves merely as an aid to song formation.   Imitation is most apparent where the style governs in externals ; it is apparent at all times, indeed, when the two central figures are not present to exercise direct stimulus upon the composer's musical-dramatic instinct.   The drama of singing voices is most forceful in Friedrich's passionate monologues and in Isabella's tearful, pleading, heroic songs.   The two are brought together in the grand duet of the first finale.   The main thread of the piece runs from Isabella's intercession to Friedrich's change of sentiment, and thence to the summoning of the mob, where there is a sudden swerve away from an expected tragic climax to clumsy high spirits.   These are the moments at which the miming impulse asserts itself most vehemently, where " word and note " become mere " expression " for the " poetry " of the theatrical scene.   By contrast with this basic intention the music as such is of very little value.   The Judge's declamatory sentence, announced in the overture, persists throughout the work as a reminiscent motif.   An anticipation of the Faith theme from *Tannhäuser*, here used to express the peace of the cloister, it is an example of the basic musical symbol invariably accompanying certain dramatic situations to hint at an essential identity beneath outward changes.

Das Liebesverbot is the complement of *Die Feen*.   In each Wagner succeeds in expressing, under the mask of a set form, something which was peculiarly his and which had nothing to do with that form.   By imitation he exercised and increased his gift for imitation, and by submitting to the spell of one impression after another in his insatiable thirst to take in and absorb, he acknowledged that the primal law of his will as an artist was *ex*pression, in the sense of reproduction of *im*pression. His art was never immediately spontaneous ; the work of others inspired him with the power of reproduction, and his *daemon* drove him remorselessly from model to model, from Beethoven to Romanticism, from Romanticism to Italian *canto*.

The emotions aroused by this latter model had now been discharged. But Wagner had produced a work with as little real survival value as that which preceded it. To the spectator imitation was still the predominant feature, and the work's individual qualities appeared merely incidental and disturbing to the general effect. The latest model's power of giving Wagner impressions was exhausted, and meanwhile practical difficulties increased amain. His debts made Leipzig too hot to hold him ; there was no chance at all of getting *Das Liebesverbot* accepted in that city. The young composer went to Berlin, hoping to get a post at the Königstädtisches theatre, but this prospect came to naught. He travelled on in high hopes to Königsberg, where Minna Planer had found employment, but there too he could find nothing. He applied to Riga and got not even an answer. Being now entirely destitute financially, he married. In the spring of 1837 the post of music director in Königsberg at last became vacant, but scarcely had he taken up his duties when the theatre went bankrupt. His young wife eloped with a lover. Wagner pursued the couple in vain, and then drifted undecidedly in the direction of Dresden by way of Berlin. Here at last a ray of hope pierced the clouds. Franz von Holtei, formerly *Singspiel* director and stage manager of the Königstädtisches theatre, had taken over the management of the Riga theatre. He collected a new personnel and engaged Wagner as Kapellmeister. Wagner entered on his new duties in the middle of August 1837, and before the year ended Minna returned to him. The last act of his life's prelude had begun.

The eighteen months between the performance of *Das Liebesverbot* in Magdeburg in March 1836 and his appointment to the post in Riga mark the lowest ebb in Wagner's fortunes hitherto. Lack of money was not his only trouble. This difficulty was to recur frequently and in even acuter form in immediately subsequent years and in later life. Moreover, on this occasion he met it with a cynicism and frivolity such as he showed once only in after years, that is to say just before his summons to Munich. The reason in both instances was not weight of practical cares, but a sudden flagging of the creative impulse. The years from 1832 to 1836 had seen the assimilation of a great number of impressions. One stimulus followed another, each providing an antithesis to that which preceded it. Wagner took increasing delight in assuming the masks of a variety of art-forms, till the carnival mood of *Das Liebesverbot* overflowed into his actual conduct of life and hurled the artist into a whirlpool of intoxicating excitements and wild escapades, culminating in an imprudent marriage. Suddenly sobriety returned. Wagner found himself completely at a loss ; his soul was barren and empty of all impressions. By comparison with earlier efforts his work at this period is hardly worth mention. A *Polonia*, sketched in Leipzig, was completed in Berlin. The *Rule, Britannia !* overture was finished in Königsberg. Both are pompous, noisy, orchestral pieces based on well-known airs. A third work, *Napoleon*, in which the emperor's fall was to be symbolised by a gong-stroke, was never executed. " I believe," runs the autobiography, " that it was my doubts as to the admissibility of this gong-stroke which, more particularly, kept me from carrying out my scheme. On the other hand my reflections on the ill-success of the performance of my *Liebesverbot* persuaded me to draft a theatrical piece in which the demands made upon the soloists and chorus should bear more suitable relation to the known conditions of the one small provincial theatre accessible to me." Wagner thus relinquished the exceptional standards in accordance with which he had designed the figures of Isabella and Friedrich. Not Madame Schroeder-Devrient but the typical provincial singer to be found in Magdeburg or Königsberg was to set the standard in a comic operatic sketch, *Die Glückliche Bärenfamilie*, taken from the *Arabian Nights*. It was a mere desperate attempt to do *something*, and it got no farther than the initial stages. The plight of genius with nothing to work upon created a wilderness for Wagner, and the de-grading embarrassment of his outward circumstances at this time only served to mirror his inner resourcelessness.

One remarkable experience, however, occurred in this time of stagnation. Wagner heard Spontini conduct a performance of *Ferdinand Cortez* in Berlin. A new conception burst upon his soul— a revelation of grand opera, not as an aesthetic idea buried between the leaves of a music-book, but as an actual, living, stage performance, a new form of theatrical art. "Though the actual performance left me cold," writes Wagner, "particularly that of the leading singers, none of whom could be said to belong to the flower of Berlin opera, and though none made an impression upon me even approaching that of Madame Schroeder-Devrient, yet the remarkable precision and fire of the production, the richly ordered *ensemble*, was something new to me. It gave me a fresh sense of the peculiar dignity of theatrical performances on the grand scale, performances in which all the details combine, through rhythmic precision, to achieve an incomparable form of art. This very deep impression survived and continued to grow in me, giving rise in particular to my conception of *Rienzi*, so that, in an artistic sense, Berlin has left its mark on my career."

Here we have a description of a new impression, both in its general and its particular effects. After harmonic expression of pictorially treated sound, and melodic expression of the dramatically personified voice, we are to get an expression of heroic action on the grand scale. In this last *rhythm* is the dominant factor, and sustains the solo voice, the choral *ensemble*, and the formal arrangement of the whole, to achieve a solemn and ardent emotional effect. The powerful new impression Wagner received from grand opera indicated a new and hitherto unknown approach to "theatre," but the impression needed time to work itself out, a slow gathering of power, before it could discharge itself with full effect. Ruthless repression and compression of Wagner's natural stream of life were needed in order that it might acquire the resilience, the spring, to shoot up from the depths to the heights.

The performance of *Cortez* took place in the summer of 1836, and the first echo of the general idea of grand opera which it presented to Wagner was a draft for a libretto after a story by König called *Die Hohe Braut*.[1] In structure this work (a love story) shows Wagner's acceptance of the new art form, but its heroics are merely external and scenic, needing the fundamental significance which only a great historic figure could give. Wagner sent his libretto to Scribe in Paris for a critical opinion. The first copy sent was lost, and further correspondence led to nothing. Ten years later Wagner's friend Kittl, of Prague, composed the libretto after Reissiger had rejected it. In the meantime, during a farewell visit to Dresden, Bulwer's novel *Rienzi* came into Wagner's hands. The picture given in this book of a

[1] *The Exalted Bride.*

popular liberator seemed to endow Spontini's *Cortez* with new, visual life. It now became Wagner's ambition to equal this work, and not merely to equal but to surpass it, and so to reach the summit of theatrical art at a single stride. All the resources of the stage and of music were to be heaped in profusion and fused through the dramatic representational emotion of vocal melody, the dynamic variety of the harmonic scene, the elemental force of rhythmic pathos. Something hitherto unheard of and unthought of was to emerge; the artist's ambitions became identified with those of his hero, reacting upon his actual life just as the sensual intoxication of *Das Liebesverbot* had done before, and forcing him to exacerbate the contradiction between the world of his dreams and the world of reality about him. The more impracticable the *Rienzi* scheme became, having regard to its composer's actual circumstances, the more grandiose waxed Wagner's conceptions. Riga stood for the actuality, but beyond Riga he saw a vision, a vision of Paris, the Mecca of the theatrical world, the home of grand opera. Wagner was busy playing a new game—the game of grand opera. But to make the game real to him he needed to *see* the city in which this art-form was centred. He needed it exactly as he had needed Schroeder-Devrient in order to create his Isabella, though now the requisite was not an actress but the theatrical-artistic idea of a distant city. Wagner's audacious will wove a magic thread between the Duna and the Seine till imagination converted dream to actuality. The more he lost hold in Riga the more closely he laid hold on Paris till the final step was taken which made the dream become real. While in Magdeburg Wagner had written an overture to a play called *Columbus*, a curious sketchy piece of work differing in form and idea from his other orchestral compositions. It is a seascape, interpenetrated by a motif expressing " intense effort and desire." Visionary fanfares of trumpets engage in dialogue, often repeated and heightened by dynamic methods till they ring out at full strength. This foreshadowing of *The Flying Dutchman* conception leapt to Wagner's mind as he read Heine in Riga. But it is also an anticipatory indication of that yearning for the distant and unknown which promises fulfilment and in which the personality seeks its true destiny and its very self.

Wagner felt the need of self-realisation. Hitherto he had played with forms, but now he would play with his own soul. He would act the hero, he would conquer that Capitol, that distant *something* promised by his dreams of Columbus and the Flying Dutchman. Paris became his Rome, the German stage a corrupt patriciate, and he himself the liberator who should lead a people to victory and glory. His first really personal masquerade begins under cover of the most solemn of theatrical forms. The gestures are those of demi-gods rather than of men, and the rhythm of the work is based on the march, now in hymn-like guise, now in a broad flow of choral song, now in pathetic monologue. The shouts of the insurgents, the peace proclamations, the impassioned, monitory or pleading speeches, each rising to and ending in climax—all are conceived in close relation to the orchestration. Orchestra, staging, choruses, solos, the whole apparatus, technical or artistic, emotions and passions as well as décor and musical phrasing, are designed on the grand scale. Bulwer's Rienzi loves a woman, but Wagner's loves Rome to the exclusion of sexual passion. His sister, modelled on Amazily in *Cortez,* is permitted to love, but even her love has to be offered up as a sacrifice. Theatrical pathos clothes a very orgy of enthusiasm, and the result is a " great tragic opera in five acts : *Rienzi, the Last of the Tribunes.*"

CHAPTER II

RIENZI is divided into two parts; the first comprises the first two acts, dealing with " Rienzi's Might," the second the third, fourth, and fifth acts, dealing with "Rienzi's Fall." These two parts, the second of which was composed nine months later than the first, were originally performed as a single whole, but the immense length of the performance suggested that the work should be re-divided into the two sections in which it had been composed and given on two successive evenings. Subsequently these sections were " cut " and reunited, and it is according to this version that the score and pianoforte arrangements were published and have come down to posterity. Whether or to what extent a return to the authentic first version is desirable is no easy question. *Rienzi* bears the same relation to grand opera as does *Das Liebesverbot* to Italian opera and *Die Feen* to German Romantic opera— that is to say, it is an imitative exaggeration. By means of exaggeration Wagner achieves the meaning, the essence, of imitation, which is the transference of musical form from the sphere of pure music to the sphere of concrete representation. Form becomes the gesture in which it finds clear expression, and the emotional effect achieved by this form-gesture governs the whole work.

The two parts of *Rienzi* differ as to the significance underlying the form-gesture, and their external separation corresponds with a real interior antithesis. The first part only belongs, or could belong, to the Riga period. It is governed by the gesture of revolt, liberation, and conquest, a gesture of might and magic power which breaks out of the sphere of " absolute " art impressions and flings open the door on " real life " impressions, making Wagner's powers of receptivity and communication free for the future of the resources of both these worlds. *Rienzi's Might* is the mighty thirst for *life*. Equipped through previous impressions of art, this desire is destined henceforth to dominate and strengthen its former resources till they achieve that high level of communicative power which Wagner calls " the only truly poetical." This power dawns in *Rienzi's Might*, but it dawns only ; full daylight comes with *Rienzi's Fall*. The setting of the latter is not Riga but Paris, in which a fresh chapter of Wagner's book of life is opened, a chapter in which dark visions of Columbus and the Flying Dutchman, beckoning into the distance, cloud the bright figure of the Roman tribune.

The music of *Rienzi's Might* is Spontini's music under Wagner's showmanship. This is not, however, a matter of external resemblance but of the harmonic, emphatically rhetorical character of the melody, the broad generality of the harmonic effects, and, most of all, of the military-march-like structure of the form. Wagner's sympathy with Spontini, which is expressed in his obituary notice of this composer and also in certain anecdotes scattered through his writings, was based on a deep elective affinity between himself and this older master of grandiose pathos and theatrical fresco. The aging Spontini may, for his part, have recognised in the young Saxon Kapellmeister a kindred spirit, wielding the persuasive magic of the born theatrical despot. Common to both is a basic conception of theatrical art as the art of evoking mimic sympathetic emotions, of music as a means of achieving this, and of the stage as presenting sight and sound in indissoluble unity. Common also to both is their concentration of every artistic faculty upon the musical stage, their scorn for non-theatrical music of all kinds, and their fanatic faith in the importance of that theatrical musical art-form to which they devoted their very lives. Until Wagner's coming no other operatic composer devoted such care, such practical study as Spontini to the dramatic element in singing. Spontini relied as much on the *singing actor* as Gluck had done on the *singer*, and what his work lost in musical substance by comparison with that of his great model it gained in eloquence and concreteness of melodic gesture. Musical gesture in Spontini is naturally " short-winded," though rounded out and carried along by the undercurrent of rhetorical movement, and it is stylised by him in march form. With Spontini everything marches—passion and mourning, triumph and despair. In such an art the triumphal march is the natural summit, the supreme manifestation of power in dramatic musical emotional gesture.

An impression of this same triumphal march forms the primal gesture in *Rienzi's Might*. In various guises it dominates the principal forms of both acts, of the introduction and of the finale. Spontini's dignified and formal gait is, however, transmuted by Wagner's youthful impetuosity and excitable temperament. It borrows thrust and buoyancy from a " will to greatness," intoxicated by its own enthusiasms and fired by the inflammable matter of its subject. Thus it gives rise to the finest piece in the whole score—one of the most beautiful things in all Wagner's work—the chorus of Peace Messengers introducing the second act. Here is coruscating youthful vigour, under the spell of the impression received from grand opera, in all its pristine freshness. Youth itself salutes and pledges the glorious future of those awakening powers which are the true subject of the first part of *Rienzi* from beginning to end. That elemental soaring motif with which *Die Feen* opens and with which it closes in the greeting to Arindal is expanded here into a sweeping, luxuriant melodic decoration. The figure of *yearning* in the overture of *Die Feen* reappears, no longer in isolated phrases but as a sustained line, while the *ensemble* for women's voices from *Die Hochzeit* flows here in harmonic euphony. The middle movement is ballad-like in its simplicity and rises to a solemn close in a melodic line which, from henceforth to the opening theme of the *Parsifal* prelude, remains Wagner's fundamental musical symbol for grave tenderness. This rich and varied chorus for female voices is balanced by the two-part " Lateran choir " which, by virtue of its chorale-like *a capella* harmonies faintly foreshadows the " Wach auf " of *The Mastersingers*.

Side by side with these two main choral pieces are other march forms in great variety, including the first finale, expressive of insurgent tumult, from which is derived the allegro theme of the overture and Rienzi's *Hymn to Freedom*, passing into the stately *Chorus of the Oath*. An effective contrast is provided in the second finale, where a ballet pantomime illustrating an attempted assassination by the *nobili* is introduced in imitation of *Jessonda*. Issuing from the vigorous and dramatic choral music of the trial scene, a great adagio *ensemble* finds resolution in the turbulent and triumphant stretto of the second theme in the overture. The whole is choral, massive, rhythmic, ecstatic. The hero as orator, leader of the chorus, and soloist appears only occasionally amidst all these powerful and elevating scenes, and is presented solely in the light of emotions of glory and power. Wagner has based the writing of this part on the dazzling qualities of the tenor voice, its physical appeal and penetrating power. The brilliant tenor, Tichatschek, made such a startling success in the rôle in the Dresden production that he would not hear of its being shortened, though this same singer failed when he was required to interpret Tannhäuser.

The few solo pieces of the first part of *Rienzi*—the terzetto for Rienzi, Irene, and Adriano, the lovers' duet in the first act, and the opening *ensemble* of the conspirators in the second act—are almost lost among these mass effects. In *Rienzi's Fall* such pieces take precedence of the crowd scenes, but in the earlier part they serve merely as connecting links. The want of a prominent female rôle (a want partly met by giving the part of Adriano to an alto) and the absence of an erotic motive in the ground-plan of the work may have had a cramping effect. Adriano's passion (modelled on Schroeder-Devrient's interpretation of Romeo) is merely touched on in the earlier portion of the work and does not become prominent till the important scenes of the second part. Wagner did not intend to emphasise this theme. The motives that occupied his mind were joy, stormy brilliance, insurrection, and he put the explosive strength of his temperament only into matters which bore on these subjects.

That temperament gave him no rest. It drove him resistlessly forward beyond the bounds of the present work upon the quest for *life*, and indeed *Rienzi* itself, from first to last, is nothing but one long cry for life. Affairs in Riga had taken a turn which was to recur more than once in Wagner's career. At first he liked his work at the theatre, but no sooner had he exhausted the immediate stimulus it brought him than troubles and misunderstandings began to cloud the horizon. Debts accumulated and there were quarrels with the manager. Various circumstances conspired to dislodge Wagner from his post. In the spring of 1839 Holtei resigned the management, but before doing so he promised Heinrich Dorn, who was then living in Riga, that he should succeed Wagner next season. Wagner did not discover this threat to his livelihood till later, and it is not even now quite clear how far the arrangement was due to intrigue on Dorn's part, and how far there was good reason for dismissing Wagner. The fact that both Dorn and the new manager assisted Wagner in his flight from Mitau at the end of June rather suggests that there were cogent reasons for Wagner's disappearance from Riga.

This turn of affairs was a hard blow to Wagner from a practical standpoint, but he was none the less conscious of its inner necessity. Neither his debts nor the intrigues of Dorn and Holtei but his own work on *Rienzi* really drove him from Riga. The moment had come for him to enter upon the larger life of which hitherto he had but dreamed. The completion of the second act of *Rienzi* carried him to its threshold. He had now imitated Beethoven, Weber, Marschner, Donizetti, and, finally, Spontini, and, thus exercised, the only really individual and independent gift he possessed—representational power —had waxed strong. Models and theories had contributed all they could contribute, but what " absolute " art could no longer supply, what all the opera composed could never give, might yet be found at the actual seat of that art, in the city whose living will made opera live. Paris and Paris alone could help him. The time was ripe for a dream to be realised, and Wagner's path lay over the sea.

CHAPTER III

RIENZI'S FALL

EACH new stage in Wagner's career opens with his precipitate flight from a present whose possibilities he has sucked dry to a future of which he already has some shadowy premonition.   In 1849 his artistic *daemon* drove him to flee from Dresden and to sever, at his own personal cost, ties which had grown unfruitful for his art.   His flight with Jessie Laussot was, indeed, never more than a project, yet even so it served to liberate creative energy.   His flight from his Zurich " Asyl " to Venice was the final step to the ecstasy of *Tristan*.   His flight from Vienna into hiding was a last desperate effort to conjure a saving miracle.   His flight from Munich to Triebschen brought him to the side of the sleeping Brynhilda.   Wagner as a man was a mere executive instrument at the behest of his art, and was thus enabled to pass from achievement to achievement.   So, in this instance, the urgency of creditors and the loss of his job were not the real reasons of his flight from Riga.   He might have found other ways of adjusting these difficulties than by a crazy Paris venture.   The demands of *Rienzi* for completion forced him to act as he did, for although he was able to conceive the urge to heroic deeds even in an isolated Russian township on the Baltic, he had as yet insufficient experience of life to conceive their fulfilment.   Wagner would never be able to understand *Rienzi's Fall* without actual contact with the world to whose threshold he had been brought by his impulse to write *Rienzi's Might*.   That world was still outside his imagination's scope, but it was for him to conquer it.

Wagner was not conscious of this chain of reasons and actions which was forged nevertheless by his artistic will that constantly wove real events into its web.   He followed the deep-seated impulses of an artistic nature to which reality was but illusion, and illusion a higher kind of reality.   It was this higher reality that stimulated his actions. Wagner saw clearly that grand opera was not a mere artistic theory

which could be practised successfully in Dresden, Munich, or Riga.
He saw that it was a living mode of expression, whose nature and
workings could only be understood in the atmosphere and amidst
the activities peculiar to Parisian life.   Just as Rienzi saw the Rome of
his day in the light of a bygone and more heroic age and tried to
resuscitate that past, so Wagner set out to remake grand opera to
become the vehicle of a new and more intensely felt art.   Subconsciously he felt that something was wrong with his plan, and made pro-
vision against it in his libretto sketch, but he was not as yet consciously
aware of it.   While his mind was still groping towards this knowledge
his soul was already absorbing the new experience.   His hazardous
journey had shown him one of the secrets of his own nature—a home-
sickness for the far horizon, a restless curse laid on him by his *daemon*
master to be forever seeking an idol to worship.   He caught the vision
but fleetingly, however, lacking as yet the power and the will to retain
it intellectually, though it had a deep psychological effect.   The yarns
of the sailors on his ship, Heine's story of the Flying Dutchman, and
his own experiences of nature on his stormy voyage, were so much
tinder which presently caught fire from the flames of the burning
Capitol.

In the meantime, however, the Capitol was Wagner's reality.   He
reached London after a passage lasting more than three weeks from
Pillau, and from London he travelled to Boulogne where Meyerbeer
happened to be staying.   Wagner showed him the score of *Rienzi*
which was complete to the end of the second act.   In September
1839 Wagner, now twenty-six years of age, reached Paris, intent
on realising his dreams for *Rienzi*.   He had introductions from
Meyerbeer to the music publisher, Schlesinger, to Habeneck, director
of the Conservatoire concerts, to Duponchel, director of the Opéra,
and to the manager of the Renaissance theatre.   These introductions,
however, did not carry him very far.   Matters which seemed easy of
attainment at a distance presented a host of difficulties on a nearer
view.   Wagner, however, was used to conflict.   If the Opéra were,
for the moment, barred to the foreigner he would force a way in.
Success in Paris was his goal, but meanwhile the rhythm of that city's
life, its contending intellectual forces and sensuous joys offered the
very kind of life he had been seeking.   The need for asserting himself
in this element provided a stimulus which no German city could have
supplied.   Wagner boldly accepted life's challenge, and set out to

carve his way by composing music for the verse of French lyricists. If *Rienzi* was a goal too high to be attained at a stride, *Das Liebesverbot* with its glorification of wanton joys might serve at least to show how well the German Wagner understood the French art of entertainment ; in fact, in Wagner's own opinion his music suited the French translation even better than the German original.

Nevertheless, this second attempt to capture the French stage also failed. Wagner paused, disheartened. All his efforts had miscarried, and he began to doubt that he was attempting the impossible. The great city accepted him indifferently and swallowed him up, leaving him to do hack work, careless of his ambitions. The few friends it brought him were all poor and failures like himself. Among them were that strange collector and librarian who disguised his past identity under the name of " Anders " and whose true name Wagner never learned, Kietz, the young painter, and Lehrs, the consumptive scholar. As to the theatres, what Wagner saw there seemed to him as trivial as the stuff he was accustomed to at home in Germany, only rather more blatantly showy and commercial in *décor*.

There was one institution in Paris, however, which was free from commercial taint—the orchestral concerts of the Conservatoire. Wagner there heard a performance of Beethoven's Ninth Symphony that exceeded his dreams, under the conductorship of Habeneck. It reawakened his youthful memories of Beethoven, and the charm of wordless instrumental music came as a new revelation. This became associated in his mind with the dream he had dreamed at sea of a mysterious Wanderer under the curse of perpetual unrest. Wagner caught a glimpse of that figure now, but not yet in the form of the sea rover, delivered at last by woman's faith. The Flying Dutchman's forerunner was a vain seeker for fulfilment. Wagner conceived his *Faust* symphony as an instrumental expression of that which the stage refused him opportunity of expressing :

> " Und so ist mir das Dasein eine Last,
> Der Tod erwünscht, das Leben mir verhasst."
> (" This doth my being so with grief oppress
> I long for death, my life is heaviness.")

The work is in D minor, the key of the Ninth Symphony. A slow introductory passage sets the contrasts—a " loneliness " theme, descending by wide intervals, and a " vision of peace " theme in D major, derived from the Peace Messengers sextolets in *Rienzi*. The allegro which is marked " very lively and full of expression " portrays the conflict between the two in a D minor theme, ascending and descending chromatically by octaves, with a second minor theme in precise, vigorous rhythms, and an F major melody in ascending chords.   Finally, the D major " vision of peace " theme is reintroduced, is depressed to the minor, and is followed by a return of the " loneliness " motif of the opening, which gradually dies away.

The work is a mere fragment.   The " feminine element," whose absence Liszt noted later, is indeed lacking, since Wagner intended to introduce it in the second movement.   The theme for this existed, but is now lost.   Did Wagner use it in the Senta ballad ?   We do not know, but clearly Wagner knew that this form of art was not for him. The *Faust* Overture, under which title he later published the one completed movement, is Wagner's last purely orchestral piece of any size or importance.   It is also his first step into the slowly emerging expressionist world of *The Flying Dutchman*.   The thematic treatment, which is still linked by the dream-like use of motifs with the melodic treatment of *Rienzi*, hints already at the musical sphere of *The Flying Dutchman* in the width of the intervals, the chromaticism of the line, the declamatory plasticity of the rhythm.   The key, too, is the same in both works.   The dramatic structure of the symphony, the concrete and objective effect aimed at in the shaping of the themes, is closer to Berlioz than to Beethoven.   The fact that Wagner heard Berlioz's *Romeo and Juliet* in 1839, and was personally acquainted with the composer whose fate was so similar to his own, may have influenced the *Faust* Overture at least as much as Habeneck's interpretation of the Ninth Symphony.   At the same time Berlioz's example was the very thing to convince Wagner that work on these lines could give, at best, but a faint suggestion of the vision he yearned to express.   That *concreteness* towards which his " Will to Expression " constantly strove could never be achieved by makeshift methods such as programmatic comments and poetic allusions.   While it might be in some degree possible to portray in purely instrumental music the lonely reveries and inner conflicts of Faust, how could he hope by this means to render the feminine element, the dawn of salvation through Woman ?

The *Faust* symphony remained an episode.   It was a cry wrung from its oppressed composer, and though unheeded by others it awoke an answering echo in his own heart.   The echo, however, was not urgent or persuasive enough to call him at once to follow it. Poverty and disappointment cast their shadows on Wagner's life in Paris, but it was not all privation and despair. He possessed a temperamental elasticity which threw off practical troubles very lightly, and a hand-to-mouth, debt-laden existence, far from seeming disastrous, appealed to him as rather in keeping with the artistic life in Paris. From time to time he met with some slight encouragement, such as the perform-ance of an overture at the Conservatoire. He was known to this and that artistic celebrity, and if their friendship had little practical result it did at least minister to his personal pride. Among his closer friends were Laube, who had recently gone to Paris, and also Heine, whose ironic turn of mind and fluent descriptive style were eagerly imitated by Wagner in his own writings in preference to the more flowery periods of E. T. A. Hoffmann who had been his model hitherto. He felt that he had much in common with Heine, and the fate of that genius, who had not only been driven into exile, but was still pursued with vindictive hate, roused him to outraged protest against the defamation of his friend. On the whole it began to appear that the first trials which overtook the newcomer to Paris and reached their climax in the autumn of 1839 had been safely weathered. Disappointment had acclimatised him, and he no longer regarded Paris with the naïve enthusiasm of his Riga days, but with a cooler, more satirical, more Parisian vision. He began to see the ordinary human qualities behind that splendid façade. He was already beginning to question his own *Rienzi* enthusiasms, and had he not put them into music while under the spell of distance they would probably never have found expression at all.

To his sobered vision the other side of that picture, *Rienzi's Fall*, now grew proportionately vivid, and he could now well imagine the downfall of a man of lofty ambitions, brought about by the failings of those among whom he lived and by his own tragic error in imputing the virtues of a bygone, heroic age to his own degenerate Rome. All this exactly expressed his own recent experiences, his ill-founded hopes of conquering Paris and the Paris Opéra, and of all the great and inspir-ing things he had expected to find in that city. Suddenly, however, Paris seemed to relent towards him. The manager of the Renaissance theatre after hearing a few pieces from *Das Liebesverbot* declared himself ready to produce it. Wagner, overjoyed at this prospective change of fortune, made the news an occasion for exchanging his poor lodgings in the Halles quarter for a pleasanter dwelling near the Boulevard des Italiens. On the very day of his move he heard that the Renaissance theatre had gone bankrupt. His last hope in Paris was shattered, his *Rienzi* dream was destroyed. He was faced at last by the dull uninspiring reality in all its brutal nakedness, the world of petty aims which is the inevitable downfall of every heroic will. *Rienzi's* dying curse on Rome was now a living experience. The failure of friendship, the emptiness and falsity of patronage cried out in Wagner for expression. *Rienzi* should indeed be finished, but not for that Paris in which Wagner had once reposed his foolish, youthful hopes and against which he now hurled prophecies of ruin. The new work was destined for Germany, in which a new temple should rise up to great, tragic art.

Rienzi was finally completed after a nine months' cessation of work upon it. Wagner had been subjected to a spiritual stress which discharged itself in the "Will to Ruin." It was the first, quite unexpected, yet quite logical, result of his sojourn in Paris. The tension found release not merely, as in the *Faust* Overture, through melancholic self-torment, but through passionate pathos.

By living experience and by study of the operas he had seen there, Paris had taught Wagner a new power of tragic climax. In those operas he had seen pathos used as deliberately for effect as any of the much-admired stage accessories of the Opera House. Meyerbeer's *Huguenots* is a most notable example of this use of pathos. Wagner's laudatory account of it, written when he was beginning to work on *Rienzi's Fall*, shows how deeply he was affected by it, how carefully he observed its methods, and how he burned with ambition to prove the equivocal nature of the prophecy that "no-one could hope to excel Meyerbeer," that "universal genius," in "a direction which he had pressed to its farthest limits."

The second part of *Rienzi* shows its connection with the first in the ground-plan as a whole, but differs from it in the conception and execution of the individual numbers. The difference is accounted for by the difference in the conditions under which the two works arose. The marching rhythm characterises the musical style of both, and in the second part as in the first all themes and forms, pathetic or passionate, are built up on this fundamental idea of the march. Climaxes, grand concerted effects, adagio movements such as Rienzi's prayer, all find musical expression in march rhythm, which ceases to dominate for a short space only in the prayer of the women during the battle finale of Act III. Here the march theme of the *Santo spirito cavaliere* battle hymn is interrupted by the women's song in three-four time, which takes up Adriano's passionate dialogue with Irene in a rhythmically shortened form and blends with it finally in an intensified repeat. It is the only movement in the work in three-four time. The grand finale of Act III opens with a fanfare of trumpets, develops in a decoratively rhythmical double march of monks and warriors, and reaches its climax in the ascending line of the battle hymn. Rienzi's progress to the Lateran (a first earnest of the march in *Tannhäuser*) sets the basic rhythmic idea for the finale of Act IV. The last finale is based on the wild clamour of the mob, portrayed in fanatically insistent repetitions in a two-part *molto passionato*.

Within this march pattern, which dominates the musical accent and therefore the style of the work, there is, however, room in the second part of *Rienzi* for important divergences from the first. The first part depended principally on choral effects, solo scenes and songs being introduced as points of repose or bridge passages. Even in the second part the most important climaxes are choral, yet the crowd as represented in the chorus does not, as formerly, take the lead, but is used only for dynamic effects, while the scenic and musical interest of the action passes to the soloists. Rienzi's speeches to the insurgents at the opening of Act III and at the close of Act IV, Adriano's great scene and aria when he swears vengeance by his father's dead body, the Cardinal's curse, Rienzi's prayer and his duet with Irene, Adriano's duet with Irene, and, as final climax, Rienzi's curse against Rome—these scenes are the pivots of the second part of *Rienzi*, and the choruses serve merely as wings and backcloth. There is an obvious tendency to stress the pathos of the individual, to go behind colouristically and dynamically conceived mass-effects and develop individual character. The work shows a notable advance also in power of musical character-isation, an advance made possible by Wagner's opportunities of observ-ing living examples of the handling of dramatic song and recitative while in Paris.

The influence of musical declamation in grand opera as practised by Auber, Halévy, and, more particularly, Meyerbeer, is traceable not alone in certain superficial stylistic echoes, such as the tendency to achieve pathetic effect by the use of melodic triplets as exemplified in

Rienzi's " Ich liebte glühend meine hohe Braut," (" Warmly I loved her, my exalted bride,") but also in the change from the simple, conversational recitative of *Rienzi's* first part to the pictorial plasticity of the declamatory line notable in the second part. Here Wagner abandons instrumentation by harmonic patterns and secures vital co-operation between song and instrumental tone. Scenes such as that of Adriano and the conspirators in Act IV, and that of Adriano and Irene in Act V, show already a dramatic vitality which, by contrast with the pathetic recitative phrasing of the first part of *Rienzi*, reveals something new in expressionist vocal representation. The gulf between the two parts in this matter of maturity of dramatic vocal treatment is so wide that it almost amounts to a genuine difference in style.

This improvement in vocal plastic expression exercises a stimulating effect in matters of declamation and structure. The overtures and finales which frame and delimit each act are more compact in proportions, and at the same time richer in variety of musical motion in the second part of *Rienzi* than in the first. Moreover, as declamation increases in dramatic significance a really new formative element enters into the structure as a whole—namely the deliberate ingrafting of the psychological reminiscent motif into the decorative form of grand opera. This very decided return to the reminiscent theme constitutes the most striking of the differences between the first and second parts of *Rienzi*. It is a clear indication that Wagner was tending to revert to the principles of Romantic opera, whose scope had now, however, to be widened through the pathos of the heroic style to comprehend a more forceful type of drama.

The reminiscent motif makes an episodic appearance even in the first part of *Rienzi*. Rienzi's meditation on vengeance, " Weh dem der mir verwandtes Blut vergossen hat " ! (" Woe unto him who shed that blood to mine allied ! ") recurs in the trial scene of Act II as a " dark warning " against himself, and again a little later as a threat to Adriano when he pleads for his father. The Conspiracy theme in the choral terzetto in Act II reappears at the moment when Orsini aims a dagger thrust at Rienzi. In the second part, however, it ceases to be episodic, and attains an expression value that governs the form. Thus the structure of the second finale is dominated by the *Santo spirito* motif. In union with the trumpet motif of the battle march, which is a reference to Rienzi's first entrance, and with

Adriano's vengeance motif, it traces a line of development that is psychological and not merely external. The Conspirators' music at the beginning of Act IV, in whose hollow C sharp minor notes and descending bass combined with the answering vengeance motif we get a foretaste of the introduction to Act II in *Lohengrin*, is developed psychologically in Adriano's vengeance motif, and finds consummation in the Monk's march from Act III. The finale of Act IV is also evolved from contrasting motifs. The *Santo spirito* theme becomes the symbol of Rienzi. There is a hint of future developments in the transposition of the Conspirators' theme from C sharp minor to E flat major after Rienzi's conciliatory speech. The chanting Monks' *Vae tibi maledicto* and Rienzi's march motif form an alternating dialogue, and the theme of the Cardinal's curse provides an impassioned climax to Adriano's fierce wooing of Irene.

Wagner's interweaving of his reminiscent motifs becomes ever more intricate and daring. In the great duo scene between Irene and Rienzi in Act V, we hear not only the *Santo spirito* theme, but, in the closing orchestral passages, Rienzi's vision of world freedom from Act II ; and the march theme which brings Rienzi to the barred doors of the Lateran is the triumph song of the last true Roman man and woman. The Curse motif, now become a weapon in the hand of Adriano, reappears in his last duet with Irene, where we get a foretaste of the wave-like chromatic sextolets of *The Flying Dutchman*. In the scene of Rienzi's death all the principal musical themes are gathered up. The Oath of Fidelity theme from the first finale ascends through a series of keys from G major through A minor to B flat major with interruptions from the chorus motif of the mob ; the Peace Messengers' theme, " Jauchzet ihr Taler, frohlockt ihr Berge," (" Rejoice ye vales, exult ye hills ! ") is heard once again in Rienzi's reminder to those who had once offered him homage. Finally, the *Santo spirito* victory motif, distorted into the minor, becomes a death motif, and to its strains, given out by the full orchestra, Rienzi, Irene, and Adriano perish amidst the ruins of the burning Capitol.

Both the ground-plan and the structure of the second part of *Rienzi* show that the interval which separated its composition from that of the first part deeply affected its organic form, and, even more profoundly, changed the composer's attitude towards his subject. *Rienzi's Fall* is grand opera in intention only. As a drama and as a work of art it abandons the sphere of historic incident for that of human passion, the emotions aroused by external events for those engendered by interior personal conflicts. On the other hand the original plan was so firmly outlined that later divergences, though they show it under a somewhat new light, cannot alter its essential character. This character is determined by the requirements of the form known as grand opera—an art of decorative, pictorial effect in which pathos is achieved by strong contrasts. However greatly *Rienzi's Fall* may differ from *Rienzi's Might* in execution, the two agree and form a single whole in this matter of tragic pathos through picturesque contrast. In both moments of greatest import depend on this fundamental conception of the form, appearing where melody rises to heroic flights, spans the wide bays of the structure, or gives character and expression to the wild, impetuous rhythms. It is at such moments that the underlying creative impulse finds clearest expression, showing itself as a desire for melodic breadth, for fiery, energetic rhythm, for impressive and passionate musical gesture. "The composer of opera must have deep and strong passions, and must be able to portray them in broad, bold strokes of the brush," writes Wagner in 1842 in his critique on Halévy's *La Reine de Chypre*, giving, thereby, the measure of his own *Rienzi*. If the passions in *Rienzi* are not very "strong," still less very "deep" as regards external action, the brush strokes are certainly "broad" and "bold"—indeed they are unforgettable. The finest moments in the work are the solemn Lateran chorus, the Oath scene with which Act I closes, the Triumph scene at the end of Act II, the sublime *Santo spirito* theme in Act III, and Rienzi's prayer in Act V. The composer's youthful enthusiasm for great deeds lives for ever in their exuberant melody. Harmony for the time is subordinate and is confined to characteristic treatment of the bass, which is usually contrasted with the melodic line and made to stand out by insistent, note by note progression, though it fails, in this two-part outline, to achieve much significance in the way of harmonic fullness and modulation.

Wagner summarises what he regards as the important elements in the work in the overture. He is not content with the mere introductory prelude usual in grand opera, but writes in accordance with the art-form to which his mind was reverting during the completion of *Rienzi* and creates an overture in semi-Romantic style that paints in broad lines a musical picture of the drama to follow. The cry for freedom, the prayer, the revolutionary *ensemble*, the peace celebrations and, high above all the rest, the *Santo spirito* victory song, combine to form Wagner's final comment on the score of *Rienzi*. The work was begotten of the yearning for action ; the struggle for accomplishment brought about its completion, and in completing his work the composer was recalled from cloudy, sentimental aspirations to the world of realities. Vague enthusiasms and day-dreams of heroism gave place to a recognition of his own apartness from, and relation to, the real world ; the march-rhythmed crowd-emotion of grand opera gives place to the personal and individual problems of Romantic opera, decorative musical gesture to a dawning realisation of music's psychological expressiveness. Wagner saw at last that his original intention of writing for Paris was a mistake ; but, even as he stood within the city he had once so ardently desired, his faith that in some far place miraculous success awaited him was no whit less strong than in the days when it had driven him overseas to France. To him the most improbable was always the most expected. A new opera-house was shortly to be opened in Dresden. *Rienzi*, obviously, was the work to inaugurate it. Wagner applied for aid to Madame Schroeder-Devrient, to Kapellmeister Reissiger, to Privy-Councillor Winkler. Meyerbeer's influence might also be useful. He at once despatched his score to Dresden, petitioning no less a personage than the King of Saxony to patronise his subject's work. There, in his own land, where grand opera was known only through slavish copies of Parisian models, Wagner hoped, with his own experience-bought knowledge of the art, to rebuild the dream Capitol destroyed, for him, in Paris. Late in November 1840, eighteen months after his first arrival in that city, he forwarded the score of *Rienzi* to Germany in the earnest hope that it would pave his way back to the Fatherland.

Wagner was still at work on the composition of *Rienzi's Fall* when, in May 1840, it occurred to him to write something for the Opéra. The management would not accept a full-length work from him, but he proposed to offer them a one-act piece, a curtain-raiser, such as was usually given before an evening of ballet. Practical good sense as well as ambition inspired the idea, for if he could get his work before the public in even a small way it might give him a market for better things. At the time he was earning a living by arranging popular operatic airs for various instruments and successful contemporary works, with and without words, for pianoforte solos and duets ; also by journalistic work for Schlesinger's *Gazette Musicale*. He wrote also for Theodor Hell's (Privy-Councillor Winkler's) *Dresdener Abendzeitung*, but the only payment he could expect for this was that the very influential editor would exert himself to get Dresden to accept *Rienzi*. These employments were not highly remunerative. Assistance from Leipzig, engineered by Laube, soon came to an end and the business of Lewald's *Europa* brought in only a very little money. Ferdinand Avenarius, who had married Wagner's youngest sister, Cecilia Geyer, was also living in Paris and acted as agent for another brother-in-law, the publisher Brockhaus, but he was not a rich man, he could lend only small sums of money, and he went in secret terror of this strange brother of his wife's who seemed to live with his head in the clouds in confident expectation of some great turn of fortune. Wagner, indeed, had no doubt at all that fortune would one day be his, and he despatched his *Rienzi* score to Dresden with as great a confidence of success as on the day when he took ship from Pillau to London.

The importance of this sense of confidence as a background to Wagner's life in Paris is very commonly underrated. The miseries of that period had for him just as much, and just as little, reality as his own romantic account of his Paris experiences implies. There is no denying that he was often confronted with the actualities of want and that he was forced to drudge for a livelihood ; it even appears that about the time of the completion of *Rienzi* he was haled to a debtor's prison, but even so unpleasant an incident as this could not burden Wagner's elastic youthful temperament with the despair his imagination has painted in his *A German Musician's End in Paris*. Wagner's nature was wholly that of the artist—that is to say, of one who selects from life's thousand possibilities the one which for the moment suits his artistic ends and who does not necessarily regard his progress to the pawnshop, or even to the debtor's prison, as an actual catastrophe. Even if Wagner's confidence in future world renown sometimes wilted slightly beneath the mute reproaches of his wife, who was obliged in time to do the roughest kinds of housework not only for themselves but for the lodger who helped to pay the rent, the least bit of luck would send his spirits soaring again and be reckoned as an earnest of the great fortune undoubtedly in store. As an artist Wagner was extraordinarily sensitive to outside impressions, because they formed the food of his art, but in matters of ordinary life he was extremely insensitive. This insensitiveness was due to no lack of what is called character, though " character " in the bourgeois sense Wagner certainly did not, and never could, possess. His central trait was not stability, but a fluid, happy-go-lucky variability of the moral nature. His sense of responsibility was limited strictly to his work as an artist. In all matters outside the theatre he showed the naïve, instinctive egotism of the actor to whom ordinary life is merely an interval between two appearances on the stage to be spent as the whim dictates, since it is only in his part that he finds his real self, and all he asks of the world is the opportunity to play that part.

Paris with its teeming life and callous disregard of the individual was a stage well adapted to the rôle which Wagner was to learn to interpret by actually living it. Its very remorselessness brought his sense of poverty and loneliness to a pitch of creative ecstasy, and its aimless multitudes increased his own sense of conscious purpose. He drew strength from the opposition he encountered. Paris had lured him once with promise of success ; it held him now by the fructifying power of failure, by the stimulus to the imagination to create unreal worlds which could only come from failure in the real one. Paris was necessary to Wagner and he knew it. He would only leave it when, having weathered every storm in that ocean of passions, he ran before the last one into the port for which he was destined. His ship was seaworthy and was, moreover, under the special guardianship of that *daemon* which had launched it on its voyage. It was an unearthly, phantom vessel, a ship of fantasy which could never put in to the shores of reality save when fantasy in another guise should offer it harbourage in faith and love and, by a willing sacrifice, release it from the curse compelling it to wander eternally.

Wagner, with his perpetual yearning for the world of dreams, his sense of the actual as a mere pathway to the non-actual, cast this fantasy in a series of novelistic sketches before he completed *Rienzi*. Rather in the manner of Hoffmann modernised by Heine, Wagner abandoned himself to the romantic satisfaction of feeling miserable and thus enlarged his purview of art. His *Pilgrimage to Beethoven* is the weightiest work as regards content, and the most successful in literary expression, arising from this phase of thought. It is an imaginatively magnified self-portrait of genius, suffering loneliness and neglect in the midst of a great city. The figure of Beethoven, as Wagner sees it here, becomes a symbol of the artist. In the spring of 1841 Wagner seriously considered writing a big biographical work on Beethoven, and he tried to interest three German publishing houses in the under-taking. The mood of depression, always accompanying the spiritual gestation of a new work, was once more upon him, and an interior expenditure of energy of which he was himself unconscious absolutely demanded a slackening of external activities. No news came from Dresden. The *Columbus* overture was given at one of Schlesinger's concerts (against Habeneck's advice, who thought the work too " vague "). It was badly performed by the orchestra and proved a failure. But Wagner's cup of humiliation was not yet full. When he submitted his sketch for a one-act piece to the management of the Opéra the manager approved it and decided to have it executed, *but not by Wagner !* Contracts of work sufficient for seven years at least had been entered into with a number of composers, and it was suggested that Wagner should cede his sketch to one of these. At first he refused, but his circumstances were desperate, and there was some danger that his sketch would be used even without his consent, thereby depriving him of a fee for which he had only to stretch out his hand.

On mature consideration he declared his willingness to cede the sketch, proposing to use the five hundred francs earned in this way to complete the sketch himself, not as a one-act piece in French but as a full-length German Romantic opera. Ten days in May sufficed him to expand the sketch into a finished libretto, of which he sent a copy to the management of the Berlin Opera. Wagner thus cast a second hawser from Paris to Germany. If Fortune seemed refractory she must be coerced. And coercion succeeded. The new libretto was sent to Berlin on June 27, and on June 29 von Lüttichau, the Dresden intendant, dictated a fateful letter to a certain German musician resident in Paris, informing him that his opera *Rienzi* had been accepted for Dresden. The clouds broke and a first ray of sun shone from the skies of home. The almost despairing artist was suddenly filled with an inexpressible sense of power ; his belief in the inner rectitude of his will had found miraculous confirmation. " As from the distance of long ages past " the blessedness of fulfilment seemed to beckon the restless wanderer. The fateful moment had come, the curse was lifted, and within seven weeks the music of *The Flying Dutchman* was complete.

CHAPTER IV

THE FLYING DUTCHMAN

MANY and various are the threads woven into the fabric of this work. Wagner learnt the story of *The Flying Dutchman* from Heine, and his own sea voyage and the ghost tales told by the sailors on board made it very real to him. He came to an arrangement with Heine about its use. The legend appears in Heine's *Memoirs of Herr von Schnabele-wopski* in the form of a description of a play seen in Amsterdam. No such play in fact existed, and the poet allows his fancy free play with the ancient saga. Wagner found all the main points in Heine's narrative—the curse laid upon the Dutchman, the promise of salvation through a woman's devotion, that woman's predestined love, and the consummation of her sacrifice when she casts herself into the sea as the Dutchman seeks, for her own sake, to leave her. "But she, with a loud voice, cries: 'I have been faithful to thee to this hour, and I know a sure way to keep that faith till death!' And so saying the devoted woman casts herself into the sea. At this the curse upon the Flying Dutchman is lifted; he is redeemed, and we see the phantom ship sink to the bottom of the sea." So Heine tells the story. He adds, however, an ironical moral to the effect that women should beware how they marry Flying Dutchmen, and that men should take care that when the women shipwreck them it shall turn to their profit! It is a method (peculiar to, and typical of the Romantic) of reviving a soul too deeply oppressed by some moving imaginative conception by means of a cold douche of wit. Heine possessed the double vision of the Romantic. He saw that dream and actuality, emotional enthusiasm and intellectual precision, were, though discordant and irreconcilable, two alternating and mutually conditioned modes of apprehension. Wagner, on the other hand, being a theatrical artist, abandoned himself unreservedly to the dream and the illusion.

For this reason he could not follow Heine's plan in its entirety. His task was to make the improbable seem probable, to place the

Dutchman and his maiden at the centre of a well-constructed plot.
He built up a plot by introducing the maiden's father and betrothed
and making them the human antagonists of the mysterious stranger.
This modification brings us to Wagner's second source—Marschner's
The Vampire—the one of Marschner's works that most interested him.
It had been performed a number of times in Würzburg, and Wagner,
while in that city, had written an allegro accompaniment to one of
the amateur tenor Aubry's arias for his brother Albert.   An episode
in this work provided Wagner with an element lacking in Heine's
version.   This was the love-sick maid's romanza about the " Haggard
man with soulless gaze " ;   her pity for him, " Wie dauert mich der
bleiche Mann wie traurig ist sein Blick ! " (" His ghastly pallor grieves
my heart.   How sorrowful his gaze ! ") ;   and the warning she receives
against the devil-possessed stranger :

> " Kind, siehst du ihn noch immer an ?
> Weh mir, es ist um dich getan ! "
>
> (" Child, still that face thou lookest on ?
> Ah woe is me, thou art undone ! ")

This suggested to Wagner the rivalry between the maid's slighted
sweetheart and her strange seducer with his unearthly charm.
Marschner's main action supplied the character of the father, who,
for selfish reasons, is willing to betroth his daughter to the phantom
stranger.   The very names echo Marschner's.   Davenaut becomes the
sailor Donald, George is actually retained as the name of the girl's
betrothed, and the heroine's own name is changed from Emmy to
Anna.   These are the characters in the first sketch.   The Dutchman
is called simply " the Stranger," and the action, as with Marschner,
is placed in Scotland.   Not only in songs, characters, names, costume,
and setting, but even in actual wording, Wagner follows his model.   The
" Ho-ho-ho " of Senta's ballad and of the Dutchman's crew is anticipated
in the " Yo-ho, Yo-ho " of Marschner's Demon chorus.   Even the distribution of the choruses resembles that of the earlier work, the male-voice
chorus preponderating in both.   Where Marschner has a drinking song
"Munter edle Zecher " (" Jolly old toper ") and a male voice ensemble
" Im Herbst, da muss man trinken " ("Autumn's the time for drinking"),
Wagner has a Sailors' chorus and hornpipe.   He tells us in his *Autobiography* that his first musical sketches, which were made simultaneously
with the first scenario, were Senta's ballad, the Norwegian sailors'

song, and the chorus of the Dutchman's phantom crew.   The links with Marschner's *The Vampire* are plain to view ; it was just at these points of coincidence with the earlier opera that the music for the new began to grow and develop.

If these debts are not to be ignored, still less are they to be over-rated.   Allow them their full value in bringing about the genesis of Wagner's opera and they are still no more than external stimuli, serving rather to show unlikeness than likeness between the two composers. The completion of *Rienzi* had prepared Wagner psychologically for a return to Romantic opera.   His experience of grand opera had brought him a renewed realisation of the importance of individual problems and of the one art-form that could give them expression.   A produc-tion of *The Freischütz* in Paris in June 1841, when Wagner was beginning work on *The Flying Dutchman*, cleared his mind once for all as to the fundamental difference between French and German opera, between historical and emotional drama.   There is a hint in the new work of the projected *Faust* symphony ; but Faust here is no longer wholly abandoned to solitary self-torment and brooding.   He has received tidings of a redemptive miracle, he has heard the call of home.   All the various influences that affected Wagner—Heine, Marschner, Romanticism, *Faust*, privation in Paris and hopes for Dresden—are fused by the heat of a new creative idea, experience of the miraculous element in things, seen not merely, as by Heine, in woman's love for man, nor, as by Marschner, in a blind, malignant, and irremediable curse on man, but as revelation in action of the miracle-working power of desire tuned to its highest pitch of intensity.   Thus the supernatural becomes natural, the improbable probable, and miracle appears, not in the form of a non-human magic, but as the logical response to faith.

Experience of the miraculous was the means by which Wagner reconquered the domain of Romantic opera.   To him music itself was something miraculous, a power that could lay bare the secrets of the soul.   He regarded it as an expressionist vehicle of things mystical and magical, and it was with growing distaste that he saw its common use, especially in grand opera, as a means of representing mere external incident.   External incident required transplantation to the sphere of the miraculous and acclimatisation in that sphere before it could be presented on a plane compatible with music as Wagner understood it. When he wrote *Rienzi*, however, he was still far from realising that the miraculous alone could give scope for music.   What, in essence, is

Rienzi ? Tenor heroics, inspired by desire for external greatness and glory, and supported by a vocal chorus that likewise draws life from notions of pomp and circumstance. *The Flying Dutchman*, on the other hand, embodies restless passion, nourished on personal experience and magnified to a supra-personal greatness through the symbolism of the sea, its natural element. By clothing this passion in the garb of individual personality and making it the pivot of his plot, Wagner succeeded in freeing opera from the discord hitherto involved in dualism of music and libretto. The older form of Romantic opera, in particular, had maintained this dualism both by the use of spoken dialogue and by the conception of the miraculous as a drama of super-natural forces. This is exemplified in the Wild Huntsman in *The Freischütz*, the enchanted ring in *Euryanthe*, the fairy world in *Oberon*, and the witches and the gnomes in *The Vampire*. This superhuman element was now to be humanised, the scene of the miraculous to be transferred to the human soul, so that, to reveal its own miraculous nature, music had no longer to embody itself in fairy-tale shapes and concepts. It could work its miracle in expressing and displaying the profundities of human passion.

A new province was thus opened to opera. If we compare *The Flying Dutchman* with Marschner's *The Vampire* (the work whence the characters in *The Flying Dutchman* were evolved and itself a Romantic offshoot of Mozart's *Don Juan*), the change is at once apparent. Even in Mozart's work the supernatural plays an immediate part in both the musical and the dramatic action, though with him the supernatural is never merely magical, but is always the symbol of a higher, magisterial power above nature, a power in the strict sense unreal and capable of embodiment only as an exaltation of the conscience. Early Roman-ticism shows a decline from this sublime imaginative concept. It gives us individual sprites, moved by their own malice and by the laws of their own being to intervene in human affairs. Tragedy in Marschner, as in Weber, is brought about by contact between these sprites and human beings, so that the fairy-tale or legendary element forms the very basis of Romantic opera. Despite some realism in detail, there can be no doubt of the unreality, the deliberately *illusory* quality of these works as a whole.

The illusory element by which early Romantic work maintained an external continuity with idealist classical music was finally abandoned by Wagner. By transferring the element of miracle to the region of human psychology he established its *artistic* truth and used fairy-tale or legendary concepts to create an illusion of the absolute reality of the unreal. In Wagner's conception of the Flying Dutchman legend, the miraculous element is in humanity itself, and a psychological process is presented in terms of concrete drama. Wagner made the work a practical success because various incidents occurred at the time which showed him how to do so ; he succeeded psychologically because his own experience had made him ripe for such a conception of the marvellous ; he succeeded artistically because he had now attained sufficient command of his magic formulae—that is to say of his music—to be able to create an illusion of the miraculous that should seem quite natural and credible.

Though there are very marked similarities between *The Flying Dutchman* music and that of contemporary works, in matters such as the three-act ground-plan of the work with its choral introductions, its solo and *ensemble* scenes, and the structure of individual pieces, which are definitely of the *Lied* or aria type, there is something about the music in itself which lifts it above the ordinary and gives it a hitherto unexampled, and occasionally almost hypnotic, suggestive power. Allowing for the fact that Wagner's mind at the time was steeped in the idea of the miraculous as actual experience, as a new type of philosophy, how was he able, without any great modification in the organic structure of music, to make it convey this sense of the miraculous, so that the very notes reveal it to the listener ? He achieved it by means of a process repeated over and over again in his later work. He could cause a world of supernatural concepts to seem natural by the magic of music, because his own contact with nature was profound. As he contemplated nature with elemental simplicity and with entire faith in miraculous fulfilment, his inner ear caught notes, tone-relations, and combinations which, passing into his music, lent it the persuasive and convincing aspect of an illusionary double of nature. The same process occurred during the gestation of the first part of *The Ring*, where the splendour of the Alps underlies the musical conception and begets the nature-symbolism of the basic motifs, and later again in its completion, in which the charms of Triebschen and the bliss of human fulfilment wake those tender nature sounds which lead the hearer to Brynhilda's rock. Similarly in *The Flying Dutchman*, Wagner's first true self-revelation, all the storms of passion pass into music by means of the nature-symbolism of the sea. The sea's elemental reality is transmuted to emotional reality, nature herself suggesting the keynote and its modifications. Wagner infuses the life of nature into the life of music, and thus achieves that intensity of expression which makes his music so extraordinarily persuasive and at the same time enriches the whole musical vocabulary.

The facts connected with this opera's origin make it clear that the music, and indeed the whole work, has for nucleus a tonal nature-symbol. Here again is a process that was to characterise all Wagner's later work. He seldom worked out his scenes and acts in the order which they occupy in his score, and in fact the series presented to us on the stage was not that which existed in his mind from the first. He begins usually somewhere near the middle of the work—at the *experience* which is its psychological root and the source of its musical expression. Thence he works *upwards* towards the climaxes of his work, and *downwards* towards subordinate characters and incidents and the ground-plan of the external plot. Thus the third, first, and second acts of *Lohengrin* were made in that order, *The Ring* grew up round the figure of Siegfried, and the germ of *Parsifal* is in the dual experience, at once musical and poetical, of the Good Friday music. *The Flying Dutchman* grows from Senta's ballad, which contains the root psychological and musical forces of the whole work and determines its general outline. We hear the Dutchman's leit-motif in the opening *Yo-ho-ho* chorus, and his ship is pictured in the first phrase of the song :

> " Traft ihr das Schiff im Meere an,
> blutrot die Segel, schwarz der Mast ? "
> (" Saw ye the ship that rides the storm,
> Blood-red the sails and black the mast ? ")

The melodic phrase is repeated in the lines describing her captain :

> " Auf hohem Bord der bleiche Mann,
> des Schiffes Herr, wacht ohne Rast."
> (" Upon the deck a ghostly form
> By day and night defies the blast.")

The image of a ship that drives aimlessly before every wind that blows dissolves the strict melody and rhythm into sliding chromatics :

> " Hui !   Wie saust der Wind !   Johoho !
> Hui !   Wie pfeift's im Tau !   Johoho !
> Hui !   Wie ein Pfeil fliegt er hin,
> ohne Ziel, ohne Rast, ohne Ruh ! "

("Hui! The whistling wind, Yohoho!
Hui! The whistling wind, Yohoho!
Hui! Like an arrow he flies
Without aim, without end, without rest!")

Imaginatively and musically the world of *The Flying Dutchman* is now outlined, and the rest is simply a matter of detail and emphasis. The contrasting world of redemption is presented as a hope only, though as a hope carrying assurance of fulfilment. The minor gives place to the major, and jagged, broken-rhythmed melody changes to long-drawn-out chanting :

" Doch kann dem Bleichen Manne Erlösung einstens noch werden,
fänd' er ein Weib, das bis in den Tod getreu ihm auf Erden.
Ach ! wann wirst du, bleicher Seemann, sie finden ?
        Betet zum Himmel, dass bald
        ein Weib Treue ihm halt' ! "

(" Yet may the spectral seaman be saved from torment eternal,
Find he a maiden faithful to death, an angel supernal.
Ah, when, poor seaman, this maid wilt thou find her ?
        Pray ye that heaven soon
        May in pity grant this boon!")

Here we have the story, and though the ballad by itself, without music and dramatisation, would have been but a fragment, it none the less contains within itself the whole development of the work as here outlined.

The crux of the work, however, is not in any external delineation of contrasts, but in the expressionist structure of the two main, contrasting themes—that of the Dutchman's plight, and that of his salvation. The Dutchman motif is neither more nor less than a nature-motif, and is built up of a sequence of lower fourth, tonic and dominant, in simple rhythmic articulation. The character of the Dutchman himself is harmonically expressed in the basic intervals, primitive tone and primitive rhythm without melodic form. The element of ghostliness in the drama finds its musical parallel in primitive tones that impress on the hearer the soullessness of nature, a tuneless immensity. Contrasted with this is the woman-motif, a melody that first descends note by note from the third, then tends upward by chords. Here a natural sequence of intervals and natural rhythm gives place to a connected melodic line. Whereas the former theme was compounded of elementary harmony and rhythm only, the latter is all melody.   Humanity, with its wealth of emotion, is thus contrasted with that which is in itself insensible.   The latter is expressed in G minor, the former in B flat major ; the two are destined to unite in D major.   Thus the musical action parallels the dramatic action and produces an impression of reality " in the round " by union of two opposite spheres of expression.   A harmony without thirds is emancipated through major-melody : nature, through the human emotions which give it sense and soul.

The importance of this work, Wagner's first great original artistic achievement, consists in this essential, absolute parallelism between scenic drama and musical symbolism.   The music successfully mirrors human passion in natural processes only because it presents a realistic picture of elemental forces in action.   Here, too, where Wagner's link with the past is closest, a vast gulf divides him from his predecessors.   Although Marschner's romanza is reproduced almost word for word in Wagner's ballad, the former altogether lacks the latter's most essential element, namely, dramatic contrast, and therewith nature-symbolism and the entire process of liberation through music. Thus Marschner's romanza is merely a lyrical and narrative piece set in a series of operatic numbers, but Wagner's ballad is the life-giving heart of a theatrical music-drama, the centre of a plot which thence derives all its strength and coherence.

The whole work develops from the ballad.   The earliest sketch, however, contains, besides the ballad, the Norwegian sailors' song and the chant of the Dutchman's phantom crew.   Step by step the emotions of the ballad are given visual and dramatic presentation. The chant of the Dutchman's crew is an elaboration of the storm picture given in the ballad, and is closely connected with the Dutchman's theme.   The words of the central stanza expand Senta's song :

> " Schwarzer Hauptmann, geh' ans Land,
>   sieben Jahre sind vorbei !
>   Frei' um blonden Mädchen's Hand !
>   Blondes Mädchen, sei ihm treu !

> *   *   *

> " Hui !   Horch ! er pfeift !
>   Kapitän ! bist wieder da ?
>   Hui !   Segel auf—
>   Deine Braut, sag' wo sie blieb ?

> *   *   *

" Sause, Sturmwind, heule zu !
    Unsren Segeln lässt du Ruh' !
    Satan hat sie uns geseit,
    reissen nicht in Ewigkeit ! "

(" Gloomy captain, go on land !
    Seven more weary years have flown !
    Seek a faithful maiden's hand !
    Faithful maid, be his alone !

      *   *   *

    " Hui ! Hark, he pipes !
    Captain bold, thou'lt try again ?
    Hui ! Hoist the sails !
    For thy bride—where is she now ?

      *   *   *

    " Howl then, storm wind, blow thy worst,
    Our good sails thou'lt never burst !
    Satan blessed them ages back ;
    Blow until the heavens crack ! ")

The fury of the storm, of which we merely hear an account in Senta's ballad, becomes present and immediate to us in these lines. The nature-motif of *The Flying Dutchman* is shown in the grip of elemental forces which leave it no rest. The Phantom chorus, treated chromatically, achieves an effect of veritable pandemonium and paints a most realistic picture of storm. Human and orchestral voices are alike employed in coloristic representation. No fairy world, such as that of the opening scene of *The Vampire*, but one of the great forces of nature is symbolised in the scenic presentation of the chorus of the Dutchman's crew.

After storm, calm ; after wild chromatics, the simple, straight-forward world of the Norwegian sailors, expressed in the clear tonality, the primitive dance-movement, the firm rhythm of their chorus :

" Wachten manche Nacht bei Sturm und Graus,
    tranken oft des Meer's gesalznes Nass :
    heute wachen wir bei Saus und Schmaus,
    besseres Getränk gibt Mädel uns vom Fass ! "

(" Many a night we've sailed the angry sea,
    Many a day we've drunk the bitter brine ;
    Now we feast and let the tongue go free :
    Sweeter drink than that is this good ruddy wine ! ")

Weber and Marschner have written very similar male choruses in *Der Freischütz, The Vampire,* and *Hans Heiling;* indeed they form a regular part of the " local colour " of German folk opera. But in *The Flying Dutchman* they stand for something more than " atmosphere." The chorus of the Norwegian sailors alternating with that of the Dutchman's phantom crew symbolises musically the strife between sea and land, between restless passion and smug physical well-being, between the chromatic and the diatonic. The Dutchman's world and that other world forever beyond his reach are emphatically contrasted in music. The Sailors' chorus with its plodding rhythm and folk-song-like C major melody serves to paint the landscape which is Senta's natural setting, just as the Phantom chorus depicts the storm that eternally harasses the Dutchman.

Thus the opera begins. The two choruses define the contrasts to be expressed, the ballad indicates the trend of the plot, the blank nature-theme portrays the hero and the redemption-motif the heroine. Thenceforward representation becomes increasingly concrete, detail more clearly defined, and we reach the Pilot's song in Scene I :

> " Mit Gewitter und Sturm aus fernem Meer—
> mein Mädel, bin dir nah ! "

> (" Thro' the thunder and storm from distant seas,
> My maiden, I am here ! "),

which forges a link between the two contrasted worlds. The plot begins to develop. The Pilot's song opens in simple, naturalistic declamation, and is without harmonic accompaniment till the second part of the phrase. It has a thematic connection with the opening phrase of the Sailor's chorus, and dies away in a refrain-like " Ho-hojo ! Hallo-ho-ho ! " In it is portrayed a first individual figure from the world in which Senta lives her everyday life, and which is illustrated further in the Spinning-women's chorus that introduces the second act and the ballad itself. This ballad was put in when the expansion of the one-act sketch to a three-act drama made a broader presentation of the main contrasts necessary. The work begins to be opera in the usual sense of the word at this point, and various details are painted in, all inspired by the conception of the sea and its movements. The sailors sing their " Yo-ho-hoes " to a wave-like motif that ebbs and flows by seconds, and this motif, on a smaller scale, forms the melodic germ of the Spinning-women's chorus.   Similarly the idea of wind and wave movements results in a predominance of sextolet formations and chromatics in the musical presentation of the subsidiary characters of the drama.   In this operatic underworld Daland's function is that of external link between the Dutchman and Senta. He is somewhat sketchily portrayed by methods which Wagner had almost discarded, and his one and only scene serves to introduce the duet between the Dutchman and Senta.   He is altogether a part of the illustrative prelude which concentrates interest on the stage presentation of the ship as she enters the harbour to the *Yo-hoes* of her crew. This picturesque incident, the appearance of the ship, her gentle rocking motion, the rattling of tackle, the casting of the anchor, the rising breeze which later heralds her departure, the dancing of the waves—all these things are minutely represented in the music.   Except in those scenes where the Dutchman and Senta occupy the scene alone, the interest is concentrated not on the human figures of the drama, but on representation of nature.   The sea, as symbolising restless passion, becomes at these times the centre of the action, and wherever the action is merely external, the *internal* drama is carried on by the sea's movements reflected in music.

One figure alone stands apart from the all-compelling spell of wave and tide, and that is the figure of Eric.   Like Daland he belongs to the external mechanism of the plot, but whereas Daland acts as mediator between the sensuous and the supersensuous worlds and is associated, unimportant as he is, with that great fundamental element in the drama which is represented by the sea, to Eric the sea, being the symbol of tragic passion, is emotionally alien and therefore incomprehensible.   He has merely a small part to play in the machinery of the story.   His task is to assist towards Senta's enlightenment by his dream-tale in Act II, and, by misleading the Dutchman in the last act, by his interference to bring about the final catastrophe.   The music assigned to him accords with this merely accidental importance, for both in the first duet with Senta and the cavatina of the third finale it has the fluent melodic style of superficial emotional characterisation. Only in the telling of his dream, where a mental picture of the Dutchman is called up, does Eric achieve any real expressionist intensity. Nevertheless, he is no mere worn-out piece of stage property taken over from earlier opera.   In Wagner's original conception—implicit in the earlier work but overlaid in the finished version—he is associated

with those forces of opposition which being untouched by the magic
of the central figure are capable of actively opposing him : such is
Wolfram in his relation to Tannhäuser and Telramund and Ortrud to
Lohengrin.   But though Wagner individualised these forces successfully in riper and richer works, he did not succeed in doing so in *The
Flying Dutchman*, where a single expression-impulse prevailed to the
exclusion of all else.   The character of Eric is faint and shadowy, not
because it is conventional, but because for its successful realisation a
more highly developed individualisation of *all* the figures was required
than the plot of *The Flying Dutchman* made possible.   In this work
any figure which cannot find its organic place in Nature is necessarily
dim and inconspicuous in the scheme as a whole.

The music of *The Flying Dutchman* is based from first to last on a
conception of life in nature which is responsible for the sombre
orchestration that contrasts so strangely with the metallic brilliance of
Rienzi, for the fanfare-like horn and trombone unisons, the wave-like
chromatic passages for the strings, and the choric treatment of the
wood-wind which, amidst the elemental tones of strings and brass,
adumbrates the singing human voice.   Realistic naturalism, moreover,
underlies this first instance of the simultaneous evolution of word and
note.   This feature is least marked in those passages which merely
carry forward the mechanism of the plot, such as the songs of Eric
and of Daland, where the words have to convey some explicit concept
and are set to music accordingly, but it is very prominent in those great
passages which determine the outline and essential features of the
whole picture.   Here we find a number of word-tone structures from
which speech-melodic phenomena are evolved, such as the theme of
the Dutchman's cry for aid in the ballad, the "*Halloho*" of the Nor-
wegians from which the Sailors' chorus is developed, and the chromatic
"*Huzza*" of the Dutchman's crew.   The simple word-tone formations
of these natural ejaculations are developed into fully formed melodies
by a process of reiterating and intensifying their basic rhythm, while
the words elaborate their underlying speech-melodic, exclamatory
impulse.   In addition to the ejaculatory-motif, Wagner uses the
movement-motif, exemplified in the wave-motif that concludes the
Sailors' chorus and is carried over into the "*Spin ! spin !*" of the
Women's chorus ; in the see-saw rhythm of the orchestral accompaniment (in the B flat major section of the first finale) to Daland's :

" Du siehst, das Glück ist gunstig dir :
    der Wind ist gut, die See in Ruh' ! "
(" Thou seest good fortune does not fail :
    The wind is fair and calm the sea ! ") ;

in the sail movement, where the last line of the Helmsman's " *Hoho !*
Ho ! Yo-ho-ho ! " is taken up by the chorus ; and the picture of
raging tempest given in Act III in the chorus of the Dutchman's crew :

" Sturmwind heult Brautmusik—
    Ozean tanzt dazu ! "
(" Ocean will dance with glee,
    Storm wind will sing for thee ! ")

These passages are not operatic libretto in the accepted sense, but
word-movement arising out of the note-movement and endowing it
with the actuality of speech ; they are, in fact, word-tone-structures.
Wagner's acute sensuous perception catches some natural sound and
recreates it in music, word, and picture, thus giving his scenes the value
of veritable experience.

Such is the basis of the work, and from it emerges—focusing,
embodying, and intensifying all the forces at work in it—the figure
of the Flying Dutchman himself. He owes his existence to these
elements, and they in their turn attain ultimate expression through him,
the expression of living emotion, a yearning for release from the aimless storm-tossed monotony of being. In this figure Wagner summarises all his earlier attempts to give form to the human experience
of suffering. *The Flying Dutchman* is the Columbus of the Madgeburg
Overture, the lustful Governor of *Das Liebesverbot,* and the hero of the
Faust symphony. He wears the very features of Beethoven as he
appears in Wagner's novel, the very aspect of his starving Parisian
artist. He is the reckless ungovernable soul that flees perpetually
from its own restlessness, seeking the haven of eternal peace, and whose
two warring impulses give rise to the two incidents that begin and end
Senta's ballad, and are developed as the scene in Act I where the sea
casts the Dutchman upon the land, and the scene in Act II where, in
his duet with Senta, he receives assurance of salvation through her.
These two scenes represent the two chief climaxes of the work. The
rest, by comparison, even the sudden tragic close, is mere padding.

Wagner has nothing to tell us about the origin of these scenes, and
we may therefore conclude that they were written later than most of

the rest, if not absolutely last. In the first draft, where he is called simply
" the Stranger," the Dutchman does not seem to have occupied a place
of leading importance. He appears to have come to the fore as the
figure of Eric receded into the background. One result was a change
in the balance of vocal characters. In *Rienzi* the tenor dominates, but
in *The Flying Dutchman* he gives place to the baritone, in accordance
with a tradition going back through *The Vampire* to *Don Giovanni*.
The whole spirit of *The Flying Dutchman* absolutely demands the deeper
tone ; its passions require a voice of more varied register, pro-
nouncedly virile and capable of ranging from sombre grandeur to
tender mystery. In thus casting his male voices Wagner returns to
the method of vocal characterisation first established by him in his
Liebesverbot, a scheme which makes the baritone interpret passion,
which is preferably expressed not in the traditional melodic line but in
naturalistic, declamatory phrases.

The Dutchman's two most important scenes show this expressionist intention. It refuses to be bound by established forms, and
extends and enlarges them, both structurally and in details of speech-
melodic handling. The broad outlines of the musical architecture
alone remain—the recitative, allegro molto agitato, and maestoso,
rising to molto passionato. Such is the structure of the Dutchman's
first scene. Visual scene, spoken word, and music are grasped as a
single whole. The Dutchman's coming ashore, the rolling bass motif
of the recitative, like a tidal wave flinging itself along the coast, the
almost flat and expressionless opening phrase "Die Frist ist um "
(" The term is past ") rising abruptly to the cry " Ha ! stolzer Ozean!
In kurzen Frist sollst du mich wieder tragen" (" Ha ! ocean proud
and strong ! A little while and thou again shalt bear me ! ")—all
show a primal unity in word, tone, and image. This unity springs
from a single basic concept—that of the momentary pause in the
march of Fate before the upflung wave is drawn inexorably back
into the deep. The Dutchman's allegro song is indeed such a storm-
driven wave :

> " Wie oft in Meeres tiefsten Schlund
> stürzt' ich voll Sehnsucht mich hinab."

> (" How oft in ocean's seething deep
> Death have I sought, eternal sleep.")

A rising and falling wave-motif, played by the orchestra in unison,
takes up the thematic lead, and on it is grafted the melodic line, in

declamatory form and with the accent of natural speech sharply emphasised, to culminate with the cry of anguish :

> " Nirgends ein Grab !
> Niemals der Tod !
> Dies der Verdammnis Schreck-Gebot ! "
>
> (" Nowhere a grave !
> Death cometh ne'er !
> This is the curse I aye must bear.")

Human longing issues from the nature-symbolism of the tempest. From sombre tremolo harmonies, mounting slowly by tenths and accentuating the suspension notes, a phrase struggles into song :

> " Dich frage ich, gepries'ner Engel Gottes,
> der meines Heils Bedingung mir gewann :
> war ich Unsel'ger Spielwerk deines Spottes,
> als die Erlösung du mir zeigtest an ? "
>
> (" Tell me, I pray, O angel sent from heaven,
> Bearing me hope of pardon and of peace,
> Didst thou but mock me with thy promise given,
> Some day the curse should lift, my sorrow cease ? ")

There is no answer but the wave-beat of the recitative. " Nowhere a grave ! Death cometh ne'er ! " echoes the orchestra. As hope dies the key changes to C minor, and note by note rises the tide of passionate song :

> " Nur eine Hoffnung soll mir bleiben,
> nur eine unerschüttert steh'n :
> solang' der Erde Keim' auch treiben,
> so muss sie doch zugrunde geh'n."
>
> (" One hope alone my heart sustaineth,
> One ray alone doth light my gloom :
> Though long the earth its form retaineth,
> Yet shall it some day crash to doom ! ")

The lost soul's last hope is in the ultimate ruin of all things. In a long-sustained unison the trumpets of the Last Judgment ring out ; higher and higher rises the C minor melody :

> " Wann alle Toten aufersteh'n,
> dann werde ich in Nichts vergeh'n ! "
>
> (" When all the dead shall rise again,
> Then shall I too find rest from pain.")

At this all the parts descend with a rush, by broad intervals, from C minor to F minor ; there is a change to diminished sevenths and a final resolution in C major to express ultimate annihilation :

> " Ihr Welten, endet euren Lauf !
>   Ew'ge Vernichtung, nimm mich auf ! "
> (" Ye whirling planets, perish all :
>   Endless destruction on me fall ! ")

A faint echo of this prayer for annihilation from the Dutchman's crew, transposed to E major, rises as though from the depths of the sea, and at last, dying slowly to the accompaniment of a drum roll on C, there resounds once again the blank Dutchman-motif.

This scene is Wagner's first great dramatic achievement.   It lives with the intensity of a passion blinded to all save itself, and the composer's skill in getting realistic effect through tone-symbolism gives strength and style to its musical embodiment.   Music ceases to be sound as such and becomes the passive instrument of a tyrannous " Will to Expression."   This same will determines the external structure, which conforms in outline to the pattern of the great outstanding scenes in the drama, and it also determines the melodic rhythmic formation in accordance with the emotions which the text conveys. The words of this text, however, are freed from conceptual limitations and serve for purely emotional expression.   There is no attempt at individual characterisation, nor at narration of a particular chain of events.   The Dutchman is nameless because he is not truly an individual.   Wagner's elemental conception of this figure is realised only by the stripping away of everything in the delimiting sense subjective. The Dutchman is the embodiment of a passion whose nature is revealed in the course of this scene ; it is seen first in the calm of exhaustion, then in a violent outburst, and finally in a " Will to Universal Destruction " generated by despair.

Contrasted with this figure of lost and errant passion is the figure of Senta.   She, like the Dutchman, is impersonal.   She is faith in the unknown, the " Will to redemption," and these qualities find expression in her only solo piece, the ballad.   Her scenes with the other women and with Eric merely affirm and explain her natural bent. Contrasted with the Dutchman, she stands for faith as opposed to passion, steadfast emotion as against unsteady impulse, melody as against rhythmic harmony.   The erotic element hardly enters into the relations of this pair.   Love, in the superficial operatic sense, has no place here, and the Dutchman himself sets it aside in the words

" Ach nein, die Sehnsucht ist es nach dem Heil."

(" Ah no ! 'tis longing, longing for release.")

In a higher sense, it is true, the relation between these two figures, male and female, becomes a love story *through the music*.   Their duet portrays the gradual growth of love, through stages of doubt and hesitation to knowledge, through assurance of fulfilment by way of wakening passion to love's full flame.

The Dutchman's part begins in a questioning, meditative vein. Each note is chosen with the most delicate perception of the expressionist values of its tone relations.   Wagner paints suppressed emotion in all its intensity.   The first melodic line starts from a low register. It is an arpeggio chord of the ninth with emphasis on the suspension notes.   From the key-note of B the voice rises unaccompanied in even rhythms to the ninth, C, and then, through tremolo harmonies in E major, finds a half close in B.   The process is repeated in quicker time, and again dies out on a questioning dominant harmony with the words :

" Wie aus der Ferne längst vergangner Zeiten
   spricht dieses Mädchens Bild zu mir :
   wie ich's geträumt seit bangen Ewigkeiten,
   vor meinen Augen seh' ich's hier."

(" Up from forgotten depths of years long vanished
   Beams now the maiden's face on me :
   Dream visions seen in days and nights eternal,
   Now turned to substance here I see.")

Here the orchestra enters softly, like a quickened pulse-beat.   The parts, ascending in chords, settle into an E major melody with a very gentle harmonic support and with rhythmic accompaniment on the horns only :

" Wohl hub auch ich voll Sehnsucht meine Blicke
   aus tiefer Nacht empor zu einem Weib."

(" Oft in the night my sighs to heav'n ascended,
   Longing for peace upon a woman's breast.")

Each turn of thought suggested by the words is sympathetically reflected in the musical line.   With the awakening of conscious passion at the words " This sombre glow I feel within my breast," there is a change from the diatonic to the ascending chromatic, and at the dawning hope of salvation : " Would but this angel bid my sorrow cease ! " the song rises to E and thence reaches a resonant major close.

A cadence of magical vibrating harmonies takes up the vocal line, the sense of inner oppression is resolved in tremolo notes on the strings, and the middle parts glisten with chromatic refraction. In both words and music there is a foretaste of *Tristan*, a first sign of the marvellous feeling for harmony which got its effects through delicate shifting tones. The progress of an emotion from the subconscious to the conscious finds spatial representation in harmony. An oboe sounds softly above the mysterious harmonies, and Senta's voice enters with the gentle question :

> " Versank ich jetzt in wunderbares Träumen ?
> Was ich erblicke, ist's ein Wahn ?
> Weilt' ich bisher in trügerischen Räumen ?
> Brach des Erwachens Tag heut' an ? "

> (" Was all a dream, a vision fair and fleeting?
> Can sight and hearing thus betray ?
> Was all till now illusion born of darkness ?
> Now dawns at last the glorious day ? ")

Slowly comes a consciousness of new life, and there is an echo of the welcome to Arindal in the

> " Er steht vor mir mit leidenvollen Zügen,
> es spricht sein unerhörter Gram zu mir."

> (" See, there he stands with sorrow wan and weary,
> His grief he pours into my willing ear.")

The melody gains a firmer outline, a surer rhythm, an increasing momentum. It rises to a chant of ecstasy, and its gathering power issues in a vocal cadence, closed by an orchestral peroration on the redemption theme.

Thus far the double monologue. The musical treatment reveals the whole inwardness of the event and is the most brilliant thing in the opera. A new magic is apparent in this unveiling of psychic processes which music alone can interpret to the emotions. It is indeed art-magic at its strongest and most characteristic. Expressionism at its most intense probes the spiritual depths beneath appearances, and brings to the light of day things concealed even from the doer in the obscurity of the unconscious mind.

The figures Wagner had created in this opera, however, were not such as could enable him to carry the psychological process a step farther. By this stage he had probed them through and through and laid bare the sources of their emotions. The line breaks off after an abrupt change to a quiet E minor passage, a foretaste of the finale of the *Tannhäuser* march. Senta and the Dutchman decline into ordinary human converse, still filled with the wonder of the vision, it is true, but using mundane ideas and tones. Verbal and musical diction alike lose their hallucinatory power and descend to condensed, realistic expression and a melody well adapted to their now intimate converse. The Dutchman-motif makes its appearance, and the storm allegro of the first scene, transposed from C minor to B minor, hints at the fate awaiting the woman who gives herself to him and at the punishment for a breach of faith. Pulsating woodwind harmonies, based on B major, which incorporate the storm theme in the major, accompany Senta's reply. Then, in a sudden orchestral silence, and with a change of key from G major to B major, Senta gives her lover the promise of salvation :

" Wem ich sie weih', schenk' ich die Eine,
die Treue bis zum Tod ! "

(" Him whom I choose, his am I only,
And faithful unto death ! ")

Emotional revelation is complete, all doubts resolved, the promise proclaimed. The duet breaks into the broad melody of the vow, the parts intermingle and the stretto is reached. Finally, the harmonies of that magical self-revelation resound once again, this time with the forceful accent of a living certainty. This is the climax and conclusion of the *spiritual* drama : the actual close, based on the somewhat weak conception of the Dutchman's mistaken suspicions of Senta's faithfulness, though vivid and picturesque in expression, is much inferior to the duet in emotional compass. It is, in fact, a not very successful working out of the first draft in which the figure of Eric occupied the central position subsequently—in the three-act version—ceded to the Dutchman. Even the Dutchman's self-revelation is in no sense a climax, for he is already wholly revealed to Senta. Heine's version, in which

K

the Dutchman is made to renounce Senta through love, reaches a nobler climax from the human standpoint than does Wagner's, where the renunciation is brought about by jealous suspicion. Wagner, moreover, was at that time incapable of coping with the clash of personalities which might have made his last act great by deepening the contrast between the Dutchman and Eric and at the same time throwing Senta's character into higher relief. It was an artistic problem which as yet existed for him only in germ. The action therefore reaches a merely external conclusion—a scenic and pictorial rounding off of matters which reached their real settlement in the duet, and which is reminiscent in its spectacular effect of the grand operatic notions underlying the original draft. Once more the two choruses, Norwegian and Dutch, Man and Nature, diatonic and chromatic, are compared and contrasted : then the dream world of *The Flying Dutchman* dissolves into the elements whence it came. The whole work, however—this ballad of love's power to calm the storms of passion—is summarised in the overture. Wagner himself gave a programmatic interpretation of this overture on the occasion of a concert performance in Zurich—of the ship's storm-tossed voyagings and her landfall, the echo of an ancient, long-unfulfilled promise of salvation for the wanderer, the cheery singing of a passing vessel's crew provoking the doomed captain to a fresh outburst of rage and despair, the wilder onset of the gale, the desperate cry for Woman from the " waste of masculine isolation," a lightning vision of the desired woman appearing like an angel from heaven, whereat the Dutchman falls lifeless, the ship crumbles into dust, and in the dawn of love Man and Woman rise united.

Such is Wagner's own conception of the programme of his overture, and such is the external sequence and internal significance he attributes to the themes in his opera. But the programme, being a condensed summary of the chief moments in the drama only, achieves a merely intellectual parallel with that drama's motive forces, which move between the two poles of blind nature and its storms and the peace of human love, of restless passion for change and the quiet of fulfilled desire, of man's longings and woman's steady faith. These opposites, which are none the less mutually interdependent in accordance with hidden laws, fulfil each other by contrast. Wagner sought and found them in the very nature of music itself. The open fifth which represents the Dutchman finds its harmonic resolution in the major

third which appears as the fulfilment of the primitive natural tones.
This most simple musical symbol, which Wagner employs here with
obvious purpose, takes us back beyond such inspiration as he drew
from Heine or from Marschner to Beethoven's Ninth Symphony.
The fifth, D–A, with which *The Flying Dutchman* opens and which
forms the ground-tone of his picture of the Dutchman, is the very same
with which Beethoven begins the first movement of his last symphony.
Wagner's development of it, however, shows from how different an
emotional standpoint he regarded it.   Beethoven's mysterious pianissimo gives place to a glaring forte, and the clamorous outcry is
heightened by a substitution of an "allegro con brio " for Beethoven's
"un poco maestoso."   The resolution in the change to the major, which
in Beethoven is but a momentary vision, is for Wagner the end and
aim of the whole.   By this shifting of the interest to a concrete interpretation of a musical process, by this elemental outburst of a Romantic,
sensual idea of music, Beethoven's idealistic musical language is given
materialistic meanings that link it up with drama, the stage, "theatre."
Some years later Wagner wrote a programme consisting of quotations
from *Faust* for Beethoven's Ninth Symphony and chose the words
"Entbehren sollst du, sollst entbehren!" ("Thou shalt *do without*, thou
shalt *want*!") as text for the first movement.   It is, yet more appropriately, the motto of his own Flying Dutchman.   In that work
Wagner, himself the perpetual seeker he saw in Faust, the eternal
sufferer he saw in Beethoven, echoes his profoundest experience of
Beethoven, and in so doing finds his own artistic independence.

The Flying Dutchman is the first example of a naturalistic opera on
the grand scale.   It is naturalistic because it does not treat passion
simply, as in earlier opera, as a pretext for formal music, but as a subject of musico-scenic drama.   Wagner finds his motive in a parallelism, both internal and external, between the movements of human
passion and the movements of the sea.   The opera is, furthermore,
naturalistic in matters of stage mechanism and scenic action, where
even the least details—unimportant save in so far as they support the
central theme—are accurately characterised.   It is naturalistic again
in the linking of word and tone and the derivation of both from
elemental phenomena, cries, and movements.   The revelation at great
dramatic moments of psychological and emotional processes is also
naturalistic.   This reaction to naturalism in the sphere of theatrical
music had its literary counterpart in the " Young German " school of

poetry which influenced Wagner greatly at this period.   It shows a revulsion against the idealistic trend of all earlier music, the operatic and instrumental music of the eighteenth century, early grand opera and Romantic opera, where musical naturalism was introduced episodically, but never as a central motive.   Wagner subordinated music to the natural expression of emotion and used it to portray the nakedness of the spirit.   Psychological events, apprehended through sensuous emotion, became subjects of art.   The soul casts aside its veils and appears on the boards with music to interpret its utterances. But the life of the senses is rooted in sex, so that research into and discovery of the secrets of the sexual relation is the kernel of the new type of art.   In *The Flying Dutchman* the contrast between the sexes is stated typically and generally.   Man asks and Woman gives, but there is no individualised man or woman.   In the next stage these simple lines were to be intricately interwoven ; the types were to develop into persons.

Wagner composed *The Flying Dutchman* in seven weeks—a proof of the vigour of the motive impulse and also of the effect of this new mode of artistic apprehension in setting free Wagner's creative energies.   " In Nacht und Elend.   Per aspera ad astra.   Gott gebe es, R.W."   ("In darkness and misery.   Per aspera ad astra.   Amen ! R.W.")   writes Wagner at the end of the score.   The way, indeed, was still dark enough, for though *Rienzi* had been accepted no definite time had been fixed for its production.   Both Munich and Berlin had already rejected *The Flying Dutchman* as " unsuited to the German stage."   In November 1841 Wagner sent the score to Berlin, where he counted on the support of Meyerbeer, then *General-musikdirektor* in that city.   He also based some hopes on the artistic propensities of the youthful King Frederick William IV.   Meanwhile the state of his Parisian affairs had become really grave, and his power of standing up to his difficulties was exhausted.   Paris, he felt, had nothing more to give him.   A drastic change in his life was imminent.   Meanwhile, he escaped actual starvation by journalistic and musical hack-work, and day by day wrote urgent letters to Dresden to hurry on the preparations for *Rienzi* and petitions to Count von Redern and Meyerbeer in Berlin to get them to accept *The Flying Dutchman*.   The spring of 1842 brought decision.   Count von Redern accepted *The Flying Dutchman* on Meyerbeer's recommendation and on account of its " musical talent " for production in Berlin ; the Dresden authorities definitely fixed the performance of *Rienzi* for the beginning of their new season.

Wagner's immediate goal was attained.   The unknown adventurer who had come to Paris two and a half years previously with the intention of conquering opera was leaving it in the certainty that two of his works were shortly to be produced at Germany's two most important theatres.   Paris had not given him what he sought there, but it had given him something different and far more important. The whirlpool of Parisian life had schooled his vague ambitions, and taught him to measure his powers against those of the world, giving him insight into the worth, or lack of worth, in the ruling powers. He had seen there the best that the art and the artists of his time could offer, and his own dissatisfaction with that best had brought him self-knowledge.   Paris had forced him to discover his own literary talent and had enabled him to complete *Rienzi* and compose *The Flying Dutch-man*.   It had shown him that his destined road led away from the false glamour of a foreign land back to his own country, away from grand opera and back to Romantic opera.   Finally, as a parting gift for his journey it gave him what was to prove a treasure for the future—an old book of sagas.   Two characters in this book drew Wagner strangely—Tannhäuser, a knightly troubadour who fell victim to Venus's wiles, and Lohengrin, messenger of the Holy Grail.   With this book and a bundle of half-finished pianoforte arrangements upon which Schlessinger advanced them money for the journey, Wagner and Minna set out on April 7, 1842, and after five days and nights continuous travel reached Dresden.

CHAPTER V

WAGNER returned to Germany at the age of twenty-nine to make his first appearance before a wider artistic public. Three years earlier he had left Riga for Paris with this end in view, but Paris had denied him his ambition, and the denial spurred him to put forth all his powers. On the crest of that effort he reconquered his own country : a people that had let him go into exile a poor music-director of no account, now welcomed him back with all the acclaim due to a successful operatic composer, gave him a secure income, and allowed him the artistic influence pertaining to the post of Kapellmeister in one of the best-equipped opera-houses in Germany.

Yet within six years Wagner had sucked dry the experience of life thus opened to him. Once more the Flying Dutchman put out to sea, challenging the storm : the first dream of fulfilment was dreamed out, and the yearning for some yet undiscovered haven prompted to more distant and more perilous journeyings. The men and women who played their parts during these years, the slowly woven net of event and circumstance, are historic facts of slight significance. The final rupture did not come about through their knavery or their pettiness. It was an inevitable consequence of Wagner's own waxing powers, of that strange *daemonic* force within which consumed and ravaged everything about him.

When Wagner first came to Dresden little was known about him. He was reputed to be still young, to have had a wild and chequered career, and to have come near starvation in Paris. His former, purely professional, acquaintance with such persons of repute in Germany as Madame Schroeder-Devrient, Heine, the *régisseur*, and Herr *Hofrat* Winkler was of the slightest. Under these conditions the fact that a work of his which was too long for a single evening and which made extraordinary demands upon soloists, chorus, orchestra, and stage machinery was actually performed for the first time, testifies, surely, to a remarkable spirit of enterprise in the Dresden intendant and leading artistes.

But their confidence in Wagner did not end here.   Ready recognition was accorded not only to the work but to the man.   About the time that *Rienzi* was first performed, Morlacchi, conductor of the Italian *ensemble*, died, and Wagner, who had proved his ability as a conductor at rehearsals, was appointed Morlacchi's successor over the heads of other well-recommended applicants.   He was given equal official standing with Reissiger (sole Kapellmeister of German opera hitherto), and after successfully conducting a performance of *Euryanthe* was exempted from the usual year's probation.   Apart from regular holidays, Wagner had no difficulty in getting leave of absence on several occasions to recommend or to conduct his operas in other towns.   He was allowed a free hand at the rehearsal of important works and, later, his wishes for the institution of regular orchestral concerts were met.   Clearly, the authorities recognised that he was an artist, and were anxious to afford him scope for work.   There can be no question but that the young and untried composer was met with kindness and consideration.   Baron von Lüttichau may not have been a man of great intellectual distinction, but he cannot be denied the credit of having helped Wagner by giving him practical confidence and by allowing him freedom to develop.

Much the same may be said of Wagner's relations with his new colleagues.   Gottlieb Reissiger, his senior and companion in office, was an able, even a talented, musician of the old school, whose sanguine temperament had hardened with time into hostility to new ideas and a fixed determination to keep his own comfortable niche in Dresden.   Reissiger, no doubt, found much in Wagner to annoy him, from the success of *Rienzi* to the younger man's wholly alien notions of musicianship.   The two conductors' equal official footing stimulated a rivalry between them, increased by the fact that they composed operas which were performed alternately.   Moreover, Wagner, brusquely and without a thought for the other's feelings, took into his own hands works which Reissiger had been conducting—a course which probably did nothing to increase the warmth of the older man's sentiments towards him.   No doubt these things led to petty intrigues, and the adherents of both parties formed the cabals so usual in theatrical life.   But Reissiger never for a moment doubted his own ascendancy over the hot-headed young experimentalist.   An indiscreet youngster who gave himself away at every turn was a far less dangerous colleague than the Italian Morlacchi had been. Reissiger rightly felt far too secure of his position with the intendant, the orchestra, and the critics to regard Wagner as a menace. The opposition in this quarter grew from a natural and genuine dislike of Wagner's methods as a Kapellmeister.

Wagner's relations with the singers were less complex. Foremost among these were two talented and commanding personalities, Tichatschek, a tenor of phenomenal vocal power, and Wilhelmina Schroeder-Devrient, a dramatic genius. Tichatschek had to be accepted as he was in all his natural *naïveté*, his excellence as a singer consisting in his feeling for rhythm and accuracy in declamation. As to Madame Schroeder-Devrient, Wagner's attitude towards her, since the days when her performance of Fidelio had carried him off his feet, and her Romeo, turning his mind to Italian opera, had inspired *Das Liebesverbot*, had ever been that of a learner. In her he found his *alter ego*. Watching her performance he experienced " a psychic commotion, at once terrible and blissful, amounting to ecstasy, through this indescribable dual life of the stage." Tichatschek and Schroeder-Devrient were pattern artists, beyond criticism, and moreover his personal friends, but even apart from these two the company, at the time of Wagner's appointment, contained, if no more geniuses, a very creditable number of excellent singers. Later, during Wagner's tenure, the personnel was strengthened by two more singers of supreme talent, Friedrich Mitterwurzer, a Leipzig baritone, and Wagner's young niece, Johanna Wagner.

Such, then, was Wagner's new environment. Before many rehearsals for *Rienzi* were over, Fischer, the director of the chorus, became his enthusiastic and devoted adherent, as did also Heine, the *régisseur*, who had been an old friend of Wagner's stepfather Geyer. Fischer's chorus was famed for its high state of training, for purity and volume of tone, and for precision. The orchestra, led by a Pole named Lipinski, whom Schumann describes as " an imposing individual," contained a high proportion of competent players both in the wind and the strings. Thanks to the persistent effects of a former training in Italian opera its tone was reputed the best in Germany. The opera-house, a new building opened only the previous year, was fitted with all the latest stage machinery. A splendour-loving and generous court with a tradition of preference for operatic art, if only on the spectacular side, took a keen interest in productions and personnel.   Choir service in the Catholic Chapel Royal formed a part of the duties of conductors, orchestra, and chorus, and this, though from a practical point of view it interrupted their work in the theatre, yet afforded the stimulus of a great realm of art other than the theatrical.

There can scarcely have been in Germany at that day another stage where conditions were so favourable for the production of *Rienzi*.   Its success was commensurable.   Preparations, notwithstanding, dragged on till October 20, 1842.   Wagner spent the intervening months of anxious yet happy expectation in family visits, journeys to Berlin in connection with a performance there of *The Flying Dutchman*, and a holiday for his health's sake at Teplitz.   He was forced to borrow money from his brother-in-law Brockhaus to tide him over immediate difficulties.   But he had won his throw.   The unknown young musician found himself lifted suddenly out of " night and misery " to a place among the celebrities of his day.   His earliest published autobiographical notes, which shortly appeared by Laube's invitation in the *Zeitung für die elegante Welt*, contributed further to surround him with something of the glamour of a prince in a fairy-tale. It was in this character and not as a great artist that he was acclaimed. In Dresden, as in all Germany, he was thought of as the hero of a story of adventure crowned with a piece of extraordinary good luck.   His success, seen not as the fruit of long struggle but as the reward of a bold stroke which " came off," filled the professional musical world with astonishment rather than genuine admiration, and caught the general public in a wave of enthusiasm for so dramatic a turn of fortune. In the few weeks before Christmas, *Rienzi* was given no less than six times, each time amidst increasing applause.   The artistes would not hear of the cuts which Wagner proposed to shorten a performance lasting nearly six hours.   The Dresden management set their hearts on an immediate production of *The Flying Dutchman*, and insisted that Wagner should get the MS back from Berlin at once.

Success, it seemed, had come.   Wagner's financial difficulties were, indeed, still pressing.   He received three hundred talers for *Rienzi*, two hundred of which went to clear off the debt to Brockhaus. Creditors in Magdeburg and Riga grew clamorous at the news of his good fortune, and further expenditure was necessary to set up house and to live in Dresden in a style suited to his new position.   If the warm-hearted Madame Schroeder-Devrient, understanding the situation, had not advanced a thousand talers, Wagner's position would have been as precarious as ever, despite the apparent turn in his fortunes. Annoyances of this kind, however, having failed to dishearten him during the bad years in Paris, were unlikely to disturb him very seriously now. Moreover, it seemed impossible that success on this scale should not continue. Other German theatres would take up *Rienzi*, and the approaching production of *The Flying Dutchman* would confirm his triumph. While in Teplitz Wagner had made a few preliminary sketches for *Tannhäuser*, and other projects crowded upon him. All he needed was time to execute them and later to produce them on the stage. The career of a successful opera composer, such as Meyerbeer, lay plain before him. His first success swept away all doubts, and the intoxication of achievement raised him to a condition of almost overbearing triumph.

Under these circumstances Wagner was tempted to regard the ties of office as a mere hindrance and a burden. This was not because he disliked the Dresden theatre as he found it. Indeed, he built all his hopes upon it. But he needed leisure for creative work. He accordingly had serious thoughts of declining the proffered post of Kapellmeister, and only the arguments of his family and of Minna persuaded him to take a more prudent estimate of his immediate prospects as a composer. Dresden's reception of *The Flying Dutchman* probably did still more to sober him. Conditions seemed even more favourable than they had been for *Rienzi*. Then he had had to prove himself : now he could reckon upon the support of a large public, a lively interest in his person and his story, and the suggestive magic of former success. It is true that he lacked the splendid figure of Tichatschek in the title-rôle, and that the singer who took the part of the Flying Dutchman could not compare in personal charm with the exponent of Rienzi. On the other hand, Madame Schroeder-Devrient as Senta was the central figure in the piece. The reception of the work, however, was so extremely bad that Wagner's friends pressed for an immediate revival of *Rienzi* to expunge the ill-effects of the failure. Performances of *Rienzi*, accordingly, continued amidst undiminished enthusiasm, though the work was now divided to fill two evenings and so to avoid either cuts or excessive length. Four performances was the most to which *The Flying Dutchman* would run.

There must be something profoundly wrong here, something of

which Wagner had had no inkling hitherto. His gradual enlightenment on the point showed the success of *Rienzi* in a new and far less
encouraging aspect. Wagner knew that *The Flying Dutchman* was not
a falling-off as compared with *Rienzi*. Rather the original, the individual, element in his work attained stronger and clearer expression
therein. He had no shadow of doubt in his own mind that it represented an ascent, and an ascent in the right direction. But he now
made the disturbing discovery that where he himself felt that he was
still in bondage to convention he was received with acclamation,
but that where he attained creative freedom he was met with astonishment and disapproval. The glamour of his former success was gone
for him. He realised that as a serious artist he disappointed people.
His first appearance in Germany might have ended in patent and
immediate failure had he begun with *The Flying Dutchman* instead of
Rienzi.

The discrepancy between merit and public response, between
expectations and results, took him aback. If he was not as yet fully
awake to the cause of the failure of his second venture, and if the
principal effect of it for the moment was to set him brooding on
the meaning of this discrepancy, he was none the less obliged on the
practical side to revise his views as to his chances of speedy and
increasing success as an operatic composer. The offer of the Kapellmeister's post in Dresden had to be taken more seriously, the exhor-
tations of Minna and the family sounded more persuasive. Wagner
himself conducted the first performance of *The Flying Dutchman* on
January 2, 1843. On January 4 he entered into serious discussion
of the intendant's proposal. On January 10 he conducted a performance of Weber's *Euryanthe* as a test, after which he went on a short
visit to Berlin to assist at the performance of *The Flying Dutchman*
fixed for the end of March, and meanwhile von Lüttichau's proposal
passed the necessary stages. Wagner took up his new appointment
on February 1. " Consciousness of the high opinion commonly held
of such an appointment, and the lustre my preferment possessed in the
eyes of others, dazzled even me at last into regarding as an extraordinary stroke of good luck what was soon to prove a source of
sufferings which wore me out. And so I became—oh, joyful day !—
Royal Kapellmeister ! "

Had Wagner been no more than he seemed—a talented young
composer and conductor—this " extraordinary stroke of good luck "

would no doubt have proved really to be so. All the conditions of success were present. And yet these very conditions helped to make Wagner other than the thing he seemed. The transplantation into new and fertile soil caused an unexpected burgeoning of seeds of development sown in the Paris years. Inevitably they burst the confines of a position which was designed for no such expansion of personality. Wagner at thirty years of age developed simultaneously in three directions : as conductor, as composer, and as man. But Dresden persisted in regarding him, under each of these aspects, as the person he had seemed to be when first he came. He, on the other hand, went to all lengths to advertise these changes in a provocative manner. The result was conflict.

Wagner's career as a conductor in Dresden was signalised by three achievements which all acknowledged to be remarkable. These were a production of Gluck's *Armida*, with Madame Schroeder-Devrient, on March 5, 1843, a performance of the Ninth Symphony at the Palm Sunday concert, April 5, 1846, and a performance of *Iphigenia in Aulis*, newly arranged by himself, on February 24, 1847. In *Armida* he had the inspiration of the great actress's power of creative interpretation ; in the symphony he relied on his own interpretive insight ; and in the *Iphigenia* he occupied the conductor's desk as *re*-creator of the work. All three, however, meant far more to him than mere exercises in interpretation. Armida's figure impressed itself deeply on his imagination, with effects which are to be seen in the Venus he was then creating in *Tannhäuser*, in his Isolda, in the later Paris Venus, and finally in Kundry. The Ninth Symphony, whose first movement had already inspired *The Flying Dutchman* overture, now suggested to him, through the bass recitative of the finale and the transition to the choral hymn, a new style of declamation, and a new idea of the expression value of the vocal word. In point of date this performance comes between *Tannhäuser* and *Lohengrin*, and forms, indeed, the stylistic link between the two works. Wagner's rearrangement of *Iphigenia in Aulis* was the immediate precursor of his *Lohengrin*. Not only does the diction of Wagner's translation and amplification belong to the style of *Lohengrin*, but so does the orchestral tone-colour, not to mention the intervention of miracle at a critical moment in the plot, and the substitution of a tragic ending for Gluck's happy one.

Interspersed with these three outstanding achievements in conducting, and leaving aside performances of his own works, his productions of Marschner's *Hans Heiling* and *Adolf von Nassau* may also be noted. Besides these there was the routine work of the usual repertory operas, among them fashionable Italian and French works of the day, Mozart's *Titus*, which Wagner rehearsed, and Mozart's *Seraglio*, *Don Juan*, and *Figaro*, in which he deputised for Reissiger.

The opposition made Wagner's manner of conducting Mozart the point of attack. This was first launched from the *Kapelle*, when in April, soon after his appointment, Wagner was called upon to take over *Don Juan* at short notice. Lipinski, the Kapellmeister, persuaded a committee of the managers to extract an apology from Wagner and a promise of amendment. What was this dispute about? Wagner had established tempi contrary to use, and improvised fantastic changes in separate movements. The singers, used to traditional methods of performance, had been unable to follow, and Wagner, to avoid disaster, was forced to give way. The result was an argument on the subject painful to public, singers, orchestra, and conductor alike. The *Kapelle* were angry; they were proud of their traditions and demanded that the young Kapellmeister should respect them. He was known, they said, for an eccentric, but Mozart, surely, might be exempted from his whimsies. Coming from Paris, he might want to introduce new methods of conducting, but they were unsuited to the Dresden stage. This, or something like this, was the burden of their reproaches, and it was to be heard again and again in the future from press, public, and individual critics.

To regard these incidents as manifestations of mere narrow-mindedness or personal spite would be to miss their essential point. Narrow-mindedness and enmity there may have been, for the Dresden critics of that day, headed at first by Schladebach, a music-director, and later by Karl Banck, whom Schumann describes as a dullard, are worthy neither of respect nor justification. But the opposition to Wagner's methods as a conductor, and to his way of conducting Mozart in particular, testifies to an instinct in his critics characteristic of that time and relatively sound. In regard to *Armida*, *Iphigenia*, and the Ninth Symphony, his opponents failed to make good their point. In these instances traditions of performance were either non-existent or insufficiently well established, so that, to less sensitive ears at least, unaccustomed elements in the interpretation were submerged in the effect of the works as a whole. But when well-known works appeared in the guise lent them by Wagner a certain strangeness was immediately remarked. Not only the journalists who backed Reissiger but Robert Schumann himself noticed " R. Wagner's incomprehensible handling of the tempo " in *Fidelio*. If objective witness were lacking we should still have a definitive and certainly not hostile or prejudiced source of information in Wagner's own statements as to his conception of the conductor's task. These form the best argument for the disinterestedness of the opposition, an opposition based, like hostility to Wagnerian composition, on the natural antagonism between two contradictory conceptions of music. The older of these conceptions required musical interpretation and performance to be tonal, formal, the newer insisted on their being expressionist, emotional.

The *formal* idea of musical performance, then generally accepted, was based on musical conceptions derived from the Viennese classics and from French and German opera. It was founded on an idea of melody as lyrically-rounded song-phrase within the manifold forms of sonata, aria, symphonic movement, or operatic *ensemble*. A too detailed pursuit of expression values, of each change of movement in the line, must destroy a view of the formal architecture as a whole, and distort the basic character of the melody. In the opinion of that day, subjectivity of expression was less important than a capacity for rendering the symmetric flow of song-phrases and displaying their structural beauties.

Wagner, too, when he set out to perform a piece of music, took song as his measure. But song to Wagner was not the tuneful aria, designed to display the charms of a beautiful voice, but declamatory song of the kind which Madame Schroeder-Devrient practised and through which she got her effects, even when the voice, as a voice, failed. It was vocal dramatic recitative. In grand opera this form was employed exclusively to introduce the arias. In German opera it was relegated to spoken dialogue. In Italian opera it was usually confined to unaccompanied recitative. For Wagner, however, it was the foundation of everything. In it he found what he calls the " Melos " of the work, and this " Melos " is expression. To him the whole purpose and nature of performance consisted in presenting expression. The vocal period, therefore, with its formal structure, melody designed to display the voice, could never, for him, be fundamental. Instead he sought the dominating and unifying principle of performance in the phrase. The phrase must determine the way in which the melody, and indeed the whole work, was to be performed. A piece of music was to be regarded as a progressive unfolding of expression, and its performance should follow every turn in that expression, every changing phase of emotion.

This was an unusual and controversial point of view, particularly when applied to Mozart's music and without the preliminary discussion and explanation appropriate to so drastic a change. Wagner's modifications of tempo were merely the most pronounced outward sign of his new ideas of performance. More important was the hostility of the performers, singers no less than instrumentalists, to an expressionist method which, as they instinctively recognised, required an entirely new technique of performance. Moreover, not habit and wont alone but genuine artistic conviction of the inapplicability of these methods to Mozart's music opposed the innovation. Matters were different in regard to Gluck and Beethoven, principally because in their case there was no firmly established tradition, but also because their music seemed better suited to an expressionist method of performance through which it gained in life and plasticity. Gluck, it is true, builds up his arias in well-defined melodic periods, and Wagner found them stumbling-blocks in his path. He accounted for them as an imperfection in Gluck caused by his bondage, through his libretti, to the " fettered pathos " of the Racine school of tragedy, and thought that in moments of strong emotion Gluck's music " left much to be desired." It did not occur to Wagner for a moment that this " imperfection " might be the result not of Gluck's era in the history of musical development, but of Gluck's considered theories of opera. A true adherent of the doctrine of evolution, Wagner saw all things, including Gluck, as links in the ascending chain by which music was to attain expressionism. But he could forget Gluck's formal aria melodies in the grand sweep of his recitatives. Here he found an intimation of something he himself had envisaged; here was free outlet for the emotional will to expression. Where Gluck's musical line was insufficiently marked it might be illuminated by orchestral emphasis and additions. Such emphasis was clearly well adapted to the note of heroic pathos underlying Gluck's operas, and of a sudden this pathos—a development of eighteenth-century vocal declamation, and musically harsh—ceased to seem stilted and tiresome and became instinct with life and meaning.

This new emphasis on expressionist values rediscovered Gluck, and the same change of outlook provided the key to that late work of Beethoven, the Ninth Symphony. Wagner's performance, however, cannot be said to have been a " discovery " of the Ninth Symphony in the sense often claimed for it. The work may have been little known in Dresden, where concerts were few, and no doubt it made little impression when conducted by Reissiger, but elsewhere, in Leipzig under Mendelssohn, and in Vienna under Nicolai, Beethoven's last symphony had been worthily played and the public had grown familiar with it. None the less, Wagner's performance was epoch-making, not in regard to the Ninth Symphony alone, but for the interpretation of Beethoven as a whole. Here Wagner's expressionist interpretation found, as it had not found in Mozart, or even in Gluck, a subject really requiring such interpretation, since the will to expression had been a factor in its creation. It is characteristic that Wagner concentrated his interest chiefly on that part of the work in which the will to expression is strongest—namely, in the finale. The bass recitative engaged his attention particularly. There he found the same problems of interpretation and performance which had interested him so deeply in Gluck's recitative, a free-flowing melody emancipated from the period, "Melos" based on the significant declamatory phrase. Here is no appeal for sensuous justification in vocal beauty, no bondage to strict tempo. In performance freedom of movement is required to reveal its meaning, and yet it is wrought with a profound feeling for song—as Gluck wrote his recitatives, as Madame Schroeder-Devrient sang, as, in Wagner's opinion, the conductor should conduct. He demanded clearness above all things, not, however, the clearness of technical precision, but rather clearness of expression springing from sympathetic understanding of every turn of phrase.

For Wagner the bass recitatives were the pivots on which the Ninth Symphony turned. In them the earlier movements found organic union with the finale; that which the recitatives *expressed* explained what had gone before, summed it up intellectually and carried it on to the climax. Wagner interpreted the three movements of the Symphony retrospectively, as preparations for the final triumph hymn. They were a programmatic sequence whose connection he explained to his audience by quotations from *Faust*. Conductors of the "formal" school were unable to understand this expressionism in

Beethoven's musical idiom—a fact which explains Spohr's, and even Mendelssohn's, coolness towards this work, particularly towards the finale. Wagner was greatly pleased, however, when after his final rehearsal, Niels Gade, a musician hitherto opposed to his methods, declared that he would willingly pay double only to hear the instrumental recitative over again. As always, the key to Wagner's interpretation was to be found in the recitatives. He was little concerned with details of the musical period, of structure. He concentrated on what was spontaneous, emotional, cataclysmic, in the inner drama as it develops from moment to moment, and this he emphasised in the spirit of improvisation. The orchestration was illuminated, the thematic web unravelled, the dynamics carefully graduated, the tonal relationships of individual groups accurately balanced. *Espressivo* was his highest aim. By means of this, in the broadest sense, naturalistic mode of interpretation based on a naturalistic conception of music as a whole, a view of the musical process as *experience*, the demiurge in the later Beethoven stood for the first time revealed.

" There was once upon a time a man who was impelled to express all his thoughts and feelings in the language of music. . . ." So runs one of those anonymous notices in the *Dresden Anzeiger* which Wagner used to rouse public interest in some forthcoming production. Was Beethoven such a man (as Wagner thought), or did he read into Beethoven's work something, present indeed in germ, even prominent and important in the finale of the Ninth Symphony, but no such dominating force as it was in Beethoven's interpreter ? That Wagner should think as he did was inevitable, for he could only conceive of music as a " language " in which to " express " all that is " thought and felt." He could only interpret and he could only create music as a language conveying thoughts and feelings. Where it failed to fulfil this function he thought it feeble, insipid, worthless. As his self-realisation increased and he came more and more into public conflict with an entirely different conception of music, he became passionately convinced that his was the only true one. The whole musical past seemed to him but a preparation for that perfect freedom of expression for which he himself strove. Where expression was intimated but not carried out, as in Gluck and Mozart, he thought he saw genius hampered by convention ; where it was consciously aimed at but not fully achieved, as in Weber's *Euryanthe*, he saw failure, due either to outer circumstance or inner weakness. Where, however,

L

it became prominent, as in Beethoven's later works, he hailed it as a foreshadowing of what he himself thought and willed. He saw everything with the eyes of a great theatrical artist for whom events, whether in life or in art, are neither static nor subject to eternal change, but continually in progress towards some climax. Wagner felt he must reveal this hidden cumulative impulse, this most fruitful cause of action, that he must explain it as the expression of the will to live. For him, therefore, the theatre must be the goal of all art, since the theatre alone could *express* with final clarity, could give artistic form to continuously changing expression. Anything but the stage, even Beethoven's symphonies, must fall short of this ever-changing fulfilment. But if the theatre were to be able to reach the goal of expressionist representation it might not tie itself down to closed forms, as in the work of Gluck and Mozart. It must break down form and must take for its only law the law of free movement, of continuous development. It must express, like Madame Schroeder-Devrient, through an ascending scale of emotion. "From the standpoint of my own capabilities, which I am more inclined to despair of than to overvalue, I regard my present and forthcoming works as mere experiments to see if opera be possible," writes Wagner to Hanslick in January 1847 on the subject of *Tannhäuser*. In what sense does he question if opera is "possible"? He is not thinking of opera as a branch of the art of music, as in Gluck, Mozart, and Spontini, but of opera as a vehicle for intense and ever-cumulative passion, as an epitome of all that Wagner as a creative artist was struggling to represent.

When Wagner left Paris he had schemes for a number of operas in mind. An old book of sagas had made him familiar with the stories of Lohengrin and Tannhäuser, and Raumer's *History of the Hohenstaufens* had interested him in Frederick II's son and his chivalrous dreams. A plot began to take shape in his mind, which was to combine the more important elements in the dramas of *Rienzi* and *The Flying Dutchman*, not uninfluenced by *The Maid of Orleans*. The effeminate Manfred, having been deprived of his lands, is inspired to fight for his throne by a girl who, unknown to him, is his half-sister, the daughter of the Emperor Frederick by a Saracen woman. Love for the stranger maid gives him strength, but Fatima will consent to be his prophetess only, no more. At the moment of parting she receives in her breast a treacherous dagger-thrust aimed at Manfred. The first sketch belongs to the final months in Paris and is rich in effective operatic moments. The Saracen heroine is unmistakably a more active counterpart of Senta. When Wagner reached Dresden this idea was crowded out by plans for *Tannhäuser*, the first sketches for which were laid down in the summer of 1842. Madame Schroeder-Devrient's interpretation of Senta, however, revived it, and Wagner finished the libretto. The great singer's personality directly influenced his work. He saw her as a sisterly prophetess of the realm of art which he sought and himself as Manfred, fired to fresh activity by her. In his enthusiasm, however, he failed to see her as she saw herself. She felt herself to be—and indeed she was—just the type of loving, self-giving woman whose strength springs solely from her womanhood, which Wagner's conception of Fatima excluded. Madame Schroeder-Devrient refused to be apotheosised on the stage as the heroic virgin. She felt the falsity in the idea, and Wagner came eventually to agree with her. Meanwhile, in February 1843, rehearsals began for *Armida*. It was produced on March 5. On April 7, five weeks later, Wagner wrote to friends in Paris that his libretto for *The Venusberg*—for such originally was the title of *Tannhäuser*—was complete.

Its plot has as many or more sources than that of *The Flying Dutchman*. The association of the old saga of the "Song Contest" and Heinrich von Ofterdingen with that of Tannhäuser, who was lured into the Hörfelberg, sprang from a suggestion of the literary historian, E. T. L. Lucas. In the final form memories of E. T. A. Hoffmann's Ofterdingen saga, Fouqué's Song Contest, and Tieck's Christianised Tannhäuser poem, all play a part. As with *The Flying Dutchman*, Heine probably provided the final impulse, in this case by his reflections on the Tannhäuser legend, published in the *Salon* in 1837. Here and there we can trace reminiscences of former plans of Wagner's own. Thus the Pilgrims' Chorus recalls a similar procession with the dead Brigitta in the *Hohe Braut*, and the love of a man for a woman above him in rank runs as a motive through both works. The influence of the figure of Armida on Wagner's conception of Venus and her kingdom of love is vouched for by the fact that he set to work on the libretto immediately after the *Armida* rehearsals, the link being Madame Schroeder-Devrient, who embodied both ideas. Armida, however, is to be regarded less as an inspiration and model than as an explanation and enrichment of the original conception.

As regards the autobiographical element in *Tannhäuser*, Wagner has told us all that he could and would in his *Mitteilung an meiner Freunde*. " My happy change of circumstances, my hopes of further fortunate developments, and most of all a sort of intoxication caused by new and congenial surroundings, fostered in me the appetite for pleasure, and distracted a soul, moulded by past sorrows and conflicts, from its true path. The instinct in every man to *live*, here and now, impelled the artist in me to courses which could not fail, after a little, to disgust and revolt me." Wagner then proceeds to describe how the conflict between sensual enjoyment and " the yearning for satisfaction in a higher and nobler element " reached a tragic intensity, whence sprang " a desire to pass out of this present world " as the only gate to love's fulfilment.

Psychologically the situation shows a striking resemblance to that which, ten years earlier, produced *Das Liebesverbot*. Then, however, the " higher, nobler element," now envisaged as " a pure, chaste, virginal, unapproachable love," played no part in the conflict. It had been hinted at in the figure of Isabella, but in the actual working out it had given place to a more sensual emotion. The central female figure in that youthful work was now to be divided into two, one embodying renunciation, the other desire. The woman who renounced was a creation of pure fancy, evoked in answer to the need for dramatic contrast. Tannhäuser's love for Elizabeth, hers for him and her will to redeem him, were the products of Wagner's unaided imagination. They echo his idea of the Saracen maid, of woman solely as prophetess and virgin. But the concept which Madame Schroeder-Devrient rejected as unreal served to emphasise the full significance and reality of the woman who is Desire—of Venus. Born of a burning sensuality, both emotional and intellectual, the figure of Venus, under the magic lighting of the stage, casts a shadow, an unreal reflection of herself, which is Elizabeth. The drama grows from the existence of this " double " of vital, *daemonic* womanhood. By the use of imaginative contrast, and by the action this contrast evokes, Wagner here finds a continual and increasing impulse to sensuous expression, lacking in *Das Liebesverbot*.

The idealised dream-figure of Elizabeth and Wagner's reference to " the desire for sensual enjoyment " in his life are, equally, symbolic of the power that moved him to create, and which is to be found in the eroticism of his plot. All other delights are felt as mere adornments to or shadows of this one. Sexual desire is the most genuinely human and the strongest force in Wagner's nature. All the creatures of his imagination are the fruit of erotic concepts, the pledges of desires so intense that they were driven to seek their objects in unearthly, ecstatic dreams and visions. To witness the truth of this neither Wagner's wild student years, nor the mood that evoked *Das Liebesverbot*, nor his early marriage, nor his subsequent adventures with women are necessary. Each frank expression of his nature proclaims it. So powerfully was he dominated by the erotic impulse that the whole structure of his thought is built upon the processes of love. Even when, in his writings, he handles apparently abstract themes, he does so by means of similes borrowed from the relations between man and woman, such as begetting, embracing, giving birth, passion, fulfilment, and lassitude. Love, at its most violent in sexual love, is for him the event underlying all events. As a man he was unremittingly pursued and tormented by the sexual instinct, so that he saw it as the curse and at the same time the highest bliss in all life. It drove him as a man to seek woman, and as an artist to portray the drama of seeking and finding, the curse of denial, and ultimate escape from the demon of instinct by the gateway of death.

The erotic impulse in Wagner found expression in the figure of Tannhäuser, who was, as none of his forerunners had been, blood of his blood, and, as none other before Tristan, an embodiment of real suffering. We see him tossed by uprushes of elemental sensuality from hot fleshly embraces to the joys of an equally sensual asceticism. He passes from one to the other, the plaything of the passions which dominate his nature. The vague restlessness with which the Flying Dutchman was cursed is seen plainly now as the curse of the promptings of the blood. Beneath that curse man must follow his fate, sometimes in voluptuousness, sometimes in pain and grief. The overmastering potency of the forces of nature require a merely passive heroism, and it is only by making these real that the artist endows his central figure with individuality. These motive forces are outside his personality, mysterious powers which drive him from the woman who satisfies the senses to the woman who gives freedom from the senses, and from her back to the first, till the voluptuousness of momentary satisfaction through sexual enjoyment gives place at last to the voluptuousness of eternal fulfilment through sexual death.

The action of the drama consists in its hero's spell-bound movements between these opposite poles, between the love that is pleasure
and the love that is death. Very significantly Wagner called his
completed libretto not *Tannhäuser*, but *The Venusberg*. The Venusberg
was indeed the kernel of the work. Wagner's vision of it had roused
the artist in him to desire to present it upon the stage. The Venusberg
and its opposite had begotten in him the expressionist impulse now
clamouring for birth. The excitement of this discovery of elemental
eroticism continued to work in him through and beyond the *Tristan*
period, for then, and not till then, was he able to realise to the full the
resistless, terrible might of his Venus. In the interval he had discovered and explored other regions of his imaginative life and had
found new spurs to expression, but nothing stirred so deeply the fires
of his being or sent the flames leaping so high as this great vision of
desire and of its twofold fulfilment in the intoxication of sensual
enjoyment, and in the ascetic ecstasy of death. "However and
wherever I touched my plot, I found myself glowing with warmth
and light. Notwithstanding lengthy interruptions to my work, I was
back in a flash in that strange, fragrant atmosphere which had intoxicated me from my first conception of it." Wagner experienced a
creative self-abandonment such as he had never known before, even
during the volcanic days when he had composed *The Flying Dutchman*.
He was even assailed by a superstitious dread that he would die
before finishing a work into which, for the first time, he could put
his whole soul.

Wagner finished the libretto on April 7, 1843, but was delayed in
setting to work on the composition by official and other duties. He
had accepted the post of conductor of the Dresden " Liedertafel," and
was asked to compose a work for a male-voice choir festival which
was to be held in the coming July. The result was *The Love-Feast of
the Apostles*. The work has the theatrical tinge inevitable in anything
of Wagner's. A solo-*ensemble* for the apostles is contrasted with
a chorus for the disciples, beginning with *a cappella* phrases ; then,
at the moment of the outpouring of the Holy Ghost, the orchestra
enters *crescendo*. The chorus which ends the work is a foreshadowing
of the knights' song that greets the unveiling of the Grail in *Parsifal*.
Another work of this period is the *Festival Song for the Unveiling
of a Memorial to Frederick Augustus I.*

Wagner did not begin to make musical sketches for *Tannhäuser*
until November 1843, and more than a year elapsed before the first
outline was finished in December 1844. The score was not complete
till April 13, 1845. The events which during these months came
between the composer and his work were not without their effect upon
it. The ill-success of *The Flying Dutchman*, which Wagner himself
conducted in January 1844, probably both humiliated and strengthened
his pride. The work day by day in Dresden afforded various stimuli.
It included a performance, conducted by himself, of the Pastoral
Symphony at a concert for Palm Sunday, 1844, rehearsals of *Hans
Heiling* and *The Midsummer-Night's Dream* that same spring, and,
in November, Spontini's *The Vestal*, conducted by the composer.
Another event of importance was the coming, in May 1844, of Johanna
Wagner, daughter of Wagner's brother Albert, to join the Dresden
company. Wagner believed this seventeen-year-old girl showed
promise of becoming in the future a worthy successor to Madame
Schroeder-Devrient. Johanna was undeveloped as yet, but she
possessed the advantage of the physical grace and vocal beauty of
early youth. " I declare that I have never heard a lovelier voice, but
what chiefly delights me is the emotion, the warmth and dramatic
ability which distinguish her performance even now. She is fortunate
in the opportunity of seeing and hearing Schroeder-Devrient so that
she may model herself on her qualities." Thus, when Wagner was
setting to work on the second act of his *Tannhäuser*, he had before him
upon the stage the very image of that Elizabeth he had imagined *for*
the stage. Johanna Wagner became the dramatic and vocal model
for Elizabeth, as Madame Schroeder-Devrient was for Venus. Again,
the appropriate mood for the *Festal March* was induced in him by the
composition of the *Gruss seiner Treuen an Friedrich August*, composed
in August 1844. Thus outward circumstances of all kinds became
allies of Wagner's creative will. His work with the men's choral
society in Dresden gave him fresh ideas on the handling of the male-
voice chorus. The varying favour with which his work was
received in Dresden and elsewhere sharpened his insight into his
own nature and taught him to endure praise and blame, and
the acquaintance of musicians of repute, whether he admired or
despised them, set him in an arena of contending personalities. Thus
he experienced the varied world to be mirrored in *Tannhäuser*. Slowly,
as befitted the gravity, the spiritual complexity of the work in hand,

and with constant nourishment from without, his imaginations took body and clear shape.

Many and various as were these influences, they served, as before, merely as nourishment to the original living germ which selected them at will and incorporated them within itself. In this case, however, the germ was not, as in *The Flying Dutchman*, a single ballad. We must seek it in the early draft made in Teplitz in the summer of 1842. It comprises not only an outline of the plot but a few musical sketches. The titles attached to these—*Venusberg, Pilgrims, Close of Act II*— indicate the points about which action and music were alike to crystallise. In Venus, symbolising sin, in the pilgrims, symbolising salvation, in the tragic close of Act II and the opening of Act III with the penitential journey, the whole work takes its rise. Together with these themes we hear also the first notes of a wood-wind melody (afterwards rejected) for the herd-boy, symbolising nature in its aloofness from both sin and salvation. Thenceforward the drama develops according to the laws of alternation. The first act is dominated by Venus, the second by Elizabeth. The curse of insatiable desire which the goddess of lust puts upon Tannhäuser as she lets him depart from her kingdom is contrasted with the self-sacrifice of a young and holy love. Tannhäuser, a merely passive figure in both these acts, bears the full weight of the third, in which the forces that contend for him join battle within his soul. The troubadours, his companions, welcome him back to their world in the first act, and cast him forth from their midst in the second. They symbolise the "world," with its tame views of man and of art, with its refusal to see or admit the *daemonic* element in life. One figure stands out from the throng, endowed with intuition, understanding, forgiveness. Wolfram, Tannhäuser's counterpart, lacking the force, is free also from the curse of passion. He loves without desire and judges without hate. The Landgrave is the neutral centre about which the action revolves. The chorus of courtiers and huntsmen and the Festal March serve merely as musical embellishments. The pilgrims' chorus, answering the wild song of the sirens, accompanies the action from Tannhäuser's first salute to the final proclamation of the saving miracle.

Such were the sources, literary, autobiographical, and psychological, which inspired the work, shaping its content and form. But the kernel was as ever that theatrical instinct in Wagner which evoked incidents, passions, revolts against passion, in order to make a stage play of the whole. The stage with all its possibilities, surprises, sensations, is his final goal. Nevertheless, the visible action there presented would remain incomplete without immediate sensation, without music to affirm, to foretell, to fulfil the psychological drama given to the eye and the mind upon the stage. This music must be such music as Gluck and Mozart desired to make, but were prevented from making by false premises, such music as Beethoven had fore-shadowed in his Ninth Symphony, music that could convey an expression of spiritual events not to be conveyed by speech and gesture upon the stage. Should it be possible, through music, to add this form of expression to the stage, a new form of theatrical art would be attained. The theatre would become as the magic garden of Armida, whose phantom shapes entrap men, change their everyday natures, endow them with immediate visions of emotions else but dimly guessed, grip their imaginations and shake their very souls. If this were to be done at all it must be done through music, and this was Wagner's meaning when he spoke of his works at that date as " experiments " to discover " if opera were possible." Music alone could solve the problem. If it could reach the goal, if it could convey to all men the glowing passion of the artist, the " possibility " of opera would be established. But what if it could not do this ?

And it seemed as if it could not. *Tannhäuser*, at its first performance on October 19, fell almost as flat as *The Flying Dutchman* had done. The scene had been most carefully prepared, the scenery painted in Paris, the richest of costumes provided. The orchestra had been considerably strengthened, and Fischer had rehearsed the choruses. Wagner himself conducted, Tichatschek filled the rôle of Tannhäuser, Johanna that of Elizabeth, Madame Schroeder-Devrient that of Venus, Mitterwurzer that of Wolfram. Yet even these singers, personally attached to Wagner and giving their very best, failed in their parts. The débutante Johanna was a mere shadow ; the expressionist significance of her part was entirely beyond her. Vocally, even, it was too much for her. Elizabeth's prayer had to be shortened, and the adagio of the second finale severely cut both on her account and on Tichatschek's. Tichatschek had a voice, but there was no " tragic emotion " in it ; Madame Schroeder-Devrient, however, was an even greater disappointment. She could not, she declared, make head or tail of her rôle ! A week was allowed to pass between the first performance and the second, which took place before a half-empty house.

It went better, however, and the audience warmed a little. It was found possible, as it had not been with *The Flying Dutchman*, to retain the piece and to give seven performances in all before the year's end. But it was not, like *Rienzi*, an unquestioned triumph. The piece was saved at a heavy price, and Wagner himself was acutely aware that such success as it had was unreal. Such as it was, it was due to passages in the work which were *operatic* in the old-fashioned sense, to set forms with an easy appeal, still fairly numerous in this work, to melodies and songs. In all that he really aimed at he had failed. He had sought to grip his hearers' souls, but they cared for nothing but the " musical entertainment " he had to offer them. The rest, where it had escaped cutting, was regarded as a tiresome admixture. The music he offered as the best he could give found no response. It was hopeless to think that other theatres would take *Tannhäuser*. There was growing neglect of, even actual hostility to, his earlier works. The sudden wild craze for *Rienzi* was most decidedly a thing of the past ; it had been succeeded by a very chilling sobriety. The critics nagged. Wagner's Dresden successes, in so far as they were successes, were now attributed to the personal interest of local cliques ; on more mature examination the works could never stand. Adventurer's luck was proving fickle. Was there nothing but malice, spite, and envy at work here, or is an explanation to be found in the nature of Wagner's art ?

Among contemporary critics a distinction must be made between those who turned against Wagner out of malice or prejudice and those whose attitude was due to genuine disapproval of a new and strange form of musical drama. What, then, lay at the root of objections for which the opposition made out a very real case ? Robert Schumann, who had no personal liking for Wagner but also no malice or envy against him, wrote a letter to Mendelssohn after reading the score of *Tannhäuser*, in which he expresses a very unfavourable opinion. He misses " pure harmonies and correct four-part choral writing." The music, he says, " is not a scrap better than *Rienzi* ; on the contrary, it is duller and more forced." Wagner " can hardly write four good bars at a stretch." There is no lack of penetration and understanding in these words. Schumann's criticism, in common with that of many a perfectly serious-minded contemporary, was valid. Wagner's music recks not of pure harmonies and correct

four-part choral writing ; it *has* a forced effect ; there are seldom four
good bars together—that is, if it be looked on as music in the sense
required by Schumann. But Schumann himself—that strange seer—
added a further and a complementary word, after having heard
Tannhäuser performed. " I have to take back a great deal," he says,
" which I wrote after reading the score, for the whole thing wears
a very different aspect upon the stage. I was gripped by much
of it."

Here, then, the contradiction is resolved. Schumann could not
have more convincingly proved his disinterestedness towards Wagner
nor his critical acumen than by these most true words. The justification of this new form of art was to be *gripping*, and the will to *grip* the
hearer explains its failure measured by the older æsthetic standards
of music. It also explains the opposition it aroused. With this
gripping quality a new factor entered art. To those who first experienced it it was something strange which they had not the capacity
to receive, and to which they were therefore more likely to give a
hostile than a friendly response. Was the music of Mozart, of Haydn,
of Rossini, of Mendelssohn, or of Meyerbeer *gripping*? All these
wrote beautiful music, and each wrote differently from the rest, but
none intruded upon the subjective, inner life of the individual hearer,
none *gripped* him. Weber and Marschner, it is true, impinged on the
emotions, the latter by a gruesome element in his romances of the
supernatural, the former by simple, popular sentiment. No one,
however, had set out like Wagner exclusively to *grip*, and each left
his hearers plenty of opportunity to enjoy the delights of pure music
and melodious singing. Even in Beethoven's work, in which, as
Wagner himself had recently shown, the *gripping* element played a
considerable part, it remained subsidiary in the general effect, illuminating, no doubt, but not supporting the structure. People were
disinclined to admit that this *gripping* quality was properly an *artistic*
quality. An art based upon it could never evoke the desired response,
since it required a *readiness* of response which did not exist, and which,
moreover, people had no intention of making.

This gripping quality, however, is as much a correlative of expressionist, as is beauty of formal, art. It is only when it can in a very
real sense infect the observer with its own mood that it can reveal
itself, through emotion, to his consciousness and so attain its object.
Music was to Wagner himself a natural expression of emotion, bound

by no laws, and it was also an illusionary reflection of emotion. It could touch his hearers, therefore, only when they realised what it strove to do and surrendered themselves freely to it. Schumann read the score of *Tannhäuser* as music in the accepted sense, and as such he found it bad. But when he heard it performed there dawned upon him, habit and use in listening to music notwithstanding, an intimation of the new will underlying this development of the art. And later it alarmed him. He saw that music, if it sought to become *expression*, to *grip*, must cease to be music in the same sense as the music of all the past. Feeling that the will to expression did not spring from music itself, he traced its origin to the art of the stage, and the musician in him revolted strongly against the idea that the art of Bach, Mozart, and Beethoven should become subject to the will to theatrical effect, for though this could no doubt teach it to *grip*, it must rob it of its own essential glories. This new music gripped him in the first moment of surprise, but afterwards he condemned it as a shameful abuse of music. Here is the true cause of the gulf that divided the musicians and many of the critics from Wagner and his art. Here, too, is the reason why the public held aloof until it had learnt to recognise the emotion-stirring quality in his work and thereafter either to enjoy it as such, or deliberately to reject it. Properly understood, the cleft was caused not by blindness and stupidity, but by a real contradiction between two irreconcilable views of art.

" Wagner is not a sound musician. He lacks feeling for form and beauty in music. But you must not judge him by pianoforte arrangements. There are many passages in his operas which could not fail to excite you profoundly if you heard them from the stage. And if the light of his genius is not bright sunlight, it has none the less a mysterious enchantment which masters the senses. But . . . the music apart from the stage is slight, often amateurish to boot, superficial, perverse. . . ." Every word in this letter of Schumann's is true, and every word is false. Only because the music *as* music was such as Schumann describes, because apart from the stage it had no real existence, could it be true *theatre*. From the theatre it borrowed new laws of form, of tonal beauty, of content, and so rose to a high level of artistic greatness.

Wagner's music grew out of scenic impulses which it interpreted to the emotions and to the mind. Scenic impulse at its simplest is the impulse to motion, and, for Wagner, music's task is to represent movement. The scenic motive impulse was not unknown in the older form of opera, for without it the musical stage-play could not have been. But there the impulse was translated from scenic into musical terms and stylised in song. This stylisation accounts for the lack of naturalism in the operas of Gluck and Mozart. They were not, as Wagner supposed, hampered by their libretti. They deliberately forewent naturalistic musical presentation of the scene, and concentrated on the primacy of the human singing voice. After Gluck's day grand opera, Spontini's more especially, ventured a first step in the direction of naturalism and stylised in a form which was an approach to real movement—namely, the march. By this means both scene and music acquired movement—they went forward. *The Flying Dutchman*, however, broke through the march convention and a starkly naturalistic idea of movement dominated the scene, and through it, the music. The march-form vanished, overwhelmed by the movement of the sea, the movement of passion. In place of regular march rhythms appeared the motion of the tides, inspiring new ideas of rhythm, harmony, melody, tone-colour, and dynamics. And the forms themselves were ruled by the ballad, the song, whence the whole drama was derived.

The change which made the song central accords with the tendency towards Romantic opera. It was marked by an alternating series of song moods, passing gradually from the lyrical to the narrative. Though these songs are not musically connected they mark moments of special emotional intensity, while the forwarding of the action of the drama is entrusted to spoken dialogue. Here, too, there is stylisation. The dramatic whole is divided into sections, conceived either scenically in dialogue, or emotionally in music. The musical moments in their song-like, narrative form suggest a national version of the Italian aria style, and like that are usually designed to display the voice attractively.

The elemental dramatic impulse behind *The Flying Dutchman* gave life and fluidity to the conventional forms both of march and song. The work was a harbinger of the coming change from stylised to naturalistic motion. This tendency, however, needed restraint if music was to acquire the power of transcending and uniting the conventionalised passion of grand opera with the lyric sentiment of early Romantic opera. The march's studied bas-relief, the isolation and lyric conventions of the song must go, and both must take their place in the ever-flowing stream of naturalistic emotion. A blend of march and song forms, each freed from all trace of stylisation and susceptible to every change of action so that they are no longer formal types of song but forms of absolute expression, sets the stage for *Tannhäuser*.

The novelty of *Tannhäuser* as a stage piece consists in the use of the interaction of two different worlds to form the plot. The two chief contending forces in the drama are the Venusberg and the Wartburg, and they predominate alternately. The first act presents them one by one, marking the contrast yet keeping them apart. In the second act they become confused in Tannhäuser's imagination. In the third act they are brought into immediate conflict. The dramatic interest is centred in the interplay of these two worlds, to both of which Tannhäuser belongs. It is heightened by abrupt transitions from a " near " to a " far away " which continually attract and repel each other, and by the resultant suggestion of three-dimensional space, now evolved from the flat, two-dimensional picture presented by the old march. Thus the scene gains depth and plasticity, an illusion of actuality, and music, freed from stylisation, acquires naturalistic truth of expression.

The music of *Tannhäuser*, like its plot, is based on the idea of conflict between two worlds of emotion and their alternate approach to and withdrawal from one another. This concept of a " near " and a " far away " fixes the main outlines of the musical dynamics— the pilgrim march in varying aspects of tonal light and shade, Venus's magic hill glowing red, or fading at the approach of the pilgrim train. Such, in outline, is the musical emotional plot as sketched in the overture. It is the first overture to show a plastic, three-dimensional picture, not a mere suggestion of mood, but an objective presentation of a plot. The spheres of action as presented on the stage, and of emotion as presented in the music, are identified, and in a preliminary survey of the illusionary emotional field the course of the forthcoming music-drama is marked out. This course is closely followed by the musical dynamics, which are seen most clearly in the overture. It is also followed by other aspects of music—by melody, harmony, rhythm, by the musical structure of scenes and forms, by the musical composition as a whole. Music such as this is not a stylisation of the march or the song, but a revelation of a continuous dramatic movement. And since it makes the laws of that movement its own laws, it is able by suggestion to sweep the listener with it into that movement. It *grips*, it moves him.

Music is used to portray the three-dimensional movements of the drama. There are emotional impulses strong enough to fill that three-dimensional space, comprising not only the conflicting elements of the Venusberg and the Wartburg, of Venus and Elizabeth, but also the significantly ranged figures of sirens, pilgrims, troubadours, the herd-boy, the Landgrave, Wolfram, and such scenes as the castle hall, the realms of the goddess of love, the countryside in spring and autumn, at dawn and at nightfall. It is a world far richer in scenes and human figures than that of *The Flying Dutchman*, and it offers a wealth of possible contrasts. Its phenomena are ranged in perspective according to their importance, and their occasional assembly in big *ensembles* is effortlessly contrived. The individual scenes accord with the general idea of the work, peopling the appointed space and endowing it with variety and colour. Emotion governs the relations of each part to the whole; every emotional utterance is clear and well defined. Could music in the old sense as form, tunefulness, skilful choral writing, have portrayed all this? Could it even have hinted at the constant growth and movement of such a drama?

Musical movement consists mainly in modulation—variation, transition, harmonic change from one key to another. Unmodulated music is static. Music that moves but in which motion is regarded merely as a mode of formal development is modulated by slow, imperceptible degrees, smoothly, with preparation in advance designed to avoid any startling change. Music, however, which is to *express* movement must modulate strongly, emphatically, because the changes denote actual movement. Music modulates not only harmonically but also dynamically, in timbre and melodic gait. Dynamic modulation was the source of the earliest three-dimensional space concepts in music, but these were intensified by tone-colouristic modulation and acquired content and meaning through harmonic and melodic modulation which peopled the space first defined by dynamics, just as the figures in a play give life and perspective to the scene.

The melodic scheme in *Tannhäuser* is based upon song and march forms. The narrative and the active forms thus hold equal sway, giving the work the double character of grand and of Romantic opera.

Both forms being freed from stylisation and endowed with plasticity, the melody also acquires a new naturalistic quality. Used to express the actual, immediate emotion accompanying each turn of events in the story, it presents a most vivid picture of the psychological drama. It does not seek to develop according to its own proper law, the law of melody : it seeks to provide immediate emotional interpretation of the words ; it has passed from the set period to the declamatory phrase. It is swayed throughout by that natural factor which underlies and regulates all oral and vocal delivery, namely, the *breath*.

Wagner's contemporaries thought him lacking in melodic inventiveness, and from their own standpoint they were right. For Wagner a melody that was complete in itself was an impediment to the naturalistic development of the action. He employed it, however, in certain instances where the moment called for a lyric climax, as in Tannhäuser's love-song, and in the song contest, and on such occasions his weakness as a melodic writer is at its most apparent. Schumann's remark about " slight and superficial music " is here more intelligible, if by no means more just. Even at such moments as these Wagner's melody, though in itself inconsiderable, carries the action forward and must be interpreted with reference to it. The festal entry of the guests in Act II is the nearest approach to a satisfactory compromise between the requirements of melody in the old sense and musical originality. Here is a simple action to be presented by simple means. Wagner's contemporaries, however, when easy, clear, melodic periods were lacking, complained of muddle, of a plethora of dissonances, of the predominance of too firmly rooted thematic material.

Wagner's melodic treatment, as may be seen as early as *The Flying Dutchman's* more critical episodes and fully developed in *Tannhäuser*, is a modulatory melodic treatment. It powerfully summarises the action at certain moments, and is at the same time a lever to release the functions of harmony. It embodies the harmonic action, and is, in fact, no more than linear harmony, articulated for declamatory purposes. This was the reason why Wagner's contemporaries failed to hear it as distinct melody : they heard it as harmony. The declamatory analysis of harmony into melodic phrases may be found as early as the opening of the great duet in *The Flying Dutchman*, " Wie aus der Ferne längst vergangner Zeiten " ("Up from forgotten depths of years long vanished "). Almost all the melodies in Tannhäuser are likewise resolutions of a basic harmonic complex, and that even where, as in Wolfram's *Star of Eve*, there is an apparent approach to normal vocal melody.

Since the set melodic phrase represented for Wagner a cessation of action, since he was unable to recognise formal tone-motion as such, his music is necessarily a music of continual modulation. The centre of interest is concentrated not on the surface melody but on the harmony beneath. It is here that the drama works itself out, for harmony by constant change of melodic line can people the space created by dynamics. The melody, however, is no longer something distinct in itself, to be discerned apart from the depths whence it emerges. It is a reflection thrust up to the surface of music by the harmonic drama beneath.

As with Wagner melody becomes articulated harmony divided into declamatory phrases which are governed by the laws of breathing, so harmony attains melodic inner intensity, consciousness, and vocal movement. This movement is best attained by chromaticism, which accordingly pervades both harmony and melody, follows each change of expression, gives notice of each least deviation. As foreshadowed in *Das Liebesverbot* it acts as a new formative power. Chromaticism dominates practically the whole melodic harmony of *Tannhäuser*. Used in the pilgrims' chorus it expresses advance and withdrawal. In the *Venusberg* music it portrays the quivering flames of sensual ecstasy, the bounding pulses of the blood. In Wolfram's song, *Star of Eve*, it expresses the most exalted sentiment, in Venus's appeal the allurements of lust, in Tannhäuser's tale of his pilgrimage to Rome, the very blackness of despair. There is hardly a melody in the work unmarked by chromatic change. It blends and ceaselessly develops melodic and harmonic expression, it unravels into melody the threads of the harmonic complex which, thus enriched, fills out the contours of dynamic tone-space. But while melody and harmony pervade this space, rhythm, being of all factors in music the nearest to speech, is used for naturalistic expression—as, for instance, in the solemn tread of the pilgrims, in the alluring gestures of Venus's bacchantes.

Thus a scenic dramatic impulse led to an entirely new way of regarding musical media. Dynamics, harmony, melody, rhythm, are conceived as tonal methods of presenting a stage-play. They are used no longer to lift the hearer above actualities into a world of

M

fair forms, but to convey, by the naturalistic expression of intense emotion, an artist's experiences and sufferings to his audience. Such an art is ultimately rooted in a capacity for emotion rather than in any special talent. Experience of the itch of the senses taught Wagner to develop a new method of stimulating the senses by scenic and musical drama.

A tale of suffering can only be effective if it convinces the hearer of its truth; therefore to be credible, to be convincing, was the aim of the new art. Stage action, in order to seem credible, must present a realistic conflict of forces, and music must use all means proper to it to express the passage of events. Again, old operatic forms must give place to more natural methods of presentation. The chorus as *ensemble* must fall into place in the musical and dramatic whole. Wagner goes some way to achieve this where, as in the entrance procession and the pilgrims' march, the set form fits the action as naturally as Tannhäuser's, Wolfram's, Biterolf's, and Walter's solos take their place in the course of events. But in other instances, where a chorus and *ensemble* are desirable from the musicians' point of view but where their use *en masse* would produce an unreal effect, he divides them into naturalistic groups. The individualisation begun in *Rienzi* is carried a step further in the septet finale of Act I, in the interjections of the chorus during the song contest, in the abrupt exclamations of the rival singers and the men's chorus at the judgment on Tannhäuser. Wagner's preoccupation at the time with a male chorus may have influenced this bold handling of the male *ensemble*—a treatment which may be noticed also in *Lohengrin*. Regarded organically, it is seen as a logical outcome of the naturalistic style which dominates the whole musical formation.

This formation shows three main types. Intimately associated with traditional opera is the set form in which the will to drama is still presented under a convention, and of which the songs, the march, and the duet between Elizabeth and Tannhäuser are examples. In the latter there seems to be an echo of the " O namenlose Freude " duet from *Fidelio*. Apart from the particularly dramatic epilogue it is superficially a falling-off as compared with the duet at the meeting between the Flying Dutchman and Senta. The septet finale of Act I, containing a stretto melody which Wagner used in *Die Feen* and *The Flying Dutchman*, is also to be classed as a set form. In addition, there are two free, fluid forms, one a development from the earlier march into the complex *ensemble* moving slowly to a dramatic climax, the other a development of the earlier aria or song form into the narrative scene. At the same time the division into numbers practised in the older form of opera and still retained by Wagner in *The Flying Dutchman* was abandoned. Just as within the individual "number" or section the declamatory melodic phrase had ousted the melodic period, so within the act the formal, self-contained musical piece was replaced by the scene, which is a breathing-pause in the action. The movement, the flux of the whole, took hold upon the greater forms as upon the lesser and welded them into a unity.

Here, too, we find the marks of transition. Elizabeth's greeting is aria of the old type, though it takes its place in the scenic plot and the musical treatment is free. It is also a striking opening to the act. And, like the old aria, it aims at effective vocal display. Elizabeth's prayer is a mingling of song and of free melodic recitation such as Weber had already employed, only more simply and effectively, in his "Leise, leise," adagio. The youthful Johanna Wagner's failure in the second half of this intentionally emotional piece would be very understandable even had she not been a beginner, and Schumann's talk of "forced" music finds its best justification here. A certain unreality in the figure of Elizabeth is reflected in her music whenever she appears alone, and is shown either by a conventional tinge, as in the aria, or by artificiality of expression, as in the prayer. The introductory conversational duet between Wolfram and Elizabeth and the epilogue are interesting for the manner in which Wagner interweaves his themes in pursuance of a method introduced in *The Flying Dutchman*. Melodic instrumental passages are interwoven with recitative dialogue in a manner which stresses their reminiscent and associative value, the orchestra thus being used to suggest feelings which supplement those expressed by the singers. Of the narrative pieces, Wolfram's "Als du in kühnem Sange uns bestrittest" ("When for the prize in song we all contended"), in Act I, retains something of the song or aria character, and the Landgrave's great speech in the second act is a narrative statement, neither being very strictly governed by the content. Thus from an artistic point of view the three most interesting pieces are the introductory duo scene between Venus and Tannhäuser, the finale of Act II, and the story of events in Rome with the orchestral prelude belonging to it at the beginning of Act III. It is no mere chance that the creative spirit asserts itself most plainly at these three

points. All three scenes are indicated in the early sketches of the
summer of 1842, and are, indeed, the most important in the whole
work. The rest exists merely to provide a vehicle for these. The
significant line of the whole expressionist drama runs through them,
and in them is chiefly concentrated that " moving " quality upon
which the success Wagner strove for depended.

Wagner's plan for the duo scene between Tannhäuser and Venus
was the boldest thing he had yet attempted. Gluck's influence is
particularly obvious here. Tannhäuser's simple, lyrical love-song is
the nucleus. Its threefold, chromatically ascending strophic repetition musically outlines the scene. Venus's first reply is a brief
recitative, modelled, like the opening dialogue, on Gluck's serious
and simple diction ; her second answer is the seductive " Geliebter
komm, sieh dort die Grotte " ("Beloved, come ! see yonder bower "),
in F sharp major, with a magical eight-part violin accompaniment
and chromatic melody with rich arpeggio harmonies ; her third soars
to the passionate climax of the love-curse :

> " Hin zu den kalten Menschen flieh',
>   vor deren blödem, trübem Wahn
>   der Freude Götter wir entflohn,
>
> *   *   *   *   *
>
> Suche dein Heil—und find' es nie."

> (" Hence to the loveless world of man,
>   from whose poor, feeble, troubled dreams
>   to godlike raptures we once fled—
>
> *   *   *   *   *
>
> Seek there for grace and find it ne'er ! ")

Thus the scene is formed of strophe and antistrophe ; song and
dramatic recitative are interlinked and steadily carry each other
forward. The duet in the old sense is no more, and there is unbroken
development from the revelation of the forces of love-magic to the
invocation of the Virgin. With the naming of that name the drama
swings violently over to the opposite of its two poles ; a few stormy
bars transform Love's grotto into the Wartburg and change passion's
notes into a herd-boy's song and a simple pilgrim litany.

Wagner wrote this scene three times in all, first for the Dresden performance of *Tannhäuser* in 1845, then, fifteen years later, for Paris, and for the third time, nearly thirty years after the first, when he composed the second act of *Parsifal*. It represents one of his basic concepts and throws light on a primal impulse in his will as an artist—an impulse to get to grips with the powers therein portrayed, to disburden himself of them by giving them artistic form, to make the theatre, through them, a faithful mirror of his deepest experience of life.

The first of these versions has the freshness and spontaneity of origins ; the second outshines it in brilliance and fervency of execution ; the third raises the scene from crude, sensual representation to metaphysical symbolism. In practice the first version was a failure. The importance of this opening scene for the effect of the whole was absolute, yet it fell utterly flat. The audience found it stiff and cold. Neither Schroeder-Devrient nor Tichatschek understood the meaning of music-drama such as this, and the public were at a loss in face of the new form of art. Not only performers and public, however, but the artist himself failed to completely understand himself. The experience he was striving to express—the Venus experience—bold as his plan was, yet remained in bondage to formal musical types, had not ripened to complete creative freedom.

This freedom, and with it success in the task he had set before him, came in the second finale. The piece is based on the march and is the counterpart of the Venusberg scene, providing a picture of the everyday external world whose forces are grouped about the central hero of the drama with the saving figure of Elizabeth above all. The whole is expressed within the framework of the march-form, from the procession of guests at the beginning to the pilgrims' choir at the end. The piece has three sections or stages. The solemn entry, the Landgrave's speech, the songs of the competitors up to Tannhäuser's hymn of love, and the flight of the women make up the first. The second consists of the threats of the knights, Elizabeth's plea for Tannhäuser, and Tannhäuser's confession and prayer for mercy. The third embraces the Landgrave's judgment and the imposition of the pilgrimage of penance—" Mit ihnen sollst du wallen zur Stadt der Gnadenhuld " (" With them to beg for mercy to Rome thou must repair "). As Venus's enticements and her curse form the core of the first act, so Elizabeth's sacrifice and promise are central in this. The march concept conveys a spiritual drama. It resolves the older type of opera into a multiplicity of form-images and places them in strict evolutionary relation to one another. Under these form-images the music develops in a way at once emotionally comprehensible and expressive, without setting the audience any unwonted problems to solve. There is real coincidence between that which was operatic in the old sense and the dramatic, *moving* quality which was Wagner's aim, so that his effect " came off " even though the greater portion of the adagio in the middle of Tannhäuser's " Zum Heil den Sündigen zu führen die Gottgesandte nahte mir (" to bring my sinful soul salvation, this angel came from heaven above ") had to be cut out. This finale, in which naturalistic emotional presentation and stylised form agree together, would seem to prove that opera was still " possible "—nay, even necessary for the building up of a great architectural *ensemble*, a picture of manifold forces to be focused and mirrored on the stage. The powerful B major adagio, " Ich fleh' für ihn, ich flehe für sein Leben " (" I plead for him, oh spare him, I implore you ! "), in which Elizabeth leads, the Landgrave and singers respond with a choral counter-melody and Tannhäuser's " Erbarm' dich mein " (" Have mercy, Lord ! ") penetrates through all in an absolutely naturalistic cry of anguish—is not this irrefragable proof of the possibility, the necessity of opera ? One might answer that the fact that the act " came off " though the very heart of the whole had been forcibly cut out is proof that opera is *not* possible ! The audience responded simply to what was formally melodic and architectonic, not to the immediate sensuous appeal of expressionist art. Essentials might be omitted without hesitation as long as externals were pleasing.

If the failure of the Venusberg scene, and the success of the mutilated finale left Wagner any doubts as to the real nature of opera, the fate of the third great moment in his work—the story of the pilgrimage to Rome—must have solved them. This scene follows from the other two, and in it the main action finds its culmination and resolution. Wholly expressionist, it is adapted neither to the strophic song-form, like the Venusberg scene, nor to the march-form, like the finale. It is a piece of free declamation, such as had before been used only in recitative introducing an aria. Marschner, it is true, had produced something not unlike it in his Vampire's (Ruthven's) story, but he had not proceeded so boldly. A similar intention underlies Eric's dream narrative in *The Flying Dutchman*. In *Tannhäuser*, however, the narrative is not episodic, as were its predecessors ; it is the centre and meaning of the whole act. All that goes before it is of the nature of emotional preparation, all that follows grows out of it. In it and through it the development of the central character is completed, the decisive battle between the forces that contend for him is fought out.

If the singing voice as such is not used in the traditional sense and is confined to expression, in the strictest sense to elucidation, the accompaniment, on the other hand, grows in importance. It is here that the musical drama, in the new sense, is worked out. The character of the themes and their interrelations portray events of which the voice tells. They do so, indeed, even before the singer appears on the stage, by means of the orchestral prelude, which was considerably fuller and more detailed in Wagner's first draft than in his final version. He cut it down later, realising that the pictures which his own knowledge of the tone-symbolism in his work made so clear to him could not be conveyed to his audience by the orchestral performance alone but must find their final expression in song. This song must transcend plastic declamation and become the immediate representation of suffering ; it must be absolute emotion rendered audible. While the orchestra in its motival portrayal of the penitent's journey, in its grand tone-picture of the Eternal City, in the harmonies of a theme of faith and hope, mirrors the singer's story, the voice itself rises to heights of expression to tell of the terror of the ban :

> " Hast du so böse Lust geteilt,
> dich an der Hölle Glut entflammt,
> Hast du im Venusberg geweilt :
> so bist nun ewig du verdammt ! "

> (" If thou these vile desires hast felt,
> if thou the flames of hell hast nursed,
> if thou in Venus' hill hast dwelt,
> thou art eternally accursed ! ")

Unaccompanied save for an occasional chord emphasising the rhythm, the voice sings on, at first in numb monotony upon a single note, then rising to a deliberately unmelodious discord. The expression of this phrase reaches terrific intensity. The song becomes a cry—a last embodiment of actual, ecstatic feeling in disregard of any kind of stylisation, creating a complete illusion of real, immediate sensation.

This piece was an utter failure. Tichatschek had a magnificent singing voice and a delicate feeling for rhythm ; he was also genuinely devoted to Wagner, but he could not overcome the singer in himself. He must *sing*, he must have melodies to shape. And his voice had no accent of pain, no expression. The audience were at a loss what to make of the wearisome, long recitative. They were more baffled still when it was followed by the, to them, dull *dénouement*—a mere arbitrary winding-up. At this point again, as in the Venusberg scene, Wagner had failed to solve his problem. Later, inspired perhaps by the appearance of the Mountain Queen at the end of *Hans Heiling*, he substituted for the leaping flames of the Hörfelberg and the tolling bells of the Wartburg, a final vision of Venus and her song of allurement as Tannhäuser dies upon the dead body of Elizabeth. He also added a new closing chorus, first omitting the previous one of the pilgrims and then combining the two. There is no work of Wagner's whose final form remained so long unsettled. The first revision of the Venusberg scene and the Song Contest took place in the *Tristan* period. We now have two authentic versions : that of the final Dresden revision in 1847, and the amplified version prepared for the Paris production in 1860.

Wagner did not, and indeed could not, bring this work to completion. He could and did finish the external drama he had built up round the figures of Tannhäuser, Venus, and Elizabeth, but the creative impulse behind those figures had forces within it which were too great for the expressive limitations of the story, or for any one work—forces which moved Wagner's whole nature and dominated all his art. The theatrical artist had found a new theatrical theme in the conflict between the ecstasy of the senses and that death-wish which is its climax, in the lacerating passion of desire which finds fulfilment only in annihilation. The Flying Dutchman's curse of vague unrest is seen plainly now as the curse of eroticism, the strongest force in all human, and therewith in all dramatic, action. The peculiar interest of *Tannhäuser* is that it is a first deliberate loosing of the erotic *daemon*, whose power was to be seen at its height in *Tristan* and, purified and redeemed, in *Parsifal*.

Thus the work could not, by its very nature, be brought to a conclusion. This accounts for *Tannhäuser's* formal incompleteness, for Wagner's insistent attempts to complete it, and for the experimental nature of the first close in which he tried to present the *Liebestod* by operatic media. It also explains the dual presentation of womanhood, the sinful and the holy, in contrast and conflict, and the development of an expressionist operatic plot from their interactions. Wagner's great achievement here was to make such a plot possible, thereby discovering the new realm of art towards which he had groped in *The Flying Dutchman* and the laws of theatrical-musical formation. It took him the rest of his days to develop the forces first recognised here.

CHAPTER VI

LOHENGRIN

WAGNER finished the score of *Tannhäuser* on April 13, 1845. On the following November 17, a month after the first performance of *Tannhäuser*, he read the libretto of *Lohengrin* at the "Engelklub," a Dresden arts society. The new work had been sketched out during a summer holiday in Marienbad, following upon the completion of a plot for a three-act comic opera to be entitled *The Mastersingers of Nuremberg*.

Years later *Tristan* was to have a similar aftermath. In both instances the excitement and strain of erotic confession afflicted the composer with a morbid dread of sudden death which passed, when he had finished his work, into fear lest he should never again find "so warm and characteristic" a subject, and was finally thrown off in a humorous reaction. But the two examples of this process show differences as well as similarities. *Tristan*, being the more mature expression of passion, produced more complete humorous reaction, for the artist's nature having been profoundly moved the pendulum swung back through its whole orbit. After his young manhood's expression of passion in *Tannhäuser*, however, the reaction was only sufficient to carry him through a *sketch* for a comedy, after which counter-reaction set in and the sketch was laid aside. *Tannhäuser* was merely a step on the way to *Tristan*, and that path had to be trodden to the end before Wagner could find his way into the realms of comedy. The truly elemental nature of the impulse behind *Tannhäuser* is, however, proved by the fact that a comic rebound did ensue. It is proof, also, of the persistence of the underlying idea that plans for a comedy thus begun were actually realised fifteen years later.

A more direct result of the new line struck out in *Tannhäuser* was that Wagner became aware of a fresh factor in the art of getting an effect, namely, *the tragic*. The tragic outlook which characterises all Wagner's work from *Tannhäuser*, *Lohengrin*, and *The Ring* to *Tristan* is the result of this fundamental determination to *grip* an audience. Wagner increasingly considered all theatrical media simply as agents to this end. For this purpose he was not content with stripping music of its proper forms and revolutionising musical interpretation; he went on to remodel the scenic action associated with music. The principle of motion required not only that action should continue to the very last moment of the play, but that after the play was over it should still sweep the hearer forward, causing the emotion it had imparted to work on in his consciousness. To effect this a dramatic subject must have no solution, no winding-up, and this was what Wagner understood as *tragic*. This alone must infallibly grip the spectator and transform him from objective witness to subjective participant.

It is here that the break with operatic tradition is most notable. Neither Gluck, Mozart, nor Spontini ever wrote tragic opera. They believed in rounding off their subjects satisfactorily, so that whatever depths had been stirred the audience might reawake to the consciousness that it was all make-believe. This was no mere convention. It was a concept inherent in the character of opera, in which action was not designed to provide an illusion of reality but to afford occasion for the display of musical forms, and as such could not tolerate a realistic pursuit of the issues of the story. During rehearsals for *The Vestal* in Dresden, Spontini insisted—to Wagner's amused astonishment—on the *chantez-danser*, which precluded the cutting of the final jolly ballet and chorus, and in so doing showed a profound understanding of the musical theatre. Again, when Lüttichau criticised the ending of *Tannhäuser*, saying that Weber " understood the job better " and " always ended his operas happily," his words, philistine as they sound, were based on commonly accepted ideas of theatrical music. A happy ending served to break the spell. Only the more modern French operas of Halévy, Auber, and Meyerbeer had at that date contravened this rule, and in these works operatic plot was subordinated to history. The *tableau* as a whole was of more importance than the fate of individual participants ; exalted heroic pathos and a leaning towards the spoken drama led to the piling-up of emotional effects. Tragedy in this form of opera is rather a matter of extrinsic need for a climax to the plot than of intrinsic emotional logic. Nevertheless, we have here the earliest indications of a tendency to endow opera with a truly dramatic plot—a tendency further expressed in the use of stage mechanism to create illusion, and in the naturalistic treatment of musical declamation.

The use and handling of tragedy in the modern French opera of his day was the point from which Wagner started. In *Rienzi* the conception of tragedy is still naïve, as in grand opera. *The Flying Dutchman's* ending is midway between the tragic and the happy, for visible external disaster brings salvation on a higher plane. *Tannhäuser* is Wagner's first tragedy in the Wagnerian sense. It deliberately *grips* up to the very last. And yet, paradoxically, while we recognise the endings of *The Jewess*, *The Huguenots*, and even *Rienzi*, as *operatic* because, though their heroes perish, their deaths complete and round off the pattern of the plot, the end of *Tannhäuser* leaves us doubting its necessity. The tragedy seems forced. The third act gives an unsatisfactory impression of *fading out rather than ending*. Without a musical understanding of the story of the journey to Rome the conclusion of the drama which it conditions cannot but seem dull, unintelligible. This imputation is just and points to a lack of artistic clarity in the tragic conception. Tannhäuser dies, and in the moment of death finds salvation. But neither his death nor his salvation are given clear plastic expression. Tannhäuser's transfiguration is not felt to be organic, like that of the Flying Dutchman; it is merely an epilogue. A sense of death and disaster still prevails, even while the pilgrims' chanting and the orchestra proclaim atonement and pardon. Thus the ending is not happy, nor is it a clear and absolute expression of the will to tragedy. It is felt to be just a dull conclusion to a tale of certain symbolic individuals.

This, however, is the point at which Wagner was now to strike out a new line. Henceforth the individual loses importance. Wagner no longer concentrates upon his story. He ceases to deal, as in *Tannhäuser*, in erotic types. Not that any other passion takes the place of the erotic, but tragedy in itself becomes the subject of drama. Built up little by little out of the lives of the various characters in the story, tragedy itself stands revealed at the close. Thus the end provokes a climax, not a relaxation, of sympathetic emotion in the audience.

Wagner himself describes " the character and story of this Lohengrin " as " type of the one and only tragic theme." The subjective truth of this is not diminished by Wagner's subsequent assertion that *Lohengrin* expresses " the essential tragedy of modern life," bearing the same significant relation to it as the *Antigone* to life in the Hellenic state. Wagner thought himself justified in drawing this parallel. He believed that an insatiable yearning " to love, to be beloved, to be understood through love " was *the* tragic problem of the modern world. It was an ethical interpretation of tragedy, and it is as inadequate as a clue to Wagnerian art as any purely musical analysis of his scores. For Wagner neither music nor ethics are independent factors ; they are aids to theatrical expression. The tragedy of *Lohengrin* is not the special tragedy of Wagner's era, nor should it be likened to the Greek drama's tragedy of fatal discord between love and the duties of citizenship. Wagnerian tragedy is the means by which the theatre is able to evoke an illusion of unending emotional tension. Thrusting in Wagner's own subconsciousness for expression, it suggested to him that conflict between desire for love and the duty of foregoing it should prove the most effective of dramatic symbols.

The tragedy of *Lohengrin*, accordingly, is not dependent, like that of *Tannhäuser*, on any particular subjective premises. *Tannhäuser* sins by concupiscence. Lohengrin and Elsa are free from such guilt : but the command *not to question* is incompatible with the nature of love, and from the moment that Elsa loves Lohengrin with a woman's love she is bound to search into the mystery of his nature. As far as the story goes *Lohengrin* is a tragedy of caprice and violence. When Wagner, upon the recommendation of his friend Dr. Hermann Franck, first studied the plot as a plot, he did not himself know quite what to make of it. He tried altering the ending, proposing that " Lohengrin should be allowed to sacrifice his higher nature, from which the veil had been torn, for the sake of remaining with Elsa." He soon saw that this solution was " unnatural." His experiment, however, had given him insight into the story's secondary meaning, revealing its significance not as a story of persons and events but as " a tremendous enrichment of our emotional impressions, and thereby of our emotional impressionability." A happy ending in the traditional sense would nullify these benefits. The crux of the whole was the inevitability of conflict, and this inevitability, presented as *tragic* in the theatrical sense, became the basis upon which Wagner worked, the new creative idea. The power to grip, in *Tannhäuser* confined to particular figures, was now to become absolute, the plot being used solely for the purpose of manifesting it. This lent a new impetus to the drama, a new interest to scene, dialogue, and music. The dramatic root of the work must be sought in the final scene, whence the whole plot was slowly evolved *backwards*. Any change in the ending would, therefore, have made nonsense of the whole.

How greatly Wagner's mind was occupied at that time by the problem of tragic expression not as a consequence of but as a basis of dramatic action is proved by his rearrangement of Gluck's *Iphigenia* during 1847, the *Lohengrin* year. With a heightened sense of the importance of the wording of a libretto, Wagner altered the translation to connect " arias and choruses, most of which stand baldly in a row . . . by bride-passages, preludes, and epilogues for the sake of getting greater dramatic vividness." These alterations, the reasons given for them, and the strengthening of the orchestration, show that Wagner thought Gluck's work sadly in need of revision. In carrying out this work he gave attention not to the music only but also to " enlivening scenic presentation in order to make the dramatic action really live," and found that the action itself " had in great part to be newly invented, so bald and dry is the arrangement of most of the scenes." Furthermore, Wagner states in his autobiography that the original " can only be explained by the purely conventional scenic treatment still obtaining in the Paris of Gluck's day." It is obvious that he was quite unaware of the true nature of Gluck's work. He simply thought it a primitive attempt to achieve his own passionate style of music-drama. His new ending shows the gulf between the two styles at its widest. The fact that Gluck did not dispense with the " inevitable marriage " at the conclusion was regarded by Wagner as a mere flourish made in concession to French taste. To his mind a drama so accented could only have a tragic ending in the classic sense. He therefore substituted Euripides' ending for that of Gluck. Artemis appears and snatches Iphigenia from home and lover to become a priestess of the gods in some mysterious, unknown realm. We see here at work the same craving for the tragic, the moving, that forms the germ of *Lohengrin*, the same notion of a divinely ordained separation that parts Lohengrin from Elsa. In the arioso sung by Artemis we hear echoes of the summons to a distant land and the promise of victory from Lohengrin's Grail story and words of farewell. Wagner has interpolated a chorus of Greeks, expressing the same emotional tension in almost the same words as the chorus which follows the Grail story in *Lohengrin* :

" Wie fühl' ich das Herz in der Brust
von selig süssem Weh erbeben,
seh' ich sie zu der Götter hohem Sitz sich erheben,
durchströmt auch mich himmliche Lust !
Wie wagt' ich noch zu klagen ?
Solche Wonne zu tragen
fühlt sich mein Sinn kaum kraftbewusst !

("How feel I the heart in my breast
With sweet and hallowed sorrow shaken !
Seeing her to the gods' high throne uptaken,
I too know joys serene and blest !
Should I then dare repining ?
Such blessedness divining,
My soul its weakness doth attest ! ")

A similar transport of sympathetic emotion was to effect, in *Lohengrin*, that " tremendous enrichment of our emotional impressions and thereby of our emotional impressionability," of which Wagner speaks. Tragedy in both *Iphigenia* and *Lohengrin* is the quality which grips the hearer, which aims at doing more, which seeks to *move* him irresistibly to emotional response.   Tragedy and pathos in this sense are interchangeable ideas, and a classical term is made to cover a Romantic concept of " sweet and blessed woe," surpassing all passions and flooding the senses with a luxurious orgy of emotion.

In his *Mitteilung an Meine Freunde* Wagner speaks of "a new, indescribably powerful craving, the craving of the heights for the depths," as the basis of the emotion which strove for artistic expression in *Lohengrin*.   This sentence, accepted literally and objectively with later metaphorical glosses set aside, gives a very clear account of the original inspiration of that work.   Juxtaposition of heights and depths is the dramatic kernel in *Lohengrin*, as was juxtaposition of nearness and distance in *Tannhäuser*, where emotional alternations, visible drama and musical structure are rendered by a hither-and-thither motion, by a suggestion of slowly reddening and dying fires.   In *Lohengrin*, on the contrary, the dramatic idea is presented in terms of contrasting light and shade, of conflict between two superimposed spheres or planes.   In *Tannhäuser* phenomena are disposed horizontally, in *Lohengrin* vertically.   Tannhäuser's desire roves from Venus to

Elizabeth, from a world of magic to a world of nature, from joyousness to sadness.　Lohengrin's stoops from the heights to the depths.
The tragedy, the emotional appeal of *Tannhäuser* lies in the guilty
emotional schism in its hero's nature which death alone can heal.
The tragedy of *Lohengrin* lies in the incompatibility of heights with
depths ; the very fact that each is impelled to love and seek out the
other involves the guiltlessness of each in guilt.

The idea of intercourse between a higher nature and a lower, of
the "guiltless guilt" resulting therefrom and of the appeal this
subject makes to the emotions is fundamental in Romanticism and
had been handled frequently before Wagner's day, notably in
Marschner's *The Templar and the Jewess*, and in Weber's *Euryanthe*.
In both these works the contrasts are presented typically.　Marschner's
Knight Templar is made to stand for the lower nature.　Over against
him is set the heavenly vision of Rebecca and in conflict with her purity,
he, like Telramund, is destroyed.　Only that aspect of the subject,
however, which Wagner presents in the first act of *Lohengrin* is herein
anticipated.　*Euryanthe* has far more in common with its successor.
In this work the world of the *depths* found such complete plastic
expression in the figures of Lysiart and Eglantine that Wagner based
his Telramund and Ortrud directly upon them.　Euryanthe herself,
with her "guiltless guilt" of misplaced trust, anticipates all the chief
characteristics of Elsa.　Even the emotional atmosphere of early
chivalry (including the good king) is to be found in the earlier work.
Yet that work was never thought out to its logical conclusion.　As a
musical composition it outgrew the older operatic form without consciously pursuing the change to Romantic expressionist opera, while
at those critical points which secure the texture of the drama, and in its
happy ending, it remains definitely fettered to tradition.　Euryanthe's
simple faith in Eglantine, Adolar's wager with Lysiart, are operatic
devices in the old style.　They have no inherent power to move the
hearer's sympathies and so fail to awake the emotional response to a
tale of "guiltless guilt" required for acceptation of music composed
on expressionist principles.　Adolar, both musically and dramatically
a purely lyrical figure without independent dramatic action of any
kind, is a plaything of circumstances which he does not understand.
Thus, though there are *heights* and *depths* in this work, though these
are contrasted, and though there is the sure touch of genius in the
conception of each individually, no real link is established between

them. The weakness of the dramatic impulse appears in that, while it allows them to reach out to one another, it fails to base its appeal to the emotions on the impossibility of their union. The very thing which was chiefly lauded in *Euryanthe* to Wagner's disadvantage, the happy ending, is symptomatic of something only half-willed, only half-achieved, in Weber's work. Ruthless logic in execution could alone have perfected it. The contrasting spheres should have been inwardly, organically, related, and their relations should have been brought to a tragic, Romantic, *moving* climax at the close.

The spark of originality in Wagner's so largely derivative work consists in his intuitive grasp of the logic of the action. In the result, his treatment of the subject has annihilated Weber's. There are few such instances of an imitative work's ousting its model. Even after Wagner had arbitrarily altered Gluck, even after he had drawn a certain stimulus from Marschner, the works of these composers retain some independent value. Weber's *Euryanthe*, however, was absorbed into *Lohengrin*, leaving no residue. Were a *purely* musical comparison of the two works possible the judgment of history in this matter might be contested; but neither work is patient of such an estimate. Both are specimens of Romantic, illusionary-theatrical art, both seek to present naturalistic emotion on the stage by means of music. They are thus alike in artistic aim and artistic media. Weber was the first to dream that such methods and effects were possible, but he failed to achieve his goal. His work, therefore, became but a stone for another's building. Wagner, less hampered by secondary considerations of a purely musical nature, was free to direct his whole will to *theatre*, and at length, with his own previous experience to aid him, he was able to perfect the work his predecessor had begun.

The close relationship between the two works is especially apparent in the ground-plan of the most important section of *Lohengrin*, the second act, and is highly significant when we consider *Lohengrin's* origins. Taken in conjunction with the first act's debt to Marschner's *Templar* it proves Wagner's skill in imitative summary. At the same time it points to the impulse which marshalled and unified these various stimuli from the beginning—that beginning, the point of departure, the root of the work, being the third act, which is all Wagner's own. Here we find the primal element, the basic idea of *the tragic*. Wagner composed the music of his third act first, and from thence set out to master the territory marked out by his predecessors. This third act, moreover, contains the germ of personal experience from which the work took its rise.

That experience was a bitter one. On the exalted plane of *Lohengrin* there is no place for Tannhäuser's simple, human cry " Have mercy on me ! " Red heat has burned to a clear white light, passion has turned to longing—the longing of the lonely soul to be dissolved in love, the longing that was the Flying Dutchman's curse. Lohengrin is a development of the Flying Dutchman idea, enriched by the Tannhäuser experience. The Flying Dutchman's utmost hope was for loyalty engendered by pity ; he put aside the thought of love as not for him. Lohengrin craves not only absolute love and loyalty but unconditional faith. The homeless wanderer and the visitant from realms of " glory and blessedness " share the basic emotion of longing, but whereas the Flying Dutchman is only conceivable as a passive figure, Lohengrin is essentially a creature of action.

The Lohengrin concept draws its vitality from this idea of action. This it is which constitutes the difference between Lohengrin and Adolar and makes intercourse possible between the *heights* and the *depths*. A creature from the higher sphere brings light to the lower at a critical moment by his *deed* ; thereby he involves himself with the lower and subjects himself to its laws, only to be repulsed in the moment of his most ardent self-giving. Such is the germ of experience from which the drama springs. It borrows the form of an old saga. Its characters have their prototypes in *Euryanthe*, whose wrongfully-accused heroine becomes Wagner's Elsa. Gluck's Iphigenia and Marschner's Rebecca supply certain theatrical traits, and Johanna Wagner serves as vocal and histrionic model. " Johanna's part, which is very important and really the principal rôle, is to be the most stimulating and touching thing in the world," writes Wagner to his brother Albert, while at work on the preliminary sketch in August 1845. Just as Lohengrin is a more vigorous version of the Flying Dutchman, so in Elsa the Senta motifs are repeated. Elsa, like Senta, has a dream vision of a lover who is also a champion. Her story of the Unknown Knight in Act I is a repetition of Senta's ballad thrown into higher relief by the structure of the plot, and like its prototype it is a dream with power to conjure reality. Nevertheless, apart from characteristics derived broadly from Euryanthe, Iphigenia, and Rebecca, apart from the tone-colour and vocal modelling sug-

gested by Johanna's young voice, other and more personal motives
were involved in the creation of Elsa. These affect the dramatic
conception of the character and are particularly evident in certain
verses addressed by Lohengrin to Elsa in the third act, and subsequently cut :

> " Wenn alle ihr zum Ruhm mich wähnt erlesen,
>   wenn alle ihr an meine Reine glaubt,
>   so ist in diesem Kreise doch ein Wesen,
>   dem Zweifel seines Glaubens Treu' geraubt.
> Das ist mein Weib, wie schmerzt mich's, dass ich's sage,
>   ein Weib, auf das ich stolz mein Glück gebaut,
>   das Weib, zu dem ich reinste Liebe trage :
>   Elsa, die Gott mir gestern angetraut ! "

> ("When all men here know me the chosen of Heaven,
>   When all men here believe me true of heart,
> One being, giving heed to doubt's slow leav'n,
>   Is robbed of faith and trust by doubt's fell art.
> It is my wife, ah, woe is me ! my nearest,
>   My wife in whom is all my joy and pride,
> The wife for whom I cherish love the dearest,
>   Elsa, but yesterday my God-given bride ! ")

If we compare this reproach with certain words spoken by Wagner
about that time—" Others are happy ; they have their enemies outside
their home, whereas I have my bitterest foe at my table "—we may
well believe that Elsa's guilty doubts are echoes of unhappy experiences in Wagner's own domestic life. Wagner's letters to Minna
until some time after he settled in Switzerland show how deeply his
emotions were enslaved to her charms, and how his masculine ardour
survived all differences and temporary disagreements—a fact of which
Minna was very well aware. It was this very sensual tie which, as
letters and many recorded words bear witness, lent such wounding
bitterness to the pair's intellectual estrangement. If Wagner as a man
had not been in love with Minna, her doubts could not have struck
him so to the soul. These doubts appeared from the time that
Wagner began to outdistance *Rienzi* and to develop the individuality
destined to bring him into conflict with his environment both as man
and artist. Minna, being constitutionally hidebound and conventional,
could not follow him here. In the struggle between her love and

her convictions, she began to doubt the integrity of Wagner's will. Lohengrin's complaint against Elsa concerns this very form of doubt, a doubt which threatens not love but confidence, which seeks to subjugate the creative artist to the canons of ordinary shrewdness, to enslave him to the every-day.   This was Wagner's own complaint against Minna—the complaint of faith-demanding action against anxious, hypercritical love.   Little as Elsa resembles Minna in general, certain characteristics of Minna's had a profound effect on the development of the character.

Lohengrin and Elsa stand for the two main forces in the drama, and the new will to the tragic and the touching was to be manifested through their interactions.   The rest was a matter of building up the plot upon the stage.   The forces of doubt are represented by Telramund and Ortrud.   Directly derived from Weber's Lysiart and Eglantine, their physiognomy is yet far more clearly defined.   They fight the natural fight of darkness against light, of the depths against the heights.   Telramund's desire for revenge, prompted by his wife's lies, is more credible than Lysiart's hollow cynicism.   Ortrud, for her part, gains, through the contrast between heathendom and Christianity, between the world of magic and the world of miracles, a *daemonic* greatness, before which Eglantine's jealous intrigue pales. The superior intensity of both conceptions—Telramund's chivalrous sense of honour and Ortrud's savage heathenish gift of prophecy— is closely connected with the historical setting of the action.   Wagner chose for his purpose that borderland between saga and history where magic and miracles still seem compatible with a historic background. He himself speaks of his endeavours to " present historic legendary incident truthfully."   He found his sources in Grimm's *Deutsche Altertümer*.   The business of the herald, and allied incidents such as the indictment, trial by ordeal, the setting of the lists, the procession to the minster, the bridal song, witness to this.   At the same time the bewitching of young Gottfried by Ortrud, the lifting of the spell by Lohengrin, the swan, the dove, the manifestation of miracle, and the ease with which the spectators accept the supernatural, surround historic truth with the glamour of a legendary remoteness.   Wagner, therefore, used historic trappings not from any interest in historical accuracy as such, but to lend improbabilities an air of probability. The plot of *Rienzi* is historical ; that of *The Flying Dutchman* contrasts realms of reality and fantasy which in *Tannhäuser*, though inwardly

united, contrasted, and clothed in the vesture of mediaeval Romanticism, are externally separate. In *Lohengrin* the two are joined,
indigenous to one soil. To achieve this Wagner harks back to a very
remote past and simplifies the human element, which seems primitive
indeed by comparison with the multi-coloured world of *Tannhäuser*,
and accordingly finds easier access to the miraculous. Contrasts of
height and depth, light and darkness, permeate the action, and a
tendency towards simplification, even in individual character-drawing,
finds its appropriate stage background in " a truthful presentation of
historic, legendary incident." The whole is given a patriotic German
setting, answering to the mood of 1845, whereby the character of the
King acquires something beyond the mere colourless goodness of
the king in *Euryanthe*.

From history and saga and old national custom, from realms of
magic and of miracle, Wagner builds up his picture of a world remote
in time and emotionally simple. Within it he sets forces of light and
darkness, whose conflicts evoke the love which draws the higher nature
towards the lower. The irreconcilability of these contrasts makes a
tragic ending inevitable, and tragedy begets that sympathetic emotion
which is the impulse whence the drama and all its figures spring and
into which they pass. The emotion of *Lohengrin*, however, *moves*
rather than *grips*, is tender rather than violent. It calls accordingly
for lyrical expansion and for this Wagner makes use of the chorus.

In *Lohengrin* the chorus has two functions. It plays a direct part
in the drama, as in *Rienzi*, *The Flying Dutchman*, and *Tannhäuser*, but
also, in and beyond this office, it serves for lyrical interpretation of
mood. By giving verbal and musical emotional expression to the
events of the drama, it emphasises the *moving* appeal. The chorus in
Tannhäuser, apart from a few set musical numbers such as the pilgrims'
march and the entrance of the guests, is used solely to strengthen
soloistic *ensemble* effects. In *Lohengrin* it becomes an independent
vehicle of expression. This use is a reversion to classic drama.
Wagner's pre-occupation with Euripides' *Iphigenia* when retranslating
and revising Gluck's opera of that name, may have influenced him in
this matter. But in Wagner's work the two functions of the chorus
are indissolubly linked. There are some purely dramatic choral
passages of a naturalistic stamp such as the short replies to the King,
a number of ejaculations strewn through the work and, chiefly to be

noted, the very realistic chorus which heralds Lohengrin's coming. On the other hand, there are numerous passages of a purely lyrical character, such as the whispered words that accompany Elsa's first appearance, the choral echo of her vain appeal for a champion, the tender passages that follow Lohengrin's appearance, the singing as Elsa enters the minster, the grand *ensemble* at the close of Act II : " Welch ein Geheimnis muss der Held bewahren " (" Oh what a secret is his heart concealing ! "), those choruses which precede and follow the story of the Grail up to the final " Weh ! " (" Woe ! ") that concentrates the whole tragedy into a single note of music. These latter have their being apart from any external incident. As mere crowd-soliloquies, expressing the emotions of the crowd, they would but hold up the action, did not this require some lyrical discursions to emphasise the primal impulse to tragic emotion. But apart from the naturalistic-dramatic and the lyrical-expository, there is yet a third type of chorus, represented in those *ensemble* passages which serve to bind or to emphasise the musical-theatrical structure, such as the prayer, the march finale to Act I, and the men's chorus in Act II. In these Wagner's experience as conductor of a men's choral society bore rich fruit. The bridal chorus in Act III also belongs to this operatic, concert-platform category. It is Weber's *Jungfernkranz* raised to a stately, heroic level, and it is one of Wagner's most characteristically German inspirations.

These choruses, whether they be dramatic or lyrical, whether they serve to introduce or to close the musical scenic action, form a living musical background upon which the musical drama is woven. The vocal group holds up a mirror to the drama which appears therein sometimes as a set picture, sometimes as fluid action, sometimes as an emotional reflex. In each of these different manifestations it imprints itself in choral song. The chorus develops from a vocal complex obeying formal laws into an expressionist individuality which may support, take part in, or supply a lyrical comment upon, the drama. A chorus so closely interwoven with the musical action requires of the latter that fundamental simplicity of mood which has been shown to be necessary to Wagner's treatment of his subject as a whole. Simple contrasts contribute to make plain the elemental tragedy through which emotional response is to be evoked. The fact that *music* is involved with the chorus which now takes a part in the dramatic action necessitates a lapidary style if the great mediator of expression is not to prove an uneasy yoke-fellow. Accordingly, the action of *Lohengrin*, unlike that of *Tannhäuser*, which depends for its effect on continual and startling changes, is built up of broad, simple situations. There are no sudden impulses on the part of its characters to surprise us. Scene follows scene in strictly logical sequence. The crises of the action—Lohengrin's coming in Act I, Ortrud's attack upon Elsa in Act II, and Elsa's question in Act III—are not unexpected but are the natural consequence of what has gone before. Not only does the strict gradation of scenes, each an emotional entity, make a choral setting possible ; it gives rise, furthermore, to a new tone-symbolic method. The reminiscence-theme of the Romantic school—at first a *mere* reminiscence and employed in *The Flying Dutchman* and, more lavishly, in *Tannhäuser* to recall particular persons and emotions—can now be used to summarise a *situation*. The themes of Lohengrin's coming, of the Forbidden Question, of Doubt, of the Swan, of the Grail, are not reminiscent echoes, still less indications of particular traits in the persons of the drama. They are *situation-motifs*. They characterise particular emotional complexes which dominate all the participants as one. They are expressionist symbols of the tragic concept underlying the whole work. Passing beyond the confines of individual characterisation they betray the emotional forces at work within. In a drama that is really worked out not in the actions of its characters but in an organised sequence of situations this type of theme affords a tone-symbolic fulcrum of scenic unity.

This use of the situation-motif to express scenic unity calls for new treatment of orchestral tone and harmony. In *Tannhäuser* the modulatory movement of sound develops from presentation of two concepts—distance in space and strong emotional contrast. The former is reflected in the composition of the orchestra through ever-varying strength of dynamic register. Spontaneous changes of emotion are expressed in chromatic harmonies, lavish use of enharmonic change, and startling chord sequences. The tone colour of *Lohengrin*, on the other hand, is based on contrasts of *height* and *depth*, of etherial spirituality and glowing actuality. The contrast is one not of strength but of brightness, not of colour but of intensity. The unity of the situation-motif establishes the harmonic formation ; its modulatory development constitutes the formal constructive task which devolves upon the artist. To the orchestra, accordingly, in the guise of instrumental complement of a pseudo-classical stage chorus, falls the double task of delineating the musical sphere of the work and of establishing a basis in harmony and modulation for the thematic action. Thus, while the chorus, exceeding its formal musical function as a vocal group, is employed to manifest tragic emotion, the orchestra, transcending its traditional function of accompanist, is made an independent vehicle of musical dramatic action.

The orchestration of *Lohengrin* is an example of extreme clarification of sound. Wood-wind, strings in the highest and lowest registers, horns, trumpets, and trombones, are chorally contrasted in groups individualised by harmony and similarity of timbre. The downward sweep of the action, as from heaven to earth, is reflected in this grouping, this vertical structure, which symbolises the vertical movements of the emotional drama. Even in details of scenic action this separative treatment is apparent. Elsa and her songs are rendered throughout in the soft colouring of the wood-wind. Lohengrin's Grail chivalry is suggested by the mystic aerial tone of the strings, Ortrud's allegiance to the powers of darkness by the dark tones of the English horn and bass clarinet, the King and his Herald by metallic trumpet-blasts. The Forbidden Question motif is announced in stern wood-wind harmonies and is answered, upon its more urgent reiteration, by the upper strings in choral echo, while remaining the property of the wood-wind. The strings are principally used for their lyrical expression-value and give soft instrumental accord to the contemplative chorus. There is an entire absence of the rushing string passages so frequently accompanying the abrupt transitions in *Tannhäuser*, and dazzling virtuoso effects of all kinds are avoided. On the other hand, the technical display of the strings in their very highest position is greatly enhanced by the legato effects and repeated changes of register of the wood-wind. The orchestration of *Tannhäuser* shows a marked tendency to theatrical effect; as for instance in the horns, the ornamental treatment of the wood-wind and the rushing passages of the strings. In *Lohengrin* orchestration is chiefly based on exploitation of tonal quality and lyrical intensity. The two most brilliant orchestral passages measured by traditional standards, the prelude to Act III and the passage which leads up to the last scene, the procession of warriors, are, significantly, the earliest parts of the composition. They stand as it were isolated amidst the swirl of the

work as a whole.   Other great orchestral passages, the preludes to
Acts I and II and the dawn music in Act II, are not designed to be
" effective " in the usual sense.   The procession to the minster,
which in an earlier work would have provided an opportunity for
a display of orchestral pomp, is, unlike the march in *Tannhäuser*,
orchestrally very simple.   It depends entirely on the crescendo fullness
and brilliance of its tonal groupings, which are finally gathered up in
the solemn tones of the organ.

This unifying treatment of the orchestra, choral in character, is
compatible with the effort for simplification which underlies, in a
scenic sense, Wagner's handling of the plot and, in a musical sense,
his use of the lyrical chorus.   The part he assigns to harmony as the
principal vehicle of expression renders this possible.   Special instrumental effects become superfluous when the individual instrument,
even if heard alone, seems no more than the wash of harmonic movement, in which latter the essence of the drama is felt to reside.   Yet
harmony could not have been thus employed unless the situation-
motif notified change in harmonic movement.   The relationship
between *Lohengrin* and *Tannhäuser* is as apparent here as is their dis-
similarity.   When the Venusberg motif breaks in upon the song-
contest, seducing Tannhäuser's imagination, when Elizabeth's song
echoes through the duet with Tannhäuser, and Wolfram's in the
epilogue to the prayer, associative trains of thought are, it is true,
suggested.   But when Lohengrin's knightly A major motif, which
dominates the whole first act of *Lohengrin*, is heard, transposed to
A minor, in Elsa's last appeal at the close of Act III and the chorus
cries its final " Woe ! " something is expressed much greater than, and
altogether different from, any reminiscent train of thought.   A *musical*
fate is here fulfilled, and similarity of theme is made to reveal an
emphatic change in harmony.   The tragic idea on which the work
is based attains direct symbolic expression in sound.   This fundamental
tragic idea is evolved, musically, by the chromatic depression of the
third from A major to A minor.

The musical essence of *Lohengrin*, namely, the contrast between
major and *minor* as expression values and its emotional appeal, is a true
counterpart of the visible drama and of the tonal progression from
the *heights* to the *depths*.   In the matter of musical symbolism and
figurative construction, *Lohengrin* bears resemblance to *The Flying*

Dutchman. A certain harmonic process is inherent in both works—the insertion of a major third in the open fifth. As in *Lohengrin*, musical and dramatic action are derived from the artist's grasp of harmonic expression-values. In *Lohengrin* the change from major to minor and its emotional portrayal is, indeed, a more complicated matter. The contrast must be fully revealed; the major key intensively, the minor extensively, and they have to be shown in conflict. The ultimate victory of the minor power must seem to be based not on harmonic change in the accustomed sense but on expressionist symbolism. Herein lies the essential thematic purpose of the orchestration of *Lohengrin*, its modulatory development, and its division into chorus-like instrumental groups to which separate harmonies are entrusted. Herein also lies the explanation of the existence and significance of its motifs. Associated neither with persons nor with moods but with emotional situations, these are few in number yet melodically and rhythmically so sharply defined that they convey immediately the pure essence of each situation. Every change of their harmonic expression becomes at once evident. They possess this penetrating quality because they are not thematic inventions but primal harmonic phenomena. The crises in scenic action occur between Lohengrin, Elsa, and Ortrud, those in the conceptual drama between Faith, Love, and Doubt, those in the musical drama between three fundamental harmonic types—the major chord, the minor chord, and the diminished seventh which connects them.

The major tonality, expressed by the peculiarly tender A major key, is the habitation of all the phenomena of the *heights*—the Grail, whose harmonies, passing easily into F sharp minor, give Lohengrin's song to the swan and his narration, and Lohengrin himself, whose rhythm dominates the whole of the first act from Elsa's narrative up to the final victory hymn. The minor tonal sphere is defined by the Forbidden Question theme. Its announcement in the minor proclaims from the first that its demands can never be fulfilled and foreshadows a tragic issue. Its ominous shadow falls over the first act. In the second it returns, significantly, during Ortrud's colloquy with Telramund and disturbs the act's stately close. In the third it rises to the height of its power in Lohengrin's final warning, " Elsa, was willst du wagen ? " (" Elsa, oh I implore thee ! "). The third fundamental harmonic formula is the chord of the diminished seventh, the musical symbol of doubt and, functionally, the method of harmonic modulation. It underlies Elsa's urgent questions in the bridal chamber. It holds most persistent and most formidable sway in Act II, where it dominates the night scene between Ortrud and Telramund and that crisis in the emotional action marked by the grand *ensemble*, "In wildem Brüten darf ich sie gewahren" ("What dark dismay upon her heart is stealing!"). It has the same significance for Act II as the characteristic major has for Act I, and similarly it is constantly spurred on by the threat of the minor subject of the Forbidden Question. Considered thematically, the effect of the diminished seventh serves a double purpose : to portray Elsa's insistence, through animated succession of intervals, and to form the sustained relationship of ever-changing sound from bar to bar. Consequently it is most prominent in the final *ensemble* of Act II and accompanies Ortrud's words, "Der Zweifel keimt in ihres Herzens Grund" ("Within her bosom seeds of doubt are sown"). As an expression of doubt and its attendant misery the same phrase had already been used in the dialogue between Euryanthe and Eglantine, following the latter's "Dein Hoffen und dein Sehnen zeigt dir als höchstes Glück nur Tränen" ("All thy hopes and fears show thee no higher bliss than tears"). But whereas in Weber's work the idea is merely episodic, in Wagner's it becomes an important vehicle of dramatic expression.

The tone-world of *Lohengrin* is thus founded on three harmonic types—the major, the minor, and the diminished seventh. The other harmonic phenomena are grouped in order of importance around the basic key of A. The A major-A minor world of tragedy and miracle is contrasted with the realistic C major world of the King and the Herald, with the royal fanfare as foundation. Ortrud's and Telramund's nocturnal conspiracy is cast in F sharp minor, the relative minor key of A major. The duet in the bridal chamber begins (like *The Flying Dutchman* duet) in E major, changing as Lohengrin hints at his origin to A major and sinking when Elsa's doubts overmaster her to E minor. In all those parts of the music which concern the inner drama as a whole the main key relationship is maintained, but in all that concern Elsa alone the flat keys prevail. The two harmonic hemispheres, the sharp and the flat keys, are contrasted, the first denoting the tonal sphere of the miraculous, the second that of unawakened innocence. Elsa's song of thanksgiving, "Euch Lüften die mein Klagen" ("Sweet zephyrs, sighs did swell ye"), is in B flat major, the procession to the minster is in E flat, the bridal chorus and victory hymn in B flat major. In these pieces the flat key predominates, but there are others which are allied through modulation with the sharp keys. Elsa's story of her dream begins in A flat major, is intensified in its course by diminution into A flat minor and passes thence into A major as her Lohengrin vision comes true. There is no reason to suppose that these key relationships are deliberately contrived. It is enough to notice that this method of harmonic structure is peculiarly effective. But Wagner's successful use of acoustic references demonstrates the importance he assigns to the organic structure of his harmonic complex. Everything in the work has primarily an harmonic basis. Plot, scene, and action might all be justly described as emotional manifestations of an absolute harmonic sense. This harmonic sense finds very complete expression in the theatrical interplay of *heights* and *depths*, since harmony in itself, as a musical acoustic phenomenon, implies the diffusion and division of tone into high and low registers.

The motif, being a crystallisation of the harmonic complex which is revealed as the action develops, obeys the same fundamental law of formal structure. Structurally the motif as found in *Lohengrin* stands midway between the melodic reminiscent theme of *Tannhäuser* and the characteristic subject of later works. It is allied to the latter by the fact that expressionism has changed its function, making it a unit in the musical action, but its song-like formation still connects it with Romantic opera of the older stamp. The motifs of the Grail, Lohengrin, the Forbidden Question, and Doubt, all alike are based on the lyrical, two-bar, rhythmical phrase, corresponding with the rhymed couplets of the versification :

> " Nie sollst du mich befragen,
>   noch Wissens Sorge tragen,
>   woher ich kam der Fahrt,
>   noch wie mein Nam' und Art ! "

> (" These questions ask me never ;
>   Brood not upon them ever ;
>   From whence I hither came,
>   Or what my race and name ! ")

The first announcement of Lohengrin's coming is given a similarly lyrical setting, with a more faithful rendering of word-values :

> " In lichter Waffen Scheine
> ein Ritter nahte da.
> So tugendlicher Reine
> ich keinen noch ersah ! "

> (" Arrayed in shining splendour,
> A noble knight I saw.
> His look sublime and tender
> Inspired my soul with awe.")

The unifying function of the harmonic motif acquires a new importance. Not only does it serve as a musical expressionist symbol of the fundamental tragic concept, but it overrides distinctions between the *set* form and the *free*, between purely periodic and purely declamatory formation. Distinctions between aria (or *ensemble*) and recitative which obtained in traditional opera and which in *Tannhäuser* were emphasised rather than abolished, are here set aside save for a few faint traces in certain objective, narrative passages such as Telramund's accusation in Act I. The new motifs, combining qualities of brevity, point, and lyrical form, pave the way for a new arioso style in which the declamatory freedom of the recitative blends with the well-defined symmetry of the *set* song-form. The form of the big *ensemble* emanates from the more constricted musical phrase. In accordance with its greater inherent strength it is susceptible of greater expansion, its framework being the march. Song and march, the basic formal types of grand and Romantic opera respectively, are here organically united. The song is the germ-cell, showing that the basis of the dramatic concept is lyrical ; the march sustains the action through all changes of expressionist characterisation. In the first act of *Lohengrin* song and march are freely interwoven ; the second opens lyrically and settles later into the solemn march of the minster procession, with lyrical interludes ; the third opens with bridal chorus and duet in march form, after which the lyrical form resumes sway in Lohengrin's song of the Grail—the true climax of Elsa's lyrical dream song with which the inner drama begins.

There is one danger in this method of construction—the danger of rhythmic monotony. Wagner did not succeed in avoiding it in

Rienzi, nor does he do so here. Like *Rienzi*, *Lohengrin* has only a single short *ensemble* in three-four time, the prayer before combat in Act I. This uniformity of rhythm is closely associated with the problematic character of the work as a purely harmonic drama and with the consequent uniformity of the movement of its phrasing. There is much orchestral syncopation, and the urgent, hurrying motion thus lent to the accompaniment may perhaps spring from Wagner's sense that rhythmic contrast is lacking. Such stylistic drawbacks are, however, outweighed by the gain of a new formative principle in which lyrical arioso, melody built of phrases of short duration—in itself nothing but the free, declamatory climax of the harmonic motif—becomes the unifying basis of the whole super-structure of performance and expression.

The tragic idea in *Lohengrin* is governed by its composer's inten-tion, not merely to grip, but profoundly to *move* his audience. It finds scenic manifestation in the interaction of two worlds, a higher and a lower, represented by simple characters on whose actions the chorus supplies a lyrical commentary. This stage drama has its musical parallel in a harmony which expresses vertical concepts in tone. The tragic appeal which the drama makes is reflected in the drop from major to minor ; the orchestration supplies a twofold exegesis by means of modulation and tone-colour processes, made apparent in the situation-motif which at the same time forms a link between scene and music. As a symbolic epitome of the contending forces of scenic-harmonic action, the situation-motif is also the germ-cell of formal structure. All media are in accord, for all spring from the same source, namely, an expressionist will to evoke tragic emotion. This emotional appeal is distinct from poetry, distinct from music, distinct, indeed, from art as such. It merely *uses* art to embody and reveal stark emotion. Wagner became by degrees perfectly aware of this, though he did not feel that in subordinating art to emotional purposes he was sacrificing it, but rather providing it with a new aim, the only one which could fully justify it. He had, however, had doubts as to the right ending for the Lohengrin story and similarly he felt that only trial could disclose if his libretto's intent could be truly realised in music, if the tragic appeal of stark emotion could find musico-scenic presentation, if, in fact, opera was a branch of art capable of being made wholly subordinate to naturalistic emotion.

The proof or disproof of this must be sought in the third act, and in the third act only. Externally the end, in reality this act is the beginning or root of the tragedy. The graph of the inner drama can be traced from the third act through the first to the second—from the self-revelation of a supernatural being through his act of grace to a lower world to his final annihilation because the lower nature fails to retain faith in him. The tragic fatality of *Lohengrin* concerns the inception and growth of unbelief. The second act, which witnesses Elsa's transition from perfect faith to a faithlessness which is only not expressed, presents, accordingly, the main problem of the work. The substructure of the other two acts is needed to bring all the creative forces into play here. From the nature of the plan the construction of the third act is more simple than that of the others, being based on a conversation between Lohengrin and Elsa and Lohengrin's story. Here the fundamental will to tragedy is most fully revealed, since it is shown only in results, not in causes. The first act links the other two. It knits up and establishes those constructive forces which are resolved in the final act, passing them on with heightened intensity to the second act, which is the most important part of the work.

Accordingly, the work's true evolutionary sequence, the movement of the action from above to below, is from Lohengrin's Grail story to the grand *ensemble*, "In wildem Brüten darf ich sie gewahren" ("What dark dismay upon her heart is stealing!"). The Forbidden Question motif in F minor, breaking in at the close of this finale, is the true climax; all that follows it is mere external winding-up. It may be that Wagner realised that the creative development of his work was not coincident with the order of the plot, and that for this reason, in his final version, he placed the essence of his third act—Lohengrin's story—at the beginning of the whole in the form of an orchestral prelude. For him this prelude summed up the whole matter, leading the listener straight to the creative sources of the work. By this device the hearer can receive the work in the order in which its creator conceived it, and the third act becomes merely an explanatory commentary upon the prelude. The circle is complete. In composition, however, Wagner followed an impulse which led from the simple to the complex, from a higher world to a lower, from his third act, by way of his first, to his second. Only so could the essence of the whole be expressed in the prelude—that essence being stark emotional appeal, independent of any particular story, and made through an expressionist miracle of ascending and descending harmony.

The third act has two scenes—Elsa's question and Lohengrin's answer. The question put in the privacy of the bride-chamber is answered publicly "before the world, the King and his lieges." The plan of both scenes is plainly derived from *Tannhäuser*, but shows a more practised invention. A prelude portrays the festive tumult of the wedding-feast, its triplet quavers being reminiscent both of the orchestral prelude to Act II of *Tannhäuser* and of the fanfare theme in the overture to *Euryanthe*. The equally spirited piece which links the first scene with the second portrays the assemblage of the knights. Stage trumpets calling in sharply contrasted keys and a martial theme in the orchestral wind form the simple outline. To these are added unison passages in the strings imitating the clatter of a troop of horse as in Liszt's *Mazeppa*. Complete realism is the composer's intention. "If we cannot have horses we may at least, whenever a captain arrives, see what can be done to imitate the sound of a rider pulling up and dismounting." The very "operatic" bridal chorus has in common with these two orchestral passages a popular simplicity which harks back to an earlier period. The melodic theme of the song, which is in B flat major, agrees note for note with the adagio in B major in the finale to the second act of *Tannhäuser*. The final scene on the Scheldt also has a short *ensemble* introduction, the vassals' greeting to the King, and the King's spirited address, based on a continuation of the march movement. These two operatic preludes are more conventional than those which introduce the acts of *Tannhäuser* and take us back to the choral preludes of *The Flying Dutchman*. When Wagner began the composition of *Lohengrin* he may have had the same sort of purpose in mind—that of making the miraculous element which is the kernel of the plot yet more impressive by the realism which leads up to it. In the first act this method of exposition is freely used. In the second act it is quite abandoned, though at the merely external change of scene from Elsa's chamber by night to the minster procession in the morning, men's choruses are inserted to form a neutral bridge-passage.

The first great scene of the composition, the dialogue between Lohengrin and Elsa in the bridal chamber, begins with the same almost hesitating touch. It is lyrical at first, like the old duet.

Introduced independently, the voices are linked together in octave formation with a broad cadence in consecutive sixths, similar to the slow E major section of the duet of *The Flying Dutchman*. The melody is founded on luxuriant treatment of line and chromatic transition, reminiscent of the lyrical quality in Schumann to which Wagner approaches very closely here. The continuation to Lohengrin's "Atmest du nicht mit mir die holden Düfte" ("Dost thou not breathe as if the scents of flowers?") in C major is also pure Schumann. Lyrical emotion here ceases, and its alternate, duet-like expression by the pair gives place to a dramatic dialogue, while instead of an orchestral accompaniment which has hitherto merely filled in the harmonies and marked the rhythm, there is now a strong independent instrumental movement. With Elsa's rejoinder, "Ach, könnt' ich deiner wert erscheinen" ("Ah! could'st thou only worthy find me"), clear melodic form is lost, being supplanted by the chromatic idiom; the Question theme is heard in the orchestra, the harmonic development becomes more complicated. Trombones heard for the first time—as in Tannhäuser's narrative when he speaks of the papal ban—accompany Lohengrin's warning, "Höchstes Vertrauen hast du mir schon zu danken" ("Trust I have shown thee, Elsa, of the deepest"). The lyricism of the opening reappears in Lohengrin's "An meiner Brust, du Süsse, Reine" ("O let my arm, sweet love, enfold thee!"). As his song continues the music intimates the secret of his supernatural origin by introducing the A major, until "Aus Glanz und Wonne komm ich her" ("My home's a land of light and joy!") gives the signal for Elsa's passionate outburst. Miracle and unbelief stand in sharp contrast face to face. The A major Grail theme calls for its immediate contrast, the Doubt theme in diminished sevenths—"O Gott, was muss ich hören!" ("Oh Heav'n, what hast thou told me!") A vision of the swan's dreaded return deepens sorrow to despair: the Forbidden Question can no longer be withheld. It is asked, and the violent entrance of Telramund and the conspirators (reminiscent of Adolar's struggle with the serpent) constitutes the dynamic climax. A faintly echoing E minor cadence closes the musical scene. The first E major melody, the Doubt theme and the Forbidden Question theme, form the epilogue.

Wagner insisted more than once on the completeness with which he identified himself with the character of Elsa whilst composing

o

Lohengrin. The process must be understood in a purely artistic sense ; its justification is to be found in this scene. Wagner's imagination, like Elsa's vision, conceived the figure of Lohengrin but dimly as one ready to reveal himself in loving response to a need. Only the fated, and fatal, question of the drama could wake that vision to real existence. It is, indeed, the creative artist's own question. Lohengrin stands for the ideal vision, Elsa for the human conditions, of art. For this reason the question had to be put at the beginning of the work and the answer had to follow immediately.

Lohengrin's story of the Grail was written some two years after Tannhäuser's story of his pilgrimage to Rome. Even its first version —the second was considerably shortened—shows a remarkable change in formative method. In contrast to free, prosodic delivery in the earlier work, the later has a song of three strophes. Each of the first two verses consists of three eight-bar phrases answering to the twelve lines of verse. A third verse of four lines and ten musical bars closes the song. The harmonic character of these stanzas accords with the meaning of the words. In the first verse A major and its directly related keys portray the mystery of the Grail. The second verse, describing the duties of the Knights of the Grail, is in F sharp major, freely modulated. In the last verse, as Lohengrin names his name, there is a return to A major. Such is the harmonic wave which carries the melodic line. Sustained at first by voice and strings alone in ascending and descending A major intervals, it is then softly taken up by the full orchestra. The gradual descending harmonic progression is encompassed by a tentative upper part and rings out suddenly in A major as the Grail is named. In the second verse the melodic upper line is firmer, the orchestral tone increases in density and volume, the violins fall silent, and the prevailing colour is that of trombones and lower strings, indicating the descent to earth of the supernatural, until the higher registers re-enter upon the command that Lohengrin shall remain unknown. Only when Lohengrin has told his name do the mystic notes become real. The words ring out free and unaccompanied ; as at the beginning the intervals march from A major to F sharp minor, now no longer veiled by the orchestra, and emphasised by powerful chords. The veil of mystery has been rent, the splendour of the higher world shines upon the lower in full glory. For the delicate A major of the opening violin notes is substituted the reality of full orchestral tone and Lohengrin's chordal major theme rings out with dazzling brilliance.

As in *Tannhäuser*, Wagner made a number of important alterations in the ending of *Lohengrin*. The first version of the Grail story was double the length of the present one. It carried the narrative further, describing Lohengrin's call and setting forth. The big *ensemble* of lamentation which ends with Lohengrin's prophecy of victory and which is still preserved in the score and in pianoforte arrangements, contained originally a special speech to Elsa. Ortrud's song of vengeance, in its first version, contained the story of the enchantment of young Gottfried. The release of the swan from enchantment—effected in the present version by Lohengrin's silent prayer—was besought in the first in repeated songs, and the swan itself sang a farewell to the waves. These passages were eventually cut, some before composition, some before the first performance in Weimar, while others were omitted entirely. There were other reasons for this besides those of economy. So much matter following the Grail story undoubtedly detracted from the effect of the story itself. Externally the plot could only end by a slow extinction of the excitement of that moment, as expressed in the words of the chorus :

> " Hör' ich so seine höchste Art bewähren,
>   entbrennt mein Aug' in heil'gen Wonnezähren."

> (" O, to learn thus his mystic name and calling !|
>   Adown my cheeks what holy tears are falling ! ")

This chorus, a dying echo of the Grail theme, is now followed by the appearance of the swan, by Lohengrin's brief sad greeting to it and his tender farewell to Elsa, by Ortrud's triumph hymn (with a reminiscence of her oath of vengeance in F sharp minor), by Lohengrin's silent prayer to the accompaniment of the Grail theme in F sharp major, and by the restoration of Gottfried, accompanied by the knightly Lohengrin theme. As this theme fades away into the distance and Elsa gazes on the forsaken shore it changes to the minor and is suddenly cut short by the wild " Woe ! " cries of the chorus.

After the completion of the sketch during the summer of 1846, the composition of this one act occupied Wagner from September 9, 1846 to March 5, 1847. With it he had a basis for the two acts which precede it in the dramatic order, for the actualisation of the Lohengrin vision renders both dream and reality plastically attainable. Elsa's doubts, which are in a sense Wagner's own, are the means of summoning Lohengrin *for him* from the heights to the real world. In the bridal-chamber scene Wagner transcends lyric sentiment and discovers the constructive intensifying power of motival expression. In his musical treatment of Lohengrin's account of his origin he formulates new principles of harmonic expression—melodic action within a harmonic setting, orchestral tone-distribution, subordination even of the human voice within the harmonic organism, association of speech with song in the free, declamatory arioso form, the harmonic lyrical phrase. The success of these two scenes demonstrated and established the fact that tragic emotional appeal might be a fruitful impulse to expression. By this means Elsa's question and Lohengrin's answer realised Wagner's artistic purpose and formed a basis for all that was to follow. The fact that he took six months to compose the third act, during which he more than once laid the work aside, is evidence that he found it difficult to penetrate to the heart of his subject. The first and second acts, on the other hand, were completed with astonishing rapidity. By August 28 the overture was finished ; during the winter Wagner worked upon the full score and finished it by March 1848, for with the completion of the third act, pent up forces which had gathered during the composer's six months' work upon it were released in full spate of creative energy.

The first act, more especially, is very clearly the product of such a flood-tide of vigour. The Herald's prologue-like opening, the King's speech, Telramund's calumny, Elsa's appearance and tale of her wondrous dream, Lohengrin's miraculous advent and his wooing, the prayer before the combat, the combat itself and the rejoicings at Lohengrin's victory—the whole act, indeed, is fresh and vivid and full of varied interest. Regarded as a unity, it is the strongest piece of work Wagner had up to that time achieved, and is structurally comparable only with the first act of *The Valkyrie*. Externally this effect of unity comes from the spontaneous flow of incident, but it is confirmed by the motival summing up. The whole course of the action, from Elsa's entrance onwards, is based on the Lohengrin theme, for Lohengrin's miracle is the central subject of the act. Each crisis, accordingly, is based upon this theme, presented in various guises. Elsa's story of her dream contains a mere foreshadowing of it in A flat major. In the chorus that hails Lohengrin's coming it attains the joyous certitude of A major. In the finale it appears again in B flat major. An approaching climax in the external drama is characterised in the sphere of harmony by a rise from time to time of a half tone, so devised that A major, the very note of the Grail itself, coincides with the final moment of revelation. Round the three principal scenic and musical crises, one of which—Elsa's narrative—passes without a break into the chorus of greeting, other scenes are grouped to fill in the external picture. Such are the scenes preceding Elsa's appearance, Lohengrin's salute to the King, his request that his name and origin shall never be asked, and the prayer before the combat. From the first the action marches boldly forward. The Herald's proclamation, the King's speech, the homage of Saxony and Brabant, Telramund's indictment of Elsa—step by step, in straightforward sequence, outward incidents lead up to the essential. From a musical standpoint this preliminary scene may be regarded as a relaxation through the antithesis of visible action and narrative of the intense lyrical emotion of the prelude. Such being the case, musical emphasis is slight, the King's speech and Telramund's have the character of dramatic recitative, and it is not until the chorus, passing from E flat minor to C minor, dies out in " profound horror " after the words :

> " Ha, schwerer Schuld zeiht Telramund !
> Mit Grau'n werd' ich der Klage kund."

> (" Ah, Telramund, how grave thy word !
> Each true heart with dismay is stirred ! ")

that we pass into the inner world of the drama to follow. This begins with the proclamation of a court of justice and the summons to Elsa to appear before it. Henceforward the plot is developed not mechanically but emotionally.

With Elsa's entry the lead passes from stage to orchestra. There begins the first of those great scenes of eloquent silence employed at times by Wagner (as in Act I of *The Valkyrie* and in *Parsifal*) when he wished to suggest some spiritual change inexpressible in words. In this instance such a change is brought about by Elsa's entrance and is reflected in the whisperings of the chorus. The orchestration suddenly assumes a new, unfamiliar colouring. In place of the full robust tones of the preceding scene, tender wood-wind passages in unison are heard in the hidden cadence of A flat minor, maintained by continuous enharmonic modulation. A broken chromatic sequence

of harmonies accompanying a melody for flutes and clarinets presents
a strange, shimmering picture of Elsa lost in a world of dreams to
which the King's questions penetrate like sounds from another
universe.   It is a repetition of the picture of Senta amongst the
spinning-women.   And as Senta sings her ballad to and for herself,
so Elsa relates her dream, not to justify herself, but for the sake of the
promise it brings to her own heart.

Like Lohengrin's Grail story, Elsa's narrative of her dream takes
the form of a song with three verses.   The first and second stanzas
are divided by a short interruption from the chorus, the second and
third by the King's decree of a trial by combat, so that Elsa's third
verse naturally proclaims her choice of a champion.   The song is
based on A flat major harmonies, and its climax is attained by thematic
treatment.   To a simple melody with soft orchestral accompaniment
the first verse tells of Elsa's appeal to heaven and her trance-like
slumber.   Here the Lohengrin theme begins to creep in—the major
triad with its characteristic rhythm just as at the close of the Grail
story.   In muted tones the orchestra foreshadows the vision, while
the voice, touching only the peaks of the harmonic range, thereafter
passes into the enharmonically changing chordal sequence which marks
Elsa's entrance and which now finds verbal expression in her words:

> " Den Ritter will ich wahren,
>   er soll mein Streiter sein ! "

> (" The Knight who thus consoled me,
>   He is my champion true ! ")

An all-pervading atmosphere of emotion heralds the coming
miracle.   The spirit of Elsa's world possesses all the spectators.   The
Herald's brief summons to combat heightens the sense of tension by
its very matter-of-factness.   It is repeated, rising by a half note (as
later the similar repetitions of the Forbidden Question in the bridal
chamber).   There is no answer; only the echo of trumpets and horns
carries on the resonant last note of the challenge till it dies away to the
dull beat of the kettle-drums.   There has been no miracle, and expectation gives place to a frozen silence.   Then faith gathers itself for a
final effort.   In the progressive intervals of the Doubt theme, an
A flat minor subject leads back to the melody of Elsa's entrance,
becoming a prayer of adjuration:

" Du trugest zu ihm meine Klage,
zu mir trat er auf dein Gebot :
O Herr, nun meinem Ritter sage,
dass er mir helf' in meiner Not ! "

(" Thou my appealing cry hast borne him,
He came to me at Thy command :
O haste, Lord, to my Knight, and warn him
How of his aid in need I stand.")

As the chorus of women joins in the prayer, the wailing minor gives place to an aspiring A flat major. Elsa's melody of trust and confidence returns, the harmonies alternate, and above them rises Elsa's voice :

" Lass mich ihn seh'n, wie ich ihn sah,
wie ich ihn sah, sei er mir nah ! "

(" As in my dream he did appear,
Send him to me, my hero dear ! ")

A major breaks like sun through clouds. Soft trumpet notes, in a shimmer of violin tremolo, proclaim the theme of Elsa's visionary champion, in the as yet distant but ever-approaching and glorious reality of the key which portrays the Grail. A stormy crescendo wave sweeps on, flooding the scene. Broader and broader swells the knightly theme, sweeping chorus and actors into its course, gathering up into itself the short, broken cries, the syncopated chromatic vocal lines. Behold the Knight, the swan, the skiff !—behold the miracle ! Limpid major harmonies and heroic rhythms rise to a dazzling brilliance until at last orchestra and chorus in full strength hail the vision as an emanation of very light.

This great *ensemble* of greeting, which Wagner at first assigned to the orchestra and double men's chorus only, then alternately to the men's and women's choruses, and finally to all in unison, is a triumph of musical dramatic art owing to its peculiar blend of dramatic-tone-dynamic and harmonic-thematic effects. For a moment stage ceases to be stage, art ceases to be art, and nought remains but naturalistic expression of an emotion so overmastering that it transcends the intellectually comprehensible. Spell-bound by musico-scenic suggestion we lose all power of reflection. Wagner succeeds here in making an impression which he might, perhaps, under special conditions and in another manner, be able to repeat, but which he could never surpass. The *ensemble* is the most important thing in the first act of *Lohengrin*. It is the revelation of miracle.　All that precedes is but preparation, all that follows mere confirmation, and the true climax is that moment when king and people together hail Lohengrin as the emissary of God.

The marvellous fact is established in the A major *ensemble* which follows.　As Lohengrin's address to the swan dies away the chorus takes up the Grail theme :

> " Wie fasst uns selig süsses Grauen !
> Welch holde Macht hält uns gebannt ! "

> (" What mystic awe is o'er us streaming !
> What power doth all hearts command.")

Lohengrin greets the King, announces his readiness to do battle, and goes on to speak with Elsa and to enjoin on all that his name must never be asked, proclaiming the Forbidden Question motif which is in the same key as the motif of Elsa's indictment.　He repeats the prohibition, this time in the key of tragic contrast, the key of A minor. There is a return to A major in Elsa's reply and in Lohengrin's avowal of his love and the scene ends with the same choral passage, transposed here from a low register to a high, with which it opened :

> " Welch holde Wunder muss ich seh'n ?
> Ich fühl' das Herze mir vergeh'n."

> (" What tender mood doth arise !
> Ah, tears of delight steal from my eyes.")

This ends the first half of the act.　The musical and dramatic treatment with which the second opens resembles that of the first.　Ascending, syncopated chords again indicate an approaching climax.　The prayer in E flat major, which bears a rhythmic and melodic resemblance to the Pilgrims' chorus from *Tannhäuser*, introduces a brief, operatic pause in the action with a broadly delineated *ensemble* climax.　The combat follows and is portrayed in the canonic form of the Trial by Ordeal motif, derived in its turn from the greeting to the King and ending in the A major Lohengrin theme.　Taken up by Elsa's triumph song this changes to a solemn march in B flat major, and leads on to the victorious conclusion :

" Dich nur besingen wir,
   dir schallen unsre Lieder !
   Nie kehrt ein Held gleich dir
   in diese Lande wieder ! "

(" Praises deliver we,
    Our songs re-echo loudly !
   Ne'er will a knight like thee
   Stand on our shore so proudly ! ")

Since it is Elsa's unshakable faith which has conjured Lohengrin's presence in the first instance, it is inevitable that her loss of faith should drive him away, that it should annihilate his reality, and Wagner uses the gradual sapping of her faith, the undermining of conviction by the operation of the critical intellect, to make his strongest appeal for tragic emotional response. Elsa is lost because she is something greater than the almost somnambulist figure of Senta, because she is, as Senta is not, a real woman in love. She becomes fully a woman in the course of the second act. This act, like the first, has two sections, a night scene and a day scene. Night gives birth to doubts which day brings to light. Ortrud and Telramund, the latter as instrument, the former as the hand that wields it, are the villains of the drama, but behind both stands the force of Unbelief itself. Ortrud's heathen fanaticism clothes the idea with a kind of barbaric splendour, but it needs no such extraneous confirmation, for it is a force inherent in human nature ; and though it may, in exceptional moments, be overcome, it will inevitably return with redoubled force after such states of exaltation as the first act portrays.

The prelude depicts just such a revulsion of feeling. It begins with the Doubt motif, which is answered by the Forbidden Question motif. A flourish of trumpets from the castle battlements dies out in the theme of Elsa's faith. In its carefully calculated motival language as in its colour this prelude resembles the C sharp minor prelude to Act IV of *Rienzi* ; the Fate motif of that opera re-echoes in the Doubt theme of *Lohengrin*. At the same time the combination of motifs and the emphasis upon their significance points to an impending change of structural method. In this act the dramatic problem is not merely psychical but psychological, and similarly, from this moment on, the music too abandons the expressionism of pure emotion. The change is conditioned by the development of the action and is at first confined to an increasing conscious emphasis upon the character significance of the motif. Not merely in its harmonic but also in its rhythmic melodic aspect it is subject to frequent variations employed, as it were, in a symphonic sense. The change is as yet confined within the harmonic organism, which is none the less noticeably disturbed by the independent life of the theme. It shows that Wagner's art was tending dramatically towards psychological subtleties and musically towards an individualistic treatment of the motif apart from the harmonic complex.

The night scene begins with the conversation between Telramund and Ortrud and proceeds to one between Ortrud and Elsa. The figure of Ortrud dominates the day scene also, for a growing spirit of unbelief governs the action, while the diminished seventh is the chief factor musically and the key of F sharp minor—the sombre relative key of A major—stands for darkness as opposed to light. Telramund's opening recitative and passionate arioso, " Durch dich musst' ich verlieren mein Ehr', all meinen Ruhm (" 'Tis thou hast sought to wreck me, and crush honour and fame "), are built up of these elements of line and tone-colour. The Doubt theme dominates the vocal declamation and, in rhythmically shortened forms, the orchestral accompaniment also. It even creeps into the recitative dialogues and attains its clearest outline in Ortrud's

> " Weisst du, wer dieser Held, den hier
>   ein Schwan gezogen an das Land ? "

> (" Know'st thou who is the knight, who to
>   Our shores was guided by a swan ? ")

which is a return to the " set " song-form in F sharp minor. The Forbidden Question theme and the theme of Doubt together assume increasing control of this piece, which is derived from the vengeance duet of Lysiart and Eglantine. As its model reached its climax in the line sung by both singers, " Dunkle Nacht, du hörst den Schwur " (" Dark Night, hear thou our oath "), so here the line ascends to :

> " Der Rache Werk sei nun beschworen
>   aus meines Busens wilder Nacht.
>   Die ihr in süssem Schlaf verloren,
>   wisst, dass für euch das Unheil wacht ! "

(" Dread powers of vengeance, I conjure ye,
   Arise within my stormy breast !
Ye with the shield of slumber o'er ye,
   Learn that revenge can never rest ! ")

and, after the interruption of Elsa's night song and Ortrud's arioso
plea, finds its culmination in Ortrud's oath of vengeance. F sharp
major, F sharp minor, and the diminished seventh unite in this wild
cry to the gods of heathenism :

" Segnet mir, Trug und Heuchelei,
   dass glücklich meine Rache sei ! "

(" Speed me, cunning and deceit,
   Assure me of a vengeance sweet ! ")

Broad harmonies with fanatical, swaying rhythms characterise this
utterance, and the thematic character of the preceding duet falls into
the background. An elemental outbreak of hostile forces, portrayed
by harmonic accentuation only, is revealed in utmost intensity. The
triumphant change of the " Night " key, F sharp minor, to F sharp
major, settles the outcome of this act, as surely as Lohengrin's A major
decides that of the first. After this, both action and music are more
really concerned with the growth of doubt than with the relations
between Elsa and Ortrud. The spirit of doubt pervades Ortrud's
whispered

" Könntest du erfassen,
   wie dessen Art so wundersam,
   der nie dich möge so verlassen,
   wie er durch Zauber zu dir kam ? "

(" Hath it never crossed thee,
   One who doth wield such magic art,
   May in some future time be lost thee,
   And as he came may so depart ? ")

in F sharp minor, in which the Forbidden Question theme also
lies concealed. Elsa repulses it emotionally in a G major melody
culminating in a lyrical outburst :

" Lass mich dich lehren,
   wie süss die Wonne reinster Treu' !
   Lass zu dem Glauben dich bekehren :
   Es gibt ein Glück, das ohne Reu'."

(" Soon shalt thou learn it,
How sweet the rapture of trust and truth.
Seek this belief, and thou'lt quickly discern it :
It is a joy that brings no ruth ! ")

The ascent from F sharp to G repels the powers of darkness for
a little, but with Telramund's F sharp minor epilogue they return, and
thence invade even the waking world of daylight.   The transition to
the world of day is effected in an instrumental interlude based on the
morning song of the Castle Watch, and the scene of the Herald and
his men which follows immediately effects a pause in the action.   The
inner line of the drama is not resumed until Elsa re-enters on her way
to the minster.   The bridal procession is treated with sustained
breadth, rising in sequential flow of harmony.   Against this background fiercer and fiercer assaults are made upon Elsa's faith and
trust.   These are repeatedly interrupted by the march until, though
externally victorious, the march itself proclaims the Forbidden
Question with the full strength of the orchestral wind.   Previous
interruptions such as Ortrud's two attacks, Telramund's accusation,
and Elsa's replies to these are simple, lyrical, emotional, and melodic in
treatment.   But when Lohengrin turns upon Ortrud with the cry,
" Du fürchterliches Weib !   Steh ab von ihr ! "   (" Thou fiend in
human form, away from her ! "), the theme of unbelief stands
revealed in all its compelling power.   Foe is face to face with foe.
The Doubt theme gains the victory in that moment of tragic crisis
when Lohengrin turns to Elsa, who alone has the right to question.
It echoes then from Elsa's own soul, and at last, closely followed by
the Forbidden Question theme, it swells to a great *ensemble* :

"Wüsst' ich sein Los, ich wollt' es treu bewahren :
im Zweifel doch erbebt des Herzens Grund ! "

(" Held I the truth there could be no revealing,
But doubt and dread within my heart have grown ! ")

The double motif casts its wide coils about all the actors.   Originating
with Ortrud, it first envelopes Elsa, emerges from the orchestra
through the voice parts, now expanding into broad harmonies, now
sinking to a soft indeterminate dimness.   Still unresolved, it dies out
in the climax of the Forbidden Question.   Unbelief has found its

way deep into Elsa's heart.   Her final reply to Lohengrin has an
equivocal sound :

> " Hoch über alles Zweifels Macht
> . . . soll meine Liebe steh'n ! "

> (" Far o'er the gloomy clouds of doubt—
> Love in my heart shall rest ! ")

This is no longer the unquestioning trust of the first act ; it is the
utterance of the girl become woman.   And it is as a woman that Elsa
crosses the threshold of the minster, hiding in her heart the Question
that is whispered after her in the F minor strains of the trombones.

Musically this ends the play, in the order in which Wagner envisioned it scenically.   A change had taken place within himself while
he worked upon it.   He had passed from the musical sphere of the
Grail-vision towards a new form of the musico-scenic problem.   In
its older form it had been exhausted, as far as he was concerned, in the
two first-composed acts of *Lohengrin*, but while he worked upon the
last, that is the second, act, it had assumed a new guise and had almost
burst its there appointed framework.   If Wagner had composed the
acts in the order of their external sequence the result might have been
a reconstruction of the third act.   As things are the fact that the
last-composed act is inserted between the first and third, which possess
a true homogeneity, makes the difference in artistic treatment less
sensible.   Moreover, the harmonic expressionist structure is so much
at one throughout with the character of the subject, that even the
alien trend, in certain details, of the second act cannot destroy the
unity of the work as a whole.   This unity was asserted once again
after the work's completion in the medium of " pure " music.   There
is a flicker of high A major notes.   As these descend the melody
emerges, slowly, hesitatingly, following the descending harmonies.
Its tones become stronger and firmer, and advancing softly in chromatic motion, approach the lower registers which give them power and
substance until they shine out at last in full perfection.   Still echoing
in the depths, the musical subject rises once more to the heights.
The miracle vanishes into unimaginable distance.   It is that miracle
which Wagner envisioned in *Die Feen*—the miracle of self-revealing
harmony—the miracle of soaring architecture in sounds and of the
secret of their union within the chord—the miracle of the emotional

application of modulatory effects and of the evolution of melody as a unifying agent in the harmonic nerve-system. Scenically this miracle is presented as the interaction of light and darkness, of faith and doubt, and, like its scenic looking-glass image, it springs from an emotional creative impulse which, having been emotionally aroused, seeks to arouse emotion.

In asserting the will to emotional appeal Wagner broke even more completely with *operatic* ideas than in his revolutionary handling of scenic and musical problems. As regards the latter, it is true that in *Lohengrin* he disregards the traditions of form in the aria, the solo-*ensemble*, and the chorus, but he does not do so arbitrarily and he uses the minutely constructed song-period as a method of piling up the formal architecture. Song, being the nearest counterpart to the accent of human speech, remains from *Lohengrin* to *Tristan* the fundamental formal unit of Wagnerian structure. Was Wagner conscious of this? It was by no means his intention to make song the basis of musical form, but rather to abolish musical forms altogether and to " raise dialogue itself to the status of principal factor, even in the musical composition of a work." Such an attempt could not but raise the question as to whether it might not be better to forego music entirely, since this could only increase the difficulties of a perfectly naturalistic treatment of dialogue. After *Lohengrin* Wagner did actually ask himself this question, and answered it affirmatively. Under the influence of the political tendencies of the day and of democratic propaganda he produced a sketch entitled *Friedrich der Rotbar.* (Frederic Redbeard). This piece was designed to answer the requirements of naturalistic dialogue in the simplest fashion—it was to be a spoken drama. Before he worked it out, however, he saw his mistake. Naturalistic dialogue could not, for him, be an end in itself, only *one* of the aids to a direct expression of feeling such as *Lohengrin* with its stark emotional appeal. This called for musically and scenically interpreted tone, and could not be effected by words which are never free from conceptual limitations. It became increasingly clear to Wagner that his task was to concentrate on *emotional effect*, isolated from all formal limitations, whether conceptual or musical, and he began to regard the elucidation of emotional problems as the fundamental impulse of his own artistic nature, and indeed of the artist nature generally.

Wagner calls this emotional quality (of which the *Rotbart* experiment first made him fully conscious) *das Rein-Menschliche*—that is to say, the purely or essentially human. In its special application the designation is pertinent. Emotion is indeed " purely " human in that it directs the mind to what is *merely* human. That new " humanism " which set out to supersede all classical and pre-classical art (which it explained away as merely an ingenious pattern of the non-human) was now to be deliberately cultivated. The first effect of the " purely-human " idea was to make Wagner strip the *Rotbart* subject of all its personal and historical accretions in his search for its emotional sources. Following the same instinct which had led him to clothe *Lohengrin* in the garments of saga, he harked back to a more and ever more remote past. The device of altering temporal perspective in order to obtain complete emotional freedom leads logically from history to saga, and from saga to myth. Elemental humanity, according to Wagner, lives a life of unrestrained emotion. When all customs and conventions have been swept away the " purely-human " holds absolute sway. Thus the results of Wagner's quarryings in the *Rotbart* subject, in search of its emotional core, appeared at length in the guise of a sketch for a grand heroic opera, *The Death of Siegfried.* Its very title betrays the fundamental will to tragedy. Even externally the story outdoes *Lohengrin* in this respect. The hero, appearing miraculously, is not merely rejected by a humanity which lacks faith, but is annihilated by active hate. An opera of the *Lohengrin* type seemed to Wagner the best way of presenting this subject. The emphasis in *Siegfried* being laid on heroic strength rather than, as in *Lohengrin*, on the awful unapproachability of the divine, a new interest was provided, and the fact that the hero's fate was to be destruction, not rejection, suggested an epic vigour and stronger contrasts as compared with the lyric mood of *Lohengrin*. In December 1848, Wagner read the libretto to a chosen circle, among whom were young Hans von Bülow and his friend Karl Ritter. To those who at that time only knew *Tannhäuser*, Wagner spoke of the narrative passage in Act III of that opera, and also of *Lohengrin* and the method of treating the words musically which he had therein attempted. Critics less particularly concerned with questions of musical structure are wont to find scenic reasons for Wagner's choice of his subjects. Thus Gustav Freitag, after hearing Wagner recount the contents of the plot, opines that " dreams of the heavens and of cloud-borne song, delighted anticipation of unprecedented scenic effects," were for Wagner " the spell which first attracted him to stories of this world of the gods." Apart from the implied reproach of spectacular theatricality, this sentence draws attention, no doubt rightly, to the influence of scenic impulses upon Wagner. To give these convincing form, however, some exceptional emotional stimulus was required.

Wagner had not yet begun to compose *Siegfried* when a new scheme obtruded itself—a yet more powerful embodiment of the tragedy of annihilation, of the victory of darkness over light. The subject dealt not with destruction as an involuntary consequence of conflict with the world, but with death self-chosen in " revolt against the loveless generality of mankind." Once again the character embodying the subject was borrowed from mythology, in this case not Germanic but Hebraic. Wagner proposed to write a *Jesus of Nazareth*. Like Lohengrin his hero comes into the world as a vision of celestial light, like Siegfried, he is slain by the world, but, in this surpassing both, he himself wills his death because he knows that the world is not worthy of him. He accepts death as a final witness against the fashion of this world. A very full sketch for this work, illustrated with numerous biblical texts, was made in December 1848. Love, as representing the fundamental craving of emotion—of the " purely-human," is contrasted with Law, as representing the demands of conventional thought, hardened into insensitive forms. The sacrifice of love is " simply an incomplete expression of that universal human impulse which drives the individual into revolt against the loveless generality of mankind—a rebellion which, for the truly lonely individual, can end only in self-destruction ; and even this is but a mere nay-saying to the loveless herd."

If Wagner's art requires by its very nature a tragic foundation, there is an equally vital connection between the artistic problem which finds utterance in *Lohengrin, Siegfried,* and *Jesus of Nazareth,* and actual events in the composer's life. Wagner needed the spur of emotion and was driven to *create* emotional conflict with others for the sake of the inspiration he derived therefrom. In his capacity as Kapellmeister, in his private affairs, and in the social and political conditions of his day he found conflicts enough for his imagination to universalise. And Wagner saw the universe in the theatre. As a creative artist he had come to reject traditional theatrical make-believe and to regard expression of the " purely-human " as both the starting-point and goal of theatrical art, so that his ideas of what the theatre ought to be as a social and artistic institution underwent an inevitable change. He felt called upon to renew, or rather entirely to re-create, opera and on the same grounds he believed that the operatic stage should be rescued from its—as he supposed—unworthy use as mere entertainment and made a vehicle of experience. He composed, he conducted, and interpreted in obedience to the demands of expressionist truth and therefore, logically enough, he began to apply the same measure in judging opera as a public institution. The result was that the word " reform " was forever on his lips. But whereas by virtue of his magnetic personality he could, in certain cases at least, impose his own point of view as a conductor, and could even maintain it—though here opposition was stronger—as a composer, his attempts to apply it to established institutions resulted inevitably in open war. Here was no mere question of use and wont nor even of aesthetic opinion but of a philosophic idea striving to gain control of real material power. This real power was defended not so much by established rights and interests as by the genuine conviction that the claims made by this " expressionist " artist were altogether beside the mark—that art is but a form of play and that the theatre, accordingly, as a human activity, must be judged not ethically, but as a place of entertainment—that even " expressionist " works of art should, after all, be classed as amusement.

It was this divergence of outlook which brought Wagner into conflict with the contemporary stage as a whole, caused him to quarrel with every theatre with which he had to do from Dresden on, and made him a revolutionary, a reformer, and regenerator. Only so can we understand Wagner's efforts to reorganise the theatre, his consequent political and social theories, his quarrel with the Dresden intendancy, and the part he played in the Dresden revolution. There is a seeming discrepancy between Wagner's writings and sayings during the revolutionary years and his later pallid account of them, but the discrepancy is superficial only. He is justified in defending himself against what might be called a " police " interpretation of his actions, even though in so doing he suppresses certain awkward facts. Wagner was merely a " revolutionary in favour of the theatre." He could be nothing else, for his life was centred there. His whole experience, whether of politics, philosophy, sociology, art, or religion, was real to him only in so far as it afforded him new sources of theatrical expression. But though it is a mistake to try to present Wagner as a practical politician it is even more unfair to impute his revolutionary aspirations to hopes of bettering his chronically disordered affairs. His reckless way of living, the failure of his hopes of speedy success for his operas, and, first and foremost, the publication, at his own expense, of pianoforte arrangements of *Tannhäuser*, had certainly increased the difficulties under which he began his Dresden career. Moreover his embarrassments were no secret and did not tend to increase the intendancy's satisfaction with a Kapellmeister whose conduct, in the ordinary social sense, was so open to critcism. There was some attempt to restrain what all regarded as his folly in money matters by raising his salary on certain conditions, and to hold him more strictly to his official duties. He was admitted to have done well on occasions and even to have shown talent—within certain well-defined limits—as a composer, but it became increasingly evident that he was out of place in a theatre which was committed to a programme of the ordinary, practicable kind. If Wagner on his part found a lack of stimulus in the repertory, the intendancy, on theirs, were dissatisfied with a Kapellmeister who might sometimes bring off a brilliant new reading of a work, but neglected his ordinary duties, spent most of his time either composing or engaging in controversy with the critics about his own operas, made himself much disliked personally, and persisted in suggesting that the causes of all these evils might be removed by " reform." Under these circumstances it did not need Gutzkow's appointment as dramaturgist, nor his mild campaign against Wagner to ensure that matters would go from bad to worse.

Wagner himself felt that his position in Dresden was insecure and turned his eyes towards Berlin. In 1844 *The Flying Dutchman* had been given there without success, but *Rienzi* was to follow under brighter auspices. Wagner hoped that the work would attract the king's notice, that he would be permitted to dedicate *Tannhäuser* to him, to read him the libretto of *Lohengrin*, and to give the first performance of the latter work in Berlin. All these schemes fell through. The king did not attend the performance of *Rienzi*, the work was judged immature, and a spiritless production rendered the whole thing a failure. Wagner's prospects of dedicating *Tannhäuser* to Frederick William were remote, since His Majesty would not accept the dedication of any work unknown to him, and it was not proposed to produce *Tannhäuser* in Berlin. Count Redern made the amiable suggestion that Wagner should arrange certain passages from his works as military music, so that the king might hear them on parade. Even this plan came to nought, though Wagner sent the introductory march to Wieprecht, the military bandmaster, for re-orchestration. Nor did the *Lohengrin* reading prove practicable. Tieck, whom Wagner asked to use his influence, held out little hope of any practical result, even should he be able to obtain an audience. " What can you expect," he said, " from a man who as hotly favours Donizetti's *Lucretia Borgia* to-morrow as he does Gluck's *Iphigenia* to-day ? "

The first performance of *Rienzi* in Berlin took place on October 24, 1847. Wagner had counted upon its success to ease his Dresden difficulties and its failure proportionately strengthened the hands of his enemies. With his Berlin expectations thus dashed he was com-pelled to come to grips with affairs in Dresden. He began by trying to mould them nearer to his wishes. During the winter of 1846, while working on the preliminaries of the composition of *Lohengrin*, he had written a detailed paper on the subject of reorganising the Dresden Court *Kapelle*. This pamphlet was submitted to Lüttichau, and by him to the rest of the intendancy. Wagner's proposal that the orchestra (and consequently himself) should be relieved of the burden of repertory was not for a moment seriously considered, but his suggestion for a series of orchestral concerts, to be conducted by him, was better received. Meanwhile, as *Lohengrin* drew near completion, Wagner was swept into the rising tide of political feeling. In the aspirations of the democratic movement Wagner imagined that he recognised a manifestation of that " purely-human " quality which was his own goal in art. All his immediate plans having failed, he was carried away by a flood-tide of sentiment which gave him hope of fulfilment in a new social order. These plans, too, drawing nourish-ment from the general hope of betterment, grew bolder and more ambitious, so that the breach with existing conditions tended to widen. The pamphlet on the reform of the *Kapelle* was followed by another on the reorganisation of the Court theatre. This Wagner placed in person before the leading Minister, who referred him to the deputies. In this way Wagner became involved in a political movement which had already taken fast hold on his friend and colleague, Röckel the music-director. Wagner became more and more convinced of the profound connection between art and politics. He thought of the revolutionary movement as an attempt to express a new, liberated humanity with an ethic based on free outlet for the natural emotions. These emotions would find their supreme demonstration in the theatre. That, indeed, was the true end and aim of revolution, which, apart from the theatre, would be as pointless as non-scenic music. At a meeting of the democratically-minded *Vaterlandsverein*, Wagner made a speech on the relation of republican aspirations to monarchy. As in *Rotbart* (the sketch for which belongs to this period) he called the king " the first and most genuine republican " and declared that republic and monarchy were identical.

This sentimental, " operatic " solution to a problem of practical politics was received with " enthusiastic applause " by the meeting in general, but with contempt by the few who look for meaning even in oratorical flights. The incident sufficed, however, to jeopardise Wagner's post. The *Kapelle* split into two parties, one for and one against his dismissal. There were some delicate negotiations with Lüttichau, who, though his personal feeling towards Wagner had steadily cooled, took the correct official way out of the situation. On July 2 Wagner received a month's leave of absence to seek another appointment. He set out for Vienna by way of Breslau, and in both cities waxed ecstatic over " the glorious life of the streets," the rich costumes and *décor* of the democratic movement. " You ought to see what these people look like," he writes to Minna from Vienna, " the National Guard, clad quite military-fashion, with wide silk tricolour sashes, the students (8000) standing guard in coats of old German cut, with plumed hats, bayonets and sabres. I have hardly seen any but handsome people. And then the richness, the life ! And the curious dress of the women—a new kind of hat with feathers and German tricolour ribbands. Almost every house flies the German flag." But his whole conversation in a city from which Metternich had just been expelled and from which the Imperial House of Austria had been forced to flee, was of the theatre. It was suggested that if he could get release from his Dresden appointment he should take over the management of the Kärntnertor theatre. Yet with this alluring prospect before him he suddenly reverted to his old view of his post as " a royal appointment—for life, and with a fine salary."

After the suppression of the Dresden rising such of its ring-leaders as were arrested were questioned, when brought up for examination, about the part played by those who had escaped. Bakunin, the Russian, stated that " he had, from the first, recognised Wagner for a visionary, and that though he had often had talk with him, frequently on political subjects, he had never entered into any practical arrangement with him." Wagner's own utterances at the time justify us in supposing that Bakunin, who had a knowledge of men, was expressing a genuine opinion, uncoloured by any chivalrous idea of sparing Wagner. His estimate of Wagner as a politician is a just one despite the fact that it ignores the positive side of Wagner's programme, the reformation of the theatre.

In August, after returning from Vienna, Wagner set out for Weimar, where Liszt had recently settled. Wagner had not seen Liszt since they met at Schumann's in the previous March, though a few months earlier Wagner, harassed by his creditors, had offered to sell Liszt all his published works for the sum of five thousand talers. Liszt had never yet heard *Tannhäuser*, and it was now arranged through Princess Wittgenstein that he should do so. In November 1848 Liszt conducted the overture in Weimar. The first performance of the whole work, outside Dresden, took place there on the following February 16, in connection with celebrations of the Grand Duchess Maria Paulovna's birthday. Wagner, however, was unable to be present. Matters in Dresden had by then become so critical that he dared not apply for leave of absence. The score of *Lohengrin* had just been returned to him. He had not, indeed, submitted it officially, but normally it would have been performed as a matter of course, and its rejection had the appearance of a public reprimand. Wagner at the time was in the despairing mood of the *Siegfried* and *Jesus of Nazareth* sketches. The ground, he felt, was rocking beneath his feet. As his prospects of getting his works performed grew more and more remote, his animus against the existing order of things increased. He went to meetings, he helped Röckel with the issue of a political broadsheet, and so slipped almost unawares into a purely political movement. He was classed already as a suspect whose doings and sayings were watched. Such was the position when Lüttichau and the Court first got wind of proposals for the reorganisation of the theatre made by Wagner to the minister Oberländer in June of the foregoing year, and Lüttichau became aware that this composer and

Kapellmeister whom he had rescued from obscurity was endeavouring by political means to undermine his position and get him replaced by an artistic committee. At this juncture Wagner summoned a meeting of the more progressively-minded members of the *Kapelle*, expounded his proposals, and consoled the dissatisfied with promise of better days to come. Lüttichau now felt that it was time to abandon his attitude of passive disapproval. Wagner was summoned to an official conference. " In all the time he has been here he has been no manner of use—slovenly performances of church and operatic music, noted with displeasure in the *highest quarter*—finances in a disastrous state— arbitrary action in handing Minister Oberländer a plan for reform of the theatre," so run phrases in the protocol, which closes with the statement that Wagner " is unsuited to his post and that he is per- mitted humbly so to inform his Majesty, as he thinks fit."

The breach was at last complete. Events were to corroborate it more speedily and more drastically than could have been foreseen at that February discussion. Even then Wagner failed to realise that a break with Lüttichau and with Dresden conditions must be followed by a break with the public stage as a whole—that his life as an ordinary citizen must be forfeited. He may have been dimly conscious—and even glad—that this was the only solution, but he first gained courage to act from the force of circumstances into whose maelstrom he was now caught up. When Beuth's reactionary ministry took office in March, liberal optimism, already hard hit by Metternich's victory in Vienna and the shootings of revolutionaries there, suffered a profound disappointment. The clash of opinion led to open hostilities. Beuth dissolved the progressively-minded Chambers and the Prussians advanced to the frontier, ready to support the reactionary government. The king and his ministers secretly left the capital. A provisory government took control, the streets were barricaded, shots were fired, the Prussians advanced upon the town, while from May 3rd to 9th the well-disposed revolutionaries endeavoured to hold their own. Wagner hurried from one to another, distributed appeals, and watched the thrilling drama of battle from the tower of the Kreuzkirche. When the provisory government fled to Chemnitz through Freiberg Wagner went with them and, chancing to spend the night with a brother-in-law living in the town, had the extraordinary good luck to escape arrest in their company. All this time his mind was occupied exclusively with his theatrical projects. He discussed them on the tower of the Kreuzkirche and on the road to Chemnitz, conscious throughout of the pleasurable excitement of a memorable experience whose *actual* significance meant little or nothing to him in comparison with the imaginative incentive he derived from it. His brother-in-law warned him against returning to Dresden, and, believing that he would be safe in Weimar, he retired there to await events.

In Liszt's opinion there was no artistic future for Wagner in Germany ; London or Paris were the only places for a nature such as his, and he wrote to his secretary Belloni in Paris, commending Wagner to him as a man of " dazzling genius." The thought of Paris, however, roused no warm response in Wagner, and for the present he decided to let things take their course. He felt a pleasurable sense of rest and freedom   He heard Liszt conduct a rehearsal of *Tannhäuser* and was amazed to find his ideas so well understood. He visited Eisenach and, for the first time, the Wartburg. A letter from Minna telling him that a warrant was out for his arrest as a revolutionary startled him in this idyllic retirement. Weimar was safe no longer. Liszt supplied him with money, and a small farm was found near Weimar to afford secure hiding for a few days. There Minna came to him secretly from Dresden, acceding to his urgent request but filled with bitter reproaches. With a forged passport he set out through Jena, Coburg, and Lichtenfels to Lindau, where the anxious moment of passport inspection passed safely, and once aboard the Rorschach steamer he was in Swiss jurisdiction. For the second time he found himself a fugitive with all retreat into the past cut off. For the second time he was a free man. His future was even more insecure than when he embarked at Pillau for London, but he was content with the knowledge that he had finally escaped from forces which had sought to enslave him.

The period of struggle with these forces had proved the most psychically fruitful of Wagner's life. The short seven years in Dresden produced not only *Tannhäuser* and *Lohengrin*, but *The Death of Siegfried*, key to the mythological world of *The Nibelungs*, and the sketch for *The Mastersingers*, a legacy to a yet more distant future. And the road which had already led him from *Tannhäuser* to *Jesus of Nazareth* was destined to lead him by way of one of the greatest works of his life to its end—from *Tristan* to *Parsifal*. Wagner's sufferings in Paris had awakened him to consciousness of self, but his Dresden trials revealed to him that particular spiritual kingdom which was his as an artist and taught him to realise his own essential unity whether as creator, as executant, or as theorist. That such a unity did indeed underlie all his actions, is proved by his conduct in the stormy Dresden years. His task henceforward was to recognise its laws, to trace its origins, and to adopt it consciously as his guide through life.

PART III
DRAMA

CHAPTER I

THE RING OF THE NIBELUNGS

WAGNER arrived at Zurich on May 28, 1849 ; but this was not to be his ultimate destination, only a break in his journey to Paris. Liszt had advised and Minna insisted on the project, and Wagner, being penniless, had to acknowledge, reluctantly, that the scheme was practical. But he did not believe that this way lay his road to power. Twice he had challenged the world ; when he fled to Paris from Riga, and again when he left Paris for Dresden. Both times he was beaten, and the third attempt was undertaken against his own convictions. Even actual success seemed meaningless to him in the circumstances. The struggle lasted for fifteen years, maintained on Wagner's part with a cheerless assiduity which turned gradually to cynicism. Useless efforts in Paris, lonely years in Zurich, Venice, and Lucerne, concerts in London to earn money, renewed hopes of fame in Paris, failure there instead of success, a return to Germany full of plans which never materialised, and, finally, despair—such is in outline the story of those fifteen years. But when on May 4, 1864, Wagner stood before King Ludwig, though he had not conquered the world, he had won one man over to his cause and that a man who could command the things that Wagner needed.

These wandering years are full of varied and picturesque incident, for a nature such as Wagner's sought the stimulus of continual change. Their interest in this respect is, however, but external ; it was human emotion which now played the all-important part, deep joys of life and love, overshadowing the transitory emotions of earlier days. When Wagner left Dresden he was thirty-six years old. His sensual temperament had led him into an early marriage. Common trials and common joys kept the couple united for over ten years, but no sooner was their regular home life in Dresden broken up than the ties of wedlock slackened. Wagner's wife hankered for the past, while he in his new-won freedom realised his true self for the first

time. Jessie Taylor, a young admirer of Wagner's and a passing
fancy of his in Dresden, was now married to a merchant called Laussot
and lived in Bordeaux. Together with an elder Dresden friend,
Frau Julie Ritter, she offered help to the needy Wagner, who, in spite
of Liszt's introductions, had met with nothing but difficulties in
Paris. He therefore left Paris for Bordeaux where he found his
disciple weary of a humdrum marriage and, catching fire from her
enthusiasm and passion, made plans for a speedy elopement. The
couple were to wander romantically in Malta, Greece, and other
out-of-the-way countries, Minna was to see him no more, he would
lose himself in Jessie's young love and satisfy his life hunger in her.
Then, at the critical moment, Jessie hesitated ; she confided in her
mother who prevented the elopement and wrote to Minna. Minna
hastened to Paris, expecting to find Wagner, but he had incontinently
fled to Geneva, where Frau Ritter joined the despairing lover and
persuaded him to return to Zurich.

This was the first storm to shake the marriage ; a second and
more severe one occurred a few years later when Mathilde Wesendonk
came into Wagner's life. The two were drawn gradually together as
if by fate. Once more it was the woman who, from a high sense of
duty, shrank from the final step. She did not, however, forsake
Wagner, but helped him as far as she could. As an artist he had
won her, and to the artist in him she belonged. Through her husband,
his natural rival, she procured him necessaries, money, a home and
comfort. She herself gave him the knowledge that she loved him
and the anguish of a creative impulse born of frustrate desire. The
apparent tragedy of Minna's discovery actually brought deliverance
from an emotional *impasse*, and Wagner's unfulfilled love poured itself
out in artistic creation.

Wagner's marriage with Minna ceased, after this, to exist save in
name, though for short periods the pair lived side by side, and his
passion remained unsatisfied. There followed a period of light loves.
Sometimes, as with Liszt's daughter, Blandine, these took the form of
wanton romping, sometimes, as with the actress Frederica Meyer in
Biebrich, " Serafinchen " in Vienna, or " Mariechen " in Penzing, of
clandestine domestic joys. But with the Venusberg tumult still
ringing in his ears he began to feel the first stirrings of a new kind of
love—a love which should be a blend of all those kinds he had tasted
separately—the domestic happiness he had known with Minna, his

soul-searing passion for Mathilde, his petty sensual amours. The awakening of this love coincides with the close of this epoch of his life and with the idea of the development of man through woman. The pale phantoms of Senta, Elizabeth, and Elsa give place to glowing, passionate types of womanhood, creatures of infinite surrender— Sieglinda, Brynhilda the dream-maid, Isolda, the Paris Venus, while Eva, the counterpart in comedy of self-immolating passion, heralds the queen of them all, the awakened Brynhilda.

During the fifteen years which elapsed between the flight to Zurich and the call to Munich, Wagner was almost wholly pre-occupied with the experience of woman and its resultant enrichment of manhood. Such practical matters as the problems of making a living, finding a home, getting his works performed and engaging in criticism and controversy were of slight importance compared with this. Till then he had not known its wonder-working power, but from about the age of thirty-five to fifty it was the dominating force equally in his life and art ; seeds sown in the Dresden period grew and flowered under the sun of love.

It was a profound spiritual revolution, the causes of which Wagner himself did not at first understand. Cut suddenly adrift from the Dresden routine, he felt free yet purposeless, and the creative fires burnt low. He had projects and plans in abundance but all seemed alien to his view of the world as seen from Zurich. Struggling against his inertia in order that the friends who were supporting him might not think him wholly idle, he applied to a French poet in Paris for an opera or translation. He planned an *Achilleus* and sketched the scenario of a *Wayland the Smith*—both designed for Paris and both undertaken in the foreboding that they would come to nothing, as indeed they did. He felt that none of those who were trying to help him, not even Liszt, could understand what was the matter with him. During recent eventful weeks he had for the first time really got to know Liszt, and in the care with which he thought of and provided for everything recognised a readiness to help such as he had never met with before. Yet even between himself and Liszt he felt some inner unbridgeable gulf.

The fact was that at this time he could not even understand himself. He was clear as to what kind of life he had discarded and why, but he had no idea what to put in its place. His future seemed a mere blank negation of his past. He floundered like a rudderless ship in the breakers. The recent cataclysm had shaken him more than he dared admit to himself. He had played mentally with the idea of a break with the old life, and then suddenly it had happened. Yet the grand upheaval, the social revolution he had counted on, had failed to come about. His affair with Jessie Laussot was a wild attempt to escape from life and the world. The failure of this attempt brought Wagner to his senses. Where did he stand? What did it all mean? he asked himself. The laws and conventions that he himself had thrown off, and had thought thereby to have swept away altogether, obtained more strongly than he had believed both in private and political relationships. During the month of May, 1840, which he spent in Geneva after the failure of his elopement with Jessie, he acquired a new sense of realities, as one awakening from a fever. The kindness and encouragement of Frau Julie Ritter, who had come there on his behalf, gradually restored his self-confidence. He set out on a walking tour to Zurich with Frau Julie's eldest son, Karl, a promising young musician. There Minna gave him a welcome which restored the broken links with the past. Recent events seemed like a bad dream. " I have found a new wife," he wrote to Liszt. He had found a new home too, lovingly prepared by Minna, inviting to rest and quiet. Through Karl Ritter he came into touch with the Zurich theatre, of which, under Wagner's tuition, Karl was to become conductor. Here they were joined by another young enthusiast of Dresden days, Hans von Bülow, whom his parents intended for the law but who was determined to study music under Wagner with Ritter.

The little circle thus formed was enlarged by acquaintances made in Zurich, among them the kindly government official, Jacob Sulzer with, later, Gottfried Keller and a few political refugees including Georg Herwegh. In these surroundings the world became real again to Wagner. The Paris projects were abandoned, but in July, shortly after his return to Zurich, a fresh enterprise was launched. He sent his *Lohengrin* score to Liszt, begging him to get it performed if possible in Weimar. Liszt agreed and kept his word. On August 28, 1850, in celebration of Goethe's birthday, the revolutionary refugee's new opera was produced for the first time at the Weimar Court Theatre. With this act Liszt brought Wagner fully back to realities. His long review of *Tannhäuser*, intended to pave Wagner's path in Paris, had already reminded him—as Liszt was always trying to do—of his vocation as an artist.   A real personal friendship grew out of the *Lohengrin* correspondence.   Light began to penetrate the chaos of Wagner's thoughts and feelings and he began to gather up the threads that link the past and the future.

Amongst the various plans which Wagner formed towards the end of the Dresden period, one only seriously engaged his attention —namely, *The Death of Siegfried*.   The libretto was already written and bore the sub-title " A Grand Heroic Opera."   Liszt was insistent that it should be composed and applied for an advance honorarium from the Weimar Court.   The musician in Wagner began to clamour for employment.   The *Siegfried* idea interested him keenly.   Yet something stood between him and the work.   He was willing to take it in hand, reason suggested no objection, yet he sensed an undefined obstacle.   The only way out of this difficulty was to turn the light of self-criticism upon the inhibition.   Wagner planned a written work to justify his career hitherto both to himself and his friends and to formulate his opinions on politics, socialism, and revolution.   Even Liszt failed to realise the inner necessity for this and spoke disparagingly about " political platitudes and socialistic gibberish."   Wagner, however, knew that it was his only way to progress as an artist ; he must prove that art, true art as he saw it, includes all the activities of life, that it expresses the whole man, that only as the expression of absolute humanity can it be true and that only this truth can justify its existence. Yet how can it be true if it is regarded from the first as *art*—a phenomenon with laws of its own foreign to the laws of life ?   It was no " socialistic gibberish," no passing mood, that had made Wagner a revolutionary.   A conception of art as a means of expression, gradually taking possession of his whole nature, drove him to formulate a philosophy.   He had to become a politician, a revolutionary, a socialist, an atheist—not because these questions as such interested him personally but because his art depended on the answers to them.

His task consisted not merely in indicating the relationship between these various spheres of thought but in revolutionising them.   He had to conceive a clear picture of the world of the future before he could discover its artistic laws of expression, and it was lack of this knowledge which prevented him from composing *The Death of Siegfried*.   The libretto belongs to the revolutionary period in spirit as well as in date. Its hero is free, natural " purely-human " man, active and forceful, as contrasted with the wholly emotional, feminine figure of Elsa. Like Elsa Siegfried is ensnared in the world's deceits, like her he is its guiltless guilty victim. But in him the story is carried further. Love overcomes the world's trickery, the Nibelungs are freed, mankind and the Ring are purified by fire. Siegfried and Brynhilda, "united in everlasting bliss," rise to Valhalla, "pledges of eternal power" to Wotan, the All-Father, who now reigns in joy over the free. The idea is directly derived from Wagner's speech in the "Vaterlandsverein" on "What is the relation between republican aspirations and the throne?" That was the political, as *The Death of Siegfried* is the artistic, presentation of the idea of kingship over a republic of free men. The chief plank in the enthusiastic artist-politician's platform was the annihilation, through love, of property, which is destructive of human rights, coupled with an anti-Christian communism, and such also is the basis of his " Heroic Opera."

In *The Death of Siegfried,* unlike Wagner's previous works, the artistic impulse does not wholly dissolve material traces of the work's origin. Three lines of approach can be distinguished. There is a human, personal problem, based on the struggle for freedom, a political problem based on the question of property, and a practical problem of artistic structure resulting from the desire to discover new sources of expression. Of the three the last is the most important, but it is over-ridden in the sketch by the other two. This it was that made it impossible for Wagner to conceive the work in terms of sound. He felt that he had no satisfactory solution of the human and political problems. The didactic, intellectual element, apparently organically inseparable from the theatrical, hampering and yet inspiring it, tended to grow stronger and stronger. It insisted on becoming predominant. Wagner therefore decided to leave his sketch alone for the present, unconscious that it was the very way to rid himself of the obstructive elements. He took to writing to clear the way for composition. He evolved theories and thought that he was laying down principles, but all was for the purpose of gaining a clear understanding of *The Death of Siegfried* and of the music hidden within it.

Wagner began to write immediately after his flight from Dresden, inspired at first by the excitement of the moment and in anticipation of that irresistible march of political events which was to herald an artistic millenium. As this expectation proved false he abandoned practical politics for cultural history, art history, and æsthetics. He concentrated increasingly upon the theory of art, particularly of theatrical art, as the highest and final goal of revolution. Again, in discussing art, he tended to pass from general problems to the particular case of an artist who, having been prompted by his instinct to probe the laws of his own will, has at last seen his way clear for further work. Such, generally speaking, is the sequence of ideas presented in *Art and Revolution*, *The Artwork of the Future*, *Opera and Drama* and *Communication to My Friends*. Wagner passes from political observation to autobiographical explanation, the intervening works serving to link up the exterior phenomenal world with the interior world of the artist. But *Communication to My Friends* was furthermore the imminent precursor of the new *Nibelung* libretti, for Wagner had at last satisfied himself as to the essential content of *The Death of Siegfried*, both in outline and in detail, and his path as composer lay clear before him.

Wagner was engaged in literary activities from July 1849 till about the middle of 1851. Towards the close of this period he had begun the libretto of *Young Siegfried*, the first companion piece to *The Death of Siegfried*. *Art and Revolution* introduces the Nibelung series and *The Artwork of the Future* is the first imaginative intimation of Wagner's artistic goal. *Opera and Drama* is an essay in æsthetic criticism, designed to cover a wide field, and *Communication to My Friends* a very revealing piece of autobiography. Besides these substantial works, the first of which was separated from the last by a period of two years, Wagner from time to time produced pamphlets in answer to the criticisms his writings had received. *Art and Climate* and *The Jew in Music* link *The Artwork of the Future* with *Opera and Drama*. *A Theatre in Zurich* promulgates the idea of a national theatre of public drama. An open letter to Liszt *On the Goethe Foundation* seeks to establish this idea on a practical basis. Wagner also published some explanatory notes on works given by him at concerts in Zurich and a number of occasional pamphlets. But whatever the subject or occasion, the underlying thought and treatment is always that of the principal writings, which form the basis of Wagner's artistic activities till his wandering years ended with the beginning of *The Mastersingers* and the call to Munich in 1864. They inaugurated that period, as the Paris writings inaugurated the Romantic operas. Incidentally they fulfilled the minor function of bringing in money quickly, though this was not their true justification. They were inspired by the desire to discover fresh sources for the expressionist purposes of the musical theatre. *The Death of Siegfried* indicated the general direction. The sketch was now to be amplified, intellectualised, and freed as an artistic project from useless literary and conceptual ballast.

Wagner based his philosophy on that of Feuerbach. He accepted Feuerbach's views on Christianity, the state, society, and man, derived the title of his *Artwork of the Future* from that writer's *Life of the Future*, and dedicated the work to him. His dependence here on Feuerbach and later, when Herwegh introduced him to Schopenhauer, upon the author of *The Universe as Will and Idea*, should be neither denied nor overestimated. The two philosophers provided him with words, ideas, and outlook, as Beethoven, Weber, and others had given him musical language. Questions as to whether Wagner was an optimist like Feuerbach, whether he acquired Schopenhauer's pessimism, and whether later he regained a happier philosophy, are beside the point. As with music neither Hegel's, Feuerbach's, nor Schopenhauer's philosophy possessed any interest for Wagner save in so far as it expressed the creative impulse that was momentarily his—an impulse always and solely directed to eventual stage representation. Optimism and pessimism alike were to him methods of getting theatrical effect, of driving home the expressionist appeal. All that the world offered him, thought, experience, the past and the future, were and could be nothing but this. Wagner's philosophy, like his poetry, composition, orchestration and stage directions, was a preparation for the theatre and had no meaning save in so far as it served the theatre. The only subject really treated in these writings is the artist Wagner and his efforts to discover new means of expression. He finds these in setting and solving the problem of " das Rein-Menschliche," the " purely-human " or natural man.

Wagner's work hitherto had led him to the idea of the " purely-human " as the basis of his art. The opposite of the " purely-human " is the conventional in its many manifestations. Convention is love-lessness, the " purely-human " is love. Elsa and Siegfried are the feminine and masculine embodiments of the " purely-human " and both are destroyed by lovelessness. It was the struggle between the " purely-human " and the conventional which made Wagner a revolutionary, for revolution, as he understood it, meant the revolt of love against convention and the victory of the " purely-human," from whose recognition all desired practical and political consequences must follow. But why did he set up " the purely-human " as the highest goal? It was because of his disposition to estimate all things, interior and exterior, solely as means of expression. He valued expression quite apart from the importance of the emotional appeal to be expressed, and the impulse to get the utmost possible from emotional appeal led him to the idea of the " purely-human." By the " purely-human " he really means the " purely-emotional," or, in other words, complete surrender to the emotion of the moment. It is a recognition of the dominance of the sensual in all beings.and in their interrelations. All that does not pertain to the sensual is valueless in the " purely-human " sense. Such is the basis of Wagner's attitude to the story of human culture, which he interprets with a fine disregard of historical fact. Such also is the basis of his estimate of the arts. The fulcrum of every and any work of art is man, man as a purely sensual being, and it must be judged according to its capacity for portraying sensual man.

For this great task the plastic arts, poetry, and even music are insufficient. At best they present but a partial picture of sensual man, never the whole of him. Only a simultaneous appeal to all the senses can do this, an act of absolute illusion, comprehending all arts, the art of staged drama. This art alone reveals " full artistic truth." In it " real life at its truest and most intelligible finds direct presentation." " Purely-human " artistic representation must never isolate a detail but must present it as part of a perpetual flux. " This is purely-human dramatic art because it presents human life in motion. The proper subject of drama is not the finished act or fact but the representation of unconscious becoming, of the begetting of deeds and characters." Only the sensual aspect of this process of becoming is taken into account, for the drama mirrors " the emotionalisation of reason." Drama is not drama in Wagner's sense unless it " materialises before our eyes " this " wholly instinctive emotionalisation."

Since it is the mission of art to communicate and interpret emotion, only that which is capable of emotional communication should be given artistic form. In the beginning speech was pure emotional communication. It springs from music and carries the mark of its origin in the sounding vowel, which is the natural musical expression of emotion. Subsequently the vowel was outlined by

consonants for the purpose of intellectual characterisation and dif-
ferentiation of the emotions. As the natural element, the "purely-
human," faded, these conceptual elements in speech became more
prominent, forming by degrees the intellectual language of prose.
It was now desirable to get back to the speech of emotion, realising
that the musical vowel-sound is its primary element, and indicating
the inner relationships of these "natural" sounds by consonantal
identity, as in old German alliterative poetry. Prose speech, conceptual speech must give place to emotional. Pure feeling is pure
melody; melody therefore springs from combinations of oral
emotional sounds. The rise and fall of accent determines the course
of the melody and the breathing determines the length of the melodic
phrase. Wagner describes the formation of language by the physiological analogy of the structure of the human body. The consonant
bears the same relation to the vowel as the flesh and skin to the human
frame. The vowel corresponds with "the whole interior organism
of the living physical man." It is bounded and shaped externally by
its consonantal integument; inwardly it is united by a second consonantal integument with the "organs" through which it derives
sustenance. The heart is represented by "the musical note in its
richest, most independent activity. The blood it sends out to
nourish the consonants is too abundant all to be wholly absorbed
and returns to the heart again to be refreshed by the living fount
of air and to proceed once again upon its course."

The analogy is doubly valuable; first for the vivid manner in
which Wagner describes the origins of musical emotional speech,
and secondly because the province to which he goes for his parable
unconsciously stresses the essentially physical nature of the Wagnerian
"purely-human" type of emotional representation. He proceeds on
the same lines to distinguish between "eye hearing" and "ear
hearing." "Eye hearing" appreciates only the conceptual or consonantal aspect of speech and it is to this sense that the poet has always
appealed. The musician, on the other hand, has written solely for
the vowel-appreciative "ear hearing." But "only perfect hearing,
hearing of ear and eye simultaneously, carries certainty to the inner
man . . . through word-tone-speech." Transitions from one emotion
to another are represented and plainly defined by the use of the
alliterative consonant, which itself now becomes a part of music.

Wagner pursues his doctrine of the naturalistic origins of speech and music to its logical conclusions, but his line of enquiry is less disinterested than it would appear, for *Opera and Drama* is a retrospective justification of the alliterative rime employed two years previously in the libretto of *The Death of Siegfried*. Having established the exclusive importance of word-tone speech, the essentially emotional character of drama, and the " purely-human " as the only proper subject of art, Wagner naturally finds the existing arts of poetry, music, and, in particular, opera, feeble and ineffective. He accounts for them as mistaken, if not frivolous, experiments of the formative instinct, explicable only on the ground of false premises in a religion, sociology, and statecraft unguided by knowledge of the " purely-human."

Naturalistic emotional representation does more than merely discover the principle of word-tone speech ; it goes on to provide it with a new grammar. " A note of music, having acquired emotional universality, forms the vehicle or channel of the poetic idea which through it becomes a direct outpouring of feeling." A sequence of such " outpourings of feeling " forms a phrase (whose length is determined by the breathing) and so constitutes a melody, in which individual notes are related in a horizontal sequence which is governed by the rise and fall of accent. The consciousness of relationships between notes is expressed through key. " The key of a melody is that which conveys directly to the emotions the relationships of the notes comprising it." The notes in a melody have also a vertical function. The key which is their emotional sphere has two dimensions —melodic breadth and harmonic depth. The manifold resultant tone-relations and combinations afford opportunity for infinitely numerous grades of melodic-harmonic expression. Moreover, the " somewhat indefinite " melodic content of horizontal melody receives " full expressive definition " through vertical harmony, which " completely conveys every important crisis to the senses." Modern music, an art expressing undefined emotion, has developed from harmony, and word-tone melody can alone give it the emotional definition it lacks. On the other hand, word-tone needs a foundation of harmony if it is to display its emotional content fully. Poets had created word-tone melody by raising conceptual speech to the level of musical emotional speech, and musicians had evolved and cultivated harmony through centuries of effort. " Only the kind of melody that modern ' harmonic ' music makes possible is the melody that the poet needs

and that can at once excite and satisfy him." A meeting-place has
at last been reached for poet and musician, word-tone melody and
harmony, horizontal and vertical musical emotion.   " The poet has
become musician, the musician poet ; together they form the
complete artist."

The vehicles of word-tone melody must be direct participants in
the drama, constantly exercising an individual influence upon it ; that
is to say they must be distinct persons.   Accordingly the chorus of
traditional opera must cease to exist as an undifferentiated group.
The only proper vehicle of harmony is the orchestra in which words
are neither possible nor requisite ; it is " a materialisation of the idea
of harmony in action," and in it " the conglomerate members of the
vertical chord manifest their common trend in a horizontal direction."
Orchestral speech, differing radically from human, oral speech,
possesses, as it were, vowels but no consonants.   It is therefore emotional without the faintest intellectual admixture, and is analogous to
the primary sounds of human speech.   The different instruments
used, however, supply the variety of sound produced in human speech
by the introduction of consonants.   These instruments may be divided
into consonantal groups, graded as are, for instance, the sounds P,
B, V, and F in verbal utterance.   Thus a differentiating principle,
comparable with that of human language, may be detected and
developed in the construction of an orchestra.

This argument, which Wagner pursues with pedagogic and
dialectic gusto, is a very through-going attempt at the tonal materialisation of emotion.   Feeling—an interior, invisible process—is to be
completely externalised and revealed as the subject of theatrical
performance.   Thus it ceases to be feeling in the original, unconscious,
sense, and becomes material for a representational art—the conscious,
objective stuff of drama.   As such it is neither more nor less significant
than, say, a historical subject, from which it differs only in that it offers
its originator the particular new artistic impulse he requires.   The
capacity of affording such stimulus is the one distinct gain offered by
an emotional view of art.

The meaning of the " purely-human " ideal becomes apparent in
this idea of the " emotionalisation " of all events.   Wagner makes
emotion the first condition of all art and adds a second—namely, that
it must deal exclusively with the state of " becoming," with " repre-

sentations of the unconscious begetting of deeds and characters," so that in the new drama *development* is the force which sets " purely-human " feeling in motion.   Feeling must not be caught and fixed in a particular phase or moment of crisis, for that would be an act of stylisation ; only when emotion is represented continuously in process of " becoming " can artistic representation impose that illusion of actuality which is for Wagner essential to all drama.   " Nothing contributing to a scene should be merely imagined or intimated ; everything should be fully carried out and perfected."   Consequently the stage should not be asked to represent anything which it cannot represent naturalistically.   To interpret emotion is the theatre's highest vocation, and it can only fulfil it by representing the emotional process as one of ceaseless evolution.   The idea of perpetual evolutionary flux is the true formative principle of drama.

The doctrine of evolution, like the idea that the " purely-human " must be pure emotion, is a fundamental concept in the " Romantic " view of life.   The evolutionary hypothesis was an achievement of nineteenth-century science which substituted for the idea of organic *change* in matter that of *advance*, and interpreted growth as progress, on the analogy of changes in the phenomenal world which it represented as changes for the higher and the better.   Wagner's thought was governed by the evolutionary theory.   He wrote an astonishing number of autobiographical studies, not from vanity nor from any external cause but because he found in himself a most fruitful example of evolution and was incapable of regarding his own life and work otherwise than as a steady upward progress.   Similarly he saw the course of history as a gradual struggle towards some high goal.   Hence his ideas of reform, and later of " regeneration," his belief in revolution not strictly as *change* but as a step towards a dream-future, his interpretations of cultural and æsthetic history, and his estimate of the art and artists of succeeding ages according to the stage he supposed them to have reached.   The evolutionist thinks of time as a tower built by progress, of which the past is the base and the future the battlements that are to crown it ; the bolder his will and imagination, the nearer he believes its completion to be.   It is a point of view that pervades all departments of life and thought.   If the idea of absolute evolution is to hold good it must be generally applied, whether in statecraft, politics, religion, the history of art and the arts, or the development of an individual.   It must also dominate the organic structure of a work of art. A clear appreciation of the importance attributed by Wagner to the idea of " becoming " is essential to a proper understanding of his æsthetic and of the emotional basis of his work. The two doctrines of sensualism and of evolution condition and complete one another. The " sensualist " artist needs the evolutionary theory as a formative principle ; the evolutionary thinker is driven to accept emotion as the supreme arbiter of life, the one trustworthy avenue of perception.

The evolutionary hypothesis involves the idea that the present is a bridge from the past to the future. It also involves the conception of the present as actual motion, even in art, upon which it thus imposes a time-consciousness. Stylised art-forms abolish the sense of real time. In music the forms of fugue and sonata have a time-dimension of their own, independent of the course of real time. Emotional naturalism in art, however, seeking as it does to represent realistically the "becoming" of emotion, requires identification with real time as a structural basis. Its forms need ideas of past and future as emotional structural elements. Emotionally regarded the past is memory and the future presentiment, and these two form the basis of an artistic presentation of emotional evolution. Memory and presentiment, however, can take account only of the more important events in the emotional life. Opera had methods of suggesting such memories before Wagner, and Wagner himself made increasing use of these, but in his work for the first time memory and presentiment were deliberately interwoven as factors in musical expressionism, mirroring the temporal, psychological process presented in the themes of the written drama. " In these fundamental motifs, which are not sentences but plastic emotional moments, the author's meaning finds its plainest emotional realisation, and the musician, as interpreter of the author's meaning, must therefore so order these motifs in full accordance with the author's intention, that their arrangement and repetition will of itself evolve a completely unified musical form."

The composer should model his motival development not on the loose operatic use of the reminiscence motif but on the firm thematic texture of Beethoven's instrumental music, for Beethoven's skill in this respect had (in Wagner's opinion) brought him to the threshold of absolute emotional representation, lacking only the word-tone melody attained through alliance with poetry for perfect expressionist verisimilitude. Word-tone melody heightened by association with action and gesture, and orchestral harmony incorporating memory and presentiment—these two opposite and yet coincident expressionist media comprise the " complete, unified art-form," in which " the widest range of human experience can be so completely and intelligibly conveyed to the emotions that each phase of it is accepted by the emotions as at once intensely exciting and utterly satisfying."

Such, in outline, is Wagner's teaching in this book. Though formulated in general terms all the important points bear in reality upon a work already planned, *The Death of Siegfried*. Alliteration, a dialogue deliberately emphasising emotional phases, a mythical subject chosen as the most appropriate and simplest milieu for the " purely-human "—Wagner used them all before searching for their theoretical justification. He propounds as general a series of propositions valid only for this particular work and those directly derived from it. Alliteration was suited to this subject, but later Wagner neglected or wholly abandoned it, and practice taught him as artist that the chorus and polyphonic *ensemble* were more important than as theorist he would allow. Even the musical formulæ he here established as fundamental did not stand the test of time. Indeed, in his very next compositions the form of the closed period served him more often as scaffolding than his theories would lead one to suppose. He was more ruthlessly revolutionary in his writings than in his music, setting down in words hard and fast formulæ which he did not endorse in artistic practice. Actually Wagner had outgrown extreme naturalism after writing his sketch for a prose drama, *Friedrich der Rotbart*, and the fact of his return to music was in itself an acknowledgement of the conventions of art. The chief use of his theoretic writings was that by developing his theories to their logical conclusions he was able to rid himself of their tyranny.

Political and doctrinaire elements which had crept into his operatic sketches were by this means eliminated and their psychological origins discovered in the desire for a wider range of expression, in the search for the impulse necessary to widen it and in the problem of giving form to this new impulse. Hence Wagner's dream of the " purely-human,"—his second dream as an evolutionary-emotional theorist. The two dreams gave birth to a third in the vision of an " art-work of the future " which was to consist in the representation of " purely-human " emotion on evolutionary lines. Sensualism had triumphed, giving rise to a materialistic conception of art, more particularly of music. It also nourished expressionist ambitions and urged them continually forward. But behind all these impulses lay the primal impulse of the will to theatre which employed the rest simply as means to evoke a fresh series of theatrical fantasies.

After *The Death of Siegfried*, offspring of the revolutionary period, Wagner became for the second time, and quite deliberately, a polemical writer. He turned perforce to æsthetic criticism in order to wrestle with ideas of the " purely-human," of freedom, and of property which had crept into the plot of his drama, and to fight his way through to the musical composition of the work. While engaged on the book, however—the three parts of *Opera and Drama* occupied him from the autumn of 1850 to February 1851—he lost sight of his point of departure. As he got rid of his revolutionary ideas in print, his drama, which had been conceived in a revolutionary spirit, tended to vanish too. The " guiltless guilty " Siegfried, the freeing of the Nibelungs, the triumph of a royalist republic, half-artistic, half-political programmatic ideas, gave place to others capable of artistic development and full of vitality. While Wagner was finishing *Opera and Drama* the figure of Siegfried had been undergoing a metamorphosis. In Dresden in the autumn of 1848, Wagner came across the old fairy tale of the foolish Youngest Son who goes forth " to learn what fear is." In the winter of 1850 he remembered this story and suddenly saw that its hero was simply a younger Siegfried. Externally the new idea seemed to fit in with the old, for it was surely desirable, even imperative, to show the world-betrayed hero of *The Death of Siegfried* in his innocent youth. Inwardly Wagner's own new-won sense of freedom made him feel nearer to the youthful hero than to the tragic victim of the world's conventions, whose lot had once seemed so like his own, for with *Opera and Drama* he had forged a sword that had cleft the old anvil in twain. The new plan ripened quickly, and soon after the completion of *Opera and Drama*, between June 3 and 24, 1851, the libretto was sketched out. Theory was now put to the proof. The experiment made with the libretto of *The Death of Siegfried* in the teeth of established conventions, was successful now that Wagner's mind was free and at peace. About this time he was joined in Zurich by a young Dresden friend, Theodor Uhlig, his colleague in the *Kapelle*. Uhlig was originally one of Wagner's opponents but had gradually become his enthusiastic supporter and an advocate of his writings and works. He was the first to see the manuscript of *Young Siegfried*.   Talks with Uhlig about the just finished libretto and the composition to follow are probably embodied in *Communication to My Friends*, in which Wagner, feeling once more on sure ground, presents a cross-section of his past experiences and opinions.

This writing, whose critical acumen is only equalled in interest by the self-revelation discernible between the lines, serves also as an explanatory introduction to " Three Operatic Poems " (*The Flying Dutchman, Tannhäuser*, and *Lohengrin*), the publication of which was retarded by the political and religious misgivings of the publishers. Before the alterations they insisted on were complete its conclusion required revision, for in it, after a critical review of the development of his work heretofore, Wagner had discussed his forthcoming *Young Siegfried* and *The Death of Siegfried*, plans for which had been greatly modified during negotiations with the publishers. The " grand heroic opera " of the Dresden sketch had now become " three dramas with a prelude." " I propose sometime to present these three dramas on three successive nights at a festival specially instituted for the purpose, with an introductory evening devoted to the prelude. . . . Anyone who approves of this plan will be, like myself, undisturbed by questions as to the when and where of its realisation, for he will not fail to discern that in this undertaking I part company altogether with our present-day theatre."

When Wagner wrote this in November 1851 the third drama and the prologue existed as yet in his imagination only.   After Uhlig's visit he finished his *Communication to My Friends* (first version) and was then eager to begin the composition of *Siegfried*.   " Something you could not possibly conceive of is simply making itself!   The musical phrases to these verses and sentences are coming without the slightest trouble to me.   They seem to grow up like wildflowers from the ground.   I have the beginning already in my head and a few plastic motifs such as Fafner's.   I am glad to work and keep working at it," wrote Wagner to Uhlig.   With Liszt he was more reserved.   Though *Young Siegfried* was intended for Weimar and Wagner had already received two hundred talers for it as payment in advance, he could not make up his mind to send Liszt the libretto.   In spite of himself he felt the need of explaining all kinds of things in it which should not really have needed explanation.   There were also other more material difficulties.   His house was cramped and very noisy and he suffered from a troublesome abdominal complaint. Uhlig, a cold-water enthusiast, suggested that he should undergo a water cure and Wagner gladly fell in with a plan that agreed with his " back to nature " theories. Such a cure could be had at Albisbrunn in the neighbourhood of Zurich, and Wagner decided to make an effort to re-establish his health before attacking the *Siegfried* music in earnest. The cure occupied nine weeks, from the middle of September to the end of November, during which time Karl Ritter bore him company. All work was laid aside, but the plan matured. On his walks and talks with Karl Ritter round Albisbrunn his problems were gradually solved, and a long letter to Liszt, dated November 20, 1851, contained a full account of this, and also two important pieces of news. Karl Ritter's mother had come in for a considerable sum of money and was now able to carry out alone the plan previously formed with Jessie Laussot of helping Wagner by a permanent and substantial yearly allowance. This made the advance on *Siegfried* from Weimar unnecessary and Wagner paid back the money he had already received. He did not do this merely to rid himself of a troublesome obligation, for about the time of Frau Ritter's offer the *Siegfried* plan had assumed proportions quite unsuited to the Weimar theatre. The plots of the two *Siegfried* dramas contained much matter that was left " either to indirect narrative or to the audience's own deductions. The things which give the story and the characters their infinitely moving and far-reaching significance can find no place in the representation ; the audience has to be told about them, merely." Now these narrative sections began to take shape as independent dramas. " Think of Siegmund's and Sieglinda's wonderful and calamitous love, of Wotan's secret connection with this love, of his estrangement from Fricka and the violence he does to his own heart in condemning Siegmund to death for the sake of the moral law. Then think of the glorious Valkyrie, Brynhilda, who, divining Wotan's inmost thoughts, defies the god and is punished by him. Imagine all this wealth of interest (as I have sketched it in the scene between the Wanderer and the Wala and—more broadly—in Brynhilda's narrative) as the subject of a drama to *precede* the two *Siegfrieds*, and you will understand that it was not mere reflection but actual inspiration that prompted my latest plan." To link the three dramas in one a prologue was necessary—*The Theft of the Rhinegold*. " Its subject is the perfect representation of all circumstances connected with the robbery—the origin of the Nibelung treasure, Wotan's theft of it and Alberich's curse, as presented in narrative form in *Young Siegfried*."

This passage is from a letter which Wagner wrote to Liszt on November 20, 1851, just before the end of the cure that was to fit him for the composition of *Young Siegfried*. Once again, however, he changed his plans. His next task must be to draft and complete librettos for the third drama and the prologue. As these new visions took shape in Wagner's mind *Young Siegfried* faded ; its music no longer sounded in his ears. In the winter of 1851–52 he conducted works of his own and of Beethoven's at three subscription concerts in Zurich. The *Tannhäuser* overture was also performed and Wagner himself was amazed at its success. " The women particularly were completely bowled over by it. Their enthusiasm was so great that they fell to sobbing and weeping. I received some curious accounts of first impressions ; with most there was a sense of overwhelming sorrow which found relief in tears and was then succeeded by an ecstasy of joy." One of these women was the twenty-four-year-old wife of an Elberfeld merchant, Otto Wesendonk, who had recently settled in Zurich as the representative of an American firm. A friendship soon sprang up between Wagner and these new arrivals. Herr Wesendonk was an amateur of the plastic arts ; his wife cared more for poetry and music. The subscription concerts, followed in April by a performance of *The Flying Dutchman* at the Zurich theatre, widened Wagner's circle of acquaintance, among whom a Dr. Franz Wille, a democratic journalist from Hamburg who, with his wife Eliza, had established a kind of patriarchal and revolutionary ménage at Mariafeld in the neighbourhood of Zurich, was particularly congenial to Wagner. Social and musical activities postponed work upon the new sections of the *Nibelung* cycle for some months, while Wagner's creative instinct drew stimulus from his delight in the favourable reception accorded to his earlier work. Not until April 1852, nearly six months after his letter to Liszt, did the scenic sketches for *The Valkyrie* and *The Theft of the Rhinegold* take final shape. A beautiful summer resort near Zurich, an inn called " Zum Rinderknecht," high in the hills, where Wagner stayed from June 1 to July 1, 1852, saw the completion of the libretto of *The Valkyrie*. Wagner was even more pleased with it than with *Young Siegfried*. " I am more enchanted than ever with the grandeur and beauty of my subject ; in it my outlook upon the world has found perfect expression. After this work I shall probably write no more poetry. It is the highest and most perfect of which I am capable."

As in the case of *Young Siegfried* the music at once took shape. A young man who visited Wagner at this time relates that he sang and wrote down the melody of Siegmund's love-song, "Winterstürme wichen dem Wonnemond " (" Winter storms have waned in the winsome May "), as he was reading him the work. After the excitement of creation Wagner felt the need of a rest. He set out on a walking tour through the Bernese Oberland to Lugano, where he sent for Minna, returning *via* Lake Maggiore, the Simplon, Geneva, and Lausanne. Several German theatres now made inquiries about *Tannhäuser* and even Berlin showed interest. For the latter, however, Wagner stipulated that Liszt should conduct and negotiations fell through. He issued detailed instructions for the production of *Tannhäuser* at other theatres, followed by a shorter article on *The Flying Dutchman*. The libretto of *The Rhinegold* was therefore not finished until November. The two *Siegfried* libretti had now to be revised to accord with it, certain abbreviations and alterations having become desirable. The diction was improved by the use of alliteration, shortened here and lengthened there. The alternate singing of men and women in the choral finale of the funeral scene in *The Death of Siegfried* was cut out, to be used years later in *Parsifal*. The most important change, however, was that made in the ground-plan of *The Death of Siegfried*. Wagner wrote it first, but the addition of three preceding pieces had placed it at the end of a series, and in it the complicated threads of all had to be gathered up and resolved. A revised prelude, the scene of the Norns, links it to the three previous works and hints by the symbolism of the breaking off of the thread that the end is utter destruction of all things. In place of the Valkyrie chorus, the germ of the first Brynhilda drama, Wagner inserts a great scene between Brynhilda and Waltraute, dealing with Wotan's expectation of the end of the world, and he casts Brynhilda's final song in a new and more revealing form. As in the first version the Rhine Daughters regain the Ring, not, however, as the symbol of freedom to live but as the symbol of redemption through love. Brynhilda's fiery death no longer raises her with Siegfried to the throne of the All-Father as " sureties of eternal power," for with a brand from the funeral pyre she sets fire to Valhalla, within whose wood-piled walls Wotan and all the gods silently await the devouring flames. The " revolutionary " drama, with its promises of joy, victory, and freedom, has become an apotheosis of love :

> " Nicht Gut, nicht Gold,
>   noch göttliche Pracht ;
>   nicht Haus, nicht Hof,
>   noch herrischer Prunk ;
>   nicht trüber Verträge
>   trügender Bund,
>   nicht heuchelnder Sitte
>   hartes Gesetz :
>   selig in Lust und Leid
>   lässt—die Liebe nur sein ! "

> (" Not goods nor gold,
>   Nor heavenly pomp ;
>   Not house nor hold,
>   Nor lordly state ;
>   Not callous commerce's
>   Treacherous bond,
>   Not evil convention's
>   Rigid rule.
>   Blessed through weal and woe
>   Let love be alone ! ")

Thus the " purely-human " triumphs over moribund, loveless convention. During Christmas 1852, Wagner read the finished libretto to the Willes at Mariafeld, and shortly after had it privately printed. At last he felt that his work was ripe for music.

In Wagner's letter to Liszt from Albisbrunn, he gives as the chief reason for the expansion of the two *Siegfried* libretti into a trilogy and prologue the fact that they are overburdened with epic narrative and explanatory passages ; the cycle is designed to substitute direct representation for these. Such an explanation might satisfy Liszt, and no doubt four dramas served better than one to present an intricate story ; but there was a deeper reason for the revision which Wagner did not express. After his recovery from the stunned condition which followed the great upheaval, the *Siegfried* libretto he took with him from Dresden and which even there had been somewhat eclipsed in his mind by the *Jesus of Nazareth* sketch, seemed to him his one available bridge to future creative work. This bridge, however, led not to music but to critical and æsthetic speculations, and Wagner emerged from these to find not a dying but a youthful and blooming Siegfried. The story which linked the two was rather a useful pretext for taking up of a new plan than an organic reality. Actually, with the birth of *Young Siegfried* the Dresden *Siegfried* sank to the status of a sketch which Wagner wished, but felt no imperative need, to carry out. Later the same fate overtook *Young Siegfried*. Wagner began on it enthusiastically, lost interest, laid the work aside and, after an interval, was full of a new plan. He was moved not by any need to complete the story but by desire to discover the real creative basis of his subject. The same process might conceivably have taken place with a series of disconnected plots, for *Friedrich Rotbart* was Wagner's real starting-point for *The Ring*.

It was not until Wagner came to *The Valkyrie* that he could be sure whether it was to be the sole lasting result of his work on *The Ring* subject, or whether the two works which had led up to it would maintain a life of their own. He believed that they would, and found a means of cementing the whole series by a prologue. This prologue is the only drama in the cycle which Wagner did not produce in the usual ecstasy and which he did not, while writing it, believe to be the greatest thing of which he was capable. Moreover it is here that links with the past become evident. There is a kinship between *The Nibelungs* and *Hans Heiling* as there is between *The Flying Dutchman* and *The Vampire*. Marschner made renunciation of love the price of power over the spirit world : " If I wish to wear your crown, earthly love I must disown." Heiling, half demon Alberich, half love-sick Wotan (and like these two represented by the baritone voice) is king of the underworld, of the dwarfs who work in gold and jewels. The similarity of subject influences even the music of *The Valkyrie*, for the minor melody prophesying death which afterwards runs through the whole cycle agrees almost note for note with the Mountain Queen's great aria, " Thou hadst else fallen prey to the cruel revenge of the spirits," and *The Rhinegold* prologue shows unmistakable traces of influences which affected the narrative passages of its distant Dresden predecessor, *The Death of Siegfried*.

Wagner was well aware of the twofold function of this prologue. It was required to pave the way for the two *Siegfried* dramas and had no significance in itself, yet there was so much that needed explanation and exposition that another almost full-length drama was necessary.

From this constructional basis, and bearing in mind *The Valkyrie* which was the fruit of his labours, Wagner turned once more to its stem and root. He had almost lost interest in *Young Siegfried*, but with some slight alterations in ground-plan and structure it could be fitted on to *The Valkyrie*. *The Death of Siegfried*, on the other hand, seemed entirely alien. He had extracted the best from it. The work was a torso. But he was anxious to complete the great cycle and the content of *The Death of Siegfried* was indispensable for this. He therefore *devised* it as he had devised the prologue. He was no longer interested in his masculine hero, Siegfried, whose tragedy did not move him, in whose death he found no sense of release. Another tragedy had taken the place of this in his mind, the tragedy of *The Valkyrie*, of woman's love by treachery made wise and finding consummation in destruction and destruction in consummation. The flame of this love now fired *The Death of Siegfried*, revivifying the old sketch. The motives of the new drama seemed to fit in just at those places where Wagner had excised large sections to form the matter of later works. The scaffolding could be retained and rearranged. Thus *The Valkyrie*, representing the fine essence extracted from the first sketch, eventually reacted upon and revivified the latter, and Wagner was able to round off his cycle. But this curious backwards process, in which the first work of the series grew out of the last and eventually reshaped it, caused a rift in the structure as a whole, dividing it into two distinct sections. Only one of these sections—that directly dominated by the idea of the Valkyrie—could at first find expression in music. The other, the province of the human woman Brynhilda, did not reveal the soul of music inherent in it until more than ten years later.

Two conceptions of Brynhilda, as Valkyrie and as Woman, are the sources of *The Ring* music. The first section comprises the drama of the dream-maid, the second that of the woman in whom that dream is fulfilled. A decade separates the two, for it was not until Wagner had had actual experience of woman's self-sacrifice that he could, like Siegfried, break through the ring of flame which Wotan had cast about Brynhilda.

From the moment that Wagner discovered a heroine for his work his Wotan and his Siegfried, two different incarnations of masculinity, took second place. Wotan is the dreamer, doomed never to find fulfilment in woman. He is a slave to moral conventions, and, therefore, the woman who really understands him can stand to him only in the relation of a daughter; she is the child of his wishes and his will, the dream-maid. Contrasted with Wotan is Siegfried, his youthful reincarnation, his second self freed from bondage to convention. He breaks the Spear of convention, and so attains that of which Wotan can only dream. There is no real antithesis between Wotan and Siegfried and the balance of the work is not upset by the interchange of the two figures. In the musical action they possess an inner identity, for they present the same character at different stages of its evolution, in bondage and in freedom. Thus, though Wotan fades as Siegfried comes to the fore, the downfall of one involves the downfall of the other. Musically neither occupies a central place, for that place is held by the woman who is the cause of the male figure's transformation and the mainspring of his being and actions.

When this woman came into Wagner's life the music for his new work came with her. She appeared first in the person of Jessie Laussot, whose home Wagner entered as a fugitive exile and with whom he would have fled as Siegmund with Sieglinda. This love-story, like Siegmund's, was shattered by convention; it raged and passed over like a storm. The second time Wagner encountered this woman she assumed the guise of the dream-maid, the confidante of his thoughts, whereupon the figure of Wotan found its musical fulfilment. The initials " G. S. M." inscribed upon sketches for the prelude to *The Valkyrie* stand for " Gesegnet sei Mathilde " (" Blessed be Mathilde "). The musical fates of Siegfried and Wotan were decided by Jessie-Sieglinda and Mathilde-Brynhilda.

" I have never been able to agree," writes Eliza Wille in her Memoirs, " with statements I have from time to time read and heard that Wagner experienced all the miseries of banishment in Zurich. The exile was held in high regard by everyone, had a settled home of his own and friends to intercede for him, among them one whose like could be seldom found. Anyone to whom Wagner spoke a friendly word felt honoured. . . . He knew nothing in Zurich of the political exile's weary lot, of his hopeless search for sympathy, of the knocking at doors often enough barred against him." Wagner himself tells a very different story. Peace, security, recognition, sympathy were his in small degree or not at all; worries were continuous and each apparent turn of fortune proved deceptive; he felt an increasing bitterness, hatred, and contempt for the world, and his personal affairs drove him eventually to desperate decisions. Was Eliza Wille's estimate a merely superficial one? She certainly heard much from Wagner himself, who was by nature very communicative, and at the beginning of his affair with Mathilde in 1852 she was the confidante of both. Or does Wagner exaggerate? His letters at least deal with facts and in them we find that he was constantly in need of money, that his earnings were always less than his expectations and in any case insufficient for his needs, that his negotiations with publishers came to nothing, and that mental conflicts made him wretched.

The truth is that both were right. Eliza Wille's account treats the practical difficulties as not insoluble and the psychological ones as inevitable, for she is merely an observer, though a sympathetic one; Wagner's words are the cry of the actual sufferer. Circumstances played a great though not a decisive part in his distress. He was reduced to begging from Liszt, from the Grand Duke of Weimar, from Otto Wesendonk, and others, but money was eventually forthcoming. His earlier operas were not taken up in Germany as enthusiastically as he hoped, but they gained ground gradually. His hardest task was the fulfilment of a contract to conduct concerts at the London Philharmonic in the spring of 1855, for the work proved more exigent, more uncongenial, and less remunerative than he had expected and hindered the scoring of *The Valkyrie*. Obstacles of this kind, however, might vex but could not seriously affect Wagner. His real troubles were of a different nature. Banishment weighed heavily upon him. He missed living contact with theatres, singers, and orchestras. Concerts and operatic productions in Zurich could not make up to him for his inability to hear *Lohengrin*. He had many opportunities for friendly intercourse, but his real musical affinity, Franz Liszt, was far away, and came to Zurich twice only, for a week in July 1853 and not again until three years later, in October 1856. Thus Wagner felt himself severed from the very roots of his artistic being, from practical concern with music and the stage, and from intercourse with like-minded companions. But he suffered at this time as man even more than he did as artist. Mathilde Wesendonk, just awakening to consciousness of her own womanhood, was the dream-maid whom Wagner's will had called to life. In her eyes he read the dawn of a love that could understand, yet he was forced, like Wotan, to cast her once more under the spell of sleep. Thus his life

was an anguished struggle both inwardly and outwardly. Where a
friendly observer saw only the richness and fullness of his life he
experienced only sorrow and the impulse to portray it. He became
himself his own artistic subject, from profound conviction mirroring
his own being in the work that was struggling to birth. He was the
Wotan of his own imagination, a splendid yet anguished figure.
Involuntarily he became his own interpreter, experiencing life in
accordance with the emotions he felt impelled to embody in his
next work.

Wagner read his finished libretto to the Willes during Christmas
1852 and afterwards prepared for composition in his own peculiar
way. At these times certain conditions were always essential to him.
Though comfort meant much to him he could, as long as he was
engaged on writing in prose or verse, live very modestly without
finding his deprivations intolerable. But this was not so when he
was composing. He prepared for it with a kind of solemnity. If he
did not feel in perfect health he took a cure. His study had to be
carefully fitted up with rich carpets, chairs, cushions, curtains, and
pictures. He was regardless of money at these times and surrounded
himself with every luxury within reach. His " Letters to an Up-
holstress " from Vienna and later from Munich show a riot of
theatrical fancy in their descriptions of such appointments. They
express neither extravagance nor ostentation in the ordinary sense,
for Wagner needed these things as suggestions when composing, just
as Schiller needed the smell of rotting apples when writing poetry.
To Wagner the act of musical creation was an act of procreation. He
entertained music as he would entertain a woman and adorned his
study as for a lover's assignation. " Stay where you are, I am in
heat," he once cried to Weissheimer in Biebrich, when the latter called
on him unexpectedly and caught sight of Wagner hastily retreating
and bathed in sweat. The tendency to pander to these demands of
the creative instinct may have grown upon him with the years, but it
had always been present. When in Zurich the time drew near for the
composition of *The Ring*, Wagner made his arrangements accordingly.
In April 1853 he took a new and pleasanter house. " You will find
everything very nice when you come," he wrote to Liszt, " for the
devil of voluptuousness has taken hold of me again and I have made
my house as comfortable as possible." The time of preparation was
occupied with business connected with the private printing of the

Nibelung libretti, while in Weimar Liszt was producing the three grand romantic operas in quick succession. Wagner himself conducted concerts in Zurich, and with the idea of improving the prospects of *The Ring*, perhaps even of getting a theatre built for it there, he gave one, twice repeated, consisting of extracts from his own works. He got an enthusiastic reception—he was celebrating his fortieth birthday —but the hoped-for results did not materialise. Soon afterwards Liszt came to Zurich. It was the friends' first meeting after years of intimate correspondence. Wagner had been deeply grieved early that year by the untimely death of Uhlig and the stimulus of Liszt's companionship provided a strong incentive to work.

He still delayed, however, needing something more. " I need some satisfaction from without in order that, by a pleasant reaction, I may happily project what I have within me. I must be entirely free to travel, to go to Italy, perhaps to visit Paris again, in order to attain that peaceful state which is just what I lack at present." After Liszt's departure he went to St. Moritz over mountain and glacier with Herwegh; then, returning to Zurich, to Bern, Turin, Genoa, Spezia, and Milan; then to Basle where Liszt rejoined him after the music festival in Karlsruhe with Joachim, von Bülow, Cornelius, and Draesecke, and the friends spent a few riotous days together. The music was coming, but it had not yet come. Wagner went to Paris with Liszt and the Princess and, when they left, sent for Minna and spent a pleasurable week recalling the past. It was now the end of October. Suddenly Wagner turned homewards. The moment had come. On November 1, 1853, the composition of *The Rhinegold* was begun.

Five and a half years had passed since the completion of *Lohengrin*. During these years Wagner composed only one small " occasional " piece, a " Sonata for the album of Frau M. W." Written shortly before he began *The Ring*, it is a summary of the past and a promise for the future, a delicate act of homage to the woman who had inspired the music which was now to flow from him in an almost unbroken stream. Illness and business worries caused pauses, but no real stoppage. Wagner composed *The Rhinegold* between November 1, 1853, and January 14, 1854, and finished the full score with the gold pen Mathilde had given him on May 28 of that year. There followed a bare month's pause. *The Valkyrie* was composed between June 28 and December 27, though in this case the full score was not completed so quickly, for Wagner's visit to London formed a trying interruption and it was not until March 1856 that he could write *finis* to the work. Several months now elapsed during which Wagner's time and attention were taken up with schemes for building a house, with plans for a new opera, *Tristan and Isolda*, and a sketch entitled *The Victors*, and with business negotiations with the publishers, Breitkopf and Härtel. Then came *Siegfried's* turn. On September 2 the first act was begun and, like *The Valkyrie*, immediately scored. Events, internal and external, then intervened. The Wesendonks offered Wagner his long-desired " refuge " in a house and garden close to their own. On the morning of Good Friday, 1857, as he took his first quiet survey of his new domain, he saw a vision of his *Parsifal* to be. *Siegfried* then reasserted itself and the composition of the second act was completed on July 30, 1857. But here the thread suddenly broke off.

External reasons for this were not lacking. Breitkopf's had finally declined to publish *The Ring*, and there was no apparent possibility of ever getting that vast work performed. Were these reasons sufficient? Were Wagner's energies exhausted by his tremendous output? Yet he had just conceived a new work. The truth is that his artistic energies were not exhausted but had found another channel. The work upon which he had been engaged, though ostensibly a fragment, was really complete in itself. The drama of the Valkyrie and her world was finished, though her creator was not yet conscious of this. The young Siegfried who reforged the sword and slew the dragon was indeed he whom Brynhilda's love had foreknown. What Brynhilda had willed as Wotan's daughter, defying his forced command, had come to pass, and the " Fearless One " of Wotan's dreams had appeared and fulfilled his mission. This was the work of the Valkyrie ; what followed was outside her world.

The first part of *The Ring*, an ideal unity by virtue of the inner meaning of the drama, and a unity also by date of composition and style of wording, properly ends here. *The Valkyrie* is its centre and the source of its music, which in the first two acts of *Siegfried* expresses that " purely-human " believed by Wagner to be the highest expression of emotion, of Nature herself. This idea of Nature determines the character of the music ; it is the purpose of the prologue to reveal the secrets of her rule over primæval forces.

The libretto of *The Rhinegold* was designed to summarise events leading up to the dramas to follow. It deals with origins and so proclaims that love is the basis of the " purely-human " :

" In Wasser, Erd' und Luft
lassen will nichts von Lieb' und Weib."

(" In water, earth and air,
Love's raptures none
Will e'er renounce.")

Water, earth, air, and fire, all the manifold phenomena of nature, are subject to the law of love, and this is manifested in the play of primal forces. One alone among these is rebellious. Alberich the dwarf curses love, for by so doing he can possess gold. Thus he blasphemes Nature's highest law. He is " The Loveless One." In a letter to Liszt of January 1852, Wagner says of the character of Ortrud that " she is the woman who knows not love. To say this is to say all—the most terrible thing that could be said. Her soul is *politics*." This was written at a time when the figure of Alberich was taking shape in Wagner's mind. Alberich, Ortrud's male counterpart, is the soul of politics, and politics and lovelessness are interchangeable ideas. Politics means strife for power, property, and gold. Gold, which comes from Nature, is the enemy of Nature's supreme law of Love, and conflict between the two brings ruin. It is only when gold returns to the womb of Nature that Love can once more reign.

Such is the kernel of the drama. There is but one crime, the crime against love. But love is the natural law of all that is, for Nature *is* Love. Wagner's antagonism to Christianity at this period was based on this conception, for he believed that Christianity taught a love contrary to natural love. In *Tannhäuser* he shook his audience by a revelation of the power of love, in *Lohengrin* he moved it by the miracle of love. Now he sought to present this love as it is in itself, showing it as a natural passion in mortal combat with the lovelessness that is its opposite. The love-emotion as a natural manifestation, believed by Wagner to be the very essence of music, thus becomes the subject not only of music but of drama. His sensuous view of music is presented in terms of a drama designed to glorify the philosophy of sensualism. The dramatic idea and the musical idea coincide exactly; the scene becomes a projection of the musical organism in a series of objective pictures and movements. Arguments for word-tone speech, presented under physiological similes in *Opera and Drama*, are here repeated more forcibly in artistic form, and a process comprehended by—and comprehensible by—the senses alone is clothed simultaneously in musical notes, words, gestures, scenes and action that all express the same idea and thus attain an expressive unity which assails all the senses at once. The sensualist principle is here fully grasped, worked out to its logical conclusions, and successfully applied.

The Rhinegold accordingly forms a prologue not merely to the events of the drama but to their sensuous musical presentation. Wagner's object is to present passionate love as the basic emotion of elemental Nature and her children. He seeks to show the profound schism in Nature caused by the first sin against the law of love. In this prologue, however, these things are expressed only in broad outline. The first task is " to find plastic nature-motifs capable of developing increasing individuality as vehicles of the passions to be expressed in this far-reaching drama and of the characters which embody them." These words in Wagner's " explanatory epilogue " throw light on the *Rhinegold* music. It is designed to convey premonitions in the natural sphere of the more developed passions of humanity. The music which takes its rise in *The Rhinegold* portrays the events of Nature and the events of passion so far as these are identical, passing from the pre-human drama of *The Rhinegold* to *The Valkyrie*, that " terrible storm in the elements and in the human soul which dies gradually away in Brynhilda's magic sleep," and thence to the world of forest and cave which is the setting for the boy Siegfried, Mime, and Fafner. But from the moment when in the bird's song Nature becomes articulate in human speech the drama of passion in elemental nature comes to an end. Human passion as such overmasters all else, forming a new " nature " outside elemental nature. Simultaneously the impulse which has guided the music hitherto fails and another is substituted for it. The first half of *The Nibelung* cycle is crystallised emotionally about the Valkyrie, Brynhilda ; it is based intellectually on the idea of a fettered god's attainment of freedom in Man ; it is linked temporally by the order of composition ; it is characterised musically by the idea of the drama of passion as a drama of nature. Nature is the symbol which guides the work throughout, establishes its foundations, marks out its boundaries, and governs the style and character of the music from first to last.

In Wagner's musical philosophy at this period harmony represents Nature. It is " the matrix which receives the fructifying seed of the poet's purpose and obedient to the law of its female organism brings it forth fully formed." Harmony, impregnated by poetic intention, brings forth melody—a melody conditioned by harmony. Its progress from one key to another is determined by the changing root note, and fusion of harmony with melody is required to establish the emotional content of the latter. Harmony is thus " the most essential element in music," the womb of melody, creative Nature herself. All vital musical phenomena are harmonic phenomena. If the passionate incidents of the drama are regarded as mirroring a natural process, this process must, for the musician, be a harmonic process. The triad, originally a device to reinforce the single note and give it definition by indicating its relative vibrations, now becomes fundamental to a comprehension of music. The melodic upper line ceases to be the most vital part and becomes merely the surface of the musical organism, whose life and power of motion are now found in the deeps of harmony. The emotional course of the drama finds its musical expression in combinations of chords and their relations.

Harmony thus becomes the vehicle of musical drama. It was so intended even in *Die Feen* and *Lohengrin*, but in *The Ring* it plays this part more effectively, more logically, more thoroughly. Pure nature is symbolised by unmodified fundamental harmony. As nature attains individuality harmony branches out into an endless variety of chords. The relations between individual phenomena are represented musically by relations of intervals. The harmonic key system constitutes a world corresponding with the emotional world of visible drama. Nature regarded as emotion, and harmony as Wagner understands it, are an organic unity. They manifest themselves differently but are moved by the same impulse, and thus inevitably coincide. As the idea of passion in nature lends increasing prominence to the composer's concept of the " purely-human " he becomes increasingly preoccupied with harmonic relations. He thinks of Nature herself as the great primal chord from whose permutations and combinations spring all the phenomena of life. The nearer these remain to their origin the more obvious are their harmonic relations with this chord and the simpler the note sequences, but the further they depart from primitive nature and approach the human and the individual the more artificial and elaborate must their musical portrayal be. Harmony is " Nature herself in her profundity and vastness, veiling the infinite and eternal ground of her processes of growth, begetting and birth from the curious eyes of mankind because those eyes can only apprehend that which growth, begetting and desire have rendered visible."

Thus harmony becomes a symbol of an infinite tone-space within which work the intervals, constructing, differentiating and relating. It becomes a time-concept through the distributive action of rhythm. This seeming metaphysical parallel between nature and harmony is really a very thorough rationalisation of musical phenomena, whose tonal basis is therein assimilated absolutely to that of the world of visual imagery. A world is established whose visible aspect is borrowed from the primitive phenomena of visible nature and whose audible aspect is taken from the relationships of harmony. It is the task of the stage to convey the visible aspect of this world to the eye with absolute realism. The audible aspect, so far as this is not represented on the stage, is entrusted to the orchestra. Wagner calls this "a realisation of the idea of harmony in supremest, most vital mobility."

He begins by presenting the twofold significance of nature— emotional and harmonic—through the elements, earth, air, fire and water, and through the scenes and landscapes associated with them, such as rivers, mountains, caverns, tongues of flame, mists and clouds, thunder and lightning, rainbows, sunsets, storms and tempests, the ripple and wash of forests, night and morning, sunshine through water. These form his dramatic settings, from the quiet opening to the violent scenes which follow. They also supply the fundamental note. The serene harmony of flowing water rises in mounting chords from the low E flat with which *The Rhinegold* opens. Leaping flames are portrayed in rapid chromatic ascending and descending chords of the sixth. Broad chords, with a peaceful, plastic rhythm expressive of the spacious freedom of mountain peaks, form the Valhalla motif. Clouds, lightning and thunder are depicted in harmonies which grow ever more compressed until they discharge themselves suddenly with a resolution upon the six-four chord and roll gradually away in the distance. The rainbow is painted in shining major tones, and the storm rages in hammering unison sextolets. Harmonisation is in accordance with the tone-colour employed. The open notes of the horns present a picture of the watery depths of the Rhine, and harp-chords colour the rainbow.   The mellow timbre of tubas and the heavier brass is used to portray the stately repose of Valhalla, and the most agile of the instrumental groups, strings and wood-wind, depict fire and tempest.   All these things form a scenico-musical background for individual figures in which the forces of nature are embodied.   Mermaids people the waters, gods the mountains, dwarfs the caverns, and giants the face of the earth.   Valkyries ride the storm, the great serpent crawls over the ground, and there is the creeping toad and the fluttering wood-bird.   Since the figures in the drama are at first little more than types, the harmonic complex resolves itself into simple set formulae.   These too are types, derived from fundamental harmony but already forming distinct melodic and rhythmic *motifs*.   Such are the C major motif of the Rhinegold itself, Wotan's " mighty thought " as he approaches the stronghold (later to become the motif of the Victorious Sword), and the clear-cut rhythm of Donner's thunderclap.   Significant chord sequences are constructed from the apposition of nearly-related harmonies.   The sustained chord of the dominant ninth, resolved in the major, becomes the symbol of the Rhine Maidens' song, and a sequence of diminished and augmented triads expresses the malice and jealousy of the Nibelungs.   These formations are not arbitrarily attached to certain figures and scenes but play the same part in the harmonic development as the former in the drama.   By their chordal combinations, their modulatory connections, they build up a musical drama parallel to that upon the stage.

As this scenico-musical duality develops and the characters in the drama gain in vitality and individuality, so the rhythmic and modulatory motion, the melodic physiognomy of the motifs which inter-penetrate the harmony become more lively and vivid.   The two spheres meet in *words*, in which music finds final utterance and which assist scenic representation.   Wagner lays great stress upon this double function of words.   His libretto is strewn even more lavishly than that of *The Flying Dutchman* with onomatopœic ejaculations, these being nearer to music than ordinary speech.   The Rhine Maidens' " Weia ! Weia ! " and " Wagalaweia," Alberich's " Hehe ! Hehe ! Hieher ! Hieher ! " Donner's " Heda ! Hedo ! " the Valkyries' " Hojotoho ! " and Siegfried's " Hoho ! Hahei ! blase, Balg " (" Blow, bellows ! ") are onomatopœic speech-formations with a motival significance.   Wagner's choice of alliterative verse was governed ultimately by a desire for realism even in verbal expression. Coupled with the use of this quasi-musical speech realistic effects are required from the orchestra. Examples of these are the wash of waves, the hiss of bellows at the forge, the crack of Alberich's whip and the groans that answer it, the snapping of Alberich's bonds, the bursting of the door of Hunding's hall, the galloping of the Valkyries, the hammers of the Nibelungs, Hunding's horn and the tramp of his feet, the hiss of steam and crackle of fire, the sound of Alberich's climbing, Mime's " waddling and tottering " gait. Even visual impressions are translated into sound. The great span of the rainbow is portrayed in a G flat major melody of overarching chords, and the approach of the serpent's scaly length in a bass passage of one-bar phrases, heavily slurred and rising by degrees. Most of these formations are something more than mere episodic tone-painting. They have a permanent validity, because they are derived from natural sensuous impressions translated directly into terms of music.

This correspondence, to the point of absolute identity, of scenic with musical phenomena establishes sensualism as a valid mode of art. Such an art inevitably takes nature for its subject, for the will to expression is essentially naturalistic in origin and finds in things natural its most perfect models. The artist reverts to nature to satisfy his realistic impulse. Wagner in his prime of manhood sets out to discover that source of expressionist art, just as his Wotan sets out to find the Wala. His reward is the discovery of Brynhilda, daughter of Wotan and the Wala—the " Nature " section of The Ring. Scenically and emotionally a drama of passionate desire, it is musically a drama of harmony conditioned by the appearance of the motifs, and these two aspects are one, for both originate in the idea of *naturalism*.

The deliberate acceptance of harmony as the basis of music forms the groundwork of Wagner's musical style in the first section of The Ring. He seeks not merely, as in Lohengrin, to exploit the expression-values of the contrast between major and minor and the distinctive characters of different keys, but splits up the harmonic complex, endows the intervals with independent significance, determines the relations of each to the key-note and to the upper melodic line, and gives them individual colour. Harmony is no longer regarded as a single entity working simultaneously in different registers, but as an association of related but independent intervals, and motif and cadence take the place of melody as formal structural elements.

Motif is harmony in the horizontal position, linking its notes by rhythmic sequence into melodic form, mediating modulatory changes and expressing the quality of an instantaneous, vertical musical structure in terms of the successive and horizontal. Motif is not melody in the sense of being a dominating melodic line, nor is it theme in the sense of being an element in symphonic structure. It can be expanded melodically or thematically, but by origin and nature it is individualised harmony, and it is valuable in that it is a means of translating the harmonic concept into linear terms. It serves as a brief, compact note of exclamation, making the harmony plainly recognisable at all times and revealing its own unbroken inner connection with it. Motif, therefore, has not, like melody, a set periodic structure. It is a phrase—usually a one-bar phrase. When rounded out to form melody it corresponds with the singer's breath ; when employed thematically, with the instrumental solo. It always assists harmonic development, and has therefore nothing in common with the independent symphonic theme which has its own logical development. It is the creature of harmony, whereas the latter, in symphonic art, forms a thematic substructure.

In *The Nibelungs* the motif represents harmony become active, linear, progressive. Derived from harmony, never dissociated from harmony, and tending to return to harmony, it is in fact the harmonic motive impulse worked out in linear music. The will, the trend, of harmony takes form in the motif and is bounded by cadence. The same laws that cause us to accept a piece of tonal architecture as a symbol of the visible world require that this world should be resolved in a closing harmony to correspond with its beginning—that is to say, they require cadential treatment. A new form of musical periodicity is thus evolved in which the harmonic period takes the place of the melodic as the ultimate unit of a harmonic group. In this period the motif provides the modulatory impulse, the cadence its limitation, and these two formative powers combine to make up the basic formula of Wagnerian music, the song.

The harmonic song-form, like the melodic, is usually threefold in structure. This is accounted for not by the melodic line but primarily by the course of the harmonic action. Lohengrin's Forbidden Question is the earliest example of this threefold harmonic song.

The first two periods form a pair, the third, being doubled in extension, leads through a rich modulatory passage to a major cadence. The equally important motif of the Nibelungs—

> " Nur wer der Minne Macht entsagt,
> Nur wer der Liebe Lust verjagt,
> Nur der erzielt sich den Zauber,
> Zum Reif zu zwingen das Gold "

> (" He who the power of love forswears,
> From all delights of love forbears,
> Alone can master the magic
> That makes a ring from gold ")

—is based on the same structural principle, though it is put far more forcibly into practice. It forms the standard type of harmonic song found in the first section of *The Ring*, uniting in one a group of motifs. The harmonic period, conditioned by motif and closed by cadence, constitutes the structural unit, and repetition of the first period conveys an impression of organic growth in the form. The third and longer period gathers up and rounds off the whole. Harmonic song of this type is the very corner-stone of the music of *The Ring*.

From it Wagner goes on to build up on a vast scale by means of small units. The lyrical harmonic phrase sets the standard. It absorbs traditional recitative or musical dialogue, interpenetrating it motivally and bringing it to a closing cadence. Free declamatory recitative is only possible in opera, for its forms, derived from the melodious phrasing proper to song, require the counterpoise of dialogue or of the pure pathos of sung speech. Harmonic drama does away with both melodic and declamatory song, setting in their place the harmonic period which, actuated by the motif, carries the whole work along. Here again there is development along lines laid down in *Lohengrin*, for the *arioso* becomes an organised, smooth-flowing delivery of song. Though occasionally the actual singing voice is treated merely declamatorily, a substructure of logical progression is always discernible in the music. Strict melody must have beginning and end, pauses and contrasts. Harmony carries all these within itself; a close at once begets a new beginning, and contrast is self-evolved. Harmony is not, like melody, an individual phenomenon. It is supra-individual and capable of inexhaustible modification. It contains the cause, whereas the old form of melody contained only the effect. In

The Rhinegold Wagner still occasionally employs dialogue closely allied to recitative, notably in Fricka's talk with Wotan as they gaze upon the stronghold.   Here involuntarily he gives way to the operatic need for supplying the contrast of plain declamation with the grandiose melody of the Valhalla theme.   But as melody loses its individual prominence, the difference between it and recitative becomes inconspicuous and the two meet midway in lyrical enhancement of a harmonic process. The narrative passages of *The Valkyrie*, such as Siegmund's story and Wotan's account of his life, are built up of harmonic phrases on a grand architectonic scale.   The simple harmonic period is developed by the motif, which is ever more sharply individualised, into a melodic, *arioso*-like type of song-delivery.   The formative process is in principle the same though externally the reverse of that of *The Rhinegold* prelude. The harmony is built up and established by the interweaving of nature-sounds used as motifs until melody appears as the nature-sound of human speech.   In the big narrative passages there is a groundwork of primitive harmony, empty as yet of motif and set in motion simply by the words.   When, however, narrative ceases to be mere description and becomes charged with emotion, harmony becomes more condensed and acquires an individual stamp, displaying the power of the motif at its highest.   The first process leads from dim stirrings of emotion to intellectual clarity, the second from intellectual concepts to emotional manifestations.   The former culminates in the spoken word, the latter begins with it.   Both constructive methods are derived from the conception of the musical process as a harmonic process, and proceed, according to the nature of the problem, either from the motival interval to the harmonic whole or from plain harmony to the development of individual motifs.

As the old recitative loses its declamatory character and passes into the harmonic period, so, simultaneously, the aria form of melody becomes a part of the basic harmony.   Recitative gains in sensuous musical charm, but melody loses its independence and becomes merely the upper line of the harmonic period.   The harmonic song, being the first symposium, shows the new type of melody evolved from harmony.   In answer to vocal requirements it is expanded into the *arioso* song which comprises a group of harmonic song-forms.   The whole musical structure of *The Rhinegold* and of the first two acts of *Siegfried* is governed by this song-form.   The song of the Rhine Maidens, Loge's story of " Weibes Wonne und Wert " (" Woman's wondrous delight "), Mime's song of the forge, Erda's "Weiche, Wotan, weiche " ("Yield it, Wotan, yield it ! "), Donner's invocation of the thunder, are high outstanding peaks in this song series. It persists, even in minor episodes, in almost unbroken sequence from Mime's opening song to the talk with the Wanderer, Siegfried's forge songs, Alberich's night song, Fafner's "Wer bist du, kühner Knabe ? " ("Who art thou, valiant stripling ? "), Mime's "Willkommen, Siegfried " ("My welcome, Siegfried ! ") and the wood-bird's song. The structure of this act is that of the old song-opera. Since the latter is the basis of German Romantic opera its appeal has to be changed from a primarily melodic to a primarily harmonic one. The ordering and inner unity of the whole structure is dependent on this. As emotion passes from the natural sphere to that of human passion, song loses its simple periodicity and becomes definitely melodic, as in Siegmund's love-song, Wotan's farewell and the antiphonal verses of the prophecy of death. This latter affords the perfect example of the harmonic song-period expanded by the impulse to motival modulation into the big scena.

With harmonic movement as the governing agent in form, a new method of unifying scene or act is discovered, so that the whole appears as a single extension of the harmonic action. Its organism is made up of period, song and *arioso*, each of these members developing directly from that which precedes it. A sense of real time in music, impossible in the set traditional melodic forms, results inevitably from harmonic drama. Continuity in musical representation at last makes it possible to liberate and give scope to all the expressionist forces of harmony. External, formal limitations, the difference between recitative and song, are abolished, and a continuous flow of music is maintained. The formal structure of the scene, the act, the whole work, the whole first section of the *Nibelung* cycle, is pervaded by harmonic "becoming." The impulse behind this "becoming," concentrated in the motif, never flags. It continually builds up harmonic structure, continually brings it to closing cadences, continually develops new forms from it and conducts it through all the changes inherent in it from the first up to the final cadence of resolution. This is the drama of music's continuous "becoming " through harmonic development—the drama of harmony. The act, the work, the cycle forms a single harmonic wave. Moved by the living indwelling force of motif, it persists through all minor incidents of period and song up to the fundamental harmonic cadence which spans the whole.

In tone-colour as in structure the work is naturalistic. In *Lohengrin* Wagner worked on the principle of using threefold orchestral wind in order to represent each chord in the same tone-colour. In *The Ring* each group is redivided into four, so that the different compasses within each register can be represented. The brass is strengthened by the addition of the soft-toned tenor and bass tubas, the number of the horns being occasionally increased to eight. The most striking characteristic of the orchestration consists in the naturalistic vigour and modelling of tone. The colours of the various instruments are not mixed, but used to enhance the harmonic development. The orchestra of *The Nibelungs* is an orchestra of chordal masses. Certain groups are employed as suitable to represent natural sounds or other natural sense-impressions, such as the heavy brass for the crawling of the great serpent, the kettledrums, tuned in augmented fourths, for the entrance of the dragon Fafner, the divided strings for the tossings and swayings of the forest trees, high trills on the wood-wind and abrupt violin runs with trombone accompaniment for the ride of the Valkyries. Extraordinary demands are made on technique and expression in the interweaving of sharply defined interjections and in harmonic reproduction. In the strings this calls for unusually high positions and fluency in chord movements, in the wood-wind for exceptional singing tone and figuration, in the brass for swift changes of note both in long slurred phrases and in dynamic modulation. The instruments of the orchestra form a chorus of nature's voices. The peculiar tone of each is developed in accordance with its affinity to natural sounds, and the united orchestra mirrors the harmonic action both in treatment of line and in tonal character.

The diction employed in the libretto is suited to the tonal character of this harmony-impelled orchestration. Emphasising as it does the transition from non-conceptual to conceptual utterance by the lavish interspersal of onomatopœic syllables, and the non-intellectual aspect even of word-sequences by the use of alliteration, its lines tend to be brief, its thought disconnected, and its object emotional rather than logical appeal. Strict sentence sequences are lacking, as are the melody of the versification of *Lohengrin* and all incidental decoration dependent on the charms of language. The diction of *The Nibelungs* is noisy, jerky, abrupt, and strictly confined to essentials ; it is like a line of posts set up to mark the course of the harmony. Individual words even are lopped of their first or last syllables. Thought is compressed

s

to ensure that the purely phonetic aspect of speech shall have precedence. The melody is of a kind suited to such speech. Derived from and impelled by orchestral harmony, it seeks resolution in the spoken word. It stands, therefore, from the first in close relation to verbal rhythm, the movement of speech. It is designed to bridge the gaps left in the text by extreme verbal economy, and is in its turn dependent on the sustaining power of harmony to accomplish its task of interpretation. Melody in *The Ring* has, accordingly, no external stylistic unity. It is its function to mediate between the two spheres of the visible and scenic and the audible and emotional, and is therefore swayed as one or other predominates, inclining sometimes to one, sometimes to the other, and serving both alike only in moments of complete equilibrium.

The skill with which a balance is maintained between verbal-conceptual and melodic-lyrical treatment of melody increases through the three works of the first section of *The Nibelungs*. In *The Rhinegold*, allied in structural detail with *Lohengrin*, song-melodic syntheses and speech-rhythmic passages are still found side by side. There is a clear line of demarcation between the lyric and the epic. The song of the Rhine Maidens and that of Alberich, the Valhalla greeting and the song of Fricka, Loge's tale and the subsequent dialogue with Mime, Alberich's songs and dramatic dialogue, the final scene and the passages leading up to it, are treated as musical contrasts. Climaxes of melodic song rise like peaks from the dramatic passages, and the subject is dissected rather than unified. The opening act of *The Valkyrie* contains the first big melodic climax in an unbroken melodic development. From the thunderstorm of the beginning, through the first meeting and Siegmund's story up to the duet, the new form of melody persists, welling up from harmony and finding its fulfilment in the spoken word. It no longer forms a lyrical pause in the midst of dialogue ; the very intensity of the dramatic dialogue passes into the eloquence of melodious song. The two chief scenes of the second act once more set up the two as contrasts. On the one hand there is the forceful music of Wotan's story, begotten by the yearning of music towards speech, on the other the prophecy of death, the stammering utterance of an overflowing wealth of harmony. Each of these scenes is splendidly one-sided, and the contrast between them reveals the twofold nature of the problem of word-tone art.

The stylistic question as to whether speech or song should predominate in dramatic dialogue had been up to this point a burning one. It was not until Wagner had wrestled successfully with the complex of ideas represented in Wotan's narrative that he found a way of uniting the two. Beginning with the nature utterance of the Valkyries' song, his skill in handling word-tone increases throughout the third act of *The Valkyrie* up to the climax of the work, the lovers' parting. In the melodic development from the elemental and natural to the human there is a parallel with the first scene of *The Rhinegold*, though that was objective and this purely emotional. Melody sprung from the union of harmony and speech gives harmony the fulfilment of form and speech its emotional tonal equivalent. Declamation becomes a line of pure melodic song, giving expressive form to scenic gesture. Melody like this ceases to be a symmetrical musical structure ; it is blood and nerve in terms of musical vibrations. It is the direct expression of an emotional overflow, and derives its penetrating power from its organic connection with this physiological process. It is the fine flower of the speech-melodic art of *The Ring*; the goal of Wagner's strivings, as hinted at in Siegmund's love-song and promised in the prophecy of death. The process culminates in the final scene between Wotan and Brynhilda. There the grand melody of expression through speech-song is achieved. In it word and tone are united, and neither is sacrificed to the other. Emotional music, intellectually interpreted, is carried on the wide arch of the harmonic period, while the orchestra lends the singing voice inner confirmation of the inexpressible.

Wagner found this solution when he had reached the heart of his subject, the point at which the gathered forces of his nature-drama were ready to burst forth in " purely-human " passion. It was the moment when interpretation of musical processes in terms of nature-symbolism gave birth to a new form of expressionist art. All the elements of music were involved, and thus, despite the apparent thinness of the plot, the first two acts of *Siegfried* teem with a happy abundance of new musical images. Wagner succeeds, as he could hardly have done in the older form of opera, in building up two long acts from a mere three and five male voices without *ensemble* or chorus. Invention and imagination endow these two acts with a wealth of melodic forms, though no hard-and-fast distinction is made (as in *The Rhinegold*) between the lyric and the epic, and no operatic high lights are emphasised. In *Siegfried* song reaches no such great passionate climaxes as in *The Valkyrie*. Indeed, it no longer needs them. Melody as natural speech, speech as natural melody, are effortless. Each character, the Dwarf, the Dragon, Siegfried, Wotan, Alberich, the wood-bird, speaks in accents of spontaneous melody, which, free from all conventional restrictions, is in itself natural sound stamped with the individuality and precision of speech. The circle is complete. Harmony, actuated by motif and rounded into form by cadence, attains melodic physiognomy through words. Individual word-tone-melody emerges from the nature-world of tone. It is at one and the same time a final expression of that aspect of orchestral drama which is beyond the province of speech, and a bridge linking this drama to the visible scene.

The meaning of the scenic process is the same as that of the musical. Like word-tone-melody, the persons and events in the scene reflect a process of evolution from primitive nature to "purely-human" emotion. The first three pieces of the *Nibelung* cycle centre round no theatrical incident in the ordinary sense, have no dramatic fulcrum. In *The Rhinegold* the action ostensibly concerns the possession of the gold. Alberich steals it from the Rhine Maidens; Wotan, with Loge's help, ravishes it from the Nibelungs; Erda gives warning that it is a fatal possession, and for its sake Fafner slays his brother Fafolt. This ends the action which centres in the Ring itself. Henceforward it is merely a symbol, and even as such does not reappear until *Siegfried*. An outward link is maintained solely by Wotan's story in Act II of *The Valkyrie*, and, apart even from this interpolation, *The Valkyrie* has two dramatic motives—the love story of Siegmund and Sieglinda and the story of the dream-maid, Brynhilda. Connected with the tragedy of the Wälsungs only by the theme of Brynhilda's defiance, the latter story is theatrically a separate subject and dominates the third act as the former does the first. Three plots thus go to form *The Valkyrie*—that of the Wälsungs, that of Brynhilda, and, intellectually linking the two, a continuation of the drama of the Ring. This last is confined to indirect narrative and externally holds up the action. In the first two acts of *Siegfried* a new plot is introduced which is linked with its predecessors by the dramaturgical expedient of the Prophecy and is, moreover, without any central incident of its own. If *The Valkyrie* is overcharged with vigorous and various dramatic motives, *Siegfried* lacks them entirely. The forging of the Sword, Mime's conversation with the Wanderer, the slaying of the Dragon, Mime's punishment, follow each other naturally. The mere fact of these events is plot enough, and the story passes from incident to incident until the song of the wood-bird recalls memory of Brynhilda, forming a link with preceding works which for two whole acts have been forgotten.

This is neither opera nor drama, for both forms demand an organised system of events springing from a common root and moving to a common end. The Ring, which is the pledge of external cohesion, is a conceptual symbol without objective importance. Brynhilda, the principal character in the emotional drama, has no part in *The Rhinegold*, the first act of *The Valkyrie*, or the first two acts of *Siegfried*, and becomes a real personality only in the two central acts of the whole work. Wotan, who plays an important though not a principal part in *The Rhinegold*, dominates the scenes with Brynhilda and subsequently exercises a purely episodic influence as the Wanderer. Alberich, the most powerful dramatic figure in *The Rhinegold*, vanishes entirely, to reappear merely as the discoverer of Fafner's lair. Mime, a secondary figure in *The Rhinegold*, plays a superficially but not inherently important part in the first act of *Siegfried*. Fafner, eclipsed by Fafolt in *The Rhinegold*, belongs exclusively to Act II of *Siegfried*, and Loge, who is a motive power in *The Rhinegold*, has a purely symbolic part to play when he reappears in the Fire Magic scene. The rest of the gods, with the exception of Fricka, who is necessary in Act II of *The Valkyrie*, have merely walking-on parts in the *Rhinegold* world. The stories of Siegmund, Sieglinda, and Hunding are finished in two acts of *The Valkyrie*, and Siegfried, who with these and Brynhilda is not hinted at in *The Rhinegold*, is the last to appear, in the third work.

This constant change of characters and displacement of the focus of action even within a single work such as *The Valkyrie* shows that strict dramatic form is neither intended nor attempted. The external action is made up of a chain of linked events. The work must not be regarded as a dramatic whole, nor has any character in it such central significance as that of the Flying Dutchman or Lohengrin. Its meaning must be looked for in this continual change of characters, scenes and subject. The *Nibelung* drama does not seek to present a plot; its subject is *successiveness*, so that there can be no central dramatic incident. It deals with evolution, with " becoming," with the inward and upward trend of the life-force. This is the process that the nature of the music demands; it is the drama of harmony. The gradual emergence of word-tone-melody from harmony carries within it the plan, characters and incidents of the scenic drama. This process of emergence is conceived in terms of a myth whose dramatic symbolism is derived from naturalistic interpretations of musical evolution. Music itself is thought of as a growing harmonic organism and is embodied in theatre, in action. From these it borrows form, character, colour and style, lending them in turn the impulse of the law of continual becoming.

This drama of evolution is worked out on two planes—from primitive musical harmony to the nature-melody of word-tone-expression, and from primitive natural instinct to the awakening of human passion and, finally, to a conception of free, " purely-human " personality which crowns the work's close, even as the slavery of convention forms its starting-point. Between the two, child of the one and dreaming of the other, stands Woman—Brynhilda, daughter of Wotan and of the Wala, of desirous creative will and of Nature the Eternal Mother, from whose womb springs all life.

The preliminaries are fulfilled—plot and method, starting-point and goal, form and technique, stand revealed at last. The task is set and the charm works. Floor-cloth, wings and back-cloth become waters, mountains and caves ; an instrumental bass becomes the foundation of the world, the zigzag line of a piccolo a flicker of fire, the costumed singer " purely-human " Man, the stage Reality. All the relations of truth and illusion are logically transposed. Nature becomes art, art presents itself as nature, not relatively but absolutely. The kingdom of absolute illusion is established. Theatre plays Life, and Life becomes but a pretext for Theatre.

The Rhinegold

In these three works the subject used for purposes of " theatre " is the gradual rise and culmination of the dramatic impulses inherent in harmony. The Rhinegold shows the assonant world of Wotan assailed by the hostile forces of chromaticism (embodied in Loge) and of dissonance (embodied in the Nibelungs) ; The Valkyrie the evolution of emotional song-melody, which is Woman ; and Siegfried the melodic development of the masculine force of rhythm. Such are the elements of drama which, blended organically, determine the character of each separate work and the mounting curve of the whole.

The Rhinegold, which has four scenes, is set externally in an instrumental framework. The orchestral prelude depicts the depths of the Rhine ; the interludes, ascent from the Rhine to the mountain peaks, descent to Nibelheim, and re-ascent by the same road to the heights of Valhalla. These transformation scenes—upwards, downwards, and again upwards—are conveyed to the eye upon the stage by scenes confirming the instrumental imagery which, on its functional side, represents a display of chordal verticality. The from-high-to-low movement of *Lohengrin*, here multiplied by sharper gradation and translated into terms of objective reality, is once more re-enacted. The harmonic uniformity of the prelude, enlivened only by an increasingly intricate interweaving of parts, serves merely to introduce the scene which follows. This prelude is built up exclusively on a primal motif of natural motion and shows the harmonic germ-cell of the whole work in the guise of a purely tonal phenomenon. A Romantic wave-and-water picture such as Mendelssohn paints symphonically in his overtures to *The Hebrides* and *Melusine*, and Weber vocally in the Mermaid episode, is here rendered in theatrical fresco. From this instrumental tone-picture emerges the song of the Rhine Maidens. As the glint of the gold appears, separate chordal motifs unite in a three-part song which is fresh and natural in melody and elemental in orchestral accompaniment. This song is central to the scene which, in the voices of the passionless children of Nature, represents the evolution of the pure triad. The introduction of the hostile voice of Alberich develops the scene on the lines of dialogue. Wooing, questioning, and threatening, Alberich's bass ceases presently to form a quartet with the trio of female voices ; it interrupts and finally breaks up the song into its separate parts, thus providing the stimulus of dramatic contrast. In a musical sense also Alberich's confused, deep chaotic notes and hard, distorted rhythms contrast with the pure harmonies and easy, flowing melodic sequence assigned to the women's voices. Alberich has no individuality, but he is introduced with that instinct for design which governs the whole scene. None of the figures stand out in the round, full plastic physiognomy being reserved for those motives of drama which they convey—the life of nature in an ascending chordal line, the glittering Gold in a C major flourish of trumpets, the renunciation of love in C minor with a B major half close. These three principal motifs are grouped, upon simple harmonies, in the song—a kind of roundelay—which the Rhine Maidens sing as they dance about the treasure :

> " Rheingold ! Rheingold !
> leuchtende Lust, wie lachst Du so hell und hehr ! "

> (" Rhinegold ! Rhinegold !
> Dazzling delight, thou laughest so bright and brave ! ")

A bridge passage of reminiscent echoes accompanies a change of scene from the waters to the clouds. The descending thirds of the Ring magic and the breaking-up of harmonic elements into melodic sequence give rise to a new and vigorous plastic concept—that of the stronghold Valhalla. Proclaimed by the brass in stately chords and majestic rhythm, it initiates and dominates the new scene musically, just as a representation of the stronghold itself dominates the stage. It stands for something complete and established both in music and scene, for those heights of perfected harmony lifted above the course of the musical-dramatic development to which, as it is unfolded, the drama must gradually ascend.

The opening dialogue between Wotan and Fricka changes by degrees from recitative to *arioso*. The entrance upon the scene in pursuit of Freia of the giants Froh and Donner and, finally, of Loge, and of their motifs into the music, brings life and movement as the work hurries on to a climax such as that provided by the trio of women's voices in the first scene. It is reached here in Loge's song of " Weibes Wonne und Wert " (" Woman's wondrous delight "). This is the centre of the scene and the first great narrative passage written by Wagner since the Grail story in *Lohengrin*. In plan and diction, in vocal lyricism, strophic form and insistence upon songful delivery, it greatly resembles its predecessor. It differs from it in the interweaving of certain very vital verbal and musical ideas borrowed from the previous action, in its less direct connection with the character into whose mouth it is put, his description being wholly objective, and in its complete subordination to the course of the drama. It serves as a first melodic rallying-point in the drama, which thence proceeds with increased impetus. The story is developed in swift dialogue—the giants' new demand, Wotan's fury, the abduction of Freia. Loge's scherzando song, " Über Stock und Stein zu Tal stampfen sie hin " (" Over stock and stone they stride down to the vale "), occasions another brief pause, after which the mists slowly close in. The gods grow suddenly old and, as in the scene beneath the Rhine, darkness envelops the stage. It clears to reveal the yawning depths of earth.

Scenic design now finds symbolic interpretation in music. Loge's chromaticism burrows into heavy descending chordal masses, a minor flourish proclaims the Gold motif, a hammering smithy rhythm passes from the orchestra to an actual anvil on the stage and back again to the orchestra. The harmony is violently cleft asunder. Beginning with sharply dissonant suspensions, a line mounts upwards from the bass and the gold's new kingdom stands revealed. The scene proceeds in abrupt and telling dialogue. Alberich and Mime quarrel over the Helmet of Invisibility to the accompaniment of the illusory harmonies of modulated interrupted cadences for the muted horns. The cry " Nibelung all', neigt euch nun Alberich " (" Nibelungs all, kneel ye to Alberich ! ") celebrates Alberich's triumph. It is vigorously realistic. In Mime's " Sorglose Schmiede, schufen wir sonst wohl Schmuck unsren Weibern " (" Free and unfettered, forged we once work to grace our own women "), there is a reversion from simple song-form to the atmosphere of the opening, and with Alberich's reappearance an emphatic close is reached.

Rhythmically organised dissonance portrays the realm of the Nibelungs as exactly as do harmonic waves the Rhine's depths and broad harmonies the mountain heights of Valhalla. Alberich's " Die in linder Lüfte Weh'n da oben ihr lebt, lacht und liebt " (" Ye who, lapped in softest zephyrs, there aloft live, laugh and love ")—a proclamation of the power of the gold and the victory of lovelessness —is the centre of the Nibelung scene, as is Loge's " Weibes Wonne und Wert " of the Valhalla scene. With but fleeting approximations to *arioso* style, this narrative passage is the first perfect example of a style of delivery differing equally from melodic song and recitative. While the accompanying orchestra dilates upon the theme, its purely accentual expressionist elements are condensed in lyric form. Dialogue now takes the place of speech supported by motif, and Loge's questions lead up to the revelation of the secret of the Helmet of Invisibility, the metamorphoses of the serpent and the toad, and the arrest. This is dramatically the most intense, and pictorially the most vivid, scene in *The Rhinegold*. More elaborate in subject and treatment than the first scene of the theft of the gold, it evokes daemonic powers and shows, in the musical as in the visual drama, the first onset of stronger passions. The orchestral interlude which follows this scene recapitulates its development in reverse order, working back through the motifs of the gold-smithy, the giants, Valhalla, Loge's ambitions, Freia's golden apples, and the song of the Rhine Maidens. Music, independent now of scene, speaks again in melody. For the second time the curtain rises on the mountain of the gods, with Valhalla invisible and wrapped in cloud. A few short sentences release Alberich from his bonds. The struggle centres in the Ring, which Wotan wrests from its fettered possessor, while the Lord of the Abyss, who has been carried by force up to the heights, calls down his curse upon the creatures of the light.

Musically, Alberich's curse—the passion of greed—represents the far-reaching effects of diminished and augmented intervals as harmony-destroying agents. It finds vocal expression in rhetorical pathos on the operatic model of the Cardinal's curse in Halévy's *Jewess*. The destructive power of dissonance, having found its way into the world of light, firmly establishes itself in chromatic distortions of chordal formations and thence begins its disintegrating work.

This completes the *action* of the Prelude. What follows is mere visual demonstration—the hurried arrival of gods and giants, the covering of Freia's form beneath a mound of gold. One last climax interrupts the even course of events when Fafner vainly demands the Ring from Wotan. The power of dissonance, of the curse, invades even the assonant world of the gods. Erda, the Earth-Mother, represented by the opening nature-motif transposed to C sharp minor, rises from the Abyss of Eternal Becoming to warn the creator god against the passion which must inevitably break up the Eternal, the Peaceful, and bring it to an end. If Wotan would keep his divinity he must not desire. Wotan thereupon casts the Ring to the giants, and Fafner falls, first victim of the curse. Dissonance is hurled down to the depths, and only the mind of Wotan sees it working on towards some far-off goal. From surging orchestral passages, shot through with Donner's fanfare-like evocation of the storm, emerges a new nature picture as the harmonies lift and clear. The rainbow's melodic arch appears and the clouds roll away from Valhalla. From far beneath rises the wail of the cheated Rhine Maidens, their once joyous song changed to a bitter cry, while Loge offers mocking consolation. High above in the heavens the gods march into Valhalla, with whose grave harmonies is now interwoven a new chordal motif for the trumpets—the motif of Wotan's " mighty thought " that greets and names the stronghold, the motif of resistance to the destructive forces of dissonance, the C major motif of the Sword which is destined to sweep away the old law and establish the new.

" Believe me, nothing like this has ever been composed before," wrote Wagner to Liszt when the sketches for *The Rhinegold* were complete. " I feel that my music is terrible—a maelstrom of horrors and heights." The words in their strict application are true, for " horrors and heights " in the expressionist sense intended by Wagner are the chief characteristics of the *Rhinegold* music. It is a world seen from without in alternate light and shade. Emotional appeal, present in all Wagner's work hitherto, is absent here. For the first time he deliberately applies the principle of expressionist formation in presenting a scenico-musical drama. The characters in this drama are seen objectively, as from a distance. The score plainly reveals the delight with which its composer grappled with a task of the first magnitude after a five years' interval. He quite forgets himself in his enthusiasm over the new interests it presents. The music of *The Rhinegold* is a work of decorative scenic art, not only in the grand orchestral nature pictures which enclose the whole in a multi-coloured frame, but in the musical climaxes within each scene, such as the songs of the Rhine Maidens which cast a gracious melodic wreath about the whole drama, Loge's story, the evil vitality of Mime and Alberich, and the twilit tones of the Erda scene. Never before had Wagner approached his subject so entirely objectively. With a wealth of invention in little things as in great, with much variety in colour, with a vast number of tonal and melodic ideas, Wagner constructs and assembles within narrow compass the foundations and materials for all that is to follow. Direct though the work is, it yet has the budding tenderness, the secret charm of something not yet wholly revealed. It is full, too, of the artist's technical pleasure in handling voices, orchestration, and individual instrumental parts with a skill never attained before. The music, taken as a whole, seems no more than an outline, yet just such an outline was required before the composer could proceed from the general to the particular, and, in a higher sense, expansive aspects of musical expression. As long as Wagner was absorbed in the *Rhinegold* composition he felt, and rightly, that it was something unprecedented in its kind, for by means of it he mastered the subject, style, material and form of the whole work. As, however, he emerged from this anteroom into a world of living persons and passions, he became acutely sensible of the difference between the introductory Prelude and the work that now lay before him. "*The Valkyrie* is begun," he wrote to Liszt on July 8, 1854, " and now at last I am really getting at the work ! "

The Valkyrie

The Rhinegold is concerned with objective representation. Its most important passages are descriptive or narrative, and find dramaturgical justification in the framework of dialectic in which they are set. The characters are necessarily numerous, for Wagner's object is to reach the kernel of the musical scene from as many view-points as possible. In *The Valkyrie*, on the other hand, dialectical development ceases to be an object, and therefore the drama requires fewer agents. Its dramaturgical basis is the duologue, events being set in motion by the intrusion upon this duologue of some third person. In the first act a duologue between Siegmund and Sieglinda is developed dramatically from a state of retarded exposition by the entrance of the hostile Hunding. In the second act Fricka takes Hunding's place as motive agent, and Wotan's scene with Brynhilda (outwardly a monologue but really an exchange of thoughts and feelings between the two) is introduced by a duologue scene with Fricka. The incident of the Death Prophecy, the second most important scene in the piece, is developed strophically between Brynhilda and Siegmund. The third act again is enacted between Wotan and Brynhilda, and is introduced by the Valkyries' *ensemble*.

There are thus three acts, each based on a duologue-duet, through which the drama and its characters are developed. The most complete unity of impulse is seen in the first act—that between Siegmund and Sieglinda. The third—between Wotan and Brynhilda—though planned on the same grand scale, is more involved in argument, and though for this reason it does not maintain such a simple upward sweep as the first act, it has great scenic-dynamic breadth. The second act links the two worlds of the first and the third and has no unity in itself. Wotan's monologue, though organically indispensable to the cycle as a whole, is a difficult piece to fit in. The Death Prophecy scene, in itself one of Wagner's most sublime conceptions, cannot carry the rest, and the unity attained is artificial, not organic. Too much is packed into the act, and musical unity is sacrificed to particular effects. Yet here, too, duologue forms the basis, and the beginning, middle, and end of the act are gathered up in the conflict between Wotan and Brynhilda, the other characters being ranged in the order of their approach to these two. In and through the duet formation of all three acts there persists a scenico-musical idea of *storm*. In the first act it is resolved in the magic of a spring night, in the second it darkens daylight with thunder, in the third it clears slowly to the solemn fires of sunset. This scenic nature-symbolism determines the course and dynamics of the music.

The most powerful embodiment of this movement occurs in Act I, which shows the composer's first eager plunge into the sphere of passion. As a piece of theatrical art it is one of Wagner's grandest achievements. He had done nothing like it before save in the first act of *Lohengrin*. The opening storm picture in the Prelude, reminiscent in its imagery of unison sextolets and rolling bass figures of Schubert's *Erlkönig*, proclaims at once a wide difference from *The Rhinegold*. Donner's thunderstorm motif, which formed the decorative opening of the *Rhinegold* finale, reappears with its chordal character changed to diminished sevenths and syncopated rhythms, lifting it from the primitive world of the Prelude to the sphere of passion. The first meeting between Siegmund and Sieglinda is a test of the virtue of orchestral expression as a mediator of unexpressed emotions, lingering glances, hesitating gestures, half-revealed and half-concealed. The first suggestion that the pair are growing dimly aware that their fates are linked is given by the orchestra, after which Hunding's questions lead up to Siegmund's great narrative. As in the introductory duologue with Sieglinda, an entirely new level is reached in the treatment of musical delivery. There is nothing of the lyric melody of Loge's story. There is more clearly-ordered periodicity in the musical strophic form, though there is no suggestion of *arioso*, and words have a free melodic and rhythmic flow, accent and emphasis have their natural place in the declamatory line and coincide organically with the musical structure. The orchestra is handled with notable restraint. Light harmonic and rhythmic points of support, interspersed with lightning sketches, form the accompaniment, which attains prominence only in moments of pause, as when the Valhalla theme enters upon the news of Wälse's death, when the tender melody of the opening scene accompanies Sieglinda's sympathetic glances, and when the Wälsung theme in the form of a dead-march in C minor brings a close.

Hunding's challenge to Siegmund forms a bridge-passage to the second orchestral interlude. This interlude begins in the mood of the end of Siegmund's narrative and leads up to Wotan's dream of victory, the promise of the Sword. Even as late as *Lohengrin*, Wagner would have given these lyrical echoes to a chorus. Now his system of instrumental motival expression assigns them to the orchestra, which acts as emotional interpreter between the characters in the drama. Memory and anticipation, which link events in temporal sequence, come at last to their own as formative elements—memory, for example, when Siegmund's cry " Ein Schwert verhiess mir der Vater " ("A sword my father did pledge me ") rings out to the accompaniment of Wotan's Valhalla greeting, and anticipation when, after the inflammatory " Wälse, Wälse, wo ist dein Schwert ? " (" Wälse, Wälse ! where is thy sword ? "), Wotan's " mighty thought " is proclaimed by the trumpets in C major. *The Valkyrie*, drama of passion, is thus linked to the Prelude by the agency of memory and anticipation. The theme of Wotan's " mighty thought," having forced an entrance, takes the lead in building up the third act—a duologue between Wotan's children.

Sieglinda's story of the Wanderer who smote the Sword into the tree, Siegmund's love-song, the winning of the Sword, the mutual recognition of brother and sister, make up the greatest duo-scene in Wagner's work hitherto. It does not move steadily to its climax, for the Spring song in its midst forms a lyrical interlude between the promise of the Sword and its attainment. The Love-song itself, which is almost Mendelssohnian in its tender curves, passes into the modula-tory Love-glance motif with which the act opens. Together the two continue into wide melodic arches, expanded into sequential progres-sions, until the Sword motif imposes a stricter rhythm upon the lyrical flow and it is established upon Valhalla harmonies and Wälsung chords. Development towards the C major is continuous. The C minor renunciation of love becomes an adjuration of love and surges stormily to a modulatory climax, whence issues the C major motif of the Sword, proclaimed in the victorious tones of the trumpets. Love-melody and Sword-harmony embrace one another, and Wotan's " mighty thought " becomes a mighty deed.

The unity between matter and form is perfect ; there is complete absorption of the subject in the medium. As a method of uniting music and scene the motival personages which embody the essential trend of the harmony reveal an unsuspected superiority over the merely objective motival characterisation of *The Rhinegold*. The use of the orchestra as choral accompanist and interpreter not only makes it possible to do without the singers' chorus usual in opera but actually surpasses it in the tenderness and persuasiveness with which it suggests emotion. Drama and music develop from a common point of departure with the inevitability of a natural process, and absolute coincidence between musical nature-symbolism and passion seems to have been attained. Here and there, unquestionably, there is an approximation to operatic style. The most important passage, the song of Siegmund and Sieglinda, is not far from the operatic duet in its bold plan and architecture, though an actual vocal duet is avoided. Both the melody and phraseology of Siegmund's love-song point clearly to the older form of song-melody. Artistically these things are of subordinate importance. They merely affirm the primacy of the theatrical impulse which, casting theory aside, permits neither composer nor audience to notice isolated divergences from the main stylistic trend.

No such theatrical impulse is present in the first half of the act which follows, though it reappears with the entrance of the fugitive Wälsungs, and, if the first and second scenes were omitted, the act would continue without a break from the end of the preceding act and would (like it and the third act) consist of three scenes—Siegmund and Sieglinda, Siegmund and Brynhilda, the combat and flight. Wagner actually outlines such a plan in the orchestral prelude, which begins with the motival formation which closes the first act, takes up the love-scene theme with great energy and carries it over into the new motif of the Valkyries' Ride, which forms the basis of the scene to come. The treatment here is terse and vigorous. Wotan summons Brynhilda to battle and is answered by her jubilant " Hojotoh ! " Her entrance is followed by that of Fricka, the enemy, and thus is initiated a development which, in obedience to the idea and plan of the cycle as a whole, leads down from the heights of great theatrical art to the plains of scenic and æsthetic dogma. " I am in the second act of *The Valkyrie*," Wagner wrote to Liszt in October 1854, " Wotan and Fricka—you will see I *must* succeed with that ! " Personal experiences, which, instead of lifting him to heaven, had dragged him down to earth, clamoured for expression in this picture of souls enslaved to convention, unfree. The two who talk and haggle with one another in this scene are portrayed without love or sympathy. Wagner summons up the rhetoric of " word-tone art " and, particularly in Fricka's speeches, develops it to artificial pathos. There is an *arioso* summing-up in the cry " O, was klag' ich um Ehe und Eid " (" O why weep I for wedlock and troth ? "), in the bitter accent of the phrase " Der Dir als Herren hörig und eigen, gehorchen soll ihm dein ewig Gemahl ? " (" He who before thee bends as his master, shall he command thy eternal spouse ? "), and the solemn closing song " Deiner ew'gen Gattin heilige Ehre beschirme heut ihr Schild " (" Thy eternal consort's holiest honour let her defend to-day ! "). Wotan's simple motival replies briefly interrupt the stream of eloquence and increase in vigour until Brynhilda's intervention and aid bring the discussion to an end.

This scene (considerably longer in the first draft of the libretto) not only gives Fricka undue importance but reveals a streak of weakness and dependence in Wotan. In reality it is because Fricka expresses Wotan's own thoughts that he is obliged to sacrifice Siegmund to her; yet the form in which the scene is cast makes his decision seem to be an act of irresolute submission. This contradiction between the inner logic of the drama and its expression in dialogue is an organic weakness in this scene and obliges Wagner to explain its meaning in another scene. Wotan's long and slowly-built-up narrative gives a comprehensive survey of the conceptual scaffolding of the whole drama, but it cannot obliterate the impression of weakness conveyed by the Fricka scene. Wagner himself pondered long over this interpolation. " In sober hours of discouragement my chief anxiety was for Wotan's big scene, and particularly for his revelation of Brynhilda's fate. Indeed, in London I was on the point of dropping the scene altogether. Before finally deciding I took up the sketch again and performed it myself with all due expression. I then happily discovered that my spleen was unjustified and that proper performance made it entirely musical and arresting."

Wagner's decision to retain the scene as of " prime importance in the development of the whole great four-part drama " was undoubtedly right—not, however, because performance proved it to be " musical and arresting," but because the story as a whole is only vitalised by music. As a composer Wagner expresses intensely something which he fails to express as a scenic artist, and that is why performance convinced him where reflection had evoked justifiable misgivings. The monologue lives not by its contents but by the passionate fount of music which bears it up. Starting from a deep fundamental bass, the harmonies slowly build up a picture of the universe. All events, represented by their motifs, are passed in review, but none can be developed, for the dissonance of the Curse motif clouds their harmonic purity. The Sword motif appears, daemonically distorted, and the Valhalla theme, transposed to the minor, assumes the rhythm of a dead-march. Valhalla must fall, Siegfried must die—" Nur eines will ich noch, das Ende " (" But one thing now I wish : the ending ").

There is a curious link between the emotions underlying the dark and splendid passion of this scene and those of an earlier work of Wagner's, the scene of the Flying Dutchman's entrance. In both the fundamental appeal is the same, for Wotan's longing for " the Ending " and the Dutchman's cry " Ew'ge Vernichtung, nimm mich auf ! " (" Endless destruction on me fall ") have but one origin—unsatisfied passion, the curse of lovelessness, which is the fate of both. The interest and significance of Wotan's monologue consist in its revelation of this emotion. In the *Flying Dutchman* scene, its first stirrings hint merely at something which is transparently revealed at this turning-point in Wagner's career as artist. *There* it could only find expression in the hard-and-fast form of the operatic scene ; *here* it is embodied in a piece of motival architecture which is expressive to the last detail. But, beyond all differences due to different stages in Wagner's human and artistic development, the creative impulse is the same in both—a cry for love, a sense of the loneliness of the masculine nature. This, setting intellectual arguments aside, constitutes the importance of the Wotan monologue to the drama as a whole, for that drama is a love story.

This interlude, thrust violently into the action for the sake of the continuation of the cycle, is followed by an instrumental prelude which re-establishes connection with the first act. Siegmund and Sieglinda reappear in a brief and most dramatic scene. During the interlude Sieglinda's intuition has sensed the turn of events, and she has become clairvoyantly aware that her love is doomed. Reminiscences of the duet are interrupted by Hunding's horn, the baying of his hounds, the sound of the breaking sword. The treatment is the very reverse of

T

that of the passionate love-scene. Form, there welded by melody, is here broken up by motif, and the abrupt accents of speech replace the fluency of song. A premonition of death envelops the lovers, slowly taking hold upon Siegmund, to whom it was unknown before. It takes shape for him in the Valkyrie, Wotan's third daughter, who now comes to her slumbering sister's side and reveals herself in Sieglinda's own love-strains :

> " Was im Busen ich barg, was ich bin,
> hell wie der Tag taucht' es mir auf."

> (" What hid in my heart, what I am,
> Clear as the day dawned on my sight.")

The urgent sequences of the love melody form a solemn prelude to the duologue between Brynhilda and Siegmund. Desire gives place to sublime peace, issuing in an ascending chord-figure in the minor which rises to a dominant half-close. Valhalla harmonies bring the full close. The new scene is based on a threefold revelation in melody —Love, Death, and Transfiguration. Unlike its predecessors, it is cast in the form of antiphonal strophes and reaches its climax by the development of variations on the main theme. The action consists of the message to Siegmund, his summons to Valhalla, his protest and eventual acceptance and bewailing of his fate, the birth of love in Brynhilda, Siegmund's resolve to die, and the Valkyrie's promise of victory. In the music a simple array of motifs finds expressive resolution in melodic, rhythmic and harmonic variations. Through an ever-increasing skill in the handling of variations, individual emotional freedom is imparted to the musical germ, and thus a primarily lyrical musical emotion is conveyed in terms of scenic action, just as in the first act dramatic events are clothed in musical lyricism.

Wagner, by a new route, has again reached the summit of his work, and what follows is swift development of the external action. The storm of the first prelude gathers again, and the rolling thunderstorm motif in the bass carries us back to the beginning before Siegmund came to Hunding's hall. Sieglinda dreams of days long past, of her mother, and of the warriors who burned her home and carried her away. In sleep she is a child again and calls for her brother. Waked by the thunder, she hears in the distance the voice of him whom for the second time she has lost. Hunding sounds his horn, the Valkyrie cries Victory, the Sword breaks upon Wotan's spear, and the Wälsung theme sinks to the minor. Brynhilda catches up the prostrate woman, whilst, amidst the shattering thunderclaps of the Valhalla harmonies, Wotan pursues the fugitives.

The action continues unbroken from the second act to the third, which opens with a magnificent nature picture—the cloud ride of the Valkyries. Chronologically, the theme is one of the earliest in the cycle, having been composed for a Valkyrie *chorus* in *Siegfried's Death*. Wagner wrote theme and words for this chorus in an album before he began to compose *The Rhinegold*. The words being now omitted, there remains only the main motif of galloping horse-hoofs, which is taken up alternately by horns, trumpets, and trombones with treble trills for the wood-wind and accompanying chords for the strings. Here again the orchestra takes the place of a chorus. The perfect naturalism of the music renders words superfluous, and they occur only in the shouts and chromatic laughter of the riders, enhancing the musical and scenic pictures with tone-colouristic effects. Short intervals of dialogue serve simply to give fresh impetus to the musico-scenic picture of racing clouds which culminates in the " Hojotoho ! " of the eight Valkyries.

When Brynhilda herself appears, a new motif, the motif of Wotan's wild pursuit, emerges from the bass. No pause in the fury of the storm accompanies Brynhilda's entrance with Sieglinda until she pleads for Sieglinda's life. When Sieglinda would refuse the boon, Brynhilda speaks of a new hope, the hope of Siegfried. In the sublime melody which follows, " O hehrestes Wunder, herrlichste Maid " (" O highest of wonders ! noblest of maids ! "), the inner meaning of all things is revealed as the triumph of love over persecution and suffering, and there is a dawning hope of the saving love for which Wotan looks, of the "purely-human" melody of absolute, unimpeded outlet for the emotions. Sieglinda then takes leave of Brynhilda, who remains alone to face the oncoming storm.

Wotan's voice is heard from afar, and presently he enters. The natural background remains unchanged throughout Wotan's words to the Valkyries, Brynhilda's simple " Hier bin ich, Vater : gebiete die Strafe " (" Here am I, father : pronounce my sentence ! "), her sentence of banishment, and the flight of the other Valkyries. The

scene ends as it began.   The storm dies with the dying echoes of the
Valkyries' steeds, and silence falls upon the scene.   Only its two
greatest figures, the Will to Law, which is the power of harmony, and
Love, which is nascent melody, are seen facing one another, once
united, now resolved to part.

It is the third great love-scene of the drama, following the duet of
desire and fulfilment in the first act, and the Death Message in the
second which sees sympathy ripen to active love.   Here desire and
action are both transcended, for the parting is accepted in the light of
love's wisdom.   The scene shows the growth of this wisdom in the
heart of man.   Wotan comes as an avenger, but when he leaves
Brynhilda he has found wisdom through love.   The child of his
dreams reveals to him a future which is not for him but for one coming
after him.   Brynhilda's punishment becomes her reward—the safe-
keeping of that Free One whose advent she divines.   Yet as he
gives this reward Wotan knows that Brynhilda's banishment is his
own punishment, for he, the love-seeker, casts out love from his
presence.

The emotional content of this scene is grander and more original
than that of any of the others, and its musico-scenic embodiment is,
appropriately, more complex.   It has a greater task than the portrayal
of the development of any single emotion, and the climax has to be
gradually approached from many aspects.   Three distinct stages may
be noted—Wotan's decree of parting, Brynhilda's warning to the
Wälsungs, and the revelation to Wotan of the new hope of love to
blossom from his race.   The musical structure corresponds with the
conceptions thus outlined.   The whole scene bears the aspect of a
gradual synthesis, embracing the duologue of the first stage, the sharp
motival individualisation of the second stage, and the comprehensive
Farewell melody of the last stage.   Perfect resolution is found not in
song but in orchestral harmony.   The line of development passes
from music bearing the impress of words to pure music, from thought
to emotion, from persons to scenic nature-symbols, from a dramatic
to a wholly musical appeal.   The curve of the drama as a whole represents a passage from the conscious to the unconscious.   The miracle
of Love, of Woman, of Melody, is ultimately revealed, and exalted
far above the intellectual, the dialectical.   Released from intellectual
fetters, the male voice expresses itself in broad phrases, becoming
naught but pure music supported by deep, rich harmonies.

Wotan alone gives expression to this full tide of emotion, for to him the miracle of love has been revealed. Brynhilda is silent : her melody, an inexhaustible well-spring of emotion, is heard once again from the orchestra. Chromatic chords in increasingly close position firmly round off the harmony. The song of parting, a farewell to love, echoes softly on in the orchestral bass as a kind of choral song, forming a wordless emotional epilogue to the drama. It is followed by a vision of the sleeping woman, in which Loge's flame motif flares up and the ring of fire closes about her :

" Wer meines Speeres Spitze fürchtet,
    durchschreite das Feuer nie ! "

(" He who my spear-point's sharpness feareth
    Ne'er breaks through this fierce-flaming fire ! ")

Flickering flame harmonies, accompanied by chords suggestive of the measured approach of the Fearless One to come, pass again into the Farewell, illuminated now by the mighty melody of love. The day with all its storms is over, and sunset sheds its glow over the world.

Siegfried

The Valkyrie is the saga of woman's love, of the power which acts and fulfils. It deals with the theme of The Flying Dutchman approached from the new standpoint of the regeneration of man by the love of woman. Both inwardly and outwardly Siegfried is the antithesis of The Valkyrie. It is dramatically its continuation and artistically its organic complement, for it is the saga of man, of the evolution of the procreative, creative force.

This fundamental difference implies important differences both in dramatic and in musical structure. Siegfried is a masculine drama. The only active agents—Mime, the Wanderer, Siegfried, Alberich and Fafner—are all male. Even the wood-bird's part is written for a boy's voice, so that the feminine timbre as such does not influence the piece. Contrast between the male and female voice, which dominates the principal scenes of The Valkyrie, is therefore wholly absent here, and its place is taken by contrast between various types of the male voice— the falsetto-like tenor of Mime with its jerky appoggiaturas and broken vocal line, the fresh strong natural tenor of Siegfried, the grave sustained baritone of the Wanderer, Alberich's harsh bass, and Fafner's animal roar.   Even apart from the important musical effect of these novel tone contrasts, the vocal characters represented in themselves demand a change of method.   The feminine voice tends to sustained melody in which the pure emotion natural to it can find expression.   It exercises a melodious, *cantando* influence on all that comes within its compass, so that the great duets of *The Valkyrie* culminate in a display of the melodic qualities of the male voice also.   A vocal drama representing the evocation of pure song from masculine vocal timbre finds its climax in the songfulness of Wotan's Farewell.   The male voice alone, deprived of the contrasting timbre of the female voice, develops on quite different lines.   It tends not to the melodious curves of emotional song but to energy, to precision, to dynamic and rhythmic expression.   On this basis Wagner lays down his male vocal types. In juxtaposition to the female voice they borrow, according to their degree of susceptibility, its melodious emotional tones, but alone they observe their own proper limitations.   Wagner regards these voices, also, as elemental forces, displaying in their development the law of their being.

An exclusively male-voice drama is possible only when it has some great melodic force for a foundation.   The eternal feminine, the vehicle of vocal sensuousness, may for a time withdraw into the background, leaving the stage to those of vocal strength and character, but it must remain amongst them unseen, it must be the ground and origin of the male vocal characters if they are to be anything more than hard-and-fast natural facts and are to become musical individuals.   In *The Valkyrie* the climax of the music-drama is the birth of sublime song-melody from the womb of harmony.   Its ultimate fruits are Love, Woman, singing melody, and these establish an inalienable basis for the drama yet to come.   They do not cease to be active and effective if for a time they cease to be visible.   Love—Woman—is not dead but sleeping, and in sleep is still the unconscious goal of the masculine development which begins in *Siegfried*.   With Brynhilda, feminine vocal melody sinks from the conscious to the unconscious, from speech to pure tone, from voice to orchestra.   Thus the orchestra itself now represents that feminine contrast which stimulates and answers the masculine voice.   While the latter seeks to express strength and character, the orchestra acts as its melody-evoking counterpart, inciting the male voice too to tuneful developments.   Sensuous melody, passing from voice to orchestra, is the basis of a drama which, musically speaking, is one of pure dynamic force.

The transference of the song-melodic impulse to the orchestra involves a change of method in the interweaving of vocal and instrumental parts and a corresponding change in the handling of motival development. *The Valkyrie* orchestra stands in the relation of explanatory chorus to the drama presented on the stage, and therefore the motifs for the most part retain their lyric form. They are transposed as occasion requires from major to minor, like the Gold and the Sword motifs, or they are altered in rhythm and harmony, like the Valhalla motif when it expresses the wrath of Wotan. They may undergo melodic change, as when the Love-glance motif, losing the tense exaltation it has in the first act, becomes the Flight theme in the second, or as when Brynhilda's love melody emerges from the question (assigned to the voice alone) " War es so schmählich, was ich verbrach ? " (" Was it so shameful, what I have done ? ") to find an E major apotheosis. In the orchestra these motival formations are merely explanatory, and the singing voices alone govern their form and structure. But with the growing importance of the orchestra as a source of expressionist song-melody it develops on lines of its own. The motifs become for the most part less complex in form, nor do they undergo the simple tone-symbolic changes which characterise them in *The Valkyrie*. They cease to act as mere interpreters of the trend of harmony and become individuals, carrying on almost uninterruptedly a motival drama parallel to the scenic drama. The range of emotions thus paralleled grows in extent and depth, and the emotional life of each person in the drama is analysed into numerous impulses, all plastically rendered. Wagner ceases to introduce those passages of dialogue with a purely chordal accompaniment which are so numerous in *The Valkyrie*. Orchestral commentary is continuous, and the singing voices are organically subordinate to it, pointing and interpreting it by means of words. The power of emotion to form words tends more and more to take precedence of the power of words to form music. This transference of the emotional fulcrum from singers to orchestra corresponds with an evolutionary impulse no longer groping its way towards melodious song but building upon it as upon something already achieved. On this foundation a primarily rhythmic and dynamic musico-scenic drama is enacted with the help of vocal expressionist media representing various types of character.

The external features of this rhythmic dynamic superstructure plainly denote its nature. Both acts advance from a deep pianissimo bass to a full orchestral fortissimo, from slow tempo to swiftly moulded rhythms, from dim indeterminate harmonies to a clear D and E major. Nascent energy—the motive impulse of the whole drama—is expressed in each detail of the music. *The Valkyrie* is the story of melody, *Siegfried* that of dynamically developing rhythm. The growth of the power of rhythm is the primal law of the *Siegfried* music, and the dark world of the dwarfs and of Mime in the first act, the dark power of nature embodied in Fafner in the second, are the contrasts which evoke it.

The prelude carries us at once into Mime's world with a drum roll. One by one the Nibelung motifs reappear—the song of the Rhinegold in distorted guise, the Sword motif, the Smithy theme, here rhythmically intensified upon the striding bass of the Hoard motif: "Zwangvolle Plage! Müh' ohne Zweck!" ("Woefullest bondage! Vain all my work!"). Then begins the first song-series of what is really song-opera on a monumental scale. The series opens with Mime's "Als zullendes Kind" ("A whimpering babe"), includes Siegfried's "Es sangen die Vöglein so selig im Lenz" ("The birds in springtime for happiness sang"), and closes with "Aus dem Wald fort in die Welt ziehn" ("From the wood forth in the world fare"). It is the first plastic synthesis in bold and vigorous rhythms of Siegfried's power. The development of the song-series is primarily rhythmic, in accordance with the rhythmic basis of the motifs. Externally these are the motifs of the preceding works, but their use here is conditioned by the new rhythmic impulse. The Smithy motif is the thread on which the series is strung, while Siegfried's horn and hammer themes provide the motive impulse. By them the Nibelung and Wälsung motifs as a body are expanded until, issuing in Siegfried's wood song, they are seen as a scherzo on a grand scale with Sieglinda's story as a lyrical trio-intermezzo.

In this strict rhythmic motival development the singing voices easily and naturally accept a subordinate place. They themselves are given independence and are neither declamatory nor recitative. They leave tune to the orchestra, emphasising everything of accentual importance. Wagner has at last fully realised the duet-relationship between voice and orchestra of which he dreamed. He has triumphed over the singer's egotism and restricted the voice to its word-tone function, leaving the orchestra free to develop on lines proper to it. At the same time greater freedom of movement in harmony is made possible, and the independence of the instrumental parts leads to richer modulatory development. The motifs are interwoven chromatically, deepened and heightened, and harmonic invention derives new impetus from them. There is an increasing tendency to progression by augmented and diminished intervals, which are considered not as dissonances but as nature-sounds by contrast with smooth combinations of note sequences. This thoroughgoing naturalism is exemplified in the augmented triad in the " Hojotoho " chorus of Valkyries, but it now spreads to chord combinations. Modulation is effected principally by chromatic progressions, and the voice, now subordinate to the new harmonic basis, approaches the accents of natural speech. All these things greatly enrich naturalistic expressionist music, and by comparison *The Valkyrie* seems almost a conventional song-opera of the old type.

Rhythm and dynamics govern not only each detail of structure but also the sequence of contrasting scenes. The solemn Wanderer scene is set against the grand introductory scherzo. In plan it is a companion-piece to the Death Prophecy scene, consisting of three strophes and antistrophes, question and answer thrice repeated. It is a duologue between heights and depths. The mystic whole-tone sequences of the Wanderer's harmonies, progressing gravely and evenly in chromatic alternation, frame the scene. All orders of beings, representing stages in a great process of liberation—Nibelungs, giants, gods, Wälsungs, " Notung," and finally Siegfried himself—are passed verbally and musically in review, the music taking a great lift at the name of Wotan and reaching its greatest rhythmic activity at mention of the Sword and its mystery, losing itself thereafter in the chromatic distortions of the opening. The solemn harmonies of the Wanderer grow spectral, and a maestoso intermezzo is resolved in vibrating augmented chords, whence the firm rhythms of the wood song re-emerge. Drama and music set out again from the point at which the first scene ends, and thence mount steadily to Siegfried's smithy songs. The rhythm is weightier than in the early fresh and sportive Siegfried motifs ; in the first song it is in three time and in the second reaches the ponderous force of four time. The accents fall closer and closer together, becoming heavier, harder and simpler in melodic garb, and are supported like ejaculations upon the principal chordal notes. The motifs, losing their melodic character, are stated in terms of movement, and they gain in dynamic force through the uniform and relentless logic with which they are treated. Mime's accompanying soliloquies interrupt the great rhythmic dynamic wave only to emphasise its main trend. Unrelaxed in tempo, it persists through the elemental nature cry, " Notung ! " and discharges itself in a jubilant passage for the horns, representing Siegfried's youthful strength. The anvil is smitten asunder—" So schneidet Siegfrieds Schwert ! ") (" So severs Siegfried's sword ! ").

Wagner called *Young Siegfried* the fairest of his dreams. It is certainly the simplest, the least dramatically complex, for it represents absolute primitive types. Light and darkness, straightforwardness and guile, are baldly contrasted in the dialogue. Only musical imagination makes theatrical characters of them. The subject is presented in the first act in terms of the development of the power of dynamics. The second act expatiates upon it by rhythmic flight from heavy deeps to aerial heights. Opening with a dull, pounding Fafner motif and Alberich's song of night, " In Wald und Nacht vor Neidhöhl' halt' ich Wacht " (" In gloomy wood at Neidhole still I watch "), it takes us immediately into the world of the deeps. The three rival claimants for the Ring—Fafner, Alberich and Wotan—meet. Daemonic nature-voices pierce the gloom. The words, their meaning and motival vesture, serve simply to call up a picture of night, which finds its elemental climax in the voice of Fafner. The Wanderer vanishes in lightning and thunder as he came, leaving Fafner to sleep the sleep of possession and Alberich to continue his weary vigil. The scene ends as it began, fading out on the deep notes of the Fafner motif.

The duologue intermezzo between Siegfried and Mime forms a bridge passage from the compact elemental rhythms of the creatures of the deeps to a picture of dawning day. Sound gradually steals upon the silence ; the forest leaves stir and whisper, and Siegfried dreams. The wordless voices of nature and of bird-song speak to him of Sieglinda's love, woman's love. A new type of rhythmic dynamic music emerges. It ceases to be massive and heavy, and conveys with ever-increasing tenderness each shade of emotion in delicate rhythmic vibrations. Fleeting memories of melody wander through the iridescent harmonies. Siegfried speaks in dreams, a twitter of bird-song answers, and there ensues a merry duologue between Siegfried's horn and the bird's pipings, which is finally resolved again into wordless music. The human voice, forgoing speech, expresses itself in a babble of rhythmic notes. Nature's answer comes from that deep world of night with which the act opens. The marvel of the talking serpent is not taken for granted but is regarded *as* a marvel— " Ei ! bist du ein Tier, das zum Sprechen taugt ? " (" Ei, art thou a beast that can speak like me ? "). A fairy-tale atmosphere in which elemental powers are simply apprehended persists until the death-song of Fafner. With this the dark motifs of the Serpent, the Ring, Envy, the Curse, sink down to the abyss, whence rises the life-spark of speaking Nature, the dragon's blood that makes the voice of birds intelligible to man. This magic works in the reverse of the usual sense, for it is not the bird which speaks with human tongue but the human listener who learns to interpret the sounds of nature—that is, to understand elemental melody, pure emotion. All music is by this resolved into quivering vibrations of harmony, and the atmosphere is free of any breath of passion. The wood-bird tells his tale to the notes that once accompanied the Rhine Maidens' " Weia ! Waga ! Woge du Welle," and indeed its song is but a " Weia, Waga," a non-conceptual nature-utterance whose expressionist import is nevertheless intelligible to the listening Siegfried.

Once again, however, dissonance creeps into this pure nature idyll. Siegfried brings the Ring and the Helmet of Invisibility out of the dragon's cave, whereupon Alberich and Mime, meeting at the entrance, begin to haggle over the spoils. The shrill, discordant, broken-rhythmed accents of the brawling Nibelungs form a swift scherzando intermezzo. Force and fraud are shown at loggerheads, neither aware that the dragon-slayer's real prize is the power to penetrate the secret processes of Nature. Not only can Siegfried understand the voice of dragon and bird, not only can he see into the heart of Nature, but he can read the thoughts and emotions behind Mime's song. Its gay lilt cannot deceive him ; he knows that every note is a lie. This is the music of falsity ; it is against Nature, and therefore it must be cast into the darkness where Fafner lies.

The melody of the singing voices is taken up by the orchestra, lifted up and up and lost in the play of harmonies which proclaim Nature's highest commandment—the promise of Woman. To Siegfried the promise comes in tones of elemental melody, and a wave of unrest surges within him. Once again to his inner ear comes the voice from the realms of light :

> " Lustig im Leid
> sing' ich von Liebe ;
> wonnig und weh'
> web' ich mein Lied !
> nur Sehnende kennen den Sinn ! "

> (" Joyful in grief
> I sing of love,
> Weaving from woe
> Gladdest of songs :
> The longing heart grasps them alone ! ")

The great cycle of " becoming " is complete. The motif that first appeared as the motif of the Rhine's depths, the germ of the whole drama, finds ultimate resolution as far above, as there below, the organic world. It is no longer a massive piece of motival architecture, built up from harmony to melody, but a final analysis of harmony-born melodic substance into aetherial, dynamic, vibrating rhythms. On this highest stage of " becoming " all phenomena are transparent ; the nature of things is revealed, and man himself becomes a pure child of Nature. The " purely-human," the purely emotional, is attained. Love and grief, song and mourning—these are Nature's ultimate answers to the longings of the heart, and only the longing heart can understand them. The fires of longing are kindled, and the law of Nature drives man to seek in woman Nature's most sublime manifestation. Energy, action, lead man from Fafner's cave to Brynhilda's rock, from the demons of the dark to the bird of light, from Nature asleep to Nature self-revealed. From that moment action becomes conscious of self and aware of its goal. Siegfried teaches man, as the Valkyrie teaches woman, to learn from Nature his natural vocation. Having learned, they are ready for one another.

Siegfried goes through fire to win his love—yet finds not the Brynhilda whom he sought and who was promised to him, but another. His light is no longer the light of the rock-fires, burning in daylight, but a midnight torch. Nature's world is shrouded in darkness, and Woe sets up his kingdom. It is not, however, Siegfried the victorious who enters that realm, but Tristan of " the death-devoted head."

CHAPTER II

TRISTAN AND ISOLDA

BETWEEN the completion of the first sketch for *Siegfried* in July 1857 and the resumption of that work in the autumn of 1864, Wagner began and finished *Tristan and Isolda*, revised *Tannhäuser* for performance in Paris, and wrote the libretto and began the composition of *The Mastersingers of Nuremberg*. When, after completing *The Mastersingers* he again devoted himself to *Siegfried*, he had travelled a vast distance as an artist and had, as a man, fought through the exterior and interior crisis of his life. The first section of the *Nibelung* cycle carried him to the threshold of these events ; the second was the fruit of his victory in the struggle. In the interval Wagner fought to assert himself as a creative and executive artist, being urged to the fray not by external events but by the interior problems of his nature, which provoked a crisis, since this was necessary to its further development. Wagner's ultimate purpose was the completion of *The Ring*, and his works in the interim, by assembling all his powers for a new burgeoning, became means to this end. They have a peculiar importance. Wagner never delved so deep into his own being as in *Tristan*, the *Venusberg*, and *The Mastersingers*, works which assured his victory as an artist and set him free to climb Bryndilda's rock. After that nothing could check his progress.

That an interruption in *The Ring of the Nibelungs* was necessary is proved by the fact that the third act of *Siegfried* is obviously the organic outcome and culmination of this apparently irrelevant and interpolated series of works. With the completion of the second act of *Siegfried* a creative impulse had worked itself out ; the composer's work was in reality finished. Wagner paused not because he was weary or discouraged, but because the musical springs for that which was still to come were as yet unrevealed to him. He had to live through a new phase of experience before he could express in music the love-story of Brynhilda and Siegfried, the awakening of Woman by Man. As the stream of *Nibelung* music dried up, however, a new fount of music appeared. Flowing in the same direction as the first and welling ultimately from the same deep source, it passed onwards into an emotional sphere far surpassing that of the forces of nature, into the sphere of human suffering, caused by recognition of the love-instinct as the ultimate law of being.

In the saga of *Tristan and Isolda* Wagner found a drama in which to embody this conception. Bound to one another eternally by a magic love-potion, the pair seek each other in despite of honour and morality, and upon their grave the ivy and the rose entwined proclaim the eternal victory of love. A dramatic experiment by young Karl Ritter brought the story to Wagner's notice while he was composing *The Valkyrie* in 1854. It quickly took root in him, seeming to have some kinship with the subject of the *Nibelungs*. The connection is to be found rather in the symbolism of the love-story than in its intellectual content. To Wagner as composer the *Nibelungs* had become a cycle of love-myths, mirrored in the life of nature. Side by side with this grand synthesis of the forces of passion there slowly grew up the idea of the magic love-curse, suggested within the series only by Siegfried's love betrayal. The idea grew stronger in Wagner as his own natural " Siegfried " desires gave place to wistful " Tristan " longings ; as Wotan's Dream-Maid and Siegfried's destined bride became that Isolda whom fate denied to Tristan.

Tristan and Isolda would seem more than any other work of Wagner's to owe its existence to real experience and real suffering. None shows so plainly the link between actual events and the artist's creative dreams. Early in 1852, shortly before beginning the libretto of *The Valkyrie*, Wagner came to know Mathilde Wesendonk and for a time basked happily in the emotional admiration and friendship of the enthusiastic young musical amateuse. As Wotan's Dream-Maid and confidante of his thoughts, as the destined loving guardian of young Siegfried, she inspired the music of *The Ring*. But a time came when the flames of passion enveloped the pair, and then, since she could not be the bride won by Siegfried, she became the fever phantom which leads a dying lover through the gates of death to the fulfilment of his desires. Wagner's letters to Mathilde prove to the hilt that, as regards the story, *Tristan and Isolda* is a frank confession, a portrayal of their relations with one another. Schroeder-Devrient had once supplied Wagner with the aspect and style of his heroines ; Mathilde now endowed them with soul : " That I have written *Tristan* I thank you from the depths of my soul to all eternity ! "

A second experience mingled with and ripened the first. At a time when Wagner's feeling for Mathilde was mounting to passion and chance brought the story of Tristan to his notice, Georg Herwegh introduced him to the writings of Schopenhauer. Schopenhauer influenced Wagner more deeply than any other philosopher. There was an æsthetic element in his philosophy and an organic unity in its presentation that captured the composer at once. Wagner found many points of contact in Schopenhauer's view of music as the symbolic reflection of will, and in his romantic emphasis upon and justification of the element of suffering in life and the universe. Wagner had outgrown his faith in external events. He had slowly relinquished the idea of participating either by deed or word in social revolution. As he saw the hopes cherished in his early days of exile deceived and fell, himself more and more under the sway of a hopeless passion, the conquering Siegfried mood died in him. Schopenhauer's quietistic doctrine of renunciation came to his knowledge at a moment when his own personal relations with society and with individuals had imposed on him a similar standpoint. He recognised his own emotional intuitions in the philosopher's reasoned arguments. The æsthetic quality in Schopenhauer's work combined with the melancholy beauty of his doctrine to subjugate Wagner. Psychological experience and rational perception coincided, explaining and confirming one another. Philosophy and Woman pointed Wagner to the same conclusions, and the creative artist, having just completed a great work, found the same future pathway marked out for him both in the life of the mind and the life of the passions. Though this pathway seemed to turn aside from the high road, Wagner recognised it as the only possible continuation of his journeyings.

Such was the kernel of experience round which the new work was built, but, greatly as it influenced its execution and completion, it neither determined, nor even influenced, the original conception. In this instance, where the link between Wagner's life and his art is clearer than anywhere else, the demarcation of the two and their interactions are also most plain to see. Wagner himself, writing to Mathilde from Venice in January 1859, during the *Tristan* period, says, " My poetic conceptions have always been so far in advance of my living experiences that I may regard my moral education as conditioned and effected almost solely by the former." In the deepest sense this is true, and confirmation is found in the organism of the Wagnerian work. With Wagner the creative process did not begin with the germ of experience from which the work sprang ; on the contrary, desire to create brought about the required experience. Wagner's art was an anticipation of his life which, far from serving, in Goethe's sense, to give human worth, was merely a means of access to art. The man was the means, the art the end, therefore Wagner was subject to art, not art to him. There was in him no personality, only " theatre " ; and to serve " theatre " personality had to shape its capacity for experience in accordance with the demands of " theatre."

This peculiar relationship between life and art, this anticipation by the creative will of the person's fate, is seen most clearly in the relations between Wagner's sketches for his libretti and their musical execution. The libretti are intuitive presentiments of the course of his life ; while they were being fulfilled the works ripened for fulfilment. This inner relation between Wagner's life and his will to theatre can be traced even in the early works, from *Die Hochzeit* and *Rienzi* to *Lohengrin*. But as his work divagates increasingly from that of his contemporaries, this remarkable creative principle becomes increasingly obvious. It is most obvious in *The Ring* conception, which is really an anticipation of an entire lifetime. It would suggest a weird premonitory gift which illuminated for the artist his own future pathway did not a less occult interpretation better accord with the *twofold nature* of the creative act in Wagner. As surely as Wagner prophesied his own life in his libretti, so surely did he require the actual fulfilment of experience before he could create as an artist. He could not find music for his words without experience ; life alone could give the reality of tone to his dramatic outlines. When an experience had fulfilled this end, when it had given him music, he had finished with it. It had caught fire, it had poured its energy into the drama, it had passed. At the behest of some vision of the stage life had obeyed and music had come into being. " Theatre " had established its supremacy as the source and origin of Wagner's art.

Remembering this, we may estimate the value of the experience embodied in *Tristan*. No woman exercised so profound and lasting an influence on Wagner's work as Mathilde Wesendonk. She was, indeed, his muse in the music for the first section of *The Ring*, in the plans for *The Mastersingers*, and even in the conception of *Parsifal*. Wagner feels this himself when he says, " That one supremest spring-tide fostered in me such a wealth of shoots that all I have to do now is the easy task of tending them into blossom." Apart from thus awakening and stimulating his genius, might Mathilde have proved the woman Wagner's manhood sought, the woman he dreamed her to be ? The answer is that she was not so in fact. She was perhaps restrained from giving herself wholly to Wagner less by a sense of duty to her husband and children than by an instinctive recognition that the profound spiritual ties between herself and the artist were closely bound up with art, even in so far as they might benefit the man. Wagner met Mathilde Wesendonk when his creative will required her ; therefore Mathilde belonged to Wagner the artist until the dangerous moment when the pair awoke to human consciousness of that relation-ship. At once, upon both sides, there creeps in a note of resignation, a slowly awakening sense of error. It is the keynote of the Wesendonk episode. In so delicate a relationship it was inevitable that the emotions of the participants, Wagner's more particularly, should stray a little beyond self-prescribed bounds. This explains why Minna's jealousy was felt as a coarse intrusion by Wagner and Mathilde and yet was no mad-woman's fancy. Conflict between the two women forced Wagner to abandon the " Asyl," the comfortable little home which Mathilde's loving care had provided for him close to her own splendid mansion. In the " Asyl " Wagner finished the second act of *Siegfried*, composed the first act of *Tristan*, drafted the second, and envisioned the " Good Friday Magic." Did Minna's interference really decide the matter, or was not the pair's human proximity a danger from which the artist's work had to be protected ? Had not Tristan's story —Wagner's poetic prevision of his own—to be fulfilled, the lover banished, in order that the love-song of the second act might be finished in the lonely, dreaming Venetian nights, the feverish melancholy of the third in the hard brilliance of Lucerne ?

Experience did not form the work, but the work evoked experience in order that the emotional drama Wagner envisioned on the stage might come to life in music. The process is the same in all his works. He protested later against their autobiographical interpretation. When told that a listener had said, " How deeply in love Wagner must have been when he wrote *Tristan* ! " he replied, " People do not understand how far apart from all experience, all actuality, these things occur.

I felt a longing beyond bounds to revel in music, to pour myself out in music as if I were writing a symphony. Some day I must write something about the mind's life, and how the poet's inner vision has nothing to do with external experiences, which can only cloud it, so that the work of art portrays rather what is *not* found in life." These remarks of Wagner's later years are supported by his first intimation of the *Tristan* plan to Liszt in December 1854. "Since I have never yet known in life the real bliss of love, I mean to set up a memorial to the loveliest of all dreams, in which from first to last this love shall be satisfied to the full. I have a plan in my head for a ' Tristan and Isolda,' the simplest and yet the most full-blooded musical conception. . . ." While he was at work on the second act in January 1859 he wrote to Minna from Venice, " One can write nothing real, particularly in drama, unless it is outside oneself, so that one can look at it, as it were ; if one is in the midst of it one is incapable of intelligible poetry."

We see, therefore, that the work springs neither from a love affair nor from a philosophy, but from the deep yearnings of Wagner's own soul. The conditions of Wagner's life, his enforced abstension from practical affairs, his banishment, the depressing lack of prospects for his works, contributed largely to turn these yearnings to melancholy. He was seething with vigorous life, yet the world gave him no place, and drove him violently back upon himself, forbade him to hear his own works performed, involved him in money difficulties, and in the winter of 1856, under the threat of Prussian invasion, left him unsure even of his Swiss refuge. When, defying fate, he turned to creative work, no attention was paid to it and no assistance was given him to get his work performed. The great passion for action which forms the motive of the *Nibelung* cycle died out under this treatment. All emotion in Wagner turned to longing, an orgy of grief for the unattainable. This objectless desire found support in a philosophy which teaches that suffering is man's aboriginal destiny and the negation of the will to live the law of an enlightened morality. It fed, furthermore, on the image of a woman who inspired love yet could never be possessed by her lover. All this found expression in the legend of Tristan and Isolda. In it the artist saw his desire reflected as an experience-expression of his new philosophy and his new love, and endowed with plastic form and objectivity.

As ever, Wagner's experiences were the means of giving shape and objective reality to his fantasies—in this instance to melancholic yearnings—and were evoked by his imagination for that purpose. Yet even the phase of emotion which thus begot experience, deeply as it affected the artist's human side, was but one of the causes underlying the new work. Wagner's first mention of it to Liszt insists that a will to music was the decisive factor, and this is confirmed by his later statement that he felt an impulse to " pour himself out in music, as if he were writing a symphony." After the *dramatic* inspiration of *The Nibelungs* a violent *musical* reaction occurred, replacing the complex nature-symbolism of *The Ring* by a simple dramatic embodiment of the change from day to night. Wagner envisages the chief problem of the new theatre, the discovery of a driving dramatic impulse, as a drama of the spectrum. When he said in later years that *Tristan* was " as it were, all violet, a deep lilac," he showed that a light-sense was the basis of his drama, not, however, as a matter of colouristic effects, but as a symbolic transition from light to darkness. In *Tristan* unhappy passion, an urge to music, and the interplay of night and day build up the whole. Speech, as the virile element in Wagner's structural system, as the medium of the concept, is identified with broad daylight. Music, the feminine element, is the night of instinct, of passion. Day seeks the embraces of night, speech is merged in non-conceptual tone, love finds fulfilment in death, in whose profoundest darkness this drama of lights achieves its goal. Thus music is held up as the highest manifestation of creative art, the driving force in all " becoming." For day, for speech, for the world, for light, death means extinction and annihilation, but for night, for music, for love, it is perfect transfiguration, endlessness of desire, whose dark dreams can nevermore be broken by intrusive life.

As the musical impulse triumphed in Wagner at the expense of the verbal, he turned inevitably from the *Nibelung* series with its verbal basis to the consciously musical *Tristan* conception. The change can be seen in the *Tristan* libretto. Alliteration is still used, freely but not insistently, and for the most part in matters of the daylight world. Even here the musical, lyrical vowel-sound predominates over the accented consonant with its more conceptual implications. Rime, which Wagner had theoretically discarded and which is absent in *The Nibelungs*, reappears in *Tristan*. It is used in two ways : in the form of doggerel to mark very simple speech, as in certain phrases of Kurwenal's, and in brief, free rhythms to express ecstasy. It prevails chiefly where night, music, and emotion prevail in the drama, as in the duet of the second act, Tristan's monologue in the third, and Isolda's death-song. Verbal repetition, which Wagner condemned in his writings as " operatic," is for the most part avoided, though in many instances it is rather *evaded* by the employment of a similar instead of an identical turn of phrase. The hard, jerky condensed diction of *The Ring* gives place to a flowing style full of fanciful allusions. Twilight emotion is deliberately substituted for intellectual logic in the choice of words, which are rather a thread on which to string musical notes than a constructive outline. They are first and foremost a channel for, not an interpretation of, the flow of melody, and at all moments of climax become as completely subservient to the latter as did the old operatic libretti.

Music is throughout the governing force. The dramaturgical economy of the work is a further aid to free musical development. Each of the three acts presents a single simple scene. The two principal characters dominate the stage almost exclusively, and their attendants, Kurwenal and Brangäne, play purely subordinate parts. Lesser characters are introduced either like the seaman and the herdsman into the musical drama as voices without individuality, or like Melot and the Helmsman into the scenic drama to assist the mechanism of the action. Mark's figure alone has importance as the lovers' opponent, and even he serves chiefly in the great closing scenes of the second and third acts to impart to the climaxes there depicted a more important musical development.

Subject, libretto, and scenic conception of *Tristan* are accordingly seen to be the result of an expansion of the musical impulse in Wagner which, occurring at a moment when the creative impulse behind the first section of *The Ring* had worked itself out, softened and changed the dramatic passion and nature-symbolism of that work into the lyric emotion of this vision of day and night. Music is the subject of the drama, music as identified with love, woman, night, and the yearning for death. His new vision of it as interpreting these things formed the basic creative impulse. Afterwards passion fostered the plan of the work. The artist's will to music, governing words and scene, drove him to seek and to find those experiences which should enable him to embody his musical inspiration in the reality of tone.

Wagner described his own change of artistic attitude when he wrote to Liszt of this, his "most full-blooded musical conception," and, later, of his "longing beyond bounds to revel in music." This longing presupposes the damming up in him of a musical creativeness which could find no outlet in *The Ring*, but the lyricism of the wood-scene in *Siegfried* was a sign of the coming change. At the close of the second act of that work, Wagner felt that he must shake himself free from the musical style of the *Nibelungs*, that he must find a sphere of musical expression unencumbered by laws organic and unalterable in the music of *The Ring*. The basis of style there is development from the natural harmonics, and in this connection also the second act of *Siegfried* contains a premonition of change in its chromatic loosening of vertical chordal and melodic structures. The increasing intricacy of harmonic development from *The Rhinegold* to *Siegfried* taught Wagner to look for expressionist sources beyond those of natural harmony. He sought them in chromatic inversion and dissection of natural harmony, desiring to evoke the expressionist possibilities therein latent, a world of purely musical phenomena, untrammelled by the exigencies of the *Nibelung* subject. From an initial vision of harmony as Nature, Nature as harmony, Wagner's harmonic sense gradually developed through his work upon the earlier *Nibelung* pieces to an appreciation of the ramifications of harmony for their own sake, of the dynamic force of modulation as an end in itself. He felt impelled to call into existence the wealth of figures latent in chromatic distortions of fundamental harmony and to satisfy the artist in him with their multiplicity and variety. To call out these figures from the modulatory element of music he required a plot or story capable of providing a suitable dramatic vehicle for a very intricately and delicately graded harmony. Psychic and actual experiences apart, Wagner clothed the story of *Tristan* in a day-and-night symbolism, in a drama of light, because these things were the scenic counterpart of his musical intentions. The music he envisaged was a chromatic derivative of the harmonic style of the *Nibelungs*, and he conceived it when the wealth of musical images therein evolved clamoured for separate development and treatment. The extent to which *Tristan* is dramatically and conceptually related to the *Nibelungs*, the likenesses between Siegfried and Tristan, Brynhilda and Isolda, are questions of small moment in view of their common origins : dramatic and conceptual similarities are but outward manifestations of organic musical union.

An incident at this time helped to accelerate the change in Wagner as a musician. In October 1856 Liszt paid a second visit to Zurich, staying this time for several weeks, accompanied by Princess Caroline Wittgenstein. The pleasure of the two friends in each other's society was spoilt by the noisy assemblage of local notabilities at the Princess's house and by discussions of artistic questions which bored and irritated Wagner. Despite this drawback, however, he gained from the visit a first real knowledge of Liszt's compositions, particularly the *Dante Symphony* and *Symphonic Poems*. Wagner is silent as to their influence upon him as a musician, and his open letter to Liszt in February 1857, upon the Symphonic Poems, discusses Liszt and his works chiefly from the standpoint of formal æsthetics. Such marked reserve in regard to musical details almost suggests that it was here that Liszt influenced Wagner most. This is borne out by Wagner's annoyance when others touched on the point. " Of course, there are things we are quite willing to admit amongst ourselves," he wrote to Bülow in October 1859, " as, for example, that since I got to know Liszt's compositions, I have become a very different sort of harmonist from what I was formerly, but when friend Pohl blabs this secret to all the world, right at the head of a short article discussing the prelude to *Tristan and Isolda*, it is, to say the least, indiscreet, and surely I am not to understand that he was authorised to such indiscretion ? "

Wagner had no doubt just cause of complaint in this instance. The links between himself and Liszt as writers of harmony by no means imply his dependence on Liszt. The important thing was that the pair met at a moment when a richer sense of harmony had awaked in Wagner. Liszt's luxuriant chromaticism and delight in modulation were different in origin from Wagner's expressionist impulses, and the former's bold virtuosity lent sudden wings to the latter's musical imagination. Much that he had dimly felt before he now saw effortlessly fulfilled before his eyes. Liszt's imagination started from a real instrument, whereas Wagner had to work his difficult way from a purely imaginative musical concept to instrumental and vocal reality. Thus the musician who invented as he played could well give the other something which he had as yet but dimly divined and which yet revealed its full value only when he had worked upon it. Liszt's compositions influenced Wagner in exactly the same manner as did Schopenhauer's philosophy. The essentials lay within himself, but another stirred them into consciousness. Thus regarded, Wagner's closer acquaintance with Liszt's work a year before he began *Tristan* and whilst he was engaged on *Siegfried* was the most important of all the external influences affecting the new work—more important than the dawning passion which was a mere psychic accompaniment of his changing attitude to art, more important than Schopenhauer or Mathilde, who did no more than give intellectual and dramatic form to the musical idea. Yet even Liszt's influence could take effect only along the lines of Wagner's own inclinations, could only induce closed buds to unfurl.

The process thus brought to ripeness consisted in an inner, organic development of the motif. In *Lohengrin* the motif is treated as an element in a purely harmonic organism, and in *The Rhinegold* as a serviceable connecting link evolving from harmony. In the course of *The Valkyrie* and *Siegfried*, however, it becomes an independent phenomenon, revealing the inwardness of harmony, analysing it by its own increasing powers of characterisation and overmastering it by degrees until not harmony but the motif itself becomes the ruling power. No longer do the motifs serve harmony ; rather is the latter made up of interwoven motival threads. The individual motif, more and more finely articulated from a more and more acute dissection of harmony, arrogates to itself directing power over the whole. Wagner's chromaticism, deriving from *Das Liebesverbot* and *Tannhäuser*, cuts across the chordal arrangement of intervals and compresses the modulatory element within the narrowest possible limits, the briefest possible formula. Melody, formerly thrust into the background by a fundamentally harmonic feeling, comes again to the fore, no longer, however, as the conventional periodic structure, but as a running thread of interwoven motifs, derived from and uniting in harmony—as " endless melody."

In *Tristan* the motif represents the inner motive force and formative element in the music, and this determines its relations to the dramatic content of the work. These are in no way concerned with intellectual interpretation of particular events in the drama. Where there seems to be a connection the scene should be regarded as accompanying the music, as " making visible " a *musical* event. For it is in the music that the kernel of the drama lies, moulding and forming it from within, so that the music gives a truer picture of it than do either scene or words. Here is the answer to the question as to how far the motival drama is conscious in a scenic, poetic, or unconscious in a musical, organic, sense.

" In these basic motifs, which are not exactly concrete statements, but plastic emotional motives, the poet's purpose is best interpreted, being made real to the emotions, and the musician, acting as realiser of the poet's intentions, must arrange these motifs, condensed as melodic moments, so smoothly and in such full accord with the poetic purpose that their well-considered mingling and repetition may give rise automatically to a fully unified musical form," wrote Wagner in *Opera and Drama* before he had begun to score *The Nibelungs*. Theoretically he sets the poet's meaning and the musico-plastic emotional moment upon an equality, but in practice, even as early as *The Ring* music, the motif, as musical formative element, is increasingly predominant, and the scenic drama is set within the musical. The *Tristan* change is actually the result of this tendency of music to predominate. Musical form itself becomes the dramatist's subject. There is no recorded theory of Wagner's during the *Tristan* period as to the relation of the musical motif to action, but he confesses the work to be the strictest test of his theoretic assertions, " since here, at last, with the most complete freedom, and regardless of all theoretic considerations, I pursued a course during which I discovered that I had far outsoared my own system." It was the nature of his subject which enabled him to do this. Freed from the objective dramatic meaning still attaching to the Nibelung subject, it was derived solely from musical motive forces and a sense of their dramatic significance. For this reason Wagner, speaking of the libretto, emphasises " the far more intimate blending of poem and music," and " the perfect anticipation of musical form in the poem," a state of affairs through which " melody and its form acquired a richness, an inexhaustibility of which one could otherwise have no conception."

The work, therefore, is but symbolically " Tristan and Isolda " ; its real title is " Music." It is, indeed, " essence of music " as Wagner understood music—music as drama, as ebb and flow, as the mutual attraction and repulsion, desire and fulfilment of musical forces, but music also as Wagner alone could envisage it, as pure tone vitalised and filled to its least member with dramatic energy. Not only complete harmonies and chords, not only allusive melodies and themes, but each little chromatic shifting, each apparently insignificant phrase, is endowed with a personality, a destiny. During the composition of *The Nibelungs* Wagner's eyes had been opened to the drama inherent in musical movement. His imagination eagerly investigated this mysterious dance of dark organic forces, but because of its visual, conceptual limitations he saw it as a mystic rite of passion, reflected in a love story, beginning in the daylight world of the intelligence and finding consummation in the fertile darkness of night. The drama is one of the utmost emotional intensity, purged almost entirely of plot, and its movement is an exact portrayal of the movement of music itself. The coincidence of scenic action and music is all but perfect here, music evolving into action, action becoming music. *Tristan* discovers the profound unity inherent in the nature of these opposites ; it is a fulfilment.

Wagner achieves this unity, this fulfilment, by his absolute grasp of the expression values of tone. This alone gives him insight into the dramatic significance of occurrences within the musical organism, and this alone enables him so to handle these occurrences that they blossom into theatrical, scenic drama. The *Nibelung* music at its best, in the love-notes that close *The Valkyrie*, the character-drawing in the first act and the expression of mindless Nature in the second act of *Siegfried*, brought Wagner to the threshold of this bodying-forth of expression, this eliciting of " theatre " from music itself. In *Tristan* this process finds its culmination : emotion is wholly externalised in order to endow music with plastic form. But because the interior processes of the musical organism are thus externalised in drama, music itself must take the laws of the drama for its own laws, must itself become a stage.

Wagner's imagination, being theatrical, begets tones which spring from a dramatic conception of the spirit of music, and are only to be understood from this standpoint. The chromaticism and enharmonics, the conflicts of parts, the suspensions and modulatory complexities in *Tristan*, the prominence of dissonant interpolations, startling harmonic turns and interrupted cadences, avoidance of simple cadential resolutions—all these no doubt have musically an empirical foundation and explanation. But the impulse behind all is the objectivisation of music. Wagner's chromatic line is not musical progression by semitones ; it expresses the ebb and flow of desire. The most drastic musical naturalism is employed in the symbolism of ascending and descending intervals, tonal concentrations and discharges, the entangling and unravelling of parts, long-drawn-out emotional flights, sudden outcries and ebullitions of temperament. The music is developed, finds resolution, retardation, discords or etherial flights in accordance with the objective expressionist significance with which it is indissolubly bound up. A complete system of physiological symbolism is evolved. Each aspect of music is endowed with particular significance, and its functions from greatest to least become on these lines an expressive language.

According to Wagner himself, the most novel and important feature of *Tristan* is the " art of transition " therein employed. " I now recognised," he says, " that that peculiar quality in my music (always, of course, in closest association with the poetic plan) which my friends now regard as so new and important is due to the extreme delicacy of feeling which shows me how to link so closely every moment of the transition of the most divergent parts into one another. My art is at its best and deepest in what I should like to call the ' art of transition,' for the whole fabric depends on these transitions : I have grown to dislike abruptness and violence, and though these are often unavoidable and necessary, they should never occur until the mind has been so well prepared for a sudden transition that it instinctively demands it." The " art of transition " described by Wagner, with special reference to the great scene in the second act of *Tristan*, consists in the complete identification of musical expression with the emotional time-processes of the drama. Each hesitation, delay, or decision is reflected perfectly in the music, which is formed in perfect accord with the emotional sequence of events. Musical and objective drama coincide without remainder. The great expressionist artist's long dream of completely naturalistic musico-scenic expression is at last fully realised.

In *Tristan*, therefore, Wagner achieves the perfect antithesis of traditional opera. The latter was built up deliberately upon the contrasts between formally separate " numbers " whose association nevertheless made a whole. From *Tannhäuser* onwards Wagner had striven against this method, bridging over the difference between the recitative and the set form, assimilating declamatory recitative to the *arioso*, dissolving the set form into a fluid lyrical periodicity allied to a recitative-like *arioso*. His attempt to render continuous " becoming " in music is reflected in his choice of scenic subjects. These, too, reveal increasingly an underlying concept of continuous evolution. Expressionist art tends inevitably to such subjects, for expressionism is by its nature concerned with the immediate present, with the tracing of every alteration, the interpretation of every change. *The Ring of the Nibelungs* shows in general form this preoccupation with a parallel evolution in nature and harmony, in scenic event and musical expression. In *The Ring* such a parallel is conceived as possible ; in *Tristan* the unity is fundamental, axiomatic. Wagner is here no longer concerned with evolving a changing sequence of characters and scenes, for transition is in the very nature of his subject, which, indeed, only becomes a subject in the revelation of transition. It is based on the musical phenomenon of chromaticism, a musical phenomenon of transition. The mystery of movement as such, of change, of continuous alteration, is revealed through a drama of pure emotion, thus setting expressionist music its highest task, the task of reflecting moment by moment the development of a dramatic situation. Wagner calls this direct and present apprehension of each least movement, unhindered by formal barriers, " the art of transition." He is right in considering it the great novelty of *Tristan*. It was the goal he had divined subconsciously up to *Lohengrin*, and which he had since aimed at with growing awareness—the idea of a music-derived theatrical drama controlling musical form. In traditional opera progress in the action delays the music, and progress in the music delays the action ; now the pair urge on and fulfil one another.

At this point, however, unmarked, the line has come full circle. From the art of transition, from an expressionist drama revealed in movement only, emerges a new form tending to synthesis, the self-subsistent music of the grand monologues and vocal duets. Tone in itself, independent of such motives as motion and visuality, sheer delight in vocal exercise and the liberation of the voice from the slavery of words in ringing musical notes assert themselves with elemental force. *Tristan* represents a rebirth of the musician in Wagner.

The story of *Tristan's* origins shows how entirely music predominates. In *Lohengrin* Wagner was obliged to compose the last act first as a means of access to the musical sphere of the work, but in *Tristan* this process is almost reversed. The music for several scenes existed before the scenes themselves were written. Wagner had set to music five poems by Mathilde, of which " Träume," composed on December 5, 1857, contains the germ of the duet in the second act of *Tristan*, and *Im Treibhaus*, composed on May 1, 1858, is a complete sketch for the prelude to the third act. The connection in these instances is not accidental as in another of the songs, " Schmerzen," of which the so-called " Day " motif is plainly though perhaps unconsciously the basis. The two remaining pieces, described by Wagner himself as " Studies for Tristan and Isolda," undoubtedly anticipate the fundamental musical subjects of the second and third acts and witness to his overflowing impulse to musical creation. He could not wait, even when it seemed only a question of writing down the words. He *must* compose. The whole history of *Tristan* shows this urgency, this vehemence, doubly astounding after four years of almost uninterrupted work on *The Ring*. On July 30, 1857, the music for the second act of *Siegfried* was complete, and by September 18 the libretto of *Tristan* was written. Wagner began to compose it at once. It took him three months, to the end of December, to make sketches for the overture and first act. The second was composed between May 4 and July 1, 1858, the third between April 9 and July 16, 1859. In the intervals of composition Wagner orchestrated his work, and by August 6, 1859, two years after he began his libretto, the full score was complete. During this period of intense creativeness, remarkable even as a quantitive achievement, work was interrupted by two removals, from Zurich to Venice in August 1858, and from Venice to Lucerne in March 1859, the first occasioned by the clash between Minna and Mathilde and leading to Wagner's separation from both. Yet none of these events really affected the progress of the work ; they merely date its sections. The same may be said of Wagner's voluminous correspondence at this time with Breitkopf and Härtel (including detailed negotiations about type for words and for music, and the proof-reading of portions printed during composition), and even of a serious quarrel with Liszt in January 1859 arising from a tactless remark of Wagner's about his own lack of funds.

The untiring energy with which Wagner worked on *Tristan* finds its only parallel in the genesis of *The Flying Dutchman*. The two works are also alike in that both were *musical* in origin, the earlier growing from the ballad, the later from the songs which anticipate the second and third acts. The three years between Wagner's first conception of *Tristan* as a subject and his setting to work upon it, though occupied by the composition of *The Valkyrie* and *Siegfried*, may have prepared the ground by unconscious critical sifting and arrangement. None the less, the vehemence with which Wagner went to work, his almost somnambulist steadiness and persistence, remain a marvel. Wagner himself realised this even in later years. After the difficult step-by-step approach to *The Nibelungs*, *Tristan* was like some elemental natural manifestation. It is a " cry " in the sense defined by Wagner later as the instinctive utterance of humanity when impelled to expression. " All things cry out," he said. " It is the same in the *Venusberg* as in *Tristan*, swallowed up in grace in the one, in death in the other—everywhere a cry, a cry of distress." The fundamental appeal of the music in *Tristan* is based on this " cry," from the overture's sigh of longing to the clamour of the second act and the death ecstasies of the third, in which "longing itself dies." The instinctive nature of the cry, the creature's impulse to seek relief in sound, underlies in a very profound sense the impulse which produced *Tristan*. The work is a single sustained note, by its nature insusceptible to external interruptions until it has spent itself. Thus *Tristan*, the organic complexity of its structure notwithstanding, is the simplest, the most straightforward, the most perfectly unified of Wagner's later works.

The whole work may be adequately summed up as an instinctive mating-call, swelling out slowly, rising to piercing intensity, dying away in the shadows. This is its basis as an example of the art of perpetual transition in perfect accord of action and music, and this also supplies the structural formula, which consists in a musical movement from night to day and back again to night. It is a scheme of development which bears a close inner relation to that of *Lohengrin*, as may be seen at once in the preludes of the two works, in which Wagner deliberately avoids the representational but goes beyond the merely prefatory, as employed in *The Nibelungs*, and reflects the inner problem of the work. Yet with the external principle of structure the resemblance ends, for darkness in *Tristan* occupies the place of light in *Lohengrin*. In the latter work creatures of light contend against demons of darkness, but in *Tristan* the splendours of night are contrasted with the pallid phantoms of day. The tone-picture is changed accordingly. In *Lohengrin* light is symbolised as pure harmony whence threads of melody gradually descend : in *Tristan* darkness is portrayed in upward-groping motival basses which but gradually evolve into melody. Both preludes have a crescendo basis, but otherwise run counter to each other throughout. *Lohengrin* moves from the heights to the depths and back again to the heights, *Tristan* from the depths to the heights and back again to the depths. In *Lohengrin* melody emerges from fundamental harmony and returns to it again ; in *Tristan* a fundamental motif develops into harmony and then regains its original simplicity. In *Lohengrin* the sense of key, and of the character of key, is axiomatic ; in *Tristan* such a sense is entirely wanting—there is a seeking but no finding. In *Lohengrin* no striving of melodic individualism clouds the revelation of perfect harmony, but in *Tristan* the sigh of the individual swells to a lament and dies away again in a sigh.

This consistency in contrast, being of the essence of the two works, prevails not only in the overtures but throughout. In *Lohengrin* the musical action may be described as an analysis of the original A major harmony, tragedy being introduced with the A minor change. In *Tristan* the musical action consists in the efforts of the opening motif to find resolution in pure harmony, whereas its structure, consisting of four notes in chromatic sequence, makes this impossible. The long groping from inflection to inflection, from concord to concord, has no result save to make it evident that the line cannot be resolved. It symbolises a longing which, by itself, can never find fulfilment, but with the entrance of a second melody, embracing and absorbing the first, the chromatic motif can and does find harmonic resolution.

The introduction of this second melodic character to resolve and to fulfil marks a decisive dramaturgical advance upon the *Lohengrin* conception. The *Lohengrin* prelude closes with a return to A major ; it forms a circle, ending where it began. As a tone-picture of the from high to low motion of the drama, the prelude induces in the hearer a sense of gravitational forces—the right mood for the story to follow—and outlines in briefest possible symbolism the subject of the work. The *Tristan* prelude also conveys to the hearer the basic impulse of the ensuing work as a rising and falling motion, but in so doing it deals with only half the forces of the drama. The action as a whole comprises a second sphere of expression, that of harmony-filled melody which contrasts with and complements the chromatic line of the prelude. There are thus two dramatic motives in *Tristan* —the desire of the depths for the heights and the force which answers and fulfils that desire. The second motive is revealed at the close of the work, and it takes that close together with the prelude to perform the function of outlining the whole performed in the earlier and simpler work by the prelude alone.

This close, under the name of " Isolda's Love-Death," is frequently added to the prelude when this is given apart from the whole work. Wagner himself linked them to express in lyrical form the beginning and end, the two dramatic motives, of his work. The name, however, is wrongly applied. In Wagner's own programmes the *prelude* is expressly called " the Love-Death " because " it expresses every phase of the hopeless struggle against the passion of the heart, from the stifled plaints of insatiable longing, from the tenderest thrills to that most terrible moment when love is seen to be hopeless and seems to be extinguished in death." It is not Isolda's death upon the dead body of Tristan that is the " Love-Death." The Love-Death is the death of love from the pangs of unfulfilled desire, and it is portrayed in the prelude. Wagner expressly names the close " Transfiguration." " Life divides the loves of Tristan and Isolda, but death, removing all barriers, glorifies them. To the dead Tristan the dying Isolda brings blessed consummation, eternal union, endless, boundless, free and indissoluble."

Wagner's poetic description of the prelude and close of *Tristan* is confirmed by their musical character. In the prelude the motif rises by chromatic steps and finds rest only in unresolved harmonies, but in the closing song the sustained melody ascends in ever-widening sequential arches, based on the six-four chord as the musical symbol of the cadence. In the prelude the ascending motif never finds the confirmation of tonality, but at the close of the work the key of B major persists through all modulatory excursions, and to this the melody periodically returns. The prelude is developed by thematic enhancement, but in the finale the individual line is resolved in a great ocean of harmonies, in which the chromatic lines of the prelude, the now fading dynamic forces of the drama, die away and are lost, even as the open fifth of the Flying Dutchman motif finds salvation and resolution in the major. A similar salvation or resolution is achieved in *Tristan*, though the basic musical idea is far more complex. Passion is no longer represented by an open fifth, but by an ascending chromatic line. It finds fulfilment not through the introduction of the major third, but in a sea of surging, onrushing harmonies. Given out in all registers at full strength, these fade in the gathering darkness, dying out in softly quivering sounds.

There is a close connection between the final song in *Tristan* and the leave-taking of Wotan and Brynhilda. Brynhilda's great love song, the passionate climax of the *Ring* music, is the direct forerunner of

Isolda's love song, in which Tristan's motif of yearning is trans-figured. Both works culminate in the song of Woman when she has learned to know love at its highest—a goal symbolised in the earlier work by sleep, in the later yet more trenchantly by death. Both are portrayals of transfiguration through love, of melody saturate with harmony and transcending the conceptual limitations of speech. But at the point where Brynhilda falls silent Isolda expresses this ultimate resolution in music in tone-drunken words :

" Höre ich nur
diese Weise,
die so wunder-
voll und leise,
Wonne klagend,
Alles sagend,
mild versöhnend
aus ihm tönend,
in mich dringet,
auf sich schwinget,
hold erhallend
um mich klinget ?
Heller schallend,
mich umwallend,
sind es Wellen
sanfter Lüfte ?

Sind es Wolken
wonniger Düfte ?
Wie sie schwellen,
mich umrauschen,
soll ich atmen,
soll ich lauschen ?
Soll ich schlürfen,
untertauchen,
süss in Düften
mich verhauchen ?
In dem wogenden Schwall,
in dem tönenden Schall,
in des Welt-Atems
wehendem All—
ertrinken—versinken—
unbewusst—höchste Lust ! "

(" Is it I
Alone am hearing
Strains so tender
And endearing ?
Passion swelling,
All things telling,
Gently bounding,
From him sounding,
In me pushes,
Upward rushes,
Trumpet tone that
Round me gushes ?
Brighter growing
O'er me flowing,
Are these breezes
Airy pillows ?

Are they
Beauteous billows ?
How they rise
And gleam and glisten !
Shall I breathe them ?
Shall I listen ?
Shall I sip them,
Dive within them
To my panting
Breathing win them ?
In the breezes around—
In the harmony sound,
In the world's driving
Whirlwind be drowned—
And sinking, be drinking,
In a kiss, highest bliss ! ")

Between its two poles of prelude and postlude, Love-Death and Transfiguration, chromatic motif and harmony-borne melody, runs the axle of *plot*, of scenic and motival action—the shortest possible line between those poles. Everything is discarded save that which links the opening motif on to the closing melody. The true subject of the action is the " becoming " of melody through the yearnings of chromaticism. Tristan and Isolda are not characters such as are found in the *Valkyrie*, symbolic forces of Nature such as people *The Rhinegold*, or contrasted emanations of light and darkness such as compose the drama of *Lohengrin*. They are embodied aspects of a single emotion, the emotion of passionate love. Wagner conveys his inner meaning by a magnificent one-sidedness which excludes character or individuality in the ordinary sense or relegates it to minor figures. Kurwenal and Brangäne have the epic and narrative function of carrying on the story, yet even they are not drawn in the round, but are each under the dominion of a single emotion which governs all their actions—blind constancy in Kurwenal, watchful care in Brangäne. They form the sole link between Tristan and Isolda and the outer world. The drama is planned in three concentric circles, graded from an outer world of daylight to an inner world of night. The outermost circle is peopled by the citizens of actuality—the sailors, the steersman, the herdsman, Melot and Mark. Echoes of this world, purged of earthliness by the intermediary figures of Kurwenal and Brangäne, reach faintly to the innermost circle in which Tristan and Isolda stand alone. The relations between the lovers are expressed in the crescendo-diminuendo structure of the whole work, but the outer setting sheds a peculiar light over them, turning joy to sorrow and love to death. The idea of " Fate " is embodied in the world, in the light of common day, in notions of honour and morality. Tristan and Isolda find themselves enmeshed in these things, and from their struggles springs a longing for the unfulfillable. Therefore the " Transfiguration " of the close must burst the barriers of this world, must point to a beyond where that world, the light of common day, honour and morality, have no more being, and where with them Fate's decree against the fulfilment of desire shall be annulled.

There is a link at this point between *Tristan* and an earlier work, *Tannhäuser*. The dramatic relations between *Tristan* and *Tannhäuser* resemble the musico-dynamic relations between *Tristan* and *Lohengrin*— that is to say, there are striking likenesses, but they are obverse likenesses, and the more mature work achieves a consummation undreamed of in the earlier. Passionate love is also the subject of the *Tannhäuser* drama, where the world and its morality stand between desire and fulfilment, and death is regarded as bringing salvation and apotheosis in the Beyond, in the " unreal." The emotional contrast in the two works is similar but the structure dissimilar. Tannhäuser's submission to law is recognised in *Tristan* as error—his " guilt " as the fulfilment of a higher commandment. The notions of morality and honour on which the world bases its laws are swept away before the claims of love. The irreconcilable contradiction which destroys Tannhäuser disappears for Tristan as soon as he is conscious of the power of love. Tristan before the love-drink is Tannhäuser penitent, in vassalage to the world, but after it he is Tannhäuser dead and freed from the encumbrance of the world's laws, which he sees now in their nothingness : " Was träumte mir von Tristans Ehre ? " (" What troubled dream of Tristan's honour ? "). He is now wholly the servant of passion—Tannhäuser in the Venusberg, having conquered his worldly fate.

This transvaluation of emotion in the man follows on a changed conception of woman. She has no longer two aspects, sinful and pure, devilish and saintly, but is wholly and indivisibly woman as the object of a passion which admits of no emotional schism. What the Flying Dutchman and Lohengrin wholly lacked, Wotan yearned for and Siegfried surmised, namely, sensual consummation, the resolution of that contradiction which destroyed Tannhäuser, was realised for the first time since Siegmund and Sieglinda knew its intoxicating premonitions. Sensuality and the hope of salvation are no longer opposites—Venus and Elizabeth are one. Brynhilda sleeping in expectation of her awakener, Woman grown conscious of her vocation to love, is the inspiration of the new work. Love fills Isolda and alone determines all her actions. Healing the wounded murderer, punishing the betrayer, wholly devoted to her lover, following him into the realms of death—she embodies all her creator's conceptions of woman and of love. Something which Wagner had yet to learn when, like Tannhäuser, he should for the second time join the bacchanalia of the Venusberg, is wanting in the figure of Tristan. His manhood and heroism have the glamour of an old tale, but Isolda is a woman fully formed, supremely fulfilling herself in her love. She is all action and strength ; he suffers and is weak, his strength consumed by desire.

She is the mistress of events, proffering the drink, extinguishing the torch, voyaging to Kareol. She is motion, she is music, she is that perfect harmony for which the lonely Tristan sighs. In Tristan there is no development—only a steady increase of anguished endurance. But in Isolda there is development from the will to revenge to the ecstasy of love and the transfiguration of death. Tristan, who is the passion which sets the whole in motion, dies as desire dies in fulfilment ; the creative impulse from which he springs has found its goal. Isolda passes on the full tide of the emotion of which she is the inexhaustible source. In Wagner's symbolism she is the " eternal feminine," here for the first time portrayed in its emotional completeness, gathering up in herself all his previous work and intimating all that is to come.

Dramatically the figures in *Tristan* are not seen in the round, and musically they are portrayed only in purely emotional expressionist moments. There are no characteristic individual motifs to build up step by step such vivid portraits as those of Siegfried or Mime, there is no pictorial tone-symbolism such as evoked a Fafner or a Loge, and there are no firmly established objective thematic formulæ to form the subject of the action, such as the Rhinegold and Valhalla motifs. Only the more superficial accessories of the drama, like the sailors' chorus, the ballad of Morold, and the description of the castle of Kareol are given decorative musical contours. In this way the contrast between essentials and non-essentials is emphasised, as at the hauling in of the rope in Act I, the realistic horn passage in Act II, and the awakening Tristan's first words to Kurwenal in Act III. When Wagner is dealing with the emotional drama he withdraws more and more from objective, naturalistic conceptions of musical expression. The notes of the horn in the second act change into the plash of a fountain and the rustle of leaves. The herdsman's mournful air carries us from the real world into Tristan's story of his dream and becomes his bitter cry for death, his curse upon the love-potion. The things of the real world become by chromatic inversion a negation of reality. The only motifs that remain unchanged throughout are those of the love-drama itself, regarded as symbols not of character but of emotion. Their significance consists exclusively in the ease with which they can be transformed and linked up, in their terseness, in the fact that they have no independent entity apart from their context. They are formed of three, four, or five single notes. They have a common derivation—the ascending chromatic fundamental line, developed by contrary motion, interchange of single notes, inversion, and rhythmic and tonal variation. These figures have nothing in common with the symbolic *Nibelung* motifs. Without rhythmic contour, settled melody, or harmonic covering, constantly changing their form, they are based on the natural tones of emotion on the borderline between speech and music, on the expansive impulse of highly concentrated tone-speech planned within the narrow limits of four closely compressed chromatic notes. The " art of transition " needs such small, such very small, phrases to mirror each shade of expression, and to carry on the line unbroken. Action is derived from this movement of the line and its involutions. It is a drama of chromatic motifs, carried through various stages of development up to musico-scenic form.

The unit of musical structure in *Tristan*, as in *Lohengrin* and all subsequent works, is the song-form. In the case of *Tristan* this emerges very clearly from the fact that the love-song in Act II and the prelude to Act III are anticipated in Wagner's settings for Mathilde's verses, of which they are no mere echoes but almost exact reproductions. Wagner himself recognised the part played by these songs. " I have come across the pencil draft of the song from which the Night scene is derived," he wrote to Mathilde in September 1861, " and God knows I like the song better than the grand scene ! Heavens ! It's the best thing I have ever done ! I quiver in every nerve when I hear it." The expression is exaggerated, and must not be taken for a critical evaluation. But it is Wagner's confession that he recognised the essence of the scene in the song, and this concentration of all that he held in the highest sense essential brought to *his* mind all the sources of the Night scene, whereas to others the wealth of images slumbering there could only be conveyed through scenic and musical execution.

The relation of these songs (the only ones composed by Wagner since the Paris *Romances*) to the *Tristan* score proves that Wagner worked involuntarily for visual representation on the stage even when he seemed to turn his back on the theatre. Where the creative impulse did not actually issue in scenic art his musicianship dwindled. The two songs so thoroughly exploited in *Tristan* are by far the most remarkable of the group. Of the three remaining, *Schmerzen*, based on a hint of the Day motif, and *Stehe still*, with the Death motif running through it and chromatic treatment of the second part, attain only here and there the expressionist ripeness of the other two. The first of the series, *Engel*, composed in November 1857, is merely a rich harmonic improvisation. Wagner was impelled to work up the two best songs scenically, and the fact that he derived from them the most important passages in his drama again indicates that drama's musical, lyrical origin. Indeed, even the stylistic character of the music is anticipated in the song.

The type of song employed in *Tristan* differs materially from those on which are based *Lohengrin*, *The Rhinegold*, and the first act of *Siegfried*. The two-bar division is retained as the basis of periodic structure, and is even shaped into *arioso* sections, but the form as a whole shows an effort towards inner expansion, towards the interpolation of more and more connecting links. Even in Mathilde's songs the song-form is broken through, so that they have the character of lyrical fantasias with a very free handling of the original lyrical conception. A desire for purely musical expansiveness, a delight in tone for its own sake, is the cause of this extension of boundaries, this bridging over of periods, this increasing lyrical development of the germ of song. There is evident delight in the actual sound of music, in the frequent repetition of short melodic phrases with changing harmonic backgrounds. The form is that of a flowing sequence of periods without a conceptual link to bind them. Love of the sensuous in tone—an insatiable thirst for sound, for melodic tone-pictures—is one of the most important formal elements in the music of *Tristan*. It characterises the musico-lyrical character of the work and displays itself stylistically as a tendency to sequence-formation at all moments of climax. It influences the general idea of the melodic expression-types, whose minutely complex structure is bound up with this preference for expansive development. Colourful harmony, constant changes of colour in modulation, a dissolution of the compact triad, also derive from a desire to increase the tonal wealth of music, to convey it as a thing in itself by means of the suggestive magic of sheer tone, of aerial vibrations.

The same desire governs both vocal and instrumental treatment. In *Tristan* Wagner wrote more effectively for the voice, more richly and passionately for the orchestra, than he had ever done before. Vocal treatment based on speech-accents employed in *The Nibelungs* was abandoned, and expression was attained principally through the tonal capacities of the vocal organ. Words merely mediate the musical structure, and only where they lend the latter violent emphasis do they play a prominent part. The voice flows on in a melodious expressionist line, but it is a melody which is made up of harmonic links which determine the vocal expression. These are discerned with a most exquisite sense of their significance within the individual chord, and also of their transitional or anticipatory significance within the harmonic drama, while at the same time they invariably give full value to the sensuous appeal of the voice. The element of character in the voice, emphasised in *Siegfried*, is here secondary to its erotic appeal. The voices are grouped with emphasis upon their tonal contrasts. In the principal scenes of the first and second acts the two leading voices are contrasted with one another, supplemented in the Night scene by Brangäne's rich contralto, which is introduced there simply for its tone-colouristic value. Mark's great scene is a lyrical display of the bass voice, designed to set forth the beauties of an organ more mellow and perfect than is often actually to be met with. The sailors' song, the chorus, and Kurwenal's ballad of Morold are lyrically conceived, and are introduced for their musical charm. Whereas the first two acts present the two principal voices side by side in various settings, the last displays them separately. There the whole gamut of appeal of the masculine voice is run through, from melancholy and wild cursing to visionary ecstasy. Since sheer tunefulness in song is excluded, the voice's sensuous appeal is elicited through continual emotional changes—the expression of suffering, of strength, of despair, of triumph. The quality of the male voice, its appeal as a vocal instrument, its place in the orchestral framework, are nowhere better exploited than in this scene. Such qualities as it inherently lacks are supplied by the female voice, of whose powers Isolda's death lament and song of transfiguration offer supreme examples. The work ends in an absolute surrender to the elemental quality of the female voice, this close having been prepared by the elemental in the male voice as exemplified in Tristan's great scene. The work as a whole may be regarded as a grand blend, union, and resolution of masculine and feminine vocal timbre, the two voices being used to develop one another's quality until feminine melody brings the close.

The orchestra as well as the voices emphasises quality and timbre in its members. The orchestra is smaller than in *The Nibelungs*. The tuba group is omitted save for the bass tuba, and the wood-wind is divided into groups of three instead of four. The eight and six horns of *The Ring* are replaced by four, there is but one harp, and the number of strings is not laid down, Wagner being content to prescribe merely " a sufficiency in strength and quality." The sense of elemental power and greatness expressed in *The Ring* scores, largely by means of the strength of the brass, is absent here, but tone-colour is more freely employed. This is appropriate to the structural technique. The intricate, iridescent fabric of the harmony demands, as compared with the music of *The Nibelungs*, more elaborate disintegration into independent parts. The opulent interweaving of parts creates a semblance of polyphonic writing, excludes accompaniments, and lends the tone as a whole an increased vitality and colour. Here, as in the vocal writing, purely tonal appeal is emphasised, as, for example, where the melancholy timbre of the English horn and the sad colours of the bass clarinet are exploited in lengthy solo passages. To the strings are assigned sustained vibrato effects, glissando and legato passages, and shimmering unison tremolos. The emotional effect peculiar to each instrument is utilised, the quivering, swooning appeal of mysterious gliding figures. In the heavy brass, more especially in the trombones, shadowy depths of colour are emphasised rather than dazzling brilliance, and the horn is re-endowed with the romantic character of the human voice. Involved, syncopated pedal effects evoke tone pictures in melting colours, and with increasing individualisation and economical solo use of the instruments the wealth and variety of their associations are increased. Sharpness and definition of accent are lacking in tone-colour as in harmonisation. A need of sound for sound's sake, a sensuous satisfaction in it, predominate, determining the treatment of voices and instruments alike. Working in and through these direct manifestations, it is, indeed, one of the basic forces from which the work as a whole derives, and it rules the visual as well as the musical scene.

A primary outburst of musical emotional expression occurs in the young sailor's song which directly follows the prelude at the opening of the first act. The line of the first two bars echoes the opening of the prelude, the timbre of the human voice serving as a bridge from wordless instrumental music to the sphere of music in association with concepts. The absence of accompanying harmony, the unreconciled conflict of rhythm and phrasings rouse tense expectation of the yet invisible ship and seascape. The curtain rises on Isolda and Brangäne in their closed pavilion. The sailor's song serves as a setting for Isolda's first outburst of passion, a pathetic, minor development of the motif of the overture. As the curtain of the tent is withdrawn the sailor's song is heard a second time, but the opening bars, reminiscent of the prelude, are omitted, as is the abrupt expression change of the lament. A descending bass tremolo supplies a harmonic foundation, and a sprightly sailors' chorus dispels the dreamlike mood. The sense of tension is relaxed, and the prelude theme emerges into the actualities of the drama as Isolda gazes on Tristan standing at the helm—" Mir erkoren, mir verloren " (" Once beloved, now removed "). The action is begun ; words come to the aid of pure tone and proceed to interpret it.

Isolda takes up the theme of Yearning. From this moment begins the revelation of its true nature—the drawing together of Tristan and Isolda by the fundamental force of ascending chromaticism. Subordinate incidents are introduced, such as Brangäne's errand to Tristan, her conversation with him, and Kurwenal's ballad of Morold. These interpolations are lyrical in form, and their plain diatonic character and formal symmetrical rhythm emphasise their unlikeness to the main theme and mark them as mere interruptions of the ascending line. In the exposition section the action consists in these external interruptions and thwartings of the main chromatic purpose. Its chief incident is the great dialogue between Isolda and Brangäne—a lament for Tristan's love-betrayal disguised as a plot for revenge. A false, descending chromatic line is developed—representing Tristan's false " double," the salvation-seeking Tantris—and above it rises the curse upon the betrayer. The declamatory pathos of this song marks it off from the inner, underlying trend of the act, for it represents love masquerading as hate. Afterwards the fundamental subject re-emerges, and Brangäne's question, "Kennst du der Mutter Künste nicht? " (" Mindest thou not thy mother's arts? "), brings into the drama an intimation of the mystery of the magic of love. The basic idea of the work, introduced into the action from the prelude by way of the sailor's song, hinted at subsequently in the Tantris motif, thrust aside by diatonic contrasts, becomes here for the first time fully manifest, establishes itself, takes command. There is a solemn and emphatic reminiscence of the prelude, and ascending chromaticism, in spite of all obstacles, takes fast root and proceeds to express itself in dramatic action.

At first hesitating and slight, it meets with a new interruption, scenically indicated by Isolda's death threat. This Death motif, though a seeming negation of the Yearning motif, has true identity with it, though its point is directed downward instead of upward. After Isolda's curse upon the descending motif of the Tantris phantom, the main theme, in this second disguise, introduces her second summons to Tristan. Chromaticism is recognised as emotionally dominant and the struggle to determine its *direction* now begins. Longing and the will to annihilation, the ascending trend of the prelude and its reverse, grapple with one another as the third phase of the musical action develops.

The true musical drama—chromatic resolution of all that is straightforward and formal in melody, harmony, and rhythm—opens with the meeting of Tristan and Isolda. Chromatic motifs crowd upon one another, superficially mutually contradictory but essentially at one in the task of breaking up diatonic, plastic movement. They have a common origin—the four chromatic ascending notes with which the prelude opens, and which are the very soul of the work. In " Tantris " guise this appears as contrary motion, and in the Death motif as a descending instead of an ascending sequence. The same formation is seen in the stately chord sequence, A flat major, A major, and F minor. These purely chromatic formations alternate with others in which the chromatic and the diatonic are mingled and the actual notes appear in changed order and rhythm. With Tristan's entrance the descending sixths of the Death motif become ascending thirds, half-tone progression gives place to whole-tone progression, and the motif is lifted out of the chromatic sphere into the diatonic, the realistic. This portrays Tristan's worldly aspect, envisaged most clearly in the oath of reconciliation, " Tristans Ehre, höchste Treu ! " (" Tristan's honour, highest truth ! "). Transformations of this character are not musical characterisations of an external drama. That drama is rather an externalisation of a musical evolutionary process which, circling continually about its chromatic base of four ascending half-tones, clarifies itself through permutations and transformations, change of direction and intermixture of diatonic contrasts, until its musical, emotional meaning finds objective interpretation, expresses itself in external drama in such terms as the Tantris, the Death, and the Honour motifs, finding its way through them to the fundamental subject, and interpreting it to the emotions and to the eye.

Such is the content of the principal scene of the act—the great dialogue between Tristan and Isolda. All that precedes this serves to build up the fundamental musical idea in its external aspect as an expression of Isolda's longing. This basic emotion, of which she is conscious, and which finds expression through her, is thwarted in its aspirations and driven *downwards*, is changed into a craving for death. Tristan falls under the domination of the same emotion, though in another form, for the line of the motif of Yearning is reversed and a hard, defiant rhythm takes the place of the softly interwoven notes. Here the fundamental idea is twice disguised—in Isolda's part as a phantom of death, in Tristan's as a phantom of honour. During the course of the scene the two phantoms are set side by side, they are unmasked, and the truth, the underlying unity of the twofold illusion, is established.

The scene falls into three parts—Isolda's first discussion with Tristan, closing with her demand that he shall drink with her the "cup of reconciliation," the actual drinking of the love-potion which both believe will bring them death, and their awakening to the knowledge that the desire for death and the desire for love are one. The first part is dominated by the illusory Honour motif, to which is added that of the threat of death, enhanced by the "Tantris" phantom. Developed in plastic motival contrasts, it fades slowly into Tristan's motif of Yearning. Chromaticism enters upon the E flat minor change of "War Morold dir so wert, nun wider nimm das Schwert " ("If so thou lov'dst this lord, then lift once more thy sword "). Tristan is overcome by the sense that he has betrayed love, his militant sense of honour is broken, but he still lacks the upward urge of will, and the descending death-desire prevails.

The first transformation has been effected, and Tristan's Honour motif has lost the rhythmic force of resistance. Isolda's demand, the Death motif, dominates the second part. Contrast with the external world is emphasised as the drama passes at this point from the light of common day into the emotional sphere. To the former belong the shouts of the seamen in sight of land, expressed in vigorous, direct sequences of seconds and fifths, and these, breaking in upon the lovers' dialogue, hasten its development towards the climax. Isolda's motif of Yearning, mockingly distorted, appears in her lyrical " Mein Herr und Ohm, sieh' die dir an: ein sanftres Weib gewännst du nie " ("My Lord and King, here is thy queen, 'twere hard to find a fairer bride "). The

Death threat is overpowered by sounds from without, which Tristan takes up in a storm of passionate emotion, " Los den Anker ! Das Steuer dem Strom ! " (" Down the anchor ! then stern to the stream ! "). With the concluding notes of the oath of reconciliation, " Trug des Herzens ! Traum der Ahnung ! " (" Traitor spirit ! Dream ill-omened "), he cleaves the Honour motif in twain, even as Isolda destroys the Death motif with the words " Verräter ! Ich trink' sie dir ! " (" Betrayer ! I drink to thee ! ").

The second transformation is thus accomplished, and honour and revenge are alike resolved into the primal motif, their artificial disguises discarded, the bonds of melody, rhythm, and harmony thrown off for the formless flow of the chromaticism whence they arose. The march of events to this point has served to unmask these themes, and everything external, objective, interposed between the prelude and this moment of release is but a means of breaking the fetters of realistic thematisation, of revealing in visible drama and in words the meaning of the idea expressed in the prelude. There here occurs a second blooming of the line of the prelude, richer than the first, broken up into delicately graded registers and endowed through the voices of Man and Woman with more complete musical consciousness.

The people's shouts of acclamation break upon the mighty crescendo of the prelude theme, forming an external interruption that cannot really impede the tempest of song which again and again overpowers all else until, with the headlong descent of the Death motif, " O Wonne voller Tücke ! O truggeweihtes Glücke ! " (" O rapture fraught with cunning ! O fraud with bliss o'er-running ! "), an abrupt close is reached. Yearning has proved its power to loosen false restraints. The prelude has found its completion, but does not this time die out on a note of question. With redoubled force the chromatic line asserts its victory against the realistic harmonies of C major fanfares.

The content and structure of the first act are concerned with the struggle to present the fundamental emotion of the work, in an external, dramatic sense, as passionate desire, in a musical sense as a chromatic basic motif. It supplies the driving force in the overture and is set free by the action from its scenico-musical disguises. In the second act there is no such development by contrast. The Love motif is no longer the goal of mutual recognition. There is instead an expansion of desire which loosens all restraints and can find fulfilment only in recognition of the impossibility of fulfilment. There are consequently no external dramatic crises, and where reminiscences of such occur they serve merely to expedite psychologically preordained events. In the scenic drama this condition is expressed as a dawning consciousness of the non-real, of night, of death as the sole fulfilment of life ; in the musical drama as a development towards melody of the chromatic fundamental sounds. Chromatic melody is formed in opposition to diatonic melody. The negation of the plastic element in musical expression leads to the embodiment of the non-real, of the non-objective—of the dream. The illusion of a world of dreams is to be conveyed to the senses so convincingly, so expressively, that reality seems phantasmal beside it. The main trend of this act is the passage from day to night, from the waking to the dreaming state, from the natural diatonic to melodic chromaticism.

It opens with a pang of awakening to the world of daylight—with the headlong descending fifths foreshadowed in the sailor's " Ostwärts streicht das Schiff " (" Eastwards speeds the ship ") and uttered in the choral refrain, " Heil unsrem Held Tristan " (" Bravo ! our brave Tristan "). Round this plastic diatonic centre are woven an ascending bass line and, opposing and answering it, a descending treble. Both contain the fundamental chromaticism. Together they enclose the plain diatonic fifths motif in an ever-tightening clasp until they unite in the fundamental motif which, swaying upwards and downwards, maintains on the whole an ascending trend. The prelude is no highly finished piece of work, but rather a rough sketch of the passions seeking expression in the act to follow and embodied scenically in Tristan's urgent seeking of Isolda. The scene opens in daylight mood with the sound of the huntsmen's horns dying slowly in the distance. Isolda and Brangäne hold the stage alone, Brangäne as representative of the " real " world in contrast to Isolda. The motif of yearning, reversed and descending, becomes the motif of the waiting Isolda's expectation, and answers Brangäne's simple recitative, but it is not until Brangäne accuses herself of having changed the potion that the motif of yearning takes its place as the driving force of the scene— " Frau Minne, kenntest du nicht ? Nicht ihres Zaubers macht ? " (" Love's goddess dost thou not know ? "). The motif of Expectation expands by wide curves into song— " Die Leuchte, und wär's meines Lebens Licht, lachend sie zu löschen zag' ich nicht ! " (" The signal, and were it my spirit's spark, smiling, I'd destroy it : hail the dark ! "). Isolda hurls the torch to earth, Brangäne vanishes in the darkness, daylight and actuality are together extinguished. As Isolda's expectant motif descends, the opposing line of the prelude rises, the counterpart of the waving of her veil. The motifs of Expectation and of Yearning, alike in origin but contrary in motion, press towards one another in shorter and shorter rhythms, with sharper and sharper accentuation until they meet in the unison of voices.

The method of musical development which, introduced by the Dusk scene, dominates the Night scene, differs markedly from that of the first act. Act I consists in a dramatic exploitation of motival impulses from which fundamental sounds emerge as unity. It forms a bridge from unconscious to conscious emotion. In Act II *apparently* similar means are employed, the polyphony being even somewhat richer than before, with the basses and middle parts sustaining the themes in all manner of guises such as strettos, augmentations, chromatic and diatonic alterations, but these themes have not the same importance as formerly, since they are relegated to the unconscious. Above them rises song, now pure lyrical, emotional expression. This departure from plastic motival expression marks the increasing dominion of the Dream world. It tends gradually to do away with motival objectivity—first in the singing voices which develop on purely lyrical melodic lines, and subsequently in the orchestration, where the motival threads are spun out thin and gradually lose even this subconscious reminiscent function, becoming but a dim vibrant accompaniment to the emotional melodic line of song. Finally, the chromatic foundation is reached again, and the expression melody of the Dream world establishes itself as reality.

Such is the interior trend of the great " Night " love scene in Act II. It has but one counterpart in Wagner's work—the love scene between Siegfried and Brynhilda. In *Siegfried* awakening and the will to live, in *Tristan* gathering shadows and the will to death and darkness, provide the fundamental appeal. The second act of *Tristan* is the only third act of *Siegfried* which Wagner could at that time create, for, emotionally, it represents the collapse of all worldly hopes, and, musically, it is an attempt to resolve all that is fixed and solid, to transcend and break up plastic contours. Harmony, seen on its " daylight " side in *The Ring*, now stands revealed as a nocturnal phenomenon in magical, melting outlines passing at length into mere tonal vibrations.

The structure of the scene, as always with Wagner, is threefold, representing a gradual release from motival thematisation by way of a harmony based on vocalism until the primal motif appears as a melody-forming force. The first section, still well provided with contrasts of idea and motif, comprises a dialogue between day and night; the second, which has a peaceful close, contains the love song of two voices and bridges the gulf from memories of the real world to the realm of night—" O Sink' hernieder, Nacht der Liebe " (" O night of rapture, rest upon us ! "); the third represents the transformation of night into the dream of fulfilment. This last contains the germ of the motif of Yearning and develops this fundamental idea of the work in ecstatic melody—" Ohne Nennen, ohne Trennen, neu' Erkennen, neu' Entbrennen, endlos ewig einbewüsst, höchste Liebeslust ! " (" Never spoken, never broken, newly sighted, newly lighted, endless ever all our dreams . . . love delights supreme ! ").

These three stages may be named " Twilight, Night, and Dream," or " motival expansion, harmonic resolution, and melodic development of the fundamental idea." In and through them, linking night and dream, harmonic resolution and the revelation of melody, is heard the motif of Yearning from Wagner's setting of Mathilde's song " Träume." Its vague melodic suspensions draw their peculiar charm from the chromatic shifting of the accompanying parts. The manifold inversions of the harmonisation, leading from one interrupted cadence to another, plunge the hearer deeper and deeper into the dark regions of formless emotional ecstasy. In this chromatic ascent and descent, this continual overlapping and divagation of melody, this expression of eternal flux, of the structural freedom necessary when chromaticism governs form, resides the peculiar charm of the *Tristan* music, of the new " art of transition." It is employed more deliberately in the second act than in the first, and finds its first concentrated expression in the Wesendonk song. This song, which lends its special character to the dialogue of the lovers in their Night scene, reappears, contenting itself with the mere expansion of its suspensions, as the song of the watchful Brangäne—the voice of Night itself finding its sonorous echo in the singer's breath.

Amidst the tremulous tones of harmonies whose words echo memories of the Daylight world, emotion seeks its final resolution. The melody of fulfilment emerges from a maze of chords—a transfiguration of the chromatic fundamental idea. Harmonically revealed by the opening interval of a fourth, it is developed by sequence. Rising by thirds, it passes through the whole cycle of harmonic changes to express an infinite crescendo. Leadership is assigned to the singing voices only. They cry to one another in narrowing repetitions, the lines cross, rising and falling. From the first solemn set form the song breaks up into arabesques. The orchestral parts are drawn into this elemental process of rhythmic, ornamental, chordal disintegration, whence, passing over from the orchestral to the singing voices, the fundamental notion rises to heights of ecstasy. Its expansive force bursts the ring of chromaticism, and Day, by whose banishment it came into being, breaks harshly through.

The goal sought by the original musical idea is not unending climax but perfect resolution. Passion leads back into " the world," symbolised by Mark. The lament for Mark's shame and Tristan's lost honour is built up on Tristan's Honour motif with the notes in inverse sequence. This protracted scene is a necessary organic link in the musical drama, for it joins two musical characters—the triumph of the motif of Yearning and its return to the form of the opening of the prelude after Mark has demanded of Fate " Den unerforschlich tief geheimnisvollen Grund, wer macht der Welt ihn kund ? " (" The unexplained and hidden cause of all my woes, who will to us disclose ? "). Between these highest and lowest points in the music, between the revelation of its power and its dim origins, stands Mark's speech. In it the fundamental idea returns precipitately to the point whence it set out. The music is really self-sufficient without the aid of words, like the instrumental recitatives in Beethoven's Ninth Symphony. It is an example of a grand soloistic interlude in which an intimate emotional drama finds expression, and which, in this instance, owing to the wide scope of the drama, is assigned to the human voice and supported by words. The motif of Yearning having overreached itself, having broken down through its own excess of force, reverts violently to its origins. Tristan falls by the sword of the powers of Day and the fundamental idea is rent in precipitate, hammering chords.

The events of the second act exhaust the expansive power of the fundamental musical idea ; it can rise no further, and, sinking by way of its origin in the prelude to the depths, it disintegrates. Its destruction, its resolution into the musical elements whence it was formed, and its redintegration into a grand chromatic melody free from the dissonant climaxes of passion, form the content of the third act. The first bars of the prelude are suggestive of this drama. The chromatic upward-striving, endless line is knit into an F minor theme in two-bar periods. The tension formerly suggested by chromatically distorted harmonisation is now modified to diatonic chords, and the ascending sequence of thirds in the concluding section is not an instance of arsis but of dissolution into the void. The music of this prelude is throughout an adaptation of the Wesendonk song *Im Treibhaus*, composed almost a year earlier, in May 1858. So profound is the agreement between verses and music that one might almost believe Wagner to have been influenced by Mathilde were not the poem itself only an echo of the *Tristan* libretto. Wagner probably caught that echo, and its lyric form no doubt suggested the music which hovered in his mind. This prelude, like all Wagner's work, originated in Wagner himself, acquired sensual reality through emotion awakened by him, and was thus, while seemingly mingled with another's contribution, his own, first and last. Alterations made by Wagner later for the prelude, though apparently insignificant, represent a real difference in the two versions. D minor, the key of the song, is replaced by F minor. Six-eight time becomes in the prelude four-four time. Of the equal quavers with which the song begins the first is broadly accentuated and prolonged in the prelude, and change in the time gives the ascending thirds increased evenness of motion, so that the expression of the first bars becomes heavier, that of the ascending figures more desolate. A chromatic sharpening of the ascending line is found in the score, and was subsequently introduced into later editions of the songs.

The herdsman's melancholy air in the third act, like the music for the horns in the second and the sailor's song in the first, forms an intermediary between prelude and action. It is wordless and is interpreted by the scene presented—the ruined castle, Tristan's motionless form, Kurwenal listening anxiously to his master's breathing. As in Mark's lament in Act II, the scene here finds utterance in instrumental, not vocal, music through the elegiac timbre of the English horn. The prelude, the scene, the herdsman's air melt into one another without abrupt transition until the fundamental theme of the prelude finds footing in the scene and Tristan awakes.

Like the motif of Yearning in the first act, the melancholy mood of the third is but gradually revealed, through continual change, contrast, and accentuation. In Tristan's first words to Kurwenal the interior and exterior worlds are directly contrasted, the fresh chordal rhythm of the Kareol motif, of home, being set against the chromatic distortion of Tristan's questions. From these there gradually emerges the outline of the motif of Melancholy : " Wo ich erwacht weilt' ich nicht; doch, wo ich weilte, das kann ich dir nicht sagen. Die Sonne sah ich nicht, noch sah ich Land und Leute : doch, was ich sah, das kann ich dir nicht sagen " (" Where I awoke—ne'er I was ; but where I wandered I can indeed not tell thee. The sun I could not see, nor paysage fair, nor people : but, what I saw, I can indeed not tell thee "). Diatonic thematisation is resolved, memories of chromatic-ism awake, and the original motif reappears. New action is imparted by Tristan's thanks to Kurwenal for the message borne to Isolda, and her image is evoked by the Night song motif, " Das Schiff ! Dort streicht es am Riff ! Siehst du es nicht, Kurwenal ? " (" Hurrah ! Hurrah ! She reaches the bar ! Dost thou not see her ? Kurwenal ! ").

There is no answer but the herdsman's melody. The motif of Yearning is incapable of further transformations. Disillusionment throws the action back to its starting-point at the beginning of the act. From a prolongation of the herdsman's melody emerges the Melancholy motif of the prelude, raised now to passionate intensity. The melody of Melancholy mingles with the melody of Loneliness, and the two become a curse upon the love potion, which their own longings created : " Den ich gebraut, der mir geflossen, den Wonne schlürfend je ich genossen, verflucht sei, furchtbarer Trank ! Verflucht, wer dich gebraut ! " (" Thou I have brewed, thou I created, to sip whose rapture I have been fated, I curse thee—cowardly draught ! Accursed is he who quaffed ! ").

The words mark the extreme of anguish, the summit of motival synthesis. All the musical formations circling round the expression of desire, of melancholy, and of death mingle to form a single expres-sionist line. It is a development which, governed externally by Kurwenal's words and musically through the motive forces these bring with them, signifies the elemental working of all the impulses towards dissonance, towards the break-up of harmony and melody, contained in the chromatic fundamental note. The musical line, though strongly impregnated with the conceptual significance

Y

associated with words, preserves throughout the tone-value of song and passes wholly into the dissonant sphere of chromaticism. It is the exact opposite of the harmony-saturated melody of the musical style found ' in the second act of *Tristan*. The fulfilment of Tannhäuser's story of his pilgrimage to Rome, it destroys the will to melodic form therein expressed, for it is the product of the basic idea directed towards negation, a transformation of the force of desire into the will to destruction. The words accompanying it are a curse upon the love potion—and this curse in a musical sense is the curse of chromaticism. After this supreme expressive effort its tonal elements disintegrate, and it dissolves into nothingness.

The destruction of the motif of Yearning by the curse and its resolution into its component parts represents the highest tension of dissonance and leads to the verge of the musically opposite sphere. Above tender vibrating harmonies rises the Yearning motif, now robbed of all its harshness. Dying out in a premonition of the song of Transfiguration, it calls to mind the music of the love-night, of dream. A return of the " greeting to Arindal " from *Die Feen*—the diatonic song of the first moment of reunion, " Barg im Busen uns sich die Sonne, leuchten lachend Sterne der Wonne " (" Hid our hearts away sunlight's streaming, bliss would bloom from star's tender beaming ") —forms an urging bass line. With the dæmonic element in the motif of Yearning cast out and robbed of its powers of dissonance by the curse, the moment of melodic fulfilment is reached. It is first announced in the joyous C major tones of the herdsman's reed-pipe. Then a storm of sound breaks loose ; the love melody emerges, all the motifs of the dream-world reappear, enlacing and spurring one another in alternating rhythms, a medley of three-four, four-four, and five-four time. Isolda's motif of Expectation is heard as from a distance, portraying the extinction of the beacon light which was to be a message to the beloved. Day and Night find embodiment in music which on Isolda's lips proclaims fulfilment—" Wie hör' ich das Licht ? die Leuchte, ha ! Die Leuchte verlischt. Zu ihr ! Zu ihr ! " (" What ! hails me the light ? the torchlight, ha ! the torch is extinct ! I come ! I come ! "). The Death motif and the Love motif mingle in solemn strains, the motif of Yearning ascends in wide arches and a reminiscence of the prelude is heard. The fundamental idea completes its course in Tristan's death cry.

Tristan's motif of Yearning has found its goal ; weary of chromaticism, it finds its way into ascending melody, and there breaks off. A second cycle, however, awaits its fulfilment. Between the two is interposed Isolda's lament and an intrusion of the " Daylight " world —Melot's death and Kurwenal's, Mark's second bewildered questioning of fate. The inner drama has wound its way from the world of passion which dominates the prelude to the fulfilment which follows the climax of Tristan's death. Tristan's curse, destroying the passion of desire, passes into Isolda's song of triumphant fulfilment which sets free the passion of self-sacrifice. The grand melody of the work—the Fulfilment melody of the second act—is heard once more and brings all harmonies into play. Gliding, hovering in inexhaustible resolution and dissolution of all that is harmonically concrete, it rises to ever new combinations and resolutions, proclaiming at last the motif of Yearning as the ultimate fact.

Wagner was forty years of age when he conceived the idea of *Tristan*. He was forty-four when he began it, and forty-six when he finished it. Thus even in outward fact *Tristan* is the central work of his life in another sense than is *The Ring*. The latter was begun earlier and finished later, linking Wagner's early struggle for personal freedom with the conscious superiority of the mature artist. *The Ring* accordingly affords a wider cross-section, *Tristan* a more concentrated impression, of Wagner's career. In *Tristan* there is perfect identity of music and scene, springing from artistic comprehension of a single element in music, namely chromaticism. Chromaticism, the natural expression of music and speech alike, is made the basic formula from which spring all the phenomena of the music and of the scene. In *The Ring*—a portrayal of the universe—a corresponding formula is found in instrumental harmony, and the drama is based on the contrast between consonant and dissonant tonal relations, as it is also in *Lohengrin* and *Die Feen*. In *Tristan*, however, as in *Das Liebesverbot* and *Tannhäuser*, song, the erotic utterance of the individual, finds its supreme concentration in the fundamental musical idea, its richest development in the whole. In each of the two great works a dream of Wagner's boyish fancy finds fulfilment; intervals appear in bodily shape. They walk the stage, they initiate and control the drama—a drama of notes and their relations—a revelation of the life in musical forms, envisaged as the scenic action of musical notes in their twofold aspect as chord and as chromatic line. It expresses the emergence into melody of both aspects of music and their resolution by means of speech in the pure emotion of song.

Such is the summit achieved. Emotional naturalism wrings from music its invisible secrets, forces it to become nakedly visible and to act out its formal developments upon the stage. Wagner's instinctive urge to nature, to woman, to love, finds its goal. A mystic intoxication lays hold on him. Transfiguration becomes an orgy—his imagination is obsessed by sensual riot—but in the midst of these things " set form," diatonic force, the controlling artist's will to form, rises again to life. He awakes from the night of unconscious emotional drama to conscious play : Tannhäuser forsakes the Venusberg.

CHAPTER III

THE VENUSBERG

WHEN Wagner laid *Siegfried* aside to begin work on *Tristan* he argued that he was turning his attention to an opera which would offer few difficulties to the producer. He hoped that he should soon see the new work performed and reap a speedy success. His earlier works up to *Lohengrin* had by now established themselves, and their popularity increased with the increase of public interest in expressionist art. To this interest Wagner now wished to appeal with a work more advanced than *Lohengrin*. Pieces from the still incomplete *Nibelung* cycle were out of the question ; Wagner's own interest in them had temporarily flagged. All his creative energies had been engaged by *Tristan*, and he felt confident of complete success. He could not rest till he saw the work actually live upon the boards. Breitkopf and Härtel had been persuaded, on promise of the opera's being practicable, to publish and even to print the score, Bülow had made a pianoforte arrangement, and all the material was ready for use almost as soon as the composition was completed. An enterprising manager, Edward Devrient, of the Karlsruhe Court Theatre, undertook to produce the new work, and the Grand Duke of Baden, a young man of liberal sympathies, seemed prepared to invite the political fugitive to Karlsruhe on his own responsibility, so that the first performance might take place under Wagner's own supervision. Nevertheless, as the expected date approached, negotiations with Karlsruhe slowed down. Wagner accuses Devrient of having secretly undermined the project, but though there may be some truth in the reproach the true cause of Devrient's opposition lay in his better acquaintance with the work itself. For such a venture he must have been a bigger man than Liszt, and, even so, success must have been doubtful. Devrient's sober practical estimate of the affair showed a lack of enthusiasm, but it was just. The score was not easy to perform ; on the contrary, it was the hardest Wagner had yet produced, though he did not realise this until after many negotiations with the theatres.

After the nervous and mental exhaustion of his great creative achievement, Wagner's first impulse was to find relaxation in external activities. Germany being still barred against him, he once more set his hopes on Paris, and having sold the scores of *The Ring* to Otto Wesendonk he took a fashionable house in that city for a period of years. There he entertained the artistic world at large, and Minna rejoined him from Dresden to manage his household, though, for the rest, husband and wife led separate lives. There was a prospect of *Tannhäuser's* being performed at the Théâtre lyrique, though Wagner's interest in that work had waned and was now centred in *Tristan*. His hopes of Karlsruhe being disappointed, he proposed to rent the Italian Opera and produce *Tristan* there with a German *ensemble*. In preparation for this undertaking three grand Wagner concerts were to be given in January and February 1860, with the object of interesting press and public in his work and providing money for his operatic projects. Wagner rehearsed the orchestra, Bülow the choruses, but the newspaper success was slight, the expenses enormous, and only an unexpected present of ten thousand francs saved the financial situation. Much the same results attended two concerts in Brussels, even though Wagner had braced himself to renew relations with his old enemy, the critic Fétis.

As the *Tristan* project faded again into the clouds a new avenue of success suddenly opened. At von Bülow's instigation, Princess Metternich attended one of Wagner's concerts, and her interest was captured by his extravagant personality. She spoke for him to Napoleon III, who in a mood of gallantry promised that *Tannhäuser* should be produced at the Grand Opéra. Thus the object which had once lured Wagner overseas from Riga, and which Liszt had recommended after his flight from Dresden, was to be fulfilled at last, in 1860. The way seemed to lie open for a European success. Everything was put at Wagner's disposal; in numbers and in all other respects, orchestra, chorus, and ballet were to answer to his requirements, singers were to be engaged on his recommendation, and there seemed to be nothing lacking for an ideal production.

One or two points only remained in dispute. Dietsch, the conductor of the orchestra (the man to whom the *Flying Dutchman* sketch had once been offered for composition), opposed Wagner's wish to

conduct himself, and was supported by the inviolable traditions of the
Opéra. Wagner, for his part, refused to interpolate the customary
ballet in the second act, though instead he expanded the Venusberg
scene into a grand pantomimic spectacle. These two points of dis-
agreement became known to the public, which was already prejudiced
against the foreign composer's work by the striking incident of the
imperial command. An opposition directed in part against the
Emperor, in part against Princess Metternich, in part against foreign
composers, in part against Wagner's work in general, found many
vantage points for attack. There was unrest and discontent amongst
the singers, and Niemann, though engaged on Wagner's own recommendation, did not as Tannhäuser fulfil the hopes set upon him.
After many delays the first performance took place on March 13, 1861,
and ended in a scandalous demonstration on the part of Parisian society
against the work thus forced upon it. Similar disturbances occurred on
the second and third nights, and the critics confirmed society's verdict.
The management were willing to attempt a fourth performance, but
Wagner, realising that it would be labour lost, maintained his decision
to withdraw the work.

Paris was clearly not to be the base of a victorious artistic campaign.
At the same time Wagner found himself obliged to leave the house he
had rented for three years, as a road was to be made over the site on
which it stood. Money difficulties attended the failure of his opera
and his enforced removal. He had already sold the score of *The
Dusk of the Gods*, not yet composed, to Wesendonk. The *Tannhäuser*
catastrophe set a seal upon the failure of his Paris hopes. One thing
only had resulted from his visit—the efforts of the Saxon ambassador
in Paris had procured him a conditional amnesty. He might return
to Germany, though not to Saxony. Direct intercourse with the
German stage was open to him once more. As he had done twenty
years earlier, Wagner, after suffering shipwreck in Paris, weighed
anchor for home.

The external incidents of this Paris episode had not, despite the
many disappointments they entailed, so strong an effect on Wagner as
had similar incidents twenty years earlier. At that time success or
failure in Paris had involved in Wagner's own mind the decision of a
lifetime. Now even the success of *Tannhäuser* could have been, at
best, but an alleviation of his difficulties. The hope of seeing his works

performed and radiating their influence in Paris, though providing a plausible ostensible motive, was not really what brought him to that city. There was a far deeper reason. As Wagner emerged from the loneliness of *Tristan* with the strain of its creation still upon him, he experienced after-effects which he could not then understand. Dimly these urged him to seek conditions favourable for work yet to come. He needed an atmosphere of full-blooded sensuous excitement, and the thought of Parisian society, with its *salons* inviting to pleasure and enjoyment, suddenly attracted him. For him Parisian life was a theatrical scene, magically lit. Even the love interest was not wanting. He became intimate with Liszt's daughter, Blandine, whose coquettish and social graces exercised the spell of delights long denied, and caused the memory of Mathilde's more spiritual charms to pale. Wagner's thoughts and actions were still concerned with *Tristan*, but was he himself any longer the Tristan of the " death-devoted head " ? Was he not rather that singer to whom the nature of love is revealed in unrestrained sensual allurement ? Was not Tristan's craving for death the very same craving that drove Tannhäuser into the magic kingdom of Armida, into the arms of Venus ? And was not that earlier work still psychologically incomplete—a mere musical sketch in its most vital emotional moment ? " It is strange ! When first I made *Tannhäuser* I was quite incapable of bringing off the spiritual, the passionate—I might almost call it the feminine-ecstatic ! I have been obliged to cut the whole and cast it afresh. Really, I am disgusted with my pasteboard Venus of those days. . . . But Tannhäuser's freshness, his vital eagerness, is all good, and there I have absolutely nothing to alter. . . . Only I have had to do a little patching here and there in passionate passages : for example, I have replaced a very flat violin passage accompanying Tannhäuser's outburst at the close of Act II by a new one, very difficult, but the only thing that satisfies me. However, I can ask anything of my orchestra here. It is the best in the world." Thus Wagner wrote to Mathilde.

There is no documentary proof that Wagner would have composed the *Venusberg* music without the stimulus of the Paris production, but there can be no doubt that he would not have made it, any more than he would consent to insert a ballet in Act II, if he had thought the change superfluous. The apparent compromise of a new scene to take the place of a Wartburg ballet was actually only the final incident in the quickening of music which had long slumbered in the composer's subconsciousness—the very music that had driven him to seek the sensual stimulus of Parisian life. The Opéra, Napoleon III, the ballet, had nothing to do with this process, which was a new creation, a revitalisation from an inner compulsion, of the work problematically conceived in Dresden. At the same time it is a completion of *Tristan*, for it represents a return to life from the night of love. The new version discloses what Wagner himself came to regard as of the essence of *Tannhäuser* and what he thought unimportant. The world to which Tannhäuser returns is unimportant ; here, therefore, the old version is retained. It represents the operatic side of *Tannhäuser*, and as such has ceased to interest the more mature composer. A few modifications in detail, a few cuts and orchestral retouchings, are all that Wagner finds necessary. As an artistic whole this world is complete. But that world from which Tannhäuser comes—the world of night, love-magic, and chromaticism into which Tristan passed—*that* is of essential significance. Tristan has wakened from the death-ecstasy of love, thirsty for reality. *Tristan* and the *Venusberg* (the original title even of the Dresden *Tannhäuser*) are closely bound up with one another, and the Paris version of *Tannhäuser* is as little dependent on the circumstances of the Paris production as is *Tristan* on Wagner's relations with Mathilde. In each case experience affords no more than a final incentive to actualisation in tone ; it does not govern the creative imagination, which for *Tristan's* sake evoked Mathilde's romantic tenderness and for *Tannhäuser's* the sensuous atmosphere of Paris.

The two conceptions are closely allied, and the second, though inferior to the first in outward compass and weight, embodies the climax of the impulse at work in both. Concerned strictly with essentials, its weight is somewhat disproportionate to that of the earlier work in which it is implanted. The Paris *Venusberg* is in reality an independent work, a dialogue between waning night and the dawn of a new day. Imbued with the impulses of the *Tristan* music, the *Venusberg* develops these on the musical and scenic lines of *Tannhäuser*, thus revealing the profound underlying affinity between the two works. The primal chromatic motif of *Tristan* was already present in the first *Venusberg* music, but whereas there it existed in germ only, it now attains luxuriant growth. The repetition of the Pilgrims' Chorus is omitted, and the scene directly following the prelude is pantomime. Clad in the ecstatic music of Isolda's Transfiguration, it is free even from those remnants of conceptualism, Isolda's music-dissolved words. Scene and action speak unaided. The link of melody is omitted equally with the words, and the motifs stand by themselves, concise, rhythmically accentuated, chromatically broken. The motif of Yearning is heard, flinging up the chromatic four-tone line in an echoing third. The wild excitement of the rhythms is enhanced by the use of drum, triangle, cymbals, and castanets. Figures for the strings forming an accompaniment to the Pilgrims' Chorus in the overture become a host of *amoretti* flying above the revels of nymphs and bacchantes, who sink to earth pierced by the arrows of the little love-gods. The inspiration of the whole is pictorial. "I wish I had some of Genelli's water-colours beside me," writes Wagner. "He renders these mythological orgies most vividly." The music rises to a climax of wild debauchery. The eroticism of *Tristan* is here, but it does not find musical resolution through words, for it develops in an exactly opposite sense, from an elemental maelstrom of rhythm and dynamic to melodic security built by words. A chorus of sirens exchanges the dual rhythm of the earlier version for more lively triple time. The second version is infinitely richer in all respects than the first. By way of graceful mythological pictures of love the siren melody introduces the second scene. The musical orgy has stormed itself out, and words again play a part.

It is only after Venus's curse that the libretto of the duologue is notably longer in the second version than in the first. The extra lines are almost all assigned to Venus, Tannhäuser's rôle remaining fundamentally unaltered, and being but slightly modified to suit with that of Venus. Musically also Tannhäuser's three verses of song are essentially unchanged. But the change in Venus's music is very great. Apart from a considerable lengthening of the music to fit the long, new verses, the old words are to a great extent newly set, with a noteworthy shifting of emphasis, even in declamatory accent. Where the old music is retained, as in Venus's melody of appeal, "Geliebter, komm, sieh dort die Grotte" ("Beloved, come! See yonder bower"), it is, like the sirens' chorus, changed from two- to three-time and transposed from the simply sensuous F sharp major to F major. The magical effect of this change is enhanced by the orchestration. Slurred tremolos, shakes, and sustained notes for the strings, which alternate in groups, take the place of the simpler combinations of the Dresden score, together with brilliant chord figures for the flutes and alternating sustained wind passages. As in the earlier version, this song of Venus affords a first melodic synthesis, but it is here spun out to ornamental chromaticism—" Schlürfst du den Göttertrank, strahlt dir der Liebesdank " (" Thou shalt drink draughts divine, drink deep of love's own wine "). The motif of Yearning is heard undisguised, the Venus melody rises in delicate curves sustained by the violins. What was once but a dream has become reality—the goddess of love, the dispenser of delights, is revealed in musical actuality. Up to this point the outline of the original conception is retained, but the Curse, with its sharply broken intervals, its contrasts of abrupt leaps and smooth transitions, altogether transcends its origins, passing into the region of the Curse in *Tristan*, though here transposed from masculine to feminine, from violent to purely sensuous song.

Wagner had at that time written no scene in which the sexual character of woman, the seductress and enchantress, as expressed in the voice, is so forcefully revealed. Isolda's notes of longing seem almost conventional compared with this song of Venus, in which the hot allurements of elemental eroticism are conjured into artistic form. Only one other scene in all Wagner's work is comparable with it, the scene between Kundry and Parsifal, but whereas that forms the centre of a very comprehensive whole, in the Paris *Tannhäuser* the contrasts are presented more simply, the work is unencumbered by the working out of a plot and is confined to the essence of the tonal drama. This drama consists in the contrast between the music of Venus and that of Tannhäuser, between the world of night and of love and the daylight world of nature, between the flowing chromaticism of instinct and measured diatonic melody. The latter is embodied in Tannhäuser's song as composed in Dresden, and this is preserved unaltered. Fighting its way against a riot of exaggerated chromaticism, it emerges into the actualities of a plastic tone-conception. The conflict of these opposites forms the substance of the scene in which the luxuriant elaborations of Venus's song alternate with the purely dynamic development of Tannhäuser's. The chromatic and the diatonic, free linear expression and shapely song-structure, naturalistic emotion, and stylised form, are at grips, " Göttin der Wonn' und Lust ! Nein, ach nicht in dir find' ich Frieden und Ruh' " (" Goddess of all delights ! No ! ah ! not with thee shall my soul find peace ! "). The cry to the Virgin, with its assertion of D major, decides the battle. Night and chromaticism are defeated, sunlight streams over the world. Tannhäuser escapes from shadows and enchantment to daylight and the world; yet the scene upon which the curtain now rises is not the Wartburg, not the kneeling penitent, but another scene, glimpsed once before from the heights of Tannhäuser and only now clearly envisaged. It is the scene of the holiday lists at Nuremberg and the Town Guilds in solemn procession. The demons of the Venusberg are transformed into the hobgoblins of a midsummer's night, and instead of the hymn to Venus there rises the " Preislied " :

" Der Erde lieblichstes Bild,
als Muse mir geweiht,
so heilig ernst als mild,
ward kühn von mir gefreit ;
am lichten Tag der Sonnen,
durch Sanges Sieg gewonnen
Parnass und Paradies ! "

(" The fairest sight my eyes did greet,
My Muse before me stood,
So holy, pure, and sweet,
Whom boldly there I wooed ;
The sunlight shone upon me,
By right of song I'd won me
Parnassus and Paradise ! ")

Wagner's transition from *Tristan* to *The Mastersingers* by way of *Tannhäuser* is the true explanation of the Paris episode, for in this odyssey creative instinct shaped external events. When he resumed work on *The Mastersingers* late in the autumn of 1861, he had conquered the artistic sphere of tonal reality. Wagner did not consciously follow the dictates of the work to be. He obeyed the inner voice, but he did so with his mind set upon an external end which ran before that new work like a shadow. This shadow was the production of *Tristan*. The amnesty had made it possible for him to negotiate personally with the Grand Ducal pair in Karlsruhe, and he was empowered by them to visit Vienna in search of the personnel for a performance in Karlsruhe. Thither he went, and there on May 15, 1861, was for the first time present at a performance of *Lohengrin*, thirteen years after its completion. He was entranced by the musical excellence of the production, over-powered by the enthusiasm of the public, and when the intendant proposed that the first performance of *Tristan* should take place in Vienna itself, Wagner agreed. He returned to Paris by way of Karlsruhe and there met Liszt, whom he had not seen for five years. During the *Tristan* period their friendship had passed through a crisis, really due to the hostility of Liszt's mistress, Princess Wittgenstein, to Wagner. Her dislike was increased by Wagner's affair with Blandine, but, apart from this incident, she rightly saw that in their human as in their artistic relations, Wagner was always asking, Liszt always giving. Her love for Liszt made her resent the one-sidedness of the friendship, though Liszt himself, with deeper insight, found an inner justification for Wagner's conduct. He refused Wagner no friendly office, but he had sensibility enough to respect the Princess's feelings.   There was thus a barrier between these two closely allied yet not entirely harmonious natures. Of themselves they could never have found the way to remove it, and removed it could not be until " Parnassus and Paradise " had been attained through the " victory of song."

While expecting the production of *Tristan* in Vienna, Wagner was continually on the move. Count Pourtalès offered him comfortable quarters at the Prussian embassy in Paris. When Minna went to take a cure at Soden, Wagner visited her there, attended a meeting of musicians in Weimar, and returned to Vienna via Reichenhall, where Cosima von Bülow was staying. He renewed an old acquaintanceship with Laube, sought an introduction, which accident prevented, to Hebbel, and formed a new friendship with Peter Cornelius, for whom he occasionally wrote an article on the Court Opera, anonymously advertising the performance of *Tristan*. With the same object in view, he opened up relations with Hanslick. In October portions of *Tristan* were privately performed for the Princess Metternich, and in November Wagner received inquiries from a firm of publishers as to his unpublished works. The *Nibelung* plan rose again on the horizon, and there seemed some prospect that it might be carried out. Wagner looked through the libretti, made certain alterations, and published them in book form.

The chief object of Wagner's stay in Vienna remained, however, unfulfilled. The performance of *Tristan* was prevented by the illness of the principal singer, and all efforts to find a substitute failed. Returning to Paris, Wagner found others in possession of his rooms at the Embassy, and was obliged to set to work to versify *The Master-singers* in an hotel. Schott undertook to publish the libretto, and in Biebrich, near Mainz, Wagner sought a retreat in which to compose the work. He began with the overture, but he progressed slowly.

Visitors came and went—Weissheimer, Mainz's busy Kapellmeister, Joachim Raff, of Wiesbaden, von Bülow and Cosima, and the singer Schnorr von Carolsfeld. Wagner realised that Schnorr was the very Tristan he wanted, and he now felt that Schnorr's wife, Malvina, whom he had rejected in Karlsruhe, was equal to the part of Isolda. A gay little artistic circle formed about him, in which the feminine element was not lacking. A Frankfurt actress, named Friederika Meyer, lived with him as his mistress, yet an atmosphere of storm seemed to brood over this outwardly light-hearted episode and it lasted only a few months. Schott, on whose advance payments Wagner was then living, began to complain of the sparseness of the instalments he received, and though temporarily pacified by the five Wesendonk songs, in August he stopped his payments. Wagner's *ménage* broke up, and he set out once more on his travels. The mirage of the *Tristan* performance continued to hover before him, and it seemed that the new work could never be completed until the tribute of production had been paid to *Tristan*.

To accomplish this purpose and to obtain the wherewithal to live, Wagner returned to Vienna. Ander, who was cast for the rôle of Tristan, repeatedly fell ill, and Mme. Dustmann, the Isolda, previously devoted to Wagner, had turned against him when he took her sister Friederika as his mistress. A legend began to grow up that the work was impossible to perform. The press took up a hostile attitude, strongly expressed at three grand concerts of Wagner's music in January 1863. The popular enthusiasm shown for *Lohengrin* in 1861 had completely died down, and the atmosphere of secret and open enmity which had surrounded the Paris production of *Tannhäuser* was reproduced in Vienna with yet more disastrous effect. While Wagner was on a concert tour in Petersburg and Moscow in 1863 news reached him that *Tristan* had been finally rejected in Vienna.

All hopes of Paris and Vienna were now at an end. In Berlin the intendant-general, von Hülsen, refused to receive Wagner, Dresden was out of the question, Munich, with Lachner in authority, equally so, Karlsruhe had been tried in vain, Weimar was without a conductor. Wagner found himself homeless, and some evil spell seemed to arrest the work maturing in his brain. He abandoned himself to the frivolity which accompanies despair. Taking a pleasant house in Penzing, near Vienna, he furnished it lavishly and settled down to a life of gaiety with a new mistress. He conducted concerts in Prague, Buda-Pesth, Karlsruhe, and Breslau, arranging to have " a jolly good

time again " on his return with his little lady " of the pink knickers "
in a " well-warmed, well-perfumed snuggery." Meanwhile he made
slow progress with the score of *The Mastersingers*, and began to look
round for fresh sources of money. He had hoped to make roubles
enough in another Russian tour to meet his ominously mounting
expenses, but no invitation came from Petersburg, and a time came
when he found himself in hourly peril of arrest for debt.

Flight was his only resource, and since the Wesendonks, distressed
by reports of his manner of life in Penzing, refused to take him in, he
sought refuge with Eliza Wille in Mariafeld, near Zurich. He passed
some weeks in hiding, his plans of composition going by the board while
he searched desperately for some means of livelihood. He even considered the possibility of getting a divorce from Minna and marrying
Eliza's sister, Frau von Bissing, a rich woman who had fallen in love
with him. Letters from Vienna told him that his household there had
been sold up. He hastened to Stuttgart, where he knew Eckert, the
Kapellmeister, to be well disposed to him, in a last attempt to obtain
help. Thence he planned to find some lonely spot in the Rauhe Alb in
Weissheimer's company, to set to work on *The Mastersingers*, and to
apply for advances from Schott. In pursuance of this scheme he was
to have left Stuttgart early on May 3, 1864, but late in the evening of
May 2 he received a visit from the young King of Bavaria's private
secretary, who had narrowly missed him in Vienna and Mariafeld.
He brought the King's ring and his photograph and the royal invitation to come at once to Munich. On May 4 Wagner stood in Ludwig's
presence. " He knows all about me—he understands me like my own
soul. He wants me to stay permanently by his side, to work, to rest,
and to produce my works. He will supply everything necessary for
these purposes. I am to complete the *Nibelungs*, and he will see it
produced as I wish. I am to be absolutely my own master, not a
Kapellmeister, nothing but myself and his friend. . . . Can this be
anything but a dream ? You may imagine my emotion ! My happiness is so great that I am quite shattered by it."

It was the supreme instance of the triumph of Wagner's prophetic
will. The closing words of his preface to an edition of the *Nibelung*
libretto published in 1862 was " Will such a prince appear ? " The
prince *had* appeared, as the result neither of chance, whim, nor influence.
Wagner himself had by his own work cast a spell upon Ludwig and

caused him to act as he did. His destined patron was neither Napoleon III nor the friendly Grand Duke of Baden, but a young enthusiast kindled and moulded by Wagner himself, and conjured out of dream into reality. The *Tristan* problem was solved ; it was to receive such a production as it could have received under no other conditions. Von Bülow was summoned to Munich to conduct, Schnorr and his wife and Mitterwurzer were to appear in the leading rôles. Three special performances were given on June 10, 13, and 19, 1865. " And now—rest ! " wrote Wagner to the Schnorrs after the third performance. " You have a right to be silent from henceforth if such should be your pleasure, for your achievement must have eternal influence."

At the King's desire, however, a fourth performance was given. A few weeks later, on July 23, Schnorr was buried, and with him—in Wagner's eyes the only Tristan—the work faded again into the shadows. " I have been a sad man since then," writes Wagner from Munich in September to Eliza Wille. " I was lonely in the mountains, and now I am lonely here." Since the Wesendonks' refusal to receive him, his relations with them had ceased, and neither of the pair came to the performances of *Tristan*. Wagner had entered on a new phase of his life, a phase in which the Muse of Dreams, the Dream-maid, the Woman of visions, had no place. With the break of day she had faded into the past. Warm, sensuous reality was to take her place, and the conception of Eva in Paradise presaged the awakening of womanhood from sleep.

Tristan had been performed, the shadow had led Wagner to his goal, and there had vanished. Yet there were still obstacles in the path of the work for whose sake that goal had been reached. Ludwig II had promised that the *Nibelungs* should be performed, and he now urged Wagner to do his part, to lay *The Mastersingers* aside and set to work on the score of *Siegfried*. Wotan conjured the Wala. Wagner's will was not left free but felt its subjection to royal favour. Storms gathered again about his path. The incidents of Paris and Vienna were to be repeated, but on a yet more formidable scale. The press, the public, the Court and political parties rose in wrath against the intruder who had ensnared their young King. Wagner's departure from Munich became a political question, and the King, shrinking from the conflict, gave way. Early on December 5, 1865, Wagner left Munich alone. The King's favour and love were still his ; the gifts they had brought him—the performances of *Tristan*, financial security, his victory as a creative artist—could never be taken away, while that of which they had deprived him—freedom of the creative will—was now restored.   In Geneva he settled down to finish *The Mastersingers*. " My star beckons, the riddle is to be answered," ends a poem, *On the Verge of the Abyss*, written by Wagner on August 12, 1865.   The Wanderer drew near his goal.   His flight from Munich, the last flight of his life, was to bring him to " Parnassus and Paradise."

PART FOUR
PLAY

CHAPTER I

The Mastersingers of Nuremberg is the first of a new series of works which may be described as "looking-glass images" of their predecessors, and in which Wagner (as in the Paris *Tannhäuser*) works backwards, solving the unresolved problems of bygone works. This explains the slow ripening process, occupying decades, of *The Mastersingers*, the third act of *Siegfried*, the *Dusk of the Gods*, and *Parsifal*. In the case of *The Mastersingers* sixteen years elapsed between the first draft in 1845 and its resumption in 1861. It would almost seem that Wagner, having fleetingly entertained the idea in Dresden, abandoned it as useless and thought of it no more until sixteen years later.

The plan of *The Mastersingers*, however, was not in any true sense the outline of a plot. It was rather an artistic *credo*, and as such could neither be set aside nor forgotten, though its formulation was a slow process. That the idea persisted is proved by Wagner's remarkably detailed account of the action in his *Communication to My Friends*, an account which already differs in certain details from the original scheme and mentions for the first time a peroration on "Sacred German Art," subsequently appended to the first draft. Thus while the plan seemed to slumber it was drawing nourishment from all that passed, and it woke to new actuality at the moment when the artist-wanderer arrived again at the point from which he had first glimpsed the *Fata Morgana* of the work. This point, twice reached by Wagner, in Dresden in 1845 and again in Paris in 1861, was the completion of *Tannhäuser*. On each occasion *The Mastersingers* project appears, but only on the second emerges from dreams into real artistic existence.

The story of this project is in reality a story of escape from the enchanted world of *Tannhäuser*, a world in which Wagner dwelt for sixteen years before he found the magic formula to set him free. The greatest achievement of his early manhood had led him into a

world of passion-drama whence arose a series of characters conceived
in a mood of tragic emotion—the pathetic Lohengrin, the death-
doomed Siegfried and Wotan, the youthful lovers Brynhilda and
Siegfried, and, finally, Tristan and Isolda with their tragic passion.
All these are metamorphoses of Tannhäuser, and only his return
in his original shape can break the spell. Amidst the pandemonium of the new *Venusberg*, a display of the forces of passion
at their height, the spell is suddenly loosed. Tannhäuser returns to
the real world. He has explored the realm of passion and has turned
his back upon it. It is a region of expression which holds no further
secrets for Wagner. He had once regarded it as the ground of all
action and all events and exalted it as the law of all true art under the
name of " the purely-human," but he sees it now as the supreme
*un*truth—as a dream-delusion. Recognition of this delusion, of the
deceptive power of passion, was the great lesson learned by Wagner
upon the road from the Dresden to the Paris *Tannhäuser*, and he now
uses it as a spell to conjure the once elusive play-world of *The
Mastersingers* into artistic form.

In the Marienbad sketch of July 1845, the idea of " dream-delusion "
" ohn' den nichts mag geschehen, 's mag gehen oder stehen " (" that
runs through all our striving, to folly ever driving ! ") is quite absent,
and Hans Sachs, shoemaker and poet, who in the finished work " holds
in his hands all the strings of delusion," is conceived merely as a
mediæval guildsman. As in *The Flying Dutchman* and *Tannhäuser*, the
first draft plainly reveals the literary sources of the work. The
shoemaker-poet is taken from Lortzing's opera *Hans Sachs*, which in its
turn is based on a play of that name by Deinhardtstein. In portraying
the life of the mediæval guilds Wagner had recourse first to E. T. A.
Hoffman's *Meister Martin und seine Gesellen* and later to Wagenseil's
and Jacob Grimm's studies of the mastersingers. The comic wooer
and the incidents of the second act come from Kotzebue's *Deutsche
Kleinstädter*. As a literary composition *The Mastersingers* is from the
outset libretto-like in character, for it is comedy adapted for musical
stylisation, and in action, characters, and dialogue it could more
nearly than any other work of Wagner's stand by itself without music
as a stage play. The Marienbad sketch was indeed the first step on
the way to *Friedrich Rotbart*, Wagner's project for a play at the close
of his Dresden career. At that time the urge to musical expansion
had transformed his dramatic naturalism into emotional naturalism—

a line of development which culminates in *Tristan* and the Paris *Venusberg.* The music of emotional expression was made the groundwork of the whole, action was derived from musical motive impulses, speech was dissolved in musical tone, was " chromaticised." A reaction now set in in which action and words were allowed a value in themselves, a new scenic self-sufficiency.

At the time of the first draft Wagner had in mind " a satire on the Wartburg song-contest." " I conceived Hans Sachs as the last incarnation of the spirit of folk-art, and as such I contrasted him with the narrow-minded bourgeois mastersingers whose quite ridiculous poetic formalism and pedantry I embodied in the person of the ' Censurer.' " The satiric intent with which Sachs and Beckmesser are brought into juxtaposition is matched by an " ironic reference to the artist with ideals faced by the stupid and hostile criticism of the crowd " in the Junker, Conrad, a re-embodiment of Tannhäuser himself. At eight-and-forty Wagner found insufficient scope for his expressionist faculties in this 1845 draft, which was built up principally on external contrasts and broadly comic situations. " The old plan offered me little or nothing," he writes to Mathilde from Paris in December 1861. " To say truth, one must actually have been in paradise to discover the inmost meaning of a subject like this." He made a second draft from memory of the first, which he did not receive back from Mathilde's safe-keeping until he had begun the libretto. Comparison reveals a shifting of the centre of gravity similar to that by which, nearly ten years earlier, the figure of Wotan was evolved from the original version of *Siegfried's Death.* Just as there, in course of revision, the tragic figure of the creative god emerges from that of the original youthful hero, so here Hans Sachs tends to supersede the young singer of the Preislied (another Tannhäuser) as the centre and pivot of the drama. Sachs is not a tragic figure, but he is instinct with knowledge and experience of the tragic, and it is through him that we are made to see passion from a new angle as dream-delusion. As regards his place in the drama, he may be said to absorb it into himself, not guided by but guiding it, not controlled by but controlling it. Thus the old comedy is suffused with the expressionist significance of this one figure, and the sketch of 1845 becomes, without prejudice to its light-hearted character, a mask behind whose fixed grimace we see the human eyes of Sachs. " Guard your heart against Sachs ! You will certainly fall in love with him," writes Wagner to Mathilde

when he sends her the Shoemaker's song. Measured against the
figure of Sachs, the scenic realism of the old play finds its level as a
mere allegory of the everyday world and its deceits without the
painful cleavage felt in *Tristan*. The re-creation of Sachs constitutes
the essential difference between the sketches of 1845 and 1861, a
difference which represents a changed conception of life and art.
Wagner has survived passion's crisis ; the suffering, creating god of
the Nibelung world has attained the serenity of wisdom, and Mark's
question, unanswered in *Tristan*, as to " the impenetrable, mysterious
basis of being," now receives the only satisfying answer—" It's just
the old delusion."

A new branch was burgeoning on the tree of Wagnerian art,
thrusting out at right-angles to one which already bore its crown of
leaves. But though a line of artistic development with power to
work back over and re-create past material could initiate a conception
and mark out the lines on which the work was to begin, obstacles to
further progress inevitably arose in the nature of the artist himself.
A change from the style of *Tristan* and the Paris *Tannhäuser* to that of
The Mastersingers could be no mere change of costume, for it involved
the exploration of an expressionist sphere hitherto unknown. Wagner
took a rapid general survey of the new territory in the instant of
discovery, but even his genius required the labour of years to map
it out exactly and enter fully into possession. The conquest of the
Nibelung world had previously cost him a similar struggle. Early
in 1862 the versification of *The Mastersingers* was complete and musical
inspiration came to Wagner while he was engaged on that work.
At Biebrich in March 1862, almost immediately after the completion
of the libretto, he began composition, finished the overture, began the
first act, and, before May, sketched out the prelude to the third act.
It was a burst of creative energy almost comparable with that which
produced *Tristan*, and Wagner believed that he would finish the work
by the autumn and produce it in Munich in November. But unfore-
seen events—Wagner's bankruptcy, the royal command to Munich,
entanglements there and, finally, his forced departure from the city—
brought the work to a standstill and he was not able to resume it
uninterruptedly until December 1865. The then existing hundred-
and-eighteen pages of the score had occupied four years, yet almost
three times that amount, reckoned by bulk, was accomplished within

the next eighteen months and the work was completed on October 24, 1867. The slow progress of *The Mastersingers* between its resumption in 1861 and its completion is most obviously to be accounted for, as in the case of *The Nibelungs*, by the catastrophic and cumulative troubles of Wagner's life at that period, yet the validity of such an explanation depends on whether the events of his inner life are to be regarded as the consequence or the cause of his circumstances ; and in Wagner's life and work each external incident would seem to have been directly dictated by the spirit of creative art. Even where his fate appears to have been influenced so entirely from without as by the royal summons to Munich, the incident was in reality the result of a daemonic effort of will which extended mysterious powers into the unknown, cast a spell over the young monarch and bound him to itself by the dark magic of personality. Wagner's will made the impossible possible for him, yet this will was not the will of his human intellect but of his creative daemon. This governed his life, making him a vessel of creative art, endowing him with a genius of obedience even where obedience conflicted with every demand of personal happiness, social morality, love, loyalty, or even of individual understanding and judgment. With a magnificent singleness Wagner submitted to his creative daemon, unflinchingly subordinating the highest human interests to the one law of art. In him the intuitive will was never broken by the human and personal, but pervaded and governed his whole consciousness as an elemental, natural force. Wagner's life was therefore really and truly independent of all external influences, and where such had the appearance of helping or hindering they did not serve a creative necessity. No external power could have prevented Wagner from finishing *The Mastersingers* any more than incidents in Zurich could prevent his completing *Tristan* or pressure of poverty could hinder his realising an artistic inspiration. Only one thing could keep him inactive—the lack of such inspiration. This confronted him now.

Wagner had woven into his new libretto, as he had woven into the libretti of *The Ring* and *Tristan*, impulses which required the confirmation of actual living experience before they could be clothed in music. At the same time he had laid down a type form widely differing from that of any of his former works, and this intuitive conception required, as the dramas of tragic passion had required, intellectual interpretation and fixation before it could take shape.

The main traits of the new expressionist style had been grasped, as it were, in a state of ecstatic clairvoyance, and when the first fever of creation was past the artist, still *consciously* inhabiting the world of *Tristan* and *Tannhäuser*, could scarcely recognise the new region as his own. Only hesitatingly could he add new lines to his work, for though the hot flame of the first conception had been sufficient to fix it, that flame could not continue to burn without fuel. Experience, intellectual clarification, realisation of a new style—three elements in conscious artistic creation—were necessary to give body to the sketch. Wagner's daemon therefore took possession of him once more and dragged him through three eventful years. Their incidents were, however, in a deeper sense unimportant, and when in December 1865, after fleeing from a debtor's prison and receiving the King of Bavaria's summons to Munich, Wagner sat in the train for Geneva, once more a banished man, it was only the end of a wild, three-years' dream. The waking record of that dream is the score of *The Mastersingers*. Life had provided the necessary fuel and the fire leapt up again. The daemon commanded Wagner to create, and another work of art was his response.

The experience which gave form and living tone to the idea of *The Mastersingers* is again associated with the name of Mathilde Wesendonk. Wotan's dream-maid, Tristan's mistress, found a third and final reincarnation as the muse of Hans Sachs. In November 1861 Wagner met the Wesendonks in Venice and his subsequent letters are full of echoes of that meeting, with Mathilde's answers to supplement the story. For the first time there is talk of complete renunciation, of renunciation for the sake of Art. " I have thrown myself again into the arms of my old love—my work has me again, and to her I pray ' Give me forgetfulness that I may live ! ' . . . I am blind to all now but changes of day and night, light and darkness. I am truly dead to all outward things, for I see nothing but mental images, clamouring only for music. Not a single passionate picture would come to me on that dreary journey—the world seemed to me a plaything indeed. And that brought Nuremberg to my mind, where I spent a day last summer. There is much that is charming to be seen there. It echoed through my mind now like an overture to *The Mastersingers of Nuremberg*. When I got back to ¦my Viennese hotel I hastily worked the plan out and was pleased to find how good

my memory was, how obedient and inventive my imagination ! It
saved me—much as incipient madness will often save life ! Then
I concluded this business and that, turned the key on *Tristan*, politely
refused a number of invitations to proceed in triumph through various
towns in my glorious German Fatherland—and came here ' to forget
that I live ' ! "

In replying to this letter Mathilde enclosed the old *Mastersingers*
sketch which Wagner had left in her charge.   " I bless the resumption
of this work," she wrote, " I rejoice as at a festival.   In Venice
I should scarcely have dared to hope it."   Wagner in his answer poured
out much that had hitherto been left unsaid.   " I answer you with a
confession.   Yet it is useless to say it.   Everything about you tells
me that you know all, and yet I feel I must give you my assurance
of it.   At last I am resigned indeed ! . . . I will still work—nothing
else . . . Of my life you will hear what is necessary—purely superficial matters.   Within—be assured !—there will be nothing, nothing
but work at my art ! "   The writer of this letter was Richard Wagner
only in name, for the artist in him had become Hans Sachs, and it was
through Mathilde that he had become conscious of the change,
involving work, freedom from dream-delusion, purpose in life,
activity.   A feeling hitherto unknown possessed him—a sense of
mastery over life and art.   Therefore he signs his letter, " Adieu, my
child !   The Master ! " and encloses with it the first draft of Sachs's
Shoemaker's song.

Did Mathilde evoke the idea of Sachs ?   Or was it not rather that
as the artist in Wagner developed the once-dreamed-of figure was
elicited from the subconscious by her steadfast love, was called from
dream into artistic reality ?   Wagner's letter of " confession " is not
psychologically true in the strict sense, for he speaks as an artist
through the new and interesting mask he has just assumed.   There
are gods whose divinity consists in their power of metamorphosis.
Such was the writer of this letter, and a new transformation
had just taken place.   From a mental image of Sachs (" I see
nothing but mental images, clamouring only for music ") a concrete
Sachs had emerged, bearing the features, living the life, speaking through the mouth of one Richard Wagner, though he did
not know it.   It was otherwise with the woman who loved him, and
as she awoke to the magic of a love purged of desire she felt a victor's
pure emotion.   " I feel that I have climbed a great height and now

gaze upon a marvellous sunset—the hymn of creation," she wrote to
Wagner when he sent her the finished libretto. She knew that the
life-cycle of her love was complete, that sunset had indeed come.

Wagner received the ultimate gift from Mathilde, the utmost she
could give him, in the character of Sachs which embodied his own
consciousness of *mastery*. Yet up to December 1863 there is much
of profound intimacy in his letters to her, and there are moments when
the new mask seems insecurely adjusted. " For you Hans Sachs
would be easy, but I still find him difficult." Thanking Mathilde for
the last little present he was to receive from her hand—the " lovely,
lovely " brown portfolio for the MS. of *The Mastersingers*—he writes
again : " I am not yet a true Master—even in music I am little more
than an apprentice. What will come of it, God knows ! Well, each
bit as I finish it shall go into the new portfolio. There it will be
nobly housed, and when I look at it I shall say to myself ' Now you
really are something of a Master—though far less so than she who gave
you the Master's portfolio.' "

The shadow of farewell lies over these letters, which grow increasingly tender as the premonition of separation strengthens. " The
web of the mysterious Spinstress who interwove our destinies can
never be unravelled—it can only be torn across," writes Mathilde in
her last intimate letter of December 1863. It was so torn. A trivial
incident was the occasion. When the Wesendonks refused to give
Wagner sanctuary on hearing reports of his manner of life in Penzing
a permanent breach was effected. Many years later friendly sympathies
and courtesies bridged the gulf in a sense, but by then all that Wagner
had gained as an artist from his relationship with Mathilde was, for
him, lost in oblivion. In his Autobiography he casually mentions
their meeting in Venice, ironically deploring the two Wesendonks'
appreciation of the pictures there. He then tells how, later, he received
a small letterweight in cast iron from Mathilde in answer to a hint
from himself that he was in difficulties for money, and his mocking
reference to this " noble exhortation to renunciation and steadfastness "
is all that Wagner, with his professions of " unadorned veracity," has
to tell us of Mathilde during the time that he was creating *The
Mastersingers*.

For Wagner the cup of forgetfulness, like the love-potion, was
simply a dramaturgic necessity. Both contributed to his power of
metamorphosis, for he makes none of his dramatic characters do

anything of which he himself as a man was incapable. For Goethe Frau von Stein was a never-to-be-forgotten experience, but for Wagner Mathilde was merely an aid to the invention of dramatic characters. To obtain means to that end he struggled and he suffered, but the end once attained he forgot both the means and the sufferings. His heart was set not on love, not on a woman, but on a work of art, and no experience meant anything to him save as it served his art. Now, equipped with the mask of Sachs and the Shoemaker's song, with a mood of resignation and of work, with awareness of delusion and consciousness of mastery, he was able to orientate the new work, but more was required for its execution. As, in *The Nibelungs*, the figure of the youthful hero Siegfried emerged from that of Wotan the creator-god, so *The Mastersingers* contained something more than Hans Sachs. The will to work and to transcend dreams, together with consciousness of mastery, gave the work cohesion and established its broad outlines, but within these outlines the " young hero " idea sprang up afresh, a figure not content, like Sachs and Wotan, with renunciation but demanding fulfilment, not overcoming dream-delusion but turning dream into reality and thus winning both woman *and* muse. This figure represents the other side of Wagner's conception, his intuitions of the future, the new, life-accepting side of his artist nature. Mathilde, standing only for resignation and lonely fortitude, was inevitably out of touch with this aspect and could not therefore call it into musical life. It was for this reason that a breach with Mathilde became an artistic necessity. Wagner's work was at a standstill until he could find some new experience to summon this figure from dream into life.

The idea of the promised Bride, whom Sachs and Wotan renounce and who, by virtue of their renunciation, is won by Walter and by Siegfried, is an instance of that will to experience in Wagner which held up his work as an artist until life brought realisation and fulfilment. At this time he himself also awaited fulfilment of a promise of public triumph as an artist. Because both were creative necessities a woman brought realisation of the first promise, a king of the second, by the agency of the performance of *Tristan*. The fruit of suffering and of darkness supplied the gifts of joy and daylight required for the work of the " Master." A veritable witches' sabbath was not lacking, but its sole effect was to lend additional life and vigour to the work. Victory was decisive and public, since a royal decree forced it on the notice of the world, while the same turn of events brought the bride who was to be muse and wife in one. Like Jessie Laussot and Mathilde Wesendonk, like Sieglinde and Isolda, she was the wife of another, but she was destined for Wagner from the beginning and her face bore the lineaments of Wagner's oldest friend, her predecessor in sacrifice on his behalf, for she was the daughter of Franz Liszt.

Such were the experiences demanded by *The Mastersingers* before it could come into being. The wheel of existence turned from Mathilde to Cosima, from Sachs to Walter, from awakening from dream-delusion to foreknowledge of fulfilment. Wagner's creative will commanded that these things should be made actual; life gave them to him, his art made them manifest.

The new work, however, demanded not only actual experience but intellectual clarification, and this accompanied experience step by step. As in *The Nibelungs*, the writing of the libretto cleared the way and broke up the new soil. The idea of a return from exile which originally inspired Wagner's choice of subject continued to mould its transformation into æsthetic form. Wagner, having fled from the theatre, now returned to the theatre. The work that lay before him had its origin in the days when he was a man of the theatre, and it could not now take shape until the contradiction between pre-revolutionary opera and the theories of his post-revolutionary writings was resolved. " There can be no doubt that we are still far from having achieved opera at its highest and best—not only in its musical aspect, but in its totality as a dramatic art-work—and from this standpoint I regard my works hitherto and those next to come merely as experiments as to the possibility of opera," wrote Wagner to Hanslick in 1847, shortly before the completion of *Tannhäuser*. Subsequently in his writings and works he decided that opera was not possible and substituted the idea of " music drama." A psychological change, however, more potent than argument and theory, now brought him back to this fundamental question of 1847. He was faced with a structural problem which could only be solved by asserting the possibility of opera, but he had to discover *how* it might be possible to recognise theatre and opera as productive forces and to blend them with what revolutionary and post-revolutionary experience had taught him of art. These things required an intellectual solution before Wagner's creative intuition could get to work.

Wagner's approach to the question now was very different from what it had been in his revolutionary years, when he had regarded everything from a theoretic, speculative standpoint. History, æsthetics, politics, and philosophy had then been called on to support the doctrine of art his work seemed to require. He was then abandoning the practice and tradition of the operatic stage and he sought to justify himself in so doing. Now, however, he was weary of isolated creation and he craved stimulus from the practice of his trade. He wanted to bring his critical faculties to bear not on speculative problems, but on the actual theatre. It was this that made him so anxious to produce *Tristan*. He wanted to test the practicability for stage purposes of a work created in total isolation from theatre and from opera, a work created, moreover, in a sort of sleep-walker's trance. He wanted to discover whether the highest kind of creative ecstasy was compatible with the operatic stage. Theatrical managers, critics, and singers all agreed that *Tristan* could not be performed, but for Wagner creation meant nothing without performance. He did not believe their verdict and therefore sought an answer from the only authority whose decision he recognised as valid, that is to say from himself. Until this question was settled the new work could never get further than its beginnings.

The struggle to get *Tristan* produced was thus a struggle on behalf of all Wagner's future creative work. He was thinking not of popular success or failure, but of whether or no the work could be actualised upon the stage. The struggle forced Wagner to examine once again the practical requisites of theatrical performance, and he found that it was in them and not in the work itself that the difficulty lay. This theme is discussed in three essays : the preface to *The Nibelungs* libretti published in 1862, a paper on the Viennese Court Opera issued in 1863, and an invitation to Friedrich Uhl, editor of the *Wiener Botschafter*, in the form of an open letter, to come to see *Tristan* performed at Munich in 1865.

On a superficial view, these short papers would seem to be occasional works of small importance. The preface, which contains a first reference to the " Festival Play " idea, has become an historic document by virtue of the question with which it ends : " Will such a Prince appear ? " The paper on the Viennese Court Opera argues that the management should follow the example of Paris by holding only three or four performances weekly, by appointing a special conductor for the singers apart from the orchestral conductor and the stage-manager, and by setting an " artistic director " over these three responsible persons. Wagner instituted such an arrangement later in Bayreuth and probably thought of himself when he made these proposals to Vienna, since he could have named no one else with the qualifications he required, either in the stage-manager or artistic director. The gravamen of the pamphlet lies in these requirements. They are touched on in the preface to *The Nibelungs* libretti, and are declared to have proved their worth in the invitation to see *Tristan*. In pointing to the theatres of Paris and London as models, Wagner abrogates his earlier complete repudiation of the modern stage. He enters into no discussion of the revolutionary ideas propounded in 1848 in *A Suggestion for a German National Theatre*, for questions of constitution and organisation have ceased to interest him in themselves and his mind is set on one thing only—accuracy in artistic rendering. If this were attained, it mattered not whether nobleman or man of business were in command of the theatre. All that mattered was ability, foresight, and willing co-operation in the artistic management, whose too common personal inadequacy and false economies Wagner believed to be the cause of the failure of the German stage. While he believed these ills incurable he clung to the idea of a special performance of *The Nibelungs*, but when *Tristan* had been produced in Munich with the Kapellmeister acting merely as the executive arm of the real director—in this case Wagner himself—he became immediately reconciled to the stage of his time. The principal objection vanishes : the theatre is not so bad—or, if so, only because it is badly managed. Proper management might, at least in certain instances, produce something good, even something excellent.

This *rapprochement* to the actual theatre afforded Wagner a strong incentive to creative work. If the theatre could play up to Wagner, Wagner could play up to the theatre. His genius was stimulated by the interest of purely theatrical conceptions of a subject, and he ceased to see opera and drama as sharply antithetical. The problem was no longer æsthetic, it was practical. He ceased to be preoccupied with the drama as a generic idea and began to consider it as a matter of scenic performance. Opera itself might become drama through perfection of the mimetic art in acting, singing, and scenic form. Perfect representation, therefore, in actual scenic and musical performance, was the be-all and end-all. Whether the subject of the plot were taken from myth or history, whether alliteration or doggerel, symmetrical periodicity or "endless melody," *ensembles* or choruses were employed, were mere incidents bound up with the organism and of secondary importance. The score was nothing : but the marionette-show might become the universe.

Wagner reached this conviction through the performance of *Tristan*, and this alone made it possible for him to go on with *The Mastersingers*. It is irreconcilable with the revolutionary æsthetic theories of *Opera and Drama*, but a fruitful source of inspiration to an art which required above all else actual realisation on the stage. Chorus, mass effects, processions, dances, vocal *ensembles*—everything, in fact, which Wagner once condemned in opera—proved by this new measure to have value in evoking scenic illusion. Wagner recommended to the King that the Munich Conservatoire should be replaced by a school of dramatic art, of which the most important branch was to be " the proper voice-training of singers endowed with dramatic talent." Lessons in composition and instrumental technique were to be matters for individual students, but vocal training was to be obligatory on all who attended the school, since " the human voice is the practical foundation of all music," and instruction in the " art of performance " was to form an important part in vocal training. Instrumentalists were to be admitted solely for lessons in " performance." The " art of performance " was concerned in the first place with a realisation of " the delicacies and profundities of passion," from which " the music of earlier days had necessarily often purposely kept aloof," although the expression of these things could alone raise music " to the eminence attained by poetry and painting in the great ages of the past." The scholars' exercises were to result in model performances of new works offering " important new problems of performance and production," and such model performances were to be a matter for national competition.

Apart from its interest as a practical scheme for obtaining singers for *The Nibelungs*, the plan bears a striking relation to the plot of *The Mastersingers* in its idea of a school, of the training of performers, of offers of prizes for original works, of systematic education for a special expressionist end, and even in the language in which it is clothed, proving it to be a bridge thrown by Wagner from the drama on which his mind was engaged to the world of realities. The stage-world of that work is translated into terms of the objective and practical in order that it may acquire imaginative objectivity. Wagner's goal was a fantastic one and therefore the Nuremberg song-apprentices could never become the actual scholars of a Munich school of song. Practical difficulties were left trustfully to " the judgment of such men " as the King should summon to carry out the plan, and the most important of these, the singer Ludwig Schnorr, whom Wagner envisaged as head and director, died at the age of six-and-twenty, a few weeks after the first performance of *Tristan*. With Schnorr to conduct the singers and von Bülow to conduct the orchestra Wagner had thought to realise his dreams, but wanting the man on whom his plans were founded all his schemes were vain. The " great granite block " on which he proposed to build must now be replaced by a " heap of bricks."

In *Recollections of Ludwig Schnorr* Wagner supplements and completes his paper on the music school. Schnorr is held up as a supreme exemplar of the qualities which such an education should aim at developing, of the art of expression in simultaneous song and speech. Wagner's acquaintance with Schnorr was one of the factors which brought about his change of opinion as to the nature and possibilities of theatre and of opera. " With the realisation of Schnorr's inexpressible value in my own art a new spring of hope welled up in me. I had found a living link between my work and this present age. I had something to teach and something to learn—the work which all doubted, all mocked and calumniated, was to become an undeniable artistic fact." Like all the external advantages afforded by Munich this promising friendship was of brief duration, but it gave the artist certain things which could never be lost, reuniting his art with the people and forms of the theatre and reconciling the conflict which once drove him into his own solitary fantasies. Neither banishment from Munich nor Schnorr's death could deprive him of these gains. A seeming impossibility had proved possible and right. Wagner was not really concerned with founding music schools and reviving *Tristan, Lohengrin,* or *Tannhäuser,* but with finishing *The Mastersingers,* and circumstances and events had but a momentary importance, save in so far as they assisted him in this.

Strangely but characteristically Wagner's general outlook in affairs, philosophy and politics was at once coloured and modified by his *rapprochement* to the theatre. Only an anarchist or a revolutionary could have written *The Death of Siegfried*, but the composer of *The Mastersingers* must renounce the idea of revolution. Thus Wagner's political convictions were on a par with his philosophy and his relations with women—that is to say, they were not really for him human interests and experiences, but devices for shaping masks for his perpetual stage-play, devices in which he himself believed— necessarily believed—so long as they were of use to him. Wagner revised his opinions on the theatre and on religion not to please King Ludwig, but for the sake of the work which he could not complete until he had cleared his mind on these matters. He therefore issued in 1864 a pamphlet *On State and Religion* in the form of a personal address to the King. " A beloved young friend," he writes, " wishes me to tell him whether and in what sense my views on the State and on Religion have changed since I wrote on the subject of art in 1849 and 1851." He begins by asserting the " earnestness " with which he regards the subject of art. It is this earnestness which has driven him to concern himself " with such apparently distantly related matters as the State and Religion. My purpose herein was simply and solely my art—this art which I took so seriously that I could not be content without finding for it a secure foundation in life, in the State and ultimately in Religion. When I could not find such a foundation in modern life I began to look for reasons. I did my best to examine the trend of the State in order to explain the contempt which I everywhere encountered in public life for my own serious ideal of art."

The paper compares and contrasts Wagnerian " earnestness " in regard to art with Schiller's dictum that " art is gay." The writer's changed conceptions of earnestness and gaiety in life and in art have modified his attitude on questions of political and religious order. Here is no change of political faith, merely a change in the artist's expressionist purpose. Wagner is himself aware of the non-political nature of his political views. They are translations into terms of real life of a tragic and passionate creative mood. Yet the tragedy of real life is governed by powers wholly different in nature from those conditioning tragedy in art. " Life is earnest—it has ever been so," and it is swayed by a ruthless conflict of egotistic interests, requiring for their restraint and regulation the stability of the State and the promises of Religion, both comprehended in the sacred office of kingship. The dream-delusion of patriotism and the dream-delusion of religious hope harness real passions for a supra-personal object and thus mitigate the tragically earnest conflict of individual interests. The dream-delusion of passion is the means by which the State and Religion persuade mankind to abandon internecine strife and to " recognise its deepest interests." In actual life it is for the King as the supreme representative of the State and the consecrated defender of the Faith to exploit this dream-delusion to ends of justice and mercy, but alongside life stands art, " life's kindly saviour," offering " a periodic refuge and retreat from the earnestness of things, ever present elsewhere." Art, too, makes use of dream-delusion, but it is " a dream-delusion that must be perfectly honest. It must from the outset own itself to be illusion so that it may be readily accepted by the man who craves the distraction of illusion in the great and serious sense postulated." Thus the fictitious picture presented by art upon the stage exerts the power most proper to it when " it sets conscious dream-delusion in place of reality." To do this art " should not go wholly aside from real life but remaining within it should transcend it and show us life itself as play, apparently earnest and terrible but really no more than a dream image, thus comforting us and lifting us above the sordid actuality of distress. . . . The nothingness of the world—here it is openly, harmlessly, smilingly admitted ; for our willingness to submit to illusion has brought us clear-eyed recognition of the truth about the universe." Such is the path by which Wagner himself, starting from the gravest departments of life, " first became fully conscious of the gaiety " of his art.

On German Art and German Statecraft, finished three years later, is a direct continuation of this argument. It holds up the theatre as the greatest manifestation in art of the German spirit. It is a form of art, Wagner says, which arose " without the aid of princes," and therefore " lacks power and fulfilment because it has not yet been able to reach the courts of princes and to reveal the German spirit to the hearts of Germany's rulers." He goes on to discuss the nature of the theatre and the character of " the Mime," through whose ideal relation with the poet realism and idealism are to become one in a " realised ideal." This paper was only completed when Wagner was finishing *The Mastersingers*, and it opens the way for a further series of writings concerning the theatrical art-work as " a fixed mimetic improvisation of supreme poetic value." The series clearly belongs to *The Mastersingers* period by virtue of the contrast established between cultivation of art among princes and among people, of the reappearance of the school idea, and, most of all, in its grandiose glorification of the theatre as " this immensity, this pandemonium." The subject of this " terrible " theatre is the kernel of these writings, and Wagner returns to it with a renewed realisation of its artistic fascination which not even the abuses of the day could wholly destroy. He proclaims his new doctrine of delusion-play, contrasting with the gravity of real life a conscious illusion which in the deepest sense is not tragic but eternally gay.

The process of intellectual clarification led Wagner to recognise theatre as theatre, above and beyond all theories bearing on the construction of works for the theatre. The opinions he evolved between 1862 and 1865, like the experiences he passed through in the same period, were but means to an artistic end. The former were as necessary to the form and structure of the new work as were the latter to its emotional realisation. Together they imply Wagner's transcendence of the naturalistic drama of tragic passion in favour of that of illusion, or conscious artistry in form. Truth, as the reflection of an " earnest " art, had caused him to turn from the theatre and to attack all those aspects of social life from whence it sprang. Now illusion, as the reflection of a gay art, brought him back to the theatre and to acceptation of the factors conditioning it. The realisation that passion is but dream-delusion and the theatre but conscious sport with this delusion supplied a new justification for opera, and its stylisation, to which he had objected as an obstacle to an illusion of actuality, he now saw to be necessary to the creation of an illusion of illusion.

Wagner had now found those future possibilities of opera which he had once vainly sought, but not by a reversion to the traditional form. He deliberately transplanted the old idea of stylisation into the new expressionism. He blended the stylistic intention he had acquired through his acceptance of delusion-play with the mastery of expression he had acquired in his naturalistic dramas of passion. He was now concerned not with the principles but with that *art* of the theatre through which the genuine artist surpasses his inferior rivals. The old and the new meet in conflict but find resolution in pure music. Never before had Wagner so strongly, so solemnly appreciated the significance and fruitfulness of the past, despite his humorous comments on its narrowness and deficiencies. The vague visions of 1845, the expressed desires of 1861, have been realised through the struggles of 1862–65. The mirage of external destiny led Wagner on until this knowledge was attained, fading at the moment when he could survey his new field of creative activity. The experience and the intellectual position postulated by the new work had been lived through and attained. Wagner was conscious of mastery over life and art, of having got the better both of passions and of theories. There was nothing now to prevent the completion of *The Mastersingers*. It was to develop not on the lines of realistic drama but of illusion-play.

Wagner's works up to and including *Tristan* are dramas of emotion. In *Rienzi* the thirst for action, in *The Flying Dutchman* unsatisfied cravings, in *Tannhäuser* and *Lohengrin* pity and pathos, in *The Ring* the gradual working out of passion, in *Tristan* the longing for love and for death, represent respectively the fundamental artistic appeal whose reduction to form determines the musical style—that of naturalistic opera in the earlier works, and that of music-drama in the later. The series ends with the Paris version of *Tannhäuser*, in which the contrast established between the chromatic world of Venus and the diatonic world of Tannhäuser is a purely stylistic one. Opera and Drama are symbolically embodied, the former in Tannhäuser's formal utterance, the latter in Venus's free expression, and the emotional problem of the plot is stylistically presented. In the plot of *The Mastersingers* there is no emotional problem at all, for it is the product of Wagner's intention to stylise action, speech and music, of his determination to re-create traditional opera in the media of a fully developed musico-scenic expressionist art. The main outlines and characters of the action, together with its tendency to blend organically the past with a fresh and vital present, are at the service of this stylistic purpose. The characters are ordered and grouped in accordance with the idea of *creative style* which dominates and interpenetrates the whole. The sequence of outward events is, indeed, realistically treated, but with a realism so light-hearted that there is no room for doubt as to the real nature of this dream-picture, this image of " the nothingness of things." Neither Sachs nor Walter, still less the Guildsmen and the populace, have the reality of realistic drama. Art alone is real, revealing itself in the various figures of the drama as the inspiration and basis of the whole. Art is the subject of the action, not in an allegorical but in an actual sense. *The Mastersingers* is a dream of art as *Tristan* is a dream of love. Chromaticism is the musical, desire the emotional, parent of the drama of love, but in *The Mastersingers* the will to form and a disillusioned gaiety combine to play a game of art. Emotional illusion clothes the drama of love, stylistic illusion the play of art. The latter is served equally by the characters of the scene, who unite at last in a common " Preislied " to art, and by music. The work is a well-considered antithesis of realistic drama ; it is intentional illusion in the game of art—in fact, it is " opera," and becomes so by virtue of the march-form, the fundamental type-form of operatic stylisation.

The march abolishes any illusion of actuality by framing the whole process in the stylised movement of a strictly constructed form, governed by laws of rhythm. In his work up to and including *Rienzi* Wagner retained this stylisation of the musical scene derived from Grand Opera, but from *The Flying Dutchman* to *Lohengrin* he had increasingly diverged from it and thereafter abandoned it. Now he returned to it. *The Mastersingers* is a march-opera throughout, set from the first beat to the last within the artifice of the marching rhythm.

Wagner's return in *The Mastersingers* to the march as the basic form of musico-scenic movement implies more than its employment for archaic effect in that particular work. It remains his stylistic fundamental impulse up to *Parsifal*. Even in " occasional " works of minor importance, such as the *Huldigungsmarsch*, 1864, the *Kaisermarsch*, 1871, and the *Centennialmarsch* composed for America in 1876, it is adopted as the expressionist-type nearest to hand. In works for the stage the only variation is in the method of its scenic distribution and development, and for this, in *The Mastersingers*, song, the second characteristic operatic stylistic medium, is employed. It is no longer the " free " song of the works from *Lohengrin* to *Tristan*, but a return to the original song-form of verse and regular musical periodicity. It provides a lyrical halting-place in the movement of the march and connotes dramatically a moment of static emotion to which the march leads up and from which it then passes on, having delicately gathered up the threads of action. Walter's songs in Act I, Sachs's and Beckmesser's songs in Act II, the Preislied in both scenes of Act III, and the less important songs of the Apprentices and of David, have the same place in the scheme of things as the songs of Romantic opera—that is to say, they are manifestations of the will to song and afford a contrast to the strict marching rhythm of the main movement.

As in the *Tannhäuser* period march and song are type-forms governing style, but whereas in *Tannhäuser* they are felt as artificial accretions from which the composer is striving to break free in *The Mastersingers* the principle of stylisation is the dominating factor. The restraints of form are used to dam up emotional expression, now regarded not as the arbiter but as the servant of structure. Wagner's sense of mastery is expressed in this power of stabilisation. Emotion here is but a means of interpreting form, in contrast to *Tristan* where form is but a means of displaying emotion. *Tristan* is all flux and transitions, *The Mastersingers* all firm, plastic contours. Its characters and scenes, forms and tones become crystallised, take on outline and stability. Direct illusion of actual experience gives place to indirect illusion of an objective spectacle. This at once affects the relation of words to music.

In the diction of *The Mastersingers* rime predominates. In *Opera and Drama* Wagner described rime as a peculiarity of the Romance languages which when introduced into the German tongue interfered (as he then believed) with the pre-eminently important " speech-accent." In *Tristan* rime is used to enhance musical expression in a flow of words unconfirmed by rhythm, but in *The Mastersingers* it reappears in strict scansion—as a form of doggerel. Such rigidity of diction corresponds with the rigid character of the march, and the constraint imposed by the suiting of melody to the measures and accents of rime (once regarded as an argument against set verse and end-rime) is now a reason for its employment. It affords the music an architectonic unit of stylisation, it compels the musical will to expression to follow a preordained rhythmic course. Once again Wagner's artistic intuition outran his intellectual grasp, for he tells us that he conceived the melodies of some of these songs before he wrote the verses. An air for one of Walter's songs sketched out in a letter to Mathilde is evidence that many early drafts, both of words and music, were rejected later, and it would seem that those early ideas did no more than indicate the trend of the work and were superseded by better versions when Wagner came to the actual execution. Thus Wagner, feeling a need for ordered melody, conceived a libretto which he later replaced with more pregnant wording, and this in its turn gave rise to the melody finally used. This order may not have been observed in every instance, but that it occurred in some cases is vouched for by Wagner's reference to the Walter songs. Such a course of procedure from type-melody to type-words, thence to particular words, and finally to particular melody, is proof of the primarily stylistic impulse of the work. In *Tristan* the fundamental impulse is organically musical and the chromatic line is the source of verbal and musical form and style, but in *The Mastersingers* the fundamental impulse is the desire to contrast certain formal style-types and it is these that govern both words and music.

Rime in association with the form of " doggerel " metre used by Wagner in the libretto of *The Mastersingers* encourages by emphasis upon the end words a compact and concrete turn of thought and speech, in accordance with which the talk, and consequently the action, tends to realistic solidity and strict precision. The talk in *The Master-singers* is common, everyday talk. The most obvious, concrete images are employed to express plain, objective ideas by the mouths of characters who are blunt, straightforward and sturdy. To Walter alone are flowers of speech assigned, perhaps not without ironic intention ; Beckmesser is his antithesis to the point of caricature.

While regular verse-forms, pointed by end-rime, impart force and directness to words and ideas, the use of long lines and short becomes a means of characterising the various figures and groups of figures in the play. Epigrammatic diction renders very forcefully the comic characters of Beckmesser and David, or of the Masters, Apprentices and populace in the Cudgel scene, and the appeal of speech-melodic rime effectively conveys the intimate sentiment of such characters as Eva, Pogner, and Sachs. This ingenious verbal shading builds up a drama full of life and variety, though it is in essence but a clever analysis and subsequent reconstruction of stylistic species, the humorous, the Philistine, the poetic, embodied in the characters of a play and acting and reacting upon one another with a semblance of life and reality, while they are none the less strictly confined within a certain stylistic framework and move in obedience to a preordained scheme. This scheme is the march which pursues its course in the guise of an interplay of individuals and receives from that interplay structural content and contrasting motion. It is the march which is the source of the strict verse metre, of the employment of rime, of the entire libretto down to the individualisation of each character in the drama, and it is the march also which determines the stylistic character of the music.

The primary characteristics of the music of *The Mastersingers* are strict rhythm and diatonic melody and harmony. Rhythmic formality of movement produces an effect of concentration as opposed to the tendency to diffusion and boundlessness in *Tristan*—a reaction foreshadowed in the contrast between the diatonics of Tannhäuser and the chromatics of Venus in the Paris *Venusberg*. Rhythm takes on the form of the march, verbal expression is clothed in concrete imagery, and the scene presents not the dream-like adventures of two souls but a number of characters realistically delineated. Simultaneously melody and harmony assume a diatonic, straightforward periodicity. The completeness of the inner revolution is seen in the fact that that portion of the work which contains the ground plan of the whole, the prelude to the first act, was conceived in October 1861 and fully scored early in the following year. In structure as in thematic and harmonic character it is an absolute contrast to the prelude to *Tristan*, like in unlikeness even in this, that it comprises merely the inspirational idea of the whole and through it lays down the stylistic basis. In the prelude to *Tristan* the opening notes proclaim the primary chromatic motif; the prelude to *The Mastersingers* begins with the firm rhythm of the diatonic march-theme. In the prelude to *Tristan* no fundamental harmony can be detected; the prelude to *The Mastersingers* rests on a plain C major. In the prelude to *Tristan* the musical forces are gradually assembled by way of recitative-like phrases, interrupted by pauses; in the prelude to *The Mastersingers* the periodicity of the march is firmly established from the outset. The contrast holds good in each detail of tonal and orchestral structure. The two works are diametrically opposed as regards both causes and effects. Restlessness is the basis of *Tristan* harmony, a measured stride, determined long in advance, that of *The Mastersingers* harmony. The latter takes none but right-angled turns into allied, clearly defined harmonies. More subtle modulations and chromaticisms are only unobtrusively introduced as technical devices except where chromatic dissonance is employed to portray the grotesque.

The most striking contrast of all, however, is seen in the handling of rhythmic material. The motif, which from *Lohengrin* onwards has been split up more and more rigorously into its elements until, in *Tristan*, it is reduced to a brief formula of four chromatically compressed notes, suddenly reappears as a theme, an individual melody. This melody, however, is not as in the *Tannhäuser* period a complete and isolated entity, which as such can only recur reminiscently, but melody with a motival organism, motif stylised as melody.   It immediately assumes thematic physiognomy in every form, having in itself the mobility of the motival germ.   Such melody's capacity for transformation is due to the fact that it is built up of a very few notes borrowed from the main intervals of the chord.   In the melody of *Tristan* the motif is based on the development of a *gliding* musical figure, that of *The Mastersingers* on a *marching* one—on the drop from the tonic to the dominant.   This fourth, being the shortest distance between the two chief notes of the tonal triad, forms the germ of a motif which from *The Mastersingers* to *Parsifal* (where it dies out in the Bells motif) governs the type-form of Wagner's melody.   Like the chromatic line in *Tristan* it is expanded into melody by continuance of the fourths movement in direct contrary sequence, by rise and fall, by substitution and mixture of particular notes and directions.   The march of the Masters, the Preislied, Beckmesser's coloratura and the Cudgel motif, the Apprentices' dance and chorus—there is not a melody in the whole work which is not based on the fourth, just as every musical structure in *Tristan* is based on the chromatic line. Here as there the motif is rounded out to thematic melody by means of sequence.   But whereas in *Tristan* sequence is the means, by virtue of the germ of movement underlying it, of conveying with heightened force a sense of boundlessness, in *The Mastersingers* sequence conveys, in accordance with the diatonic and plastic impulse underlying it, a sense of delimitation, of modelling and periodicity.

The melody is built up into a harmonic whole in accordance with its derivation from the interval of the fourth, motivally articulated and sequentially developed.   The harmony of *The Mastersingers*, clear and transparent as regards its main characteristics, is not the music of nature but of motival stylisation.   It is in a sense a return to polyphony, but its connection with pre-classical polyphony is more apparent than real.   It makes use of the stylistic impulses of polyphony in order to get back to a harmonic way of writing.   Harmony, after being split up and divided into interacting motifs in *Tristan*, is once again unified by a polyphonic collocation of parts, yet the newly acquired freedom of movement in the individual parts is not lost and the motival line retains a relative independence.   The spirit of expressionism vitalises a musical organism which is no longer bound up with primitive chordal accompaniment.

The evolution of motival expression begun in the purely harmonic motif of *Lohengrin* is thereby completed. The motif becomes once more a part of harmony, a part with a life of its own conceived and shaped in relation to the music as a whole. Polyphonic technique is the device by which the individualistic motif of expressionism is amalgamated with the harmonic complex ; it is made serviceable by the particular physiognomy of the motifs themselves. These being composed of harmonic fourths are seen at once to be parts of a harmonic whole, and their rhythmic derivation from the fundamental march and song types points back to the original " Romantic " idea of motival expression through *reminiscence* and *premonition*.

Form thus becomes expression, and expression takes shape under the symbol of a drama of stylised forms. In *Tristan* Wagner dug down to the roots of his own musical emotion and made musical movement the subject of dramatic representation. In *The Mastersingers* he attained the summit of his constructive genius. Each movement represents evolution towards form, and the idea of evolution towards form lies at the back of each character and circumstance in the work. The style of the libretto, rhythm, harmony, and melodic typification in the music, every detail of the workmanship, is evolution towards form, not in the general sense of the concrete realisation of an artistic vision, but in the special sense of a deliberate, expressionist, stylistic archaism. Archaising elements are used not merely to give appropriate colour but to build up a mask which determines the character of the whole. The great change marked by *The Mastersingers* consists in the creative artist's own recognition of the mask, of play-illusion, his grasp of the actualities of theatre. Forgetting the " truth-illusions " of his passion-charged revolutionary years, Wagner attains the clear vision of maturity, a secure sense of competence and mastery. Fully awake to the magic of dream-delusion, of illusionary drama, he produces his master-work, he becomes at last " the Master."

Form implies restraint, and restraint characterises *The Mastersingers* throughout. Rime restrains diction, the diatonic restrains the chromatic, the period restrains " endless melody," harmonic unity restrains motival exuberance, and the stately rhythm of the march restrains the free flow of expression. Restraint also characterises the drama, an easy-going affair whose crises are treated in a jesting spirit.

The orchestration is restrained as regards both disposition of instruments and tonal volume. The wood-wind is divided into two groups instead of three, and the English horn, bass clarionet, and double bassoon are omitted, for there is no longer any desire to imitate nature by great variety of timbre in the wind. The wood-wind is once more regarded as a closed group, and as a four-part double chorus it supplies a sufficient volume of tone. Three trumpets, trombones, and bass tubas suffice for metallic colour, the timbre of the brass being reserved for effects of solemn splendour and for dynamic climaxes as in the pre-*Nibelung* period. Stress is laid on the idyllic, lyrical quality of a group of four horns, and harps and lutes accompany the singers. The determination to restrict the volume of sound to a minimum seen in the choice and number of instruments employed is paralleled by perfect economy in the details of their use and combination. The parts are interwoven to form a far more open fabric than in *Tristan*, the orchestration is light and transparent, individual parts are plainly discernible, excessive covering is avoided, delicate, ethereal accents prevail. Even the intentional confusion of the Cudgel scene at the close of Act II is far removed from crude naturalism and achieves its effect by hurrying rhythms, dissonant clash of parts, a contrapuntal stylisation of the gathering tumult represented in the libretto.

The demands made by Wagner on his singers are also more moderate than formerly. The lyrical rôles of Walter and Eva are substituted for the grander dramatic types of heroic tenor and dramatic mezzo-soprano. There is no insistence on vocal power but rather on light and easy melodiousness, softness and flexibility in the voice, which must have tone, must be able to express the sensuous sweetness of song. Here again *naturalistic* expression is subordinated to form in order that it may become *artistic* expression. In a letter to Schnorr before the performance of *Tristan*, apropos of Mitterwurzer's doubts about Kurwenal, Wagner writes : " Can he not see that in my work the high notes must be sung not with the voice, but with enthusiasm ? " Now, however, his requirements are different. Though enthusiasm is still important, first importance is assigned to actual vocal capacity. Beckmesser alone—a dwarfish, grotesque caricature of the wicked Alberich—can dispense with real vocal equipment. His part is, as it were, deliberately mangled to contrast with the lyricism of the others. Beckmesser's parody of Alberich's malice lies outside the mood of sheer tunefulness and is expressed in speech-tone. David, as a re-embodiment of the Mime type, rises above verbal characterisation to vocal lyricism and even finds a place in the quintet of Act III. Ortrud, Fricka, and Brangäne reappear in the guise of the old-maidish Magdalene, whose part is merely episodic, being introduced musically as accompaniment, and scenically to make up the *ensemble*. As regards the bass characters, Hunding, Fafner, and Mark take shape in the very human and lyrical character of Pogner, and the Herald of *Lohengrin* is seen again in Kothner. The Telramund-Wotan type alone, the heroic baritone, is new-minted in Sachs, not by extending its expressionist scope, but by a process of lyrical gradation. Pathos and declamation are omitted, and occasional touches of tragic irony, such as those in the Shoemaker's song and in the principal scene of Act III, are speedily resolved into the formal, steady rhythm of *work*. The melancholy meditation of the Lilac song, the grave solemnity of the Dream monologue, the exaltation and noble loftiness of Sachs's final speech, go to form an ideal typification of the masculine voice. The notes of strength and passion which characterise it in foregoing works are still present, but they are subordinated to a vocal line in which all the tender emotional tones inherent in the vocal organism are given prominence in a picture wherein tonal beauty determines form.

All these voices are *vocal characters*, fundamentally tonal in nature and derived from Wagner's earlier works. Having shed their old individualistic garb, they now appear as vocal types, stripped of all save vocal quality. An expressionist interpretation of the values of these vocal types gives rise to the characters represented on the stage. They are embodiments of the parts into which the musico-scenic action is analysed in the search for form—visual form on the scenic side, tonal form on the musical. No single vocal organ can cover the entire range of the human voice, and the male and female voices with their natural limitations are but parts of a whole in this particular musical domain. When thought of, as here, primarily as pure tone, an instinctive desire arises to hear them in conclave, to construct a tone-picture in which each type of voice from highest to lowest plays a part. It is this idea which underlies the vocal *ensemble*. It forms a background from which the individual voice can then be picked out and into which it can be resolved when its particular attractions have been elicited and displayed. This is the meaning of traditional opera-form, in which between a choral opening and a choral close play is given to the individual voice, sometimes alone, sometimes in soloistic combinations of various kinds.

The desire to portray passion naturalistically led Wagner for a time to reject the traditional lore of operatic composition and to treat his voices on the lines of dialogue ; but with a revival of interest in form as such, he returned to operatic tradition in this matter as in others. The opening of Act III excepted, each act in *The Mastersingers* begins and ends with a chorus, or, in the case of Act I, with a choral solo *ensemble*. Choruses and *ensembles* in the course of the acts are not felt to detract from the mock-realism of the action. The first scene ends with a trio for soprano, alto, and tenor voices. The Apprentices' chorus and the Masters' *ensembles* after Pognor's speech, at Walter's entrance, and after Beckmesser's interruption of the trial-song, denote a grand architectonic musico-scenic scheme. The following acts are also constructed on the idea of homophonic and polyphonic contrast, of interior and exterior vitalisation through contrasting groups. All three acts close with conventional mass finales. That in Act II is dynamically developed by the continual accession of fresh tone groups, from Beckmesser's serenade to the tumult of the Cudgel scene. In the finale of Act III a dance is actually introduced. Opening upon the lively scene of the Guilds in procession, it passes on to the " Wach' auf " chorus and finds its *dénouement* in the hymn in praise of Art. In so predominantly choral a structure, the songs of Beckmesser, Walter, and even Sachs, seem little more than bridge-passages, and in this scene the choral group plays the part of protagonist in the musical action. A corresponding *ensemble* of solo voices closes the preceding scene in the shoemaker's shop. The great quintet here succeeds in linking up the individual voices to the musical whole, thereby bringing the development of these voices to a close and preparing the way for the last finale, which unites and gives utterance to all the registers employed in the work.

The tonal structure as a whole is one of gradually increasing dimensional scope. The soloistic male-voice *ensemble* of Act I, supplemented by the boys' voices of the Apprentices' chorus, is further developed in the Cudgel scene which concludes Act II. Development of the solo voices culminates in the lyrical quintet in Act III and passes thence to the grand summing-up of the last finale, whose exalted mood establishes a spiritual connection with the chorale heard " off " at the beginning of the work. This handling of *ensemble* and chorus is, again, not confined to *The Mastersingers*. Like all the stylistic acquisitions of that work, it was to remain henceforward a constant feature in Wagner's art, and it appears, suitably modified, in *The Dusk of the Gods* and in *Parsifal*. In conception and workmanship *The Mastersingers* is no isolated episode, differing by its subject, its humour, from the rest of Wagner's work. It has an effect on the compositions which follow it comparable in importance with that of *The Ring* conception on those which preceded it. Its humour has less connection with its particular plot than with the new creative phase into which Wagner was entering and which involves a quasi-humorous recognition of the stage-play *as* play, of dream as dream. In *The Mastersingers* Wagner smilingly looks back over his phase of absorption in the expression of tragic realism, sees that it is closed, turns it into a game, fixes it as form. The man who can control form is a " Master," and his work is " art "—art not as representation of passion, but as a piece of work, an end in itself, a conquest of delusion—art for the work's sake—art hammered by the master-shoemaker upon the last of form into something sound and good. *The Master-singers* is exceptional in that nowhere else has Wagner so clearly grasped, so rigidly maintained, this idea of the purposelessness of art, of art for art's sake, of art as a pure game, and it thus takes its place at the centre of Wagner's work beside *Tristan*, the most complete example of drama *with* a purpose. *Tristan* is a procession of musical expressionist characters, *The Mastersingers* a procession of stylistic form characters. Their contrast, interaction, and conjunction afford a perfect reflection of the musico-scenic action.

The march and the song are the fundamental type-forms of *The Mastersingers*, which is kept in motion by contrast between the two. The former is the form-symbol of regular motion, law and tradition, the latter of free expressionist inspiration, of creative improvisation. The aim of the musical " plot " is to absorb the song into march-rhythm, at the same time infecting the march with the buoyant energy of song, and to develop both to their utmost capacity by blending their forces. This aim is briefly summarised in the prelude. It contains three march themes, beginning with the principal theme, the march of the Masters. The strings have the principal share in it, and the broad opening rhythms are resolved in striding quavers. The theme is actually a rhythmic scale, descending in the upper parts, ascending in the lower. It is followed by the motif of the Guilds' march. Unlike the first, this is rhythmically uniform, and its stately, full crotchet chords ascend by intervals of the triad. It is announced by the wind with harp accompaniment and is urged on by brief accelerating unison passages on the strings. It is heavier and more circumscribed than the first and offers the contrast of chordal masses to the sliding scale. The two themes are joined by a third, which works out an idea borrowed from the first. Translated from staccato to legato phrasing, it loosens the regularity of the rhythm in melody, and its ascending line leads away from the compact, formal opening to a gay and festive close.

There are thus three types of march, based on the scale, the chord, and the melodic coda. Between scale and chord a short interpolation provides the first hint of song. Lyrical wood-wind soli interrupt the dynamic line with an almost recitative-like independence of anything but melodic expression, and die out softly on a questioning turn of phrase. This song-theme is at first overpowered by the chordal march-theme, but reappears after the grand march cadenza.

This is introduced in E major in the form of a strictly periodic melody for the strings with chromatic accompanying parts. It reaches no close, but is carried on by modulation until an E flat major change cuts it off. The principal march-theme then reappears in the form of a parodistic diminution of its former self, its rhythms shortened by half, staccato, and assigned only to the wood-wind. An increasingly heated dialogue is carried on between song and march, strings and wood-wind, until they are reconciled in a long-drawn pedal point in G. The march ascends in its original form from the basses ; the song, resolved into figuration, descends to meet it, and the two join in C major with the march as fundamental bass and the song as an air for the violins. Weary of strife, the song submits to the strict march rhythm, leading it melodically and led by it rhythmically and harmonically. The two absorb the second march-theme, which in diminished motion now occupies an intermediate position between the upper and lower lines of the principal march and the song. The march coda reappears and strict form gives place to a free play of the fundamental characters. The principal theme is heard again in full harmony and rhythm, and trumpet flourishes bring it to a close. Song and march, melody, harmony, and rhythm are in perfect accord, for art has reconciled their contradictions.

The prelude provides the ground plan of the whole work to come. This as it develops confirms the prelude in leading the march from constraint to freedom, the song from excessive expressionist licence to set form, uniting the two in mutual fulfilment. The aim laid down in the prelude is consciously attained.

The form of Act I is based on the idea of contrast between march and song. In the opening scene this is only faintly intimated, but a hidden chorus and an orchestral accompaniment to Walter's dumb wooing of Eva which alternates with it contain the two forms in germ. The chorus maintains the measured rhythm of the march theme, the orchestral interludes the free declamatory song motif with which the prelude opens and which issues here in the dialogue between Walter and Eva. The march theme, rhythmically shortened, heralds the entrance of Magdalene and David and is developed in playful fashion in the talk between Eva and Magdalene, and Magdalene and David. Like the prelude, the scene culminates in fully formed melody, but here the musical-dialogue form makes greater elaboration possible. Passing from Walter to Eva this melody contains a promise ; it is taken up in the orchestral finale and there dies out.

This scene follows the prelude without a break, for it merely develops the latter's contents in dialogue form, translating them into drama and drawing out inherent possibilities of contrast. On the same lines the matter compressed in the short section of the prelude between the opening of the E major air and the final long pedal point is expanded dramatically in the remainder of the first act and the whole of the second act, constituting the " development section " of the work. The use of this sonata-term is justified by the character of this development, and similarly the third act may be described as a " repeat." The " development " idea determines the working-out of themes and form-characters alike. Each of the two fundamental type-forms is surrounded by a group of allied phenomena whose ascending sequence denotes ascent towards perfection of the type, and the composer's power of structural development is seen in the ingenious variety of these symbolic thematic phenomena.

The Apprentices' scene, the second section of the " exposition," expresses the march characters in terms of the dance, for the lads are partly conscious, partly unconscious, miniatures and parodies of their masters, and therefore their melody and rhythm takes the form of a light-hearted counterpart of the latter's grave demeanour. The march, when thus resolved in the dance, gives rise to a secondary line of development which, issuing from the Garland dance and chorus of the first act, finds its way through the Midsummer's Day scene of Act II to pure dance-form in the Apprentices' ballet of the last scene of the work. The dance, with its easy, humorous loosening of rhythm, prepares the way for the entrance of the march-characters and forms the substance of a scene between Walter, David, and the Apprentices, dramatised as the latter's account to Walter of the nature and quali-fications, as they see them, of a mastersinger. Walter himself plays no prominent part in this scene and the song idea appears only in questions which are introduced to help on the action until it breaks out in the words " Muss ich singen, kann's nur gelingen, find' ich zum Vers auch eig'nen Ton " (" I must duly sing them, truly sing them, of my own invention free "), and so brings the scene to a close. David's long speech, in which Wagner reveals a great zest for decoration and ornament, is a pot-pourri of march-characters in miniature. The fundamental rhythm is rendered less weighty by transformation from two-time to six-eight time, the melody approaches the strict movement of the Masters' theme, decks it in gay colours, transposes it to the minor, and dies out in the solemn closing change of the march of the Guilds. A background is supplied by the dance rhythms of the Apprentices' choruses, the mocking air which greets David's entrance, " Was der sich dünkt ! " (" He fancies himself ! "), with its crossed falsetto strains, the giggling parody of the Masters' theme, " Aller End' ist doch David der allergescheit'st " (" He's the knowingest boy in all Nuremberg town "), and the Garland song which leads up to a final dance.

Such is the first actualisation of the contrast between march and song, the former being intimated partly in caricature and partly in the looser form of the dance, which has the effect of stimulating the song to careless abandon. Both are envisaged from a purely external and objective standpoint. The " development section " is begun, and the fundamental types confront one another in the dance, but their forces are not seriously engaged until the following scene, which contains the entrance of the Masters, Pogner's address, Walter's presentation, his trial-song, and the finale of the act.

The Masters enter to a formal march which, changing to three-time rhythms, gathers these up in four-time period groups. The character of the piece is fixed by a vigorous, rolling bass figure, repeated and expanding from bar to bar. Suggestions of the march theme appear in the upper parts without accentuating the gliding, peaceful motion. Pogner is the first to speak, to Beckmesser and then to Walter, whose song motif is subordinated to the prevailing rhythm. Kothner declares the session open, and Pogner is the first Master to stand out as an individual from a strictly objective background portrayed by dynamic heightening of simple movement motifs. With the words "Das schöne Fest, Johannestag, ihr wisst, begeh'n wir morgen " (" Our joyous feast, Midsummer day, ye know we keep to-morrow "), the blunt rhythmic contours give place to lyrical *arioso*. The march-theme emerges in simple grandeur from the deliberate restraint of the entrance scene. The proclamation that the hand of Pogner's daughter is to be the victor's prize calls forth the first free march movement, and the further declaration that the victor must be a mastersinger brings the main theme, fully formed, into the action. *One* of the two basic elements of the work has now been called into being ; its exposition forms the substance of the discussion between the Masters, Sachs seeking the theme's emotional expansion, the others its abbreviation and diminution, while Beckmesser takes up the melody of the Apprentices' chorus in a spirit of persiflage.

Into this contentious march scene the song is introduced. It appears in new guise, without lyrical emotion, clad in chivalric rhythms and adapted by a new disposition of the notes to present a picture of Walter's outward appearance. The finale begins when Pogner leads Walter before the assembly, and in its new guise the song dominates the first group of the concluding section—the Masters' whisperings, Kothner's question as to the stranger's origin and Pogner's conciliatory answer, until, as Sachs sweeps the question aside, the song motif flashes out in its original form. The same motif prefaces information given to Walter about the Masters, the school, and the preparations necessary for a trial-song. As a first instance of song that is free and follows no law but the whim of the moment, consisting of three stanzas, the first two alike, the third irregular, it breaks in on the conventional world of the " professional " singers, represented by Beckmesser, the " Censurer," with his dissonant caricature of the knightly song. The contrasts are sharply drawn. The march-idea appears in strictest and soberest guise as Kothner reads from the " tablature," while the song is overcharged with emotionalism.

At the general cry of " Fanget an ! " (" Now begin ! ") the singer begins, taking up the cry and improvising upon it.   His emotion becomes tinged with passion as he passes from melodious praises of spring to a declamatory expressionist denunciation of winter's cruelty. This is met by the opposing force of rhythm in strict four-four time. Beckmesser's voice is raised in an angry confusion of motifs and figures : " Doch dass der Junker hier versungen hat, belag' ich erst noch vor der Meister Rat " (" But that this gallant here deserves his fate, I will engage to show the Masters straight ").   Slowly, in meditative quaver rhythms, the Masters give assent, adding their voices one by one in canon form, like the Knights in the Wartburg Song-contest scene : " Man ward nicht klug * * * wer nennt das Gesang ? " (" What did it mean ? * * * Who calls that a song ? ").   Sachs's intervention introduces a pacific, lyrical movement, and the march theme becomes again perceptible.   Its internal rhythmic conflicts, begun after Pogner's address, are more acute than ever and lead, by means of sharply pointed, nagging speeches, alternating with more songful ones, into the third verse of Walter's song.   Rhythm is dissolved in violin tremolos, the wind proclaims chromatic dissonance, the voices of the Masters interrupt one another in vehement dispute, and that of Sachs alone maintains its placid, measured line.   Over all soars the melody of the song, praising Nature and Love.   The Apprentices dance and sing their Garland chorus, and the scene which opened in order and solemnity closes in tumult and laughter.   Song is resolved in the accents of passion, march becomes a parody of itself.   Walter and the Masters vanish, while in Sachs alone there lingers the note of longing from " Lenzes Gebot " (" Springtime's behest ").   This is joined presently by the march theme.   Softly but unmistakably proclaimed by the bassoon, it finds embodiment in the Master—in the man who has *mastered* the truth about song.   With the march, therefore, transposed from C major to the more sombre F major, assigned at first to a single voice only but swiftly gathering up the rest into the final chord, the act comes to an end.

In the first act the opposing forces of the work have been set up with emphasis upon their differences ; in the second a way is opened for their reconciliation.   This reconciliation is first accomplished in Sachs himself as he gradually grows conscious of the contrasts involved and of a higher ground of union, conceptually envisaged as *art through work*, as craftsmanship and inspiration combined. The idea takes form in Sachs's songs, which, as the counterparts of Walter's, maintain the latter's lyricism while at the same time reconciling his enthusiastic flights with the steady rhythm of the Shoemaker's hammer. The song that, expressing the spirit of youth, breaks through the Masters' march theme has awakened longings in Sachs's breast. Now he, the Master, takes it up and endows it with the freedom of plastic form. Sachs's two songs, the lyrical Lilac soliloquy and the Shoemaker's song in praise of his craft, form the central points in the first and second halves of the act respectively, the external action being designed to lead up from the former to the latter. They reveal that the contrasts which brought to pass the crisis of Act I were merely illusory.

The second act is thus a playful inversion of the first. The master-shoemaker takes over command from the knightly troubadour and sets the emotional mood, the " Censurer " sings the trial-song and the young knight judges the professional, the night-watchman plays the part of the dignified Kothner, the uproar in which the Masters' assembly closed finds its counterpart in the midsummer night's riot of the Cudgel scene, the boy beats the Town Clerk, and the would-be abductor is himself abducted. Everything is topsy-turvy, the action is shown as in a conjuring mirror, and the drama is developed by inversion of all relations, characters, and forms. The first act begins with a chorus and ends with an Apprentices' dance, the second begins with an Apprentices' dance and ends with a chorale-like intoning of the Serenade by a mass *ensemble*. An atmosphere of misunderstanding prevails. David misunderstands Lene, Eva, Sachs, Walter mistakes the meaning of the night-watchman's horn, Beckmesser mistakes Lene for Eva, and David believes that Beckmesser is his rival. One mistake leads to another, until affairs are so entangled that only force can cut the many knots. This chain of misunderstandings is reflected in the musical form, which represents the second part of the " development section." The themes and type-forms, after being brought together and contrasted, are ingeniously interwoven.

The opening scene takes up the thread from the close of Act I by echoing the Garland song and continuing it in the Midsummer Day's chorus of the Apprentices. The lyrical characters, Pogner, Eva, and Sachs, stand out against a background of humorous characters. The exterior link with past events is soon followed up by an interior one, forged by song. The sense of longing—" Es schwillt und schallt, es tönt der Wald " (" To furthest bounds the wood resounds ")—and with it the harmonic thirds of the air, " Da fühlt' ich's tief sich regen, als weckt' es mich aus dem Traum " (" I heard the ardent greeting ! from dreams it bade me awake "), echo in Sachs's memory and clamour for utterance in song. " Lenzes Gebot, die süsse Not " (" Springtime's behest, within his breast ") are words found by Sachs's own heart for the new air, though he cannot yet fully explain their meaning. Thus the song passes in its new form into the dialogue with Eva, and thereby the development of the germ of the song motif is completed, for this talk tells Sachs the secret of the song melody, the meaning of its transition from Walter's lips to Eva's. The door stands open from dream to reality, and the first, the lyrical, section of the act is brought to a close. In its course it has evoked the song motif from Sachs's unconscious to his conscious mind. The dialogue with Eva has shown the form towards which the seemingly formless is striving, and this form and order must now be actualised : " Das dacht' ich wohl. Nun heisst's : schaff' Rat " (" I thought as much ! She'll need be strong ! ").

The " Rat " (counsel), which has to be sought in the dramatic process, is the counterpart of form in the artistic process. Form makes the work, and accordingly the ideas of work and form together dominate the shadow play of the second half of the act. Walter's entrance forms an intermezzo between the two halves, supplying in the drama a bridge from a lyrical to a humorous sphere, while musically it represents a passionate irruption of the song motif. As the spirit of expressionism wrestles with resistant form, this passion threatens to pass from mere longing into real action. " Aufgepasst, das darf nicht sein " (" I'll keep watch ! This must not be "), for the work of art is destined to replace the work of passion. But the abduction plot is barely intimated before it is turned into farce ; the Shoemaker's lantern shines suddenly out upon the dark alley. In the first section Sachs has listened to the gospel of youth and longing ; he must now proclaim his gospel of creative form to the two contestants, Mastersinger and Junker, the conventional pedant and the anarchic pedant, the latter scorning law and order in his determination to carry off his bride, the former trusting to the persuasive powers of a serenade in strict march time. Upon these two, uniting air and march in one, breaks the song of the Shoemaker, set to the rhythm of his craft, to the rhythm of art—a hymn in praise of the shoemaker's last, that *form* upon which he hammers out his leather :

> " O Eva !   Hör' mein' Klageruf,
> mein' Not und schwer Verdrüssen :
> Die Kunstwerk', die ein Schuster schuf,
> sie tritt die Welt mit Füssen !
> Gäb' nicht ein Engel Trost,
> der gleiches Werk erlost,
> und rief mich oft ins Paradies,
> wie ich da Schuh' und Stiefel liess !
> Doch wenn mich der im Himmel hält,
> dann liegt zu Füssen mir die Welt,
> und bin in Ruh'
> Hans Sachs, ein Schuh-
> macher und Poet dazu ! "

> (" Oh Eva ! hear the cobbler's moan ;
> His grief's beyond all bearing !
> His works of art are trod upon,
> And ruined past repairing !
> Did not my weary soul
> An angel oft console,
> And call me up to Paradise,
> I'd leave this work that I despise !
> But when with him to heaven I go,
> This world of care I leave below ;
> Peace fills me through,
> Hans Sachs is shoe-
> Maker and a poet too ! ")

The idea of the shoemaker's craft as the symbol of art makes its appearance early in Act I in the dispute with Beckmesser, but here it is expanded into song, the plastic basis of its blunt rhythm is supplied by four-four march time, its harmony is derived from the extension of the augmented triad into a pure major cadence, its melody, based on the simple fervour of folk-song, is touched with solemnity.

The second section of the act, in the form of a grand finale, is concerned principally with this trio of characters—the two wooers, and the Shoemaker standing between them.   The light of the lantern forces Walter and Eva to stay their flight, while Beckmesser carries the mark of the Shoemaker's hammer.   His stiff, halting song is made up of the tuning of the lute-strings in fourths. The principal notes of the melody are a reiteration of the fundamental open notes of that instrument, and constitute at the same time a parody of the type-form of melody based on fourths. At first interrupted only by Sachs's hammer strokes, the " Censurer's " serenade changes from an attempt at a love-song into an invocation of malicious spirits of disorder, the *cantus firmus* of an incessant and inimical mass *ensemble*. The principal theme of Beckmesser's song is joined presently by a second, also derived from the melody of fourths and cast in monotonous semi-quavers. Other characters as they arrive on the scene take up this theme. They mount above one another chromatically, and the two themes draw close together in fugal treatment. Apprentices, journey-men, men and women of all trades, and, finally, the Masters themselves, are involved in the inextricable medley of voices. Beckmesser's song is sustained by the basses in chorale form with long pauses at the cæsura in each line, above them is a tumult of fourths, with tremendous crescendos and crashing discords, until at a piercing note on the watchman's horn the riot dies down as quickly as it arose. The scene closes as it began to the hammer strokes of the Shoemaker's song. David flees to his house, Eva is forced into hers, Walter is drawn in by Sachs, and Beckmesser, well beaten, limps away along the alley. Walter's song and Beckmesser's serenade die softly away in an E major moonlight theme.

The second act or " development section " having dissected the type-forms into their motive elements, the third act builds them up again into a higher unity. This unity is first achieved in the soul of Sachs himself. The prelude to Act III is based on contrast of the two main types, of which the song first appears in free monologue assigned to the orchestral bass alone. It is song indeed, the fundamental emotional and musical line of the Shoemaker's song, woven already into the closing scene of the previous act and now displayed by it-self as the essence and type of melodic song. Transfiguring *form* is opposed to the polyphonic texture of "endless" song. On the ana-logy of the march of the Masters it is based on the scale. It is set to the stately measure of the chorale, like a religious march, beginning with an ascending fourth. Upon this basis rises the melody of the Shoemaker's song, rhythmically and harmonically resolved, and to this basis it returns, dying out in the fundamental line.

This prelude is one of the earliest parts of the work. Wagner mentions it when writing to Mathilde on his forty-ninth birthday, May 22, 1862. " Now for the introduction to Act III, in which, when the curtain rises, Sachs is discovered sitting lost in thought. I give the bass instruments a soft and very melancholy passage, full of profound resignation. Then, announced by the horns and sonorous wind instruments, comes like a gospel the solemn yet cheerful melody of the ' Wacht auf ! Es rufet gen den Tag : ich hör' singen im grünen Hag ein' wonnigliche Nachtigall ' (' Awake ! Full soon will dawn the day ; I hear within the coppice grey a rapture-laden nightingale '), and is increasingly taken up by the orchestra. I am convinced now that this work will be my most perfect masterpiece—and that I shall finish it."

In this passage Wagner supplies a poetic and dramatic interpretation of the musical and formal ideas first stated in the prelude. In setting up these contrasts the prelude to Act III completes the work of the first prelude. Things there presented under the symbol of movement and thematic development are here traced back to a lyrical conception of the two fundamental type-forms, which are heard in their emotional essence, stripped of the disguise of external activities. They are no longer contradictory—they supplement one another in organic sequence. This latter prelude, accordingly, contains the basic idea of the whole work, the idea of expressionist impulse evolving into form, of the control of anarchic emotion by structural laws, envisaged no longer as conflict but as an *ascent* from actuality to the imaginative world of art.

In the subsequent act the ideas intimated in the prelude are worked out. The act is again divided into two scenes, set in the Shoemaker's narrow shop and in the wide meadow where the folk assemble for the contest, and these represent respectively the inner and outer worlds of the artist and of art. The first scene is based on the fundamental motif of the prelude to Act III, the second on that of the first prelude. Dream-like echoes of the riot in Act II are heard at the opening. David's greeting to the day begins with the melody of Beckmesser's serenade, after which it is transposed to a variation on the chorale verse of Act I and of the march of the Masters—that is to say, of ordered form. The Guilds' march theme also returns, foreshadowing the final scene—" Sollst mein stattlicher Herold sein " (" Thou my herald must be to-day ! "). These themes, however, occur only in the shortened rhythm characteristic of the Apprentices' utterance, and they rouse in Sachs a sense of contradictions still un-resolved. The " soft and very melancholy passage " which was the original form of the Shoemaker's song is heard to the words " Wahn, Wahn, überall Wahn " (" Mad ! Mad ! Everyone mad ! "). March and song as they appear in the " development section " mingle, wrestle with one another, and fall back abruptly into Sachs's song. A new march theme appears, consisting of the ascending fourth, expanded to a powerful sequence melody :

> " Wie friedsam treuer Sitten,
> getrost in Tat und Werk,
> liegt nicht in Deutschlands Mitten
> mein liebes Nürenberg."

> (" Thy peaceful ways pursuing,
> Serene thou dost abide
> Far from the clash of nations,
> Dear Nuremberg, my pride ! ")

The march becomes a symbol of the communal spirit. It tends towards a major close, when suddenly the motifs become distorted, the rhythms confused, and the fourths, in a dissonant version of Beckmesser's serenade, echo the rebellious shout : " Gott weiss, wie das geschah ? " (" God knows how that befell ! "). The song, resolved into the moonlight motif, makes reply :

> " Ein Glühwurm fand sein Weibchen nicht ;
> der hat den Schaden angericht't,
> Der Flieder war's : Johannisnacht !
> Nun aber kam Johannistag ! "

> (" Some glow-worm sought his mate in vain ;
> 'Twas he who wrought this bitter bane,
> The elder's scent ! Midsummer eve !
> But now has dawned Midsummer day ! ")

There is a return to C major, and the solemn march in fourths brings with it a promise of the Preislied melody. Expression has passed beyond the lyrical and contemplative and has attained firm rhythmic and plastic contours. The master-mind has read the true meaning of the song of dream-delusion and can show that its true end is *form*. Amidst the wild events of the night Walter has dreamed a dream, which he dares not interpret, but Sachs interprets it for him : " Was gilt's, es

gab der Traum Euch ein, wie heut Ihr solltet Meister sein ? " (" But did
your dream suggest a way, by which you might be Master to-day ? ").
The dialogue leads up to the very crux of the work—the transmutation
of song from haphazard emotional improvisation into masterly artistic
form :

> " Mein Freund !　In holder Jugendzeit,
> 　　wenn uns von mächt'gen Trieben
> 　　zum sel'gen ersten Lieben
> 　die Brust sich schwellet hoch und weit,
> 　　ein schönes Lied zu singen
> 　　mocht' vielen da gelingen :
> 　　der Lenz, der sang für sie.
> 　Kam Sommer, Herbst und Winterszeit,
> 　　viel Not und Sorg' im Leben,
> 　　manch ehlich Glück daneben :
> 　Kindtauf', Geschäfte, Zwist und Streit :
> 　　denen's dann noch will gelingen,
> 　　ein schönes Lied zu singen,
> 　　seht, Meister nennt man die ! "

> (" My friend, in youth's enchanted days,
> 　　When warm the blood is flowing,
> 　　And hearts with first love glowing
> 　Find life a rapture and amaze,
> 　　The gift of song is given
> 　　To all by kindly heaven :
> 　'Tis Spring that sings, not we.
> 　But summer, fall, and winter chill
> 　　Bring much the soul to sadden,
> 　　With love of wife to gladden—
> 　Children—business, strife, ill-will :
> 　　Then, methinks, he who can fashion
> 　　A song of noble passion
> Is Master high and free ! ")

The doctrine thus put into words has now to be substantiated in
musical tone.　Sachs takes up Walter's melody.　The Masters' march
catches up the song and carries it along with its own fundamental
motion, clarifying the motifs and strengthening their rhythms, so that,
made pliable and adaptable, they develop into concrete musico-verbal
entities.　The improvised expressionist phrase becomes a motival

individual, obedient to a controlling will. Upon this principle a new type of song is evolved, which is both improvisation and formal device, dream inspiration and product of the inventive intelligence. The stormy emotionalism of the first act gives place to something durable and well-considered. Instead of an impetuous expressionist torrent of harmonies and intervals, there is steady progress in C major, with a single excursion towards the dominant in the middle section. From a simple basic motif of chordal fourths a plain, concrete and even line of song is developed.

Thus song attains form, and the dream-delusion of the love impulse becomes subject to the control of rhythm. The converse picture is presented in Beckmesser's distorted march motif as it struggles towards song. The air of the serenade has been destroyed in the tumults of midsummer's night, and the melody of the Knight's song in its new and purified form forces itself upon the fancy. Introduced into the scene through the production of the written verses given by Sachs to Beckmesser, the song undergoes a further transformation, the lyrical three-four time giving place to a waltz in fourths which, grotesquely accelerated, issues in the Apprentices' Garland song and dance. The theme which on Walter's lips expresses lyrical emotion, becomes in Beckmesser's mouth a dance tune. The true nature of each wooer stands revealed ; each has found the form which expresses him, and has thereby laid down the law which governs himself. This law is absolute, and causes the same embryo to evolve in the one case into song, in the other into dance, for it is the law of artistic mastery, and this compels the inmost nature of things to reveal itself.

The revelation reacts again on Sachs himself. Two stanzas of Walter's song are based on Sachs's teaching, but the third, expressing a dream realised, is inspired directly by the sight of Eva in bridal array. The same vision rouses in Sachs the passions he had overcome. The spirits of the young man and the old meet at this moment, when mastery over form for the former must mean sacrifice of emotion for the latter. The story of Wotan and Siegfried is re-enacted with a clearer understanding of its implications. Sachs's dream motif reappears in the third verse of Walter's song, now no longer lost in dreams, but filled with irresistible power, accompanied by the song motif and upborne by the rhythm of the march. It no longer aims at pathos, but seeks release from pathos, and it passes finally into the Shoemaker's song. On Eva's lips Shoemaker's song and Dream

motif are transposed from man's voice to woman's, and thus find
release and transfiguration :

> " O Sachs ! mein Freund ! Du teurer Mann !
> Wie ich dir Edlem lohnen kann !
> Was ohne deine Liebe,
> was wär' ich ohne dich,
> ob je auch Kind ich bliebe,
> erwecktest du mich nicht ! "

> (" Oh Sachs ! my friend ! most kind and good !
> How can I thank thee as I should ?
> Safe in thy loving keeping
> What were I but for thee ?
> A foolish child once sleeping,
> Hadst thou not awakened me.")

Playfulness and passionate earnest meet here on the frontiers of their
respective domains ; two great cycles of Wagnerian art are in close
contact and old echoes are inevitably wakened in the music.
Reminiscences of the chromaticism of *Tristan* and of Mark's great
" Why ? " are heard in the words :

> " Mein Kind,
> von Tristan und Isolde
> kenn' ich ein traurig Stück :
> Hans Sachs war klug, und wollte
> nicht von Herrn Markes Glück."

> (" My child,
> Of Tristan and Isolde
> The grievous tale I know ;
> Hans Sachs was wise and would not
> Through King Marke's torments go.")

Attention is momentarily drawn to the human aspect of the story to
which drama and music are here brought so close by intensity of
emotional expression that they touch the borders of that other realm,
the realm of passion.   Then, with a vigorous movement, the direction
is changed.   The inner drama is complete.   Each detail of expression
has found its appropriate form, and song has discovered its own
structural laws.   It has yet to find the higher unity of supra-individual
harmony in a final unison of many voices—in the quintet which brings

the work to a close. The Master prepares the way with his Master motif. The march themes reappear, freed from the narrow pedantry of Kothner's speech, yet retaining their steadfast character. Song is acclaimed by women's voices in the chromatically ascending Spring and Love motif, which is then taken up by the three principal voices, accompanied by David and Magdalene. Amidst the interweaving of the lines melody continues to give point and direction, though it is left for harmony to interpret the tonal mystery contained in melody, dividing and resolving the voices amidst continual change of motion till they blend in the full chord of open harmony.

The inner drama of the evolution of song ends with the interpretation of the melody of homophonous song in terms of its harmonic content. The assimilation of march and song, of form-giving rhythm and expressionist melody, begins with Sachs's assent; their final union, in which the predominant function of the march is acknowledged, is reserved for the closing scene. A bridge-passage is formed by the arrival of the Guilds in procession, each to its characteristic march tune, that of the Tailors being sustained by a bleating tenor chorus, parodying Rossini's *Tancred* cavatina. The gaiety of these march-types finds eventual expression in a dance which summarises all the humorous formal elements in the work, the Apprentices footing it to the waltz in fourths of the fundamental motival subject. The themes of the Masters, heard at first singly, unite later in a grand crescendo and forge an inner link with the first prelude, though what there supplied an undefined atmosphere or background has since been endowed with the most vivid scenic actuality. The march in all its different type-forms—in the Guildsmen's processions, the Apprentices' dance, the Masters' march, the "Wach' auf" chorale, symbol of artistic achievement, the festival motif of Sachs's address to the people—has come to symbolic life. Next comes song, in which again and again the steady rhythm of the march generates the melodic impulse—individual song which the march requires to vitalise its own external continuity. The wooers enter. Beckmesser, the first, is heralded by an abbreviated version of the Apprentices' march; the staccato notes of the prelude accompany his actual appearance. The device used to express confusion amidst the mad pranks of a mid-summer's night evokes only mirth and jollity in the light of a mid-summer's morning. Song, deprived of the generative, expressionist impulse of emotion, passes into laughter, and once again, as in the Shoemaker's shop, Beckmesser finds his appropriate finale in the dance-form. The fool is made to reveal his natural folly in an involuntary dance—and that is the end of his wooing and his singing alike.

Two songs now take the place of dance in the guise of a knightly theme based on the Love motif of Act I. Endowed with the compelling power of regular, formal rhythm, the singing melody wakes response in all hearts :

> " Gewiegt wie in den schönsten Traum,
> hor' ich es wohl, doch fass' es kaum !
> Reich' ihm das Reis, sein sei der Preis,
> keiner wie er zu werben weiss."
>
> (" Upborne on wings of song I seem,
> Yet scarce can comprehend the dream.
> Give him the prize, his be the prize ;
> No one could woo in nobler wise.")

All voices unite beneath the melodic arch of song, Masters and people alike obey its spell, while high above all soars the voice of Eva with its promise of fulfilment.

Song and march are at length perfected, each in itself, each realising to the full its special nature. The world of the march gives the victor his prize, but he cares only for the prize, and not for the world whence it comes. Therefore once more the Master of the Dream intervenes, asserting the greatness and value of the march as an organising force, revealing the nature of *mastership*. Constructive form towers above mere emotion, and though the external world may destroy it, it retains its creative virtue in the imaginative world of art. Without the firm lines of the march there can be no song and no prize for song, without form no expression, and only when the two are united can they live and give birth to a living art. The finale of the first prelude—melody enfranchised by the rhythm of the march and based on the support of the Masters' march—reappears in the chorus of Masters and people. The bass sustains the main theme, while the Guilds' march in diminished form supplies the accompaniment. The Will which has begotten the whole is mirrored in the symbol of all-embracing form. Words and music together celebrate Art as the true subject, the true heroine, of a musico-scenic drama, telling of expression made perfect through form.

CHAPTER II

WHEN Wagner completed the score of *The Mastersingers* at Triebschen in October 1867, he had realised not merely art's promise but life's. He was no longer a lonely seeker; the Wanderer had found home, wife and children, for his artistic yearnings had conjured apparently unrealisable dreams into real existence. "When we are young we get obsessed by art, we know not how," he writes to Röckel in 1852, "and it is not until we have explored art through and through that we find, to our grief, that what we lack is—life." He had indeed spent the years before his summons to Munich in "exploring art through and through," and when that exploration was complete, life presented its prize of fulfilment in happiness, not as a merely human end in itself, but as art required it for its own further development.

Wagner took Cosima von Bülow under the compulsion of life for art's sake. It was the third time that he had looked upon another man's wife as the bride of his dreams. He had thought in this way of Jessie Laussot and Mathilde Wesendonk, and the fact that his love for these two never reached consummation was a matter not of personal choice or circumstance, but, in a very real sense, of Wagner's own standpoint as a tragic artist. Cosima united in herself the spheres of passionate art and of the serener heroic idyll. The transfer of Wagner's affections to her was prepared for by changes in himself as an artist. In search of the new nourishment he needed for the new artistic phase he made a ruthless incursion into another man's life.

In Cosima, "marvellously like Liszt, though intellectually his superior," Wagner found union with that side of Liszt's nature which he had always felt belonged to him. She was Blandine's sister, she was by virtue of her talents, knowledge and personal culture a far more perfect embodiment of the idea of the Paris Venus even than Blandine, and she resembled her father in her genius for self-devotion

—a genius fostered by her first husband, who himself renounced self in the service of a great creative artist. In all things she seemed the true and perfect fulfilment of Wagner's earlier loves, but even her tremendous value to Wagner as a person could not have brought affairs to a crisis had Wagner's art not been ripe for fresh contact with realities. Isolda had passed from mortal sight in heavenly ecstasy, the abyss had closed over the Goddess of Love, but the sleeping Dream-maid still awaited her destined awakener. The singer of the " Preislied " had been rewarded with " Muse and wife in one," and Eva was now to be conjured from dreams into reality.

The story of this fulfilment runs parallel with the completion of *The Mastersingers* and begins with the news of Minna's death early in 1866. Minna spent the last ten years of her life living quietly in Dresden, dreaming of the past and keeping a room ever in readiness for Wagner's visits. Her death opened new prospects for Wagner and Cosima, who had long been lovers in secret. She had been his confidante and mistress from Munich days ; now she joined him and the pair found a home on the island of Triebschen, near Lucerne. Bülow, trustful hitherto, learned the truth from a letter accidentally opened, went at once to Triebschen and, while consenting to the dissolution of his marriage as inevitable, asked Wagner and Cosima to separate for two years. This wish, dictated by Bülow's injured sense of honour, was not acceded to, and in May 1866 Cosima moved to Triebschen with her children. For a time Bülow tried to keep up the fiction that his marriage survived. He was Wagner's guest at Triebschen, entered on his duties in Munich as Court Kapellmeister and Director of the School of Music, superintended the new rehearsals of *Lohengrin* and the Paris version of *Tannhäuser* and conducted the first performance of *Tristan* on June 21, 1868. By a violent effort of will he tried to keep the idea of service to Wagner's genius separate from personal considerations, hoping for some solution which would not involve the total moral annihilation of his own life. But the car of Juggernaut passed over him. Liszt's intervention on Bülow's behalf proved fruitless, and the resultant breach between Cosima and her father and between Wagner and his friend shook the lovers' resolution no more than the alienation of the King or the condemnation of society. They remained together in Triebschen, and two years later, in 1870, after Cosima's reception into the Protestant church, a divorce was obtained and their marriage took place on

August 25. On June 6 in the previous year, a son, Siegfried, had
been born to them only a few weeks after the completion of a draft
of the new third act of *Siegfried*.

This work was indeed the true cause of the upheaval in Wagner's
life ; in getting what was necessary if it were to take form he was
driven to defy opposition, to betray friendship, confidence and common
truthfulness, and to cast prudence to the winds. " Until I was
thirty-six," he writes, " I did not guess the real nature of my artistic
impulse, but thought that art was the end and life the means " ; but
in actual fact this was as true in 1869 as in 1849. Life for Wagner
was always a " means," even when it began to *realise* wishes whose
non-fulfilment had hitherto stirred the creative instinct. The relationship between life and art did not change, though the great turning-
point of *The Mastersingers* gave the creative impulse a new direction.
Life provided happier and more serene experiences than before—not,
however, to make the man happy but to satisfy new artistic requirements. At one time Wagner spoke of his art as " the song of the
blind nightingale's yearnings," and declared that " it would cease to
have *raison d'être* from the moment that I am allowed to embrace
life's realities," but events at Triebschen show that he deceived
himself. The transition from dreams to realities did not rob his art
of its driving force, for it was never the outcome of life but moulded
life according to its own needs. When his creative will needed
relaxation instead of tragic tension it provided him with human
happiness, and so enlisted all his powers for a new effort in the decline
of life. At the heart of the matter stood not Cosima, not the love idyll
of Triebschen nor the supplanting of von Bülow, but the creation of
the third act of *Siegfried*. The stake at issue was the completion or
non-completion of the *Ring* cycle.

The third act of *Siegfried* is one of Wagner's most notable achievements. He first conceived the idea in 1851, when *Young Siegfried*
was the artistic outcome of his wrenching himself free from the bonds
of convention, but with the formulation of the will to the " purely-
human," that is, to revived, naturalistic form, there was mingled a
deep-seated ideological preconception of the *awakening of womanhood*.
Even at the time Wagner was aware of the importance of the idea.
" In those ardent discussions in Dresden," he writes to Röckel, " we
came to the conclusion that we (that is, human society) can never be

what we might be and should be until woman is awakened." He saw the goal before him, but the road to it was not so straight as appeared in the first vision of *Young Siegfried*. Woman could not be awakened until the nature of woman was understood and consciously envisaged as the power underlying artistic creation—not as an individual but as natural instinct, as the direct embodiment of emotion in contrast to the masculine power of construction and of form—as the music which lends wings to the drama of objective, visible action.

Wagner's deepest conceptions of artistic creation caused him to think of the ultimate bases of the creative act under the symbolism of sex. Word and tone, drama and music, conceptual and emotional action are regarded as respectively masculine and feminine types, and man and woman as he presents them on the stage are but the final expression of a sex-conditioned idea of art. The notion of word-tone art, of emotional drama endowed with substance and visuality, is rooted in the idea that the two formative elements, music and action, bear a quasi-sexual relation to one another. The evolution of Wagner's conception of the female character in his works mirrors this idea. Senta, Elizabeth and Elsa are fantasies on the longing for relaxation of tension, for release through woman. The Venus of the Dresden *Tannhäuser* is a sketch for the Brynhilda of *The Death of Siegfried*, while the awakening Brynhilda in the *Young Siegfried* of 1851 is a first faint foreshadowing of woman as the power that fulfils. As yet she evades embodiment in music, yet she points beyond the uncertain sketches of Freia and Wotan's Dream-maid, beyond the masterpieces of feminine expressionism, Isolda and the Paris Venus, to the " Preislied's " dream of " Muse and Bride in one." Wagner's human desire for love carved out his experience under guidance of his artist's instinct to create. His goal was the liberation of the feminine as the force that bears and brings forth expression.

Hitherto Wagner had portrayed the sexes, whether in tragedy or comedy, as contrasts, forcibly separating them or bringing them together. He now achieves portrayal of their actual union. Male and female, form and emotion, are ripe for one another. All external hindrances have been surmounted, and the two fundamental creative principles are envisaged elementally, in their essences. Not desire, not passion, but an exalted sense of a destiny beyond either tragic or comic conflict draws them to one another.

The third act of *Siegfried* resembles the Paris *Venusberg* in its lack of real plot and its abstract typification of the two sexual characters. There are other links between the works, each of which is in reality a one-act piece. Each forms a link between a past and a newly found present artistic phase, and as the Paris *Venusberg* completes the *Tristan* series, so the third act of *Siegfried* forms a postlude to *The Mastersingers*. The Paris *Venusberg* is the climax and *dénouement* of chromatic expression, the third act of *Siegfried* that of the diatonic will to form. In the Paris *Venusberg* Man is awakened, in the third act of *Siegfried*, Woman. Not alone Brynhilda the Dream-maid, but with her Isolda and Venus have been sunk in a darkness of surrender to emotion, for Woman, as portrayed in Wagner's works from the Dresden Venus on, always finds her emotional climax in a kind of waking sleep, but now the conquering power of stylised will to form comes to rouse the expressionist power of emotion out of its spellbound dreams. Such is the symbolism underlying the plot of the new act.

Wagner turns to symbolic drama in turning from a naturalistic to a symbolic conception of art, and thus finds his way into the world of the third act of *Siegfried*. It is a world whose figures have no dramatic actuality. " Thou art not he whom thou call'st thyself ! "— Erda's words to Wotan are true of every one of these characters. All are mere phantoms, conjured up from figures in earlier dramas ; they are symbolic masks. Stylistic symbolism in the third act of *Siegfried* goes much further than in the Paris *Venusberg*, for whereas in the latter the two fundamentally opposite types are contrasted, in the former the whole evolutionary process of Wagner's work hitherto is passed in review. It is a great retrospect, made when Wagner had reached his life's meridian and had attained a sublime consciousness of fulfilment. He calls up, surveys, sets in order all his experiences of life and of art. He is no longer the servant, the voice merely, of the spirits conjured up by the spells of his art. He has become their *master* ; he understands their significance ; they are the creatures of his deliberate creative will and move according to his behests. Brynhilda's awakening by Siegfried does not, therefore, constitute the whole content of the act. Two preparatory scenes lead up to it : firstly, the awakening of Erda by Wotan, signifying the evocation and rejection of the past, and secondly, the meeting between Wotan and Siegfried, signifying the transformation of age into youth, of the old forces into the new, the annihilation of the Wanderer by one who is destined to *find* the goal. This latter scene, like that of the awakening

of Woman, could not be realised by Wagner until he had experienced
the transformation in himself, until he had ceased to be the tormented
god of *wishes* and had become *doer* of the deed. When this was
accomplished what had been merely a sketch for a dramatic plot
revealed to him its symbolic meaning ; it transcended commonplace
fact, acquired a new luminosity and became susceptible of being
stylised through music as *play*.

The three great scenes which in this act form a work complete
in itself did not arise in direct succession. Wagner worked upon
Siegfried at Munich from September 1864 to the late autumn of 1865,
during which time he began the score of Act II and the composition
of Act III. How far he progressed is not known, but since the chief
work of composition occupied a full year at Triebschen (from the
autumn of 1868 to August 1869) he can hardly, in the busy Munich
period, have accomplished more than the first and second scenes in
addition to orchestrating the newly composed portions of Act II.
The contents of these two scenes accords with such a supposition.
In the first Wotan conjures up the Wala—that is to say, the artist
exerts his power to re-awaken the slumbering *Nibelung* idea :

> " Dein Wecklied sing' ich,
>   dass du erwachest ;
>   aus sinnendem Schlafe
>   weck' ich dich auf !
>   Allwissende !
>   Urweltweise !
>   Erda !   Erda !
>   Ewiges Weib !
>   Wache, du Wala !   Erwache ! "

> (" By song I call thee
>   From time-long slumber ;
>   From world's wisdom brooding
>   Wake to my song,
>   All-knowing one.
>   Wisest Wala !
>   Erda !   Erda !
>   Woman thou most wise !
>   Waken, awaken, thou Wala ! ")

The words are a conjuration of the powers of motherhood, uttered by the will to new fulfilments.   The Wala cannot but obey :

> " Stark ruft das Lied ;
> kräftig reizt der Zauber ;
> ich bin erwacht
> aus wissendem Schlaf :
> wer scheucht den Schlummer mir ? "

> (" Strong is the call ;
> Mighty magic binds me.
> Broken my dream :
> My brooding is o'er :
> Who scares my sleep from me ? ")

The two fundamental forces of the ancient world-order—the Wanderer-god as Fatherhood and Nature as Motherhood—confront one another, as do later the two fundamental forces of the new world-order, Siegfried and Brynhilda, their rejuvenated selves.   In *The Rhinegold* Erda appears unsummoned, pronounces on passion the doom of destruction and self-annihilation and so breaks Wotan's will to action, but here Wotan, the Creator-god, himself calls upon her :

> " Der Weckrufer bin ich,
> und Weisen üb' ich,
> dass weithin wache
> was fester Schlaf verschliesst."

> (" Thy sleep-breaker am I ;
> By spells I bring thee
> That all things waken,
> Though firmly sealed in sleep.")

He now knows his own will ; his mind is set on destruction, yet he will destroy not by annihilation but by metamorphosis.   The old world of passion is doomed to pass, but the Nibelung shall not be its heir :

> " Der von mir erkoren,
> doch nie mich gekannt,
> ein kühnester Knabe,
> bar meines Rates,
> errang des Niblungen Ring :

liebesfroh,
ledig des Neides,
erlahmt an dem Edlen,
Alberichs Fluch :
denn fremd bleibt ihm die Furcht."

(" One who nowise knows me,
Though chosen by me,
The bravest of striplings,
Free of all my counsel,
Has won the Nibelung's ring.
Warm with love,
Knowing not envy,
No power over him
Has Alberich's curse :
For fear ne'er has he felt.")

Experience of the kingship here foretold was for Wagner a first necessity if the work was to be completed, for only such experience could give musical form to the scene between Wotan and Erda. Not alone the Nibelungs are summoned from the abyss, for in this scene Wagner's creative will as a whole flames up afresh, as it does in the world-weary Wanderer, enabling him as he consigns the past to destruction to evoke from its ashes a rejuvenated future. The scene is the most powerful piece of autobiographical revelation in all Wagner's work, though it is not an autobiography of external events but rather a dramatised prophetic vision of the great change in his fortunes, of the fulfilment of his longings as an artist which his creative will was soon to bring about.

If the first scene is vitalised and informed by the new will to create the second, that between Wotan and Siegfried symbolises a rejuvenation of power. The Man of Wishes and the Man of Deeds are brought face to face, Wotan bearing the Spear of the old law, Siegfried the new-forged Sword, which is form hammered out by his own hand. Spear and Sword, arbitrary law and new-forged, individual form meet in conflict, and law is shattered. Wotan is destroyed with the world to which he belongs ; the god of wishes vanishes and the power that once dwelt in him passes into the youthful god of deeds. New form forces a path to where dreaming emotion awaits its coming.

Although in reconstructing this act Wagner's attention was concentrated on the principal scene, that of Brynhilda's awakening, the symbolic import now attached to the characters lent new meaning, new justification to the two scenes which lead up to it. As dramatic characters Erda and Wotan could offer Wagner no further stimulus at this stage of his development. They belong to the past ; their interest as individuals has been exhausted in the first section of the *Nibelung* cycle, transcended in subsequent works. But as reminiscences, as allegorical masks of a past which through them finds a link with the present, they emerge once more from the shadows in which they have been lost and which symbolise the no-man's-land between the two great spheres or phases of Wagner's work. Whether both these introductory scenes date from the Munich period or whether only the first preceded the completion of *The Mastersingers* is, therefore, a matter of comparatively little interest, for both are more significant for Wagner's career as a whole than for the third act of *Siegfried* in particular. In relation to the latter, though they provide an external link with the past, they serve but as substructure for the grand final scene between Siegfried and Brynhilda. Here form and expression are perfectly at one, and Wagner reaches the summit of his constructive genius, the heights of his vision. He was fifty-six years of age when, his conflicts past, life and art chimed for him in perfect accord.

The new symbolic interpretation goes beyond the incidents of the drama, for the symbolism of the libretto is paralleled by a symbolism of musical style expressed in the composer's handling of his old musical material. The original spontaneous impulse was exhausted, and this new development could not have occurred had not the old expressionist methods been superseded together with the whole conception of art to which they belonged. A mere *completion* of the Nibelung cycle after the manner of the first section by the use of outworn motival material would have been a mechanical feat, not a creative work of art, but the new *Siegfried* is only an apparent continuation of the old and is really a new creative effort, so that the use of old motival formations is no more than an external link with the past. These motifs, like the characters of the earlier dramas, reappear with a changed functional significance. They were designed once, as Wagner says in *Opera and Drama*, as " plastic emotional moments," as " pillars of the dramatic edifice," from whose " carefully calculated recurrences a highly unified musical form arises spontaneously," but they now lose this organic and formative function and become means of characterisation appropriate to a milieu conceived stylistically. No trace of realism remains even in the nature-myth itself, which becomes the all but transparent vesture of drama conceived in terms of intellect and will. The whole Nibelung world of the Zurich period—words, tones, drama and musical types—is used as a mask. A new spirit is infused into story, characters and motifs ; they have become merely costumes or disguises and their further development proceeds on lines of melodic expansion by means of sequence, with the old motifs used only to provide the initial impetus.

The melodic form of the sequence, already employed in *Tristan* and *The Mastersingers* as a means of attaining melody, now becomes the basis of a new method of melodic formation. The motif persists in the sequence, but in so doing sacrifices its independent existence, and the " plastic emotional moment " of the past becomes but a single member in an organism. As a separate entity it is lost in the bold sweep of the wide melodic arch thrown up by the will to architectonic form. As a single stone in the melodic build, it adapts itself easily to the harmonic scheme required by such melody. The reactionary process initiated in the polyphonic compressions of the harmony of *The Mastersingers* still continues, imparting to the baroque motivation of *Tristan* harmony the smooth and even surface of earlier Romantic harmonic writing. The result is a simple system of auxiliary parts, rooted in harmony and apparently resembling the melodic homophony of earlier operatic writing. Yet motival polyphony survives in these inner parts, no longer, indeed, as an expressionist object, but as means towards form. Such parts have assimilated the flexibility of the motival line, its capacity for a subtler interpretation of the harmonic drama and the relations between the intervals, and they move with easy adaptability, inwardly free. The modulatory purpose which from *Tannhäuser* to *Tristan* resulted in the break-up of harmony gave place in *The Mastersingers* to a new emphasis on tonal unity. Formerly Wagner regarded the key in the light of " the disposition of its individual members to blend involuntarily with other keys " ; now he regards it in the light of its power of synthesis, as " a family group within the genus." This enhanced sense of key corresponds with his new idea of symbolism. He thinks of his art no longer in terms of space-tone peopled with three-dimensional tonal characters, but in terms of dynamic bas-relief expressing purely decorative and stylistic movements.

As in all artistic stylisation, petrifaction had set in as instinctive passionate creation gave place to conscious construction and emotional predominance to intellectual comprehension of the will's impulses. In *The Mastersingers* this process created *masks of dramatic characters* ; here it goes further and creates *masks of types*. The main characteristics of these types had been laid down, dramatically and musically, in the earlier *Nibelung* works, but they now lose all vestiges of realism and become symbols set up by a " Master " who is not (as in *The Mastersingers*) himself involved in the play but supervises and directs it from without. He has ceased to trust in the real power of the emotions he once embodied in his characters, for those emotions have invariably led him into a world of darkness. He trusts instead in the real power of the will which brought him back from darkness to daylight, and to this will those earlier embodiments of emotion are now no more than illusionary schemata, symbolic masks of a hidden life-force. It is this life-force which he seeks, and to this end Will must awaken Emotion from her dreams—first in the past, in order to shake off its shackles, and then, self-rejuvenated, in a new present, that Will may lead Emotion out of night into day as true helpmeet and spouse. From their embrace Melody must be born, and this evocation of melody from dream-emotion into form is the true subject of the drama of *Siegfried*.

The fact that the awakening of melody is the principal subject of this work indicates Beethoven's Ninth Symphony as the " model " which in this instance fired Wagner's imagination. The first movement of that work suggested to him the type of harmonic drama first exemplified in *The Flying Dutchman*, the instrumental recitative of the finale assisted his development on lines of expressionist prose music, and now this same finale again shows the path towards awakened melody. The very process used by Beethoven when he conjures up themes from previous movements until they issue in the " Joy " melody is also Wagner's structural basis in the first and third scenes of the third act of *Siegfried*. One by one bygone motifs are called up, until from their utmost intensification and rejection the new Siegfried melody is elicited, is announced by the orchestra in Siegfried's scene with Wotan, and finds verbal utterance in his scene with Brynhilda.

It is *the* melody of expression embodied in form, the theatrical counterpart of Beethoven's " Joy " melody, the melody of supreme art. Music as well as dialogue reviews figures and events of the past. The first scene is based on G minor, rising at the close to the more hopeful G major when Wotan foretells Siegfried's advent. The root idea of the prelude to *The Rhinegold* supplies the framework within which the primal motif of harmonic evolution reappears, now compressed into chords and expanded into a long-drawn minor period. The ascending movement of evolution gets interlaced with the descending movement of decadence, involving with it the scale motif of Wotan's Spear and supported by the dotted rhythms of the Valkyries' Ride. It is the obverse of that picture of accordant elemental forces with which *The Rhinegold* opens. Wotan and Erda, restless Passion in the guise of harmony motivally disintegrated and passive Nature portrayed in a sequence of the chromatic chords designating slumber, confront one another. In vehement dialogue the two draw nearer to one another. The phenomena of harmonic evolution—Valhalla, the slumbering Brynhilda, the Curse of the Ring—emerge from Erda's chords of sleep, and even as Wotan rouses in Erda harmony-forming tones, so Erda wakes in Wotan those that tend towards melody. The Storm motif changes in turn into the Wanderer's motif, Siegmund's greeting to Spring, the shout of the Valkyries, and the melody of Brynhilda's Farewell. The old world-order with its forces, the children of Wotan and Erda, conjured up by the storm, has reached the end of its developmental potentialities. The dialogue leads nowhere, its thoughts are aimless, its tonal symbols without faculty of growth, of expansion. Then, through Wotan's last words, there suddenly shines the Promise of Siegfried—a new hymn-like orchestral melody. It assimilates the accordant motifs of Siegfried's strength, of the Sword, of Valhalla and the Ring, and it echoes the Love motif from Siegmund's greeting to the Spring. Rising to G major and assigned to the orchestra only, it dies out upon Wotan's blessing : " Dem ewig Jungen weicht in Wonne der Gott " (" To the ever-young the god in rapture doth yield ").

The scene is without development in the thematic sense, for its presentation of phenomena is merely successive. None is susceptible of further development until the Siegfried melody emerges. This is no new motif or theme, but rather the gospel of a new method of melodic formation. Its clear-cut contours lack expressive character as hitherto understood. There is no modulatory tendency in the four-bar melodic line. It keeps within the key and takes its character from energetic rhythm and the vigorous movement of the intervals. The new principle of melodic stylisation consists, in essence, in substitution of the interest of structural character for the emotional appeal of relations between intervals. A resemblance to the thematisation of *The Mastersingers* may be traced in the stress laid on formal movement rather than on expressionist sensibility. The Siegfried melody represents a return to the scale-like march-theme of *The Mastersingers* with the initial fourths expanded to heroic sixths. It is a melody of the Will to form, whose diatonic clarity and simple plastic rhythm indicate its derivation from a non-emotional sphere. By contrasting it with the motifs of an earlier period Wagner builds up a scene which shows the old creative order in the act of pouring out its dying energies to proclaim the new.

In the first scene it is foretold that the natural will shall break the shackles of emotionalism, and in the second, where the two forces are set face to face, this prophecy is fulfilled. Wotan, who is passion's slave, confronts Siegfried, who is free. As in the scene between Wotan and Erda, question and answer evoke a new cycle of memories—memories of Fafner, Mime, the smithy, Sieglinda's glance of love—and these pass from Wotan's mind into Siegfried's. Contrasted with them are the Woodbird motif, representing nature in its simplicity, and the Valhalla harmonies. The structure is determined by the latter's dissolution of expressive songfulness into brief, speech-like phrases, which merge at last into the rapid figuration of the Fire magic. The close harmonic texture is loosened, the flourish of Siegfried's horn is heard, the motif of the Spear—the pivot of the old accordant world—tries to overpower it, but is itself struck down by the Sword motif. The ascending and descending motifs of harmonic evolution and harmonic decadence which led up to Wotan's prophecy to Erda of Siegfried's advent now sweep Wotan himself away into the limbo of the past.

Functionally this scene portrays the breaking up of accordant harmony by insurgent rhythm, which, waxing ever stronger under the symbol of the leaping flames of the Fire magic, overpowers the highest citadel of melodic emotion. A magnificent march-scene is unfolded. From the midst of the flickering fire harmonies the sleeping Brynhilda's Love melody cries out to Siegfried, and the answering flourish of his horn—the symbol of power—supported by the Nature motif of the Woodbird, breaks through the flames. The interlaced double and triple rhythms of the Fire music, the resolute triplets of the Horn motif, penetrate the unbroken chromatic chords of sleep. A climax of rhythmic and dynamic tension is reached, the four-four time of the march is expanded by the triplets to twelve-eight time, and every note is calculated to express sheer energy. Comparison with the outwardly similar scene at the end of *The Valkyrie* reveals that whereas *that* is an imaginative portrayal of a lyrical, emotional climax which finds release in music, *this* represents an extreme concentration of the rhythmic will. This will to rhythm interpenetrates and loosens out the harmonies until it sets free the fundamental melodic impulse—the Love motif promised in the Woodbird's song. Here all movement ceases, for Will, led ever onwards and upwards by the Nature motif, has attained the summit. The Unknown—the world of dreaming emotion, of sleeping passion—is unknown no longer.

A perfect synthesis of Wagnerian art is here achieved. The forces underlying it are seen to be two—drama and music, form and expression, will and emotion, rhythmic strength and melodic dream, Man and Woman. Each is as yet a prisoner within the sphere in which it has grown to full stature, but each now cries out for the other— the waking Will, obedient to Nature's behest—dreaming Emotion awaiting Will with love's inherent foreknowledge. The pair are now, however, stripped of all human attributes ; they have become elemental phenomena, proclaimed as such through the deepest mystery of the sexual character—the voice. The one instinct of the voice is to sing, and perfect song is melody. Therefore the melodic development of the two voices in a duet, to which the man's voice contributes the power and form of rhythmic will, the woman's the rapture and warmth of emotion, forms the subject of the scene. Its climax outsoars all former climaxes, attaining through a blend of the musical powers of both sexes, perfect, androgynous melody.

A long introductory passage precedes the awakening. Old themes recur, and the motif of " Weibes Wonne und Wert," the basis of Loge's story and description of Freia, forms an ascending violin monologue until the modulatory influence of the motif of Brynhilda's greeting to Siegmund forces it to descend and it is finally lost in the

Love melody of Wotan's daughter. This sequence of themes is in itself no more an organically musical process than that presented in the two preceding scenes. Memories of the Siegfried prophecies play about his figure, all purely emotional. Then, amidst this medley of feelings, the Will is moved to action, and, finding contact at last with dreaming Emotion, discovers the musical domain in which it can reveal itself—the C major key of " real life " which crowns *The Mastersingers* and is now to become the fundamental key of the supreme heroic vision of Brynhilda's awakening to the light of day and to Siegfried.

Wagner has constructed the great duologue which follows in a number of sections very clearly differentiated as to content, structure, and theme. It has not the stormy headlong impulse of earlier duologues, for the conceptual architectonic scaffolding lies plain to view. The middle section, more particularly—Brynhilda's memories—has a reflective, meditative quality until suddenly illuminated by the melody of the destined Siegfried (a melody heard in the prophecy of the Erda scene)—the very end and aim of Brynhilda's existence :

> " Dich lieb' ich immer :
>   denn mir allein
>   erdünkte Wotans Gedanke,
>   der Gedanke, den nie
>   ich nennen durfte ;
> *   *   *   *   *
>   Denn, der Gedanke—
>   dürftest du's lösen !—
>   mir war er nur Liebe zu dir."

> (" I loved thee ever,
>   For I alone
>   Divined the secret of Wotan,
>   That I dared not shape to thought,
> *   *   *   *   *
>   For what possessed me—
>   How mayst thou prove it !—
>   Was, dear one, longing of love for thee ! ")

The words proclaim the goal towards which the whole work strives— the transfiguration of the love-idea from a mere conception to an ecstasy of surrender. These two states or stages are marked by the Siegfried melody, and the scene moves from the first to the second.

In later years Wagner constructed a similar antithesis in the great scene between Parsifal and Kundry. There is a very profound connection between this final work and the third act of *Siegfried*. It is apparent in the scene—reminiscent of that between Wotan and Erda—in which Klingsor conjures up Kundry, and in the duologue between Parsifal and Kundry, in the lesson Parsifal learns from Woman, in his memories of his mother, in the moment of the kiss. In the earlier work Wagner awakens Woman, in the later he gives wisdom to Man. *Parsifal* and the third act of *Siegfried* spring, indeed, from one source. The first detailed draft of *Parsifal* dates from the period when Wagner resumed work on *Siegfried*. Yet the different manner in which these scenes are developed points to a real difference in the underlying conceptions. Parsifal repulses the very emotion that Siegfried seeks and through which he comes to knowledge of his own will, and while the trend of Parsifal is against the liberation of spirit experienced in love's consummation, the drama of *Siegfried* is activated wholly by desire for such consummation. The *dénouement* in *Siegfried* is heightened by feminine Emotion's resistance to the domination of masculine Will—a resistance which brings back the E major key of dreaming emotion, shut apart, intact. The Fire magic music changes to a pastoral bass, above which rises a new, even-paced, singing melodic line :

> " Ewig war ich,
> ewig bin ich,
> ewig in süss
> sehnender Wonne—
> doch ewig zu deinem Heil ! "

> (" Ever was I,
> Ever am I,
> Ever in sweetest
> Rapture of longing,
> Yet ever to make thee blest ! ")

This melody, blending upper dominant and tonic by gentle stages, is both in its key and in its soft flexibility of movement the obverse of the Siegfried melody. It is the melody of the feminine voice, self-revealed in perfect symmetry, enflaming Will which reaches out towards it and spurring it by a display of its inherent beauty and charm to exert its utmost powers :

" Ein herrlich Gewässer
wogt vor mir :
mit allen Sinnen
seh' ich nur sie,
die wonnig wogende Welle ! "

(" A glorious flood
Before me rolls ;
With all my senses
Only I see
The sweet surge of its billows.")

The words barely hint the meaning of the great surge of music, upon which breaks the imperious motif of the Siegfried prophecy : " Erwache, Brünnhilde ! Wache, du Maid ! " (" Awaken, Brynhilda ! Waken, O Maid ! "). The surging rhythm passes over into Brynhilda's answer and the Siegfried prophecy enters in C major : " Dann bist du mir, was bang du mir warst und wirst ! " (" Then art thou to me, what aye thou hast been and will be ! "). The Nature motif of Wotan's daughters—the *Hojotoho* of the Valkyries—is heard, and the rhythm settles into hammering triplets issuing in a prolonged stretto on a dominant pedal. In Brynhilda's surrender the Siegfried prophecy is perfectly fulfilled : " Mir strahlt zur Stunde Siegfrieds Stern " (" O'er my head now streameth Siegfried's star "). An accompaniment consisting of a crotchet movement of continuous fourths sequences (which appeared as early as the " happy shepherd's dance " in the third act of *Tristan*) recalls the Preislied melody. Untrammelled by lyrical form, it interpenetrates the song of Woman as the triumph cry of masculine Will : " Sie ist mir ewig, ist mir immer Erb' und Eigen ' " (" She is for ever, is for aye my wealth and world "). The two voices, more and more closely interlaced, blend into one, dying out in the C major key of the prophecy of Siegfried.

CHAPTER III

BEETHOVEN : A RETROSPECT

THE *Siegfried* period may be said really to have ended in 1870 with the appearance of Wagner's essay on Beethoven. This work is a supplement and companion piece to the *Autobiography*. Information about himself there suppressed by the autobiographer may be found here under the guise of a portrait of the great classic composer. The words *under the guise of* are used advisedly, for Wagner's *Beethoven*, though ostensibly a tributary discourse in celebration of the centenary of Beethoven's birth, has actually no bearing whatever on Beethoven, either æsthetically or historically. It is a piece of artistic self-portraiture, the name " Beethoven " thinly disguising the sitter as elsewhere the names " Hans Sachs," " Wotan," or " Siegfried." No longer under the symbolism of staged music-drama but in ideas and words, Wagner speaks of himself and his own work, and, like the characters in the music-dramas, the portrait of Beethoven is formed and adapted to reflect the personality of Wagner.

When the idea of melody which came into being in *Siegfried* had been isolated and concentrated in the *Siegfried Idyll*, the new vision of art embodied in the symbolism of the work called for intellectual formulation. Thus the relation between the written and the musical work is here the reverse of the usual. Wagner wrote as a rule to prepare the ground for a creative effort, but in this instance because the symbolism of a completed work called for commentary. He describes his essay as " a contribution to musical philosophy " and labels it with the name of Beethoven.

It must not be thought that Wagner deliberately identified himself with Beethoven in order to glorify himself and his art under pretext of homage to the master. The process was at once more vital and more objective. Wagner believed that he had attained the summit of his art. In the writings of the " revolutionary " period he had envisaged his goal from afar, in the subsequent period of production he had grasped the reality, and now a final creative grace had brought fulfilment. Music as he understood it—as the ultimate force of life and consciousness—had led him to this height, therefore the way he had taken was the way all creative musicians should have traversed before him. He sincerely believed that they had seen it and had only been prevented from following it by certain obstacles, interior and exterior. None of them had come nearer to the truth than Beethoven, and in Beethoven's evolution Wagner saw the immediate precursor of his own. Thus Beethoven became for him the typical musician. In him the mystery of music had reached not full revelation, but the very threshold of revelation. Because this final fulfilment was lacking Wagner extolled not Beethoven's work but his " feat."

This " feat " was " the passage from instrumental to vocal music " in the last movement of the Ninth Symphony. Wagner had no special praise for the movement itself as a musical composition. It was " a formal choral cantata with orchestra," and he declared elsewhere that he did not think it the equal of its predecessors in musical content. The " feat " consisted solely in the transition from instrumental to vocal expression, whereby Wagner recognised Beethoven as of all composers the one who had most nearly reached his own goal. It was this that made it possible for him to express his own experience in terms of Beethoven's personality and art. Conscious that he himself had achieved, he embodied the struggle for achievement in Beethoven's story.

It was thus from genuine conviction that Wagner made Beethoven's art the mask of his own. His essay is really a re-examination of the arguments of *Opera and Drama* in the light of subsequent artistic experience, and it is cast in the form rather of prophecy than of criticism. He used not only Beethoven's art but his character and physiognomy to body forth his own image as his fancy conceived it. His description of Beethoven's gruff exterior, his rebellious masculine nature, his blend of violence and tenderness, his unsatisfied emotional cravings, " the proud spirit with which he sustained an immense belief in himself," was simply a stronger version of the romantic portrait of genius, suffering, struggling, dreaming, in the Beethoven novel he had begun in Paris. Even in its very revealing account of Beethoven's " possessed," " convulsed " expression of countenance the work gives a picture of Wagner as he wanted to see himself, as he strove to present himself in his character as artist.

There is more in this than the inevitable projection of the portrait-painter into the portrait, for Wagner makes of his sitter but a glorified reflection of his own imitative, subjective temperament.

Mention of Beethoven's " masculine strength of character " gives Wagner an opportunity for launching into a sketch of the ideal artist. This was necessary to explain the nature of the music which strove in Beethoven for expression. As not Beethoven's work but his "feat" was to be celebrated, he proceeds to examine the causes which led up to this feat, and, by reading a great deal of Wagner into Beethoven, arrives at the conclusion that all his work was but a preparation for the finale of the Ninth Symphony, and that it found its goal for a moment only, the moment of song's entry, after which there was a relapse to commonplace choral cantata form. The question of the relation of this " feat " to works written later than the Ninth Symphony, notably the great string quartets, is left unsolved. A glance at the argument, however, shows that Wagner's " Beethoven " is a purely imaginary figure.

Wagner's real intention was to elucidate the mystery of the union of word and tone on the basis of a comprehensive survey of his own work, and he used Beethoven's alleged " feat " and his career as man and artist, simply as symbols. The word-tone problem, which includes the problems of organic union of action and music, sound and gesture, the audible and the visible sensuous appeals, is not merely the principal but the sole content of the essay. Clothed in a Beethoven parable, this problem is presented as the attainment of " interior self-contemplation, the clairvoyance of the deepest world-dream," only to be fully experienced by the artist " when he has reached the goal of his self-development "—when, in fact, he has finished the third act of *Siegfried*.

To explain what he means by the attainment of " interior self-contemplation, the clairvoyance of the deepest world-dream," Wagner builds up a fairy-tale world of fantasy, bearing a general resemblance to one of Plato's philosophic myths. He even borrows certain ready-coined ideas from philosophy, though the connection will not bear over-stressing. From Schopenhauer he takes names and terms rather than actual ideas. Freely using the philosopher's tokens, he uses them in his own way and to his own purpose in presenting a concrete, artistic picture.

A musical cosmology based on the idea of music as a direct revelation of the soul of the universe denotes a real change in Wagner's thought. In a parallel disquisition in *Opera and Drama* the vowel stands for the inner organism of the human body, the consonant for its integument, and " the musical note with its rich, independent activity " for the heart. In *Beethoven* the earlier physiological simile is expanded to become an allegory of the cosmos, in which the artistic process is symbolised not by the physical constitution of the individual but by the whole universe, with music as Universal Will and revealer of the true nature of things.

To justify the attribution of such significance to music Wagner distinguishes between two spheres of perception—namely the sound-world and the light-world. The light-world reveals phenomena in their multiplicity, and has therefore become subject to illusion. All perceptions derived from it serve only to establish illusion and to confound knowledge of the true nature of things. The sound-world, on the contrary, is (Wagner holds) not subject to illusion. Through its intimations man is at one with nature. The cry which marks awakening from an oppressive dream is a direct expression of will. Man recognises the cry as the utterance of weal or woe and has the same intuitive understanding of all that reaches him through the gate of the ear. The sound-world reveals to the consciousness the identity of all that is, focussing the multiple rays of the picture presented by the light-world. This identity is Universal Will, which proclaims itself through the sound-world, making music the revelation of the one Will behind all things. Echoes of Siegfried are heard here. " So the bird's magic song is intelligible to the eager heart of youth, and the cries of the beasts, the breezes, the roaring hurricane, speak to the man as, musing, he falls into that dream-state in which the sense of hearing tells him the truth of that which his eye perceives as illusion and distraction—the truth, namely, that his inmost soul is one with the inmost soul of all that he thus perceives, and that only through this perception can he know the true nature of things outside himself."

The creative musician, therefore, *as* musician is not fettered by the limitations of an individual will, for in the act of musical revelation his will is identified with the Universal Will. " The sense of hearing is the door by which the world passes in to him and he to it. In this great flood which sweeps away the limitations of the phenomenal world the inspired musician experiences an ecstasy with which naught can be compared, for in it the will knows itself for the Almighty Will of the universe." A rude shock comes with the relapse from this state of rapturous somnambulant clairvoyance into the state of individual consciousness, following awakening from the ecstasy of musical creation.

To the critic there are obvious objections here—as that the sound-world is as subject to the senses as the light-world, that the whole stylistic process separates natural sound from musical sound, and that the musical composer is bound like any other artist by the limitations of his own mind. Yet Wagner's words have positive if not polemic value. Though unimportant in themselves as an account of the nature of music, they constitute a self-revelation of Wagner's own psychology as a creative artist. The illusion that he was *en rapport* with the World Will fructified his imagination. He could only think of the musical process as a world-process, and it was thence he derived the laws of form through which he externalised his own inner musical dream.

Musical composition is a revelation of World Will, freed from personal and individual limitations. In the illusory light-world the motions of this Will are manifest in a multiplicity of phenomena, and it is the task of music to mirror these motions, freeing them from the illusion of the visible. The laws which move the phenomenal universe are also the laws of music, whose notes are shapes and persons. Both worlds are manifestations of Will, and thus musical forms necessarily correspond with the forms of the phenomenal world, even though free from their material limitations. The inner identity between the motive laws of the light-world and the sound-world, of visible phenomena and sound, finds expression in music as *rhythm* and in the phenomenal sphere as *gesture*. Music is linked with the objective visible world of phenomena by the rhythmic arrangement of notes, and the obedience of both to the behests of the World Will gives rise to musical forms. " The external expression of the laws by which this union (of music) with gesture and ultimately with all the motions of life is effected is rhythm, by means of which the composer constructs periods of contrast and motion."

Such correspondence with the processes of life is the one true basis of form, and it is therefore meaningless and perverse to ascribe inherent form to music apart from its union with gesture. The cultivation and development of music " by a systematic linking of rhythmic periodic structure " had been a grave error. " It was the work of our great Beethoven to delve beneath these forms to the inner heart of music and to communicate the vision he saw there to us, revealing thereby the true meaning—long lost—of those forms themselves. . . . And in raising up music, which had sunk to the level of mere entertainment, to fulfil its sublime destiny, he has given us an art which can interpret the universe to every man's consciousness as clearly as can the deepest philosophy to the most expert thinker."

Thus Wagner establishes the position that music is the interpreter of the universe, not through concepts but through its own world of forms. These forms move in correspondence with those of the objective light-world with which they are connected temporally through rhythm and spatially through gesture. The musician is " the Universal Essence embodied in transitory man." He expresses " not his view of the universe but the universe itself with its alternations of joy and sorrow, weal and woe." He is thus identical with the Creator, from whom he differs only in that his (the musician's) participation in the creative process is of the nature of dream. Dreaming, there is revealed to him the concept of the *good man*. Faith in the original goodness of human nature, shaken by the experiences of the light-world, revives and finds musical expression in " the melody of the good man," which " Beethoven freed from the influence of fashion and changing taste and set up as an eternally valid ' purely-human' type." As the melody of primal innocence it denotes a return to natural simplicity. " It stands for absolute human goodness which, wedded to Divine Love, concentrates in itself all the graces and splendours of exalted emotion . . . even as all existence is concentrated in the ultimate revelation of Perfect Love."

In this account of the " melody of the good man " and its marriage with Divine Love we catch a glimpse of the great scene from the third act of *Siegfried*; indeed it is the allegorical interpretation of that scene. Yet Wagner is ostensibly speaking not of his *Siegfried* but of Beethoven's " Joy " melody, in the establishment of which melodic type he professes to acclaim " the first evolutionary advance " won for music by Beethoven. Herein music passes beyond the limitations of the beautiful into the region of the sublime, where, rid of all formal restrictions, it can inform all forms whatsoever with its own spirit. The simplicity of nature is an inexhaustible well-spring of melody, and melody is the primal form in music because through it is revealed that "purely-human" which is the supreme manifestation of Will.

The universal significance here assigned to melody shows a profound change in Wagner's outlook, a change further emphasised by the ideal he attributes to Beethoven in composing the "Joy" melody. In *Opera and Drama* he uses this piece as a standard example of "patriarchal melody," in "constructing" which the composer "deliberately limits his own powers of melodic invention for a moment in order to come at those musical rudiments whence he can reach out a hand to the poet. As soon as, by this simple little melody, he feels the poet's hand in his, he proceeds . . . to bolder and more complicated tonal structures." The melody thus instanced as a "limitation . . . within very narrow compass" of Beethoven's melodic powers is now extolled as "the melody of primal innocence," the "perfection of artistic simplicity." This contradiction affords further proof that the "Joy" melody, like Beethoven's personality and "feat" are, as Wagner treats them, but figments. All that matters is the lesson he draws from the example, for it expresses his own views on the nature of melody. These he derives not from the Ninth Symphony but from *The Mastersingers*, the third act of *Siegfried*, and the *Siegfried Idyll*, and he here sets up, retrospectively, the æsthetic formula of the melodic type established in those works. For Wagner has turned from "dramatic, endless melody" to simple melody— the direct musical projection of the "purely-human." His former aim of "arousing the hearer's sympathies not by melodic expression in itself but by the emotion expressed," now becomes an attempt to crystallise the "emotion expressed" in pure melodic expression. His old "revolutionary" intention was thus fulfilled in a manner which could never have been guessed at the time, but which came naturally about when the cycle of Wagner's artistic evolution was complete.

The "purely-human" melody is the first step to that form of music which Wagner calls "the sublime" because it is free from the convention of beauty. The next step consists in the assignment of "a new importance to vocal in relation to purely instrumental music," and follows upon the discovery of the connection between music and poetry. Wagner does not at this point enter into the question of the physiological basis of accent, the root-syllable idea, or the relation between vowel and consonant. At one time he would have pursued this line of argument in support of his alliterative theories with their various bearings on speech and song. Now, having long transcended all these in his own practice, he is content to state the contrasts in general form as *vocal* and *instrumental* music, the former with a basis in drama, the latter in " pure " music.

As type of the creative playwright Wagner chooses Shakespeare. Shakespeare is no poet in the ordinary sense but " a tremendous dramatist . . . not to be understood by analogy with any poet whatsoever." His fellow in music is Beethoven. Drama, not as poetry but as dramatic action, portrays the absolute soul of the universe in the mirror of the phenomenal world. Music does not portray ; it is itself the Universal Will which is but partially revealed in the concept. Consequently drama from the first inheres in music, and the laws which govern the musical theme are the *a priori* laws of dramatic action. The *Coriolanus* overture is made to serve as example here, Wagner failing to note that Beethoven composed it not to Shakespeare's but to Collins's very different tragedy. But, as in the case of the " Joy " melody, the example is of no real importance. What is important is the revelation of the laws underlying the action of *Tristan* and *The Mastersingers*. *Here*, truly enough, " musical themes reveal the inmost soul of all the phenomena in the universe," here " the music wholly comprehends the drama " and the drama expresses " the only idea of the universe adequate to the music." Only, be it noted, this " universe " is not the veritable universe but the particular universe of Wagner's imagination—an individual world which encompassed him more and more completely the more he endeavoured to extricate himself from its limitations by a system of sham philosophical generalisation.

Wagner's fictitious portraits of Shakespeare and Beethoven are true revelations of the æsthetics of his own art. " Shakespeare shows us a drama in which he makes us all but direct participants, and Beethoven conveys to us the quintessence of this same drama, for Shakespeare's drama is based on its natural characters, and Beethoven's on the musical themes which are identical with, because they are the inmost souls of, those characters. The two spheres differ only

in the laws of expansion and movement which govern them . . . and
are separated only by the formal conditions set by the methods of
apperception pertaining to each.   A perfect art-form, accordingly,
must start from the point at which these laws coincide."

This point of coincidence Wagner finds in the *dream*.

Starting with Schopenhauer's hypothesis of " the dreamer and the
visionary," Wagner's imagination constructs a grandiose theory of
his art.   He begins by distinguishing two kinds of dreams—the deep
and the less deep.   In deep dreaming the soul is wholly absent from
the world and all sense-perceptions are extinguished ; " the organism,
busied in profound slumber with its own inmost affairs, is susceptible
to stimuli analogous to " the sense-perceptions offered to the waking
mind by the ordinary world.   The deep dream is incommunicable,
for it is wholly outside consciousness.   It may be best expressed as
the mysterious act of artistic procreation and conception.   Between
deep dreaming and waking there is a lighter form of dreaming in
which the content of the deep dream takes objective shape in the form
of scenes based more or less on the common experiences of life.   The
lighter type of dream is in fact allegorical and is expressed in the song
of Erda when Wotan invokes her :

> " Mein Schlaf ist Traümen,
>   mein Traümen Sinnen,
>   mein Sinnen Walten des Wissens ! "

> (" My sleep is dreaming,
>   My dreaming brooding,
>   My brooding weaving of wisdom ! ")

The musician accordingly is " a clairvoyant somnambulist who,
through the medium of tone, projects the immediate image of his true
dream " into the outer world.   He does this by embodying a primarily
tonal process in an allegorical picture of the external world.

The poet, on the other hand—by which Wagner means only the
miming dramatist—is not a somnambulist but a visionary.   His eyes
are open to the visible world but his vision of it is " depotentialised,"
and his soul, " speaking through that state of consciousness which
immediately precedes waking," uses this faculty of " depotentialised "
vision " to embody the truths seen in the deep dream."

Such is the process by which the power of music begets visible drama.

"Beethoven's melodies convey the same truth as Shakespeare's phantom figures : the two would be one could the musician command not only the sound-world but the light-world. . . . Then Shakespeare's phantoms would speak with the awakened inner voice of music, or, conversely, Beethoven's themes would inspire the depotentialised vision fully to recognise those phantoms. . . . In each of these two essentially identical cases only a very deep need can engender the tremendous power which here moves against the natural order, from within outwards in forming these phantom phenomena."

In these words Wagner expresses all that a great artist can express of the secret of his creative processes.   Light- and sound-worlds are united : Siegfried, spirit of light, weds Brynhilda, spirit of sound, wooing her from her dreaming wisdom to the light of day.   Together they sing " the melody of the good man "—good in that he is free, strong, and beautiful—the simple, natural melody of the " purely human," engendered by its creator's " deep need."   The discovery of this " deep need " in Beethoven's " feat " is, like the whole essay on Beethoven, an allegorical dream of Wagner's.   It was his own experience that " only an art-work inspired by and based on this feat could bring the perfect art-form," in which music, as glorified Universal Will, would be not only a revelation of perfect love but " a new religion, a world-redeeming gospel of sublime innocency."   For *Siegfried* was finished, and the star of *Parsifal* rose above the horizon.

Wagner's *Beethoven* occupies a place apart among his writings. It summarises the ideas contained in these, but does so in a manner that though found elsewhere in isolated passages of allegory never as here dominates the whole conception and execution.   The essay should be regarded as primarily a work of art.   It is no scaffolding of theory but a revelation of the laws of architecture as revealed in the completed edifice.   For the first and only time in his life Wagner expresses an artistic inspiration in the medium of words and ideas, thus disclosing the nature of his own creative activity.   This act of " self-contemplation, the clairvoyance of the deepest world-dream," occurs when his interior struggles have ended in artistic fulfilment and he knows that the summit is attained.   Wagner sees the eternal joy of the artist as the deepest wisdom, the play-instinct as universal law, the creative impulse as an inexhaustible well-spring of the play-instinct. " Joy in the exercise of this power becomes humour : all the pain of the universe is powerless against this infinite delight of playing. Brahma the Creator laughs to himself because he knows the illusion about himself. Innocence regained sports light-heartedly with the pangs of sin atoned, and the liberated conscience jests with the torments it has passed through. High above all the Great Player, master and exorcist of all things, leads the way proudly and unerringly from the vortex to the abyss—laughing to himself, for to him all the magic is but play."

An exception amongst Wagner's writings, as is its musical counterpart *Siegfried* amongst his music-dramas, the *Beethoven* was written in Triebschen when *The Mastersingers* and *Siegfried* were finished and new work lay ahead. Royal favour had lifted Wagner above sordid cares. He was as happy as a man may be in his wife, the daughter of his oldest and closest friend, and she had borne him a son. He lived in retirement, giving himself up to the pleasures of creative work. A few friends, amongst them Friedrich Nietzsche, young, enthusiastic, and devoted, came to visit him and to share the fairy-tale atmosphere of his seclusion. Wagner pictured this seclusion as " deafness to the outer world," thus rounding off the symbolic parallel with Beethoven. " Those of the master's works which are almost wholly imbued with the spirit of sublime gaiety . . . belong for the most part to that period of blessed isolation when total deafness seems to have taken him entirely out of the world. There is no need to account for irruptions of a less cheerful mood in certain of Beethoven's greatest compositions by the supposition that this inner joyousness failed him, for it is an error to think that the artist can ever conceive save in a state of profound spiritual happiness. These moods must therefore be but a part of that idea of the universe which the artist conceives and manifests in his work."

In Wagner himself, at least, the " less cheerful mood " was no more than a " part of his idea of the universe " now to be manifested in a work. The universe was the universe of the Nibelungs, and the work, tragic in conception yet the fruit of " profound spiritual happiness," was his final drama of that world—*The Dusk of the Gods*.

CHAPTER IV

THE DUSK OF THE GODS

WAGNER spent six years, from 1866 to 1872, at Triebschen. They were six very fruitful years, though unmarked by the ecstasies and upheavals of the *Nibelung* and *Tristan* periods. Wagner's artistic faculties were operating powerfully yet serenely, and he was conscious of a sense of dominion over creative forces, of mastery over the spirits, which enabled him to meet tasks imposed on him from without in a mood of philosophic calm. He could look upon the scoring of *Siegfried* as a merely secondary task, and only a few months after completing its composition he began a new work on a grander scale than any since *Rienzi*. This work was *The Dusk of the Gods*. The drafting of the first act was Wagner's main preoccupation during 1870; he began it on January 9 and finished it on July 2. Next year, in addition to completing the score of *Siegfried* and composing the *Kaisermarsch*, he drafted the second act between June 24 and November 19. After six weeks' interval he began sketches for the third act on January 4, finishing it on July 22. The whole work was thus drafted within two years and a half, and a further two years and a half saw the full score completed. On November 21, 1874, Wagner wrote *finis* to *The Ring of the Nibelungs*.

During this period the once Utopian-seeming dream of production reached the verge of fulfilment. The failure of King Ludwig's Munich plans and the performances of *The Rhinegold* and *The Valkyrie* in that city against Wagner's own wishes reawakened his old dream of a distinctively German theatre. Having humorously celebrated the outcome of the Franco-Prussian war in a comedy entitled *Ein Kapitulation* and, more seriously, in the *Kaisermarsch*, he felt that he might hope for national interest in his work. We first hear mention of Bayreuth in 1870, when Wagner was composing the first act of *The Dusk of the Gods*. In April 1871 he paid the town a visit of inspection, and in the following December the municipal authorities made over to him a site for his theatre. A committee of patrons and sponsors, organised by Karl Tausig and the Countess von Schleinitz, was responsible for funds, while in Mannheim Karl Heckel founded the first German Wagner Association, which drew support from all classes of society. On May 22, 1872, Wagner's fifty-ninth birthday, the foundation-stone of the new theatre was laid. At first he hoped to be able to announce his Festival Play for 1873, then for 1874, but again the date receded. Money was still lacking, and to raise it became increasingly Wagner's chief material preoccupation. Nevertheless, despite this anxiety and its effect on his circumstances, his theatre was now an actual fact in bricks and mortar. As his great work drew towards completion so did the edifice which was to house it, while at no great distance from this palace of art rose for the man the home where " his dreams were to find peace."

In 1872 Wagner moved to Bayreuth, leaving Triebschen, "far Isle of the Blest," where he had succeeded in completing *The Mastersingers* and *Siegfried*, had composed *The Dusk of the Gods*, and had found a solution to the conflict between art and life, a fulfilment of his love dreams. In Wagner's two self-portraits, the *Autobiography* and *Beethoven*, he had solved to his own satisfaction the riddle of his own life and art. He considered that his own daemonic impulses had contributed unconsciously to his art in the past, and that now, having attained serenity and enlightenment, he was able to master them. He believed that he had attained the summit of achievement in the third act of *Siegfried*, and that his work in the future would not be to create as heretofore, but rather to bring to fruition. *The Dusk of the Gods* represents a free application of the fruits of experience, fired by the idea of performance. As the work took form this idea drew near realisation. The idea underlying the work and the idea of performance are parallel in more than an external sense—they have a profound mutual interdependence which forms the basis of the creative impulse behind all Wagner's subsequent works.

For the fourth time Wagner turned back to the past. In *The Venusberg* and *The Mastersingers* he had done no more than take up an old sketch and evolve a new stylised form from its transmutation; in the third act of *Siegfried* he had used a libretto whose full meaning he had not understood as a musician until a later stage in his life's pilgrimage; and in the two latter works we can see how the " play " idea sprang from a detached, objective contemplation of earlier dramatic sketches, in recasting which he became fully conscious of his own absolute mastery of the art of musical representation and performance. But in *The Dusk of the Gods* this awareness of representational genius becomes pivotal, and the creative impulse itself is supplied by the idea of mimetic, plastic representation in stage action. Not the *written* but the *performed* work is Wagner's object, and to this conception of the act of performance the music of *The Dusk of the Gods* owes its existence.

The germ idea of the whole *Ring*, now complete save for its final section, is to be found in Wagner's project of " a grand heroic opera." Indeed, not the *Ring* only but *Tristan* was evolved from the original *Death of Siegfried*. In essence *Tristan* is to be identified with this early work, and has for this reason usurped its place as a continuation of the second act of *Siegfried*. " They are precisely similar, for Tristan, like Siegfried, is constrained by magic to woo on another's behalf the woman destined from eternity for himself and is destroyed by the wrong relations that ensue," writes Wagner, affirming an inner connection between the two works in his " explanatory epilogue " on the origins of *The Ring of the Nibelungs*. As an artistic problem the substance of *The Dusk of the Gods* had been absorbed into *Tristan* and merely the hollow shell of a libretto remained. Like other sketches of Wagner's, notably that of *The Saracen Maid*, the impulse behind it had been a powerful one but had evaporated from it and passed into another work. Only the fact that this sketch was connected with *The Ring* cycle secured for it a more vital remembrance.

That very quality in the libretto of *The Dusk of the Gods* which had formerly caused Wagner to seek his basis elsewhere now afforded him the stimulus he needed, for the external framework of " grand heroic opera," which alienated him when he believed that he must abandon opera for ever, had acquired for him a fresh significance through *The Mastersingers*. All that was organically musical in the subject had passed into the emotional drama of *Tristan*, and what was left was all the better adapted to consciously artificial, representational ends. The old sketch was a libretto, a " set subject," in the old-fashioned sense and, in addition to the poetic ground plan, the past supplied a quantity of material in musical and stylistic expressionist gesture for its treatment. This material was welded together, moulded and scenically projected by the theatrical impulse. A number of causes contributed to this new fruition. Expressionist problems of music, word, and scene had already been recognised and solved, and the " purely-human " had found perfect embodiment in the third act of *Siegfried*. The intentional stylisation of visual drama therein achieved had led Wagner to recognise the primary importance of the *theatrical*. Simultaneously the approaching realisation of his plans for a theatre of his own had directed his attention to still unsolved problems of production and performance. Thus his artistic development, coupled with the new practical tasks confronting him, had brought to the fore his idea of art as " fixed mimetic improvisation," and anticipation of performance became a most active formative agent in the work on which he was at the time engaged.

The notion that " scenic improvisation " is the ideal dramatic form was not new to Wagner. He had discussed it in *Opera and Drama* apropos of a suggestion for a co-operative body of artists, one of whom was to assume control as *improvisator*, while the others were to subordinate themselves to him for the purposes of the theatrical work in hand. He had applied the idea to amateurs in a pamphlet on a theatre for Zurich. But in these earlier writings the notion was merely touched on incidentally with quite fanciful details, whereas it was now to form the mainspring of a work of art. The process by which it became so may be traced in the written works immediately preceding and accompanying the composition of *The Dusk of the Gods*. Wagner's writings in the revolutionary years deal principally with organic structural problems of artistic form ; those of *The Mastersingers* period pass beyond the conception of art as the sole reality to a more objective discussion of it as transfiguring *play*. The paper on *Beethoven* is a psychological, allegorical interpretation of the creative process. The new series of writings, however, is concerned exclusively with problems of performance—not with practical difficulties, but with the central idea of the close connection between a work's creation and its performance. Wagner deals with performance, the nature of mimetic art, and the theatrical artist—all subjects affecting the work of art in actual being upon the stage.

This living work consists in a synthesis of the activities of musician, singer, and writer. Wagner unites these in the character of the " mime," regarded as the ideal of German racial genius, and he believes (as he says in *A Communication to the German Wagner Associa-*

tion) that it is his mission to discover the secret of German art by evoking such genius, just as it was Bismarck's mission to initiate his people into the secret of political power. The secret of German art, according to Wagner, was its vocation, by virtue of the German racial character, to *truth of expression*. In these writings Wagner's ostensible purpose was to bring home to the artist his responsibility as a vehicle of expressionist truth. " Looking in the first place at the musician, I drew encouragement from the fact that I found him quick to grasp the right as soon as it was adequately pointed out to him. Next to him, though more hampered by deleterious conventions, I found the musical mime, who, however, wherever real talent was present, speedily recognised the true domain of his art and willingly entered upon it in response to right suggestion."

Thus Wagner ceases to seek the expression-impulse in creative art and looks for it in executive art. A creative artist himself, he deliberately goes for inspiration to the art of the mime, examines its workings, and attempts on this basis to mould its practitioners to his own purposes, just as formerly he moulded the verbal and musical material through which he fixed his ideas on paper. His outline of the æsthetic of theatrical performance serves a double purpose; ostensibly it is a justification and explanation of the will to performance, while for Wagner himself it forms the basis of a new development of expressionist art.

The three principal works in the new series are *On Conducting, The Destiny of Opera*, and *On Players and Singers*. The first appeared in 1869 and is addressed particularly to musicians, consisting for the most part in practical lessons drawn from the author's own observations. Its real interest, however, consists not in the examples drawn from a wide experience of conducting, but in the discussion, which these examples illustrate, of the rival merits of a formal and an expressionist æsthetic as applied to the conductor's methods of performance. Orchestral performance is ultimately based on the laws of vocal performance. Nothing but a true understanding of " Melos " in song can ensure appropriate tempo. The orchestral conductor, however, must look for his model not in vocal display as such, but in such singing as Madame Schroeder-Devrient's—in the song of expression, which is dramatic speech enhanced by vocal music. For such performance Italian indications of tempo are quite insufficient, since it needs the *continuous* modifications suggested by German indications. The question raised by Wagner here (and much discussed throughout the nineteenth century) as to the difference between Italian and German marks of tempo and expression is based on a very real difference between the two. The Italian system of directions is essentially *formal*, the German *expressionist*. Each is applicable to a particular type of music. The mingling and enrichment of the two which Beethoven began reflects the growth of the expressionist impulse. Wagner's statements on the subject are confusing simply because, with a deeper and clearer grasp of the phenomena in themselves, he yet regarded expressionism as necessarily an advance upon, an emancipation from, formal music and was unable to see that they are two fundamentally different aspects of art, each with its proper laws. He therefore proceeds, borrowing Schiller's terminology, to distinguish between the " naïve " character of Mozart's allegro and the " sentimental " character of Beethoven's. The true distinction is between formal and expressionist music, but Wagner discusses them in their historic sequence as though the second were an " advance " upon the first. Beethoven had lifted the " sentimental " type into " an eternally valid art type," and Wagner regarded it as the conductor's duty to convey this " sentimental " expression in accordance with the laws governing the performance of dramatic song. He explains the opposite view as a feeble desire for " a shallow compromise with the terrible and serious aspect of life," whereas expressionism has made " the serious and the terrible " the true domain of art. This constitutes the difference between the mere *beauty* of formal art and the *sublimity* of expressionist art. Expressionist methods in performance, moreover, offer the one hope of achieving a distinctively German style. As an original style this can be apparent only in expression.

" Sentimental," " expressionist," and " German " are thus made interchangeable terms. A " German style " in Wagner's sense, moreover, necessarily implied a *theatrical* style. It must aim at musicoscenic art as the one form in which the *expression* intended by the author and composer can be unalterably and unmistakably caught and fixed for all time. In music melody constitutes " irrefutable, determining form, and this may be fixed infallibly for reproductive purposes, whereas written poetry is at the mercy of each whim of the reciter. It was a practical impossibility for Shakespeare to interpret each one of his rôles himself, but this feat can be achieved absolutely by the composer in that he speaks to us directly through the mouth of each executive musician. The soul of the creative artist is infused into the body of the performer through the immutable laws of a rigid technique."

The same fallacious yet fruitful conception underlies the next important paper, on *The Destiny of Opera*. The notions laid down in *On Conducting* are now applied as maxims in a discussion of the musical stage. They are fallacious in a practical sense, for the musical apparatus, however faithfully the composer's directions are followed, does not guarantee that exact reproduction of the author's intentions presupposed by Wagner. The executive artist's personal and unconscious leanings have the same scope as in spoken drama. Yet the idea proved fruitful and significant despite the self-deception underlying it. It prescribed the direction and aim of the creative impulse. The work and the record of the work are regarded simply as means of fixing musical mimetic expression, as choreographic and choregic directions for a scenic improvisation with the author himself as " improvisor "—as the real, eternal player and actor. He holds the executants of his work on the strings of his musical and scenic directions, and through these he preserves the improvisatory character of his work across gulfs of space and time. Absolute, immediate expression through the illusion of scenic improvisation is rendered possible by means of music—and this is " the destiny of opera."

In this paper, first read as a lecture before the Berlin Academy of Arts, Wagner intended merely to summarise the ideas of *Opera and Drama* and to introduce a few new points of view, but the new points of view are so important that they completely reverse the fundamental propositions of the original. It is argued that the problems of musico-scenic structure are an outcome of the problems of mimetic-expressionist structure, which latter is deliberately enthroned as the creative force underlying the work of art. Had it not always been so ? Was Shakespeare a poet in the literary sense ? Was he not rather " a player and man of the theatre ? " Lope de Vega wrote in direct contact with actors and theatre. Molière was himself an actor. " We should study, not the poet, but the dramatist if we wish to throw light on the nature of drama, and drama stands in no closer relation to the poet than to the mime whose peculiar qualities give it birth." Shakespeare's dramas are not literary poetry, but " fixed mimetic improvisations of the highest poetic value." Their poetic value, however, is merely an

accidental adjunct.   Essentially Shakespeare's plays must be classed
" as specially effective theatrical pieces " whose " poetic value "
distinguishes them from others of less worth.

If drama at its greatest is mimetic improvisation ennobled by poetry,
the development of drama must consist in the development of the
methods by which the creative mime fixes his improvisations.
Shakespeare is inevitably dependent on the individual talent of his
players, for he has command only of words, and these are an insufficient
means of determining and fixing his intention.   This difficulty is
solved where acting is governed and accompanied by music.   Music,
by prescribing to a nicety each turn of expression, renders the executive
actor a mere passive instrument, compelled to render mechanical
obedience to the musical directions, and thus by the aid of music the
mimetic genius of the artist-improvisor can directly project itself at any
time and in any place.   As long as the musical directions laid down are
faithfully followed it will remain the same, undisturbed by the will of
others.   The use of music as a means of fixing mimetic expression,
represents, therefore, an advance on Shakespeare.   The music of expression-melody evolved by Beethoven, contains within it the laws of
mimetic art.   Music constitutes the difference between the Shakespearean
stage and the new operatic stage—a difference as great as that between
the Shakespearean stage and the stage of classical antiquity.   These
three divergent ideas of the nature of the theatre vary with the culture
of their times, but agree in regarding the art of the theatre as mimetic art.
Differences of method—chorus and dithyramb in the first type of
drama, spoken dialogue in the second, and music in the third—are
merely different ways of presenting an essentially unchanging art.

The Destiny of Opera agrees with *Opera and Drama* in regarding
music as a method of expression, though in making it the principal
medium of mimetic art and accepting as an axiom that all drama is
simply mimetic theatrical improvisation, it throws a new light on this
basic idea and transforms it to accord with Wagner's recent practice.
It is remarkable that in this pamphlet Wagner makes no attack upon
the designation " opera," and even uses it in his title.   He no longer
regards the " art-work " as the contrary but rather as the fulfilment
of opera.   Neither does he regard it as " drama," but as the musical
counterpart of drama, as a mimetic idealisation of reality achieved by
its resultant *twofold* reflection in the mirror of art.   This deeper vision

contrasts with the theory built up in *Opera and Drama* upon the speech-tone idea. Wagner's views had matured, for he had discovered a basis and foundation for them in that world of the theatre to which they essentially belong. This reacted on his general philosophy of life, though in his first account of a system of thought, ruled by the mimetic idea, he touches only occasionally on general political or cultural subjects. This self-restraint was the easier for him in that at this time his young friend Friedrich Nietzsche was enthusiastically applying his ideas in general philosophy. The two men influenced one another mutually. Nietzsche, inspired by Wagner, awoke from the study of classical philology to the knowledge that he was an artist, while Wagner, carried away by Nietzsche's imaginative flights, borrowed from him a new philosophical system.

This give-and-take between the pair was, none the less, based on a profound mutual misunderstanding. Nietzsche failed to recognise that Wagner's nature and the nature of his art were purely theatrical. He regarded the man and his work in an abstract and ideal light until the realities of Bayreuth showed him his mistake. Wagner, for his part, adopted Nietzsche's terminology rather than his thought, as he had done in the cases of Feuerbach and Schopenhauer and was to do later in that of Gobineau. Wagner's mode of apprehending whatever came to him from without, whether politics, religion, philosophy, or other men's art, was not rational but imaginative, and whatever idea corresponded with his own imaginative desires, whether it were an axiom, a concept, a work of art, or a philosophical system, had to be suitably transformed and adapted for existence in Wagner's own interior world. It might retain an appearance of independence, but it actually passed wholly into a nature that knew nothing outside itself and could understand nothing that would not admit of such transplantation. Nietzsche's mistake was to deceive himself on this point, to misunderstand Wagner's clearly expressed identification of drama with mimetic art in *The Destiny of Opera*. With his ideas of the " Apollonian " and the " Dionysiac " and their derivative, the idea of " the birth of tragedy from the spirit of music," he supplied philosophical illumination to Wagner's own conceptions of a mimetic art conditioned by music, and at the same time stimulated him to develop an æsthetic of the " mimetic art-work." This led Wagner, continuing the argument from *The Destiny of Opera*, to hail a partnership in mimetic art of player, singer, and composer as the one hope for the drama of the future. He had said what he had to say to the musician in his paper *On Conducting*, and he now followed it up with observations on the nature of the " mime," to whom he ascribed the capacity for supreme theatrical and dramatic art.

" Close consideration must convince us that the actual art in a theatrical performance is simply the art of the performers, and that the author participates in it only in so far as, when building up his poem, he has calculated in advance upon the effects of mimetic representation." With the enunciation of this principle *On Players and Singers* opens. Creative work in the author consists in the invention of a dramatic subject, which he must embody by preparing in advance its mimetic effect. Artistic form must always tend to this object, so that the art of the author or composer is organically determined by the art of the mime.

The style of such a mimetic art is fixed by the actual structure of theatre and stage. Shakespeare wrote for a stage which was visible from all sides and upon which the actors moved in all directions, as in real life. This circumstance alone is sufficient to explain the naturalism of Shakespeare's theatrical style. Subsequently this form of stage was abolished and was replaced by an imperfect reproduction of the stage of classical antiquity, with an orchestra forming a focal point in front of a raised platform upon which the play appeared as a two-dimensional picture. Such a stage is properly an *operatic* stage, bound up with the laws of operatic effect, and to compress the stage-play within it is to rob it of the conditions, such as the Shakespearean stage afforded, indispensable to naturalistic mimetic art. Even opera, however, for which this form of stage was really designed, could not reach the norm of the mimetic style until the inner relations of these conditions were properly understood. These relations turn upon the interposition of the orchestra between the public and the stage. " In the theatre of antiquity the orchestra was veritably the seat of magic, the teeming womb of the ideal drama whose heroes . . . were presented in the flat upon the stage while the enchantment proceeding from the orchestra was in itself sufficient to portray exhaustively all imaginable heights and lengths, breadths and depths, in the personalities thus presented." Wagner, therefore, holds it right that this theatre should have triumphed over the theatre of Shakespeare, and that opera should triumph over the spoken drama, which should be absorbed into it. Yet such a victory would never be really satisfactory until its artistic possibilities had been exploited to the best effect. A new naturalism had to be found for the operatic stage—a naturalism not resembling the naturalism of Shakespeare in externals, but of at least equal artistic rank.

This new naturalism could come only from proper relations between the effective factors. The orchestra must not, as in traditional opera, be regarded as a mere accompaniment to the singer's virtuosity. Its place within the artistic organism must be in accordance with its architectonic position as the centre of the theatre. " Thus it should be : *here* the orchestra with its inestimable influence, *there* the dramatic mime : *here* the matrix of ideal drama, *there* its visible embodiment, sustained on all sides by music."

Wagner next turns his attention to the mime himself, thus " music-sustained." Since the modern stage, no matter to what use it is put, is properly an *operatic* stage, the nature of modern mimetic art should be studied in the nature of the operatic mime. His activities are based on three premises, viz. : unaffected naturalism as seen on the Shakespearean stage, an adaptation of this naturalism to the operatic stage in which the orchestra is the determining factor, and the recognition of the indissoluble connection between such mimetic art and the orchestra, which is its basis and which gives it the plasticity and naturalness that the two-dimensional operatic stage, as compared with the three-dimensional Shakespearean stage, must otherwise lack.

Wagner takes as his model, for treatment of dialogue at least, the first performance of *The Mastersingers* in Munich, where the singers were " trained to interchange dialogue with natural speed and verve and to proceed thence imperceptibly to pathetic effect." This reference to *The Mastersingers*, however, merely assists Wagner's unconscious purpose of studying the structure of the new work with which his mind was occupied. What *was* this score which grew under his hands ? Was it a record of musical form accompanied by scenic directions ? Was it an attempt to ensure a brilliant performance by minutely detailed instructions ? Wagner replies by pointing to the effect of the directions in his scores on the performances both of instrumentalist and singer, who, " with unerring instinct, discover in them the very picture the author desires them to reproduce." His scores, his libretti, his stage directions and notes as to performance are dictated not by caprice, but by the deepest intuitions of the mimetic instinct, and all serve the sole end of "fixing the manifold life of the dialogue in the most definite manner possible."

Such a score really parallels the choreographic apparatus of the works of classical antiquity which a purely literary judgment would condemn as overloaded. Fundamentally Wagner's score is not a written record of a self-subsistent work, but a set of instructions for a cast of actors. By fixing his mind on this idea of performance, Wagner has created quite a new type of work—a work of mimetic art. His scores "must be a riddle to æsthetic critics until they have actually fulfilled their purpose—that is to say, until they have served as technically exact models for complete and faithful dramatic performances."

The creative artist's sole object is a living mimetic art ; notes and words have merely secondary significance as musical and verbal indications. They are properly but the hieroglyphs of miming, which is the true inspiration and object of the creative imagination. Essentially the proposed innovation consists in the use of music and speech simply as symbols in the miming art, in denying them their own proper organic life in order that they may become media for the expression of theatrical effect. The dramatic music of *Tristan* must give place to the tone-play of *The Dusk of the Gods* with its deliberately mimetic intention. Expression is still the basic principle, but the means and method of its application in these two works—so closely allied in content—are poles asunder. When, formerly, Wagner adopted a new view of the musical medium he found a new and appropriate subject in which to express it : in this instance a subject fully worked out and ready to hand gave him a new idea as to its treatment in musical miming.

This idea, pursued to its logical consequences, caused a new self-revelation on Wagner's part. He rejected both the specifically poetic and the specifically musical, for neither was essentially of the theatre. These things were of use to him only in so far as they served for miming. To produce perfect mimetic art, to force the performers to complete self-surrender by offering them a perfect model in this kind, the dramatist himself must become mime—not, of course, by appearing in person on the stage, but by assuming the rôle of the Punch and Judy showman who, while he hides himself from his audience, speaks in assumed voices and moves his figures on strings, is at once *all* and *nothing*. He is governed by "the dæmonic impulse to pour himself out which is the root of the miming instinct," but at the same time he can bring cool reflection to bear upon his state.   He is like an improvising mimic watching himself in a mirror. He is fundamentally related to the mere interpretative performer through the self-emptying faculty, but he is master and superior by virtue of the reflective capacity.   He hovers like a disembodied spirit above the actual mime, who feels and knows that all the wealth of the dramatist's imagination has been put at his disposal.   " Thus the two become one, and the poet, seeing his other self in the mime, exults inexpressibly in the latter's appeal to the sensibilities of the public."

This paper (which contains more incidental polemic and is less terse and concentrated than *The Destiny of Opera*) is dedicated " to the memory of the great Wilhelmina Schroeder-Devrient." From her Wagner received his most vivid experience of the art of acting, and on her example he bases his treatise on the nature of the executive artist.   " She was capable of inspiring a composer to compose as he must compose if his work is to be worth such a woman's singing, and she did it by what I have called an ' example,' given in this instance by her, the mime, to the dramatist. . . . Not only this example, however, but all my knowledge of the nature of the mime I owe to this great woman."   The passage establishes beyond doubt that it was from Schroeder-Devrient's acting in the early Dresden days that Wagner took the idea of the great heroine of *The Death of Siegfried*, of the love-betrayed Brynhilda.   A Brynhilda inspired by theatrical appeal was later transformed by new ideas of passionate musical expressionism into Brynhilda the Dream-maid, into Isolda, into the Paris Venus, and, finally, into that fulfilment of the musician's longings for " purely-human " melody—the awakened Brynhilda.   Now that the cycle of musical-expressionist phases was complete, Wagner returned to that first, that *theatrical* figure whose inherent mimetic life was to shape and people the domain of the new work.   Words and musical tones are still the servants of representational appeal, and the dramatist himself becomes actor, accepting the task as his highest vocation.   Wagner's conviction of the truth of this view of art became unshakable as the score was written, the theatre built, in which his mimetic world was to assume actual life.

The Dusk of the Gods is an example of the mimetic art of a musician and scenic artist.   Its basic idea—that of an enforced betrayal of love—

had found expression in Wagner's work even before *Tristan*. It is to be found in his earliest operatic experiment, the 1832 fragment entitled *Die Hochzeit*. In *Die Hochzeit* Cadolt loves Ada, who is the bride of Arindal. There is a struggle of the kind which ends the first act of *The Dusk of the Gods*. Cadolt enters Ada's bridechamber by stealth, and Ada in defending herself throws him from the ramparts into the courtyard below, but her own act awakens her to the knowledge that she is really his, and, fleeing from her bridegroom, she shuts herself up in a turret of the castle. " There she remains until night, when the funeral is celebrated with all solemnity, and she appears, pale and silent, amongst her maidens," to fall lifeless upon her dead lover's corpse. The quotation is taken from a sketch in the *Autobiography* for the last scene of *The Dusk of the Gods* (first draft), and goes to prove that the struggle in the first act of that work, the final scene, and the very motive of the plot had been foreshadowed, though the forces are somewhat differently distributed, in an operatic project of the composer's nineteenth year. To what degree he was influenced by E. T. A. Hoffmann, Immermann's *Cardenio and Celinda*, or Heine's *Ratcliff* is of less importance than the fact that he so early adopted this particular dramatic idea as his own. The special emotional complex it embodies was one of the principal preoccupations of Romanticism. It expresses a conflict—felt as tragic—between an outer world of fact and an inner world of emotion, regarded as a mysterious and uncontrollable force which wins Pyrrhic victories over actualities. This Romantic notion of " the world " as inimical to emotion and of emotion as in a mysterious sense superior to fate, was for the first time embodied by Wagner in his sketch for *Die Hochzeit*. During the Dresden period, inspired by Madame Schroeder-Devrient and by revolutionary doctrines, it took scenic shape in the draft for *Siegfried*, subsequently (as a musical rather than a primarily dramatic impulse) gave rise to *Tristan*, and eventually, when Wagner had mastered all expressionist media, led him back again to his original sketch. *The Dusk of the Gods* is accordingly something more than the closing work of *The Nibelung* trilogy. While summarising in it all the expressionist possibilities developed hitherto and placing them at the service of miming, Wagner also takes up and fully works out the basic concept of Romantic art and philosophy—the idea that the world of things seen is an illusion which may be unveiled and so annihilated by the power of emotion, which is music.

The very form of the libretto in its final state represents a return to this idea. The revolutionary vision of freedom which illuminated the first version became, in 1852, a panegyric on love : " Selig in Lust und Leid lässt die Liebe nur sein" ("Blessed in weal and woe, let love be alone "). This second "final " version, made in accordance with the ideas of the first section of *The Nibelungs*, which was then ready for composition, was again modified in 1862 when the libretto was prepared for publication. The hymn to love was replaced by a prophecy of destruction. Based on the philosophy of Schopenhauer and of India, it reflects that desire to flee from the world which took hold of Wagner in Vienna shortly before the summons to Munich, and which is expressed in the title *Gotterdämmerung*, first adopted at that time :

> " Führ' ich nun nicht mehr
>   nach Walhalls Feste,
> wisst ihr, wohin ich fahre ?
> Aus Wunschheim zieh' ich fort,
> Wahnheim flieh' ich auf immer ;
>   des ew'gen Werdens
>   off'ne Tore
> schliess' ich hinter mir zu :
>   Nach dem wunsch- und wahnlos
>   heiligstem Wahlland,
> der Welt-Wanderung Ziel,
> von Wiedergeburt erlöst,
> zieht nun die Wissende hin.
>   Alles Ew'gen
>   sel'ges Ende
> wisst ihr, wie ich's gewann ?
>   Trauernder Liebe
>   tieffstes Leiden
> schloss die Augen mir auf :
> enden sah ich die Welt."

> (" Fare I now no more
>   To Valhall's feasting,
>   Wist ye whither I wend me ?
> From Wish-home fare I forth,
> Dream-home flee I forever,
>   Eternal Becoming's
>   Gaping gateway
> Bar I behind me fast.

To wishless, dreamless,
Holiest Will-land,
Of world-wandering goal,
 From birth and death redeemed,
Made wise at last, I wend me.
Blest, eternal
End of all things—
Wist ye how I it won ?
Mournfullest loving,
Bitt'rest anguish,
Opened at last mine eyes—
Ended saw I the world ! ")

Three different endings, each the fruit of a particular mood, were
alike rejected when the actual time for composition came. The hymns
to freedom, love, and destruction never attained to music, and only
the thought of the lovers, at one in feeling, destined for one another
from the beginning and parted for a time by the deceitfulness of
outward things, found tonal expression. Brynhilda, mounted upon
Siegfried's steed, rides into the burning pyre which consumes
his body :

" Fühl' ich meine Brust auch,
 wie sie entbrennt ;
helles Feuer
das Herz mir erfasst,
ihn zu umschlingen,
umschlossen von ihm,
in mächtigster Minne
vermählt ihm zu sein !—
Heiajaho ! Grane !
Grüss' deinen Herren !
Siegfried ! Siegfried ! Sieh !
Selig grüsst dich dein Weib ! "

(" Feel too my bosom,
Aglow with fire ;
Flames are leaping
About my heart ;
Siegfried enfolding,
Held fast in his arms,
In love unending
Made one with my own !

Heiajaho !   Grane !
Go we to greet him !
Siegfried !   Siegfried !   See !
Brynhild' greets thee in bliss ! ")

Wagner explains the eventual omission of the Prophecy of Doom by the assertion that " its meaning had already been clearly conveyed in the music-drama." The music of the finale, to which he refers, unites most ingeniously the principal themes of the entire work, namely, the song of the Rhine Maidens, the Valhalla motif, and the Siegfried motif, sustained and illuminated by the melody of Love's miracle, first heard on Sieglinda's lips in the third act of *The Valkyrie* : "O hehrestes Wunder, herrlichste Maid " (" O highest of wonders ! noblest of maids ! "). Sieglinda's dream passes, at the close of *The Dusk of the Gods*, into Brynhilda's clear vision that lovers belong to one another by right and necessity of love. Further than this neither the words nor the music can go ; comment and reflection, struck out of the libretto, are employed in the music simply to develop the one supreme theme of union, scenically presented in the vision of burning Valhalla as the symbol of that world of power and violence and illusion which victorious emotion has annihilated. The *semblance* of philosophy underlying the libretti of *The Ring* and especially prominent in the several endings of *The Dusk of the Gods* is thus almost imperceptibly discarded in the final act of composition. No sooner had Wagner rediscovered his original attitude to the subject as an expression, in mimetic art, of the conflict between emotion and illusion than he forgot the speculations of the interim and revealed the pure essence of his thought, purged of all doctrinaire accretions.

Emotion and the cheating of emotion through the deceitful world of appearances constitute the forces of the drama, for they are by their nature fundamental postulates of mimetic theatre whereby this is allied to music. Emotion is presented under the guise of Woman, who is portrayed in every phase of feeling, in triumph and in despair, in love-surrender and in the will to annihilation, in ruthless savagery and heavenly ecstasy. Every expressionist possibility of the feminine soul is explored, so that the resultant character is in the human sense improbable. Wagner's heroine is regarded as a purely emotional being presenting the whole gamut of imaginable mimetic appeal. She is a mimetic elemental, in whom we must not look for individual

psychology since she embodies a tremendous imaginative effort towards
spectacular emotional expression.

Opposed to her stands Hagen, master of deceit. Emotionless and
without the faculty for joy, he offers a perfect contrast to the feminine
embodiment of emotion. Hagen, like Brynhilda, is no *person* in the
human sense but the typification of a mimetic principle—the sinister
power which brings sorrow into the world, the dæmon of the phenomenal world, even as Siegfried is its genius. Where Brynhilda is
characterised by the many-sidedness and mutability of feminine appeal,
Hagen represents the gloomy steadfastness of the male, standing like
a rock in the rising tide of emotion which may overwhelm but can
never move him. He is a figure conceived on grand lines, apparently
without passion yet with power to summon up all the passions. The
nocturnal Watch song, which affords us our one glimpse into Hagen's
soul, was introduced as an after-thought. Theatrical emphasis is laid
again and again upon this terrific quality of reserve ; man's power
of repression is contrasted with woman's insurgent temperamentalism.
The tremendous figure of Hagen is felt to be the very source of the
powers of darkness which reach out from him to engulf all the
creatures in the drama.

Brynhilda and Hagen represent the two poles of the action and the
plot is so designed that the gulf between them is widest at the beginning of the drama and at its close. Pursuing diametrically
opposite ends, their paths cross midway. They are the dominating
forces throughout and the external events of the story are mediated
through figures which have no wills of their own and are mere pawns
in the game played by these two. Such are Siegfried, Gunther and
Gutrune. The very slight characterisation of the two Gibichungs
shows from the first that they are mere cogs in the mechanism of the
play. They display the sources of the libretto very clearly. Even
Siegfried himself is devoid of real initiative. At first he is wholly
Brynhilda's ; falling later under Hagen's sway he is robbed of his own
will by the magic drink, and Hagen's use of him to win Brynhilda's
trust brings about the tragic climax, but as an independent factor in
the action he is unimportant—a mere stage illusion of the Siegfried
who forged the Sword, slew Fafner, and awakened the Dream-maid.
So purely theatrical a creation would have spelled failure in earlier
works, but it embodies the true inner law of the style of *The Dusk of
the Gods*—a style that *requires* a looking-glass figure, devoid of individual

will, as the subject of representation. The same necessity which makes Brynhilda and Hagen, the two main forces of the drama, suprapersonal types embodying the elemental contrasts of mimetic musical expression, deprives the figure for whom they contend of the personality it once possessed. The magic drink which masters Siegfried's senses is ostensibly a symbol of the deceitfulness of the world, but for the purposes of this work it destroys his individuality and reduces him from a living man to a mere mimetic mask. He becomes a puppet as Gunther and Gutrune are puppets, guided by wills not their own. This is a sphere in which true characters cannot exist ; its figures are mere reminiscent shadows, advising, commenting, warning, pleading— never acting spontaneously. The Rhine Maidens, the sinister Alberich, once active and self-determinative, are but passive mementoes of their former selves and wills. The three Norns recall Erda, now lost in the abyss, and Waltraute remembers Wotan, whose will was shattered with his Spear. One by one the earlier figures return, either in person or on the lips of others, but all are mere phantoms, symbols of themselves—conscious " theatre " directed to " theatre's " one attainable end—mimetic appeal. Writing of the difference between opera and spoken drama Wagner says that the latter's idealisation of life is redoubled by the addition of music. He has accomplished that process in this work. Passion-expression, form-expression, melody-expression are no longer living forces in the musico-scenic organism, for, undergoing a second idealisation, they become mimetic reproductions of themselves—they become opera.

The Dusk of the Gods is indeed opera, not merely because in it, as in The Mastersingers, operatic means are used for the sake of an expressionist stylisation of form, but by virtue of the principles underlying its origins and structure. It is a composed libretto. It is true that words and music are the work of one brain, but the composer was able to regard the librettist objectively across a wide gulf of twenty years. It contains not characters with a life of their own but carefully thought-out rôles. Its hero is not an artist's vision of a man but a singing actor, and the author applies his skill to giving this singing actor such tasks as will best display his mimetic powers. The work differs from older opera principally in the fact that whereas the latter emphasises vocal virtuosity, The Dusk of the Gods emphasises chiefly representational virtuosity. This accounts for the novel treatment, in certain respects, of the libretto and rôles, not affecting the *genre* of the work. External resemblance to opera is very striking in the *ensembles* of the Norns and Rhine Maidens (the second of which becomes a quartet-like interchange with Siegfried) in decorative male-chorus effects, and in the trio of Brynhilda, Gunther, and Hagen, which sums up and closes the second act. A lavish use of purely picturesque effects—such as sunrise and sunset over Brynhilda's rocks, nightfall and day-break on Hagen's watch, the Rhine Maidens' dances, the mist-wreathed landscape of Siegfried's death, the funeral pyre, the flooded Rhine, burning Valhalla—testifies to the direct derivation of the scenario from opera. Orchestral treatment emphasises the picturesque element. Yet even more than by these tendencies to lyrical decoration, to *ensemble* formations with and without chorus, and to theatrical treat-ment of character, the operatic stamp is impressed by the form and diction of the music.

The music of *The Dusk of the Gods*, like the action, makes play with masks from the past. These masks are not used, however, as in *Siegfried*, as reminiscent symbols conjured up to create a new present, for they remain of the past which becomes a means of characterisation. The music is in the march-form with song groups interwoven, but these type-forms (march and song) are not the organic expression contrasts of *The Mastersingers*, sustaining the action by their interplay, for they too have lost individuality and inner fertility and have become a framework for a looking-glass drama of motifs and thematic phenomena. All is adapted to Wagner's fundamental purpose, which is conscious mimetic appeal. The music's purpose is to intensify to the uttermost this conscious mimetic expression, to "fill out" the two-dimensional picture of the stage until it assumes all the richness of actuality, to make its figures tonally concrete and alive. For such a task the strictly organic functions of music are not only dispensable but actually disadvantageous, for they would tend to dispute the primacy with mimetic expression and subject it to themselves. Music is here required to follow, to serve, to interpret, and to these ends must employ its full equipment of expression-formulæ, advancing them as they are needed. Its originality must consist not in novelty of substance but in the art with which it blends things given into an organic musical whole.

The music of *The Dusk of the Gods* is synthetic and choreographic. In all its critical moments it rests upon old material, taken not only from the earlier works of *The Ring* but also from *The Mastersingers*. In so far as it can be regarded independently *as* music its special features may be said to be development, transformation, and summation, hence a tendency to structural combination, favoured by the wealth of decorative scenes. The change from the darkness of the Norns' scene to the light of day, Siegfried's journey from Brynhilda's rock to the hall of the Gibichungs, Waltraute's appearance in the thunderstorm, the Fire magic, brightening as day declines, red dawn on the waters of the Rhine, the marriage procession, Siegfried's funeral train, the finale—all these afford occasion for symphonic expansion. They offer a new formative impulse to the art of thematic transformation. Tone-pictures cross and recross as the flames leap up at the nightmare dream of Siegfried's betrayal. They constitute a tone-poetic narrative at Siegfried's journey up the Rhine, and at his funeral they are combined polyphonically, as also in the splendid, high-vaulted thematic architecture of the finale.

This kind of symphonic association affords, in the first place, room for intellectual interpretation. It doubtless also embodies an intellectual impulse in a mimetic psychological sense. Apart from this, however, it amalgamates the separate motifs with the harmony whence they arose, and a process initiated in the pseudo-polyphony of *The Mastersingers* and carried a stage further in the motival reminiscences of *Siegfried* here reaches completion. Above and beyond the use of the motif as a means of intellectual characterisation it is fitted into place in the fundamental harmony under pretext of ingenious combinations. This reveals the original blood-relationship of great motival groups, such as the Valhalla and Ring motifs with their sequences of accordant ascending and descending thirds, and the actual identity of certain individual formations, such as the melodies of the Rhine Maidens, of the Woodbird, of the Love motif, and the Fire magic. Because these motifs possess a primal harmonic unity, it is now possible to adapt them to mimetic expression, at the same time binding them into the cast-iron rhythmic form required by opera. It is also possible to take from the motif its former actuality and to reduce it to the same condition of undisguised illusoriness as the figures on the stage. Both stage-picture and motival fabric are no more than choreographic media necessary to the actor in order that he may catch the author's vision and reproduce it—the vision in this case being the elemental contrast between true emotion and deceptive emotion. Scenically this contrast is embodied in the figures of Brynhilda and Hagen, for the rest are simply passive subjects of illusion; musically it is expressed in the clouding of the pure harmony of Brynhilda's love by the force of dissonance, whose briefest formulation is to be found in Hagen's "Woe!" interjection taken from the Lament of the Rhine Maidens. The musical contrast governs change in motif and harmony just as the scenic contrast gives rise to the incidents of the visible drama. The two correspond, for both reflect the same fundamental impulse—a will to mimetic expression fired by the idea of illusion-play.

In scenario and in plot the earliest version clearly betrays its origin in the *Lohengrin* period. In both works the central incident of the first act is the longed-for arrival of a stranger from afar, in both the second act opens with a dialogue between the villains of the piece and culminates in an interrupted bridal procession, and in both the third act has two scenes, the first precipitating the catastrophe, the second, lyrically conceived, bringing a solution on a higher plane of being. This coincidence still remains as regards the second and third acts, but the first act of *The Dusk of the Gods* has been changed. In the draft of November 1848 it had two scenes, the court of the Gibichungs and Brynhilda's rock, with a chorus of Valkyries as introduction. The need for a prelude soon became apparent and Edward Devrient (held afterwards in small account, though his writings contain a considerable proportion of the thought material for Wagner's revolutionary pamphlets, even to his definition of the "mime") urged that one should be added. This was done in 1849 and constituted a first step in the revision to which the whole cycle was subject before its completion. At the same time an important double scene—the song of the Norns and Siegfried's farewell to Brynhilda—was added to the first act. Later, as the cycle evolved, Wagner saw no possibility of lightening this act. The chorus of Valkyries was replaced by the long Waltraute scene to form a link with what had gone before, and this first act in its final form actually exceeds the entire *Rhinegold* in compass and length. Like the latter, though there is frequent change of place, unity of time is preserved by the fiction that the action occupies a single day. It is a prefatory act which is really a separate work in itself. It is not an exposition but a complete drama representing the invasion by hostile forces of

Brynhilda's life of love. The two subsequent acts deal with her revenge and her transfiguration.

Regarded as a work within a work, like the third act of *Siegfried*, the scenic structure of the prelude and first act of *The Dusk of the Gods* finds justification. They deal dramatically with the subject of love-betrayal, a subject introduced only indirectly in *Tristan* in the " Tantris" episode. The form, therefore, is that of a complete drama, beginning with the scene of love and farewell on Brynhilda's rock, ending with the forcible wooing and enclosing a picture of the world which causes this act of betrayal. The introductory scene of the Norns, which was originally designed to provide a synopsis of the previous story, is no longer so required and becomes a prophetic vision of the illusion-play to come. The thread of fate, once woven in sure foreknowledge of the destined hero, becomes entangled and breaks off, and, like Erda in the third act of *Siegfried*, the Norns sink down into the abyss. The threat of treachery disturbs the process of eternal Becoming : "Der Welt melden Weise nichts mehr" ("The world hears us wise ones no more ").

Wagner clothes this scene in the form of a ballad with three strophes, twice repeated. Its separate verses pass briefly from the original motif of Becoming to the challenge of Siegfried's horn, resembling, in this summary of the motives of the drama, Wagner's use of the ballad in *The Flying Dutchman*. The Norns' scene, like the ballad, is a lyrical paraphrase of the musico-scenic action, the song-form whence the drama springs. At its heart is the accordant motif of movement. Transposed from major to minor it is made the symbol of melodic Becoming, of the emergence of melody from the succession of harmonic intervals. In the Norns' song all the motifs are reviewed in compressed sequence as revelations of this primal motif melodically individualised. In their midst, as an incentive to ever-further Becoming, is the modulation motif, symbol of the harmonic Question "Weisst du, wie das wird ? " ("Know'st thou what will be ? "). The note of query is struck by the modification of the tonic triad into a remote dominant harmony. From the musical aspect a formula of modulation which leads harmony from phase to phase, this Question motif represents from the dramatic viewpoint the urge to change which leads from phenomenon to phenomenon. It is the fundamental question of the work, even as the accordant motif-type is the fundamental form of the thematic answer. In bringing the two into prominence the Norns' scene stands apart from the work like the old-fashioned prologue. In a ballad-like prelude it reveals the motive forces of the drama before the curtain rises, thus contributing further to the atmosphere of unreality and make-believe.

The first scene of this dramatisation of drama shows the leave-taking of Siegfried and Brynhilda. A stately bridge-passage portrays sunrise, not naturalistically as in *The Rhinegold*, but with grand decorative expressionist effects. A pathetic phrase with a turn, reminiscent of Rienzi's prayer, is developed by crescendo sequence, the harmonic structure towers above the dominant in a formation of thirds to the ninth and eleventh, whence it changes into the theme of Siegfried's horn in march-form and the curtain rises upon Siegfried and Brynhilda. The scene has a duet character but is quite unlike anything of the kind done by Wagner before. The music is a music of gesture, of expressionist gesture, finding resolution solely in the actor's voice and movements. It is masterly, it perfectly fulfils its purpose, because the gestures are themselves conceived in accordance with all the resources of voice and stagecraft. The fact that these gestures are *mere* gestures is necessitated by the plot and manner of treatment. A symphonic interlude opens with a similar easy flow of music, portraying Siegfried's Rhine journey and leading to the Gibichung scene with which Act I begins. The motif of Brynhilda's Farewell absorbs and intensifies that of the Wälsungs' Love glance, eventually giving rise to a melody which advances in a sequence of fourths and is a direct echo of the Apprentices' dance. The simple Nature motif of Siegfried's horn reappears and is tossed as a song motif from voice to voice with easy motion until it is at last confined to a pastoral bass, passing from a dance movement into the Wave theme of the Rhine. The voices of nature cry their warnings, echoing the Rhine Maidens' song of the Gold and the Curse of the Ring, and, suggesting the proximity of a world of evil, they become increasingly sombre in tone. The opening phrase of the Song echoes on significantly and alone, and its chromatic depression casts a first cloud upon the hitherto pure flowing harmony. With the Rhine Maidens' song, now a lament, dissonance invades the harmonic world—the dissonance which Hagen takes up in his " Woe !" motif. It is first heard at the moment when the deceitful world of illusion becomes visible, and thereafter, ever gathering in intensity, runs through the whole work as the symbol of betrayal.

Musical gesture becomes increasingly lucid, tonal choreography more marked, as Gunther, Gutrune, and Hagen make their appearance. The marionette-like quality of the Gibichungs is stylised musically in the dance-form of a minuet in the minor, accompanying Gunther's speech. Hagen's story of the Wälsungs, the hoard, and Brynhilda alternately slackens and tightens up the dance, to which the Gibichungs move like puppets in obedience to some external power. The scene suggests a ballet accompanied by dialogue, in which the ballet master, keeping hold on his dancers, dances with them the prescribed steps and from time to time breaks off to narrate. Again *gesture* is dominant and governs the style and course of the music in accordance with the mimetic quality of the characters. It is a gesture of unfree, passive natures, unable to express themselves save in the prescribed rhythm of formal periods.

Siegfried is brought into this unfree world much as Lohengrin is brought into that of Telramund and Ortrud in response to Elsa's longings. But for Siegfried the magic of a pure love is replaced by the selfish claims of natures incapable of true emotion, and therefore the music which expresses his coming is merely a deliberate decorative representation of the musical gestures of climax. Instead of Lohengrin's sudden A major there is a colourless minor seventh, and in place of the accordant theme of Lohengrin proclaimed by chorus and orchestra, we hear the thirds of the Curse motif as Hagen sings " Heil Siegfried, teurer Held " ("Hail, Siegfried ! hero, hail ! "). The note struck is that of essential untruth, of deception within deception. A drama on so frankly illusory a basis *can* only develop as a mimetic puppet-play. Siegfried needs the cup of forgetfulness no more than Tristan needs the love potion, for he is a changed man from the instant he enters the world of the unfree—changed through the fact of contact with it. This change is apparent in the first words he utters, in which his heroic motif suits itself to the unfree rhythms of the preceding scene though it expands them from three-bar rhythm to four-bar. The minuet becomes a formal march, against which background the characters continue to act out their parts as mechanically as ever, even though they make the *gestures* of free action. The melody of the Love greeting to the awakening Brynhilda, the motif of Siegfried's Destiny, is heard, only to be transformed by the harmonic change of the Cup of Forgetfulness motif into a chord of the minor seventh—into the harmony, based on the diminished triad, of Siegfried's arrival at the court of the Gibichungs, Hagen's greeting, the Curse and the Betrayal. Tonally and dramatically the process is the inverse of that in the love potion scene of *Tristan*. *There* the external drama emerges from the music, *here* the music is organically adapted to external circumstance and untruth is given modulatory confirmation. The drink in *Tristan* changes slavery's illusions into real freedom, but the drink in *The Dusk of the Gods* changes an external semblance of freedom into a servitude to conceptually motivated design.

Hagen's prophecy in the introductory dialogue is fulfilled from the moment that dramatic expression has been given to the change in Siegfried's nature. Siegfried's wooing of Gutrune, Gunther's questions about Brynhilda, the oath of blood-brotherhood, and the departure for Brynhilda's rock, follow in swift dramatic succession without elaborate musical characterisation. In the original version, Gutrune's gentle greeting closed the scene, but later, when the figure of Hagen had gained in stature, Wagner added the Watch song which quite eclipses the externals which lead up to it. The figures of the play vanish, and, as in the Norns' prologue, the composer himself seems to come before the curtain and to speak in his own person, though a semblance of dramatic continuity is preserved. A prolongation of the Lament motif gives rise to a new and mournful legato melody, " Ihr freien Söhne, frohe Gesellen, segelt nur lustig dahin : dünkt er euch niedrig ihr dient ihm doch, des Niblungen Sohn " (" Ye sons of freedom, lusty companions, laugh as ye sail on your way ! Base though ye deem him ye both shall serve the Nibelung's son "). The song rises to a pitch of dæmonic pathos and for a moment the mimetic mask falls. The supreme power of deceit reveals itself, recognises itself, in the mirror of a world which it rules and upon which it is to bring the inevitable doom of all deceit—downfall and annihilation.

As the Watch song dies away the figure of Brynhilda is brought a second time before us. The scene upon which the curtain now rises bears an external resemblance to the first scene of the third act of *The Valkyrie*, though the Thunder-cloud theme is compressed and abbreviated—a mere echo of the original—and Waltraute appears without her sisters. She comes to tell of Wotan's doom, of the tree Ygdrasil, hewn in pieces for the firing of Valhalla, and to plead for the return of the Ring to the Rhine. The scene is a dramatic representation of the first intrusion of sorrow's dissonance into the pure harmonies of Brynhilda's love, of a first assault upon this emotion in the guise of a demand for its willing sacrifice. Waltraute's speech, working up to this appeal, reaches dissonance in the anguished plea, " Hör' mich, hör' meine Angst " ("Hear me, hear my distress ! "). In musical dramaturgy and vocal treatment the dialogue which follows is the counterpart of that between Isolda and Brangäne before Isolda extinguishes the torch. Here as there the passionate plea for restraint upon emotion reveals for the first time to the latter its own unique value. Therefore Brynhilda's answer to the gods is a refusal : " Die Liebe liesse ich nie, mir nahmen nie sie die Liebe, stürzt' auch in Trümmern Walhalls strahlende Pracht " ("While life doth last will I love, from love they never will win me ; fall first in ruins Valhall's splendour and pride! "). But, unwittingly, she sings her hymn to love to the strains of the Renunciation motif, even as Isolda dashes the torch to earth accompanied by the chords of the Death motif.

The grand climax of the Waltraute scene, in which feminine emotional appeal is exploited to the uttermost, stands, like Hagen's Watch song, outside the action, strictly speaking. The two great songs are designed to reveal the inmost hearts of the two great forces here in conflict—man's conscious manipulation of the powers of illusion, woman's blind surrender to emotion, with the Lament motif as a mysterious link between them. Hitherto each has grown within its own separate sphere to a moment of unequivocal self-revelation. Now Siegfried brings them together. Brynhilda's Fire harmonies, glowing softly in the dusk, flame suddenly into fury. The major theme changes by chromatic sharpening into augmented chords, Siegfried's Horn motif breaks in, Brynhilda's melody reaches out towards it in sweeping curves as she rises in the midst of the flames. There is a sudden change as the harmony of illusion, of minor sevenths, takes the place of the major motif, which is lost in the modulations of the motif of the Helmet of Invisibility.

The scene which follows—the conquest of Brynhilda and the rape of the Ring by Siegfried disguised as Gunther—is presented with weird dramatic effect, and Wagner here realises with the cool deliberation of age an idea of the fantastic which had inspired the earliest works of his youth. He is a " mime " playing with himself the play of tragic delusion. Siegfried and Brynhilda alike have now ceased to be masters of themselves—he because an alien will has been imposed upon his own, she because she is bewildered by events. Suddenly cast down from the heights of love ecstasy reached in the scene with Waltraute, she is beside herself. She has been victim of a rape of the ego, not unconsciously, like Siegfried among the Gibichungs, but consciously. In this tremendous and paralysing crisis not a melody stirs in the music. The accordant, forthright harmony of Brynhilda's world is arrested and modulatory harmony, with its ever-shifting tone-relations, establishes the dominion of deceit, precluding clear melodic formation. The modulation of deceit, scenically represented by the motifs of the Helmet of Invisibility and of Forgetfulness, governs and shapes the scene until there breaks from Brynhilda an elemental cry of anguish. The power of emotion, Brynhilda's loving nature, is invaded by the forces of dissonance and deceit. As Brynhilda's eyes meet those of her conqueror the Siegfried melody is heard for a moment. Then the Love motif sinks down, broken, and fades away in the harmonies of transformation and forgetfulness.

Brynhilda, too, is now among the unfree ; she cannot but follow Siegfried even here, and has become like him a mask of her former self. But there is a difference between their states, for whereas Siegfried is wholly a slave, Brynhilda remembers that she has been robbed of her soul by violence. She now has a dual personality, torn by conflict, tossed hither and thither between truth and falsehood, and the enforced change turns her love to hatred. There is but one thing she can do—she can win love back by slaking hate. Brynhilda must become the Isolda who gives Tristan the death-drink. The action centres now in the conflict in Brynhilda's heart between love and hate, truth and falsehood, and in the power of Will, embodied in Hagen, which has caused the struggle. Like Ortrud, Hagen is an emanation of the powers of darkness. He is driven by the thirst for power as Brynhilda by the need for love. Alberich lives on in him, and appears to him, phantom-like, in dreams. Hagen's dream introduces the second act. The later version of this scene shows an important variation from the earlier, for in *The Death of Siegfried* Hagen promises Alberich the Ring—" Den Ring sollst du haben, Nibelungenfürst, frei sollst du sein " (" The Ring will I win thee, Nibelung Prince, free thou shalt be "), but in *The Dusk of the Gods* this promise to Alberich is omitted—" Den Ring soll ich haben : mir selbst schwör ich's " (" The Ring will I win me. To myself swear I ! "), and it is made clear that Hagen is in dream-converse with himself. Alberich is not the actual Nibelung of the first draft, but an unreal dream, a nocturnal phantom of Hagen.

The weird atmosphere of the last scene of Act I persists here—that is to say, it prevails in the two scenes in which the utmost is made of the diametrically opposed mimetic appeal of the two principal forces of the drama. The climax in which they are to measure their strength approaches and forms the chief content of Act II. Siegfried's return and his story of the combat is the signal for Hagen to act. The Lament motif, which entered into the Waltraute scene as a warning of evil to come, now takes charge of real events : " Not ist da, Not. Wehe ! Wehe ! Hoiho, hoho ! " (" Need is here ! Need ! Danger ! Danger ! Hoiho ! Hoho ! "). Hagen's summons to welcome the bride is set to the strains of his " Woe ! " motif. He knows his own dark schemes, but his followers take the grimness of his mood as an amusing accident. The call to the marriage concludes with a solemn prayer to the gods to bless the pair. A grand declamatory passage for full chorus and orchestra proclaims the Gibichung motif, portraying in solemn strains the return of the travellers. As Brynhilda, escorted by Gunther, sets foot on land, Siegfried steps forward to meet her, and the two unreal masks confront each other. A scene upon which darkness descended at the close of Act I is here repeated in broad daylight. Brynhilda, with her dual consciousness, recognises Siegfried, but he, having by his own act fallen victim to the world, does not know that she is his. The moment has come predicted at the end of the Norns' scene—the thread of the known breaks off—the future is all dark—a tremendous question.

From this moment begins the drama of the two who are no longer themselves, who have become bondslaves of deceit. Hagen, who has silently awaited his hour, now enters the arena. Brynhilda is in his power and must speak as he commands, and it is therefore on her lips that the Revenge motif of the Nibelungs, whispered to Hagen's dreaming ear by Alberich, re-reters the drama. Brynhilda sees on Siegfried's hand the Ring which her conqueror wrested from her—in a flash she knows the truth and hurls her accusation :

> " Betrug ! Betrug !
> Schändlichster Betrug !
> Verrat ! Verrat !—
> wie noch nie er gerächt !
> Heil'ge Götter !

Himmlische Lenker !
Rauntet ihr dies
in eurem Rat ?
Lehrt ihr mich Leiden,
wie keiner sie litt ?
Schuft ihr mir Schmach,
wie nie sie geschmerzt ?
Ratet nun Rache,
wie nie sie gerast !
Zündet mir Zorn,
wie nie er gezähmt !
Heisset Brünnhild'
ihr Herz zu zerbrechen,
den zu zertrümmern,
der sie betrog ! "

(" Betrayed ! Betrayed !
Shamefully betrayed !
Deceit ! Deceit !
Vile beyond all revenge !
Gods most holy,
Ruling in Heaven !
Was this concealed
In your decree ?
Saved ye this sorrow
Too great to be borne ?
Doomed me to shame
And bitterest dole ?
Teach me a vengeance
Too dire to be told !
Stir me to wrath
That may never be stilled !
Break in pieces
The heart of Brynhild,
May but this traitor
Taste bitter death ! ")

In magnificence of theatrical appeal Brynhilda's cry for vengeance as far surpasses Isolda's curse as the latter excels it in truth to human nature. Isolda expresses the madness of unrestrained and unrestrainable emotion, Brynhilda the pathos of carefully calculated mimetic effect. Musically, therefore, it is based entirely on tones either alien to Brynhilda's nature or in themselves distorted—motifs of the gold-lust of the Nibelungs and a chromatic distortion of Brynhilda's farewell to Wotan, rhetorically phrased, and with Hagen's " Woe! " motif creeping in. Constrained by the forces of illusion, Brynhilda gives a totally false account of her own nature and is swept along on a tide of purely theatrical passion to hurl her accusation against Siegfried.

Siegfried is called on to clear himself by oath and Hagen is to be witness of the oath. The course of events hitherto has lent his " Woe ! " motif the *value* of truth, and it now gains, through Brynhilda's accusation, predominance in appeal. In this way the power that has gone out from Hagen returns to him from all hands to be concentrated symbolically in the point of his treacherous spear. The oath pronounced by Siegfried and repeated by Brynhilda as an accusation of perjury carries further the work of deceit. The Lament motif and a distorted version of Brynhilda's motif accompany Siegfried's song, which contains no note of the true Siegfried, but is mere empty declamation, expressing an alien will. Yet on Brynhilda's lips even this song is caught up into a world of passion and pathos which endows the same notes with a quite contrary meaning and concludes in a tempest of Valkyrie chromatics.

This second theatrical climax reaches the height of pathos, and the contending forces of the drama are seen in sharpest contrast. Events are ruled not by Siegfried and Brynhilda as they *are* but as they *seem* to be. At this point there is an abrupt break ; Siegfried's speech makes a digression into the superficial, brushing aside what has just occurred and leading straight on to the wedding music in accordance with the operatic tradition by which, when the climax has been reached, the conflict is glossed over by the unconcerned exit of one or other contending party. Siegfried, Gutrune, and the chorus depart, leaving Brynhilda with Gunther and Hagen to ask who is the author of this treachery : " Welches Unholds List liegt hier verhohlen ? " (" What craft of demon dread here lieth hidden ? ")—sure that " there is something in this more than natural," though she has no clue to the mystery. Had the subject been treated as literary drama the unravelling of this mystery must have followed here, but mimetic treatment glides away from this question and advances towards a fresh climax of representational expression. Brynhilda, robbed of her true self, undergoes a further transformation as Hagen's " Woe ! " motif, invading and changing the Lament, enters into her soul, and she expresses *his* will and *his* purpose who has ensnared her as she asks : " Wer bietet mir nun das Schwert mit dem ich die Bande zerschnitt ? " (" Who bringeth me now the sword wherewith I may sever my bonds ? "). She is at last wholly Hagen's—the eye that is to guide his weapon to its mark. Hagen moves towards her, taking up his own theme from her lips. The central moment of the drama has come, the moment when the two great antagonists, falsehood and emotion, take hands. Each thinks he is using the other for his own ends, yet each betrays the other. Brynhilda's treachery is proclaimed to the motif of the gold-lust of the Nibelungs : " Doch träfst du im Rücken ihn . . . an ihm spart' ich den Segen " (" Yet if at his back thou strik'st . . . and so no spell there set I "). The Hagen motif triumphs, bearing along with it the distorted Brynhilda motif, and, sweeping onwards, the two great fundamental themes draw Gunther too into their ever-widening curves. Hagen's purpose on Brynhilda's lips—" So soll es sein, Siegfried falle " (" So shall it be : Siegfried falleth ! ")—dominates the line, which is presently resolved in the trumpet flourishes of the festal train. Like the Forbidden Question motif at the end of Act II of *Lohengrin*, the dual Hagen-Brynhilda motif breaks in upon the wedding music and is repelled only to re-assert itself triumphantly in the closing bars.

The only way in which this act differs from traditional opera is in the conscious and deliberate association of the illusory character of the dramatic motive with the self-deception of the characters of the play. The self-renunciation regarded by Wagner as the fruitful ground of all mimetic art is here itself the subject of representation. Self-renunciation is here the germ-idea of the drama, as is chromaticism in *Tristan* and alternation and contrast of forms in *The Mastersingers*. The characters are not dramatic realities but dramatic fictions, and the plot is so designed that they seem to lose their freedom of will and to become, as the genius of the work would have them, *play-actors*. The scenico-musical process as such is unaffected by this artistic illusion of a drama of illusion, this deliberate metamorphosis of natures into their opposites. The non-actuality of stage representation when music lifts it into its own non-actual sphere and the puppet nature of the characters in such drama—taken for granted in traditional opera—have here been intellectually formulated and embodied in a work of art. The *result* is the same, and Wagner, well aware of the parallel, considered that in this type of illusion play opera had achieved its

destiny and that at the same time the very forms of traditional opera—
not the forms of *arias* and *ensembles* designed for vocal display but the
scenic forms of opera as a whole in contradistinction to spoken drama
—had found new justification.   In some preliminary remarks to a
reading of the libretto of *The Dusk of the Gods* in Berlin, he states that
he has introduced his most important innovation in making " the
dramatic dialogue itself the chief subject of the music," whereas
traditional opera had assigned to the music " only static lyrical
moments."   The second act of *The Dusk of the Gods* has the rhythm
typical of traditional opera—a regular alternation between scenes of
expository dialogue and scenes of emotional crisis.   Thus between
the opening Night scene and the assemblage of Gunther's lieges
there is a connecting link of dialogue between Siegfried, Hagen, and
Gutrune, while in the second half of the act Brynhilda's accusation,
the oath, and her decision to bring Siegfried to his death, stand out as
high lights.   The peculiar disposition of the work makes these climaxes
theatrical rather than lyrical, so that the aria's place is taken by a climax
of representational effect, and this is followed by interpretive dialogue,
just as recitative follows aria in traditional opera.

In Act II an essential resemblance to traditional opera is disguised
to some extent by technical differences required by representational
expressionism, but in Act III the parallel is complete.   The subject
of the drama as such has been exhausted, for that subject is the power
of the lie, and this has been fully explored in Act II.   All that remains
is to bring the work to a close, and this is accomplished by song.   The
last act of *The Dusk of the Gods* satisfies the operatic demand for an
action so arranged as to give scope for music and song—satisfies it so
completely that the actual " cast-iron " forms of operatic song are
reproduced, and the lines of demarcation between these lyrical form-
organisms and the connecting passages of dialogue are left plain to
view.   Siegfried's death is the only external event still to be portrayed,
and even this incident has been discussed and plotted to the last detail
in the foregoing act.   The remainder of Act III is concerned with
those " static emotional moments " which are of the essence of opera—
scenic pictures framed in song.   Such are the three principal scenes
of the first half of the act—the scene of the Rhine Maidens, Siegfried's
story of his life, and the Dead March which forms a symphonic bridge-
passage to the second half of the act.   This is completely dominated

by Brynhilda's final arioso monologue, which is prolonged into a lyrical scena addressed to a chorus arrayed in the operatic manner. Between these four chief scenes of the act there are connective passages in which the last theatrical touches are added to the characters on their purely puppet side.

The last act provides not only a theatrical finish to the work but a retrospective survey of the whole *Nibelung* cycle. Memories are awakened of the depths of the Rhine whence all arose. The Lament motif, purged of its dissonant sharpening, becomes again the opening phrase of the Rhine Maidens' song and advances with a chromatic wave-like motion, through which the Rhine Maidens, in their weaving dance, rise from the depths to the water's surface. In two verses of the women's trio—the lyrical melody alternating between simple diatonics and chromatic involutions, the fresh limpid soprano voices, the orchestral background of shimmering waters—a new picture is painted of nature's blissful awakening, but as Alberich once came to ravish the Rhine's treasure, so now comes Siegfried, unwitting robber of the hoard. The Lament motif, with Hagen's motif emerging from it, supplies the outline of the Rhine Maidens' next song, which is both a story of the past and a warning of the future. But the note of solemnity soon dissolves in pure lyricism, the Threat motif takes on a merry rhythm and becomes once more the original dance melody in which the voice of Siegfried joins, forming a quartet. Musically the scene depends on vocal display, while its mimetic significance consists in decorative pictures of the Rhine valley, the Water Maidens, and Siegfried.

The opening of the second scene is equally peaceful. Siegfried, encamped in the forest with Gunther and Hagen and a following of huntsmen, tells the story of his life. The scene is the conventional "narrative" scene of opera. An introductory hunting chorus is taken up by the orchestra, which, as the huntsmen are revealed, strikes into a vigorous march, and this, passing on from the Siegfried motif to the siren-song of the Rhine Maidens and thence to the Gibichung theme with the motif of Hagen's threat interwoven, dies out on the Woodbird motif. Siegfried's story follows—at once a retrospect and a final self-metamorphosis, for through this tone-picture of his life he comes to remembrance of his own proper nature. Music strips away the mask, Siegfried knows himself, and the annihilation of his present false existence brings—death.

The second scene, like the first, closes in song, and the third opens with a solemn march rhythm. Words are unnecessary : the oncoming mists into which all the figures of the drama must vanish creep up round Hagen as the dead Siegfried is borne behind him. Music alone speaks, calling up memories through which Siegfried, released from the life-story told in the song, rises from the ashes of himself. In *Siegfried* melody builds up a living man, and in *The Dusk of the Gods* the formative power of rhythm performs a like miracle. In a non-actual world music itself becomes actor, lifting Siegfried out of the deceptive world of things seen and restoring to him his pristine emotional verity.

The second half of the act shows how Brynhilda follows whither Siegfried has gone. The two halves are linked by the Dead March and the return of the funeral train, announced by Hagen to the combined strains of the now triumphant " Woe ! " motif and the distorted Brynhilda motif. Hagen admits that it is he who has killed Siegfried : " Ja denn, ich hab' ihn erschlagen. Ich, Hagen, schlug ihn zu tot " (" Yea, then ! 'Twas I that did slay him. I, Hagen, sent him to death "). Hagen's goal is all but attained—the false magic of appearances has subdued all the forces of emotion. Gunther too must fall, and the Master of Illusion reaches out for the prize. But he is arrested in the act, and by the dead hand of Siegfried. The power of illusion is broken *because* it has annihilated the seen ; it is itself the victim of the illusion that the power of emotion is destructive. But emotion, once freed from bondage to the visible world, has attained enlightenment, and in its light the false pageant of seeming vanishes away. Brynhilda's question at the swearing of the oath— then silenced by the power of illusion—the question of questions about the mystery of " becoming," is again asked and this time finds its answer : the whole visible universe is but a make-believe play.

This question and this answer form the kernel of Brynhilda's grand final monologue—a counterpart on a much vaster scale of Lohengrin's narrative. The fable of universal " becoming " and passing away constitutes the resolution of the drama, which now returns to its origins. The scene is a companion piece to that of the Norns—an epilogue spoken by the poet behind a tragic mask. The fiction of identity between the drama and the real scheme of things is preserved up to the last word and note. The illusion of mimetic action becomes an illusion of the world-process, and the poetic mime's final act is to proclaim, in the pathos of dramatic speech, that the truth of the stage and the truth of the universe are one.

This speech achieves form by a mighty structure of combined fragments. A solemn introduction is provided by the measured strains of Brynhilda's words to the mourners and her repulse of Gutrune, issuing in the original harmonic Question of the Norns. Brynhilda's command to prepare for the burning relaxes the rhythm, and in fulfilment of the Norns' prophecy and Waltraute's the ascending scale-motif of Wotan's Spear builds a tone-picture of the towering pyre in whose flames she and Siegfried are to find union. The imperious accents of the command evoke a vision of the dead hero— a true vision as opposed to that false appearance which, having brought about betrayal, could bring emotional enlightenment only at the cost of illusion's torments : " Mich musste der Reinste verraten, dass wissend würde ein Weib " (" My woe must he work all unwitting, that wise a woman might grow ! ").

The play's appeal, the world's appeal, are recognised at the last as illusion. The god of passion goes to his rest ; the Ring, symbol of the play, must return to the depths whence it came, and with it vanishes that world of appearances which it has conjured up. The motival and modulatory formations evoked from harmony by the Lament dissonance must return to the fundamental chord. Brynhilda hurls the torch into the pyre, the flames of chromaticism are unleashed, the storm rhythms of the Valkyries, sweeping with them the ascending chords of the Siegfried motif, fan them into fury. All the rhythmic and harmonic forces of the world of *The Ring* are let loose, but above them hovers unifying melody, the melody of Love's promise, soaring ever higher : " Siegfried, Siegfried ! Sieh ! Selig grüsst dich dein Weib " (" Siegfried ! Siegfried ! See ! Brynhild greets thee in bliss !").

In a region where words fail music carries fulfilment. Hagen alone finds the solution incomprehensible. Still bound fast to illusion, he thinks he may yet recover the Ring, the magic of the world of appearances, and so he is sucked into the maelstrom of forces which are resolving earth and fire into water. Above this conflict the aboriginal melody of the " Weia-waga " motif rises triumphant, while from it flash out the stately chordal masses of the Valhalla motif, and high above all, emblem of the one thing which does not " pass away," soars the melody of the Love-promise—of Emotion, lord of fate and of the universe.

The completion of *The Dusk of the Gods* concluded a work which covered Wagner's artistic development from his thirty-fifth to his sixty-first year. He began it in Dresden, the scene of his first artistic success, and he finished it when he had attained his life's ambition in Bayreuth. Conceived from a dim intuition of his own creative powers, it set him to survey the whole realm of personality, while its execution necessitated all the multifarious experiences through which he passed between its initiation and completion, and, in addition, certain curious inversions of sequence. The origin of the whole is to be found in its close, and the work is cleft into two sharply defined sections. Two great works outside the cycle intervene between these sections, the second of which did not become ripe for execution until Wagner had surmounted all the interior and exterior obstacles of his career. A creative work so broken up cannot be expected to possess stylistic unity in the ordinary sense, and indeed a cleavage of style is necessary in view of the multiplicity and range of the whole, for by contributing a series of fresh creative impulses to the work it supplies that variety in detail which makes it an organic structure of a high type and justifies artistically the immense length of the form chosen. The controversy as to whether, given favourable outward conditions, Wagner could have completed *The Ring* without a break is a barren one, for during the intervals imposed by circumstances Wagner received new formative impulses which have made his work the living thing it is.

No order of merit can properly be assigned to the several works of the cycle. *The Rhinegold* must always hold pride of place for its picturesqueness, fresh naïveté, and wealth of fantasy. *The Valkyrie* and the first two acts of *Siegfried* make a strong and direct appeal by their passion and musical full-bloodedness. The third act of *Siegfried*, an heroic idyll, marks the summit of artistic perfection. *The Dusk of the Gods* is a stylised compilation in which Brynhilda and Hagen stand out as more than life-size representational types, in which the once naturalistic musical impulse is replaced by a deliberate gesture of theatrical appeal, and in which the dramatist, appearing consciously as mime, speaks the epilogue which explains the whole cycle as a fantasy of " becoming " and " passing away."

The Ring, therefore, regarded as a whole, mirrors an artistic evolution in all its phases. It originates in accordance with a theory of " word-tone art " and ends by finding " the destiny of opera " in the

" singing mime." It begins in revolutionary yearnings and ends in nihilism. It begins in flight from the theatre and ends in a return to it. Such a whole would be impossible without stylistic differences in the parts—differences which illuminate the inner meaning. This great work of art is not dependent on unity of content between its parts, nor indeed on objective content in any or all of them. Comparisons, therefore, with other attempts to shape the matter of the *Nibelungenlied*, and questions as to the relative value of mediæval and mythical versions of the story are unfruitful, as are any lines of investigation starting from the *subject-matter*. For Wagner subject-matter is merely a medium which he handles neither for philosophic nor for poetic ends, but solely for the purposes of " theatre," which, under the *mask* of a subject, runs in progressive sequence through all the possibilities of a many-sided will to expression. The fundamental impulse behind this will to expression is presented under the dynamic symbolism of "becoming" and "passing away"; it finds musical embodiment in the synthesis and analysis of motivally formed interval relations in the chord and in their modulatory intertwining and unravelling until they find resolution in the matrix of fundamental harmony, and scenic representation in a nature-myth of never-ending birth from and re-absorption into the ground of all " becoming."

The inner connection between the four works of the *Nibelung* cycle must be sought in this peculiar conception of Wagner's will-to expression and quite apart from any interpretation of the story as such. The greatest organism within the larger organism of Wagner's work as a whole, *The Ring* is from first to last a representation of harmonic development. Saga, erudition, critical and æsthetic considerations have simply supplied media for its execution, and though they contribute to the unity of the work, brilliantly maintained even in details, they have no closer connection with its essence than have the laws of chordal combination, form, and tone. The drama is not derived from Wagner's interpretation of the myth—rather the myth supplies a scenic symbol for a representation of the evolutionary harmonic life of music, conceived by the composer as a totality. Upon this basis all has been developed with an inner logic which has realised Wagner's faith in " theatre " as a creative art in a veritable work of art.

This faith was responsible for something more than the work, for as always with Wagner art moulded life. *The Ring of the Nibelungs*

not only set the theatre its greatest task in the drama of " becoming "
but actually built the theatre which could accomplish the task—
a theatre apart from other theatres which remain theatres of form,
of opera in the old sense—a theatre of Expression.   Expression had
shown Wagner the task which lay before him, and he had now to erect
a building in which he might become (like any owner of a puppet-
show) improvisor, manager, and actor in one, or, as he supposed
Shakespeare to have been, " a play-actor and theatrical *entrepreneur*."

Shakespeare had found no incompatibility between the stage of
his day and his own creations, but Wagner's expressionist will, with
its deliberately rigid conceptions of the laws of theatre, refused to
adapt itself to the stage as he found it.   He was therefore forced to
build his theatre for himself, and he did so through the agency of his
works.   When the great work that embraced the entire world of the
theatre reached completion the theatre too was complete, and eighteen
months after the conclusion of *The Dusk of the Gods* the first " Festival
play " was enacted on the stage of Bayreuth.   " Musical acts made
visible " was Wagner's description, in default of a better, of his own
works.   Expression had to become visible, had to become act and
fact, since only so could it proclaim its existence and exercise its effect.
The *final* expression of expression was the Bayreuth theatre—an " act
of music " made visible indeed.

PART V
SACRED FESTIVAL-PLAY

CHAPTER I

PARSIFAL

" I AM quite clear now as to the choice which lies before me ; I do not yet know how I shall choose—but then the choice probably does not lie with me but with *It*, the Brahma, the Neuter. The question is this : whether I am to produce my works or to make new ones. . . . The choice itself when made will show which of the two was the more necessary. If I alone can produce my own works, so it will be ; of that I am sure ! If I alone can write the works I still have in my brain, *so* it will be. Well, which is the harder task ? Which is the more important? The first, I am inclined to think. Whether or no a few more works of this type are to be given to the world is probably of less account to the World Spirit than that some one representative work of this type should be fully and perfectly revealed to the world. . . . For in a certain very deep sense, intelligible to the World Spirit alone, in any new works I might make I should only be repeating myself—I have nothing more essential to reveal. Put like this there would seem to be very little choice, and I cannot consult my own wishes in the matter. But here too there is help, and I have a sweet delusive vision that I might perhaps be able to combine the two—to find rest and quiet in the intervals of the struggle, or after it, and be able to finish my works. Oh, *It* does not let me lack alluring fancies ! But I know my dæmon ; there are solemn hours when I know all, when no alluring fancy beguiles me and I—am still resolved to endure all ! "

So runs a letter written from Paris to Mathilde Wesendonk in May 1860. It proves how consciously Wagner envisaged his own life's course as the operation of the creative dæmon, of the " Brahma," of the all-overruling " World Spirit." It also proves that he recognised his creative instinct as the twofold instinct to *make* and to *produce* his works. He considered these two activities equally important

—or the second, perhaps, more important than the first. It was important not for the sake of any one particular work but for the sake of the type of art which was his. He believed that this type was so clearly represented in the series of works culminating in *Tristan* that there was " nothing more essential to be revealed." The great point now was to make men recognise this essential, and that could only be accomplished by proper production. And Wagner had his dream of what production might and should be—a breathing of the breath of life into a choreographic sketch from whose symbols only the composer could conjure the vision he had seen. As a man of the theatre to whom the written word or note was but a makeshift, he rebelled against a purely literary existence. He could not endure to live on paper only. He preferred to sacrifice this rather than deny his imperative need to see his work performed. But might it not be possible to do both—to produce what he had written and then write further works for production?

It did indeed prove possible. His creative dæmon had strength to fulfil both tasks, since the two were in reality one. After the completion of *Tristan*, Wagner's own realisation of the close connection between them became so acute as to leave him no rest. Previously the work of creation had involved only complete surrender to his subject, but now the thought of production stood like a remorseless slave-driver over each new work. Therefore *Tristan* became an engine of assault upon the contemporary stage in general; the *Venusberg* was designed to conquer the Paris Opéra; *The Mastersingers* was written for the German theatre. Yet over and over again the apparatus of production proved inadequate and attempts at reform or even compromise came to nothing. At last *The Ring of the Nibelungs* built for itself the theatre it needed in order to take living form. The " delusive vision " of the letter to Mathilde had come true; the unity of creator and producer was not broken. The two interdependent vocations were fulfilled simultaneously; pauses in practical activity allowed leisure for fresh creative work, wherein Wagner was stimulated by the knowledge that it would find its fulfilment in production and performance.

Wagner believed it essential to theatrical art that creator and producer should be one. It was the idea of all others for which he fought. No then existing theatre, however, could have adopted it, since it involved abandoning a many-sided programme and submitting the stage to the sole control of a single personality whose ideas of drama, moreover, were not those of the majority. Of the two alternatives, total transformation or compromise, Wagner demanded the former; the theatres could offer, at most, the latter. One solution remained—that this strange creator-mime should have a theatre of his own where his will could have free scope. This stage would not be simply a place for the scenic representation of literary works; it would itself be the subject, the content, of the performance, with the written word to serve merely as a jumping-off place. Wagner dreamed of his theatre as " a giant," as " pandemonium," as " an abyss of all possibilities from the lowest to the most sublime." It was to emerge from the narrow sphere of reproduction and become a universe in itself, a true vision of the nature of reality revealed to the expressionist mime, and, in the ecstasy of the representational urge, passed on by him to others.

To create a stage with such representational possibilities was Wagner's ultimate aim in and beyond his works as such. It was an ambition bound up with no one work but with the creative development of the representational impulse in itself, of the instinct to exploit the resources of sensuous dramatic representation to the uttermost. The stage was not to be a means of exhibiting a work; the work was to be a means of exhibiting the stage. In relation to this stage any one play would be simply " an example," whereas the stage itself was to stand for the sum-total of all such examples, for the full possibilities of drama. Thus the Wagnerian stage which, from the time of his flight from Dresden and amidst all his speculations, interests, and experiences, took increasingly clear shape in Wagner's mind, was not merely a special kind of theatre in the ordinary sense of the word. It represented rather the pure conceptual content of his whole life's work, the essential will to drama which is common to all his works. Stripped of accidentals, the active principle in this will to drama now became so pronounced that, in accomplishing a new act of synthesis, it materialised an actual theatre out of the world of dreams. Here at last the artist could improvise as he pleased, manipulating his puppets on music's strings while his audience listened and believed. Yet his very improvisations were themselves conditioned by the hidden laws of that stage which, under each new mask, could but embody the same unchanging play-magic inherent in it.

Wagner knew how greatly the structure and conditions of the stage influence the work that is to be presented upon it.   After the revolutionary period this subject recurs very frequently in his writings and he lays great emphasis upon it when speaking of his own ideal theatre.   Wagner's attacks on the stage in general had less effect in reforming that institution than in clearing his mind as to his own requirements.   His very one-sided criticism of the modern theatre had little influence upon it but proved most revealing as to the particular nature of Wagnerian drama.   His idea of drama, as he explains in his *On the Destiny of Opera* and *On Players and Singers* (both expositions of *The Dusk of the Gods*), is based on those two concepts which, in his opinion, underlie classical and Shakespearean drama—namely, naturalism and idealisation.   Naturalism is of the essence of theatrical action, and idealisation is conditioned by music.   But these two must be combined ; naturalism must be sought within, not outside, the proper sphere of musical expressionism, and music must become naturalistic.   The magic of the stage consists in the twofold illusion imposed by a music which is dramatic in conception and form and a drama in which action is musically idealised.   Neither the dramatic nor the operatic stage can fulfil these reciprocal conditions.   The dramatic stage presents action with faithful realism, the operatic stage a frankly idealised tone-picture whose unreality is rendered obvious from the outset by the orchestra stationed in front of the stage and by virtuoso singers.   The gulf between these conditions and those which Wagner envisaged was so wide as to make " reform " impracticable.   The idea of opera as dramatic illusion which underlies his peculiar dramatic requirements, his strange powers of improvisation, could never be realised in an existing framework.   No amount of revolutionary, controversial, or educative criticism—no royal mandate even—could alter this.   A stage seen only in the flat yet producing a plastic effect, a stage offered clearly to the eye yet set at that distance which lends enchantment—this unreal reality had first to be actualised to the creative power of its inventor before others could even conceive it.   Till then it was as unimaginable as would be the score of *Tristan* from a mere verbal description.   Moreover, not until he had realised his own vision of a theatre did its inventor possess a true measure of his own capacities as a dramatist.   While Wagner's theatre was but a project, a hope, his fancy hesitated between dreams of a stage of his very own and flattering notions of ennobling and transforming the

common stage. No sooner, however, was his own stage built than
the ordinary stage vanished from his mind, ceased entirely to offer
him its incentives. The "Festival-Play" idea revealed the requirements of the "Festival-Play Stage." As soon as these were fulfilled
the actualities of that stage reacted again upon the creative imagination,
and the instinct to exploit the resources now indeed available spurred
it to new heights of improvisation. The result was the "Sacred
Festival-Play."

In a pamphlet entitled *Das Bühnenfestspielhaus zu Bayreuth* (The
Festival-Playhouse at Bayreuth) which Wagner wrote in 1873
and dedicated to his benefactress Frau von Schleinitz, he enters
exhaustively into the special resources of his stage and the possibilities
of dramatic representation which these afford. Purporting to be a
description of the laying of the foundation-stone at Bayreuth and of
the general character of the undertaking, the paper is in reality an
aesthetic treatise on the "Festival-Play" conception. Wagner explains
that the central idea has been to "make as perfect as may be that part
(of the building) designed to create sublime illusion." Emphasis is
thereby laid upon the structure of the stage and not upon the adorn-
ment of the auditorium which, both as a place of social amenity and as
forming the greater part of the architectural whole, was wont to claim
the chief attention of the theatrical architect. Such considerations
are now to be swept aside and space and seating arrangements are to be
regarded solely in relation to the stage. The clarity of the scene and
the mystery of the music will thus between them transport the spectator
to an ideal dream world where he may receive "the absolute reality of
a sublime art's most complete sensuous illusion." In contrast to the
simplicity of the auditorium there must, as regards the stage, "no
longer be anything makeshift or sketchy, but perfection must be
required both in the scene and in the acting so far as the artistic
resources of the age allow."

The great difference between Bayreuth and the ordinary theatre
consisted in this attempt to produce complete illusory effects. In the
ordinary theatre the stage was obviously unreal. The solid reality of
the auditorium was emphasised by the architectural and decorative
care lavished upon it to contrast with the flat, two-dimensional
picture which the stage presented. At Bayreuth, on the other hand,
all memory of this reality was so far as possible to be obliterated, while

singly and as a body the assembled audience was to lose consciousness of self save for senses keyed to grave attention in anticipation of the hypnotic magic of the scene which for the time was to be the only valid reality for them. Nothing less than this attitude to the theatrical process as a dream-experience could stimulate the creative improvisator to produce his play, or his play to develop its possibilities. Again, one thing was essential if this dream-experience hypnosis were to be induced—the orchestra must be invisible. This fact, therefore, now governed the plan of the auditorium and its architectural and emotional relations to the stage. Starting "from this new-realised necessity for concealing the orchestra, technically the seat—the dwelling-place—of the music, we gradually arrived at a total rearrangement of the auditorium in our new European theatre."

Wagner first discussed the idea of a concealed orchestra in 1862 in a preface to the libretto of *The Nibelungs*. It was based on two considerations, on early practical experience of the clarifying and unifying effect upon sound of the interposition of a screen, and on desire to conceal the actual orchestra from the view of the audience because it hindered ocular illusion. An acoustic observation and a scenic expedient were thus both taken into account, but the second carried more weight and decided the issue. The resultant muting of orchestral tone in favour of vocal tone, and the muffling of incidental noises, had practical value, but as far as Wagner's work is concerned the effect is not wholly advantageous. It takes from the individual tone of the various instruments and justifies itself only where, as in *The Ring*, the orchestral compass is very wide. In *Tristan* and *The Mastersingers*, on the other hand, orchestral tone, whether solistic or choric, loses the requisite intensity and immediacy through this artificial muting. The scenic consideration, however, decided the question. The dream-magic at which Wagner aimed was impossible so long as the orchestra remained visible. That conscious emphasis upon the non-actuality of the stage-show which justified the visibility of the orchestra for the ordinary stage, made it inappropriate to the Wagnerian stage whose purpose was "to cause the eye to take in a scene as true, which can only be if it can be induced to pass over interposing actualities such as the technical apparatus used to present the scene."

With the accommodation of the orchestra in a pit concealed from the eye of the beholder not only was a hindrance to illusion removed but certain conditions were set for the architecture of the theatre as a whole, for scenic mechanism, and for the plane of the auditorium. This latter was now divided from the stage by an apparently empty space—the orchestral cavity. The spectator must not be able to see into this cavity. The traditional arrangement of seats in directly superimposed tiers had therefore to be abandoned in favour of the amphitheatre form. But the classical amphitheatre, enclosing the stage, could not be used. This had been purposely designed to surround the chorus which was situated in the orchestra and behind which the scene was thrust forward as a flat picture. The object of the Wagnerian stage was to conceal the orchestra from view and to present itself as real, three-dimensional space. It must therefore be visible from the front only, constituting a segment of the circle formed by the amphitheatre. The stage was to convey the impression of a space receding from the spectator's eye, visible to all in the auditorium, and at the same time set apart by the pit in which the orchestra was concealed so that the actors in the scene should appear magnified, superhuman. Tricks of perspective were employed to complete the spatial illusion of the stage. From the footlights backwards the sizes of things were proportioned to their supposed distance from the spectator. Thus all methods of pictorial illusion were directed to the single end of producing a complete illusion that the events on the stage were real. The spectator was " actually in a ' theatron '—that is, a space designed for the one purpose of *looking*, and that in the direction suggested by the orientation of each seat. Between the spectator and the scene towards which his eye is turned nothing is clearly discernible, but a sense of distance lends the scene the remoteness of a dream, while music, rising phantom-like from the ' mystic Abyss ' (like those vapours which ascended from the sacred womb of Gaia beneath the throne of the Pythoness) induces in him a clairvoyant rapture in which the scene before his eyes becomes for him a true mirror of life itself."

The simile used by Wagner in this passage is not chosen at random. It has a bearing on the fundamental idea underlying the new type of theatrical architecture and planning. Wagner's theatre was to resemble the Temple of the Oracle, with a congregation assembled in darkness, with a priest proclaiming in mystic trance the decrees of destiny, with an altar upon which the priest's visions are symbolically revealed in a series of magical pictures. In this temple the god-inebriated soothsayer is the theatrical artist himself. He no longer imagines himself a showman, manipulating his puppets on strings of music, but a priest, enveloped in music as in vapours from the Abyss of Being. The figures on his stage are no longer corporeal beings but remembrances of things seen in the spirit and made to pass across the magic circle of an unreal reality. No longer is the stage the actor's platform but the altar of the seer, and this sacred character henceforth determines the rhythm, the gesture, the nature of the play.

The dream theatre of Bayreuth fulfilled the aspirations of *The Ring*; the real one, tested and perfected by the production of *The Ring*, begot a new work, supplying the necessary creative stimulus and determining the form in accordance with the new conditions it offered. The motive behind this new work was neither the expression of passion, nor the drama of musical form, nor melodic characterisation, nor theatrical appeal as such; it was the stage itself as both subject and actor in the play. *Theatre* itself is here manifested in its primal character as space endowed with life and moving in obedience to the laws of the miming art. All those factors which define or people that space —playhouse, spectators, dramatic plot, scenic presentation, actors, music—are but devices to make it seem living and real. Theatre *plays* theatre. It masks itself as a *temple* in order to borrow the interest that belongs to the sacred, to claim belief in the reality of what is unreal, to dignify its make-believe laws as the laws of a world above and beyond the actual world. Creation and production—the seeming alternatives of choice in Wagner's letter to Mathilde—were here absolutely at one. Creative art made production its subject, and the miming instinct which underlay all Wagner's work was *itself* to be presented on the stage. Improvisation—the most absolute manifestation of the music impulse of the stage—became the subject-matter of the drama.

Thus the stage, regarded as the sum of all mimetic possibilities, as the final expression of the art of creative representation, as a living organism, delicately differentiated and sensitive in every nerve, as a work, not as a building—this stage now begins to play of itself. Playing so, it reveals the laws of its being—a being conditioned by music. At the same time the elemental sources of this music are also laid bare, for they alone can explain the stage. The task assigned to the music is determined by the character of the stage to which it belongs and which gives it scope. It is the invisible might of music which creates the required "remoteness" whence the things of the stage are convincingly conveyed to the charmed senses, which lends sensuous life, an illusion of spatial reality, to figures and pictures presented two-dimensionally to the eye. In this art of a self-miming stage, of a life-endowed space, it is music's mission to interpret both character and scene, to give them body and shape in tone. Ocular illusion is rendered practicable, reasonable, acceptable, by aural illusion. All the functions of the senses are exploited to this one end of absolute illusion. The laws of perspective are used to deceive the eye and the auditorium is arranged accordingly, as is also the stage and the scene upon the stage, which, by the device of the sunken orchestra, "seems to hover in the distance." The tone-picture also "hovers in the distance." Its invisible power masters the senses and lends tonal confirmation to what the eye seems to see. Moulding itself in each detail to the perspective spatial picture, it endows it with the indefinable yet convincing plastic quality of objective reality. Music becomes living, moving space; tone makes us sensible of space as an active force. The method used to lend this tone-space the same illusionary power as the visible scene, the method by which tone is translated into terms of emotional concepts of "near" and "far" with intervening stages graded according to the laws of perspective, is dynamic harmony.

Harmony in modern music is the art of building in tone, storey by storey, by splitting up the fundamental note. It produces its æsthetic effects by making us conscious of the relations between notes. If the fundamental note holds first place its acoustic neighbours interest us in the ratio of their distance from it. The essence of harmony, its æsthetic purpose, consists in its revelation of this drama of tone relationships with their entanglements and resolutions, and the peculiar emotional interest latent in all harmonic music depends on this quality.

As long as harmony remained subservient to the laws of musical form it was able to interpenetrate and develop these forms emotionally without rebelling against the primal laws of form, but when emotional concepts began to enter in, the laws proper to tone were more and more frequently ignored. Tone-relations and the emotional appeal bound up with them were increasingly emphasised as the emotionally interpretive power of music was more keenly felt—indeed as emotion generally was assigned increasing importance in life and thought. The first volcanic outbreak of emotion in music occurs in Beethoven's work, where, however, it is chiefly confined to the language of loud and soft dynamic. But when composers of the Romantic school clarified and particularised Beethoven's broad emotional expressionalism, the inner relations of harmony grew more intense, and the union of emotional, objective ideas with the forms of harmonic modulation became closer. Music ceased to be the art of formal tone and became the art of expressing tone relationships which act on, and are acted upon, by the emotions. It came to be used as a symbol of the emotional life, whose processes projected themselves into the processes of tone and governed its organic movements.

Wagner was aware of the growth of this harmonic sense of music and of its importance in the expressionist presentation of emotional processes. The more visual and objective his emotions became, the more consciously he translated visual processes into harmonic. He came to realise their ideal identity in that both were emanations of the same sensuous impulse which in them made two different yet mutually confirmatory appeals to the senses. As a composer he worked with an ever-growing objective perception of tone-relationships and their interest, and the interpretation of these relations from a variety of emotional standpoints developed his musical style. He regarded himself as a master of harmony. He believed that the element of harmonic form was the basis of music and that its chief task was enrichment and multiplication of tone-relations. Therefore the musician must also be a dramatist, for it is the objective activity of drama that rouses the active powers of musical harmony and endows their motions with meaning.

In an article *On the Application of Music to Drama* written for *Bayreuthe Blätter* in 1879, Wagner speaks of the reciprocal action of drama and harmony and of harmony in itself as the principal elements of form in modern music. He points out that it is generally agreed that " Beethoven's innovations occur more plentifully in the sphere of rhythmic co-ordination than in that of harmonic modulation," whereas Mozart " surprised his contemporaries by his tendency—arising from a deep need of the soul—to bold modulatory expansion." This difference reveals the difference between the symphonist and the dramatist. The symphony, in Wagner's view, derives from the dance-form and develops on lines of rhythmic invention ; an effort to transcend this limitation and to achieve the richness of harmonic expression resulted in the adoption of " programmatic " ideas. Thus many new possibilities were discovered in harmony, yet when purely instrumental music attempted to incorporate these with the programmeless symphony, æsthetically meaningless and technically hybrid musical forms were the result. The conquests won by " programme " music in the realm of harmonic expression cannot be developed to the best purpose unless they are employed in conjunction with drama where the interaction of events affords natural justification for the invasion of the rhythmic dance-form of the symphony by the complications of harmonic action. The bold modulation which seems empty and superficial in post-Beethoven symphonic writing finds complete justification when connected with scenic dramatic conceptions. The fusion of the thematic web of symphony with the harmonic development rendered possible by drama offers the one hope of a new and really living art-form.

Following this line of argument Wagner recognised harmony as the governing factor in his musical forms. For him the harmonic process was directly linked up with the scenic process, which in its turn finds emotional corroboration in harmonic modulation. Each incident in music-drama is a scenic-harmonic incident, but while only harmony can convey full sensuous comprehension of the scene which it accompanies it requires the scene in order to develop. Harmony is action and action is harmony : neither can exist alone. Conceptual ideas underlie tone-relations, yet the former, in accordance with the expressionist possibilities of musical tone, must never be other than emotional and " purely human."

Wagner's conceptual tonal world is the result of his objective grasp of tone-relationships based on the artistic phenomenon of harmony. For him harmony stands for the basis of all being. As he wrote in *Opera and Drama*, " amongst mankind's artistic capabilities it has no fellow. It is like a natural force which a man can be aware of but cannot understand." Modulation is the motion of harmony ; scenic action governs and justifies modulation. All dramas are dramas of modulation. The impulses, however, which may give rise to modulatory action or drama are of two kinds. Either some given, pure harmony may be broken up by dissonance, may conquer the disturbing elements and so reassert its pristine purity, or, alternatively, some given discord may find harmonic resolution. The former is the type of chordal action—the drama of the chord—such as underlies *Die Feen, Rienzi, Lohengrin, The Ring,* and *The Mastersingers* ; the latter is the type of chromatic action—the drama of chromatics—exemplified in *Das Liebesverbot, Tannhäuser, Tristan,* and *The Venusberg.* There is yet a third and simpler type—the supplementation of the open harmony of keynote and fifth by the complementary third—which Wagner uses only in *The Flying Dutchman* where he exhausts its possibilities. The other two types of plot, however, dominate his work from first to last as the many and various interpretive possibilities inherent in them demand formulation.

Wagner's chordal dramas are universal dramas. The fundamental harmony from which they emanate symbolises a complete, harmonious world, such as is first intimated in the introductory harmonies of *Die Feen* and the ringing A with which *Rienzi* begins : the A major key of *Lohengrin* builds a world far above this world, full of light and purity, and the E major key of *The Rhinegold* prelude identifies harmony absolutely with the world of nature. The chromatic dramas, on the other hand, are individual dramas. The searching chromatic line is an emotional portrayal of the incomplete single note's efforts to find cadence and consonance. In chromatic drama the motive of action is yearning for salvation in harmony, whereas in the drama of consonance a motive is provided by the introduction of some element of dissonance which breaks up harmony. Thus in consonant, universal drama, the incentives to modulation appear in the guise of antithesis—such, for instance, as the diminished chord which symbolises Ortrud and the Nibelungs, and the discords of Hagen and of Beckmesser. When these intrude upon the pure fundamental chord modulation becomes necessary. The two types of drama, however, are always perfectly distinct ; each basic impulse preserves its integrity within the work it dominates. It would be impossible to confuse the chromatic drama of *Tristan* with the consonant drama of *The Nibelungs* whence it was evolved. The particular harmonic sphere laid down at the beginning determines the dramatist's attitude throughout.

A time came, however, when this viewpoint was changed and enlarged to comprehend all the various forces of both the dramatic and the modulatory impulses. Wagner had experienced and embodied the stimuli to consonant and chromatic, universal and personal drama. From these, slowly gathering force from work to work, had finally emerged the idea of the harmonic-space-drama of the stage. But just as this *stage* was no longer regarded as a mere external place of performance but as a completely realised synthesis of all the forces of representation, so harmony was now thought of as the absolute tonal counterpart of this scenic picture of three-dimensional space. And just as the latter no longer assisted drama but used it in order to exhibit itself as space in action, so harmony no longer required the objective incentives of consonance or chromaticism; these became mere aids to representation, losing their significance as incentives to action and therewith their determining influence in a work. They were now regarded objectively and employed side by side as the two fundamental and converse types of modulation. Consonant and chromatic motion, the universe and the individual, the modulation that breaks up harmony and that which restores it, each hitherto alternately constituting the ruling force of a work, were now united to present a comprehensive picture of all the diverse phenomena of harmony. This complete system of tonal-relationships has the effect of presenting a complete picture of the world of objective phenomena. The universal framework of space and each individual thing contained therein is informed by music. Every motion gives forth sound; every motion is a tonal and a spatial vibration simultaneously. The visible becomes music and music becomes visible. The mystery of the theatre is here reduced to its simplest, and at the same time to its most secret, formula, and the absolute antithesis of the real becomes real. This too fades away—the senses exchange their functions, eye becomes ear, and ear, eye, space becomes sound, and sound space. Here is the illusion of illusions—imposed by an art which thus reveals the full magic of the stage and makes musico-scenic theatre seem the verity of verities.

If the stage itself was, for Wagner, the basis of this grand conception he yet required the written word to interpret it to the intellect. Step by step he surveys his new theatrical territory until the way lies open for constructive activity and he has achieved the creative mood in which to improvise his mystery-play of space and tone.

In a letter to Mathilde written in November 1859 Wagner speaks of the mistaken construction put on something which he had said, and adds conciliatorily " Then I thought, ' Well, she will be glad to discover this truth, that when I am discussing, say, politics, I am thinking of something quite different from the ostensible theme.' " This remark applies to all Wagner's writings that have not directly to do with art—they are all about " something quite different from their ostensible theme." It applies even to what he says about art when this does not concern his own art, and indeed even here when it does not bear on the immediate work in hand. Wagner not only regards the universe from the standpoint of art and art from the standpoint of his own work but sees his own work solely from the standpoint of the work on which he is momentarily employed. All his mental processes are a part of the improvisatory process and serve no other end than to stimulate the creative urge and direct it to the purpose in view. Thus his writings on social and political reform in the revolutionary years were but a means of clearing the ground for *The Ring* and *Tristan*. Political and pedagogic writings heralded *The Mastersingers*. *Beethoven* was a backward glance from the heights of the third act of *Siegfried*. Discussions on performance and production accompanied *The Dusk of the Gods*, and, finally, the Bayreuth papers were signposts to, an elucidation of, Wagner's last work. They must not be read in the light of their ostensible theme. They are attempts, under pretext of intellectual argument, to present a new point of view. Wagner proposes to revolutionise the stage. He assembles, tests, instals new stage devices, costumes, decorations, scenery. Every detail of importance is firmly laid down, inter-relations and effects are worked out, till the whole is established, each imagined mechanism functions perfectly and all is ready for the play to begin. All these matters are unimportant in themselves ; the point is to consider how they may be useful to the play, how all may contribute to this one end.

The scaffolding of the stage was now built—of a stage endowed with the magic power of making the unreal seem real. The eye was to hear, the ear to see at the behest of an art that claimed to be life—life in the highest sense of realistic idealism. This art had performed a stage miracle, but one thing alone could make that miracle effective, and that thing was *faith*. There must be faith both in the wonder-worker and in his audience. The genius is a wonder-worker by virtue of his intuitive faculty ; yet he can work no miracle unless a miracle is required. Mankind must have fallen before it needs the miraculous or is ready to accept it. Therefore Wagner writes : " The idea that the race of man is degenerate, contrary as it may seem to the theory of progressive evolution, is seen, seriously considered, to be the only one which can give us a sure foundation of hope." The mirror of the human race is that theatre-going public upon which the acceptability, the spatial and temporal influence, of the artistic wonder-worker depends. But the more keenly the need for miracle is felt the wider must be the gulf between the wonder-worker and his public. Wagner demands faith in the religious sense of the word, for the theatrical public must represent fallen humanity, the artist the divine saviour. An art that can demand such faith must be self-identified with the holy of holies, and must regard itself as confronted with the deepest degradation. It must accept this order of things as the great tragedy of the universe in order that its demand for faith may be absolute. It must seem to be the sole possessor of divine strength in a universe lost and accurst in order that it may stoop in pity to the weak. It must become a religion that it may establish its claim upon faith— faith in the truth of illusionary art.

Such are the ideas underlying *Religion and Art*, Wagner's most important work at this period. " It may be said that where religion becomes artificial it is the vocation of art to rescue the soul of religion, to take those mystical symbols religion would have us believe actually true, and, by the ideal presentation of their symbolic values, to reveal the profound truths which they conceal."

The central idea in this passage is that of art as the saviour of religion. Underlying all religions is conviction of the perishableness of this world and hope of a way of escape from it. The founder of a religion mediates this idea to his followers by inventing myths and allegories which may lead them, by faith, to accept his teaching. But the Church has complicated a simple doctrine by piling up dogmas and myths ; and Art alone can, by its revealing forms, evoke faith-giving symbols from the welter of dogma. Such works as Raphael's Madonnas and Michelangelo's Last Judgment clothe the doctrine of the Church in idealised objectivity. Mediæval poetry, as compared with these examples of plastic art, was enslaved by the " concept." Then music came with power to dissolve the concepts fixed by speech. " A pure form, embodying a divine content, wholly freed from the concept, we may look to it as a world-saving birth of divine teaching from out of the nothingness of the visible world." While religious dogma became the plaything of Jesuitical casuistry or of a pettifogging rationalism, true music gradually freed itself from the word until, as the Church decayed, music alone was left, " noblest heir of Christian thought " and embodying in Beethoven's symphonies " the most perfect religious flowering of the Christian revelation."

What was the cause of the decay of religions and of the culture dependent on them ? War and rapine, two sins of carnal-mindedness, had proved the ruin of humanity. The Church had failed to promulgate the one saving rite of Christian thought, the Lord's Supper, the feeding upon bread and wine. " Called on to uphold a state built upon rapine and violence, and responding inevitably to the spirit of history, the Church came to believe that its success depended on lordship over empires and kingdoms." In pursuance of this end she relapsed from the New Testament to the Old, from faith in Christ to faith in Jehovah. The consequent infusion of Judaism transformed the spiritual culture of Christianity into a pragmatic civilisation with its consequences—natural philosophy, chemistry, vivisection. In such a world Art forsook its divine mission and became a plaything, an entertainment. Music, poetry, painting were delivered over to the connoisseurs.

This decay of man's spiritual life was " a hard school of suffering which the blind will imposes upon itself in order to learn to see." One thing alone could prevent relapse from even this small measure of sight, and that was a revival of the religious sense through experience won in these ages of decadence. The religious consciousness might begin anew with a sense of compassion for the degenerate past. But not even a future regenerate humanity could end the " monstrous tragedy of this world," nature's endless tale of annihilation. The artist alone, by revealing an absolute life-instinct, could transform this tragedy, " ruthless in its sublimity," into " something acceptable to humanity." Such " poet-priests—the only ones who never lie " had always existed in the race, even during its most terrible aberrations. Thus the decadent Athenians possessed the " sublime examples " of their great tragedians, and Shakespeare had held up the mirror of his improvisations to a world of violence and terror. But both had been without effect, for humanity did not then know its own degradation. Now it had awakened to its decadence and had begun to seek regeneration. The classic tragedians and Shakespeare had been misunderstood, but now " the works of these martyrs shall lead us, shall be ours, while the deeds of the men of action of their days shall be remembered only in their words. . . . Then shall the pure call of nature ring in our ears—yearning for peace, fearless, full of hope, all-appeasing, world-redeeming. The soul of man, by sorrow unified and made conscious of its high calling to redeem all nature that suffers together with it, shall thus rise above the abyss of being, and loosed from the terrible chain of birth and death shall master its own restless will, shall be free from itself. . . . Now the Redeemer himself bids us sing and make music of our aspirations, our beliefs, and our hopes. The noblest heritage of the Christian Church is the soul of music in the Christian religion, pleading all things, expressing all things. Out-soaring temple walls, life-giving, free and holy, music permeates all nature, teaching lost mankind a new language in which the infinite and incomprehensible can be perfectly expressed."

Wagner makes of art a religion—*the* purified religion of a future humanity that only such religion and such art can call into being. The tragedy of life in the natural order shall not be abolished, but the poet-priest shall exalt it by revealing to the initiate a new and purified life-impulse. Such is the promise for which is exacted the price of faith—faith in the miracle of the stage. The priestly mime intensifies expectation to a point which only the boldest could dare. The whole history of man, all the problems of the mind, the Church, the State, politics, the past and future, are to be surveyed. Schopenhauer provides the metaphysical terminology, Christianity the symbolism, Gobineau the racial theories. Vegetarianism and colonisation are Wagner's practical guideposts, so far as any exist beyond the theatre at Bayreuth.

Such is the basis of Wagner's scheme for ennobling the human race. Yet " What does this knowledge avail ? " It avails not at all in respect of political, artistic, ecclesiastical or social life, whose leaders are scarcely conscious of decadence, still less of the possibilities of regeneration. Even the best brains—those above the level of the common herd—are as yet enslaved by platitudes, by unclear conceptions of the true bases and aims of existence. Goethe doubted Christ but believed that the existence of God was fully proven, "retaining, as regards the latter, freedom, at any rate, to seek Him for himself in Nature." Schopenhauer was the first to grasp the moral meaning of the universe, and if he could not get beyond a sense of the hopelessness of things or point the way to restore them, he had yet suggested that way in the words " Perfect contentment, the truly desirable condition, is apprehended by us in images only—in art, poetry and music. Indeed, one might therefrom derive assurance that they must, after all, exist somewhere."

This, then, was Wagner's aim—*art as a release from life*. The Mosaic decalogue, being but the negative injunction of a penal code, could not point the way to this " somewhere," but it might be found through the three theological virtues—Love, transmuted by the sufferings of the world to compassion, Faith, which is " conviction that the universe has a moral meaning," and Hope, which is " the blessed knowledge that this conviction cannot be a delusion." Love, Faith, and Hope may be one in a noble work of art which " by its compelling power over the soul plainly shows us the image of that ' somewhere ' which can only be apprehended by our non-temporal, non-spatial inner selves when these are instinct with love, faith, and hope."

The series of writings which begins with the notes on Bayreuth and ends with the abstract philosophising of *Religion and Art* is plainly an intellectualisation of a world of ideas in which the artist is envisaged as possessing intuitive knowledge of suffering and as exercising a healing, saving office, through compassion. The fate of such an artistic genius is inevitably tragic. Involved with a given world of time and space, he is doomed himself to err where he comes in contact with it. He cannot fulfil his true mission unless he sets his will against the trend of this world. But the fate of the world itself is tragic. As part of the natural order it can never know peace, but if it perceives its own decadence and has faith in the religious work of art it may hope to attain to a purified life. The tragedy of the world is its own blind, desirous will. Until it awakes to a sense of the error of its blind lusts, it is condemned to suffer eternally the torments of desire. In the Christian gospel the way of purity by abstention from fleshly lusts in the two forms of appetite and sex is symbolised in the Last Supper. Both involve suffering. Opposed to the Christian doctrine is the non-Christian, the cult of the God of desire, of power, of war, of joy in this world—and this God is Jehovah, Lord of the Jews. God needs the devil in order to reveal His Godhead, the holy the unholy to manifest its holiness, the genius his dæmon to prove his genius.

And the devil, the unholy one, the dæmon who has caused all the suffering of the world and now, as decadence incarnate, is the enemy of regeneration, is the Jew. He is that dramatic antithesis which sets in motion the forces of the world of love, faith, and hope.

Wagner began his campaign against Judaism when in 1850, shortly after his flight from Dresden, he published anonymously his *Judaism and Music*. Remarks on the subject are scattered freely through subsequent writings, but in 1869 he reissued his pamphlet with the addition of *Explanations of Judaism in Music*. This was followed by a short essay entitled *Modern?* Wagner frequently introduced the subject in his later writings and expressed himself upon it with increased vehemence in two supplements to *Religion and Art*, entitled *Know Thyself* and *Heroism and Christianity*.

It would be difficult to determine how far this attitude may have been due to personal experience, to jealousy of the success of Mendelssohn and Meyerbeer and practical enmity to a form of art which was not only essentially opposed to Wagner's own but constituted an external obstacle to its acceptance. No explanation on these lines, however, could affect the deeper reasons for Wagner's anti-semitism. Schumann disliked Meyerbeer's work as much as Wagner did, but he hated the work only, not the man nor his race. With Wagner it was rather the other way ; and his hate increased, finding expression as the years passed in unmeasured abuse. While Wagner was in Bayreuth he found fresh support for his views in the racial theories of Gobineau. Fortified by Gobineau's writings he looked upon the historic Jew as the type of all that is low, despicable, and corrupt, as " the embodied dæmon of mankind's degeneracy, sitting triumphant and secure." In his hatred of " this one-time man-devourer, the successful commercial magnate of our modern society," Wagner hails the revival of political anti-semitism in his day as " an instinct noble in origin and exalted in purpose, the spirit of pure humanity."

In all this there is something more than personal or interested hostility. It was a habit of thought that persisted and increased throughout the second half of Wagner's life though it was not present in the first, a fact which seems to suggest that it was connected solely with his artistic development. Wagner's idea of the Jew is based, as his writings show, on that same need for visual images to assist the processes of abstract thought which is characteristic of his critical and speculative processes generally. His anti-semitism was as far removed from practical politics as the " communism " of his Dresden days. It was necessary for him to transfer his theatrical vision to the real world in order to be able to present it more convincingly ; the Jew, therefore, must stand for dissonance, for the element which breaks up harmony. Dissonance, which Wagner introduced into his plots in the shape of cunning, greed of power, desire for money, malice, or insensibility, required furthermore some actual human embodiment. The simple " Romantic " embodiment of the power of darkness in Ortrud (inspired by Weber's Eglantine) was insufficiently trenchant and characteristic. Wagner looked round for a living model to act the part of evil dæmon. What better model could he find than the Jew as he has existed for centuries in the popular imagination, endowed with an exaggeration of all the less worthy characteristics of his race ?

This idea of Judaism, adopted simply for its practical artistic use, gave rise to the figures of Alberich, Logi, Hunding, Mime, and Hagen, and served to express the dark side of the world of Wagner's imagination, which was, indeed, part of his own soul and as inseparable from him as was Mephistopheles from Faust. He was pleased to call this dark phase of his nature " Jew," just as he called the bright phase " Hero." The imaginary Jew whom he made responsible for all he thought detestable (including all musical critics and vivisectionists) helped also to shape his notions of a regenerate mankind. He could only make these notions objective and intelligible if the forces of decadence were clothed in a form as concrete as that of the hero-genius and saviour. It was the Jew, therefore, who had turned the Church from her true mission, the Jew who had vitiated the political world with hate, greed, and chicanery. The spirit of Judaism had adulterated the Church—" the blood of Christendom has been polluted in the semitic-Latin Church." And not only had the blood of Christendom been polluted, but the blood of the race elect to rule, the blood of all mankind in those who were by birth its noblest representatives. This racial pollution, which had been brought about as much by the race's neglect of its natural nourishment as by degenerate intermixtures, could only be cleansed by the blood of Jesus, by the blood, that is to say, not of a higher individual but of a new species, able " to save humanity, perishing in its noblest races," and constituting a " divine sublimate of the breed itself." Through this blood, "symbolically taken in the one true rite of the Christian religion," even lower races might "enjoy divine purification. Therefore was this antidote prepared against racial decadence by interbreeding; the globe itself, indeed, perhaps bore life only for this saving dispensation." Equality there could never be, but possibly " a general agreement in ethical matters " in the mind of a true Christendom. The sufferings of the world were revealed by the widespread yearning for such a moral agreement. In higher natures knowledge of the world's suffering impelled the mind to seek out the meaning of the universe. " We call those natures in whom this process culminates in some revelation to us, hero-natures." This " hero-nature," however, was very far removed from the heroism of mere strength ; that involved slaughter and bloodshed without true heroism. The true hero " contends in righteous anger for the preservation of his race, of his customs, of his honour, and, when his misdirected will has been miraculously converted, finds his true self in the saint, the divine hero."

An almost incalculable number of thoughts and concepts are here represented and Wagner continues to spin them out with ever-growing conviction. Becoming apparently a more and more abstruse amalgam of philosophical, sociological, æsthetic, political, and religious categories of thought, the work ends with a fragment of sex-philosophy entitled *Upon the Woman Element in Humanity*. In its intellectual and logical aspects this discourse alienates the reader by its arbitrariness, by the *naïveté* of its assertions, by the omission of all that appears to oppose its line of argument and the exaggeration of all that appears to support it. Quotations from Schopenhauer and Gobineau are sprinkled through the work with an effect—particularly as regards Schopenhauer—sometimes of misapplication, sometimes of unoriginality. But this fog of confusion, contradiction, and animosity clears for us when we remember that Wagner told Mathilde he had always " something quite different in mind " from his ostensible theme. Here this " something different " was a plan for a work whose intricate and luxuriant conceptual and harmonic relations might serve to confirm its author's own faith in the reality of the stage. A resplendent erection of conceptual " sets " and lighting effects, and the illusion of illimitable vistas of historical perspective, were to make him feel at home in this world of ideas, to give him confidence in himself. Never before had Wagner stood in need of so vast a speculative apparatus. Even the revolutionary writings of the *Nibelungs* period pass from the general to the particular in the problem of artistic form ; those connected with *The Mastersingers* and *The Dusk of the Gods* are practical throughout, and the *Beethoven* is an artistic allegory in philosophical guise. The Bayreuth papers, on the other hand, press further and further into the region of general speculative thought ; structural problems are never mentioned, while speculation itself loses itself in infinities.

In all this, however, Wagner was simply laying the foundations for a new work where a critical examination of the minutiæ of his plot would not have served him. On the other hand he had a twofold need of just such a phantasmagorial substructure. He required it to convey a highly involved complex of conceptual relations to his dramatic instinct, and also to enable him to base upon this subject, when dramatised, a musical structure of highly elaborate harmonies. By dint of speculative brooding he obtained concrete images in which to manifest the primal characters embodying the motives of his drama. No such analysis of conceptual relations had been necessary in the case of *Rienzi*, for then the spring had gushed fresh from its natural source and the artist's own naïve sensuous fancy had boldly and carelessly shaped his figures. Now, however, he was no longer handling the stuff of direct, concrete experience. His task was the abstract interpretation of his own past active life under the guise of a quasi-historic plot, the sympathetic observation of the results of that former activity. He had to conjure up his memories of himself as creative artist. The sole element of novelty was in the way in which these memories were made to appear, their interrelations, the stage gestures, the world built for them to dwell in. These were the things which made possible a concrete manifestation of the vapour-shrouded spokesman of the oracle. In sacerdotal ecstasy he proclaimed his mystic visions and demanded nothing in return but that men should believe in the truth of his message.

So the temple was built, the faithful assembled about the incense-wreathed altar. All was ready for the mime become priest to improvise upon his lifetime of experience as a creative artist. Shades of the past rose up, veiled in the incense of the rite. They had no longer any life of their own, but moving at the behest of a philosophically ordered system of relations they enacted the artificial semblance of a drama. They were the servants of the stage which through their movements

and gestures presented a living image of itself, played at being space
by virtue of the illusion of perspective they afforded, and found further
confirmation of its " reality " in the illusion of music. Thus Wagner
created a phantasmal world of sounding space, of visible sound, of
acting schemata, of singing concepts and conceptual tones. He
called it *Parsifal*.

Parsifal is in part a reversion to the plans of former works—
the *Venusberg*, *The Mastersingers*, the third act of *Siegfried*, and *The
Dusk of the Gods*—but it is also something far more than this. Wagner
first conceived it soon after he came to Dresden, in the *Tannhäuser*
and *Lohengrin* period, and in the two distinct worlds of which it treats
—the Grail kingdom of the first and third acts and the Magic Garden
of the second act—it forms a sequel to these two works, reconciling
the therein contrasted spheres of genius (or chordal music) and the
dæmonic (or chromatic music) as dramatised in the *Venusberg*. *Tannhäuser* and *Lohengrin* are directly concerned in it, but indeed all Wagner's
operas before and after these, from *Die Feen* to *The Dusk of the Gods*
supplied him with matter for his last work. *Parsifal* is linked with
Die Feen through the musical similarity between it and *Lohengrin*,
and with *Das Liebesverbot*, through the musical similarity between it
and *Tannhäuser*. The basic idea of the Fairy Queen who suffers
beneath a cruel spell and whose salvation is wrought by Arindal's
steadfastness serves to link Wagner's first work with his last. Verbal
and conceptual echoes may be caught in Arindal's words, " O seht,
das Tier kann weinen ! Die Träne glänzt in seinem Aug' ! Oh, wie 's
gebrochen nach mir schaut ! " (" O see, the poor beast weeps ! Its
eyes are bright with tears ! Heart-broken, it looks after me ! ") More
striking yet in *Parsifal* are variants upon themes from later dramas.
Valhalla, stronghold of the gods, becomes the Temple of the Grail,
the treasure of the Nibelungs becomes the Grail itself, the Ring of
authority becomes the Spear. Thus the basic symbols of the drama of
the Nibelungs are projected into the world of the Grail and inter-
penetrate the now united spheres of *Lohengrin* and *Tannhäuser*. By
this means these two forerunners (including the *Tannhäuser* sequels—
Tristan and the *Venusberg*) are assimilated and Wagner thence proceeds
to base the second act of *Parsifal* upon the third act of *Siegfried*.

In *Parsifal*, however, not only are the main tendencies of Wagner's
life's work represented but even his incomplete, half-finished projects

find their fulfilment. The *Love-Feast of the Apostles*, composed in Dresden, lives again in the " Lord's Supper " theme of *Parsifal* and helps to shape its choruses. Both the unfinished sketches for a *Jesus of Nazareth* find resolution there. *Parsifal* draws on the stored-up wealth of all its predecessors ; it is a compendium to which all Wagner's earlier works contribute something. Scattered seeds of thought sprang up as a single harvest when the accomplished fact of the Bayreuth stage induced them to germinate in music. The dream of *Parsifal* had in truth been the guiding star of Wagner's life. His " stronghold " idea, first embodied in Lohengrin's story of the Grail and later in the vision of Valhalla, grew in intensity until Wagner was able actually to walk in the temple of his own building, and strengthened the " home " idea until Lohengrin's dream came true. All these things had to be fulfilled for the sake of *Parsifal*. A synthesis of all earlier works, not only does it develop to its utmost capacity each several impulse embodied in it, but it reveals that essence in which they all are one.

The recapitulatory and retrospective significance of *Parsifal* is in complete accordance with its conceptual basis, which is that of a drama of pure thought ; it accords also with the external history of its genesis. From Wagner's study, begun in Paris and continued in Dresden, of the Tannhäuser, Lohengrin, Parsifal, and Titurel saga-cycle and his reading, in 1845, of Wolfram's poem, the figure of Parsifal had taken life in his imagination. It influenced—scarcely consciously—the atmosphere of the *Love-Feast* and *Jesus of Nazareth*, but with the first sketch for *Tristan* it suddenly gained vitality and shape. " Parsifal, in his quest for the Grail, is to come as a pilgrim to Kareol where Tristan lies dying in his desperate love-agony." These words foreshadow the first meeting between Parsifal and Amfortas, between the spirit of desire and the spirit of renunciation, and an outline of visual form is given to one of the fundamental ideas of the work to be, the idea of the inversion of the *ascending* chromaticism of *Tristan* to the *descending* chromaticism of *Parsifal*. This idea lived on into the period of the second act of *Tristan* (1858) and in May of that year Wagner wrote a letter to Mathilde containing a musical sketch for a Parsifal motif. Though this sketch was never carried out either verbally or musically it contains a first hint of the Faith theme to be, and the ascending final progression betrays already a characteristic kinship with the Grace theme of *Tannhäuser*, and, through it, with *Das Liebesverbot*. In 1856, however, before *Tristan* had ripened from a mere plan into an actual first draft, philosophical studies suggested to Wagner an idea for a work to be entitled *The Victors*. It contained a new character, that of the maiden Savitri, " who, in the second act, while awaiting the coming of Ananda, throws herself in rapture amongst the flowers, absorbing into herself in the joy of living sun, forest, birds, water—all nature." As woman she is spurned by Buddha when she appeals to him to give her as wife to Ananda. " But his growing sympathy with the maiden, the story of whose previous existences he reveals to himself and to the gainsayers, eventually causes him to receive her (who has now experienced in her own sufferings the whole tremendous chain of world sorrows) into the company of the blessed."

A woman is here the central figure in the drama and the men—Buddha himself and Ananda his disciple whom Savitri loves—are but passive observers. The idea of " the salvation of woman " dominates the whole. " Nothing but a very profound acceptance of the doctrine of the transmigration of souls could reveal to me that blessed moment when all shall at last attain the same summit of salvation and in which lives that *in* time have run parallel yet separate, shall meet and understand one another *beyond* time. According to the beautiful Buddhist belief, the simple explanation of Lohengrin's stainless purity is that he is a reincarnation of Parsifal, who won that purity for himself. Similarly Elsa, through rebirth, would reach up to Lohengrin. Thus my project of *The Victors* seemed to me to supply the sequel and conclusion of *Lohengrin*. For here Savitri becomes fully the equal of Ananda. And so all the awful tragedy of life exists only in the separations of time and space ; and since time and space are only our ways of looking at things and have no reality apart from us, so to the perfect vision the greatest tragic suffering is due merely to the error of the individual. Indeed, I believe it is so ! "

While this plan continued to live in Wagner's mind and was still spoken of as a separate project up to the *Parsifal* period, light was thrown on the *Parsifal* subject itself from a number of different angles. We read in the *Autobiography* that on Good Friday morning, 1857, Wagner for the first time entered the " Asyl " given him by the Wesendonks and that the artist in him was stirred at the sight of spring's awakening. " The garden was breaking into leaf, the birds were singing, and at last on the roof of my little house I could rejoice in the fruitful quiet I had so long thirsted for. I was filled with it when suddenly it came to me that this was Good Friday, and I remembered the great message it had brought me once as I was reading Wolfram's *Parzival*. . . . That ideal figure now came into my mind with overwhelming force, and, setting out from the Good Friday idea, I quickly conceived an entire drama, the main features of which I immediately and very briefly noted down in three-act form."

Shortly after the " Good Friday " idea two more important figures of the work took plastic shape, the first coming from the *Lohengrin*-world of *The Victors*, the second from the *Tannhäuser*-world of *Tristan* ; these were Kundry and Amfortas. " I have been thinking a lot about Parsifal," Wagner writes from Venice in 1859, " especially about one strange conception, that of a marvellous, world-demoniacal woman (the *Grail-herald*) which becomes ever more vital and interesting to me." It was not till a year later, however, when Wagner was preparing *Tannhäuser* for the Paris Opera, that he recognised the identity of this creature with Venus, who is Kundry. " Did I ever tell you that this fabulous and wild Grail-herald is to be one and the same person with the seductress of the second act ? Since realising this I have almost wholly cleared my mind about my subject." Yet before Wagner had attained an absolutely concrete vision of this character and while he was still occupied with the third act of *Tristan*, " the entirely new invention " of Amfortas suddenly came to him and immediately concentrated the interest in himself. " Careful thought shows Amfortas to be the centre and subject of the whole. A pretty kettle of fish, indeed ! Consider, for Heaven's sake, what this means ! It was revealed to me as in a flash of lightning that he was my Tristan of the third act, only immeasurably intensified. With his spear wound —and another wound also, the wound in the heart—the poor wretch is in terrible anguish and desires nothing but death. In the hope of obtaining this greatest boon he yearns perpetually for sight of the Grail. The vision of it may at least close his wounds . . . but no, the Grail's gift to him is ever the same—an incapacity to die. The sight of it increases his sufferings by rendering them immortal."

By comparison with this figure of suffering, offspring of the Lucerne *Tristan* period, the original hero of the work threatened to fade in significance. Yet Parsifal " is indispensable as the longed-for saviour of Amfortas : but if Amfortas is to be set in the light he deserves, his tragic interest becomes so great that it will be more than difficult to place a second hero by his side.   And yet the chief interest *must* be concentrated in Parsifal if he is not simply to come on at the end as a cold, uninteresting *deus ex machina*.   Therefore Parsifal's development, his divine purgation, even though predestined by his whole contemplative and compassionate nature, must be restored to the foreground.   I cannot use for this purpose, however, any such diffuse form as was at Wolfram's disposal—I am obliged to compress the whole into three main situations, each brimful of content and yet plainly revealing all the profundities and intricacies of the subject. For so to work, so to represent, is the nature of my art."

Wagner here shows penetrating insight into a weakness in his plan as it then existed—the pallid conception of the title figure. Amfortas embodies the Tristan of the third act.   Kundry is a blend of the Grail-herald idea with that of Savitri and borrows certain distinctive features from the Paris Venus.   Parsifal himself does, it is true, round off the subject emotionally, and through the Good-Friday-magic theme and the idea of renunciation which he opposes to the desire embodied in Tristan, he opens up a new sphere of music. At the same time he lacks sufficient individuality and definition to make him convincing as an active and not as a purely lyrical element in the story.

Wagner's plans had matured to this point when, after the beginning of *The Mastersingers*, he was overtaken by a catastrophe which for the time swept these and all other plans aside.   Then it was that Wagner himself experienced the miracle of the healing of Amfortas. His hero, Parsifal, the " blameless fool " whose only knowledge is sympathy, actually appeared to him in the royal person of Ludwig of Bavaria—a youth called to a throne.   Ludwig had learnt to know and love Wagner through *Lohengrin*.   Among his friends he actually bore the name of " Parsifal " and he was destined now to give his prototype—as a beloved woman had once given those creatures of desire called Brynhilda the dream-maiden, Isolda, Venus, Eva, Brynhilda the woman—the gift of real existence.   Thus were Wagner's ideas realised through the experiences which they themselves had evoked.   At sight of its embodied reality Wagner's *Parsifal* project emerged at once from the shadows into the light.   Furthermore, the sudden death of the singer Schnorr had tinged the artist's mood with

2 I

sacred exaltation. Schnorr's memory gave Wagner's hero vocal form, just as King Ludwig had given him a dramatic mask. In August 1865 the first fully worked out scenic sketch was put on paper, while at the same time, by the King's wish, Wagner set again to work upon the third act of *Siegfried* and strove to throw off the personal shock of Schnorr's death. " Well, this was help in time of need," writes Wagner at the end of his manuscript.

With the full exposition of his story Wagner had entered into complete possession of the new territory. " Now at last the time has come for the greatest and most perfect works to be created," he writes, forwarding his manuscript to the King. An assurance of fulfilment possessed him, and with it came a magical power of creating for himself the necessary external conditions—first and foremost among them that stage whose actualities were to embody the new musical vision. When, in 1876 at the festival performance of *The Ring*, the new theatre first revealed its enchantment, the *Parsifal* plan came to maturity. Wagner's writings had tilled the soil ; now the emotional world of the Grail began to grow nearer and brighter, gathering ideas and concepts into its orbit. In January 1877 Wagner set to work ; in February he sketched his dialogue ; by April 19 the whole libretto was complete. The music of number after number came with the ease of ripe fruit plucked from the bough. The sketch for the prelude was finished by September, and those for the first, second, and third acts by January 29, 1878, October 13, 1878, and April 26, 1879, respectively. On August 7 Wagner began to work on the full score finishing the first act on April 25, 1881, the second act on October 19, and the whole work on January 13, 1882. The first performance was fixed for the following June.

From the first sketch for the dialogue to the completion of the full score the work took five years. To those same years belong the writings connected with *Parsifal*, business disagreements and worries in Bayreuth, fantastic travel projects, money-making journeys in England and Germany, travel in Italy for the joys of art, voluminous correspondence with artists, publishers, theatrical managers, and friends, the painful episode of Nietszche's alienation, a new friendship with Gobineau, the establishment of Wagner's own newspaper, the *Bayreuthe Blätter*, of which he had dreamed for years, and, in addition, preparations for the performance of *Parsifal*, questions of *décor* and costume, choice and rehearsal of singers, while Wagner, then in his

middle sixties, began, continued, and completed his great new work.
All this exemplifies his extraordinary power as an artist of gaining
dominion over life's forces, of taking from them all that he needed to
realise his artistic will, whether storm or peace, suffering or happiness,
a wife when the plot required one, a King when one was due to appear,
a playhouse when his work demanded it. All these things came as if
at the summons of a genie from the world of fantasy into the world of
reality. Even enemies and difficulties seemed to exist merely to
display Wagner's will and increase its force by exercise. The will
itself was unassailable till having fulfilled itself, obeyed its own laws,
and realised itself in the mirror of its own creations it found its final
release. Then the magic broke and the magician perished.

The origins of *Parsifal*, in Marienbad, in Dresden, Zurich, Venice,
Lucerne, Paris, Munich, and Bayreuth, show two distinct complexes
of ideas. The first of these is the " Grail " idea, originating in *Die
Feen* and developing through the figures of Rienzi, Lohengrin,
Ananda, and the Buddha to culminate in the Good-Friday-magic
and Last Supper themes ; it represents a world of painless peace.
Opposing it is the second, the " Pain " idea, originating in *Das
Liebesverbot*, developing through the figures of Tannhäuser and the
dying Tristan to culminate in Amfortas—and through those of Elsa
and Savitri to culminate in Kundry. The harmonic, or universal,
viewpoint is thus contrasted with the chromatic, or individual, view-
point, while between the two is set Parsifal, who belongs in part to
each and wholly to neither. A stranger at first to the kingdom of
the Grail yet ignorant also of the world of suffering, he unites the two
through the knowledge born of compassion and is the destined king of
both. The main problem of *Parsifal* was to make this figure the
centre, yet not the living centre, the developmental and unifying yet
not the motive force, of the drama. What Wagner calls Parsifal's
" compassion ". is, philosophic interpretations apart, the device by
which he sets his whole work in motion. It is a device which offers
the dramatist his one opportunity of combining purity with passion,
and it serves the musician as a modulatory link between the harmonic
and chromatic spheres of expression. It is thus artistically necessary
that Parsifal's chief quality should be sympathy—that he should
suffer passively *with* both spheres without belonging wholly to either,
that with twofold receptivity he should be able to absorb the

fundamental characteristics of both. He stands between two worlds that oppose yet intensify one another. Only a passive, not an active, medium, could unite the pair. The ethical formulation of this idea is but a symbol of its functional significance as the impulse which draws these two expressionist spheres together—fundamentally, the artist's impulse to re-unite the divided halves of his own nature—two separate methods of apprehension and expression which have hitherto held the ascendancy by turns—and once again to feel and express himself as a unity. The work embodies an effort to unify two contrasting yet interdependent spheres of expression and it does so in the figure of Parsifal, who participates through sympathy in this effort.

The figure of Parsifal, accordingly, is a mirror in which the two hemispheres of the drama are caught and reflected as a single image. The dramatic, conceptual symbol of this function is *sympathy*. Similarly all conceptual structures built up by Wagner in writings associated with *Parsifal* should be interpreted as dramaturgical allegories in the guise of philosophy. They were useful in formulating his idea of a passive, not an active, hero, for only such a hero—a type of acceptance, passive amidst the flow of external dramatic events—was practicable here. As such an one Parsifal stands both within and without the action ; inwardly its pivot, he is outwardly its mirror, and it is from this peculiar dramaturgical significance that the figure takes dramatic and musical shape.

Parsifal does not know his own name. " Once had I many, but ne'er a one can I recall." As a symbol he reincarnates the earlier, active, figures of Wagnerian drama, more particularly the greatest of them all, Siegfried—Wagner's most tremendous embodiment of will. But as a factor in the new drama he supersedes his heroic prototype, for " when his (the hero's) misdirected will has been converted he finds his true self in the saint, the *divine* hero." Siegfried, naïvely delighting in his own strength, is a slayer of beasts, but Parsifal thinks it sin to kill a swan. Siegfried forges a sword, but Parsifal breaks the bow he has made. Siegfried wakes the sex instinct in woman, but Parsifal flees from her embraces. Siegfried is avid of fresh deeds, but Parsifal wanders sadly through this world. Siegfried in his fearless freedom of will despises the prophecy of death, but Parsifal knows only one commandment—total surrender of his own desires. He is the absolute converse of his prototype, embodying the change from affirmation to negation, from strong individuality to abrogation of the personal. He represents an inversion of all the past. No warm-blooded living impulse but an artificial impulse gives him being—an artificial impulse which adopts the artificial device of inversion in order to take appropriate form. An inversion of the idea of construction gives that of negation.

Both scenically and musically the figure of Parsifal is based on inversion. As he is without vital actuality, being merely an embodiment of a passive receptivity, so he lacks distinctive musical physiognomy. The motif that characterises and accompanies his appearance is not an individual motif like that of Siegfried. Its full significance does not appear until it blossoms into the melody of the Good-Friday-magic. From this earlier theme the chordal Parsifal motif is built up by means of rhythmic and harmonic compression, to form a personified symbol of the expiation and self-redemption of the creature through suffering. The melodic idea in itself, however, belongs to that great family of sequences in fourths such as Walter's *Preislied* and Siegfried's love-song, which Wagner composed while still at work upon the third act of *Tristan*. That in *The Mastersingers* is an intense lyrical expression of the hopes of the lover and artist, that in *Siegfried* a triumph hymn of the all-conquering will, but in *Parsifal* the sequence in fourths expresses nature's wordless cry for salvation. Thus a melody first shaped to express a most intense sense of personality becomes an expression of the abrogation of personality and outlines the musical figure of Parsifal. The second idea associated with him, the prophecy of the Blameless Fool who knows through sympathy, is expressed in the same tone-symbol changed by contrary motion and inversion into an ascending sequence of fifths. In the accompanying chromatic line we recognise an inversion of the Tristan motif. Thus the wills of Siegfried and Tristan are made one through a musical inversion of both ; and the " miraculous conversion of the misdirected will " by which the hero becomes the saint finds appropriate tonal expression. By means of this union of the will to action at its strongest with the will to aspiration at its highest in defiance of the native tendencies of both, both are abrogated and transformed to a new modulatory and comprehensive impulse of contrary motion—of musical negation.

The figure of Parsifal is the most artificial of Wagner's creations. It has no proper qualities and subsists solely by virtue of antithesis. Yet because this artistic antithesis is so perfect, because its structural working out by inversion of its prototypes is as careful as that of a Bach fugue, its artistic success is justified. It is an instance of musico-scenic counterpoint. The theme runs backwards and by this backward movement casts a looking-glass image of itself which, while resembling the first and mysteriously inseparable from it, has the semblance of being its absolute contrary. Those elements expressed philosophically as " sympathy " and " renunciation of the will " are truly such in relation to scenic and musical form, to technical and organic structure. But their ethical interpretation is simply an allegorical paraphrase of the conditions necessary to bring this work into existence. Only an artist who had finished his life's work, who had done forever with the world of objective drama, could have dared to conceive, undertake, and carry through such a figure as Parsifal—the mirror-image of all his own past work. Again, only the ripest experience could have grasped the multiplicity of associations and relations here premised, and represented them by reducing them to their few fundamental and determining characters. And now this artist, having subordinated his whole experience of life to the demands of his art and having thereby conjured up a whole world of figures, takes this world of his own making as the subject of a new and comprehensive work of art. He gets his formula by reversing the types in which his imagination has worked hitherto and by this inversion achieves an organic unity of contrasts. This he terms " conversion of the will through the knowledge born of sympathy." It is a formula that expresses the truth, if one remembers that this truth is the truth of the stage.

The drama is thus reversed and its central figure acts in an exactly opposite manner to his predecessors. But the principle of counterpoint goes further still. All the other Wagnerian characters reappear, the Sufferer, the Evil Dæmon, the Woman. Each plays the old part in the old way, but each evokes a response which is the reverse of the old. Expression takes on all kinds of shades, for the principle of inversion has robbed the central figure of the drama of all initiative, and this affects all the rest. Things are but reflections of their former selves, the artificial semblances of direct artistic intuitions. Reality becomes dream-like ; the individual has no more than a semblance of actuality acquired by visual and tonal suggestion.

The source of this enchantment is in the figure of Parsifal ; he alone makes it possible and requisite. Parsifal embodies an idea of in-

version that gives new actuality both to scene and music and endows
the other figures in the drama with form and utterance.   These are
all familiar Wagnerian types, now summoned to exhibit their natures
in action under the eyes of the central figure in the drama.   Amfortas
is the unhappy lover, wracked by the torment of desire—the Flying
Dutchman, Tristan, and Wotan in one, man's passion, tossed helplessly
between sensual lusts and immortal longings.   Klingsor is Alberich
and Hagen, the thief of the Ring, the thrower of the Spear, the Jew,
the enemy of all that is holy, the " lord of the world " and of its
sensual pleasures, the " embodied dæmon of degeneracy, triumphant
and secure."   Kundry is queen of the magic realm of love, the
experienced woman of the third act of *Siegfried,* the wild Valkyrie who
rides the storm, the awakening Valkyrie, who is Erda rising from the
primæval abyss, Savitri, the Magdalene, essential womanhood needing
salvation from emotional thraldom to man, the soul of dramatic music
as Wagner describes it when, in describing Madame Schroeder-
Devrient, he speaks of " the terrible blissful ecstacy of this indescribable
double life upon the stage."   With these we have Gurnemanz, the
onlooker and commentator, a more evangelistic Wolfram, Kurwenal,
or Pogner, and the sepulchral voice of the primæval King Titurel
which is the voice of nature, of Fafner, transferred to the mystic
precincts of the Sanctuary.   Wagner originally thought of putting
Isolda amongst the Flower Maidens ; he might well have named
the others Senta, Elsa, Sieglinda, and Brynhilda.   These spiritual
identities are, however, left unexpressed, save for the hint contained
in the words of the Flower Maidens' song, " Im Lenz pflückt uns der
Meister " (" In Spring the Master plucked us ").

The figures in *Parsifal* have nothing of that which gave previous
Wagnerian figures true character and individuality ; they are but types.
But while they are without dramatic character they have a recognisable
vocal character.   They are indeed living voices, embodied tones,
each a supreme representative of a type.   Wagner has found his way
through scenic mimetic fantasy back to opera.   Voices take the place of
individuals by virtue of their characteristic expressive capacity.   The
figures who tread the stage and act and interact upon one another are
not truly Amfortas, Parsifal, Kundry, Gurnemanz, and Klingsor, but
baritone, tenor, mezzo-soprano, lyrical and declamatory bass.

Here, as the sum total of his experience, the ageing composer establishes a vocal æsthetic which covers the whole ground of scénic-vocal expression. He now employs the female voice to express passionate emotion only. It becomes the vehicle of all degrees of passion from tenderness to wild ecstasy, but in grave and solemn moments it falls silent. No stylised harmonic development is possible for the vocal instrument of melodic chromaticism, nor is it, as in traditional opera, assigned to different registers, but is represented solely by the middle range of the soprano voice which is extended in both directions at times, but only for the purpose of heightening appeal. The upper and lower registers of the male voice are also little used. The heroic tenor expresses power and violence ; the lyrical tenor, whose tones are well-adapted to express either sudden and painful emotional stress or grave brilliance, is regarded as the norm of expression for that voice. Titurel's impalpable, mysterious utterances and the contemplative, narrative rôle of Gurnemanz are both assigned to the deep bass. The middle registers are used as typically masculine, whether in Klingsor's high, vehement bass or in Amfortas's lyrical passionate baritone. It is a register capable of every shade of ecstatic expression. What the third-act Tristan achieves only through a violent strain upon the vocal powers, is here realised by the composer's very complete understanding of the typical characteristics of the male voice. In the old " song-opera " both the baritone and the middle register of the female voice were neglected and assigned to subordinate rôles because they lacked the specific charm of virtuoso singing. Expressionist opera, on the other hand, gives these two chief prominence, because in them the elemental sexual character finds its clearest vocal characterisation and because they lend themselves very readily to emotional utterance. Of this use the rôles of Kundry and Amfortas are most complete examples, each character being strictly limited to the essentials of its vocal type. Vocal appeal alone is alive and active in these two, and the songs of Amfortas in the first and third acts and of Kundry in the second act constitute lyrical vocal images that serve as character-masks to the rôles.

Parsifal is actually a drama of vocal types, embodied in the established scenic types of Wagnerian art. This drama of voices has a choral setting. The solo female voice is supported by an elaborately subdivided chorus of women's voices, surpassing all previous *ensembles* for the realism with which each charming turn and inflexion of the

female vocal character—flattering, seducing, or inviting—is set forth.
Whatever the leading solo part may lack in coloratura, softness,
sensuous richness, is amply compensated in the choral accompaniment.
As in the second act women's voices support the woman, so in the
first and last acts, male choruses provide a setting for the man. These
voices represent the various ages of man, from basses and tenors
through the middle registers of the youths up to the high notes of the
boys. The whole is a piece of vocal architecture. Planned like a
dome, the parts of the harmony are built up from "old" to "young"
voices to correspond with the harmonic conceptual world of the tone-
spatial temple. In this vocal setting the sexual character and appeal
of the voices is totally excluded. Amfortas alone speaks the chromatic language of passion ; the other voices are subject to the grave
constraint of the harmonic sphere. In the second act the chorus is
used to support and enhance the musical charm of the leading female
voice, but in the other two acts Amfortas's pleading is emphasised only
by contrast with the rigid, ascetic austerity of the chorus. Once only
a woman's voice is heard singing of promise from on high, but it is
not distinctively feminine, for the deep alto tones give it a sexless
character. Kundry's few words in the expositional score of the first
act are spoken ejaculations rather than song, so hard and declamatory
is the emphasis ; they are really outside the tonal drama and serve
simply to explain certain ideas.

Thus baritone and soprano, the natural vocal expressions of sex,
are placed in choral settings which, in one case by harsh contrast,
in the other by alluring grace, help them to give complete expression
to their respective emotional contents. Between these two voices
stands the tenor voice which by virtue of its seraphic timbre becomes
the tonal symbol of passionless purity. In *Parsifal* these three voices
form the basis of the whole vocal structure, grouping, individualisation and characterisation. The male and female voices are not
separated as in *Lohengrin* ; they do not as in *Tannhäuser, Tristan,* and
the *Venusberg* reach an imperfect close in the expression of unsatisfied
longing ; nor do they, as in *The Mastersingers* and *Siegfried*, embrace
each other in union. A third voice comes to rob them of their
passionate sexual character, whereupon they simply fall silent. The
desire of womanhood perishes, the passionate longings of manhood are
transmuted to passionless contemplation. Expressionism itself passes
into a pure stylistic gesture.

The orchestral accompaniment is in full accord with this vocal drama. This may be seen by the way in which fourfold division of the wood-wind groups (with the exception of the flutes) is combined with threefold division of the brass. In the first and last acts a choral piling up of harmonies is preferred, in the middle act the appeal of the solo voice and colouristic effects. The soft tremolo of the strings as the Flower Maidens dance, together with the singing wood-wind, forms an appropriate counterpart to the scenic picture of spring's enchantment in the blossoming meadows—a far-away echo of the wood-whispers heard by Siegfried under the lime-tree. As with the technical treatment of solo voices and choruses, so in the orchestration distinct tonal characters are evoked by division of the orchestra into tonal groups. These individual tonal groups are built terrace-wise into a whole. A fresco-like technique of broad contours only is manifest in the score and expresses the wise economy of age. It corresponds also with the thematic treatment itself. In all the most important themes—those of the Grail, of Amfortas, of Kundry, and Klingsor—this consists of linear contours, the outlines of chords.

The chromatic interweaving of parts in the second act, and the chordal harmonic structure of the first and third, are alike remarkable for a peculiar transparency of colouring in the orchestration. This is obtained principally by the old-fashioned treatment of tone in which the groups are not mingled but set one above the other in layers. This is rendered additionally effective by the device of the sunken orchestra. Moreover, instruments and players being thus rendered invisible, tone acquires an unreal, discarnate quality which strips it of its sensuous appeal. Just as the characters upon the stage are without individuality, so the tone of the orchestra is without actuality ; the eye being unable to trace its source the ear accepts it as non-material. The orchestra is no longer an orchestra in the accepted sense but a refracted image of orchestral tone-rays.

Thus all the conditions help to make the work a fantasy of tonal vision, a representation of this tonal vision in a light-and-colour tapestry of spatial illusion. The fundamental idea of the external drama, that of abnegation of the will, determines the creative and æsthetic laws of the whole. All is negation—the orchestra whose presence is denied to the eye and whose tone reaches the ear stripped of reality, and the characters on the stage, who are nothing but music made visible and in whom not the laws of individual action but the abrogation of those laws constitutes the motive of the drama, for they are but the spectres of once active wills, the phantasmal antitheses of their former selves. The idea of negation is omnipresent; it is the active creative principle which constructs a new, ingenious present by inverting the past. Thus the plot itself may be characterised as a laying bare of the hidden springs of the artistic impulse behind the work.

This idea, however (above and beyond accidental intellectual accretions), is conditioned from the first by the " impulse to theatre " in an artist whose apprehension of music was scenic. This impulse sought its last and final manifestation in a permutation of the elemental forces of construction. The scene, that spatial element by means of which the expressive capacity of music had been heightened to the point of becoming visual and pictorial, was in its turn exhibited as a musical, temporal phenomenon. The music, that temporal element by means of which the expressive significance of the scene had been intensified to the point of absolute emotional revelation, was now exhibited as a spatial pictorial phenomenon. Gurnemanz expresses the principle of *Parsifal* when he says " Du siehst, mein Sohn, zum Raum wird hier die Zeit " (" Thou seest, my son, here time is one with space "). The stage moves in a visual time-rhythm, while music becomes a plastic image of space, erects edifices in tone, moves to and fro and presents characters in the medium of vocal timbre. The artistic significance of the negation-concept is expressed in these permutations, this reciprocal mimicry of the elements of construction which makes the visible invisible and the invisible visible. The result is an inversion of all correlatives based on a natural relation between these two factors ; the active principle of will becomes renunciation, the clamour of desire is stilled, passionate frenzy becomes passionless contemplation, sensual love becomes seraphic compassion, and there is an abrogation of the dæmonic forces of destruction, a state of salvation expressible only through the mystic unity of harmonic tone-space, of the grand cadence which resolves all dissonance.

Parsifal, the drama of inversion, is an exploitation of the ultimate possibilities of drama, and forms the climax of the *Dusk of the Gods*— that drama of fierce self-assertion which immediately precedes it. It could only be produced on a stage which had itself evoked the bold idea of a play upon itself, of a reflection of its own activities in a looking-glass image of themselves.

With *Parsifal* the gestatory period was a long one, covering from the first stirring of the idea to its complete expression some thirty-seven years, and this fact, as in the case of *The Ring*, had a considerable influence upon the plan and economy of the work. This influence was particularly striking in *Parsifal*, for whereas *The Ring* developed organically from a single basic idea, *Parsifal* was a complex of many tendencies originally foreign to one another. Each of the three principal characters as first conceived belonged to a different world. Parsifal himself originated in the story as a whole and as the visual symbol of the Good Friday idea of 1857. Amfortas was suggested in 1859 by Tristan, martyr of love. Kundry represents a blend of the Savitri of 1856 and the Paris Venus of 1860. To unite these three spheres in one so many conceptual links were necessary that for clear expression they required epic narrative form, with the result that the exposition section of the first act is somewhat overburdened. The action remains at a standstill while the characters are presented pictorially or descriptively and their natures expounded. Oratorical description thus exercises from the first a dominant influence upon the diction, which retains something of this character even in the critical scenes such as Amfortas's monologues and Kundry's story. Here again there is a note of purely lyrical representation almost wholly divorced from the violence of direct action and tending to substitute passive contemplation for immediate experience. This character determines the wording of *Parsifal*. The plastic vehemence of the diction of *The Ring* would here be as inappropriate as the rapturous exclamatory style of *Tristan* or the ingenious realism of *The Mastersingers*. For *Parsifal* a new form of utterance was evolved from the elements of these. It alternates between the short, aphoristic metre of the Grail chorus, the narrative iambics of Gurnemanz, and the free ejaculatory rhythms of Amfortas and Parsifal; on the very few declamatory dramatic occasions alliteration is used, but end-rime is more general. The effect is that of vocal scansion of the accents of speech. The libretto is remarkable for the prominence given to song-speech values, the melodic, musical rendering of words and sentences. All is subordinated to the primal requirements of vocal self-expression, of the voice as an instrument of song. The singing voice burgeons from the scene, as the scene from the mystery of wordless tone. Accordingly, the instrumental prelude to the first act is not a prelude to the external drama but a charm to conjure up that musical imagination which creates the scene, the song-speech characters of the drama, the living space they inform —in a word the theatrical miracle by which the invisible is made visible.

This process of awakening the imagination and concentrating it upon the miraculous events to come, shapes and conditions the themes as well as the general character of the prelude. When a separate performance of the prelude was to be given before the king in Munich Wagner supplied a programmatic commentary headed " Love—Faith—Hope ? " The first soaring theme is described as a twofold repetition by angel voices of the words of Jesus at the Last Supper. The second striding chordal theme, designated " firm and re-solute," stands for the Creed. The Love theme, returning in chromatic guise, portrays " the Agony and Bloody Sweat of Gethsemane, the Divine sufferings of Golgotha," and introduces Amfortas, " sinful guardian of the Sanctuary." The half-question, half-promise of the close suggests the hope that he may find salvation.

References to the allegory of the story apart, this interpretation indicates the musical factors which correspond with a concept borrowed from Christian symbolism. The two subjects which Wagner calls " Love " and " Faith " are represented musically by melody and rhythm, both regarded as revelations of diatonic harmony. This melody is formed from the chordal relationship of the graduated notes in the scale. Beginning as a solo awakening call it is taken up as by a full chorus, and, alternating between the major and the minor, assumes the guise of soaring harmonic flight. Flowing on in a legato syncopated movement it is contrasted with a steadily-paced rhythm, which in extended sequence of shifting chords constitutes the rhythmic and dynamic harmonic structure. Diatonic harmony, determined both by melody and rhythm, is, however, shaken by the invasion of chromaticism. Chordal structure loses its tonal integrity, plastic rhythm passes into quivering tremolo, the melodic call gives place to a lament. Finally it dies out, still unresolved, in dominant harmonies, in the question which it is the task of the work itself to answer.

The form of the prelude is purely and organically harmonic, being built upon melody and rhythm and the resultant contrast of the diatonic and harmonic, the two elements of musical harmony. The presentation of harmony under these two aspects is the structural basis of the prelude and of the work to follow. There is a corresponding real identity between the two contrasted spheres of the drama—between the realm of the Grail and the realm of enchantment. Their difference is not one of thematic contrast but of harmonic attitude, and this alone constitutes their dramatic opposition. In thematic character they are alike and therefore they tend to unite. The prelude leaves this problem unsolved, nor does it even suggest the way to a solution, for the idea of modulation, embodied in Parsifal himself, is not yet introduced. Only actual, visual representation of the contrasts expressed emotionally in the prelude can lead to its discovery. With the incarnation of these contrasts in their appropriate vocal characters the scenic drama begins.

Act I presents the world of the Grail—of diatonic harmony. It is developed from the Awakening call of the prelude, which now rings from the stage in the form of a true reveille and echoes in the dome of the Grail chorus. The march-form takes charge, and the forces of the drama are marshalled and assembled upon the stage to its rhythm. The fortress, the Temple—full resonant harmony—is the composer's aim, as it was in *The Nibelungs* and as he attained it in the second *Rhinegold* scene. There it was actually represented upon the stage and as actually conveyed to the ear in the full plastic tones of the chordal theme, but here it remains veiled to the gaze and, musically, is but faintly hinted at in the melodic line of the Awakening call. This line is actually the reverse of the Valhalla motif; *that* stood for the idea of a stronghold of might which sank down to perdition, *this* for the Grail-challenge which rises up to heaven. The symbol of dawn in the second scene of *The Rhinegold* is used again in the corresponding scene in the first act of *Parsifal*, though what was once dramatic and immediate is now oratorical and allusive. The bass voice tells the story and the rhythmic Faith theme, transformed to a march, provides an accompaniment. It is then that we get our first hints of the contending forces of the drama—the descending augmented triad which as harmony that has lost its integrity symbolises Amfortas—the promise of redemption conveyed in rising modulation which unites the chromatic and the diatonic—Kundry, embodied in a rhythmic intensification of the chromaticism of *Tristan*. Then description gives place to direct representation. Amfortas appears, and the line of the augmented triad is developed in elegiac mode. The conversation between Gurnemanz and the squires conveys a vivid impressional Kundry, and her ascending Tristan line passes into a chromatic distortion of the Grail theme, indicating an inner connection between this transformation and Kundry herself. Through the symbolic figure of Titurel, the ancient " hero," the Faith rhythm is strengthened to express masculine, formative power. In solemn and tender guise it reveals a spiritual vision of the heavenly embassy, of the trust of the sacred vessels, of the building of the Temple, of pure harmony. In contrast with this appears a vision of the powers of dissonance, embodied in Klingsor who represents the destructive force of chromaticism, for over against the Temple of harmony, Klingsor has set up his Magic Garden of the passions, of the allurements of sensual melody. Amfortas has fallen beneath his spell, and therefore the Spear, the symbol of creative power, has passed to Klingsor. Original perfection, absolute harmony, can never again be restored save by one whose unassailable purity can absorb and resolve the chromaticism of desire.

The prophecy of redemption is repeated thrice—by Gurnemanz, by the voice of Amfortas in anguish, and by the chorus of the Squires in four-part harmony. The Parsifal theme is now announced and comes like a promise of spring—the ultimate symbol of fulfilment in Wagnerian melody. Youthful in rhythm and vocal line, as though unaware of its great destiny, it breaks with dramatic effect into the solemn Grail music. It is as though Lohengrin's swan had sung him back to the home which he cannot as yet recognise, and it shatters the simple nature-melody of Parsifal which passes into the descending chromatic lament. Upon this, in the form of narrative and with vitalising effect, steals Kundry's galloping chromatic rhythm. As it comes in contact with the natural Parsifal theme its elemental instincts are wakened, the chromatic wave rises in flood, intoxicating, persuasive, seducing the resistant, harmonic will. Chromaticism falls back, however, as diatonic harmony advances. The static scene changes to one full of life and action ; the drama develops with a solemn steady rhythm. The powers of harmony are marshalled in march-rhythm and established on a basis of progression in fourths. Instead of forests, gates and walls of stone arise, while the marching Grail harmonies press ever onwards and upwards. Suddenly the chromatic lament breaks in upon these harmonies, passionately repelling them until it is outsoared by the solemn call. Rhythm alone is maintained, sinks to the deep tones of the bells, and thence ascends with gathering force. The great dome that crowns the pillared hall—the Temple of pure harmony—rises before our gaze. Above the solemn march-rhythm and accompanying orchestral groups, the male-voice choruses build a living picture of a temple of moving sound. The deep tones of the men's voices, the lighter ones of the youths', the boys' notes in the heights answer each to each antiphonally. The strong, homophonic men's chorus proclaims the rhythmic and now declamatory Faith motif. The three-part youths' chorus intones the chromatic lament, now instinct with promise. The boys sing the Faith theme in its original simplicity, yet transfigured by that celestial timbre.

Thus rises the Temple of Harmony, from crypt to dome an edifice in musical imagery and visual music. Wagner's memories play a part in its architecture; he recalls the Dresden Court chapel with its cupola'd galleries; he echoes the resounding *Amens* of its choir in his melodies, and in the archaic harmonic sequences of the messages from on high. From these heights the gaze is carried in a single sweep to the depths whence rises the voice of Titurel, like the boys' high notes, unaccompanied. The wide difference of vocal register represents *height* in musical architecture, and the listening eye passes from the boys' voices high in the vaulting to the dark crypt whence issues the unseen bass, and thence again to the central anguished figure of Amfortas, passion's sole victim in an edifice of perfect, self-subsistent harmony. For from this moment the essence of chromaticism —passion incarnate in the voice of man—takes command. The Awakening call is modulated into the augmented triad, into a descending chromatic lament. Kundry's seductive gestures entrance the senses and the voice is inveigled deeper and deeper by the allure of the phantoms of dissonance till, robbed of all its force, it perishes.

Despite all this the great harmonic edifice stands intact; as sole answer to the incursion of passion, there rings from the heights of the dome promise of a saving power which shall absorb the chromatic lament and transmute it to pure harmony. This annunciation, first proclaimed by boys' voices, gains in assurance when it passes to the men's choruses in their call for the Grail to be unveiled. Rhythmic motion is the power which has built the Temple, and it now seeks melodic fulfilment. From mystic harmonies emerge the words of benediction—melody fulfilling harmony and giving it form. It is sustained by the march-rhythm, which returns in the boys' chorus, and passing thence to the youths', and so to the men's choruses, achieves such force that it interpenetrates the harmonic whole in all its parts, endowing them with the richness of the vocal line. Once more the Faith theme ascends from the depths to the heights, and then the whole edifice of tone dissolves in the order in which it arose, from the foundations upwards. The march-rhythm, following the progress of outward events, fades into the silence whence it came. Amfortas's lament finds faint echo in Parsifal's tones, and only Gurnemanz, as he casts him forth, hears the voice of promise from on high. The boys' voices answer it with the Faith theme ; then they too die away in strains of pure harmony.

This first act is merely a framework ; its earlier and longer section consists of a series of musical and scenic explanatory sketches, while the second section summarises and works out the fundamental idea of harmonic architecture. This purely tone-symbolic idea determines the whole character and style of the music. Preference is given to all that emphasises the harmonic effect ; interest in the individual, the characteristic, is comparatively slight. The persons of the drama are outlined merely ; they are embodiments of abstract principles and the structural idiom of the tone-symbols applied to them accords with this character. In *Tristan* the natural function and effect of an ascending chromaticism intensifies the sensual emotions. In *Parsifal* the descending chromaticism which underlies the figure of Amfortas is no mere conceptual antithesis to *Tristan*, for its natural development issues inevitably in tone-formations which are inimical to the expansive impulse inherent in music. Thus a sensual representational device is used to represent the non-sensual. This strange process of putting a tool to the opposite of its proper use has the effect of making the chromaticism of *Parsifal* seem but a looking-glass image of expressionist art, altogether outside the natural sphere of music. The same looking-glass quality predominates in the harmony and tone-formation of the Grail sphere in *Parsifal*. It appears in the choice of archaic forms for the Grail choruses, and in the contrast of simple homophonic with artificial polyphonic methods of orchestration. The stiff, stylised gravity of this music sacrifices the living appeal of tone, while at the same time it makes the tone-*picture* more real and vivid. The purely introductory nature of the act accounts both for the schematisation of the music and the dim, merely suggestive, presentation of

2 K

scenic events. Wagner's purpose there was not to present drama but by inverting the devices of illusory drama, both musical and scenic, to reveal *music itself* as the true subject of the piece—music, moreover, not artificially adapted to certain ends but in the boundless effluence of its pristine nature. When this drop-scene lifts, the centre, the creative impulse of all his art appears in the person of Kundry. She it is who reveals the meaning of all that has gone before—of the great conflict between the worlds of intellect and of emotion. Hitherto we have had but a hint of her in the Lament theme as *That which must be denied*. Her appearance is to explain the meaning of this abnegation.

The second act—Kundry's act—is not only the central scene of *Parsifal*; it is in an absolute sense *the* Wagnerian scene. In it are comprehended and summed up all the Armida-ideas which obsessed Wagner from the first and which he wove into a variety of plots—the *Tannhäuser* of his Dresden days, *Tristan*, the *Venusberg*, the third act of *Siegfried*—and to which he gives final and complete expression here. For Wagner, Woman, Passion, and Music are interchangeable concepts. From their interaction and from his sense of music as the language of passionate emotion Wagner evolved his whole life's work. At the last he saw in music the essential image of essential womanhood ; and the vision was incarnate for him in the person of the actress from whom he confesses to have learnt the laws of his art, in the woman whose genius was begotten by the spirit of music, and round whose image all that Wagner as artist ever discovered of womanhood was now to be grouped and garlanded. Thus the stage is set for a monodrama of Woman—Woman, origin of the sorrows of the world, herself a victim suffering beneath and struggling to be free from the curse of her dual nature as woman and as human soul., It is a monodrama of music under the constraint of emotion and expressionism. It is a monodrama of passion cursed with the curse of desire. In this monodrama Wagner strikes down to the heart of his subject and whatever but touched upon it in his earlier works is here gathered up and fulfilled.

In outline the scene corresponds with that in the third act of *Siegfried*—that is to say it shows womanhood in bondage to the Lord of the World of Appearances. But the identity of Erda and Brynhilda, which is but hinted at and symbolised in *Siegfried*, is in *Parsifal* pro-

claimed unequivocally.   There is but one Woman—not an individual,
for the individual is never Woman, but that sexual being who alone is
Woman and as such is condemned to err throughout all ages.   Her
womanhood is the curse which makes her the bondslave of desire.
Yet through desire she becomes goddess of the enchanted realms of
love—she becomes Venus, seducer of man, winning him in Tristan
and Amfortas, and losing him in Tannhäuser and Parsifal.   Like
Brynhilda, omniscient, she reveals to man all the hidden things
of the past.   Even as mother she is Woman to Man, stimulating
the emotion, the womanhood in man's nature.   Her sole aim is
to give herself.   To her as to Venus, as to the Brynhilda of the prelude
to *The Dusk of the Gods*, the non-sexual aspect of man's nature is an
incomprehensible mystery.   With Venus and Brynhilda, therefore,
she must curse man when he repulses her, for through his repulse
her very being *as woman* is annihilated.   These are Woman's fundamental characteristics ;   the rest are unimportant, for these alone are
elemental, these alone are conditioned by music, these alone characterise Woman as the embodiment of musical expression of passion.

Both scenically and musically Klingsor is a silhouette—a dark
featureless dæmon of instinct and magical illusion and so, like Hagen,
lord of the passions.   As Wotan's spear was broken by Siegfried so
must Klingsor's go down before Parsifal.   Siegfried because he lacks
fear, and Parsifal because he lacks passion, are beyond the reach of the
enemy who challenges the frontiers of nature.   But the conceptual
explanation applied to the fate of Wotan is unnecessary in the case of
Klingsor.   "Why—he simply flies head over heels.   Do you think I
am going to make any ceremony with *him* ? " said Wagner when his
stage-manager asked him what should be done with Klingsor at the
end of Act II.   The jocular tone conveys a true and serious meaning.
Klingsor's existence is bound up with Kundry's passion; he is annihilated when that is overcome.   Kundry is defeated because her emotion
overreaches itself and shatters itself against masculine resistance.
Tannhäuser resists because he longs for action, Parsifal through
desire for suffering, passivity being the law of his nature.   The motives
are different but the effect is the same : the Woman's passion begins
in maternal tenderness, and passes through loving self-sacrifice to
an ecstasy of desire, to despair, to cursing of the beloved object, to
self-destruction.   Once again Wagner introduces the masculine
character simply as a means of evoking the full gamut of feminine

emotion, of displaying the monodrama of passion under the spur of all possible external incentives.

With a story thus simplified it is possible for this scene to become the kernel of the whole work. The "Venusberg" scene was a prelude, the third act of *Siegfried* a conclusion, but here the same scene becomes central, with the two acts which form its emotional context arranged symmetrically on either side. Any lack of real independent life in these latter is fully made up in the central scene—and the centre of the centre is Woman. "The nature of Woman is love—a love that takes into itself, that conceives, and, in taking, gives without stint," writes Wagner in *Opera and Drama*. And again: "I cannot conceive the spirit of music save as Love." It is this " spirit of music as love " which is so plainly manifested in the second act of *Parsifal*. The great Enchanter—the creator of phantoms that deceive the senses—calls it from its sleep, and it wakes with that " awful cry " in which, according to Wagner's *Beethoven*, the worlds of sight and hearing are one. Music herself becomes Queen of the drama and an intensely allegorical dream finds sensuous representation.

The real action of *Parsifal*, therefore, opens with this scene of invocation. The musical embodiment of this illusion of the senses is derived from *Tristan* and consists of the Grail theme deprived of its characteristic intervals and changed in diminution of discord. As with the Valhalla and the Ring themes these are but two aspects of a single idea. *There* descending chord sequences, *here* an ascending harmonic line are made to symbolise the powers of evil by the change from the natural triad to the diminished. In alternate ascending and descending motion the Grail theme becomes the spell by which Klingsor conjures Kundry's presence. Amfortas's cry of desire becomes Kundry's prayer for peace in the descending chromatics of " Oh, ewiger Schlaf, einziges Heil " (" Oh, ne'er-wakening sleep, only release "). The notes of suffering, common alike to Amfortas and Kundry, are also interwoven with the Promise motif of " the Blameless Fool " wherein they find their resolution. In Klingsor's mouth this Promise serves as a spur to action: " Ha! Wer dir trotzte, löste dich frei: versuch's mit dem Knaben, der naht " (" Ha! He who spurn'd thee setteth thee free . . . "). Here the naïve Parsifal theme appears, its limpid, major character and firm rhythm rendered provocatively in Klingsor's description, and works

with growing effect upon the flowing, formless chromaticism.   The
dæmonic phantom becomes Woman at the challenge of this portrayal
of Man ; rhythmical harmony subdues chromaticism to its spell.
Klingsor vanishes and the Magic Garden of the senses, the emotional
melody of Woman, dominates the scene.

There follows the most important scene in the work, and externally
Wagner has made it one of his most exquisite and graceful pictures.
It is the Kingdom of Flowers, living Nature herself clothed in the
tenderest tones of expressionist music by the chorus of girls' voices
which herald the Woman's.   A similar effect of ethereal youth is
obtained in the boys' terzet in *The Magic Flute* and the " Jungfernkranz " (Wreath of Maidens) which contrasts with the men's chorus in
The Freischütz.   Wagner, too, uses it frequently, as in the Pages'
quartets in *Tannhäuser* and *Lohengrin*, the Young Pilgrims' chorus in
Tannhäuser, the Rhine Maidens' terzet, the choruses of Valkyries and of
Apprentices, but nowhere does he attain such purity of expression,
such perfect correspondence with the scene, as in this three-part double
choral *ensemble* led by two solo trios.   There is some borrowing from
the past, and the Venusberg chromatic theme, its rhythmic emphasis
reversed, forms an orchestral counterpoint to the singing voices.
This contrast, interrupted by the gradual entry of the Parsifal
motif, sustains the exposition scene until the voices are generally
united.   The harmonies rise and fall in close curves, and an exquisite
chromatic melody emerges, rising gradually from lyrical playfulness to
the verge of passion.   A sudden transformation then occurs ; the
many give place to the one, and from the maidens' song emerges the
Woman's, proclaiming that name which is life's first cry, reminding
Man of the Mother-Woman who bore him.

The first true *song* is formed out of this melody of mother-love.
But it is entirely unlike the song-melody of Isolda, Venus, or Brynhilda.
The air itself is sustained by the orchestra, while the voice rises and
falls in ejaculatory expression.   Then all that is plastic in the instrumental melody is stripped away and the song, like that of the Paris
Venus, becomes direct emotional utterance—though here it all but
transcends music, revealing the essential tones of feminine emotion
through resolution of the melodic line into sheer sound.

Kundry is born from a cry, and in a cry she passes.   The cry,
the primal element of expressionist art, awakes her to life, and with
a cry she sinks to earth and expires.   Between these two cries, the

coming and the passing of music, the expressionist emotional impulse
runs its full course. Roused by the first cry, it seeks to discharge
itself, and so to find its way back to the blankness of sleep. Such an
emotional impulse is dominant in the figure of Kundry. Her passage
through its phases forms the inner motive of the drama and shapes the
musical structure through successive stages of maternal love, the kiss
and the curse.

The effect of this process is heightened by Parsifal's ejaculations.
Disarmed at first by remembrance of his dead mother, his soul submits
in stunned passivity to the invasion of woman's tenderness. The
chromatic wave overwhelms him, draws him into the deeps, and
thence lashes itself into the storm of frenzied desire typified in Tristan.
This is the moment of crisis in which all the elemental forces of
passionate music, of both kinds of chromaticism, are gathered together.
Desire and sorrow meet in a kiss. The ascending chromatic Desire
theme governs the upper parts, the descending, the bass, and both rise
crescendo until at the height of the contest the descending movement
prevails over all. Then comes Parsifal's second cry, the cry of descending chromaticism, " Klage ! Klage ! " (" Alas ! Alas ! "). A vision
of Amfortas appears in the augmented triad, the lament of the Grail
harmonies, the Klingsor Illusion theme, and all are drawn into the
Lament. Kundry exercises her wiles in a wordless, tender appeal for
love, the expression of Parsifal's voice changes from emotional
repression to passive endurance, finally rending the notes of Illusion
with the words " Verderberin ! Weiche von mir ! " (" Destroyer vile !
Get thee from me ! ").

Kundry now begins to reveal the Venus aspect of her nature.
Her soft persuasions change to the violent accents of passion, and
in her " Bist du Erlöser, was bannt dich, Böser, nicht mir auch zum
Heil dich zu einen ? " (" Art thou Deliv'rer, what lets me, harsh one,
that I too should share thy salvation ? ") the Tristan motif finds its
culmination. There are fleeting reminiscences of Tannhäuser's story
of the curse, of the laughing woman on Golgotha and the Saviour's
glance of repudiation, and from the midst of these, like a distorted
version of the love-songs of Walter and Siegfried, breaks the cry of
instinct clamouring for satisfaction : " Lass mich an seinem Busen
Weinen, nur eine Stunde mich dir vereinen " (" Let me upon his
breast lie weeping, be but one hour with thee united "). It meets
the resistance of the diatonic line. To the tones of the Blameless

Fool theme, which absorbs and overcomes the chromaticism, are heard the words " Auf Ewigkeit wär'st du verdammt mit mir für eine Stunde Vergessen meiner Sendung " (" Eternally wouldst thou be damned with me if but one hour unmindful of my mission "). The Grail Faith motif goads chromaticism to its final ecstasy. The Flower Magic melody re-enters with rhythmic abandon, yet it is overpowered by Kundry's voice which rises to the pitch of ecstasy as it hurls the curse of Venus, the curse of Tristan, the chromatic curse of eternal restless lust—" Und flöhest du von hier, und fändest alle Wege der Welt, den Weg, den du suchst, dess' Pfade sollst du nicht finden " (" For fleddest thou from here, and foundest all the ways of the world, the one that thou seekest, that path thy foot shall find never "). The full gamut of passion has been traversed and the cry which called Kundry into being echoes now from her own soul in the words " Irre ! Irre ! " (" Wander ! Wander ! "). It is the cry of magic illusion and conjures the presence of Klingsor. He appears and hurls his spear, but the solemn Grail harmonies arrest its flight. Kundry's death cry rings out ; with the dying note of magic illusion the world of passion sinks and fades, and we hear the words of Parsifal " Du weisst, wo du mich wiederfinden kannst ! " (" Thou know'st where thou may'st find me when thou wilt ! ").

The emotional impulse has run its course ; the work as such—that drama of music which is the principle of emotional impulse—ends, as indeed it began, in its materialisation. But as the first act was needed to serve as prelude and, by showing the contrasts, to explain the struggle, so an epilogue is necessary to depict its issue. The epilogue or third act is a symmetrical counterpart, as regards external structure, of the first act in the scenico-musical change from the Grail landscape to the Grail stronghold, in lack of dramatic action and in harmonic basis. In the third act, however, the harmonic impulse is in itself richer than in the first, for it has been nourished by what has gone before and has the task of gathering up all the threads. The manner in which these are intertwined shows a close connection with the quartet style of the later Beethoven and with the polyphonic structure of Bach, though it is still true expressionist theatrical pathos, with but the *semblance* of restraint and reserve. There are three main crises in this last—this very last—act. The first of these is the orchestral prelude which reappears later in Parsifal's narrative. The theme may be traced back to the similar prelude to the third act of *Tannhäuser* (where also it reappears in Tannhäuser's story of the pilgrimage to Rome) but here, instead of the decorative plasticity of the earlier work, there is the harsh harmony of contrapuntal chromaticism. The entrance of the " Black Knight " (a reminiscence of *Euryanthe*), the resurrection of Kundry to silent service, Gurnemanz's story of suffering, the establishment of the Grail theme as the theme of the anointing of the king, the ceremony of the Washing of Feet, sustained by the Seduction motif in altered guise —these form bridge-passages to the second climax, that of the Good-Friday magic. The Parsifal theme is therein transfigured to a vision of springtime in nature. A reminiscent counterpart of the chromatic melody of the Magic Garden, it brings fulfilment of the diatonic fourths under the scenic symbolism of a sacred idyll.

As in the plan of the third act of *The Mastersingers*, the grand march-structure of the Transformation music (here transposed to the minor character as for a funeral march) leads back again to a world of external events. There is a further echo from the past in the scenic structure, for the antiphonal singing of two choruses was foreshadowed in the closing scene of the work first entitled *The Death of Siegfried*. Eventually omitted there, they serve here as a setting for Titurel's obsequies. As in the first act Amfortas's lament forms the centre of the edifice, so here Amfortas's augmented triad and Klingsor's diminished triad are accentuated to represent a last evocation of the primal forces of dissonance. These are resolved in the Grail harmonies, from which the grave Parsifal theme is slowly built up. The Grail theme, carried upwards from the deep men's voices to supernal heights, once again vaults the great temple of tone-space in which at last dissonance and passion, suffering and desire, are transfigured and purified in perfect harmony. Kundry sinks lifeless to earth, Amfortas does homage to Parsifal. Expression gives place to pageantry, and music becomes purely pictorial as Parsifal raises the Grail to bless the assembled worshippers. The great tone-space rings and shines with a myriad heavenly harmonies which die away at last in the ethereal tones of the harps.

CHAPTER II

" In many of my writings I have repeatedly stated the lineage of our art ; it descends from the car of Thespis, from the Shakespearean theatre," said Wagner in an after-dinner speech on July 25, the eve of the first performance of *Parsifal*. He was himself ever mindful of these origins, yet in order to fulfil in his life and in his work the task they imposed, he was obliged to seem to deceive himself and others as to their nature. His power as an artist depended on the deception, and only in practising it without stint could he fulfil his vocation. This strange contradiction led in its application to consequences as paradoxical, for the effect of the illusion on others was two-edged. Those who recognised it as such regarded it as the mark of a spurious art, whereas those who accepted it for truth misunderstood the artist's real intention. The former school of thought found its bitterest exponent in Nietzsche when he turned against an art-form he at first thought genuine and later came to regard as " play-acting." Supporters of the latter school, whose acknowledged centre was Bayreuth, looked on Wagner less as an artist than as a reformer, the religious founder of a new order of society. Yet it was this same application of the suggestions of a dramatic art to the business of real life that caused Nietzsche and like-minded critics to call Wagner a " play-actor." The epithet is just, save that it was bestowed with the idea that play-acting is degrading and without value in the ethic of art. As against these two mistakes—a mistakenly literal interpretation and a mistaken imputation of dishonesty—stands the fact that while Wagner never denied either his own play-acting instincts or the theatrical origin of his art, he always insisted on his personal and artistic integrity, asked men to believe in his work, and even sought ultimately to invest this claim with religious sanctions. Is there not here some profound paradox which justifies a partial giving and a partial withholding of the faith he demanded ?

Wagner willed theatre, he believed in theatre. He preached its creed because the theatre was the foundation of his art. He knew illusion *as* illusion and gained a practical mastery of its technique even in mechanical details, and yet, though conscious of its unreality, he asked conviction of its reality. He adopted a philosophy which taught that the phenomenal world was all " illusion," because on such a basis he could ask the world to believe in the trustworthiness, the " reality " of his theatre. He pushed this doctrine to its logical extremes because only absolute faith in its truth could enable his art to fulfil its function of imposing illusion. He knew himself for a play-actor, yet he could only be so before an audience which would consent to think of him not as an actor but as that which he enacted. And because his art was twice-illusory, requiring not belief in the play but belief in the reality of the play, it was the one art for him ; for its sake he became a mime and learnt the lore of illusory drama.

Wagnerian art, therefore, is one whose manifestations must not in the first place be submitted to ethical canons. It should first be recognised and criticised for what it is in itself. Strange contradictions, which are none the less essential to each other's existence, occur in Wagner's music as in his drama. Wagner himself knew that music was an integral part of his art, yet he refused to be called a musician, realising that his music was not the art of tone-formation in the ordinary sense. As he denied the possibility of a theatrical art apart from illusionary drama, so he denied the possibility of a music shaped according to its own inherent laws. Yet facts were stronger than his arguments, and he could not make the world forget the existence of a formal musical art, in comparison with which his own mimetic music seemed to many a mongrel affair, subject to externals, organically spurious, of a piece with the " play-acting " character of his art as a whole. This " spurious " music was none the less to direct the course of musical evolution for half a century and more.

Wagner was persuaded that hostile criticism of his art was due to misunderstanding of the great art and artists of the past, and that he was the first to interpret these aright. He believed that he was as a dramatist the direct successor of Shakespeare, and that as' a musician he carried on the work of Beethoven. In view of the magnitude of his achievements these claims have a certain justification, for no dramatist since Shakespeare, no composer since Beethoven, had shown such vast powers of synthesis and execution. At the same time the comparison has only to be made to show how profound is the difference between the laws governing the art of Shakespeare or Beethoven and those governing Wagner's. The claim seems incongruous because Wagner's greatness is so wholly different in kind from that of these two giants.

In his *On Players and Singers* Wagner points with keen insight to the influence exercised by the stage of Shakespeare's day upon Shakespeare's art. He derives Shakespeare's naturalism from the natural effect with which objects were presented upon the Elizabethan stage, but in recognising differences between this and the stage of a later day he fails, strangely enough, to note the most essential—namely, the difference between natural light and artificial lighting. The latter, presenting as it does the scenic picture with magic-lantern-like effects of illumination and colour, is the determining factor in modern stage conditions. In Shakespeare's day artificial illumination was occasionally employed to suggest alternation of day and night or to indicate such natural phenomena as fire and lightning, but the use of lighting effects as a structural element in the drama was quite unknown. Once artificial stage lighting had been invented and the eye had become accustomed to its colours and shades, the fundamental condition of the Shakespearean theatre had passed entirely away. Under artificial light figures lose their natural forms and become illusory. For natural contours are substituted effects of artificial light, colour, and perspective. Shakespeare does not ask his audience for belief. He thinks of his drama *as* drama, but where a measure of faith is required as an aid to the imagination it is freely given, because character and situation are natural. Shakespeare, accordingly, is unconcerned with the problem of credibility and non-credibility—a problem which did not arise until artificial illumination endowed the stage with illusionary power, making it, instead of an ordinary, a *magic* mirror.

The problem of this magic-looking-glass stage has two possible solutions. The element of illusion may be openly recognised and an artificial drama may be developed in accordance with it. This idea underlies the opera and classical drama of the eighteenth century. Opera, by substituting singing voices for men and women, added a final touch of non-actuality to an artificially lighted and coloured stage, and French " classical " drama, by means of the poetic diction and ethical sententiousness which Wagner attacked so fiercely, removed dialogue from the sphere of probability into a mimetic make-believe world which was frankly illusory and very far removed from—indeed, entirely opposed to—the naïve whole-heartedness of the Shakespearean stage.

A second possible solution of the problem is the substitution of illusionary reality for conscious illusion. This was beyond the scope of opera or drama ; it could only be achieved by the addition of a new formative element to those of artificial colour and lighting, this third element being *tone*—tone not in the sense of sung music (as in opera) but as a means of making the scenic picture emotionally convincing— as its tonal *expression*.

Beethoven's music shows a tendency to expressionist actualisation through tone. Beethoven is an expressionist composer, as Shakespeare is a plastic dramatist, and his music is the formulation of emotion. The tendency to attach vital emotional meaning to the formal element in music drew Wagner to Beethoven. Yet as the naturalness of Shakespeare's drama is based on an acceptance of natural lighting conditions, so Beethoven's expressionist modelling presupposes a purely ideal interpretation of its emotional content. For Beethoven it is the law, not the limitation, of his art to express only the non-material. In the Ninth Symphony he approaches the frontiers of actuality, but neither there nor elsewhere does he cross them. He is essentially a musician, and the essence of music is sound. He enriches the possibilities of form in sound by an expressionism which endows form with poetic soul, making its pattern, its architecture, the vehicle of thoughts, but these thoughts are never objective, material. He is faithful to pure sound, which is for him the basis of his art, as was natural light of Shakespeare's. Like Shakespeare he does not ask for " belief," but when he requires it he gets it, as does Shakespeare, because of his grasp of the realities which underlie the make-believe.

Shakespeare and Beethoven came upon Wagner in youth with the force of revelation and they remained throughout his life the poles and guiding stars of his art. Yet he could not reveal character as could Shakespeare nor emotion as could Beethoven. His was a receptive nature in which these two powers were mirrored. His art is the art of the mime and its basis is receptivity. It is the nature of the mime, as he himself says, to be *re*productive. Nature teaches him to imitate, skill to refashion. For this he needs an " example," and Wagner's examples were the art of Shakespeare and the art of Beethoven. In order to blend the two and to *refashion* rather than merely imitate, it was necessary to interchange their effects, and for this he required yet a third " example "—the example of an art which should not merely reproduce but *make anew*. This he found in the acting of Madame Schroeder-Devrient. She was a *mediator* of Shakespeare, a *mediator* of Beethoven ; she was a body charged with emotion, an embodied emotion ; she taught Wagner the art of evolving selves out of the self—the magic of the mime. With this great actress for " example " Wagner " played " Beethoven by counterfeiting Shakespeare's art and Shakespeare by counterfeiting Beethoven's. He called this musical miming " drama " and " music made visible."

Faith—faith in the power of a theatrical art to make light audible and tone visible—is the primal requisite of this visual music-drama. It is an art in which the natural laws of the various media concerned are abrogated, in which visual phenomena govern musical forms and tone determines the actions of visual phenomena. In this dual activity mimetic art becomes creative, for in reproducing it actually *makes anew*. At the actual moment of representation it seems to stand on an equality with truly original creative work. The spirit informing it is transfigured in the likeness of genius ; it demands that we shall believe that it *is* genius, for from our faith it draws power to appear so and thus to fulfil its work of mimetic improvisation. The theatre " has the value of," not " is," the real world. When the illusionary light-colour stage becomes an illusion of light, colour, *and tone*, the illusion of light acting within the illusion of tone determines the character of the forces of the drama—of light with its correlative *object* and of tone with its correlative *emotion*. These two—object and emotion—are necessary to each other, attract one another, since they become manifest only in the motion which draws them together. The subject of the drama, therefore, is the contrast between object and emotion, between the visible and the invisible, between light and sound. The existence of this contrast or contradiction makes tragedy the norm of drama ; no deviation from it is possible save in the form of parody or idyll. It is a type of tragedy, however, derived not as in classic drama from a tragic philosophy of life but from an organic conflict between its own elements of object and emotion, light and tone.

The recurrent clash between these elements in Wagnerian drama is paralleled by what one is tempted at first to regard as Wagner's own personal system of æsthetics, his philosophy, his temperament. Yet if one attempts to study this personality as one might, say, Goethe's, one finds only a hollow mask—a mask which is creative simply because it is capable of endless metamorphosis, and is susceptible to every stimulus to expression. As a mask, as an embodiment of music in the mimetic genius, Wagner is indeed great. The governing factor in his growth, the one which lends his philosophy a semblance of consistency, is his truly consistent theory of the theatre. His apparent "development" is no more than a mimetic artist's capacity for showing endless reflections of the dramatic conflict between object and emotion in the mirror of his fancy. The *form* of these reflections is modified by his passage through life from youth to age, so that the earlier works, including *Rienzi*, do not equal his greatest; but if we look behind this natural gradation for improvement in subject and treatment in the absolute sense, we shall be disappointed. Is the Peace Messengers' chorus in *Rienzi* less impressive than the Grail chorus? Is *The Flying Dutchman* duet at all excelled by *Tristan* or *Siegfried*, or the second act of *Tannhäuser* by the second act of *The Dusk of the Gods*, as should, surely, be the case if a philosophy of life really governed these works?

Some light will be thrown on the evolution of the artist and of his works if we watch the recasting of forces which precedes the creation of each. This is the only way of gaining a true understanding of their peculiar nature. An externally organic process suggests development where in reality there is only change. Life and effort are lavished not on the subject, not on its intellectual garment, not even on its artistic workmanship, but solely on an idea of a theatrical process and its forceful representation. Representational methods vary with the nature of the process, and therein *Tristan* differs from *The Flying Dutchman*, and *Parsifal* from *Tristan*. Yet process and methods being in all cases essentially theatrical, any attempt to estimate the value of a work upon the basis of its subject or of the manner in which that subject is treated must be mistaken. In making our estimate we should not ask whether the subject presented be that of the redemption of the world or the song-contest on the Nuremberg Vogelwiese. We should not think of Wagner's work either as sacrosanct or as impious. We should ask only what is the theatrical value of that which he gives us and place the work according to the degree of force with which he has understood and handled the theatrical process.

From this point of view Wagner's life-work is seen not as a line which ascends to the end but as one which rises in the middle and then declines. During the earlier half of his artistic life he was engaged in the struggle to understand the drama from the peculiar standpoint imposed by his own mimetic, receptive nature. This made him a revolutionary, forced him to form intellectual conclusions and to investigate the laws of drama. During this period *the* fundamental Wagnerian drama, the drama of Object and Emotion, found presentation only in isolated scenes and acts—and that, until *Lohengrin*, only in and through opera of the traditional type, to which a tragic bias was imparted. A group of works followed, comprising the first half of *The Ring* series, in which the same drama was presented, though obscured by the intellectual difficulties of a dramaturgic theory which failed to recognise the will to theatre as such, mistaking it for the will to creative drama. This period was also marked by cessation of interest in the practical problems of the theatre. It was counter-balanced later by a period of absolute devotion to the theatre, the theatre of Bayreuth, when conscious miming, neglected in earlier works, became of first importance, in *The Dusk of the Gods* dominating representational expression, and in *Parsifal* appropriating light and sound, object and emotion, as mere tools of the will to theatre.

Between these two groups stand the high peaks of the Wagnerian range, comprising *Tristan*, the *Venusberg*, *The Mastersingers*, and the third act of *Siegfried*. In these works the drama of Object and Emotion, their conflict, their mutual dependence, and their union through the scenico-musical process, is presented with absolute success. The theatrical appeal of this primal conflict is expressed in tragedy, in comedy, in heroic idyll, in each case free of all theoretic or conceptual idiosyncrasies, and the essential qualities of the light-tone stage are fully established and exploited. Here Wagner as mimetic artist attains the summit of his genius, receiving, so far as is possible within the sphere of theatrical art, the chrism of the creative spirit. " If his genius does not shine like clear sunlight it has none the less a mysterious magic which masters the senses," said Robert Schumann, with prophetic wisdom. It is the profoundest comment ever made upon Wagner.

A true critical understanding of Wagner can never be attained by those who begin either by disputing his greatness on the ground that his art is "spurious" or by asserting, in blind admiration, that his greatness is of the elemental creative type of a Shakespeare or a Beethoven. The critic should concern himself with revealing the peculiar nature of this greatness, thereby denoting its sphere of operation. In studying this central problem he will survey the whole critical ground and may then pass from consideration of the work itself to its effect upon contemporaries and upon posterity. Wagner created a new stage and a new stage art. His stage was neither for the artist in words nor for the musician; it was the stage of the musician-mime, who, working in light and sound, achieved unprecedented theatrical effect. It was the triumph of a unique mimetic genius, and it had two results. It made the theatre, the operatic theatre no less than the dramatic, *musical*, and it made music, whether vocal or instrumental, *theatrical*. The union of two naturally alien art-media to a common end required an intermediary. That intermediary was expression. Through it sound became audible, light visible, emotion objective, the objective emotional. This interchange of the natural functions of visible and tonal drama is the basis of the art of the musical mime, of the magical power of his stage, and of the miracle which formed the centre of Wagner's conceptual world. But it meant that the art-media concerned were robbed of their true nature. They had to seem what they were not, to exchange their primary characteristics. Upon the stage walk sounds, not people, who do not speak but sing words, do not think but feel. Similarly, in musical form, people, not notes, move about, not sounding, but conversing in tonal relations, not forming patterns but acting. This art of juggling with the functions of the senses, being received as true in the absolute sense (and indeed demanding belief in its truthfulness as a moral duty), infected the other, separate, arts with its magic and dominated and interpenetrated the general intellectual life of an age. A "magical" art gave rise to a culture, the culture of the Romantic cast of mind which absorbs what is without in order to project what is within and, having no inherent content, lives in the interchange of internal and external. This is the culture of the mime, this is Expressionism, ever alternating, as the ages pass, with its great contrary, the culture of Form. The latter reveals matter by shaping it and gives form to the formless, but Expressionist culture, receptive and feminine and in itself uncreative, gives birth to the seed which is planted within it. Richard Wagner is one of its greatest representatives for all time. He dominates the latter half of the nineteenth century. He is the heir and fulfilment of Romanticism, the expressionist mime, the creator and perfector of the light-tone stage and of drama in music. He is the *imitative* counterpart of the elemental creators, the artists in form, the discoverers, the geniuses of mankind.

"Alles weiss ich" ("I know all things"), sings Brynhilda. Wagner himself knew all. Knowledge was his because his whole life was a fulfilment of his dæmon's behests. He knew that he would be victorious, that he would build his theatre in Bayreuth, that he would create and produce *Parsifal*. He knew beforehand of his death, if only in a presentiment, a dream. At a time when his intuitive powers were acutest he saw it in a vision, as an actor the rôle he is to play. In 1858, on the way to Venice from Geneva, he wrote to Mathilde describing his last night at the "Asyl." "Before I closed my eyes I had a vivid vision (for I used always to send myself to sleep there with the thought) of how one day I should die there—how I should lie when you came to me for the last time and, before the eyes of all, took my head in your arms and received my soul in a parting kiss! It was such a blissful dream of death and all the circumstances fitted with the actual arrangement of my bedroom. The door on the staircase was shut—you came in through the curtains from the study— you threw your arms about me—and so gazing on you I died." This death scene, evocation of imagination and desire, did indeed come to pass, though Wagner died not in Zurich but in Venice, not in sleep but at work, not in the "Asyl" but in a palace, and though not Mathilde but Cosima came to the dying man's side. Yet events occurred as he had foreseen in his dream. On the Christmas day before his death, in Venice, where he had been resting since September from the fatigues of the *Festspielen*, Wagner heard his early symphony performed before his household. Ill-health had been forgotten in Liszt's visit, in happy converse with friends and in the delights of reading on many subjects. He had planned a book *On the Feminine in Man* to carry on the train of thought expressed in *Religion and Art* and *Heroism and Christianity*, while preparations for a revival of *Parsifal* in the new year kept him busy with a vast correspondence. On Shrove Tuesday he went to the solemn burning of "King

Carnival" in the Piazza San Marco, and returning on Ash Wednesday morning (February 7) he said to the house-porter, " Amico mio, il carnevale e andato." In the evening of February 12 he played to his family the lament of the Rhine Maidens—" Traulich und treu ist's nur in der Tiefe " (" Tender and true 'tis but in the waters "). On February 13, as he sat at work, he succumbed to a heart attack.

Thus died Richard Wagner, in the city of *Tristan*, the city of desire and the rapturous dream of life. There the last discord was resolved and the Kundry-cry of music died away. He lies buried in the city of *Parsifal*, the city of fulfilment and the Festival Playhouse, in the garden of the house called *Wahnfried* (*Dream-Peace*), where all his dreams found peace.

THE END

INDEX OF WAGNER'S WORKS

INSTRUMENTAL AND VOCAL WORKS

LITERARY WORKS

PROJECTS AND FRAGMENTS

INDEX OF NAMES